Unearthing the Past to Forge the Future

Studies in British and Imperial History
Published for the German Historical Institute London
Editor: Andreas Gestrich, Director of the German Historical Institute London

Volume 1
The Rise of Market Society in England, 1066–1800
Christiane Eisenberg
Translated by Deborah Cohen

Volume 2
Sacral Kingship between Disenchantment and Re-enchantment
The French and English Monarchies, 1587–1688
Ronald G. Asch

Volume 3
The Forgotten Majority
German Merchants in London, Naturalization and Global Trade, 1660–1815
Margit Schulte-Beerbühl
Translated by Cynthia Klohr

Volume 4
Crown, Church and Constitution
Popular Conservatism in England, 1815–1867
Jörg Neuheiser
Translated by Jennifer Walcoff Neuheiser

Volume 5
Between Empire and Continent
British Foreign Policy before the First World War
Andreas Rose
Translated by Rona Johnston

Volume 6
Unearthing the Past to Forge the Future
Colin Mackenzie, the Early Colonial State and the Comprehensive Survey of India
Tobias Wolffhardt
Translated by Jane Rafferty

Unearthing the Past to Forge the Future

Colin Mackenzie, the Early Colonial State and the Comprehensive Survey of India

Tobias Wolffhardt

Translated by Jane Rafferty

berghahn
NEW YORK · OXFORD
www.berghahnbooks.com

Published in 2018 by
Berghahn Books
www.berghahnbooks.com

© 2018 Tobias Wolffhardt

Library of Congress Cataloging-in-Publication Data

A C.I.P. cataloging record is available from the Library of Congress

British Library Cataloguing-in-Publication Data

A catalogue record for this book is available from the British Library

ISBN 978-1-78533-689-8 hardback
ISBN 978-1-78533-690-4 ebook

CONTENTS

List of Illustrations   vi

A Note on the Text and Sources   vii

List of Abbreviations   ix

Acknowledgements   x

Introduction   1

Chapter 1. Scottish Experiences   23

Chapter 2. Building an East Indian Career   50

Chapter 3. On the Route: From Military Imperatives to the Tasks of Government   86

Chapter 4. Mackenzie's Survey   117

Chapter 5. Mapping History, Producing Territory   153

Chapter 6. Knowledge for the Future   180

Chapter 7. The Past in the Present   215

Chapter 8. The Surveyor General   255

Epilogue   285

Bibliography   292

Index   331

ILLUSTRATIONS

0.1. Thomas Hickey, Colin Mackenzie, 1816.   3

0.2. Title page of the *Saturday Magazine*, 28 June 1834.   5

3.1. Colin Mackenzie, 'The Roads from Hyderabad to Culboorga, Toljapor-Ghaat & Feroseabad on the Beema River, Fort St. George', 10 December 1797.   90

3.2. Detail from Mackenzie, 'The Roads from Hyderabad'.   92

5.1. 'Plan of the Districts of Hunda-Annantapur, Durmawaram, Taudamurry & Taudaputree'.   167

5.2. Detail from 'Plan of the Districts of Hunda-Anantapur'.   168

A Note on the Text and Sources

In the period covered by this book, Europeans did not follow any uniform system of transcribing Indian place names. Not only did this cause problems for surveyors such as Colin Mackenzie, but it also complicates the identification of places mentioned in the sources for today's historians. To reach some degree of uniformity, in this book, wherever possible, place names are spelled according to Walter Hamilton's *Geographical, Statistical, and Historical Description of Hindostan* published in two volumes (London, 1820). While Hamilton's spelling certainly does not come up to the standards suggested by Mackenzie, these two volumes do present the most comprehensive contemporaneous work of reference.

Even more problematic is the transcription of Indian personal names. Divergent spellings are not only to be found in the sources but, following them, also in historiography. To give just one example, one of Mackenzie's best known co-workers is alluded to in different works as 'Letchmyah', 'Letchmiah', 'Lutchmiah', 'Lakshmiah', 'Lakshmaiah' or 'Lakshmayya'. As a general rule, in all cases where a person is mentioned in historiographical publications, I have decided to follow the spelling given in the most recent work quoted. In all other cases a deliberate choice had to be made from the differing versions found in the sources.

For reasons of comparability, in some instances the conversion of the currencies used by the East India Company, particularly pounds sterling, pagodas and rupees, was necessary. The rates used are those detailed by M. Edney, *Mapping an Empire: The Geographical Construction of British India, 1765–1843* (Chicago and London, 1997), xvii.

A good part of the archival material used for this book is bound up in large volumes not indexed, in many cases containing several hundred pages. Therefore, wherever possible, I have provided page or folio numbers in the notes to give general orientation and make the identification of particular documents easier. It must be said, however, that the handwritten numbering in some of the original volumes is not consistent, and in a few cases even conflicting. In these cases the numbering that seemed most reasonable has been followed.

The list of the Survey of India records kept on site at the National Archives of India offers simultaneously two systems of reference. As the system termed 'old' seems to be generally more logical, it is followed in the references given in this book. All records could be ordered using this numbering. If necessary, however, 'new' numbers can easily be identified by using the archives' list.

As a general rule, all extracts from original texts have been quoted as exactly as possible and so may include archaic spellings and syntax. However, as the transcription of handwritten archival material was in many instances challenging, some quotes may contain slight changes and modernizations in orthography and punctuation.

ABBREVIATIONS

Actg	Acting
Adj.	Adjutant
Aud.	Auditor
B	Board
CD	Court of Directors
CinC	Commander in Chief
Dep.	Department
DNB	*Dictionary of National Biography*
EIC	East India Company
FSG	Fort St George (Madras)
FW	Fort William (Calcutta)
FWIHC	*Fort William – India House Correspondence*
Gen.	General
Gov.	Government
Mil.	Military
ODNB	*Oxford Dictionary of National Biography*
Pol.	Political
Pub.	Public
Rev.	Revenue
Sec.	Secretary

ACKNOWLEDGEMENTS

The history of this book began as a research project on British surveys in India around the turn of the eighteenth/nineteenth century. My aim was to take a fresh look at them, focussing not only on the cartographical activities but also on the many small-scale projects of knowledge production investigating objects such as natural history, social realities, archaeology or history. The deeper I went into the topic, and especially after a research trip to the National Archives of India, however, I became convinced of Colin Mackenzie's overwhelming influence on the systematization, expansion and institutionalization of such projects. More than that, in their comprehensiveness Mackenzie's surveys united many of the different forms of knowledge production experimented with by the British at that time. So I began to focus on his project, seeking to understand its underlying motives and aims. The rich documentation of his activities found in Scottish, Indian and English archives seemed to make such a focus promising even though the amazing amount of material took its toll in terms of time. The more I found out about Mackenzie's background the more I became convinced that much could be gained from a biographical approach. So this book starts off with the circumstances of his youth in Scotland and, though not intended to be read as a 'classical' biography, follows his life and work until his death in 1821 in a roughly chronological way.

Like every work of this length this book has benefitted from the support of many persons and institutions. I have to thank the Ludwig-Maximilian-University (LMU) in Munich for supporting early research through a grant. I am grateful to both the German Historical Institute London (GHIL) that made possible a first four-month research trip to England and to the German Academic Exchange Service that provided scholarships for a one-year research visit at SOAS and archival research in India. The friendly staff of the Delhi Branch of Heidelberg University's South Asia Institute helped me to organize that trip.

Archival research in India, England and Scotland was a pleasure. I would particularly like to thank the helpful staff of the National Archives of India and it was exciting to work in the scholarly atmosphere of Scotland's National Library. The professionalism and kindness of staff in both the National Archives of Scotland and the British Library should also be mentioned. Mr Weatherly Stephan of the New York Public Library gave me access to documents from the

Alexander Johnston collection in electronic form. And I should not forget to include in my thanks the many other archive and library employees, many of them unknown to me, who had to handle my requests.

Professor Eckhart Hellmuth at the LMU supported the project from its beginning. I have profited not only from his personal advice but also from his research seminar that offered a stimulating atmosphere where ideas, theories and historiographical work could be freely discussed. At SOAS Professor Peter Robb was truly generous in sharing his extensive knowledge and also in giving me advice on the project at a critical period. Professor Nicholas Phillipson discussed the project with me during my stay in Edinburgh and gave me much insight into the worlds of the Scottish Enlightenment. I also want to thank the GHIL for making this publication possible. I should particularly mention here the Institute's director, Professor Andreas Gestrich, Dr Michael Schaich and Dr Markus Mößlang. And of course I am especially grateful to the translator of this book, Jane Rafferty, not least for thinking up the title.

My friends Dr Mathias Wallner and Manuele Deho read earlier drafts of many of the chapters and made helpful suggestions. My parents supported the project throughout but above all in more critical times, which I will never forget. Finally I want to thank Lucia and Kristin, my loved ones. Lucia, my sunshine, was sometimes astonishingly patient in accepting her father being occupied. Kristin not only accompanied this project from the beginning but also read drafts of all chapters: her encouragement and critical attendance through the years proved to be invaluable for this book. Thank you!

INTRODUCTION

Mary Mackenzie's funeral in Stornoway in the Outer Hebrides was, as later reported, 'one of the last of the great funerals of the old style … a relic of the olden days' in Scotland.[1] Shortly after the old lady's death a wake was held where the mourners refreshed themselves from a cask of Madeira wine. The house remained brightly lit throughout the night and then, on the following day, a long procession made its way to the cemetery outside the town of Stornoway. Without any great ceremony the coffin was lowered into a prepared grave, and then the real festivities began, in a tent put up a few metres from the graveyard for which, according to reports, cartloads of food and drink had been brought in. After some short prayers and a sumptuous meal the 120 or so guests then got stuck in to the whiskey and wine, and the wake soon turned into such debauchery that the clergy decided to go home as quickly as possible. More and more people now poured into the tent to take part in the festivities and the shindig took on such proportions that it only came to an end when the participants ran out of steam. Many of the guests just lay down where they were, while one of them even had to be taken back into town on Mary's own bier.[2]

When she died, in 1827, at the age of seventy-nine[3] Mary Mackenzie was not only by far the richest inhabitant of Stornoway but also one of the most popular, known especially for her generosity. During her last years she had repeatedly given large sums of money to charity and, under the terms of her will, a foundation was set up for the poor of the town and a further bequest supported a girls' school. What is more, she left about a hundred of her fellow townspeople sums of between twenty and fifty pounds, thus establishing a reputation as a benefactor of the town of Stornoway.[4] She was not, however, born with a silver spoon in her mouth; on the contrary, she had grown up in an impoverished and highly indebted family which barely had the means to give her an adequate education. It was not until the 1790s, when she started

Notes from this chapter begin on page 16.

to receive regular transfers of money from her brother Colin, in India, that her situation substantially improved, and it was his legacy that in 1821 made her a rich woman.[5]

Although a monument to Colin Mackenzie was erected next to his sister's grave, he is not remembered so much for his beneficence to Stornoway as for what he did as a scientist and officer in the East India Company (EIC). He is known in particular for his massive collection of manuscripts, copies of inscriptions and other material in various Indian languages and alphabets that he put together during the last twenty-five years or so of his life, and which is regarded to this day as one of the most important collections on the precolonial history and culture of South India.[6] At the time of his death his Scottish roots were, of course, not quite forgotten: 'the Highland may justly consider him', one of his obituaries pointed out, 'one of their brightest Ornaments, for to the Qualities of a gallant soldier and Gentleman, he united the attainments of a man of profound science'.[7] Memories of Colin Mackenzie are marked above all, however, by the importance and uniqueness of his collection, and he himself would certainly have agreed with the remarks made about his life's achievements by his friend John Seely a few years after his death: Mackenzie, said Seely, had been a 'victim to science'. It was, according to Seely, to men like him, who alongside their often numerous public duties and sacrificing their own personal interests had dedicated themselves to research, that the British owed virtually all their knowledge of India.[8]

A portrait by the Irish artist Thomas Hickey, painted in Madras in 1816, (Figure 0.1) shows how Mackenzie himself wanted to be remembered.[9] At the time it was painted Colin Mackenzie was at the zenith of his career. A year earlier he had been appointed as the first Surveyor General for the whole of India and, after almost twenty-five years' service in the EIC's army, had been promoted to lieutenant colonel and was one of the first of its officers to be appointed to the Order of the Bath.[10] The painting shows Mackenzie as a confident British officer who, although leaning comfortably on a cane, does not look his age of about sixty-three. What is particularly interesting, however, is the background and the people surrounding him, whose depiction in the portrait can certainly be seen as a programmatic statement on Mackenzie's life's work. The three Indians surrounding Mackenzie can be identified as long-standing co-workers who played an essential part in his research projects.[11] On the left-hand side of the picture is the 75-year-old Dharmaiah, a Jain and expert in ancient languages whom Mackenzie had described as an 'old man worthy of veneration'; behind him is Kavali Venkata Lakshmayya, Mackenzie's chief interpreter and friend – to him he later left part of his fortune; and finally, to the right of him, his *harkara* Kistnaji, who by this time had already worked for him for seventeen years.[12] As *harkara*, or specialist in geographical issues, Kistnaji is holding a telescope, a reference to Mackenzie's cartographical work,

Figure 0.1 Thomas Hickey, Colin Mackenzie, 1816.
Source: © The British Library Board.

while the object in Dharmaiah's hand must represent a rolled palm-leaf manuscript, referring to his literary activity. Finally, in the background is the holy Jain site of Sravana Belgula in Mysore, with the seventeen-metre high statue of Bahubali, symbol of the discovery of the Jain religion, which Mackenzie considered to be one of his greatest achievements.[13]

In his later years Mackenzie increasingly came to regard his contribution to research on Indian geography, culture and history as his life's most important achievement. He himself contributed to the construction of a myth that depicts his life as geared to one single goal – entirely in the sense of a 'biographical illusion' as delineated by Bourdieu, who sees behind every autobiography the writer's desire to give their life meaning. In this process the person's life is described as a series of necessary steps that are as coherent as possible.[14] 'We do not *live* stories,' Hayden White once wrote in his deep insight into the narrative structures of historiography, 'even if we give our lives meaning by retrospectively casting them in the form of stories'.[15] The story of his life that Mackenzie told in the years before his death was that of a selfless researcher whose life's work was discovering and collecting Indian history, culture and geography. So the only autobiographical retrospective he ever wrote is primarily a look back at the history of his collection. His life before he arrived in India, in 1783, is only mentioned in a few subordinate sentences; and his first thirteen years on the subcontinent, which were of little importance for this collection and are described only in passing, seem to represent a period of almost inexcusable failures.[16]

Even though initially written as a private letter to his friend Alexander Johnston, just a few years after his death this autobiographical report became a kind of 'official' version of his life. Johnston published it for the first time in 1822 as a sort of obituary for his friend and, as it was reprinted in a number of respected periodicals in the following years, it influenced the public image of Mackenzie more than any other obituary.[17] This was not, of course, by any means Alexander Johnston's only contribution to the 'biographical illusion', which is what memory of Mackenzie's life increasingly became. In a parliamentary hearing in which Johnston, as co-founder and vice president of the Royal Asiatic Society, sought public funds in order to carry on Mackenzie's research, he set up another central building block of his story by declaring that his friend went to India exclusively because of his orientalist interests. In Britain, Johnston declared, he had already begun to research into Hindu culture and his employment in the EIC was therefore just a logical step towards further research.[18]

This new detail, not added until more than ten years after Mackenzie's death, was now published as well – in versions not entirely free of contradiction but reprinted in learned books and journals;[19] the most accessible to the British public however was the popular *Saturday Magazine,* which also

Figure 0.2 Title page of the *Saturday Magazine*, 28 June 1834.
Source: Universitätsbibliothek Tübingen

carried a print of Hickey's painting on the title page (Figure 0.2).[20] By the time Mackenzie's assumed early interest in Asia was included in the *Dictionary of National Biography* in the 1890s, it had become an established component of his biography.[21]

The problem with this image of Mackenzie's life as a series of logical steps solely directed towards his great project of research on India is not that he did not devote a large part of his life to extensive research work, but the persuasive power that this narrative gains from its inner logic has distorted the view of many other aspects of Mackenzie's life, which are made to seem fairly incidental or insignificant. For instance, the fact that in his youth Mackenzie was denied any formal higher education for financial reasons, and only acquired the means that were later to make his sister the richest woman in Stornoway during his career in India, has hardly attracted any attention. Indeed his connections with Scotland, on a social and intellectual level, have hardly been dealt with at all even though, in my view, they were of great importance for his work in India.

Above all, however – and this is not without a certain irony – Johnston's narrative often led to a distorted view of Mackenzie's scientific project itself by implying a pretty clear dividing line between public duties and private interest in his research on Indian culture and history. From this perspective his activity for the EIC becomes merely a means of achieving goals that had been set long before and at the same time, paradoxically, a permanent obstacle to achieving them because of the time and energy it took up. Robbed of any agenda other than personal curiosity and fascination, Mackenzie mainly appears to be an obsessive collector, driven by an 'almost demonic urge to reveal to the West the history of South India'.[22] This book will show that Mackenzie's project would have been inconceivable without his own initiative, great personal commitment and even a degree of obsession – but this does not mean that it should be seen in isolation from his personal ambitions within the Company or his other responsibilities as a surveyor.

'The dead', as Thomas Trautmann puts it, 'have no rights over the narratives they appear in'.[23] Still, the aim of this book cannot be simply to replace a 'biographical illusion' by a version of Mackenzie's life for which there is more evidence. A biographical narrative inevitably creates a certain coherence – but it can also discuss the breaks and turns, as well as the historical constellations, that are what make Mackenzie's long career in the EIC and the part he played in forging the colonial state comprehensible in the first place. The biographical approach here is not intended to produce a psychologizing description of a life but rather to shed light on the personal experiences and intellectual influences that lay behind Mackenzie's activities. This seems to be particularly useful because, in the EIC's transitional phase on the path to becoming a state administrative apparatus, ambitious climbers had great influence on shaping certain areas of the administration. So concentrating on a man who, from humble origins rose, during a career of forty years in India, to become head of a central administrative department, is ideally suited to discussing certain key questions surrounding the genesis of colonial statehood.

This book's protagonist is certainly not unknown to historians of South and Southeast Asia. It profits from a number of earlier works dealing with individual aspects of Mackenzie's career. As India's first Surveyor General he received considerable coverage in historiography on British surveying projects in India, foremost among them Reginald Henry Phillimore's profound, multi-volume *Historical Records of the Survey of India* and Matthew Edney's *Mapping an Empire*.[24] His activities on Java, where he played an important role during the British occupation from 1811 to 1813, were dealt with in detail by John Sturgus Bastin around the middle of the last century.[25] David M. Blake, Bernard S. Cohn and Nicholas Dirks have made valuable contributions on the origins of his collection,[26] while Peter Robb in his important essay on the Mysore Survey has emphasized Mackenzie's pioneering achievements in terms of how knowledge is produced for the state.[27] Phillip Wagoner examines in even more detail Cohn's and Dirks' central theses about the forms of cooperation between Indians and Europeans in the context of epigraphical research under Mackenzie's leadership,[28] while Jennifer Howes has examined the rich visual material produced by Mackenzie and his co-workers during his forty years in India.[29] A collection of essays edited by Thomas Trautmann deals with the connections between Mackenzie's collection and the Madras School of Orientalism.[30] Finally, Rama Mantena has looked at the accumulation of Mackenzie's collection as one of the starting points for 'modern historiography' in India.[31]

The only specifically biographical work on Mackenzie, however, is much older and was written by a Scottish local historian, William Cook Mackenzie.[32] This work is not without its problems since the author gets many of the details wrong.[33] What is even more difficult for the academic reader, however, is the author's claim to have written a 'popular biography',[34] which means that the main themes it deals with are those that would appeal to a broad contemporary public. Mackenzie's war experiences, for instance, are dealt with in epic proportions while the broader context of his career is barely mentioned. What is more, this work deals with roughly the first thirty years of Colin Mackenzie's life, which he spent in Britain, on just a few pages, borrowing heavily from Alexander Johnston's account.

Robb's article on the Mysore Survey makes a more valuable contribution to an understanding of Mackenzie's career even if it concentrates on the years after the institution of the Mysore Survey in 1799. Robb paints a picture of a man who, driven less by personal ambition than by a deep conviction that his project made sense, overcomes all obstacles and realizes his vision of the survey as an instrument of the state. Of abiding importance in Robb's view are, firstly, the connection his project established between knowledge production for the state and the government's objectives and, secondly, the restructuring of the territory on the basis of supposedly 'objective' and 'universal', yet ultimately European, criteria.[35] Robb's ideas about the importance of the survey for the state are the key starting point for my view of the project, even if my interpretation differs in some respects, for instance regarding the question of Mackenzie's personal ambitions or the significance of abstract criteria in relation to his cultural sensitivity for his project.

The focus of most recent publications is on Mackenzie's impressive collection of documents on and artefacts of Indian history and culture. In particular, recent authors have subjected Dirks' older view, namely of Mackenzie as a sort of solitary, virtually quixotic fighter trying to assert his vision of historical research on India against an obstructive colonial apparatus,[36] to fundamental revision. Wagoner was the first to point out the manifold connections between Mackenzie's project and the Orientalist School of Madras,[37] and in the meantime it seems clear that Mackenzie's project should certainly not be looked at in isolation but against the backdrop of his multifarious relations with orientalists in various parts of India.[38]

At the same time, dealing in more detail with Mackenzie's co-workers – it was undoubtedly a valuable achievement by Cohn and Dirks to have emphasized their key role for the first time – has led to a reassessment of their importance; they were far more than passive informants and made an intellectual contribution of their own. Wagoner emphasized their active role in developing a methodology for historical epigraphy in India,[39] while more recent works look at their intellectual activities in Madras after Mackenzie's death, in 1821.[40] All in all recent research conveys an image of Mackenzie's collection that depicts it as an independent part of a broader collective research project on India's history and culture that was carried along by various European orientalists but was based on cooperation with Indian intellectuals to a degree that should not be understated. Furthermore, it is becoming increasingly apparent that his collection was by no means a 'beached whale' without any great consequences but a valuable source that had a lasting effect on the development of historiography, archaeology and philology in South India.[41]

Focussing on the collection leads, quite understandably, to an image of a project in which Mackenzie's main aim was to acquire material. Howes, for instance, argues that Mackenzie collected 'raw material' that he wanted to make available to orientalists and the British public for further assessment.[42] Mantena gives fascinating insights into how Mackenzie's cooperation with his Indian co-workers led to new historical methods, but in her narrative Mackenzie also sometimes appears as a 'colonial antiquarian' in the tradition of European antiquarianism: 'The antiquarian is by definition excessive; he collects for the sake of collecting and is driven by the belief that various sources of knowledge would contribute to a better understanding of the past'. In marked contrast to the historian who profits from his work, the antiquarian however is much more interested in 'the particularity of the object itself' than in developing a 'general historical narrative'.[43]

In situating Mackenzie's collection within the context of contemporary European amateur antiquarianism, Mantena offers a valuable perspective for a better understanding of his project, and it would be tempting to take this perspective as the basis for a biographical narrative. It would be the story of a man who, from fairly humble origins, lacked the classical education and thus the philological knowledge on which to base orientalist research, but who, since he did develop an interest in such research, and furthermore yearned for the reputation connected with it, decided to serve the project of researching India in a different way. In this version he uses his extremely advantageous position as a surveyor who not only travels extensively in the country but also has a large number of co-workers available to him in the various regions of India to collect material that will not only be given to others for further assessment but that will also guarantee Mackenzie himself a place amongst the learned elite of the British in India. What then developed over the years would be a passionate chase after manuscripts and artefacts that make him into the prototype of the 'colonial antiquarian' who increasingly sees his collection as an end in itself.

Although such a narrative would contain pertinent and quite accurate explanations for the motives behind Mackenzie's collection – his interest in Indian culture and history, his desire to acquire 'cultural capital',[44] and finally the documentary impetus behind his activities – it does not really do the project justice, especially given the value that Mackenzie himself attached to it. He stressed, for instance, that his investigations should not be misunderstood as 'dry investigations into remote & obscure periods of antiquity of Legend & of Fable', but should be regarded as 'procuring authentic information of the condition & sentiments of Millions of subjects'. Of his research into the Jains in South India, who had ruled a large part of the area 'under a spirit of administration not unfriendly to the comforts of the people', he says that it was a 'subject of interest superior certainly to mere antiquarian Research to which however I have not been indifferent'.[45] Such statements suggest that Mackenzie's antiquarianism was by no means an end in itself.

One of this book's central arguments is that Mackenzie's surveys – including his collection – should be seen as an integrated project that was in line with his view of what British rule should be like, and was based on a comprehensive vision of the connections between past, present and future. Mackenzie certainly did not bring with him to Madras a 'ready-made' project for documenting Indian history; nor can this vision be considered as the 'starting point' for his activities there. For most of the nearly thirty years that Mackenzie spent, with short breaks, in the Outer Hebrides in Northern Scotland a career in India was nowhere in sight. I will argue, however, that this period nonetheless represents an important background for deeper understanding of his activities in India. This is particularly true since it was here that Mackenzie was able to see at first hand the consequences of radical modernization, connected with an attack on Gaelic culture, which led to some appalling social consequences. This space of experience, one could argue, in an individualizing (and quite possibly also trivializing) version of Reinhart Koselleck's view, structured his horizon of expectation,[46] specifically as regards his ideas about a good government for India.

Emphasis on Mackenzie's Scottish background links this book with a number of works that look at the specifically Scottish contribution to building the Empire.[47] However, such works – the most important for India are by Martha P. McLaren and Jane Rendall – mainly concentrate on the intellectual influences of the Scottish Enlightenment and the curricula at Scottish universities in whose orbit their protagonist moved during certain phases of his life.[48] Mackenzie, however, came from relatively humble origins in the Highlands, never went to university and spent most of his time in Britain far from the cultural and economic metropolises. So looking at his biography presents a new perspective in this respect as well, and leads to focussing less on the theoretical drafts of the Scottish Enlightenment than on the actual experiences concomitant with the modernization of Scotland in the eighteenth century.

Ironically, from a biographical perspective Mackenzie's career loses much of its aura of uniqueness. In some respects it can be regarded as typical of the EIC's transition from trading company to colonial administrative apparatus. Although he joined the EIC comparatively late, at the age of almost thirty, the motives and ambitions, difficulties and setbacks connected with his career in India were the same as those experienced by many of his contemporaries. Like so many others, he had to find his way through the jungle of relationships and patronage and look for a niche within the apparatus that would make personal advancement possible without London's support; and like the majority of the Company's employees he too regarded India primarily as a chance to improve his financial position. It was not until five years after his arrival that, in search of promotion, he started to establish himself as a surveyor, and it was another seven years before he began to develop the concept of a detailed survey, and thus also of his collection, along with his friend Kavali Venkata Borayya. The image of an almost obsessive researcher who subordinated all other personal interests and ambitions almost exclusively to his scientific life's work applies, if at all, only to the last third of his life.

The period between about 1780 and 1840, into which Mackenzie's Indian career fell, can be considered as a phase of 'colonial transition'.[49] During this time the EIC – due to its spectacular military successes especially in South and Central India and subsidiarity treaties with many nominally still independent states[50] – emerged as the undisputed leading power on the subcontinent. At the same time not only did the Company's apparatus become more closely tied to the British state, but also attempts were made to control the corruption amongst its employees, increasingly regarded as problematic, through a series of internal reforms, and to set up a more efficient administrative system. A number of measures were taken to regulate the conquered territories internally. Since the time of Warren Hastings, attempts had been made to establish a regular legal system, and the Permanent Settlement in Bengal sought to settle the key issue of revenue on a lasting basis.[51] As corporate bearer of sovereignty rights, even before 1757 the Company was not totally unprepared for its new role as an administrative apparatus,[52] but there is no denying that the internal expansion of the emerging colonial state also represented a phase of experimentation in which there were various competing ideas about what form British rule should take, without any uniform and established colonial ideology to draw on. Both at the ideological level and in practice the position of those in charge oscillated between seeking to maintain precolonial structures and customs and a more far-reaching transformation of the political system and social norms.

At a more abstract level David Scott, along Michel Foucault's lines, has described the transition from the eighteenth-century trading company to the colonial state of the later nineteenth century as a sort of breakthrough from the 'political rationality of mercantilism', designed simply to extend and secure power, to modern 'governmentality'.[53] This was no longer characterized by a direct connection between sovereign and subjects in the form of power and obligation. The 'population' was now increasingly regarded as an object of intervention and tactics were developed for influencing the conditions in which the people moved, in order to influence the social field's own dynamics. This new form of government, he said, implemented in Europe around 1800, found its colonial expression in India with the attempts by liberals and utilitarians at modernization. These, he went on, had conceived of the Indian 'society' as an object of intervention and had aimed to transform it radically by changing its fundamental conditions on the basis of abstract norms, in contrast to earlier 'defensive' and 'conservative' ideas.[54]

Scott's theoretical approach is certainly too schematic to understand the phase of colonial transition in its own right. Even in Foucault's work the dividing line between mercantilism and modern governmentality seems much more fluid, and even in the colonial context the transition from mercantilist to governmental rationality was probably far slower and less rigidly defined than Scott would suggest. These days, for instance, the notion he puts forward, going back to Stokes, of Munro's policy as purely 'conservative' and 'defensive' has rightly been called into question.[55] At the same time, if the militarism of the Company-state is taken as an indicator, the 'mercantilist rationality' of securing and extending rule existed far beyond the break Scott posits. Military fiscalism, understood as aggressively levying revenue to finance the military, and the influence of military elites in all spheres of political and administrative decision making, remained characteristic of most of British rule in India, even if its intensity varied from region to region.[56] And finally, as Gyan Prakash argues, in the colonial context authoritarian and governmental forms of exercising power were never mutually exclusive.[57]

If, like David Scott, we want to regard 'colonial governmentality' as an attempt at a 'systematic redefinition and transformation of the terrain on which the life of the colonized was lived',[58] then little more than embryonic precursors of such aims will be found in the approaches to government during the transitional phase. In fact, many of these approaches point in the opposite direction by seeking continuities and gradual change in harmony with what were supposed to be India's cultural norms. Nonetheless the concept of 'governmentality' does seem well suited to describe certain changes during the transitional phase since new political-administrative perspectives open up here that go beyond an interest simply in retaining power, and within which new government responsibilities were defined. This is precisely where Mackenzie's surveys – starting with the Mysore Survey, where the focus was by no means on military and fiscal interests but on intensive research into India's history, culture and society – should be located. On the one hand they aimed, by producing knowledge for the state, to define the government's objectives – but on the other they established knowledge production itself as a task for the state. The broad support his project enjoyed shows that many of those in charge shared Mackenzie's ideas, but at the same time the enduring opposition he encountered, from the military in particular, is evidence that they were by no means universally accepted.

The conditions that made it possible to carry out this expensive project comprised not only the restructuring of administrative responsibilities in India, but also the emergence of a new relationship between state and science in the decades around the turn of the century. Although there was no state institution for the sciences in Britain, unlike the countries of continental Europe, with their academies, here, too, private scientific initiatives and semi-official establishments such as the Royal Society gained increasing influence over the administration. Joseph Banks played a particularly important role in this. As president of the Royal Society he had been an advisor to various governments and had taken on the role of 'unofficial minister for science'.[59] The great opportunities for science offered by the British Empire were always the focal point of Banks' interest and, via his parliamentary contacts and as an advisor, he exerted considerable influence on the EIC.[60] The British state and the EIC increasingly made funds available for science. During the decades of war between 1760 and 1815 this was initially motivated by neo-mercantilist considerations against the backdrop of international competition, and successes in science were supposed to bring Britain prestige and accelerate its economic growth.[61] In the final years of the century the EIC in particular extended its commitment to science and around 1800 was regarded as one of the most important patrons of scientific projects. As Richard Drayton argues, in keeping with mercantilist logic imperial actors such as the EIC could derive military, economic and also propagandistic advantage by supporting scientific projects: 'Service to the cause of knowledge lent dignity to an enterprise which might have appeared otherwise as mere plunder and rapine'.[62]

This essentially pro-science climate within the EIC not only made the Mysore Survey possible, but also provided an important basis for Mackenzie's successful career as a surveyor. At the same time, however, his surveys demonstrate a new development in the relationship between state and knowledge production which, in the medium term, implied that the colonial state was no longer exclusively interested in narrowly defined projects that would serve its military and economic ends, and no longer took the position of an early modern sovereign – as the patron of individual scientific enterprises. In fact, under Mackenzie's leadership a project for producing knowledge for the state was set up for the first time in India in systematic and increasingly institutionalized form which, due to its breadth of content, was supposed to become the basis of the government's policies.[63] Mackenzie and his co-workers had a major impact on how the project was conceived, in terms of organization and content, and his determination and belief in the value of his surveys played a big part in their success. However, it was a long path from surveying routes for military purposes at the start of his career to becoming Surveyor General with a professional apparatus at his disposal and the ability to investigate huge sections of South India using a uniform system. How this came about can only be understood against the backdrop of the specific historical constellations within which Mackenzie's career ran its course.

Although the emergence of a new understanding of 'government' and the increasing perception of science as a potential instrument of state had many parallels in Britain itself, it is hardly surprising that the first state-funded project of this size, including the administrative structures, was carried out in India. During the nineteenth century the permanent problems arising from lack of knowledge about things Indian continued to produce veritable 'information panics' within the administration,[64] even though since the time of Warren Hastings, if not earlier, various initiatives had been started to overcome these shortcomings, at least in part. Of course, the knowledge produced here went far beyond simply acquiring 'information' since it was the selection, ordering and structuring of the data that gave it any actual significance.[65] It is hardly necessary to mention that Mackenzie's surveys also produced 'orientalist' knowledge, if the very general definition of 'orientalism' as put forward by Breckenridge and van der Veer is accepted: a 'way of conceptualizing the landscape of the colonial world that makes it susceptible to certain kinds of management'.[66]

So this book can also be read as a contribution to the debate on the nature of 'colonial knowledge' that recent researchers have embraced with such intensity,[67] and in which the processes of knowledge production are given attributes ranging from 'epistemological violence' to 'dialogue' and 'conversation'.[68] If it looks at the processes of knowledge production in detail this is not only to emphasize the manifold forms of cooperation, but also to demonstrate the way in which precolonial knowledge formed a basis for the surveys' results, such as maps and statistical descriptions. However, it seems to me to be less important to make a distinction between two fundamentally divergent knowledge systems that arguably even finds expression in concepts such as 'fusion',[69] than to illustrate the basic compatibility of certain attitudes which makes differences seem surmountable and clearly suggests a sphere beyond ideas of 'cultural incommensurability'.[70] This is all the more important since the debate about the nature of 'colonial knowledge' is partly characterized by the image of two integrated, largely homogeneous cultural blocs that come together in the asymmetrical power structure of the colonial situation.[71]

The power relationships in the process of knowledge production were by no means as clear as a perspective of this sort implies, and it is Mackenzie's project that shows the boundaries of the respective knowledge systems to be far more fluid. From the point of view of personnel, Mackenzie's surveys were anything but a purely European project; many were carried out by Indo-European and Indian co-workers. They can be seen as an expression of the specific characteristics of colonial transition in South India, as David Washbrook has described them: the relatively open contact between the diverse ethnic groups; hierarchies that were far less racist than in later phases of British rule in India; and the power basis, by no means solid despite military dominance of the British, who represented a vanishingly small minority compared to that of Bengal.[72]

Placing less emphasis on differences during the phase of transition should not, however, disguise the fact that, around 1800, the EIC's apparatus for rule clearly had colonial structures – the most obvious example is perhaps the fact that Indians were excluded from all high offices.[73] Even in the case of Mackenzie's surveys, putting a non-European in charge would have been inconceivable. Although Washbrook rightly warns against over-simple teleologies when looking at the phase of transition, and against being too quick to apply the attribute 'colonial',[74] there can be no doubt that during this phase, characterized not least by war and violence, the foundations were laid for the colonial state of the later nineteenth century. Nonetheless, a certain caution is called for when describing Mackenzie's project as 'colonial' if this attribute is meant to signify content rather than context. This applies not only because his surveys can be compared with similar projects for mapping and inventorizing territories in Europe itself, but also because the aims and motivations behind this project cannot simply be reduced to the same interests of the colonial state of the later nineteenth century. In fact, during the last years of his life in Calcutta, Mackenzie himself was very sceptical as to whether his superiors understood his project and his ideas about British government in India that were bound up with it.

All the same, Mackenzie's surveys represent an important starting point for the mid-century colonial state, which could benefit not only from their results but also from the administrative structures set up with them. Paradoxically, in some ways Mackenzie's project pointed to something beyond itself: if it created a body of knowledge based on assessment of precolonial archives and collaboration with Indian intellectuals and local administrators, then in consequence it made these strategies for producing knowledge seem less indispensable. The project was supposed to document, not bring about any sort of direct changes – but this documentation did bring change in many ways, for instance by slotting local knowledge into the new contexts of statistical and historical memoirs, or concepts of territorial order into the strict framework of cartographical logic. Mackenzie wanted his surveys to create a body of knowledge that would guarantee continuity between the British and their predecessors and, on this basis, facilitate cautious changes that would improve the population's living conditions in a way that harmonized with their own interests. But at the same time, he created the basis for more stable and more self-assured colonial rule in which, because greater knowledge of India supposedly existed, it was also possible to draw stricter dividing lines between the colonizers and the colonized. In this respect, too, Mackenzie's project embodied the phase of colonial transition.

This book is based on sources from archives in India and Britain. The most important individual collection is the *Survey of India Records* held in New Delhi, containing the correspondence and reports of the Surveyor General's departments in Calcutta, Bombay and Madras; this also provides a good overview of Mackenzie's surveys. Although many of these files are not listed in the collection's published catalogue,[75] there is a sort of transfer list, possibly drawn up when the material was moved from Dehra Dun to New Delhi after Indian independence, and this makes it possible to assess the material systematically. These sources, which are essentially administrative, were supplemented by using the India Office Records in London. Apart from the official correspondence between India and London they also contain numerous copies of documents produced in India. What proved to be particularly useful here was the *Board's Collection* consisting of dossiers on many individual projects put together for the Board of Control.

Along with these files concerning Mackenzie's official activities for the EIC, other material was consulted that provides further information about the circumstances of his career. His collections held in the *Oriental and India Office Collections* were particularly useful. They contain not only translations of Indian manuscripts but also his own, often fragmentary reflections on certain topics;

likewise his private correspondence, held today in various collections, for instance in London and Edinburgh, in the Scottish National Library and Scottish National Archives. The latter also contains valuable holdings covering Mackenzie's youth in Scotland that throw new light on the background to his career in the EIC.

Mackenzie does not make life easy for the historian. His handwriting, often virtually illegible, and his predilection for leaving no square centimetre of paper uncovered, are the least of the problems; they do at least have the positive side effect of making the conditions in which he wrote most of his letters and reports more accessible – writing by candlelight in a tent after a strenuous day's work somewhere in South India, I imagine, and always with the threat that the paper supply might run out. Another difficulty is Mackenzie's habit of writing copious official reports, some over a hundred pages long, detailing the occurrences of just a few weeks of survey. Many of them are highly repetitive, and contain information that could have been summed up on just a few pages. The reader does not fare much better with his correspondence. His letters are overlong and, as the popular biographer W.C. Mackenzie complained: 'The real trouble is the absence of private as distinct from official or semi-official that the reader of biographies demands above all others'.[76] And Nicholas Dirks is quite right in characterizing his official correspondence as 'voluminous, detailed and dry'.[77]

Still, although it is not easy to gain access to Mackenzie's thinking on the basis of individual manuscripts, taken together they do provide a fount of historical information, especially on his surveys, the like of which exists for no other contemporary British project in India. Furthermore, the very fact that Mackenzie's official correspondence exists at all, due to his insistence on correct filing and archiving, points to his extraordinary bureaucratic abilities and the great attention he paid to the transparency of certain administrative processes. On closer inspection his massive reports that official committees had to deal with turn out to be a sharp weapon in the bureaucratic battle for certain objectives. There can be little doubt that he was disinclined to commit theoretical reflections to paper, but this does not mean that it is impossible to reconstruct certain key elements of his thinking from his writing. And finally, his letters and memoranda are by no means as devoid of content as a superficial inspection might suggest; on the contrary, studying them in greater detail also reveals the contribution to the project of a detailed survey made by those whose voices have long been thought to be lost.

Notes

1. E. McIver, *Memoirs of a Highland Gentleman Being the Reminiscences of Evander McIver of Scourie*, ed. George Henderson (Edinburgh, 1905), 200.

2. Cf. J. Shore, Lord Teignmouth, *Sketches of the Coasts and Islands of Scotland and of the Isle of Man: Descriptive of the Scenery of Those Regions*, 2 vols (London, 1836), vol. 1, 182–87; and id., *Reminiscences of Many Years*, 2 vols (Edinburgh, 1878), vol. 1, 347–50; McIver, *Memoirs of a Highland Gentleman*, 199f.

3. Mary Mackenzie died on 2 September 1827. Cf. the death notice: 'Deaths', *Blackwood's Edinburgh Magazine* 22(133) (December 1827), 768.

4. Cf. *The New Statistical Account of Scotland, by the Minsters of the Respective Parishes, under the Superintendence of a Committee of the Society for the Benefit of the Sons and Daughters of the Clergy*, 15 vols (Edinburgh, 1845), vol. 14, 125; McIver, *Memoirs of a Highland Gentleman*, 199f.

5. Her inheritance is estimated by various sources to have been thirty thousand pounds. Colin Mackenzie had left her a little under half his estate, but calculating the amount she received was complicated by the fact that he made various different wills, the last of which was incomplete. Cf. versions of the will in BL/IOR/L/AG/34/29/33, 249–53; Mary Mackenzie to Mrs. S. Mackenzie of Seaforth, 24 June 1822, NAS/GD/46/15/25; *New Statistical Account*, vol. 14, 125; McIver, *Memoirs of a Highland Gentleman*, 198f.

6. The only catalogue of the whole collection, albeit with gaps, is by H.H. Wilson, *A Descriptive Catalogue of the Oriental Manuscripts and Other Articles Illustrative of the Literature, History, Statistics and Antiquities of the South of India, Collected by the Late Lieut.-Col. Colin Mackenzie, Surveyor General of India*, 2 vols (Calcutta, 1828).

7. 'Colonel C. Mackenzie', *New Monthly Magazine and Literary Journal* 3(12) (December 1821), 642. Other obituaries were published in the *Gentleman's Magazine* and the *Asiatic Journal*. The first is a very short description of his career as officer and scientist while the second mainly discusses his publications. 'Col. Colin Mackenzie', *Gentleman's Magazine* 91(2) (October 1821), 378; 'Biographical Memoir of Colonel Mackenzie, C.B., Late Surveyor General of India', *Asiatic Journal and Monthly Register for British India and its Dependencies* 12(72) (December 1821), 537–40.

8. J.B. Seely, *The Wonders of Elora, or The Narrative of a Journey to the Temples and Dwellings Excavated out of a Mountain of Granite and Extending Upwards of a Mile and a Quarter*, 2nd extended edn. (London, 1825), 226.

9. For Thomas Hickey see M. Archer, *India and British Portraiture, 1770–1825* (London, 1979), 205–33.

10. Cf. 'The Late Colin Mackenzie C.B', *The East India Military Calendar Containing the Services of General and Field Officers of the Indian Army. By the Editor of the Royal Military Calendar* 3 (1826), 311. The medal itself is not in the portrait.

11. The painting has often been discussed. See for example M. Edney, *Mapping an Empire: The Geographical Construction of British India, 1765–1843* (Chicago and London, 1997), 154; S. Jaireth, 'Close Encounters of the Colonial Kind or Looking for Colin Mackenzie's Pandits', *Social Alternatives* 20(4) (2001), 55–60; Archer, India and British Portraiture, 232f.

12. Cf. Colin Mackenzie, 'General Report on the State of the Surveying Department at Fort St. George and Draft reports of Progress for 1817', NAI/SIR/REP/3, Appendix 3 (1 August 1816), 37–76, here 73; 'Detailed List of the Establishment attached to the Superintendant of the Mysore Survey for the Month ending 30th April 1809 per Order of Government of 28th February 1809', NAI/SIR/SGO/90A, 213.

13. Mackenzie dealt extensively with the history of Sravana Belgula and published some of his material. Hickey possibly used an illustration from Mackenzie's collection as a model. See Kavali Venkata Borayya and C. Mackenzie, 'Account of the Jains: Collected from a Priest of this Sect; at Mudgeri. Translated by Cavelly Boria, Brahmen, for Major Mackenzie', *Asiatic Researches* 9 (1809), 244–86, esp. 262–65; John Newman, *N. view of the hill of Sravana*

Belgola (Mysore), with statue of Gommatesvara. 17 August 1806. Copied by Newman in 1816 from an original sketch by Benjamin Swain Ward taken in 1806, BL/OIOC/WD/576.

14. P. Bourdieu, 'Die biographische Illusion', in id., *Praktische Vernunft: Zur Theorie des Handelns* (Frankfurt/Main, 1988), 75–83, here esp. 76f.

15. H. White, 'The Historical Text as Literary Artifact', in id., *Tropics of Discourse. Essays in Cultural Criticism* (Baltimore and London, 1986), 90. Emphasis in the original.

16. Published by Alexander Johnston in connection with a description of his collection written by Mackenzie himself: 'Statement of the Literary Labours of the Late Colin Mackenzie, C.B. (Originally Communicated to the Asiatic Journal)', *Asiatic Journal or Monthly Register for British India and its Dependencies* 13(75) (March 1822), 242–49; and 13(76) (April 1822), 313–25. Of the first thirteen years Mackenzie wrote here (13(75), 243): 'on the whole of this period ... I look back with regret; for objects are now known to exist that could have been then examined; and to traits of customs and of institutions that could have been explained, had time or means admitted of the inquiry'.

17. Ibid. Reprinted twice in a slightly edited version: 'Biographical Sketch of the Literary Career of the Late Colonel Colin Mackenzie, Surveyor General of India; Comprising Some Particulars of his Collection of Manuscripts, Plans, Coins, Drawings, Sculptures &c. Illustrative of the Antiquities, History, Geography, Laws, Institutions, and Manners of the Ancient Hindus; Contained in a Letter Addressed by Him to the Right Honourable Sir Alexander Johnston V.P.R.A.S &c. &c.', *Journal of the Royal Asiatic Society of Great Britain and Ireland* 1(2) (1834), 333–64; and *Madras Journal of Literature and Science* 2(8) (1835), 262–90 and 2(9) (1835), 354–69. An abridged version is already to be found in 'The Late Colin Mackenzie C.B', 311–31. Wilson quotes the letter extensively in the introduction to his catalogue, as does a later catalogue of the part of the collection brought to Madras. Wilson, *Descriptive Catalogue of the Oriental Manuscripts*, vol. 1, ii–xvi; see, also, W. Taylor, *Catalogue Raisonnée of Oriental Manuscripts in the Library of the (Late) College, Fort St. George, Now in Charge of the Board of Examiners*, 3 vols (Madras, 1857–62), vol. 1, iii–ix.

18. See A. Johnston, 'Statement by Alexander Johnston, 19 July 1832', in *Minutes of Evidence Taken before the Select Committee on the Affairs of the East India Company and Also an Appendix and Index*, 6 vols [London, 1832], vol. 1: Public, 254–57, para. 1930. In his autobiographical letter, as edited by Johnston, Mackenzie does indeed mention that he was interested in Indian culture before his departure from Britain but does not claim this to be the reason for his entering the EIC. Cf. 'Of the Literary Labours of the Late Colin Mackenzie', 242.

19. Johnston's statement was reprinted in full: 'Copy of Sir Alexander Johnston's Evidence Relating to the Mackenzie Collection', *Journal of the Royal Asiatic Society of Great Britain and Ireland* 2(2) (1835), xxx–xxxiii. In this statement he dates Mackenzie's plan for his collection to his (wrongly dated) visit to Madura in 1783, but in the same volume of the journals he gives the date for this as 1796, which is what Mackenzie himself stated. Cf. Johnston's contribution at the society's meeting: 'Proceedings of the Anniversary Meeting of the Royal Asiatic Society Held on Saturday, the 9th of May 1835', ibid., ix–xvii. See also M. Napier, *Memoirs of John Napier of Merchiston, his Lineage, Life, and Times, with a History of the Invention of Logarithms* (Edinburgh and London, 1834), vi–vii; Taylor, *Catalogue Raisonnée*, i–iii. See also the reprinted excerpts of Johnston's statement in 'The East Indies', *London Literary Gazette or Journal of Belles Lettres, Arts, Sciences &c.* 817 (15 September 1832), 586–88. The fact that Johnston's narrative was reprinted in academic journals meant that it also reached an international readership, for instance in C. Ritter, *Erdkunde von Asien*, vol. IV, I, Section 2 (Berlin, 1836), 422–24.

20. 'Importance of British India to the Merchants and Manufacturers of Great Britain', *Saturday Magazine* 127 (28 June 1834), 241–43. The engraving under the title 'Colonel Mackenzie and the Brahmins' was modelled on a drawing privately owned by Johnston. The *Saturday*

Magazine, published weekly by the Society for the Propagation of Christian Knowledge, between 1832 and 1844, was one of the first cheap widely distributed magazines of the nineteenth century that tried to popularize the sciences from a distinctly Christian point of view. Cf. A. Fyfe, *Science and Salvation: Evangelical Popular Science Publishing in Victorian Britain* (Chicago and London, 2004), 48–50, 63.

21. H.M. C[hichester], 'Mackenzie, Colin (1753?–1821)', *DNB*.
22. B.S. Cohn, 'The Transformation of Objects into Artifacts, Antiquities and Art in Nineteenth-Century India', in id., *Colonialism and its Forms of Knowledge: The British in India* (Oxford, 1996), 88.
23. T.R. Trautmann, *Aryans and British India* (Berkeley, Los Angeles and London, 1997), 40. Trautmann is referring to his reassessment of William Jones' role in the history of linguistics.
24. R.H. Phillimore, *Historical Records of the Survey of India*, 4 vols, (Dehra Dun, 1949–58); Edney, *Mapping an Empire*. See also I.J. Barrow, *Making History, Drawing Territory: British Mapping in India, c. 1756–1905* (New Delhi, 2003), 76–80, 88f; C.R. Markham, *A Memoir on the Indian Surveys*, 2nd edn. (London, 1878), 73f, 80; T.B. Jervis, 'Memoir on the Origin, Progress, and Present State of the Surveys in India', *Journal of the Royal Geographical Society of London* 7 (1837), 138f.
25. J.S. Bastin, *Raffles' Ideas on the Land Rent System in Java and the Mackenzie Land Tenure Commission* (Verhandelingen van het Koninklijk Instituut voor Taal-, Land- en Volkenkunde, vol. 14) (s-Gravenhage, 1954).
26. Cohn, 'Transformation of Objects into Artifacts'; N.B. Dirks, 'Colonial Histories and Native Informants: Biography of an Archive', in C.A. Breckenridge and P. van der Veer (eds), *Orientalism and the Postcolonial Predicament. Perspectives on South Asia* (Philadelphia, 1993), 211–32; id., 'Guiltless Spoliations: Picturesque Beauty, Colonial Knowledge and Colin Mackenzie's Survey of India', in C.B. Asher and T.R. Metcalf (eds), *Perceptions of South Asia's Visual Past* (New Delhi, 1994), 279–313; id., *Castes of Mind: Colonialism and the Making of Modern India* (Princeton and Oxford, 2001); D.M. Blake, 'Colin Mackenzie: Collector Extraordinary', *British Library Journal* 17(2) (1991), 128–50.
27. P. Robb, 'Completing "Our Stock of Geography" or an Object "Still More Sublime". Colin Mackenzie's Survey of Mysore', *Journal of the Royal Asiatic Society* 8(2) (1998), 181–206.
28. P.B. Wagoner, 'Precolonial Intellectuals and the Production of Colonial Knowledge', *Comparative Studies in Society and History* 45(4) (2003), 783–814.
29. J. Howes, *Illustrating India: The Early Colonial Investigations of Colin Mackenzie 1784–1821* (Oxford, 2010). See also J. Howes, 'Colin Mackenzie and the Stupa of Amaravati', *South Asian Studies* 18 (2002), 53–65.
30. T.R. Trautmann (ed.), *The Madras School of Orientalism: Producing Knowledge in Colonial South India* (Oxford and New York, 2009). See also id., *Languages and Nations: The Dravidian Proof in Colonial Madras* (New Delhi, 2003).
31. R.S. Mantena, *The Origins of Modern Historiography in India: Antiquarianism and Philology, 1780–1880* (Palgrave Studies in Cultural and Intellectual History) (New York, 2012).
32. W.C. Mackenzie, *Colonel Colin Mackenzie: First Surveyor-General of India* (Edinburgh and London, 1952). W.C. Mackenzie died before it was published so the town of Stornoway took it over. Cf. A. MacLeod to Reginald Henry Phillimore, 12 June 1953, BL/OIR/354.54.
33. For example, he reported – probably following a mistake in the index to Mark Wilks' history of Mysore – on a work by Mackenzie on the Third Mysore War unknown to him, but which was actually by Roderick Mackenzie; and a piece that he discusses as Mackenzie's concluding report on his tasks in Java is, according to Bastin, a document with which a Dutchman answered a query from Mackenzie. See Mackenzie, *Colonel Colin Mackenzie*, 209; M. Wilks, *Historical Sketches of the South of India in an Attempt to Trace the History of Mysore*, 3 vols, (London, 1810–1817), vol. 3, 525; R. Mackenzie, *A Sketch of the War with Tippoo Sultaun;*

or, a Detail of Military Operations, from ... 1789, until the Peace ... in February 1792, 2 vols (Calcutta, 1793–1794); J.S. Bastin, 'Colonel Colin Mackenzie and Javanese Antiquities', *Bijdragen tot de Taal-, Land en Volkenkunde* 109 (1953), 273–75.

34. William Cook Mackenzie to Reginald Henry Phillimore, 29 April 1940, BL/OIR/354.54.
35. Robb, 'Completing "Our Stock of Geography"', 192, 198–206.
36. See, however, Dirks' own relativization of this position: N.B. Dirks, 'Colin Mackenzie: Autobiography of an Archive', in Trautmann, *Madras School of Orientalism*, 29–47.
37. Wagoner, 'Precolonial Intellectuals', 799–804.
38. For the manifold influence of Mackenzie's collection on the work of Indian intellectuals and European orientalists see the essays in Trautmann, *Madras School of Orientalism*; for connections with individual orientalists also Howes, *Illustrating India*, Chapter 2.
39. Wagoner, 'Precolonial Intellectuals', 788f, 810f.
40. See esp. L. Mitchell, 'Knowing the Deccan: Enquiries, Points, and Poets in the Construction of Knowledge and Power in Early-Nineteenth-Century South India', in Trautmann, *Madras School of Orientalism*, 151–82; R.S. Mantena, 'The Kavali Brothers. Intellectual Life in Early Colonial Madras', ibid., 126–50; ead., *Origins of Modern Historiography*, Chapter 3.
41. T.R. Trautmann, 'Introduction', in id., *Madras School of Orientalism*, 1–25, quote 13; Mantena, *Origins of Modern Historiography*, 84; Wagoner, 'Precolonial Intellectuals'.
42. Howes, *Illustrating India*, 8, 52 (quote), 75.
43. Mantena, *Origins of Modern Historiography*, 51.
44. For the concept of 'cultural capital' see P. Bourdieu, 'Ökonomisches Kapital, Kulturelles Kapital, Soziales Kapital', in R. Kreckel (ed.), *Soziale Ungleichheiten* (Göttingen, 1983), 183–98, esp. 185–90.
45. Colin Mackenzie to William Bentinck, 23 June 1805, BL/OIOC/Mss Eur/F/228/39, 15, No. 11.
46. See R. Koselleck, '"Space of Experience" and "Horizon of Expectation": Two Historical Categories', in id., *Futures Past: On the Semantics of Historical Time*, Translation and Introduction by Keith Tribe (New York, 2004), 255–75.
47. See T.M. Devine and J.M. Mackenzie (eds), *Scotland and the British Empire* (Oxford History of the British Empire Companion Series) (Oxford, 2011). See also T.M. Devine, *Scotland's Empire 1600–1815* (London, 2003); J.M. MacKenzie, 'Essay and Reflection: On Scotland and the Empire', *International History Review* 15(4) (1993), 714–39; and *Empires of Nature and the Natures of Empire: Imperialism, Scotland and the Environment* (East Linton, 1997).
48. M.P. McLaren, *British India and British Scotland, 1780–1830: Career Building, Empire Building and a Scottish School of Thought on Indian Governance* (Akron, Ohio, 2001); Jane Rendall, 'Scottish Orientalism: From Robertson to James Mill', *Historical Journal* 25(1) (1982), 43–69. See also A.A. Powell, *Scottish Orientalists and India: The Muir Brothers, Religion, Education and Empire* (Worlds of the East India Company vol. 4) (Woodbridge, Suffolk and Rochester, NY, 2010), 6–10.
49. See esp. the *Special Issue* of *Modern Asian Studies* 38(3) (2004) including essays by Ian Barrow, David Washbrook, Michael H. Fisher, Susan Bayly and Robert Travers. Summarizing: I.J. Barrow and D.E. Haynes, 'The Colonial Transition. South Asia, 1780–1840', ibid., 469–78.
50. For these forms of indirect rule see M.H. Fisher, *Indirect Rule in India: Residents and the Residency System 1764–1858* (Delhi, 1991).
51. These processes have been examined most thoroughly in the case of Bengal. See for example R. Travers, *Ideology and Empire in Eighteenth Century India* (Cambridge, 2007); M. Mann, *Bengalen im Umbruch: Die Herausbildung des britischen Kolonialstaates 1754–93* (Stuttgart, 2000); P.J. Marshall, *Bengal: The British Bridgehead: Eastern India 1740–1828* (The New Cambridge History of India pt. 2, vol. 2) (Cambridge, 1987).

52. Cf. P.J. Stern, 'From the Fringes of History: Tracing the Roots of the English East India Company-state', in S. Agha and E. Kolsky (eds), *Fringes of Empire: Peoples, Places, and Spaces in Colonial India* (New Delhi, 2009), 19–44; and in more detail J. Stern, *The Company-State: Corporate Sovereignty and the Early Modern Foundations of the British Empire in India* (Oxford, 2011).

53. D. Scott, 'Colonial Governmentality', *Social Text* 43 (1995), 191–220. Fundamental for Scott is M. Foucault, 'Governmentality', in G. Burchell, C. Gordon and P. Miller (eds), *The Foucault Effect: Studies in Governmentality* (Chicago, 1991), 87–104. See also M. Foucault, *Geschichte der Gouvernementalität I. Sicherheit Territorium, Bevölkerung: Vorlesung am College du France 1977–1978*, edited by M. Sennelart (Frankfurt am Main, 2004).

54. Scott, 'Colonial Governmentality', 204f. He refers explicitly here to E. Stokes, *The English Utilitarians and India* (Delhi, Bombay, Madras and Calcutta, 1959).

55. See McLaren, *British India and British Scotland*, 249–54.

56. See for example D.M. Peers, 'State, Power, and Colonialism', in D.M. Peers and N. Gooptu (eds), *India and the British Empire* (Oxford History of the British Empire Companion Series) (Oxford, 2012), 16–43; and *Between Mars and Mammon: Colonial Armies and the Garrison State in India 1819–1835* (London and New York, 1995); D.A. Washbrook, 'India, 1818–1860: The Two Faces of Colonialism', in A. Porter (ed.), *The Oxford History of the British Empire, vol. 3: The Nineteenth Century* (Oxford and New York, 1999), 395–421.

57. G. Prakash, *Another Reason: Science and the Imagination of Modern India* (Princeton, 1999), 126, 260 fn 11.

58. Scott, 'Colonial Governmentality', 205. U. Kalpagam, 'Colonial Governmentality and the "Economy"', *Economy and Society* 29(3) (2000), 419, talks in this context of a 'process of "normalizing" the colonial terrain' on the basis of universalist norms.

59. J. Gascoigne, *Science in the Service of Empire: Joseph Banks, the British State and the Uses of Science in the Age of Revolution* (Cambridge, 1998), 23. See also J. Gascoigne, 'The Royal Society and the Emergence of Science as an Instrument of State Policy', *British Journal for the History of Science* 32(2) (1999), 171–84.

60. Cf. Gascoigne, *Science in the Service of Empire*, 135–45; R. Desmond, *The European Discovery of the Indian Flora* (Oxford, 1992), 44–46. Banks' influence is also manifest in many individual projects in India. See for example A.P. Thomas, 'The Establishment of Calcutta Botanic Garden: Plant Transfer, Science and the East India Company, 1786–1806', *Journal of the Royal Asiatic Society* 16(2) (2006), 165–77; S. Sangwan, 'The Strength of a Scientific Culture: Interpreting Disorder in Colonial Science', *Indian Economic and Social History Review* 34(2) (1997), 217–49; and 'Natural History in Colonial Context: Profit or Pursuit? British Botanical Enterprise in India 1778–1820', in P. Petitjean and C. Jami (eds), *Science and Empires: Historical Studies about Scientific Development and European Expansion* (Dordrecht, Boston and London, 1992), 281–98; A. Grout, 'Geology and India, 1775–1805: An Episode in Colonial Science', *South Asia Research* 10(1) (1990), 1–18.

61. The term 'neo-mercantilism' was taken up especially by John E. Crowley for British economic policy towards the end of the eighteenth century, when economic liberalism combined with economic nationalism. John Gascoigne's argumentation in relation to Banks follows this approach, but mainly stresses the national element. Cf. J.E. Crowley, 'Neo-Mercantilism and the Wealth of Nations: British Commercial Policy after the American Revolution', *Historical Journal* 33(2) (1990), 342; Gascoigne, *Science in the Service of Empire*, 65–110, 213, fn 101.

62. R. Drayton, 'Knowledge and Empire', in P.J. Marshall (ed.), *The Oxford History of the British Empire, vol. 2: The Eighteenth Century* (Oxford and New York, 1998), 249; see also id., *Nature's Government: Science, Imperial Britain, and the 'Improvement' of the World* (New Haven and London, 2000), 107f, 115–20.

63. The institutionalization of the project distinguished Mackenzie's survey from similar enterprises, especially Francis Buchanan's surveys. This meant that it went beyond what Arnold described as the Company's 'fitful flirtation' with the sciences: D. Arnold, *Science, Technology and Medicine in Colonial India* (The New Cambridge History of India, pt. 3, vol. 5) (Cambridge, 2000), 25.
64. C.A. Bayly, *Empire and Information: Intelligence Gathering and Social Communication in India, 1780–1870* (Cambridge, 1996), for example 171–73, 316.
65. Cf. N. Peabody, 'Knowledge Formation in Colonial India', in Peers and Gooptu, *India and the British Empire*, 89; and ibid., fn 40. This criticism of Bayly originally comes from Dirks. See Dirks, *Castes of Mind*, 309f.
66. C.A. Breckenridge and P. van der Veer, 'Orientalism and the Postcolonial Predicament', in eid., *Orientalism and the Postcolonial Predicament*, 6. Obviously they refer to E. Said, *Orientalism* (New York, 1979).
67. See the recent summary in Peabody, 'Knowledge Formation in Colonial India'; also helpful is the discussion in Wagoner, 'Precolonial Intellectuals', 783–86.
68. N.B. Dirks, 'Foreword' in B.S. Cohn, *Colonialism and its Forms of Knowledge*, xii; and *Castes of Mind*, 9; Trautmann, *Aryans and British India*; and *Languages and Nations*; E.F. Irschick, *Dialogue and History. Constructing South India, 1795–1895* (Berkeley, Los Angeles and London, 1994).
69. A similar objection could, of course, be raised against the term 'precolonial' as opposed to 'colonial', which I have used for lack of suitable alternatives. What is meant is the chronological significance, in other words, 'from the time before British rule'.
70. On this important point about the compatibility of certain attitudes I agree with Wagoner, 'Precolonial Intellectuals', 798f. For a valuable discussion of the concept of 'cultural incommensurability' see S. Subrahmanyam, *Courtly Encounters: Translating Courtliness and Violence in Early Modern Eurasia* (Cambridge, Mass, 2012), 1–30.
71. See Cohn, *Colonialism and its Forms of Knowledge*, for example 4, 18f; and the criticism by W. Pinch, 'Same Difference in India and Europe', *History and Theory* 38(3) (1999), 389–407. For colonialism as 'cultural project of control' see N.B. Dirks, 'Introduction: Colonialism and Culture', in id. (ed.), *Colonialism and Culture* (Ann Arbor, 1992), 3.
72. D.A. Washbrook, 'The Colonial Transition in South India, 1770–1840', *Modern Asian Studies* 38(3) (2004), 481–83.
73. Cf. Marshall, *Bengal. The British Bridgehead*, 101, 138f.
74. Cf. Washbrook, 'Colonial Transition', 482f.
75. National Archives of India (ed.), *Catalogue of Memoirs of the Survey of India, 1773–1866* (New Delhi, 1989).
76. W.C. Mackenzie to Henry Reginald Phillimore, 29 April 1940, BL/OIR 354.54.
77. Dirks, *Castes of Mind*, 100, 306.

Chapter 1

SCOTTISH EXPERIENCES

The Attraction of India

In May 1785 the Edinburgh periodical *The Lounger,* prone to moralizing, published a letter by a certain John Homespun,[1] who had previously described himself as a 'plain country-gentleman, with a small fortune, and a large family'. In *The Mirror,* the forerunner of *The Lounger,* Mr Homespun had repeatedly expressed severe criticism of what he regarded as the decadent, fashionable life-style of the nouveau riche rural upper classes. He had warned against too close contact with 'Dukes, Earls, Lords [or] Nabobs' because they could have a cor-rupting influence on the character of simple people.[2] In his letter of May 1785 he was now able to report a particularly serious state of affairs. After twelve years in India the son and daughter-in-law of his neighbour, Mushroom, had moved back to the area where Homespun lived with his wife and daughters. The younger Mushroom had brought with him from India not only a fortune of a hundred thousand pounds, but also completely new customs. For instance, the first time the family 'appeared in church … their pew was all carpeted and cushioned over for their reception, so bedizened – there were flowered muslins and gold muslins, white shawls and red shawls, white feathers and red feathers'. The Mushroom daughters, extravagantly dressed, repeatedly sprayed themselves with perfume during the service and even the returnees' old father had not been able to resist the new style: 'their father, like a fool as he was, had such a mix-ture of black sattin and pink sattin about him, and was so stiff and awkward in his finery, that he looked for all the world like the *King of Clubs*'.[3]

In fact, Mr Homespun could have laughed at such posturing, but he feared the influence of the inhabitants of Mushroom Hall – as the Mushrooms'

---

renovated abode was now called – on his own family, all the more so since they were some of the few neighbours with whom the nouveau riche clan still had contact: 'Mrs. Mushroom has forgot most of her old acquaintance in the parish and associates only with us and one or two more of her neighbours, who have what she calls *capability*, that is … as I understand it, who will listen to all the nonsense she talks, and ape all the follies she practices'. Their extravagant lifestyle and tales of suppers with Indian 'Nabob[s] with half a dozen hard names' were not without their effect so that Homespun feared not only for the morals of his wife and daughters, but also for his money. His wife, for instance, gave orders 'to purchase one [shawl] at a sale in town, which she got a monstrous bargain, tho' I am ashamed to tell, that it stood me in two fat oxen and a year old cow'.[4] But even the Mushroom family itself suffered the effects of the new lifestyle introduced with their new wealth, as the returnee's sister explained later, also in *The Lounger*. After a hard struggle, she said, the father had had to give up his spittoon, while the whole family wrestled with staff they had brought with them from India and new table manners: 'we must sit quiet during a long dinner of two courses and a dessert, and drink wine and water, and never touch our meat but with our fork, and pick our teeth after dinner, and dabble in cold water, and Lord knows how many other things'. All in all, she maintained, Mr Homespun had far less reason for envy than he thought – in fact, the wealth acquired in India brought with it many new worries and unpleasantness: 'it is so troublesome an affair to be fashionable!'[5]

However satirical these sham letters to *The Lounger* may have been, and however much they reflect the scepticism of their actual author – Henry Mackenzie, the editor of the periodical – about the social developments of his day,[6] they certainly point clearly to the common view held in Britain in the second half of the century regarding the opportunities connected with a career in India. Despite all scorn and prejudice against the extravagant lifestyle of the nouveau riche 'Nabobs' – as the returnees were called in a distortion of the title 'Nawab' given to Indian rulers – during those decades employment by the EIC was much sought after since it was regarded as extremely lucrative. The vision of the fantastic riches to be gained in India was founded not least on the success of many employees who, since the 1760s, had returned as rich men and who had stood, often with success, for seats in Parliament.[7] The fact that a career in India could facilitate social and economic advancement is also demonstrated, for instance, by the example of the Englishman James Rennell. Semi-orphaned, he had been brought up by a vicar's family and had gone to India during the Seven Years' War. He had started his military career as a ship's boy at the age of fourteen. Since he regarded India as a 'fine country for a young Gentleman to improve a small fortune in',[8] he had taken up a position with the EIC and in later years had a brilliant career as a surveyor and geographer. When he returned, in the 1770s, Rennell was not only accepted by London's academic elite but had also – due especially to private trade – amassed sufficient financial means to sustain himself without difficulty and to support his relatives.[9]

The fact that wealth acquired in India could also be used sensibly like this was stressed in another article in *The Lounger*, which by no means coincidentally represented a counterpart to its small series on the role of the Nabobs in contemporary Scotland.[10] The author of this article, signed with the pseudonym John Truman, was the Edinburgh Professor Alexander Fraser Tytler, Lord Woodhouselee, whose son-in-law James Baillie Fraser was himself employed by the Company.[11] Fraser Tytler, who obviously wanted his report to serve as a model, told the story of a young Scotsman who goes to India as a doctor in order to escape his impoverished family's financial problems. In his twelve years there, some of which he spends at a small outpost in Bengal, he manages to acquire a fortune of twelve thousand pounds. Upon his return, conscious of his responsibilities, he invests it for the good of his family and local community: he buys back and renovates the family home, pays his poor sister an adequate allowance and, as a gentleman farmer, devotes himself to the sciences. Finally, being a doctor, he treats the poor of the region without charge.

Even if Fraser Tytler is portraying an idealized image here, he is still describing the hopes and dreams that whole generations of middle- and upper-class Scots associated with a career in India. The figure he presents – of a young doctor from impoverished but decent stock – can be regarded as representative of the Scottish applicants since the overwhelming majority of them were well-educated members of the local elites. On the other hand, the lower classes, for whom the only options were joining the rank and file in the King's or the EIC's army, had hardly any chance of becoming rich in India. This is why military service on the subcontinent, whose climate was considered to be thoroughly unhealthy, was very unpopular with them. So the Company itself recruited ordinary soldiers almost exclusively from south of the Scottish border and Ireland, while the Highland Regiments, attached to the Royal Army, mutinied on an almost regular basis if they heard they were being posted to India.[12]

As research in recent decades has shown, Scottish patronage networks that can be traced back to the beginning of the eighteenth century were firmly anchored in the EIC in the century's last decades.[13] Even though the exact proportion of Scots within the EIC continues to be disputed,[14] it seems clear that, in certain spheres in India, Scotland, compared to its proportion of the British population, was hugely over-represented. From sheer numbers this is most clearly obvious in the Company's Officer Corps[15] and the private trade it licensed within Asia,[16] while in the civil administration a disproportionately high number of Scots was appointed to important positions.[17] Undoubtedly networks based on family connections, traditional clan loyalties and above all a common Scottish identity played a major role here, and not only in the case of the trading houses, which by the turn of the century dealt with a not inconsiderable proportion of world trade.[18] However, the administration of the EIC in London continued to be dominated by Englishmen, particularly the twenty-four-man Court of Directors that was dominated by the capital's rich traders and in which Scottish members only gradually started to gain influence from the mid century onwards.[19] The Directors were responsible for employing people and granting licences, and they appointed on the basis of relationships – familial, political or social: on occasion they also sold positions for large sums of money.[20]

There were clearly various factors contributing to the fact that Scottish applicants for jobs in the Company were so successful despite serious competition from other parts of Britain. An explanation often given is the real or supposed quality of the applicants. Their proportion in the Officer Corps, for instance, is hardly surprising since Scots also played an important role in the Royal Army. Many of the Scottish applicants, in the civilian branch as well – though by no means all – held a higher rank in the social hierarchy of their country than their English counterparts. In some sectors better professional qualifications also played a part, particularly as regards academic education. The EIC doctors were almost exclusively Scottish; what is more, many of them were able to make a name for themselves as natural historians, aided by the fact that at Scottish universities there was a close connection between the curricula of natural history and of medicine.[21] What also points to the good and very practice-related education of many Scots is that a disproportionate number of them were employed in technical jobs, for instance as surveyors or engineers.[22]

The high number of qualified Scottish applicants was also due to the specific situation in Britain after the Scottish–English Union of 1707, which tended to restrict the career opportunities in Britain of many well-educated Scots from the middle and upper classes. Even though the English labour market increasingly opened up to the so-called 'North Britons', especially after the virtually definitive defeat of Jacobinism in 1745, equality of opportunity for Englishmen and Scots in the southern part of the island was still a long way off. In particular, jobs in the British administration in London were hard to come by so the Company established itself as a source of patronage whereby Members of Parliament used their influence on the Court of Directors to satisfy the Scottish demands. So the opportunity of working for the EIC also functioned as a sort of safety valve for tensions arising from the economic and social discrepancies between the various parts of Britain.[23]

In the 1780s the prospects for Scotsmen in India seemed particularly rosy. Not only did the number of Scottish applicants accepted under Warren Hastings in Bengal reach unimagined heights, in Madras too the political climate for Scots under Governor Campbell was obviously very favourable.[24] It was not only the careers of people like Thomas Munro or John Malcolm, who rose from being simple officers to become governors, that started here, but also that of Colin Mackenzie. Like his two future friends, he came from an impoverished family and, like them, he had to realize his ambitions in India without any strong support in the jungle of patronage and interests that was characteristic of the EIC and influenced every career in India.[25] Above all, however, like them he brought with him to India experiences and ideas that were to have a lasting impact on his behaviour there.

An Island in Transformation

Colin Mackenzie was born in 1752 or 1753 and grew up in Stornoway on the island of Lewis in the Outer Hebrides.[26] His father, a trader called Murdoch Mackenzie known as 'Carn', was undoubtedly part of the local elite since he belonged to the extended family of the Seaforths and their locally important relations.[27] He seems to have been active as a merchant in Stornoway harbour before, being the owner of a ship, he took on the job of Postmaster, in the 1770s.[28] A contract dating from 1767 indicates that a 'Murdoch Mackenzie Senior Merchant in Stornoway' extended the lease on a property on the South Beach for an indefinite period.[29] Here, right next to the old school house, was probably the house where Colin Mackenzie was born, which he was later to describe as the 'the only thatched house on the South Beach' at the time. In his correspondence from India this simple, one-storey house, which he had extended and renovated for his sister Mary, constantly plays a role; and it possibly speaks of happy childhood memories and a certain sentimentality that, when planning alterations, he was keen to retain the largest possible part of the old building.[30]

The closeness of his lifelong relationship with his homeland is evidenced by the fact that, even after years of living in India, he still spoke of Scotland as 'our happy native land to which we [Scots] here are ever desirous to return'.[31] In his correspondence with Scottish friends he contemplated his origins in the Highlands and reminded them of his Gaelic mother tongue.[32] Yet his links with Scotland are not only to be found in sentimental musings and private memories, since Mackenzie grew up in an environment where radical social and economic change was both visible and tangible; and there are good reasons to assume that many of the views he later put forward in India were connected with these experiences.

Since the early seventeenth century, Lewis had been one of the extensive estates of the Mackenzies of Kintail, who were *caber feidh* (hereditary chiefs of the Mackenzie clan) and were given the title Earl of Seaforth during the time of James I/VI.[33] The history of this family exemplifies the changing role of the Scottish peers in the Highlands, who evolved during this period from traditional chiefs with the respective rights and obligations into modern proprietors.

They orientated themselves increasingly to their English counterparts, thus becoming part of the larger land-owning British elite. After the Jacobite uprising of 1715, in which the fifth Earl took part, Seaforth was stripped of his title and his lands forfeited. By the early 1720s, however, he had managed to buy back most of his possessions. As in many other cases of the Scottish elite, around the middle of the century the Seaforths' relationship with the British state started to change. The son of the fifth Earl, who himself had only been partially pardoned, became a loyal supporter of the House of Hanover. He converted to Protestantism, became a Member of Parliament in London, and during the Jacobite uprising of 1745 stayed on the side of George II.[34] Once the title was reacquired, by the next generation, the link to the London Court was sealed. Later representatives of the family such as Francis Humberston Mackenzie, who inherited the estates in the 1780s, preferred to live in London townhouses and had dreary Brahan Castle, the Seaforths' ancestral seat, converted into a modern country house that would even have been acceptable on the other side of the Anglo-Scottish border.[35]

The new orientation of the land-owning elites in the Highlands, now proprietors committed to commercial interests, also signified a redefinition of the relationship between them and the inhabitants of their large estates. As a result the significance of the intermediaries known as 'tacksmen' declined, small lots were leased directly to a new class of part-time farmers who could be employed in other spheres at the same time, and visible changes came about to traditional settlement structures. In the final third of the century in particular this process accelerated as demand for the Highlands' agricultural products in England and southern Scotland increased. The landowners now sought increasingly to skim off the profits resulting from higher prices by raising the rents to previously inconceivable levels.[36]

These processes can also be traced in detail on Lewis. Here Seaforth and his estate manager George Gillanders, who was responsible for the island, developed an ambitious programme in the 1760s that was supposed to promote the further economic development of the island and to increase the profits of the Seaforth family, which was under enormous financial pressure. The measures suggested by Seaforth and Gillanders in a memorandum, and doggedly implemented in the following decades, were supposed to reform fundamentally what they regarded as old-fashioned social economic structures.[37] These included doing away with the tacksmen, dividing up the land with far higher rents, promoting fishing and agriculture through a premium system and boosting kelp production, a sort of alkali acquired from algae that was much sought after for the production of soap and glass.[38]

Many of these measures affected Colin Mackenzie's home town of Stornoway, which around the turn of the century owned the only major harbour on the Outer Hebrides – a naturally protected dock with a sort of quay – and had several hundred inhabitants.[39] Now and again ships from Holland, Ireland and north and east Europe docked at Stornoway and did a small amount of trade in various consumer items, but the harbour functioned mainly as a fish exchange; the large herring fleets docked there, not only offering employment for the local population during the summer but also serving as an important buyer for independent local fishermen. However, the island, which despite fishing was largely agricultural, had a chronic shortage of capital and this had prevented any sort of major independent economic development; so most inhabitants of Lewis, just like those on the other Hebridean Islands, were dependent on a highly precarious subsistence economy.[40] In the 1790s, according to its minister, the parish of Stornoway was still dependent year round on imported foodstuffs, despite the introduction of potato growing, and this was all that prevented famine.[41]

Therefore Stornoway's development as a centre for trade was of particular importance for the authors of the programme of improvement. They planned, for instance, to attract 'useful' (that is, wealthy or well-educated) immigrants by building houses and providing loans, and to build roads connecting the settlements, many of which were quite remote, with the planned town.[42] Along the South Beach, where Colin Mackenzie's family lived, an area was designated where roads were planned and lots were allocated, on condition that a stone house was built, with a long-term option of compensation for the expense. In order to attract immigrants this offer was displayed in both Scottish and English newspapers.[43]

John Knox, who visited Stornoway in the 1780s, found a town divided into two. Along the coast was the traders' town, consisting of about fifty stone houses with gardens built according to an orderly plan; and a certain distance away was the fishermen's and artisans' town, composed of simple small huts, likewise surrounded by small gardens.[44] And indeed, the town was not only divided geographically. Just like in other areas of the Highlands, on Lewis a relatively small English-speaking elite formed around the factor (Seaforth's agent on the island) Gillanders.[45] They not only dominated the Gaelic-speaking majority in economic terms, but also believed themselves to be culturally superior and wanted radical reform of the island's society. What they saw as the inhabitants' obvious backwardness was particularly connected with their language: Gaelic must first be replaced by English; only then could civilization be spread.[46]

It would perhaps be an exaggeration to describe the new cultural and economic regime that developed during these years as 'internal colonialism',[47] and it seems highly questionable whether the whole of Scotland, including the Lowlands, can be seen as a 'victim' of this 'colonialism'.[48] Nonetheless many of the programmatic statements regarding the concept of general 'improvement' based on external cultural norms and ideas – as represented by the elites

– could indeed be regarded as an 'ideology of improvement'[49] that in some ways mirrored ideas of Britain's civilizing mission in its Empire. Language policies anticipated a similar position taken by some in the debate on education in India just a few decades later.[50] This is apparent in the policy of the Society in Scotland for the Propagation of Christian Knowledge (SSPCK), whose strategy as the 'shocktroops of Presbyterianism'[51] since the century's early decades was to spread the English language by founding schools.[52] Let us consider, for instance, the following passage from Gillanders' and Seaforth's *Proposals for Improving the Island of Lewis,* in which they stress the need to work together with the SSPCK:

> the Inhabitants of that Country are at present extremely ignorant, and for the want of language can not have any Communication or Correspondence with Strangers, without which it is impossible to reform the people. It is therefore expedient for the Proprietor to make application for two more Society Schools as well as two Itinerant Preachers in order to instruct the people and teach them the English language. It is to be observed that no strangers, either Preachers or Schoolmasters, will agree to go to that Country without adequate Salaries & that the natives, who might serve for less can never answer the purpose.[53]

It is hardly surprising that this programme of 'improvement' led to serious social tensions. The island's small merchants, for instance, were strictly against bringing in immigrants, as the Inspector General for Fisheries in Scotland discovered when he talked to them, because they saw the new competition as a threat to their business.[54] The local lower classes did not put up with the social and economic changes passively either but tried to use their opportunities for disobedience and sabotage. For instance, when a spinning school was set up, intended to promote the island's economic development, it met with resistance right from the start.[55] Many of the island's inhabitants decided to turn their backs on their homeland. Emigration to North America, which increased dramatically in the Highlands from about 1765, was regarded by many landowners as a problem: in pre-Malthusian terms it represented a particular danger to prosperity – especially since, due to the costs involved, it was less of an option for the poorest section of the population than for the small tenants, who were confronted with higher rents and rejected the new economic regime. A growing population, however, was still regarded as the basis for economic growth. Nonetheless, the often badly thought-out modernization policy of the landowners and their representatives on the ground was, paradoxically, one of the main reasons for emigration, as the situation on Lewis confirms.[56]

The first great wave of emigration from Lewis took place after the famine years of 1772 and 1773, when the crops failed in large areas of the Hebrides. The food crisis may well have stimulated mass emigration, but for most of the emigrants the new tenancy conditions also played a role. John Downie, then minister at Stornoway, observed for instance that only a section of the population wanted to emigrate because of desperation and hunger. In fact, many of the tenants wanted to use the threat of emigration to get 'the Lands at their own price'[57] Since their additional demands to be compensated for inflated rents and for Gillanders to be dismissed from office were not fulfilled, in 1773 between seven hundred and eight hundred people left the island, followed by about another hundred a year later.[58] Initially Mackenzie of Strickathrow and Gillanders wanted to stop the families leaving at any price and even planned to employ troops for this purpose. Since Seaforth would not agree to this, however, and in their eyes concession in the question of rents was out of the question, they were ultimately unable to halt the wave of emigration.[59]

In the 1780s the landowners' right to drive out tenants who would not pay by means of a summons of removal, used systematically during the Highland Clearances,[60] served primarily as a form of pressure on tenants to pursue the programme of improvement, for instance by implementing the cultivation of potatoes or by attending the unpopular English-speaking schools.[61] What is more, it offered an opportunity to get rid of the 'troublesome people' who vociferously led the opposition to the changes introduced.[62] There were quite a few of these as in the 1760s and early 1770s Gillanders and his small clique of likeminded people established a corrupt regime which appropriated all the positions of power on the island one after the other and used them unscrupulously for their own economic advantage. As Seaforth's estate manager Gillanders was responsible for setting and collecting the rent and, as *baron baillie* (magistrate), he had a great influence on the local jurisdiction. He also had considerable control over raising the excise – particularly significant were the profits from illegal whiskey production[63] – and over the postal service, the most important means of communication with the mainland.[64] As a former resident of Stornoway was later to report (one whose views are passed on only from the pen of John Knox, who was generally highly critical of factors) the combination of these various powers meant that for a time Gillanders had a virtual monopoly over trade in certain types of fish and cattle.[65] It is certainly typical of his behaviour that he had to be warned against unleashing a wave of unrest by seeking to increase the price of tenancy agreements during the famine of 1772 and 1773 in an attempt to extend his own estate.[66]

Colin Mackenzie never forgot the brutality with which the new economic and social regime was imposed during his childhood and adolescence. This, for instance, is what he wrote years later to Gillanders, when he feared a similar wave of emigration: 'I hope my friend the times you & I have seen of a popular ferment as in 1773 will never disturb the Lewis – you then saw with what facility a few worthless adventurers could spread among an ignorant people principles subversive of their true interests & future peace; you have seen families sold by the head to pay the expense of their passage to America who might have lived by their industry at home'.[67] Although Mackenzie held the emigrants' ringleaders responsible here, he implied quite clearly that responsibility also lay with the island's landowner. These experiences from his youth were also the ones that were to shape the ideas he later came to hold about what the British colonial state in India should be like.

Public Service at Stornoway

Colin Mackenzie's childhood and adolescence coincided with a turbulent phase in the history of the island of Lewis. However, it was not just his experiences with radical modernization that stayed with him all his life, but also, as he put it himself, that here too 'early seeds of passion for discovery and knowledge' were sown.[68] Like his siblings – apart from his sister Mary, who was six years older than him, he also mentions at least two brothers[69] – Colin Mackenzie, who spoke Gaelic at home,[70] presumably attended the local parish school, where for a small fee children from the local upper class were taught not only English but also reading, writing and basic arithmetic.[71] For an additional fee it seems that Latin and algebra could also be learned, but for most pupils the curriculum was restricted to acquiring basic knowledge and in only a few cases was designed to prepare the pupil for university. As Mackenzie later wrote of his time at school: 'In my time this was a great deficiency in the education of our young people; none were allowed to go any length in the Classicks except such as were meant to be Clergymen, & the rest were sent young to sea whence they returned not much improved in morals'.[72]

In later years Mackenzie regarded his relatively limited school education as a great drawback that hindered his career.[73] Nonetheless in Alexander Anderson, who taught children aged five to fifteen at the SSPCK school from 1763,[74] Stornoway seems to have had an inspirational maths teacher who is said to have motivated not only Colin Mackenzie but also Alexander Mackenzie, who was later to give his name to the Mackenzie river in Canada.[75] How exactly Anderson could have influenced Colin as a teenager is not entirely clear, but it is by no means unlikely that they knew each in the small town of Stornoway. Colin seems to have been exceptionally gifted and was thus able, presumably with Seaforth's backing, to continue his education for a while. A later source states that he profited from the fact that his father occasionally also traded in books, which meant that he had plenty to read. Later on, according to the source, he was sent to London for further education, with Seaforth's help.[76] Alexander Johnston provides the information that the mathematically gifted Mackenzie, again with Seaforth's help, made contact with his great-grandfather Francis, the fifth Lord Napier.[77] This seems at least to fit in with a longer stay in

England for Mackenzie since Francis Napier, despite his family seat being near Edinburgh and his being, since 1761, one of the Lords of Police in Scotland,[78] spent most of his life in England and on the European mainland.[79]

Although Johnston's account is in many cases misleading, close contacts between Napier and Mackenzie are not improbable. After discovering various hitherto unknown manuscripts by his ancestor John Napier, one of the most famous mathematicians of the sixteenth and seventeenth centuries and regarded as one of the discoverers of logarithms, Francis was working on John's biography.[80] In doing so he had gained the impression, as Johnston reported, that his ancestor believed that the so-called Arabic numbers were initially invented in India and from there exported via Arabia to Europe. Francis Napier had, according to Johnston, wanted to pursue this theory further and, following the tracks of his famous ancestor, had travelled to Venice, where he had acquired the writings of famous Jesuit missionaries. These he had forwarded to the young Colin Mackenzie who, as his assistant, was supposed to advise him in mathematical matters and also to collect further information about the Indian tradition of mathematics.[81] There are, however, no parallel sources to support Johnston's version and, as Johnston himself declared, the material collected by Francis Napier for the planned biography was lost in a shipwreck in 1809.[82] In any case, they can only have worked together for a few years at most since Napier died in 1773 or 1774, at which point Mackenzie was only about twenty years old.[83] Almost exactly from this time onwards, however, there are clear traces of Mackenzie in Scottish archives, which suggests that the young man had returned to his home town.

Thus, as already mentioned, he experienced at first hand the first wave of emigration from Lewis in 1773. In the same year a Colin Mackenzie is mentioned in a tenancy agreement on Stornoway.[84] Since the name is very common it is impossible to say whether this actually was the son of Murdoch Carn Mackenzie. Be that as it may, from the mid1770s onwards he seems to have helped his father occasionally with the post office accounts, evidenced by his signature on various documents at this time.[85] It was obviously a time when Carn Mackenzie's family was mixing in the highest circles in the small town of Stornoway. Colin himself, for instance, writes of a close friendship with Alexander, son of George Gillanders, and of a long stay with him at Brahan Castle, where Gillanders occasionally sorted out his employer's business affairs.[86] He also knew Francis Humberston Mackenzie, later Lord Seaforth, who was roughly the same age as him and with whom he shared memories of mountaineering on Lewis.[87]

Like his father's employment in the postal service, so vital to Gillanders, Colin's appointment as Comptroller of Customs in early 1776 can also be regarded as evidence of this close relationship with the most important families on Lewis.[88] The job in the Stornoway Customs House had been a constant problem for Gillanders ever since it was set up in 1765 because the then collector, Archibald Smith, and his four colleagues had clearly retained a degree of independence from the estate manager.[89] After a series of controversies, including over the poor state of the Customs House which Gillanders was supposed to repair and maintain, Gillanders and Mackenzie of Strickathrow tried for a long time to get rid of these 'troublesome people'.[90] Even though they could not prevent Reid from succeeding Archibald Smith when he died, they did at least manage – probably with Seaforth's support[91] – to appoint their trusted Colin Mackenzie to the second most important position, that of comptroller.

Mackenzie's appointment was by no means unusual as in Scotland, like England, people were appointed to the Customs Service from the extended middle class, to which the traders in Stornoway also belonged. Apart from a certain ability with figures, a particular condition for appointment to the post was adequate knowledge of spoken and written English and some knowledge of bookkeeping; the support of an influential patron was also needed.[92] Seaforth had clearly lent such support to Mackenzie, and he was appointed as comptroller on 8 February 1776 by a Warrant of the Lords of the Treasury. After paying the required deposit and taking his oath of office he began working for the Scottish Customs in the summer, thereby entering one of the most modern and centralized branches of the British administration.[93]

From about the middle of the century the organization of the Scottish Customs system had been largely analogous to that of England.[94] The central organ was the Scottish Board of Customs in Edinburgh, which on the one hand was responsible to the Lords of the Treasury in London and on the other supervised a number of outposts in the various harbour towns. The establishment in Stornoway can be seen as typical of one of the smaller outposts: it was headed by the collector, who, amongst other things, negotiated with the captains, was responsible for most of the correspondence and compiled, along with the comptroller, the quarterly reports to the Board in Edinburgh. The comptroller himself was mainly responsible for the accounts. He calculated the import and export taxes, was responsible for general bookkeeping and occasionally deputized for his boss. The staff also consisted of an inspector, a surveyor and landwaiter as well as two tidesmen, who were responsible for checking the data provided by the captains, inspected ships, and made sure that no goods were landed secretly.[95]

The busiest times at the Stornoway Customs were late summer and autumn, when the large herring fleets arrived at the harbour, all the more so since the Customs Service was also responsible for raising taxes on salt, vital for the preservation of fish. But during the rest of the year, too, they were kept busy and the battle against widespread smuggling presented a great challenge. The correspondence between the Customs House in Stornoway and the Board in Edinburgh gives a good impression of the tasks undertaken by this small outpost. Combatting the usual forms of smuggling – the false declaration of goods or the secret removal of loads at night – was effected largely by exact inspection of the ships upon arrival and again before departure. This was not always so easy since the smugglers had vivid imaginations. For instance, the collector and comptroller were obliged to taste the imported wine themselves in order to prevent Spanish wine being declared as Portuguese, as was apparently quite common.[96] It was particularly difficult to control the ban on exporting weapons and saltpetre during the American War of Independence because many of the captains had special permissions, and in some cases weapons were needed to protect their own ships. Even the import of books had to be checked once the Board had received information that a pirate edition of Robertson's *History of America* was to be imported from Ireland.[97]

Another responsibility of Customs was to requisition the cargo of stranded ships, which were often simply plundered. In 1778, for instance, the wreck of a ship originally carrying firewood was found empty on Uist by Customs officers. Although there were rumours that the cargo had been secretly transported to Ireland, the local population could not or would not give any information about the perpetrators.[98] A few years later Mackenzie, as comptroller, had to spend three weeks with a tidesman on a remote beach on Lewis in order to supervise the unloading of another stranded ship.[99] The Customs House correspondence indicates that despite their best efforts they could not completely wipe out smuggling and plundering even though the disciplinary measures available to them were by no means pleasant for the traders: ships that were used to evade customs and smuggled goods were confiscated. With the exception of tobacco, which was burned, the ships and goods were auctioned off and the money paid into the state's coffers.[100]

Sometimes working outside Stornoway Mackenzie had, of necessity, not only to learn how to present himself as public servant to a mistrustful population, but was also confronted by the needs and problems of the island's rural inhabitants, who were often desperately poor. During his seven years in the post, however, his main job was bookkeeping and internal documentation of the Customs' work.[101] Here he developed abilities that were to distinguish him during his later career in India: it was his duty, for instance, not only to produce scrupulously exact accounts, but also to archive the incoming and outgoing correspondence. The various books kept by the comptroller, tidesmen and landwaiter all had to correspond exactly with one another; the Board in Edinburgh picked up on every mistake.[102] John Brewer has shown that in the eighteenth century a sort of professional ethos for revenue officers developed in the English tax and customs administration, based not least on skill, industry and exactness, correct behaviour in public and a loyal relationship with superiors and colleagues.[103] This observation can undoubtedly be applied to the Scottish Customs staff as well and Mackenzie's subsequent administrative work in India shows the extent to which he had internalized these bureaucratic virtues. So his employment at the Customs House did not only represent a stepping stone on his career path but also an experience enabling him to develop capabilities that were to prove extremely valuable later, when he was tasked with building up a government department.

A New Direction

Although it offered a certain security, employment with Customs could never offer any great future for an ambitious young man like Mackenzie as there was a very limited prospect of promotion. With his comptroller's income of eight pounds per quarter he was by no means a big earner and the best case scenario was that after many years he might succeed Reid as collector, which was not much better paid.[104] So even after just a few years he seems to have decided to look for a better paid job elsewhere. This fact alone can hardly disprove Johnston's assertion that Mackenzie's decision to go to India was based purely on interest in the Orient he developed when working with Napier.[105] Yet there are more important reasons to question Johnston's assertion – precisely because he gives only one single factor as the basis for Mackenzie's decision. Admittedly in his report of 1817, which sounds fairly autobiographical, Mackenzie himself mentions that his interest in Indian geography and history had been aroused before he left England; but then he adds that his actual research work did not start until some thirteen years later.[106] What is more, there is no indication that Mackenzie pursued his alleged original interest in Hindu mathematics (based on the work he did for Napier) once he was in India.[107] But above all, Mackenzie's own correspondence from the 1780s contradicts Johnston's version: it may well be that before he started work for the EIC Mackenzie had found a certain interest in India, but the main reasons why he left for India were far less unusual.

His father's financial situation was clearly crucial. Since the early 1770s rumours had already been circulating about Murdoch Carn Mackenzie's imminent bankruptcy. However, Gillanders and Mackenzie of Strickathrow, who seem to have been creditors, decided not to take any hard measures against him – even a summons of removal may have been an option – because he was obviously far too deeply involved in their business.[108] At this point in time Carn clearly already had large debts and his situation does not seem to have improved in the following decade as he cannot have made any great profit from his job as Deputy Postmaster. For an annual income of seventy pounds he was obliged to organize a weekly packet boat from Lewis to the Scottish mainland, whence runners made the connection to Inverness – not a particularly lucrative business, as evidenced by various submissions by Gillanders and Mackenzie.[109]

Carn's sons apparently saw little chance of a job in Britain that would solve their father's problems. Colin Mackenzie's older brother Alexander, for instance, had already left Scotland by the late 1760s to try his luck in the West Indies – though with little success, so that, when he returned in 1801, he was dependent on his brother's support.[110] In the 1770s another of Carn's sons seems to have joined the Highland Regiment recruited by Thomas Humberston Mackenzie.[111] Ultimately his father's debts also seem to have been crucial in Colin Mackenzie's decision to apply for a cadet post in the EIC at the relatively advanced age of twenty-nine – most of the cadets were half his age.[112] Even though, as he later wrote, the various creditors never took the 'rigid measures' against their debtor that would normally have been imposed, this was for him a 'subject ... which sits as heav[il]y on my mind as the appropriation of the National finances does on the minister'.[113] In the 1790s he was still transferring money to his family in Scotland on a regular basis. A substantial proportion of it was used, apart from looking after poor relations, to reduce his father's debts.[114]

For all this, however, it was by no means easy for him to leave his Scottish homeland and his correspondence from this time shows that he was far from wildly enthusiastic about service in India. In November 1782, when his professional future was still unclear, he made this quite obvious in a letter to George Gillanders from London, where he states his hope 'of being either placed here or at least *transported*; tho' perhaps you will tell me I need be at no loss for the latter in London'.[115] Perhaps not too much should be made of his choice of words here since he did, after all, want to convince Gillanders that the only option was to leave his Customs job, a job Gillanders considered important. However that may be, there can be no doubt that Mackenzie wanted to work in India mainly for financial reasons. As he wrote some years later, he wanted to use the time there to save 'a little bit against a rainy day in the West Highlands'. What he meant was a sum of ten to fifteen thousand pounds that would enable him to live the life of a financially independent gentleman.[116]

Precisely when he conceived the plan to give up his job with the Stornoway Customs permanently is not entirely clear. What we do know, however, is that in 1779 he took paid leave of absence for the first time in order to attend to his 'private affairs'. Originally granted just for July, at Mackenzie's request the period of leave was extended by a month, on condition that he provide a suitable replacement.[117] After some discussion a further two-and-a-half months' leave was granted between February and April 1781.[118] Finally, in January 1782, he approached the Scottish Board of Customs again requesting a month's leave from March onwards 'on account of the state of his health & to attend his private affairs'.[119] As before, this leave was granted, and indeed an extension initially of one month and later a further six months from May 1782.[120] In order to gain permission for these somewhat unusual absences he was not averse to using private channels. Although this was by no means uncommon, it could also meet with rejection. As on earlier occasions, the members of the Board of Customs – including Adam Smith – granted his leave in January 1782, but stated that in future they would not accept requests of this sort: 'in future those applications are to be made with the knowledge & concurrence of the Collector & immediately to the Board not through any private channel'.[121] After that Mackenzie applied directly to the Treasury in London for a further absence of one year, so that the Scottish Board could only signal its agreement.[122]

Exactly what Mackenzie did during his absences in 1779 and 1781 is not entirely clear, but from 1782 onwards he seems to have been actively seeking a position in the EIC. The extent to which he relied on the support of influential friends and acquaintances to achieve this becomes clear in a letter to George Gillanders of November 1782. At this moment in time Mackenzie was in a desperate situation. Even though he had spent most of the year trying to get a job with the EIC he had so far been unsuccessful and the six-month extension of his paid leave of absence had already run out on 20 November, even though he had tried to use every available connection to Parliament. But without the right letters of recommendation there was little that even the Scottish MPs could do:

> My leave expired 20th of this month & I did not know what to do to have it prolonged; I was not recommended to any patron to apply & it was awkward to apply to members without introduction. I applied to Mr Sinclair of Ulbster[123] upon very light grounds & he recommended to me to go to Genl. Ross as Member for the North Burghs;[124] Genl. Ross very justly observed that it was no Burghs affair & said the Lord Advocate [Henry Dundas][125] as Lord McLeod's[126] Agent was the proper person; this I could not do & returned to Mr Sinclair who very humanely sent my Petition to the Treasury; I have attended six days there & no answer – this is the way I am situated.[127]

Mackenzie's lack of success, and the fact that he did not dare to approach Dundas without direct recommendation, highlights his dependence on his patrons. At the same time, the patronage relations also required reciprocation from the client and involved obligations that might sometimes run counter to the client's short-term interests.[128] That is why, for example, he was unable to accept the offer by an MP to buy his job at the Customs from him for six months' wages; because he had promised a successor acceptable to Seaforth and Gillanders his hands were tied. This was all the more unfortunate since now that his leave was over he seems no longer to have received any wages and had not so far managed to find even temporary employment in London.[129]

The situation does not appear to have changed until the arrival in London, in winter 1782/83, of Francis Humberston Mackenzie, whose brother Thomas Frederick had bought the Seaforth estate three years earlier from their heavily indebted cousin Kenneth Mackenzie.[130] In the meantime Thomas Frederick had been posted to India as an officer, where he died, in April 1783, so at this point

Francis Humberston Mackenzie was the most important representative of the Seaforth family in Britain. The contacts his brother had fostered in Parliament were also available to him, especially with the influential Charles Francis Greville,[131] who had worked with Thomas Frederick Humberston Mackenzie in recruiting the *Seaforth Highlanders* in 1778/79 and had later maintained close contact with Francis for years due to their common interest in botany.[132] As Colin Mackenzie said himself, in the course of the following two decades Greville remained one of his most important contacts in London.[133] Initially, however, it was mainly his influence in the Treasury that was important: since 1779 Greville had been talked of as a possible Treasurer of the Household – he was appointed to this position in 1783 – and so it is quite possible that he put in a word for Colin Mackenzie at Francis Humbertson Mackenzie's request.[134] In any case, given Humbertson Mackenzie's presence it is not all that surprising that in December 1782 Colin Mackenzie was retrospectively granted a three-month extension of his leave.[135]

His appointment at very short notice as a cadet in the EIC's army seems also to have been due to this influence as Francis Humbertson Mackenzie had friends on the Court of Directors.[136] This was also greatly significant as the final decision about most applicants lay with the Directors, who in the 1780s divided up vacant positions amongst themselves. Given the high number of applicants it is unlikely that Colin Mackenzie would have been considered without the direct intervention of a significant personality. It is even possible, as Reginald Henry Phillimore suggests, referring to a note in the appointment commission's files,[137] that his application was initially rejected, but the name Colin Mackenzie was so common that the identity of the rejected applicant cannot be reliably established. What is quite clear, however, is that Mackenzie was only appointed shortly before his departure date. Although he is mentioned in the list of cadets in the military registers for 1782, his appointment date is given as 17 January, which can only mean 17 January 1783.[138] His patron is named as the ship owner Charles Boddam, a Director of Scottish origin who had maintained connections with his homeland.[139]

Colin Mackenzie only had about two months before his departure – military training in Britain was not envisaged[140] – and on 12 March he put to sea heading for Madras.[141] He was never again to see the British coast and the Scottish Highlands where he had spent most of his first thirty years. But this does not mean that he broke off all relations with his homeland. The patronage relations that had made his appointment to the EIC possible in the first place were to remain very important in India as well. Likewise his desire for the financial means needed for an undisturbed life in Scotland remained a motive for his career on the subcontinent, a motive that at least in the first decade or so of his life there seems to have been more important than any sort of orientalist interests.

Certainly, when Mackenzie was living in Scotland he hardly thought of his life as a 'prehistory' of his Indian career, even if in retrospect it can be argued that his Scottish experiences shaped the course his Indian career was to take. Two of these experiences should be singled out to make his Indian activities more understandable: firstly, his work with the Scottish Customs that made it easy for him to perceive his function in the EIC as that of a loyal 'public servant'; and secondly, his experience of the radical modernization of the Highlands, to which he retained a very ambivalent attitude throughout his life. On the one hand he was genuinely convinced of the logic of 'improvement', but for all his enthusiasm for reform he was also in favour of moderation; he believed that changes should always be in the interests of the local population, paying due respect to their cultural notions. Seen in this way, Mackenzie's youth and adolescence in Scotland appear to be much more than an inconsequential era that had little to do with his later activities in India before an 'orientalist awakening', however conceived, took place: in many ways his ideas and actions, as the following chapters will show, were directly connected to these Scottish experiences, even if there was still a long way to go before Mackenzie would develop his project of knowledge production in all its breadth.

Notes

1. 'Influence of the Neighbourhood of a Rich Asiatic, in a Letter by John Homespun', *The Lounger* 17 (28 May 1785). All articles from *The Lounger* are reprinted in and quoted from *The Lounger: A Periodical Paper, Published at Edinburgh in the Years 1785 and 1786. By the Authors of The Mirror*, 4th edn., 3 vols (London, 1788), vol. 1, 156–63.
2. 'Consequence to Little Folks of Intimacy with Great Ones, in a Letter from John Homespun', *The Mirror* 12 (6 March 1779). This first contribution signed 'Homespun' was followed by another in *The Mirror*: 'Description of a Visit of a Great Lady to the House of a Man of Small Fortune, in a Second Letter from Mr Homespun', *The Mirror* 25 (20 April 1779) and a 'response' by his 'daughter': 'Behaviour of Great Ladies in Town to Their Country-Acquaintance, in a Letter from Elisabeth Homespun', *The Mirror* 53, (26 July 1779). All articles in *The Mirror* are reprinted in and quoted from *The Mirror: A Periodical Paper, Published at Edinburgh in the Years 1779 and 1780*, 3 vols (Edinburgh, 1781), vol. 1, 89–96, 193–203; vol. 2, 146–55.
3. 'Influence of the Neighbourhood', 158–160; quotes: 159f, 160.
4. Ibid., quotes: 159, 161, 160f.
5. 'Narrative of a Country Family Raised to Sudden Affluence by the Arrival of a Son from India, and of the Taxes to Which the Enjoyment of Its Wealth Is Subject, in a Letter from Marjory Mushroom', *The Lounger* 36 (8 October 1785) (Published in *The Lounger: A Periodical Paper*, vol. 2, 1–8, here 3f). There were two more letters under the pseudonym 'Marjory Mushroom': 'Marjory Mushroom's Account of Her Life in Town. Hardships to be Endured by a Disciple of the Ton', *The Lounger* 56 (25 February 1786), ibid, 200–08; and 'Third Letter from Marjory Mushroom, Giving an Account of her Feelings on Her Return to the Country', *The Lounger* 62 (8 April 1786) ibid., 253–262.

6. Cf. H.W. Drescher, *Themen und Formen des periodischen Essays im späten 18. Jahrhundert: Untersuchungen zu den schottischen Wochenschriften The Mirror und The Lounger* (Frankfurt am Main, 1971), 36–40, 44–47, 103–06. On Henry Mackenzie see also H.W. Drescher, 'Introduction', in id. (ed.), *Literature and Literati: The Literary Correspondence and Notebooks of Henry Mackenzie*, 2 vols (Frankfurt am Main, 1989–1999), vol. 1, 29–39.

7. Cf. P. Lawson and J. Phillips, '"Our Execrable Banditti": Perceptions of Nabobs in Mid-Eighteenth-Century Britain', *Albion* 16(3) (1984), 225–41; P.J. Marshall, *East Indian Fortunes: The British in Bengal in the Eighteenth Century* (Oxford, 1976), 214–17.

8. James Rennell to Rev. Gilbert Burington, 7 November 1763, BL/OIOC/Mss Eur/D/1073. Cf. Lawson and Phillips. '"Our Execrable Banditti"', 227.

9. Amongst other things Rennell traded in cotton and had his own warehouse in Dacca. See Rennell to Rev. Gilbert Burington, 30 October 1770; 2 November 1770; 16 October 1776, BL/OIOC/Mss Eur/D/1073. By 1771, six years before his return, he had already amassed a sum of about seven thousand pounds, from which he expected interest of 350 pounds per year. James Rennell to Harry Verelst, 1 January 1771, BL/OIOC/Mss Eur/F/218/103. What is more, in 1776 the EIC granted him a pension of six hundred pounds per year. Rennell to Burington, 21 December 1776, BL/OIOC/Mss Eur/D/1073. For Rennell's career see also: C.R. Markham, *James Rennell and the Rise of Modern English Geography* (London, Paris and Melbourne, 1895); and C.A. Frenzel, *Major James Rennell, der Schöpfer der neueren englischen Geographie: Ein Beitrag zur Geschichte der Erdkunde* (Leipzig, 1904).

10. 'Narrative of the Happiness of a virtuous and benevolent East Indian; in a Letter from John Truman', *The Lounger* 44, (3 December 1785), vol. 2, 74–84. Cf. K. Datta, 'James Mackintosh, Learned Societies in India, and Enlightenment Ideas', in J.J. Carer and J.H. Pittcock (eds), *Aberdeen and the Enlightenment* (Aberdeen, 1987), 41f.

11. On authorship see: Drescher, *Themen und Formen*, 45; and Datta, 'James Mackintosh', 41.

12. Cf. G.J. Bryant, 'Scots in India in the Eighteenth Century', *Scottish Historical Review* 64(1) (1985), 24f; A.N. Gilbert, 'Recruitment and Reform in the East India Company Army, 1760–1800', *Journal of British Studies* 15(1) (1975), 89–111, esp. 92.

13. See, for example, A. Mackillop, 'Locality, Nation, Empire. Scots and the Empire in Asia, c.1695-c.1813', in Devine and Mackenzie, *Scotland and the British Empire*, 60–65; G. McGilvary, *East India Patronage and the British State: The Scottish Elite and Politics in the Eighteenth Century* (London and New York, 2008); Devine, *Scotland's Empire*, 250–70; MacKenzie, 'Essay and Reflection', 714–39.

14. This applies in particular to the generalization of the figure from the Hastings era. See: Mackillop, 'Locality, Nation, Empire', 64; and J. Riddy, 'Warren Hastings: Scotland's Benefactor?', in G. Carnall and C. Nicholson (eds), *The Impeachment of Warren Hastings: Papers from a Bicentenary Commemoration* (Edinburgh, 1989), 30–57.

15. Between 1758 and 1834 about a quarter of the officers in the Company's army were Scots. Cf. P.E. Razzell, 'Social Origins of British Officers in the Indian and British Home Army, 1758–1962', *British Journal of Sociology* 14(3) (1963), 250, Table 3; Bryant, 'Scots in India', 23; Riddy, 'Warren Hastings', 42.

16. Of the 371 licenses granted between 1776 and 1785 about sixty per cent were to Scots. Cf. Riddy, 'Warren Hastings', 42.

17. In the 1780s, under Governor Archibald Campbell, about half of the most important committees in the Madras government were peopled by Scots, even though they constituted less than ten per cent of the civilian employees at this time. Cf. A. Mackillop, 'Fashioning a "British" Empire: Sir Archibald Campbell of Inverneil and Madras', in A. Mackillop and S. Murdoch (eds), *Military Governors and Imperial Frontiers c1600–1800: A Study of Scotland and Empires* (Leiden and Boston, 2003), 205–31, here esp. 218–28. See also McLaren, *British India and British Scotland*, 25.

18. Cf. B.R. Tomlinson, 'From Campsie to Kedgeree: Scottish Enterprise, Asian Trade and the Company Raj', *Modern Asian Studies* 36(4) (2002), 769–91; J.G. Parker, 'Scottish Enterprise in India, 1750–1914', in R.A. Cage (ed.), *The Scots Abroad: Labour, Capital, Enterprise, 1750–1914* (London, Sydney and Dover, 1985), 198–203.

19. Cf. Devine, *Scotland's Empire*, 262; Parker, 'Scottish Enterprise in India', 191–98; H.V. Bowen, *The Business of Empire: The East India Company and Imperial Britain, 1756–1833* (Cambridge, 2006), 274f and the prosopographical study by J.G. Parker, 'The Directors of the East India Company, 1754–1790' (Ph.D. dissertation, University of Edinburgh, 1977).

20. Cf. Peers, *Mars and Mammon*, 47; J.M. Bourne, *Patronage and Society in Nineteenth-Century England* (London, 1986), esp. 28, 62f; R. Callahan, *The East India Company and Army Reform, 1783–1798* (Cambridge, MA, 1972), 17.

21. See Desmond, *European Discovery of the Indian Flora*, 45–80; MacKenzie, *Empires of Nature and Natures of Empire*, 65–70; and 'Essay and Reflection', 716; and Arnold, *Science, Technology, and Medicine*, 60.

22. Cf. McLaren, *British India and British Scotland*, 26, 33. For the curricula at Scottish universities see P. Wood, 'Science in the Scottish Enlightenment', in A. Broadie (ed.), *The Cambridge Companion to the Scottish Enlightenment* (Cambridge, 2003), 94–116.

23. Cf. Devine, *Scotland's Empire*, 260–70; L. Colley, *Britons: Forging the Nation 1707–1837* (London, 1994), 128f; R.M. Sumpter, *Patronage and Politics in Scotland, 1707–1832* (Edinburgh, 1986), 9.

24. Cf. Riddy, 'Warren Hastings'; Mackillop, 'Fashioning a "British" Empire'.

25. For the family background of Munro and Malcolm see McLaren, *British India and British Scotland*, 16–20.

26. The date of birth, 1754, given (without evidence) by W.C. Mackenzie seems very dubious as contemporary sources and his gravestone agree that he died in May 1821 at the age of 68. See Mackenzie, *Colonel Colin Mackenzie*, 1; *The Bengal Obituary or, A Record to Perpetuate the Memory of Departed Worth, Being a Compilation of Tablets, and Monumental Inscriptions from Various Parts of the Bengal and Agra Presidencies, to Which is Added Biographical Sketches and Memoirs of Such as Have Pre-eminently Distinguished Themselves in the History of British India since the Formation of the European Settlement to the Present Time* (Calcutta, 1851), 135; and 'Asiatic Intelligence. Calcutta Miscellaneous: Deaths', *Asiatic Journal and Monthly Register for British India and its Dependencies* 12(71) (November 1821), 505f.

27. Colin Mackenzie [to John Mackenzie?], 18 February 1798, NAS/GD/46/17/4, 530f. When considering having a signet ring made, Colin Mackenzie claimed in this letter that he was directly descended from the Mackenzies of Fairburn and the Mackenzies of Achilty, two branches of the Seaforth line of the Mackenzies of Kintail. Both branches went back to the eighth and ninth Baron of Kintail. By the time Colin Mackenzie was alive this close relationship was already about eight or nine generations back, but according to his own statements there were also connections to the Seaforth family via his grandfather Kildin. He had married a niece of Roderick Mor Mackenzie of Coigeach, who as Tutor of Kintail had functioned in the early seventeenth century as official advisor to his nephew, the second Lord Mackenzie of Kintail and first Earl of Seaforth. Via this connection he was also related to some other important branches of the family, the Mackenzies of Kintail and the Earls of Cromarty, who also went back to Mackenzie of Coigeach. For the Mackenzies of Achilty and Fairburn and the Tutor of Kintail see A. Mackenzie, *History of the Mackenzies with Genealogies of the Principal Families of the Name,* new revised and extended edn. (Inverness, 1894), 108, 177, 225f, 235–37, 505–7, 513–16.

28. Officially the estate manager, George Gillanders, also held the office of Postmaster, but had delegated it to Murdoch Carn Mackenzie. The first account signed by Carn is dated August 1774. Cf. 'Deputation by Robert Oliphant Esq, Deputy Postmaster General of Scotland

to George Gillanders as Postmaster of Stornoway', 1776, NAS/GD/46/13/99/5, and the account in NAS/GD/427/91/4.

29. 'Charter in favour of Murdoch Mackenzie Senior Merchant in Stornoway', 17 August 1769; NAS/RS/38/12/23.

30. Cf. Colin Mackenzie [to Francis Humberston Mackenzie], 31 January 1792, NAS/GD/46/17/4, 316–23, here 318 (quote); also 21 July 1794, ibid., 440–47, here 444; Colin Mackenzie to Alexander Gillanders, 25 July 1794; ibid., 448–55, here 449f.

31. Colin Mackenzie to Alexander Gillanders, 25 July 1794, NAS/GD/46/17/4, 448–55, here 455.

32. Colin Mackenzie to John Leyden, 9 October 1810, NLS/Ms 3380, 136–39, 140–43 (two letters).

33. For the following see also T. Wolffhardt, 'Inseln am Rande Europas: Zeit, Entwicklung und Tradition auf Lewis und Harris, Äußere Hebriden', in A. Fischer-Kattner et al. (eds), *Schleifspuren: Lesarten des 18. Jahrhunderts. Festschrift für Eckhart Hellmuth* (Munich, 2011), 242f.

34. Cf. R. Mitchison, 'The Government and the Highlands, 1707–45', in R. Mitchison and N. Phillipson (eds), *Scotland in the Age of Improvement* (Edinburgh, 1996), 32, 34–36, 40f; and A.I. Macinnes, *Clanship, Commerce and the House of Stuart, 1603–1788* (East Linton, 1996), 196f.

35. Cf. Colley, *Britons*, 158f. For the ambivalent role of Francis Humberston Mackenzie, who on the one hand pursued a policy of radical modernization, but on the other felt committed to traditional notions of his role as *caber feidh*, see F. McKichan, 'Lord Seaforth and Highland Estate Management in the First Phase of Clearance (1783–1815)', *Scottish Historical Review* 86(1) (2007), 50–68.

36. Cf. T.M. Devine, *Clanship to Crofters' War: The Social Transformation of the Scottish Highlands* (Manchester and New York, 1994), 32–53; id., 'Landlordism and Highland Emigration', in id. (ed.), *Scottish Emigration and Scottish Society* (Edinburgh 1992), 87–94; C.A. Whatley, *Scottish Society 1707–1830: Beyond Jacobitism, Towards Industrialisation* (Manchester, 2000), 24–54.

37. George Gillanders and Kenneth Mackenzie, 'Proposals for Improving the Island of Lewis, the Estates of Kintail and Lochalsh, with other matters relative to the right management of the Estate of Seaforth', Edinburgh, 19 February 1765, NAS/GD/427/150/1. See also Wolffhardt, 'Inseln am Rande Europas', 246f.

38. In the second half of the eighteenth century, kelp production became one of the most important sources of income for landowners on the Outer Hebrides. For instance, at the beginning of the nineteenth century, Seaforth's estates produced about nine hundred tons per year, bringing a net profit of over ten thousand pounds. Cf. M. Gray, 'The Kelp Industry in the Highlands and Islands', *Economic History Review*, 2nd ser., 4(2) (1951), 203. See also L. Rymer, 'The Scottish Kelp Industry', *Scottish Geographical Magazine* 90(3) (1974), 142–52.

39. In 1703 Martin Martin talks of a village in which about sixty families live. The 'Statistical Account' of the 1790s lists 760 inhabitants. Campbell's claim of 2,000 inhabitants in 1774 is probably a mistake based on Webster's census of 1755 which gave the inhabitants *of the whole parish* as 1812. Cf. M. Martin, *A Description of the Western Isles of Scotland: Containing a full Account of their Situation, Extent, Soil, Product, Harbours* (London 1703), 30; J. Sinclair, *The Statistical Account of Scotland Drawn up from the Communications of the Ministers of the Different Parishes*, 21 vols (Edinburgh, 1791–99), vol. 19, 245; vol. 20, 616; vol. 21, 476; and J. Campbell, *A Political Survey of Britain: Being a Series of Reflections on the Situation, Lands, Inhabitants, Revenues, Colonies, and Commerce of this Island*, 2 vols (London, 1774), vol. 1, 622.

40. Cf. Campbell, *Political Survey*, 616–22; J.R. Coull, 'The Development of Herring Fishing in the Outer Hebrides', *International Journal of Maritime History* 15(2) (2003), 21–42, esp. 22–26; R.A. Dodgshon, 'Coping with Risk: Subsistence Crisis in the Scottish Islands and Highlands, 1600–1800', *Rural History* 17(1) (2004), 1–25.

41. Cf. Sinclair, *Statistical Account of Scotland*, vol. 19, 249.

42. Cf. Gillanders and Mackenzie, *Proposals for Improving the Island of Lewis*, 1765, NAS/GD/427/150/1.

43. Cf. [Member of the Highland Society in London], *The Necessity of Founding Villages contiguous to Harbours for the Effectual Establishment of Fisheries on the West Coast of Scotland and the Hebrides* (London, 1786), 19–22. See also John Mackenzie to Daniel MacLeod, 16 June 1762, NAS/GD/427/226/3.

44. J. Knox, *A Tour through the Highlands and Hebride Islands in MDCCCLXXXVI* (London, 1787), 182f.

45. In 1763 John Walker reported that of the roughly seven thousand inhabitants of Lewis about six thousand did not have command of either written or spoken English. Cf. J. Walker, 'An Oeconomical History of the Hebrides or Western Islands of Scotland', *Transactions of the Gaelic Society of Inverness* 24 (1899–1901), 125. See also R. Mitchison, 'Scotland 1750–1850', in *The Cambridge Social History of Britain, 1750–1850*, 2 vols (Cambridge, 1990), vol. 1, 181.

46. Cf. C.W. Withers, *Gaelic Scotland: The Transformation of a Culture Region* (London and New York, 1988), 110–12.

47. For the problems and opportunities of this concept, which has hardly been worked out theoretically, see R.J. Hind, 'The Internal Colonial Concept', *Comparative Studies in Society and History* 26(3) (1984), 543–68.

48. The blurring of the social and cultural boundaries between the Highlands and the Lowlands is one of the main criticisms made of Michael Hechter, who introduced the concept of 'internal colonialism' in the British Isles. Hechter refers mainly to economic, not cultural, processes. M. Hechter, *Internal Colonialism: The Celtic Fringe in British National Development, 1536–1966* (London, 1975).

49. See P. Womack, *Improvement and Romance: Constructing the Myth of the Highlands* (Basingstoke and London, 1989), esp. 3, 5, 11, 174f.

50. A good overview is L. Zastoupil and M. Moir, 'Introduction' in eid. (eds.), *The Great Indian Education Debate: Documents relating to the Orientalist-Anglicist Controversy, 1781–1843* (London Studies on South Asia 18) (Richmond,1999), 1–72.

51. Macinnes, *Clanship, Commerce and the House of Stuart*, 178.

52. Cf. Devine, *Clanship to Crofters' War*, 113f; C.W. Withers, *Gaelic in Scotland 1698–1981: The Geographical History of a Language* (Edinburgh, 1984), 120–37; id. *Gaelic Scotland*, 121–45 and 'Education and Anglicisation: The Policy of the SSPCK toward the Education of the Highlander, 1709–1825', *Scottish Studies* 26 (1982), 37–56; and D.J. Withrington, 'The S.P.C.K. and Highland Schools in Mid-Eighteenth Century', *Scottish Historical Review* 41(132) (1962), 89–99.

53. Gillanders and Mackenzie, 'Proposals for Improving the Island of Lewis', 1765, NAS/GD/427/150/1.

54. D. Loch, *Essays on Trade, Commerce, Manufactures and Fisheries in Scotland: Containing Remarks on the Situation of most of the Sea-Ports*, 3 vols (Edinburgh, 1778), vol. 2, 180f.

55. Cf. 'Memoir of Dr Walker', in W. Jardine, *The Naturalist's Library, II: Ornithology, vol. XII, III* (Edinburgh, London and Dublin, 1842), 25. See also, in general: J. Symonds, 'Toiling in the Vale of Tears: Everyday Life and Resistance in South Uist, Outer Hebrides, 1760–1860', *International Journal of Historical Archaeology* 3(2) (1999), 101–22; and E. Richards, 'How Tame were the Highlanders During the Clearances?', *Scottish Studies* 17(1) (1973), 35–50.

56. Cf. Devine, 'Landlordism and Highland Emigration', 91; R.E. Tyson, 'Landlord Policies and Population Change in North-East Scotland and the Western Isles', *Northern Scotland* 19 (1999), 63–74; J.M. Bumsted, *The People's Clearance: Highland Emigration to British North America, 1770–1815* (Edinburgh, 1982), 45–47.

57. John Downie to John Mackenzie of Strickathrow, 4 March 1773, NAS/GD/427/216/17.

58. Various magazines reported that the people emigrated due to the 'oppressions they laboured under'. See, for instance: 'Chronicle', *Annual Register, or a View of the History, Politics, and Literature, for the Year 1773*, 2nd edn. (London, 1775), 121; 'The Monthly Chronologer: Scotland', *London Magazine: Or, Gentleman's Monthly Intelligencer* 42 (July 1773), 363. See also D. MacDonald, *Lewis: A History of the Island* (Edinburgh, 1978), 165.

59. See John Mackenzie of Strickathrow to George Gillanders, 10 April 1772; also 16 November 1772; 17 November 1772 and 10 December 1772, NAS/GD/427/214/17, 26, 27, 28.

60. The Seaforth estates played a pioneering role here as well. Another great migration in 1781/1782 was followed by the expulsion of more than three hundred people on Lewis and Skye in the early 1790s. All in all about three thousand people were expelled between 1780 and 1832, many in the name of Francis Humberston Mackenzie as head of the Seaforth family. McKichan stresses, however, that most of these cases of expulsion were caused by new proprietors. Cf. E. Richards, *A History of the Highland Clearances: Agrarian Transformation and the Evictions, 1746–1886*, 2 vols (London and Canberra, 1982–1985), vol. 1, 200; and McKichan, 'Lord Seaforth and Highland Estate Management', 66.

61. See the report in the minutes of the SSPCK meeting of 1799. Cf. W. Bennett, '*The Excellence of Christian Morality': A Sermon preached before the Society in Scotland for Propagating Christian Knowledge at their Anniversary Meeting* (Edinburgh, 1800), Appendix, 20–22.

62. See for example John Mackenzie of Strickathrow to George Gillanders, 7 October 1772, NAS/GD/427/214/24.

63. He had received a patent as 'Surveyor, Inspector & Gager of the Excise in the whole of Lewis Island'. John Mackenzie of Strickathrow to George Gillanders, 14 February 1772, NAS/GD/427/214/14.

64. Gillanders was entitled to appoint the Postmaster. John Mackenzie of Strickathrow to George Gillanders, 20 August 1771, NAS/GD/427/214/6.

65. Cf. Knox, *Tour through the Highlands and Hebride Islands*, 92f.

66. John Mackenzie of Strickathrow to George Gillanders, 7 October 1772, NAS/GD/427/214/24.

67. Colin Mackenzie to Alexander Gillanders, 25 July 1794, NAS/GD/46/17/4, 448–55, here 452f.

68. Mackenzie, 'Statement of the Literary Labours', 242.

69. According to W.C. Mackenzie (*Colonel Colin Mackenzie*, 1), Mackenzie had at least three brothers and one sister; Phillimore (*Historical Records*, vol. 1, 349) and, following him, P. Robb ('Colin Mackenzie', *ODNB*), say two brothers and one sister.

70. Cf. Colin Mackenzie to John Leyden, 9 October 1810, NLS/Ms 3380, 136–39.

71. This was probably the school supported by the Royal Bounty (a yearly donation from the King), which, in comparison to other schools in the Highlands, had a fairly good reputation. It seems to have been more suited to Mackenzie's social environment than the alternative SSPCK school. For the schools see MacDonald, *Lewis: A History of the Island*, 141–45, and the reports by John Walker for the Commission of the Annexed Estates (1763) printed as Walker, 'An Oeconomical History', 124 and for the Assembly of the Church of Scotland, printed as J. Walker, 'Report to the Assembly 1765, concerning the State of the Highlands and Islands', *The Scots Magazine* 28(12) (1766), 682.

72. Colin Mackenzie [to Francis Humberston Mackenzie], 21 July 1794, NAS/GD/46/17/4, 440–47, here 445.

73. See Colin Mackenzie to William Bentinck, 23 June 1805, BL/OIOC/Mss Eur/F/228/39 (11), 13–16, here 16.
74. Cf. the report by John Walker to the SSPCK 1763, printed in 'Memoir of Dr Walker', esp. 36.
75. Cf. Mantena, *Origins of Modern Historiography*, 61, 211f, fn 7.
76. A.M. Macleod, 'A Highland Parish of the Last Century', *Good Words* 32 (1891), 238. These are the recollections of one of the author's friends about his grandfather (John Downie?), a clergyman in Stornoway.
77. Johnston, 'Statement by Alexander Johnston, 19 July 1832', 254, para. 1930.
78. 'Domestic Transactions', *Royal Magazine or Gentleman's Monthly Companion* (October 1761), 214.
79. Cf. J. Shaw, *The Management of Scottish Society, 1707–64: Power, Nobles, Lawyers, Edinburgh Agents and English Influence* (Edinburgh, 1983), 11. In the years before his death Francis Napier lived in a house in Seaford, Sussex. Cf. M.A. Lower, 'Memorial of the Town, Parish and Cinque-Port of Seaford, Historical and Antiquarian', *Sussex Archaeological Collections Relating to the History and Antiquities of the County* 3 (1854), 124; and A. Johnston to 'My Dear Daughters', 1 July 1836, in M. Napier, *The Life and Times of Montrose Illustrated from Original Manuscripts, Including Family Papers; With Portraits and Autographs* (Edinburgh, 1840), 501–6, esp. 503.
80. Napier, *Memoirs of John Napier*, vi–viii. As regards Mackenzie's collaboration with Francis Napier this author also, of course, refers to Johnston's statement, while another biography of the mathematician from the 1780s makes no mention of it: D. Stewart, Earl of Buchan, and W. Minto, *An Account of the Life, Writings and Inventions of John Napier of Merchiston* (Perth, 1787).
81. See Johnston's long contribution to 'Proceedings of the Anniversary Meeting of the Royal Asiatic Society held on Saturday, the 9th of May 1835', *Journal of the Royal Asiatic Society of Great Britain and Ireland* 2 (1835), ix–xvii. This story was reprinted several times: see for example 'Proceedings of the Anniversary Meeting of the Royal Asiatic Society held on Saturday, the 9th of May 1835' *Madras Journal of Literature and Science* 4(12) (1836) 168–77; 'Proceedings of the Anniversary Meeting of the Royal Asiatic Society held on the 6th of May 1837', *Journal of the Royal Asiatic Society for Great Britain and Ireland* 4(2) (1837), xxxiii, fn 10; M. Napier, 'Introduction', in id. (ed.), *De Arte Logistica Joannis Naperi Merchistonii Baronis Libri qui supersunt* (Edinburgh, 1839), lvi–lix.
82. Napier, 'Introduction', lixf.
83. The year 1773 can be found in most reference works. Cf. for instance J. Debrett, *The Peerage of the United Kingdom of Great Britain and Ireland*, 13th improved edn., 2 vols (London, 1820), vol. 2, 870–72; W. Anderson, *The Scottish Nation, or the Surnames, Families, Literature, Honours and Geographical History of the People of Scotland*, 3 vols (Edinburgh, 1862), vol. 3, 239f. However, the year is stated as 1774, just a few years after Napier's death in E. Kimber, *The New Peerage; or, Ancient and Present State of the Nobility of England, Scotland, and Ireland: Containing a Genealogical Account of All the Peers*, 2nd edn., 3 vols (London, 1778), vol. 2, 219.
84. 'Set of Acres in and about the Town of Stornoway for six years from whitsunday next made by the Right Honourable Kenneth Earl of Seaforth at Seaforth Lodge upon the sixth day of September one thousand seven hundred and seventy three', NAS/GD/427/44.
85. Cf. the accounts in NAS/GD/427/91/5.
86. Colin Mackenzie to Alexander Gillanders, 25 July 1794, NAS/GD/46/17/4, 448–55, here 451.
87. Colin Mackenzie to Francis Humberston Mackenzie, 9 August 1796, NAS/GD/46/17/4, 485–95, here 492.

88. 'Warrant', 8 February 1776, NAS/CE/3/13/3. There can be no doubt that the Colin Mackenzie mentioned was the future Surveyor General of India as is evidenced for example by Charles John Shore, who spoke to some of the family's acquaintances. See Shore, *Reminiscences of Many Years*, vol. 1, 347–49.

89. For building the Customs House see 'Instructions for George Gillanders Factor of Lewis by Doctor John Mackenzie, Comissioner for Lord Fortrose', 1767, NAS/GD/427/153. The Customs employees had come to Stornoway in June 1765 (John Mackenzie of Strickathrow to George Gillanders, 2 November 1771, NAS/GD/427/214/11). From this time independent Custom Accounts (NAS/E/504/33/1) and letter-books (NAS/CE/86/2/1) were kept for Stornoway.

90. John Mackenzie of Strickathrow to George Gillanders, 2 November 1771, NAS/GD/427/214/11.

91. There is evidence that the Seaforth family kept on influencing appointments to the Stornoway Customs House in later years. See Adam Smith and David Reid to Francis Humberston Mackenzie, 23 January 1786, NAS/GD/427/225/8.

92. For the very similar entry requirements for the English Customs service see J. Brewer, 'Servants of the Public', in J. Brewer and E. Hellmuth (eds), *Rethinking Leviathan: The Eighteenth-Century State in Britain and Germany* (Oxford, 1999), 128f; for the complicated processes for influencing appointments see A. Murdoch, *The People Above: Politics and Administration in Mid Eighteenth-Century Scotland* (Edinburgh, 1980), 18–20.

93. Board of Customs to Stornoway, 10 July 1776, NAS/CE/86/2/3; 'Warrant', 8 February 1776, NAS/CE/3/13/3.

94. Cf. R.C. Jarvis, 'The Archival History of the Customs Records' in F. Ranger (ed.), *Prisca Munimenta: Studies in Archival and Administrative History* (London, 1973), 209; E. Evelynola, *The Organization of the English Customs System 1696–1786* (Newton Abbot, 1968), 56f.

95. See G.M. Anderson, W.F. Shughart II and R.D. Tollison, 'Adam Smith in the Customhouse', *Journal of Political Economy* 93(4) (1985), 740–59, esp. 742–45; and T. Donnelly, 'The King's Custom Administration in Aberdeen, 1750–1815', *Northern Scotland* 16 (1996), 187–98. For appointments to Stornoway in 1773–1775 see 'North Britain Customs Establishment Book', NAS/CE/3/13/2.

96. Board of Customs to Stornoway, 8 February 1777, NAS/CE/86/2/3.

97. Board of Customs to Stornoway, 7 June 1777, NAS/CE/86/2/3.

98. Stornoway to Board of Customs, 30 May 1778 and 27 July 1778, NAS/CE/86/2/2, 10 November 1778, NAS/CE/86/2/3.

99. Stornoway to Board of Customs, 13 December 1781 and Board of Customs to Stornoway, 18 April 1782, NAS/CE/86/2/3.

100. Cf. Board of Customs to Stornoway, 27 September 1776, NAS/CE/86/2/3; Donnelly, 'King's Custom Administration', 196f.

101. See esp. the 'Customs Accounts' 1776–1781: NAS/E/504/33/1 and NAS/E/504/33/2, both of which he worked on.

102. See Board of Customs to Stornoway, 19 June 1776, 17 September 1776, 10 October 1776 and 19 April 1779, NAS/CE/86/2/3.

103. Brewer, 'Servants of the Public', 135–47.

104. Cf. 'North Britain Customs Establishment Books', NAS/CE/3/13/2. Mackenzie drew this salary from February 1776.

105. Johnston, 'Statement by Alexander Johnston, 19 July 1832', 254, para. 1930.

106. Mackenzie, 'Statement of the Literary Labours', 242f.

107. According to Wilson's catalogue his collection contains not one single translated text on arithmetic. Cf. Wilson, *Descriptive Catalogue*. Although Wilson's catalogue contains a

relatively small number of scripts on natural scientific subjects, according to his descriptions only a few smaller scripts (0.2 per cent of the total) deal with arithmetic in the narrower sense (vol. 1, 129f, No LIILIV; 160, No. XXXV and XXXVI; 254, No. X; 356, No. III, vol. 2, 141, No. LXXIII).

108. Cf. John Mackenzie of Strickathrow to George Gillanders, 14 February 1772, NAS/ GD/427/214/14: 'I observe what you write about Carn his Bankruptcy is what I long ago suspected but as we are now so far in for it with him I think the method you propose yourself the best for Procuring redress that is if possible to find a Cautioner for what is pass'd before he is turned out of office'.

109. 'Deputation by Robert Oliphant Esq, Deputy Postmaster General of Scotland to George Gillanders 1776', NAS/GD/46/13/99/5; 'Memorial' by Gillanders [1778], NAS/ GD/46/13/99/6; Murdoch Mackenzie, 'Memorial in Regard of the Lewis Packet and Post Office', 26 September 1787, NAS/GD/46/13/99/7. The payment was raised to 85 pounds between 1787 and 1789. Cf. NAS/GD/46/13/99/17A.

110. Cf. Colin Mackenzie to William Kirkpatrick, 16/19 November 1801, BL/OIOC/ Mss Eur/F/228/19; Colin Mackenzie to Henry Trail, 2 August 1805, BL/OIOC/Mss Eur/F/228/39.

111. Colin Mackenzie to George Gillanders, 16 May 1780, NAS/GD/427/211/6.

112. Cf. G.J. Bryant, 'Officers of the East India Company's Army in the Days of Clive and Hastings', *Journal of Imperial and Commonwealth History* 6(3) (1978), 205.

113. Colin Mackenzie to Alexander Gillanders, 25 July 1794, NAS/GD/46/17/4, 448–55, here 450.

114. See for instance Colin Mackenzie [to Francis Humberston Mackenzie], 13 February 1792 and 2 March 1793, NAS/GD/46/17/4, 434, 435–438; and John and Alexander Anderson to Mackenzie of Seaforth, 7 February 1797, ibid., 498f.

115. Colin Mackenzie to George Gillanders, 23 November 1782, NAS/GD/427/211/27. Emphasis in original.

116. Colin Mackenzie to Francis Humberston Mackenzie, 9 August 1796, NAS/GD/46/17/4, 485–95, here 492, 494. In the same letter Mackenzie mentions that Seaforth was not particularly happy about his departure from Stornoway: 'These [return after mastering ten thousand Pounds to fifteen thousand Pounds] are views which I have never dropped in my worst of fortunes, and which I can now venture to tell you I could entertain even (when influenced by motives which I shall ever honour) you did not fully approve of my Indian Voyage – Views for which I perhaps paid dear in tearing as under those ties which attached me to affectionate relatives, the prudence & regard for them will justify it, while my heart tells me I did no injustice to my feelings' (Ibid., 494f).

117. Colin Mackenzie to Board of Customs, 22 March 1779 (quote) and Board of Customs to Stornoway, 26 July 1779, NAS/CE/86/2/3.

118. Mackenzie had postponed his period of leave here without permission. Stornoway to Board of Customs, 14 October 1780; Board of Customs to Stornoway, 8 November 1780; Colin Mackenzie to Board of Customs, 13 February 1781; Board of Customs to Stornoway, 1 March 1781; 21 March 1781; 11 April 1781, NAS/CE/86/2/3, Minutes, 20 March and 9 April 1781; NAS/CE/1/17, 62 and 78.

119. Board of Customs to Stornoway, 24 January 1782, NAS/CE/86/2/3 (quote); Minutes, 24 January 1782, NAS/CE/1/17, 261.

120. Board of Customs to Stornoway, 15 April 1782 and 27 May 1782, NAS/CE/86/2/3; Minutes, 15 April 1782 and 23 May 1782, NAS/CE/1/17, 317 and 348.

121. Board of Customs to Stornoway, 24 January 1782, NAS/CE/86/2/3.

122. Board of Customs to Stornoway, 27 May 1782, NAS/CE/86/2/3; Minutes, 23 May 1782, NAS/CE/1/17, 348.

123. At this time the agricultural reformer John Sinclair (1754–1835) was MP for Caithness. Cf. J. Brooke and L. Namier (eds), *The House of Commons 1754–1790*, 3 vols (London, 1964), vol. 3, 440f; R. Mitchison, *Agricultural Sir John: The Life of Sir John Sinclair of Ulbster, 1754–1835* (London, 1962), 32–36.

124. Between 1780 and 1784 Major General Charles Ross (1729?–1797) was MP for the Tain (Northern) Burghs. Cf. Brooke and Namier, *House of Commons*, vol. 3, 377f.

125. Since the 1770s Henry Dundas, Viscount Melville, had expanded the position of Lord Advocate into a sort of ministry for Scotland. See M. Fry, *The Dundas Despotism* (Edinburgh, 1992), 34f, 54–95.

126. From 1780 to 1784 John Mackenzie (1727–1789), known as Lord MacLeod, was MP for Ross-shire. From 1779 to 1782 he was in India, and so was not available as the MP responsible for Colin Mackenzie. Cf. Brooke and Namier, *House of Commons*, vol. 3, 86–88.

127. Colin Mackenzie to George Gillanders, 23 November 1782, NAS/GD/427/211/27.

128. The anthropologist James Scott, for instance, stresses the mutual obligations in the patronage system when he describes it as a 'largely instrumental friendship in which an individual of higher socio-economic status (patron) uses his own influence and resources to provide protection or benefits, or both, for a person of lower status (client) who, for his part, reciprocates by offering general support and assistance, including personal services to the patron'. J.C. Scott, 'Patron-client politics and political change in Southeast Asia', *American Political Science Review* 66(1) (1972), 92. For a detailed discussion, referring explicitly to this definition of Scott's, see Bourne, *Patronage and Society*, 4–9.

129. Cf. Colin Mackenzie to George Gillanders, 23 November 1782, NAS/GD/427/211/27; Board of Customs to Stornoway, 22 May 1783 and Stornoway to Board, 2 June 1783, NAS/CE/86/2/3.

130. See H.M. Chichester and G.J. Bryant, 'Thomas Frederick Humberston Mackenzie (1753–1783)', *ODNB*.

131. For Charles Francis Greville (1749–1809) see Brooke and Namier, *House of Commons*, vol. 2, 550f.

132. See Greville's correspondence with Thomas and Francis Humberston Mackenzie from the years 1778 and 1799 to 1806: BL/Mss Add/42071, 67, 101, 195, 197–99, 204–07, 209–12, 213–16 and with Francis Humberston Mackenzie BL/Mss Add/40715, 165–68; 211f.

133. Colin Mackenzie to Henry Trail, 2 August 1805, BL/OIOC/Mss Eur/F/228/39.

134. Cf. Brooke and Namier, *House of Commons*, vol. 2, 550f.

135. Board of Customs to Stornoway, 16 December 1782, NAS/CE/86/2/3; Minute, 16 December 1782, NAS/CE/1/17, 496.

136. Cf. Colin Mackenzie to George Gillanders. 23 November 1782, NAS/GD/427/211/27.

137. BL/IOR/B/98, 767; Phillimore, *Historical Records*, vol. 1, 349.

138. See 'List of Cadets appointed in the Year 1782', BL/IOR/L/Mil/9/255, 65Z and 74Z. This is clearly Colin 'Carn' Mackenzie, as the name of his ship, *Atlas,* is mentioned.

139. Cf. Parker, 'The Directors of the East India Company', 25–27; and G. McGilvary, *Guardian of the East-India Company: The Life of Laurence Sulivan* (London and New York, 2006), 139.

140. Cf. Callahan, *East India Company and Army Reform*, 18f.

141. Cf. the *Atlas* logbook: BL/IOR/L/Mar/B/27/Q. Here too the frequency with which the name Colin Mackenzie occurs has caused confusion. However, Peter Robb's suggestion that Mackenzie possibly went to India as early as 1782 with the *Deptford*, though probably not until August 1783 with the *Argos* (Robb, 'Colin Mackenzie', *ODNB*) is clearly contradicted by a letter from the Board of Customs in Edinburgh stating that its former employee sailed on the *Atlas*. Board of Customs to Stornoway, 30 June 1783, NAS/CE/86/2/3.

Chapter 2

BUILDING AN EAST INDIAN CAREER

Madras

On 2 September 1783, the day that the *Atlas* dropped anchor at Madras, it was stormy and rainy. After a relatively uneventful voyage of almost six months – from Portsmouth, via the Cape Verde islands, then through the Atlantic to Cape Town, where the ship stopped to stock up on water and food, then sailing round Madagascar and Ceylon – this was the ship's first port of call in East India before carrying on to Calcutta. To start with, however, the bad weather prevented passengers and crew from disembarking and the repairs needed after such a long voyage from being carried out. All that the passengers could do was spend the whole day and another night on board until on 3 September they were eventually transported to the beach and stood on terra firma once again after more than six months at sea.[1]

What they saw during their enforced stay on board must have really piqued their curiosity, at least that of those passengers who had never been to the subcontinent. The artist and former round-the-world sailor William Hodges, who a few year earlier – under perfect blue skies – had taken the same route to Madras, describes the view that confronted the observer of the city from the sea in his travelogue: from a long, flat coastline, and the light sand of the beach, Fort St George reared up and beyond its walls the impressive buildings of the EIC, many adorned with colonnades. Most of the passengers were particularly impressed by the gleaming white of the buildings, often compared to marble, achieved using a technique typical of Madras, that of polishing the house walls with *chunam*, a sort of shell lime.[2] North of the Fort, at some distance from its walls, came the much larger black town, likewise walled on the land side, where Chinese, Portuguese and Armenian traders initially lived alongside the

Notes from this chapter begin on page 73.

original indigenous population. Finally, to the south was the former Portuguese settlement of San Thomé.[3]

The *Atlas* was certainly not the only ship to drop anchor at Madras on that September day in 1783 as at this time the city – Britain's most important naval stronghold in South India, and vital for controlling the Gulf of Bengal – was at war. Despite its imposing appearance from the sea, until well into the nineteenth century it had no actual harbour. So the ships that stopped there had to drop anchor one or two miles away and wait for the local catamarans and *masula* boats to collects goods and passengers. Given the strong current and high tide, which still today make Madras beach one of the most dangerous in the whole of India, loading and unloading ships was far from danger free and there were often tragic accidents leading to the loss of goods or passengers.[4]

On this 3 September some of the new arrivals, employed by the EIC as writers or cadets, must have gone straight from the beach to the interior of the Fort in order to report for duty and to move into their accommodation. In many cases, however, the first thing was to pay the boat people and to organize transportation of their luggage, which was generally piled up on the beach after arrival. During this time traders tried to sell their wares to the new arrivals while all sorts of servants and the agents so indispensable to a European staying any length of time in India, known in Madras as *dubashes,* offered their services.[5] For many of the passengers this first contact with the indigenous population was quite stressful and their reports make it clear that here they were confronted for the first time with the sensation of being in an environment that felt culturally quite alien. Even an experienced traveller like William Hodges was struck by the surroundings, and for him the first contact with Indians was 'the moment in which an European feels the great distinction between Asia and his own country'.[6]

The insecurity suffered by the new arrivals as a result of this experience can only have been overcome to any extent once they entered Fort St George through the Sea Gate. Of course, if Francis Swain Ward's drawings are to be believed, there were plenty of new and unusual things to see here as well – such as the bazaar not far from the gate, where servants in white linen and traders in turbans swarmed around, and Europeans being carried along on the customary palanquins – but the dominant feature was the EIC's representative buildings. In particular, beyond a large open space, Fort Square could be seen: a walled square with the Governor's house in the middle, the town's power centre whose façade, in keeping with the style of the town, was brilliant white, structured with pillars and balconies. All round Fort Square various buildings such as the Admiralty residence, quarters, arsenals and shooting ranges emphasized the military significance of Fort St George, while the EIC's civil servants were quartered in a former Catholic monastery, partially built by the Portuguese, at the side of the large parade ground. The town's mercantile character was revealed by the numerous traditional trading houses, generally called 'go-downs', whose lower floors were used for storage, with the traders living upstairs.[7]

In 1783 Madras already had a history stretching back over 140 years. Founded in 1639 as a modest stronghold on the Coromandel Coast, it had developed into one of Britain's most important trading centres in India, initially due to the flourishing textile trade.[8] The town was not so much a 'colonial port city',[9] as an agglomeration of settlements that existed before the British arrived. Here too, however, as in Bombay or Calcutta, warehouses and administrative buildings had grown up around the Fort, and indeed houses for the European population; while local traders, attracted by the financial opportunities, had settled in the neighbouring black town. The image of the city that confronted the observer in the 1780s had largely developed in the 1740s after three years' occupation by French units. It was this experience of military vulnerability in particular that had led to the Fort being extended; it was more or less completed by 1783 under the direction of the engineer Patrick Ross.[10] With its characteristic form – semi-octagonal, following the principles of the French architect Vauban – it still dominates the city to this day.

As the town made progress, its population also grew and before long the limited space within the Fort was no longer adequate as a residential area for the European inhabitants. Madras was characterized by the heterogeneity of its population, made up of the most diverse ethnic and religious groups: Tamils and Telugus, Gujaratis and Marathas, Sunni Muslims from North India and Shiites from the Deccan, Armenian and Syrian Christians, Catholic Portuguese and French, as well as Protestant Dutch and British. Compared to many other colonial towns in India this had led to great cultural openness and plurality.[11] Thus from the mid century onwards the northern section of the black town was increasingly used as a residential and business area by the European population. Furthermore, in the 1760s, between and in the villages surrounding Fort St George, which gradually became a formal part of Madras in the course of the eighteenth century, a series of villas were built as residences for well-healed Europeans, typically known as 'garden houses'. So the city of Madras gradually grew together from a number of different settlements which for a long time had their own independent administrations.[12]

Politically, too, Madras – as one of the three British presidencies in India at that time – had gained a certain importance. Restitution of British rule in Madras, with the Peace of Aix-la-Chapelle of 1748, had been followed by further conflicts with the French in which local rulers increasingly became involved as well. The British, especially after the Seven Years' War, had eventually gained the upper hand and had pushed the French back to their original stronghold of Pondicherry. Not least due to the sepoy armies formed during these decades[13] the Company, along with its great military success in Bengal, was also able to establish itself as a territorial power in the south of the subcontinent. Around

1780, on the southeast coast, they ruled not only over the Madras Jaghire – the area around the Fort, which the Company had gradually acquired from its ally, the Nawab of Arcot – but formally at least over the Northern Circars as well, an area south of Orissa that was occupied for a time by the French. British possession was confirmed by the Mughal in 1765.[14]

Nonetheless, the impression of great power that may have imposed itself on many travellers when they first saw Fort St George was not a true reflection of the Company's actual standing in South India. It had acquired its new position as a territorial power in competition with the aspiring states of the region, especially Mysore under the Muslim ruler Haidar Ali, who had risen from the administration of the former Rajah and pursued an aggressive foreign policy.[15] The deteriorating relationship between him and the British had led to conflicts and, between 1767 and 1769 and again since 1780, to wars. The last of these especially, still going on in 1782, shows how insecure the Company's position in South India was at this time – despite the abundance of power on show in Madras. The widespread corruption, disputes within the governing council, as well as the corruptibility and incompetence of Governor Thomas Rumbold had led to the emergence of an anti-British coalition consisting of all the significant powers in the region: Mysore, the Nizam of Hyderabad, the Marathas and the French. Haidar Ali's armies had plundered their way through the Jaghire in order to cut off the Company's supplies and had reached the outskirts of Madras. The British units that opposed them had suffered a devastating defeat in the Battle of Polilur. Although this had no serious consequences for the EIC – Haidar died in 1782 and under his son, Tipu Sultan, the coalition fell apart, while the British armies enjoyed their first successes under Sir Eyre Coote, who had rushed in from Bengal – the Battle of Polilur remained a traumatic experience. Not least, the financial problems arising from the war exposed the need to reform the trading company's internal structures. Thus the war almost lost in South India was certainly an important impetus for the changes made in the 1780s and 1790s.[16]

Above all, the military defeat can be seen as an expression of a far deeper crisis affecting the internal structure of the EIC and caused by the fact that many of its employees were far more concerned with their own interests than with those of their employer. What had become particularly notorious were the networks of its ally, the Nawab of Arcot, who took out enormous loans in order to protect and extend his military and political independence. With great skill he managed to play off the interests of his creditors, many of whom were themselves Company employees and even had a lobby in the London Parliament, against the interests of the trading company. While the Directors were primarily interested in an atmosphere of political stability that favoured trade, his creditors supported the Nawab's expansive policy that was supposed to enable him to service his debts. Thus Rumbold's predecessor, Lord Pigot, had been summarily removed by his colleagues in Madras when he sought to reinstate the Rajah of Tanjore, whose territory had previously been annexed by the Nawab.[17] Lord Pigot died a short time later as a result of his imprisonment, and the scandal caused in London's political circles by these events was intensified when it became known that in 1780 Rumbold had returned from India with a fortune of three-quarters of a million pounds, a large proportion of which came from the Rajah's coffers.[18]

At this time the American War of Independence was shaking the British Empire and overshadowing all other events, so the initial reaction in Parliament was fairly muted. For instance, a parliamentary commission of enquiry into the war in South India, which investigated Rumbold, ended without any concrete results. Even so, when the first rumours about his machinations reached London, Lord Marcartney was appointed as Governor, the first not to have made a career for himself within the Company and therefore viewed as far less susceptible to traditional practices, which were increasingly being regarded as corrupt.[19] At around the same time massive criticism of Governor General Warren Hastings started, led by Edmund Burke and eventually leading to his impeachment, and new concerns were raised about the Company's poor financial state.[20] Eventually it became ever clearer, bearing in mind, too, the loss of a large section of the North American colonies, that Lord North's Regulating Act of 1773 was no longer adequate to control Britain's Indian possessions effectively, possessions that were now more important than ever. So the India Act of 1784, based on a draft by Henry Dundas, finally subjected the EIC to control by the British Parliament.[21]

Above all, however, the administration in India needed to change. So in the 1780s a long phase of internal transformation began within the Company, which represented an important turning point in the history of British rule in India. From a trading company, designed primarily to make a profit for private investors, a colonial administrative apparatus emerged during the decades to follow, subject to control by the British political system. In the process the Company's employees, originally lured to India by the prospect of personal wealth, gradually developed into civil servants, some of whom had long careers helping to build up the administrative apparatus. It is only in retrospect, however, that this becomes clear. The young men who docked at Madras on that September day in 1783 had no idea of the changes that were gradually to take place. They still dreamed of returning home, after a few years, as rich men.

Changing Prospects

One of the passengers who docked at Madras on 3 September 1783 was Colin Mackenzie, who boarded ship for India as an officer cadet but had already been made an ensign before arrival. Probably he had in his luggage a letter of recommendation from Humberston Mackenzie to Governor Lord Macartney,[22] which was quite common for new arrivals in India and opened many a career door by facilitating appointments to advantageous positions. However, Mackenzie soon had to fulfil his military duties. The war against Mysore continued until early 1784 and Mackenzie was sent with a corps of sepoys to the southern provinces of Coimbatoor and Dindigul,[23] where the British had had considerable success with an invasion of Tipu Sultan's provinces.[24] It seems that he was already involved in examining more closely the fortifications of Dindigul and Palighaut occupied by the British, a task that was to recur quite frequently during his career as an engineer. Six years later, during the Third Mysore War, his knowledge of these fortifications, handed back in 1784, was of great importance as they were stormed again, an attack in which Mackenzie himself took part.[25]

In June 1784 Mackenzie probably visited Madura, where Samuel Johnston, a civilian employee of the Company, lived with his wife (daughter of the fifth Lord Napier) and his son Alexander as a number of dated drawings made by Mackenzie indicate Samuel Johnston's house.[26] Alexander Johnston, then still a child of about eight years, later tried to claim that this visit was a key moment for Mackenzie's future cooperation with Indian intellectuals – his mother, he said, had introduced him to 'Brahmins and literary natives', as a result of which Mackenzie had conceived the plan for his collection.[27] Apart from other inconsistencies, this contradicts Mackenzie's own account and Johnston, who himself had published that account, must have noticed this as he corrected himself on this point only a few years later.[28]

Mackenzie's interests during his first years in India seem to have been quite different from what Johnston suggests. Mackenzie had probably only committed himself as a cadet because there was little chance of a job in the civil branch[29] – now he was searching for ways to accelerate his career and applied for a position with the Madras Engineers. The appointment, for which apart from a suitable recommendation all that was needed a simple test of basic mathematical knowledge, seems to have been retrospectively granted in May 1786.[30] This was certainly not unusual as, unlike in France, in the eighteenth-century British army, as in the Company, practical in-service training was seen as more important than previous academic education.[31] The engineers corps offered the chance to avoid a purely military career. Within the EIC army the engineers held a special position that put them in a sort of halfway house between the civil and military authorities and was based on the fact that the engineers, originally civilians, had not been integrated into the military until 1759.[32] So the Commander-in-Chief of the army had no independent right to give the engineers orders, and could only do so with the agreement of the civil government. At the same time, the corps, as one engineer put it in the early nineteenth century, was a 'skeleton corps', made up exclusively of officers to whom the pioneers were only regularly subordinated in the event of war. In peacetime, on the other hand, even the Chief Engineer was forbidden to take over an independent commando.[33]

Since the early 1770s the Madras Engineers had been led by an experienced officer, Patrick Ross, who had previously done many years' service in the Royal Army in the West Indies, and whose name today is primarily associated with the rebuilding of Fort St George.[34] Less well recognized, however, are his achievements as head of his department, which in some thirty years as Chief Engineer he purposefully built up, making it more independent of the military command structures. In 1775, for instance, his staff consisted of only about eight officers, but eleven years later the number had risen to twenty-one.[35] The centrepiece of his reform programme was the creation of administrative structures within which the engineers could embark on a regular career and, connected with this, increasing professionalization and specialization of the staff, following the French model.[36] Along with remuneration for his staff that reflected their qualifications, his most important demand was that all engineers should fall under the exclusive responsibility of the Chief Engineer. In his view the practice approved by the government up to this point – of subordinating officers from the corps to the commander on the spot – made it largely impossible for them to work in a coordinated and efficient way.[37]

Mackenzie, the new arrival, was greatly influenced by his superior's ideas. Years later he still remembered Ross as one of the people whose integrity and talent he most admired,[38] and when he himself became head of a department it was Ross's leadership style that he used as a model. Above all, however, in Ross he had found a superior who encouraged his ambitions and helped him to pave the way for his future career. In peacetime the corps of engineers, which despite the problems highlighted by Ross was regarded as one of the most professional groups in the Company's service, functioned as a sort of 'public works department' that performed numerous technical and architectural tasks in both the civil and military branches.[39] The Chief Engineer's books from this period, nowadays to be found in the Mackenzie Collection, indicate that the engineers were concerned with: maintaining and extending barracks, fortifications and public buildings; drawing maps for military purposes; road building; and even with producing gunpowder in the mill at Egmore.[40]

In 1787 Mackenzie carried out work on quarters and fortifications in several of the presidency's garrison towns.[41] But at an early stage he began to look for a chance to distinguish himself beyond the ordinary activities of an engineer in order to accelerate his career. During these years his prospects in India changed fundamentally because he was forced to recognize that, under the new conditions for EIC employees, the likelihood of making a huge fortune within a few years was remote. Above all, the usual eighteenth-century practice of saving a small sum during the first years in India and then investing it in the lucrative inland trade had been curbed, since it had long had the reputation of encouraging corruption and abuse of office amongst the employees, of plundering the country, and of provoking armed conflicts.

So in the second half of the eighteenth century the opportunities for involvement in private trade were continually reduced: from 1767 all governors in Bengal had to swear an oath that they would not indulge in private business,[42] and the Regulating Act of 1773 forbade all members of the newly formed Supreme Council and employees of the tax and justice administration any involvement with trade.[43] What is more, new monopolies on salt, areca nuts, tobacco and opium limited the trade opportunities open to other employees.[44] The ruling that members of the Council were not allowed to involve themselves in private business was extended to Madras in 1785 and a year later officers were forbidden to take part in any sort of financial transactions.[45] At the same time, the appointment of governors such as Macartney, Cornwallis and Archibald Campbell, who had not previously been employed by the Company and were thus hardly embroiled in trading activities in India, meant that adherence to these regulations was more strictly supervised.[46]

So around the mid 1780s Colin Mackenzie found himself in an unexpected situation. Without the opportunity to make a fortune within a few years in the time-honoured way, he had to get used to the idea of a long career with the Company, as he later told Humberston Mackenzie in a long letter:

> This (for us) unfortunate system you have adopted at home of sending out Governors only distinguished for the uprightness of their conduct & disinterestedness prevents our acquiring money ... the good old times when everything could be bought & sold here are now no longer. [But] ... notwithstanding the System of Publick Oeconomy on the expenditure, the Appointments by Gouvernment here are accompanied with handsome Salaries which will be always objects to moderate men who have devoted their time & health to the service of the Company & as there will now be the reward of long service & merit it encourages thinking men to persevere in the strict line of duty seeing it the only road to preferment, the cheque to rapid fortunes also has chequed the tendency to extravagance & expense what prevailed much in India, so that moderate fortunes will still attend a long residence in India in any eligible situations.[47]

Mackenzie clearly had no difficulty in adapting to the new conditions. The role of the loyal employee, conscious of his duty, who gave personal commitment and followed a 'strict line of duty', was familiar to him from his time with the Scottish Customs. Furthermore, he clearly thought that the chances of a rewarding position within the Company were not bad, especially since in his compatriot Patrick Ross he had a superior, friend and champion who was encouraging him in his future career. Ross presented Mackenzie with a model for the course of his career: on the basis of professional qualifications and irreproachable behaviour it was possible to attract attention by personal commitment and achievement, for which, of course, appropriate remuneration could be expected. Mackenzie internalized this meritocratic principle of achievement and recognition to such an extent that in later years, when he thought his activities were not being sufficiently recognized, he had no hesitation in demanding the salary he thought he deserved, 'which so many years ago I was taught to look up to as the honourable owed recompense of my exertions'.[48]

In particular, Ross encouraged Mackenzie to specialize as a surveyor. The time seemed to be favourable for a career in this sphere because, since the 1770s, the Directors in London had been asking for maps of the presidency in Madras, the last urgent request being in 1783. All previous attempts had failed, however, due to lack of continuity in personnel, the transfer of already existing sketches and maps in private ownership, and above all failure to coordinate the various projects.[49] Although Ross's initiative to appoint a Surveyor General for Madras who should coordinate the surveying work and be responsible for archiving and duplicating maps failed because it was rejected by London on grounds of cost,[50] the Board in Madras had signalled its agreement so that in the medium-term it seemed fairly likely that this position would be created.[51]

So Mackenzie, who had had some initial experience of cartography while working as an engineer,[52] started to specialize in surveying. To start with, in 1787/1788, during an inspection trip to the fortifications in the north of the presidency, he took the opportunity to make maps of the lines of communication between them.[53] His first significant surveying job dates to 1788, when he was sent with a military unit to Guntoor, one of the Northern Circars, which after 1765 had initially remained under the control of the Nizam of Hyderabad's family and only now was taken possession of by the Company.[54] Mackenzie accompanied the unit on its tour through the region and, following orders, made maps of the routes they had taken.[55] Before this he had already shown how seriously he took Ross's promise that special services would be rewarded. Without being commissioned to do so, and at his own expense, Mackenzie had, en route to his posting, surveyed roads and passes that were of military importance and had made maps and journals that he made available to the government. These were later published in the *Oriental Repertory* by Alexander Dalrymple, the hydrographer and geographer.[56]

And Ross, too, kept his promise: when Mackenzie was promoted to lieutenant in 1789 Ross congratulated him with 'infinite pleasure' and promised to give him vigorous support in his future career, support he considered richly deserved.[57] And indeed, just a few months later he wrote a memorandum for Governor John Holland, in which he once again emphasized the service Mackenzie had given and sought appropriate recompense:

> As ... [these] are works of great labour and of great merit, undertaken by that Gentleman on his own expense through zeal to the service ... I flatter myself you

will think him deserving of some mark of approbation and that you will be pleased to grant him such a compensation as may place him on a footing with Surveyors employed in such Service.[58]

Mackenzie was officially recognized as a qualified surveyor in 1790, when he was commissioned by the government to carry out a full survey of the Circar of Guntoor.[59] It was not until twenty years later,[60] however, that this project was completed under his supervision as his military commitments had priority – as was often to be the case in the years that followed. At the start of the Third Mysore War he was ordered to the front, in April 1790.[61]

Officer and Engineer

The fact that Mackenzie was called away from a surveying project, something that was to recur repeatedly in the following decades, shows the extent to which he, as an officer, was dependent on military orders, despite the special status of the corps of engineers. But there was little chance of a glorious rise within the army in this corps. In keeping with the Company army's general practice, promotion was strictly according to seniority.[62] From 1770 onwards engineers could only make progress if there were vacancies within their own unit and, furthermore, they had no way of getting back into the regular army.[63] So the small size of the corps was a great impediment to a rapid rise through the various ranks. Although a joint initiative by Patrick Ross and his Bengal colleague[64] in the 1790s led to the decision that henceforth engineers could be promoted to the army's highest rank (colonel),[65] for middle-ranking officers in particular the prospects remained limited. The number of engineers in Madras, an average of twenty in the previous decade, may have risen to twenty-seven by 1796, but only three positions remained available of a rank above that of captain.[66]

However, expansion of the corps, but above all the large number of officers who left due to death or illness,[67] did introduce a certain dynamic even though promotion was often still connected with a long waiting period. The corps' official lists between 1789 and 1800 reveal that the average wait for promotion from ensign to lieutenant was three years; from lieutenant to captain about five years; from captain to major ten-and-a-half years; from major to lieutenant colonel, again, another twelve or so years; and for promotion from this rank to that of a colonel a further thirteen years.[68] Of course these are only average waiting times and since the careers of individual officers depended on vacancies that happened to come up, the waiting times could vary considerably.[69] Colin Mackenzie, for instance, had to wait six years for promotion to lieutenant, but was then made a captain after only four years; but it was another thirteen years before he was made a major, in 1806; just three years later he was promoted to lieutenant colonel; and in 1819, after another nine years, to colonel.[70]

Only the salaries of the higher ranks offered the opportunity to make the savings required for a financially independent life in Britain.[71] In 1793, when he had already reached the rank of captain, Mackenzie was still writing that an imminent return to Britain, even only temporary, was out of the question for the time being because the poor prospects of promotion in his corps and the high living costs, due to the constant change of location while surveying, made it impossible to save any decent sums.[72] There were, however, various other opportunities for making money more quickly, even as an engineer, but in the EIC's system of patronage these basically depended on the good will of a superior.

A particularly good opportunity for attracting the decision makers' attention was presented by a war. The relatively small strength of the corps of engineers and the importance of their tasks meant that even low-ranking officers often came into direct contact with important superiors and had the chance to distinguish themselves. In his thirty-eight years' service with the EIC Mackenzie took part in numerous wars and, as he himself stated, before 1796 in more than any other officer in the presidency.[73] From 1790 to 1792 he served in the Third Mysore War and a year later in the siege and conquest of the French stronghold in Pondicherry; from late 1796 to early 1797 he was involved in the conquest of Ceylon, also perceived as a threat to British rule in India because of the French conquest of the Netherlands.[74] An expedition to the Philippines, for which he was summoned to Madras in summer 1797, was called off at the last minute[75] but two years later he was again involved in a war against Mysore, which was to lead to the ultimate defeat of Tipu Sultan.[76] In 1811, now a man of about sixty years of age, he took part as Chief Engineer in the conquest of Java, previously a Dutch possession.[77] A year later he was involved again, this time in the victory over the Sultan of Yogyakarta, who until then had exercised largely independent rule.[78]

In times of war, engineers were responsible for numerous technical and logistical tasks. Thus Mackenzie, who was in command of various engineers, craftsmen and pioneers for this purpose and whose activities are very well documented beyond his own journals, was involved, for instance, in reconnoitring roads and landing sites,[79] in uncovering weak spots in enemy fortifications and in planning and organizing subsequent attacks,[80] as well as in bridge building and the construction of technical aids.[81] W.C. Mackenzie has described his hero's experiences during the wars so extensively that there is no need to go into all the details here.[82] Suffice it to say that here, too, Colin Mackenzie distinguished himself by unusual diligence and courage that was constantly cited. From 1792 onwards he was personally mentioned on an almost regular basis in General Orders conveying thanks to the troops.[83] Arthur Wellington, who commanded Mackenzie in the Fourth Mysore War, is supposed to have cried out years later in Spain, when there were problems with the siege of Badajoz: 'Oh, that old Mackenzie were here!'.[84]

Whatever credence should be given to such anecdotes, it is clear that when he took part in wars Mackenzie always managed to attract the attention of his superiors in a way that was to further his career when peace returned. Perhaps the two most important steps in this career – his appointment as Surveyor to the Nizam's Detachment in 1792 and as Superintendent of the Mysore Survey in 1799 – occurred directly after the two wars against Tipu Sultan and were intended as rewards for his services. At the same time, participation in wars could also be worthwhile financially as after victories huge sums were usually divided up between the soldiers and officers.[85] The amounts allocated to the middle ranks were not a fortune, but for those who had held positions of responsibility the sums involved were not inconsiderable. For the expedition to Ceylon in 1796, for instance, in which Mackenzie had taken part as Chief Engineer, he expected to receive prize money of about a thousand pounds.[86]

Various factors determined the amount of prize money that could be expected. As was common practice, in the EIC army it had been determined, since 1758, that the public funds and treasures – though not the private money of individuals – found in a conquered fortress or town should be divided up between the members of the victorious army; the Commander-in-Chief generally decided who should get what.[87] Although in principle the money was divided up according to rank,[88] those in charge did have a certain room for manoeuvre and could allocate money as a reward for special services.

In the case of the EIC this also meant, of course, that personal connections played a role in the distribution of the money and the officers with good connections often received disproportionately large sums for their achievements. For example, Mackenzie complained that the Third Mysore War could have been really lucrative for him if the money had been allocated purely on the basis of his achievements, but this had by no means been the case, despite Cornwallis's appreciation of his work: 'the vast number of competitors well supported by parliamentary interest', he wrote to Scotland, 'does not leave the C in C at full liberty'.[89] This was certainly not the only case where he felt he had been disadvantaged when it came to dividing up the prize money, and it is typical of him that he was not prepared simply to accept the situation. Years after the conquest of Ceylon, for instance, he was still complaining about unfair treatment, while his own claims went far beyond what was a regular captain's share.[90] Nine years after the Fourth Mysore War he was still demanding money he thought he was owed as commander of about five hundred men, including cadets and Indian artisans.[91] Often accompanied by statements from colleagues confirming the services he had performed,[92] entries of this sort can be found again and again in the official files. But in the shadow of this official correspondence Mackenzie himself also moved in the grey area of patronage structures, within which the right connections were often far more valuable than personal achievements.

Networks of Patronage

Although Mackenzie was officially part of the military, and war service played a major role for him (especially in the 1790s), most of his career took place in the quasi-civil sphere that was accessible to him because he belonged to the EIC's corps of engineers. His career, unspectacular but nonetheless long and generally successful, was based on his specialization as a surveyor, which he had already embarked upon in the 1780s. The career steps he took can by no means be described as the regular ones within a prescribed structure; in fact he was constantly appointed to new positions, often created for him personally. After the Third Mysore War, in 1792, he was appointed as the official Surveyor to the Nizam's Detachment in Hyderabad, and seven years later as superintendent of a survey of newly conquered Mysore. After another eleven years he took on the job as the first Surveyor General for the presidency of Madras, and finally in 1815, marking the high point and final post in his career, for the whole of India.

In later years, in particular, Mackenzie constantly stressed the degree to which his career was based on personal commitment and service – and with some justification. However, this should not be allowed to disguise the fact that his career would not have been possible without external influence – after all, the most important decisions about financial claims and appointments to lucrative positions were made in corridors behind the official correspondence. 'In this Country, as at home, everything is done by influence',[93] Mackenzie wrote to Seaforth, adding in one of his next letters that 'the manner of carrying on business is in India the same as elsewhere & ... interest & ... influence are very necessary to give weight to every claim of whatever nature'.[94]

So beyond the official correspondence a battle for posts and careers took place that was sometimes hard fought. Among the civil servants, prestigious positions in the administrative sphere, for instance in one of the government's central secretariats, were just as sought after as staff positions amongst the low- and middle-ranking officers.[95] Connections within the Company's patronage system were essential and many of the most glorious and rapid careers in this period were due almost exclusively to good connections. 'Those without influential patrons', as Martha McLaren aptly sums up the situation of the decades around the turn of the century, 'could either resign themselves to a lackluster career or seek ways to beat the system'.[96]

Mackenzie's specialization as a surveyor represents just such an attempt. But his correspondence with Seaforth in the 1790s also demonstrates how hard he tried to build up an informal network of supporters and what a key role his patron played in this as the central point of family and clan relations. This is true, for instance, of the Third Mysore War, when Mackenzie managed to make his way into the close circle around the Governor General and the Commander-in-Chief, Charles Cornwallis. Initially appointed as personal adjutant to the Chief Engineer, for the six months between August 1791 and February 1792 Mackenzie deputized for him.[97] A position of this sort, but above all the introduction it brought with it to the 'Cornwallis family' as insiders called the small circle around the Governor General,[98] could not, of course, be attained without the right connections, and in his letters to Scotland Mackenzie wrote quite freely about the personalities who had helped him in this: his most important supporters, he said, were Colonel Maxwell, Commander of the 74th Highland Regiment in the 1790s,[99] Alexander Mackenzie, temporary Commander-in-Chief of the Bengal Army,[100] as well as Major William James Madan, Cornwallis's nephew and adjutant.[101] It comes as no surprise that all these people turn out to have had direct connections with the Seaforth family: Alexander Mackenzie of Coul came from a branch of the Seaforths and was thus related to Colin Mackenzie himself;[102] as a member of the Maxwell family of Monreith in the Edinburgh region Hamilton Maxwell was part of the Scottish elite and may well have been personally acquainted with Francis Humberston Mackenzie;[103] and Madan, though not a Scot but the son of the English Bishop of Peterborough,[104] was well acquainted with Mary Proby, Humberston Mackenzie's wife and later Countess Seaforth,[105] a childhood friend of his sister Charlotte.[106] Just how valuable these contacts were becomes apparent in Mackenzie's subsequent appointment as surveyor in Hyderabad, in which Madan in particular used his personal influence.[107]

It is hardly surprising that in his letters to Seaforth Mackenzie mainly emphasizes common acquaintances as supporters, while other people who probably played just as important a role are not mentioned.[108] Despite these omissions, however, the correspondence presents a clear enough picture of the patronage structure within the Company; its relative complexity arose from the fact that certain decisions – in Mackenzie's case appointments, creation of new posts, and remuneration – could be influenced from various different power centres. From the point of view of the engineer in the Madras presidency, the civil government on the spot and the military there were very important, but these by no means always pursued the same objectives. From 1773 onwards they were subordinate to the Governor General or the Commander-in-Chief in Bengal,[109] so that support in Calcutta was also of great interest. Finally, however, most important of all were supporters in London, either amongst the Directors or, from 1784, in the influential Board of Control, since appointments and salaries were approved by these bodies, or occasionally also rejected or modified.[110]

While at the higher levels – especially in London but also in Calcutta – the support of an influential patron was of fundamental importance, on the level of the Madras presidency personal acquaintances made in India played the key role. But what is striking here too is that at the start of his career Mackenzie's most important friends and supporters came from Scotland – his superior Patrick Ross; Dr James Anderson, Surgeon Major and Physician General of Madras and from 1786 chairman of the government's Medical Board founded in that year; and James Brodie, a civil servant who held important positions in the 1790s, such as military secretary to the government. With the exception of Brodie,[111] however, Mackenzie's family connections with Seaforth do not seem to have played a role.

In Bengal personal acquaintances were far less important for Mackenzie. Although, as already mentioned, he had friends and acquaintances in the military throughout India following the wars, these were mainly in the Royal Army, which had little relevance for his career and whose officers often only stayed in India for a few years. As regards the power centre in Calcutta, a man in his position could generally only hope for the recommendation of high-ranking supporters. Ultimately, as far as decisions made in London were concerned, in the first two decades of his career his Indian contacts played virtually no role, a situation that was only to change at the beginning of the nineteenth century, when some of his friends had returned home after a successful career in India and occupied key positions in the decision-making bodies in Parliament and the Company. Initially, of course, he could not exert any sort of personal influence on the decision makers there unless someone respected in these circles intervening on his behalf.

Against this backdrop the fact that he had relatively few important contacts in Britain became a big problem for Mackenzie. In the first two decades of Colin Mackenzie's stay in India Francis Humberston Mackenzie, soon to be Lord Seaforth, was the only influential man whose support he could hope for in London, though he had no doubt that Seaforth's intervention could greatly enhance his career prospects. 'I believe I have now laid a tolerable foundation in this country by ... service & application', he wrote to him in 1792 after he had already made a certain amount of progress, 'if you lend a hand (which I am convinced you will) it will be of very essential consequence to me & you can always depend on my grateful remembrances'.[112] His own willingness to make an effort could provide the basis for a promotion, but the decisive impetus had to come from others: 'It happens often in this country, as I have too much experienced', he wrote four years later to underline the urgency of an intervention by Seaforth, 'that for want of ones' friends at home being circumstantially apprized of matters here, opportunities are irretrievably lost of effecting what might otherwise within the reach of persons constantly present & indefatigable in the execution of their duty'.[113]

In order to secure Seaforth's support, in a number of letters he stressed his loyalty to the head of the Mackenzie clan. In full accordance with the customs involved in patronage relations he also made clear his intention of intervening himself on behalf of the clan if ever he were in a position to do so: 'As it may be possibly sometimes in your power to lend a helping hand ... I submit whether it might not be useful to your own interests to have a friend, sometimes near you, willing & able to follow the Cabberfey [*caber feidh*] Interest from old fashioned principle & attachment, as well as from personal obligation'.[114] Such assurances and regular long letters notwithstanding, he received no reply for years, so finally in 1797 he sent Humberston Mackenzie a cask of Madeira wine via the agent Tulloch, Brodie & Co.[115] When in the following year he learned that his patron had been given the title Lord Seaforth, Baron Mackenzie of Kintail, he planned to have a dinner service made in China decorated with the Seaforth crest as a gift for his patron.[116] Now and again he tried to attract Seaforth's attention via middlemen, for instance via his friend John Mackenzie ('of the Temple') in London or via his agents John and Alexander Anderson.[117]

Even though Mackenzie received hardly any personal letters from Seaforth, in the 1790s he did in fact intervene on Mackenzie's behalf several times – though with little success. This may have been because he had little real interest in his far-off relative or it could be that his long absence from London – he was Governor of Barbados from 1800 to 1806 – meant that there was nothing much more he could do. Above all, the fact that he generally intervened at a late stage presented a major problem as, ideally, letters of recommendation were supposed to reach designated important Company office-holders before they left Europe. 'Governor & Commander-in-Chief', Mackenzie asserted, for instance, 'now seldom stay 3 years, & those that are first with them have the only chance of succeeding'.[118] Indeed the six Governors under whom Mackenzie served between 1785 and 1805 only held office for an average of three years and four months.[119] But only rarely – for instance in Wellesley's case[120] – did Seaforth's letters of recommendation turn up on time, as Mackenzie later recalled: 'I could never get an introductory letter sent out', he wrote to Seaforth's heiress Mary Stewart Mackenzie, 'till the Governors were going home so that I have still lying by me Letters to Lord Cornwallis, General Meadows[121] &c &c sent by your father's directions by his political friend Mr Adam[122] & others but still too late to be of use'.[123]

Nonetheless, as he later reported, Mackenzie did manage to get to know all the Governors General, though often only just as they were about to leave, so that the effect of these connections was fairly limited – totally frustrating for him bearing in mind the efforts involved in attracting their attention. Once they were back in Britain he could hardly reckon with support from these 'great men'. In 1809, when he felt once again that the then Governor Lord Minto was not giving him adequate support, he expressed his frustration very openly in a letter to his friend John Leyden in which – as far as I can see the one and only time in his extant correspondence – he quotes the Bible:

> I have indeed such experience now of all the Great men from Europe in the course of 23 years'[124] service that I have *no hope* & *no desire* to cultivate further knowledge of their ways; a few years ago I had indeed a little acquaintance & I imagine I might be just as useful now as then – but now I may apply a Phrase you may have once read per- haps 'and then arose another King in Egypt who knew not Joseph nor his Brethren'.[125]

The greatest problem in the first twenty-five years or so of his service in the EIC was that, despite occasional interventions by Seaforth, he had no long-term and stable support in London. Seaforth's long absence and the fact that he was not involved in the Company's affairs prevented his patron from having any direct influence, and Mackenzie's requests that Seaforth engage his political friends in Mackenzie's cause[126] remained largely unsuccessful. How little could be achieved under these circumstances is illustrated by Mackenzie's unsuccess- ful application for posts as Surveyor General in 1796 and 1804. Although he was supported by the government in Madras in both cases – in 1804 by Arthur Wellesley as well[127] – these applications were rejected in London. It was of little help that Seaforth – a good year after the first rejection! – supported his plans in a memorandum to Charles Grant, an extremely influential Director.[128] Both attempts were rejected; the first Mackenzie found somewhat surprising, the second less so.[129] It was only thanks to his doggedness that in 1810, at the age of more than fifty-five, he was finally appointed to a post that he had been applying for since he was a young man.

By contrast, what was possible with the right connections is illustrated by the career of his long-time competitor Alexander Beatson, one of the sons-in-law of Charles Oakeley, who was Governor in Madras from 1790 to 1794 and for his part also cultivated very good connections to Pitt and Dundas in London.[130] Since 1776 – although Beatson had never officially belonged to the corps of engineers[131] – he had been carrying out tasks similar to Mackenzie's as an engi- neer and surveyor, and in 1792 was appointed Town Major of Madras. After returning to Britain between 1795 and 1798 for health reasons, a time he used for successful lobbying, along with his well-paid job as commanding officer in the Corps of Guides he was appointed to the position of Geographical Surveyor in the Madras presidency, which is presumably what prevented Mackenzie's appointment as Surveyor General.[132] The Fourth Mysore War, which started shortly after his return to India and during which he was part of Wellesley's closest advisory staff, turned out to be so lucrative for him that by 1800 he was able to return to Britain and buy several farms. A particular distinction he was given was that Wellesley allowed him personally to convey the news of the victory over Tipu Sultan. Finally, it was also thanks to his good contacts in the

EIC that seven years later he was appointed Governor of St Helena, an island controlled by the Company.[133]

Another example of rapid advancement is the career of Mackenzie's friend James Brodie who managed, along with a successful career with the Company, to amass a great amount of money in just a few years. A member of the Brodie of Brodie family that owned estates in Moray, northwest of Inverness, he had come to India in 1789 at the age of about twenty as a writer.[134] He was probably following the example of his uncle Alexander Brodie, one of the most well-known nabobs in London, who had worked in Madras in the 1770s and 1780s, had made a great fortune there, and upon his return had taken a seat in the House of Commons – from 1785 to 1790 as MP for Nairnshire and from 1790 to 1802 as MP for the Elgin Burghs.[135] Not only was Alexander Brodie regarded in Parliament as a friend of Dundas and influential leader of the Moray Association, but he also maintained his contacts in Madras, where he continued to exert considerable influence and, for a time at least, owned a large number of shares in the EIC.[136] He supported his nephew's career, amongst other things through his close contacts to Henry Dundas.

So even though, strictly speaking, the seniority principle also applied in the civil departments, James Brodie advanced rapidly. After a short spell in the public and revenue department from 1794 to 1797 he held the influential post of secretary to the government in military affairs, before eventually being appointed Garrison Storekeeper and Import Warehousekeeper. At this point, however, he only had marginal interest in his official duties because within a few years he had managed to amass a fortune through illegal private trade.[137] On the banks of the Adyar that flows through Madras he had a magnificent villa built, known as Brodie Castle,[138] and was still regarded as one of the up-and-coming men in the Madras administration when he drowned in this very river in 1802.[139]

Compared with the careers of these men Mackenzie's progress within the EIC was fairly slow; but taking into account the forty or so years he spent in India, all in all he was very successful. For a long time he refused to give up on his original goal of making as much money as possible as quickly as possible – but external factors forced him to develop new strategies for achieving it. The prospect presented to him by his superior, Patrick Ross, of advancement on the basis of professional qualification and personal commitment ultimately brought success. But the fact that he had too few reliable connections in London meant that his career progressed far more slowly than he had originally hoped. Of course, without any connections it would scarcely have been possible at all, but the very fact that they were insufficient to remove all obstacles from his path and that his dream of accelerated promotion remained beyond his grasp forced Mackenzie to take a course that to some extent could be regarded as a model within the colonial administration.

The Value of Knowledge

Mackenzie's career as a surveyor was based on his personal ambitions in an environment in which he was trying to compensate for lack of patronage by personal qualifications and achievement. This in itself, however, does not explain the enthusiasm and commitment with which he generally fulfilled his duties in posts specially created for him. What must be his most important contribution to building up the colonial state – the establishment and institutionalization of a survey that went far beyond cartography as an instrument of the state – was essentially founded in his conviction that his activities were of value, a conviction that cannot be explained simply by personal interests and which relativizes the image of an ambitious careerist. Peter Robb describes this aspect of Mackenzie's career as follows: 'There was an intellectual excitement in his inquiries, a lively curiosity and the pursuance of scientific method. Thus such efforts as his helped establish a pattern which was followed in many other aspects of government and investigation in colonial India'.[140]

Although the Company was trying to make a name for itself, around 1800, as a patron of the sciences, many of its scientific projects in India would not have been possible without the initiative shown by its employees on the ground. The alliance between science and colonial state was not formalized until a later period. The term 'state scientist', used in the anglophone sphere, did crop up in the colonies but not until the second half of the nineteenth century.[141] So, with few exceptions, it was not so much professional scientists as amateurs, mainly civil servants and officers of the EIC, who contributed to its research projects of the eighteenth and early nineteenth centuries. For this reason, despite all the officials' rhetoric, David Arnold sums up the EIC's rule by saying that it was more of a 'fitful flirtation' with than a 'rule of science'.[142] Nevertheless, and this was crucial for Mackenzie's career, within the EIC an environment existed in which scientific activity was not only highly regarded but also, for certain projects, provided with the necessary financial resources.

Mackenzie did not go to India with any sort of 'pre-formed' concept of knowledge production. Many of his ideas, especially those he put into practice in the second half of his life in India, were not developed until he arrived there. If we want to trace the influences that were crucial here, what necessarily attracts attention to start with is the town of Madras. As a surveyor Mackenzie's life was characterized by a 'restless, itinerant lifestyle' to an even greater degree than that of many other Britons in India.[143] However, the very fact that he had to move about so much for his job and was unable to stay for a longer period in any of the smaller British strongholds in the presidency meant that for almost thirty-five years after his arrival Madras remained for him a sort of home from home. This is where he regularly returned for longer stays and where he kept the possessions he did not need in the field. What is more, from the 1790s onwards he most likely owned his own garden house in the suburbs.[144]

Above all, however, Madras is where Mackenzie did most of his socializing with Europeans. When he moved to Madras in the 1780s, after living for a long time in fairly provincial Stornoway, this had meant a move from a sleepy backwater in the most remote part of Britain to a cosmopolitan metropolis. But even though compared to other presidencies there was a relative openness in the contact between the different social and cultural groups in Madras, the British elites still developed their own independent social structures that followed similar cultural rules to the ones in Europe.[145] As in other strongholds in India the size of this elite in Madras, consisting of officers, civil servants and independent traders, was relatively small. They formed a community within the metropolis that perpetuated certain aspects of life in a British town with its inevitable Freemasons' lodges,[146] theatrical and musical events, balls, receptions and drinks parties, sporting events or joint evening excursions. Despite all the hierarchical divisions within this elite, their divisive social and cultural mechanisms were aimed less at internal inequalities than at the European lower classes – above all soldiers in barracks – and parts of the indigenous population from whom the British inhabitants of Madras were, as elsewhere in India, becoming increasingly isolated.[147] So the young officer Mackenzie, despite his modest background and lack of formal education, came into close contact with the presidency's administrative and cultural elite. It was clearly thanks to his superior, Patrick Ross, with whom he developed a personal friendship that went far beyond professional contact, that he quickly became an accepted member of this 'society'. Mackenzie was a regular visitor at the Chief Engineer's house and lived with him for several months at a time when visiting Madras before buying a house of his own.[148] Ross, a cousin of Adam Smith,[149] was one of the most respected personalities in the British social life of the town. For quite some years he was a member of the board responsible for government business,[150] was active in the Theatrical Society that was seeking to set up a theatre in Madras,[151] and through his professional dealings had connections to almost all high-ranking civilian and military employees in the town.

Then there was Dr James Anderson, whom Mackenzie mentions as the second crucial personality during his early years in India and describes as a 'Gentleman distinguished for his philanthropy'.[152] Anderson, Surgeon Major and Physician General of Madras,[153] was a central figure in the network of natural historians that emerged in South India at this time. Amongst his scientific friends were, for instance, the German Johann Georg König, one of Linné's pupils who had come to India to work for the Dutch East India Company and since the late 1770s had been employed by the British as a naturalist; another was the Scottish doctor, William Roxburgh, who like Anderson had studied in Edinburgh and later became head of the botanical gardens in Calcutta.[154] Most important of all were Anderson's contacts in London with Joseph Banks and Charles Francis Greville (the latter being a friend of Seaforth and influential natural historian), since via these connections South India was also included in the imperial system of British botany, with its headquarters in Kew Gardens.[155]

This new, often highly educated environment made a profound impression on Mackenzie. It made him more aware than ever of his shortcomings in terms of formal education and years later he was still bemoaning 'the disadvantage of the want of these early academical acquirements that prepare the mind for Scientific Investigations'.[156] In the 1780s and 1790s he did all he could to catch up on what he had missed, either by teaching himself or with the aid of his new acquaintances. Patrick Ross, for instance, encouraged him to gain experience of astronomical observations in the Madras Observatory whenever possible – important for a good surveyor[157] – while Dr Anderson not only pointed out the usefulness of natural historical observations but personally took 'the trouble of giving [him] some instruction in Mineralogy & the art of classing the different species of earths, stones, & minerals'.[158]

Above all, however, it seems fairly certain that in the 1780s Mackenzie embarked on an intense phase of studying by himself. In Madras books were a scarce and, due to the long transportation distances, an expensive commodity. Since the mid century a small library had existed in Madras and people also often swapped books with one another. In the early 1790s attempts were made to formalize this practice by setting up a sort of book club in the form of a mobile bookshop.[159] From this time at the latest Mackenzie had books sent from Britain once a year, via his agent,[160] and all his life made use of his friends' libraries.[161] He also acquired some of his books from Calcutta and showed great interest in auctions where the collections of those who had returned to Europe or had died were on offer, and also those of merchants who had gone bankrupt.[162] Reading, he wrote to a friend, was his favourite occupation after a hard day's work and when he was busy surveying far away from the social life of the presidency his hunger for new reading matter seems to have been virtually insatiable.[163]

His interests were not confined to the natural sciences. Just how broad they were is illustrated by a list of books of which he mostly had two copies and which in 1815, before he departed for Calcutta, he sold to the newly founded College of Fort St George.[164] Among the more than seventy volumes, which presumably constituted only a small part of the library he had at the time, there are books on British and international history, on current affairs, on mineralogy, biographies of well-known personalities and informative, learned and political journals. Hardly surprisingly many of the books are about geography or are travelogues, for instance Humboldt's *Travels in Latin America*, or are about the history and culture of India, such as Robertson's *Historical Disquisition*. Since 1805 the Oxford professor and orientalist Richard Heber had been supplying Mackenzie with new literature; when Mackenzie asked him for a list of new publications, in 1816, Heber replied politely – and probably not exaggerating all that much – that he could hardly imagine a title that Mackenzie did not already know.[165]

Mackenzie clearly felt a particular need to catch up in the sphere of the Latin and Greek classics; lack of such knowledge had earlier proved an impediment to studying at university. So in the early 1790s he read the *Illiad* and the *Odyssey* in a translation by W. Cowper.[166] Then came authors such as Pliny (presumably the Elder), Diodorus Siculus or Arrian, extracts of which at least were likewise available in translation.[167] In later years, in particular, reading these and other ancient authors also served the purpose of learning more about India's historical geography, which he tried to reconstruct by comparing places and rivers he had located with those mentioned in the texts. His lack of knowledge of Greek caused him certain difficulties here since he sometimes felt the translations were unreliable. So, as he wrote to his friend Leyden, he had to rely on the help of acquaintances in order to decipher 'the accurate meaning of the texts of Strabo, Mela, Ptolemy & the Minor Grecian Geographers'.[168] In the case of Herodotus he even had recourse to Larcher's famous French translation. He had borrowed it from a friend and carried it round with him for several years.[169]

Mackenzie's efforts to broaden his educational horizon by self-teaching can, of course, be seen as an attempt to acquire cultural capital intended to earn him recognition and ultimately to promote his career. Thus, for instance, he prefaced one of his first major works, a sort of memoir dealing with technical and cultural irrigation plants in South India, with a few verses from Homer, basically designed to demonstrate his educational credentials.[170] Yet despite examples of this sort, which crop up repeatedly in Mackenzie's writings and correspondence, it would be wrong to see his hunger for education and interest in the sciences simply as a sort of social and cultural mimicry orientated towards the ideals of his superiors. On the contrary, he was convinced of the value of knowledge and the sciences, a conviction that went far beyond his own personal interests. As he summed up his efforts to Seaforth: 'I have much to regret myself the want of early initiation to the Sciences; I have struggled hard to get the better of this great want, & have just learned enough to see its value, & the loss the Publick … sustain[s] by [not] taking it up'.[171]

This unconditional belief in the value of knowledge and science to the world in general was undoubtedly influenced by his new environment as Mackenzie was now confronted by actors who saw the sciences as an instrument that could help to bring about a general improvement in living conditions. This was particularly true of the group around the natural historian James Anderson, who generally sought to achieve their goals through private initiative. Anderson himself, for instance, along with his duties as a doctor, was seeking to introduce new agricultural crops in the presidency. In a garden on the edge of town – provided for him by the EIC[172] – he was experimenting with the cultivation of mulberry and apple trees, promoting the planting of cotton and sugar cane as well as silk production, and attempting to generate cochineal, a dye produced from the dried remains of a South American insect.[173]

Anderson was an enthusiast who sent his suggestions for enterprises of this sort to many famous people in Britain and regularly published this correspondence[174] in order to gain further support, especially from the decision makers in the EIC. For instance, he personally approached Governor Hobart and appealed to his genuine interest in promoting 'every investigation connected with [the] public welfare'.[175] Such appeals were not without some success and Anderson's attempts at silk production were promoted without reservation by those responsible in London: 'we shall cheerfully consent to your rendering ... pecuniary assistance to the ... laudable undertaking', the Directors wrote to the Madras government, adding that they would not only cover the costs incurred so far but wanted to give Anderson 'more substantial proof of the sense we have of his abilities and zeal', in other words, financial remuneration.[176]

Of course, the Company's own economic interests played a role here,[177] but Anderson's concept of the 'public welfare' was by no means related solely to these interests. In order to encourage Indian landowners to take some initiative of their own, it seems, he had his texts on the possibility of silk production translated into Malayalam by Teroovercadoo Mootiah, a Brahmin who occasionally advised him on the cultivation of certain plants and who also worked as a translator for other Company employees.[178] The incentive here was not to increase the Company's profits but to spread 'useful knowledge' that should ultimately serve the good of all. For men like James Anderson or Joseph Banks 'useful knowledge' of this sort should certainly not be separated from 'pure science' – on the contrary, it was precisely the utilitarian character of the sciences that constituted a major part of their value, and for this very reason it was in the government's interest to promote scientific activity.[179]

For Mackenzie too, who embraced this argumentation in many of his official entries, this did not of course mean that science should only be judged by its utilitarian value. He justified the value of mineralogical research in India not by its economic advantages, for instance from mining, but by the fact that it could shed 'much light ... on the Theory of the Earth'.[180] Naturally, general scientific knowledge did not exclude usefulness, either in the sphere of the natural sciences or in researching Indian history and culture, which was to play a prominent role in Mackenzie's later project of a comprehensive survey. This was the spirit in which he later claimed, still very modestly and possibly due to his lack of formal education, that his research was of 'advantage to Government & to Science in General'.[181] He hoped that the results of this research 'may be found useful, at least in directing the observation of those more fortunately gifted to matters of utility, if not to record facts of importance to philosophy and science'.[182]

Notes

1. Cf. the *Atlas* logbook: BL/IOR/L/Mar/B/27/Q. See also A.J. Farrington, *Catalogue of East India Company Ships' Journals and Logs 1600–1834* (London, 1999), 39; R. Hackman, *Ships of the East India Company* (Gravesend, 2001), 63; and J. Sutton, *Lords of the East: The East India Company and its Ships 1600–1874* (London, 1981), 166.

2. Cf. W. Hodges, *Travels in India, during the Years 1780, 1781, 1782 & 1783* (London, 1793), 1f; and E. Fay, *Original Letters from India (1779–1815)*, edited by E.M. Forster, 2nd edn. (London, 1986), 161–65.

3. For the turbulent history of San Thomé, which became a British possession in 1749, see C.S. Srinivasachari, *History of the City of Madras: Written for the Tercentenary Celebration Committee* (Madras, 1939), 68–76; and for the emergence of the 'Black Town' ibid., 17, 41f, 115–117,123.

4. Cf. W. Nichelson, *Sundry Remarks and Observations, Made in a Voyage to the East-Indies … with the Necessary Directions for Sailing to and from India, and into the Several Ports and Harbours thereof*, 2nd edn. (London, 1773), 47f. See also G.G. Armstrong, 'The Port of Madras for Three Hundred Years', in *The Madras Tercentenary Commemoration Volume* (London, Bombay, Calcutta and Madras, 1939), 209–16. For details of the role of the boatmen for ships travelling to Madras and the gradual regulation of their working conditions see R. Ahuja, *Die Erzeugung kolonialer Staatlichkeit und das Problem der Arbeit: Eine Studie zur Sozialgeschichte der Stadt Madras und ihres Hinterlandes zwischen 1750 und 1800* (Beiträge zur Südasienforschung 183) (Stuttgart, 1999), 69–124.

5. For the *dubashes*, who as agents were the South Indian equivalent to the *banians* in Bengal, see S. Neild-Basu, 'The Dubashes of Madras', *Modern Asian Studies* 18(1) (1984), 1–31. See also P.J. Marshall, 'Masters and Banians in Eighteenth-Century Calcutta', in B.B. Kling and M.N. Pearson (eds), *The Age of Partnership: Europeans in Asia before Dominion* (Honolulu, 1979), 191–214.

6. Hodges, *Travels in India*, 2. A much less positive and romanticizing picture of this first contact is in Fay, *Original Letters*, 162.

7. Around 1785 the artist Francis Swain Ward did a series of illustrations of the Fort's streets and squares that was published at the beginning of the nineteenth century and seems topographically reliable. However, in such drawings fictitious picturesque detail was often added. Partly reproduced with abridged description in H.D. Love, *Vestiges of Old Madras, 1640–1800: Traced from the East India Company's Records Preserved at Fort St. George and the India Office and other Sources*, 3 vols (1918; reprint, New York, 1968), vol. 3, 277–80; see also the 'Plan of Fort St. George as completed', ibid., 156.

8. For the history of the town see Srinivasachari, *History of the City of Madras*. Love, *Vestiges of Old Madras* and the various essays in the *Madras Tercentenary Commemoration Volume* of 1939 also provide a wealth of material.

9. For the somewhat debatable suggestion that Madras could have been a model for this type of town see for example M. Kosambi and J.E. Brush, 'Three Colonial Port Cities in India', *Geographical Review* 78(1) (1988), 32–47; and P. Mitter, 'The Early British Port Cities of India: Their Planning and Architecture circa 1640–1757', *Journal of the Society of Architectural Historians* 45(2) (1986), 95–114. See also the fundamental criticism by R. Ahuja, 'Unterwegs zur Kolonialmetropole: Madras in der zweiten Hälfte des 18. Jahrhunderts', in D. Rothermund (ed.), *Periplus 1996: Jahrbuch für Außereuropäische Geschichte* (Münster, 1996), 62.

10. See his report: Patrick Ross, 'Confidential Report of the State of the Defence of Fort St. George', 11 March 1783, Chief Engineer's Books, BL/OIOC/Mss Eur/Mack Gen/68.

11. Cf. R.E. Frykenberg, 'The Social Morphology of Madras', in K. Ballhatchet (ed.), *Changing South Asia*, 5 vols (London, 1984), vol. 3, 21–41; and Washbrook, 'Colonial Transition', 494. Ahuja, 'Unterwegs zur Kolonialmetropole', esp. 68f, warns against an over-harmonious interpretation of the mutual dependencies that towards the end of the eighteenth century were marked by an imbalance of power in favour of the British.

12. In 1791 the population of Madras and its surrounding villages was estimated to be about 300,000. Cf. C.W. Ranson, 'The Growth of the Population of Madras', in *Madras Tercentenary Commemoration Volume*, 319. For the difficulties in defining the exact boundaries of towns in the eighteenth century and the various villages and settlements with autonomous administrations see S.M. Neild, 'Colonial Urbanism: The Development of Madras City in the Eighteenth and Nineteenth Centuries', *Modern Asian Studies* 13(2) (1979), 217–46.

13. For the sepoy army in Madras see C. Wickremesekera, *'Best Black Troops in the World': British Perceptions and the Making of the Sepoy 1746–1805* (New Delhi, 2002), 88–95. See also G.J. Bryant, 'Indigenous Mercenaries in the Service of European Imperialists: The Case of Sepoys in the Early British Army, 1750–1800', *War in History* 7(1) (2000), 2–28.

14. For details of this see M.S.R. Anjaneyulu, 'The English Acquisition of Chicacole Circar', *Journal of Indian History* 56(1–3) (1983), 127–34; R.E. Frykenberg, *Guntur District 1788–1848: A History of Local Influence and Central Authority in South India* (Oxford, 1965), 28–31; Love, *Vestiges of Old Madras*, vol. 2, 594.

15. Cf. I. Habib, 'Introduction: An Essay on Haidar Ali and Tipu Sultan', in id. (ed.), *Confronting Colonialism: Resistance and Modernisation under Haidar Ali and Tipu Sultan* (London, 2002), xvii–xlvii.

16. Cf. esp. Irschick, *Dialogue and History*, 16–18. See also H. Furber, 'Trade and Politics in Madras and Bombay', in A. Siddiqi (ed.), *Trade and Finance in Colonial India, 1750–1860* (Oxford, Delhi and New York, 1995), 80f. How threatening the situation was for Madras is conveyed in the lively description by Hodges, *Travels in India*, 5–8.

17. Cf. C.A. Bayly, *Indian Society and the Making of the British Empire* (The New Cambridge History of India pt. 2, vol. 1) (Cambridge, 1988), 57–61; F. Noyce, 'A Ştriking Episode in Madras History', in *The Madras Tercentenary Commemoration Volume*, 97–106.

18. Cf. J. Phillips, 'Parliament and Southern India, 1781–1783: The Secret Committee of Enquiry and the Prosecution of Sir Thomas Rumbold', *Parliamentary History* 7(1) (1988), 81–97.

19. Cf. L.S. Sutherland, 'Lord Macartney's Appointment as Governor of Madras, 1780: The Treasury in East India Company Elections', *English Historical Review* 90(356) (1975), 523–35; T.G. Fraser, 'India 1780–86', in P. Roebuck (ed.), *Macartney of Lisanoure, 1737–1806* (Belfast, 1983), 154–215, esp. 158–65; and Phillips, 'Parliament and Southern India'.

20. In 1785 the Company's debts in India and the City of London amounted to more than 19.5 million pounds. Cf. S. Förster, *Handelsmonopol und Territorialherrschaft: Die Krise der East India Company 1784–1813* (Kleine Beiträge zur europäischen Überseegeschichte 9) (Bamberg, 1991), 9.

21. H.V. Bowen, 'British India, 1765–1813: The Metropolitan Context', in P.J. Marshall (ed.), *The Oxford History of the British Empire*, vol. 2: 'The Eighteenth Century' (Oxford and New York, 1998), 540–44. For the Hastings trial see P.J. Marshall, *The Impeachment of Warren Hastings* (Oxford, 1965); G. Carnall and C. Nicholson (eds), *The Impeachment of Warren Hastings: Papers from a Bicentennary Commemoration* (Edinburgh, 1989); and P.J. Marshall (ed.), *Writings and Speeches of Edmund Burke*, vol. 6: *India, The Launching of the Hastings Impeachment, 1786–1788* (Oxford, 1991) and vol. 7: *India, The Hastings Trial, 1789–1794* (Oxford, 2000).

22. Cf. Johnston, 'Statement by Alexander Johnston, 19 July 1832', 254, para. 1930. Lord Macartney was a friend and promoter of Alexander Johnston's father, Samuel, and had acquired for him the lucrative post of Paymaster in Madura. See Macartney to Sir John Macpherson, 11 January 1782 and Macartney to [George] Johnstone, 12 January 1782, in C. Davies (ed.). *The Private Correspondence of Lord Macartney, Governor of Madras (1781–85)*, (London, 1950), 18–20, 178f.

23. Cf. Colin Mackenzie to Chief Sec. FSG, 1 August 1816, NAI/SIR/REP/3, 37–76, here 43; id., 'Statement of the Literary Labours', p. 243.

24. For these operations cf. W. Fullarton, *A View of the English Interests in India; and an Account of the Military Operations in the Southern Parts of the Peninsula, during the Campaigns of 1782, 1783, and 1784: In Two Letters* (London, 1787), 156–66, 283; *The Annual Register, or a View of the History, Politics and Literature, for the Year 1783* (London, 1785), 107, 295; and H.H. Dodwell, 'The Carnatic, 1761–84', in id. (ed.), *The Cambridge History of India*, vol.5: *British India 1497–1858* (Cambridge, 1929), 287.

25. Cf. Mackenzie, *Sketch of the War with Tippoo Sultaun*, 81–84. See also Colin Mackenzie to Henry Trail, 2 August 1805, BL/OIOC/Mss Eur/F/228/39; and 'Memorandum on the Duties Colin Mackenzie has been employed since 1790' (Copy of a Paper given to General Harris 14 August 1798), NAS/GD/46/17/4, 538–40.

26. It seems that Johnston had it renovated during Mackenzie's visit as one of his drawings shows the building 'before it was repaired' – however, it is by no means clear how far Mackenzie was involved in the works. See Colin Mackenzie, 'Fort Defiance and the Landscape near it, near Madura, in 1784. Originally sketched by C McK', BL/OIOC/WD/633; id., 'Fort Defiance near Madura before it was repaired by Mr John(n)s.', June 1784, BL/OIOC/WD/634; and id., 'Fort Defiance: 1784', BL/OIOC/WD/736. Johnston's biographer James Rutnam mentions that he was involved in the construction of an apartment block, a well and various other buildings but his work, being fragmentary and giving no sources, seems not very reliable. Cf. J.T. Rutnam, *The Early Life of Alexander Johnston (1775–1849), Third Chief Justice of Ceylon* (Colombo, 1988), 6.

27. Johnston, 'Statement by Alexander Johnston, 19 July 1832', 254, para. 1930.

28. Johnston even errs in the date of the visit. For his new version see 'Proceedings of the Anniversary Meeting May 1835', xiii.

29. In the second half of the eighteenth century a position as a writer with the Company was regarded as about three times as valuable as that of a cadet. Cf. P.J. Marshall, 'British Society in India under the East India Company', *Modern Asian Studies* 31(1) (1997), 98.

30. For the circumstances of the appointment see Phillimore, *Historical Records*, vol. 1, 349. In the official lists the date of Mackenzie's appointment to the corps of engineers is given as 16 May 1783. Cf. *The Bengal Calendar for the Year 1789: Including a List of the Hon. and United East-India Company's Civil and Military Servants on the Bengal Establishment, &c. Including Also Those at Madras, Bombay, Fort Marlborough, China, and St. Helena*, A New Edition, Corrected at the East-India House ([London] [1789]), 54.

31. This was true despite the establishment of *the Royal Military Academy* in Woolwich in 1741. Cf. S. Jayewardene-Pillai, *Imperial Conversations: Indo-Britons and the Architecture of South India* (New Delhi, 2007), 57f; Phillimore, *Historical Records*, vol. 1, 266.

32. For the history of the Madras Engineers see H.M. Vibart, *The Military History of the Madras Engineers and Pioneers from 1743 up to the Present Time*, 2 vols (London, 1883).

33. See Thomas de Havilland's description of the state of the Corps in 1821, which he sent to the government with a number of suggestions for improvement. Summarized in detail in Vibart, *Military History of the Madras Engineers*, vol. 2, 3–25, quote 5.

34. For Ross see A.W. Massie, 'Patrick Ross, c. 1740–1804', *ODNB*; Phillimore, *Historical Records*, vol. 1, 382; R.G. Thorne (ed.), *The House of Commons 1790–1820*, 5 vols (Warburg, 1986), vol. 5, 55f.

35. Cf. 'Return of the Corps of Engineers under the Command of Lt Col Ross', 1 May 1775, Chief Engineer's Books, BL/OIOC/Mss Eur/Mack Gen/68; and 'List of Engineers in the Madras Establishment from their Formation on a Military Plan in March 1770 to the last Return from India in 1794', BL/IOR/H/91, 175–77.

36. Patrick Ross to Alexander Wynch, 29 May 1775; Patrick Ross to George Stratton, 28 December 1776 and 27 June 1777, Chief Engineer's Books, BL/OIOC/Mss Eur/Mack Gen/68.

37. Cf. Patrick Ross, 'Confidential Report of the State of the Defence of Fort St. George', 11 March 1783, Chief Engineer's Books, BL/OIOC/Mss Eur/Mack Gen/68.

38. Colin Mackenzie to Henry Trail, 2 August 1805, BL/OIOC/Mss Eur/F/228/39.

39. Marshall, 'British Society in India', 97; Jayewardene-Pillai, *Imperial Conversations*, 70; Vibart, *Military History of the Madras Engineers*, vol. 2, 18.

40. Cf. 'Extract of a Letter from the Chief Engineer to the Honorable Alexander Wynch Esq., President and Governor of FSG', 27 February 1773, Chief Engineer's Books, BL/OIOC/Mss Eur/Mack Gen/68; Patrick Ross to Robert Stewart, 17 June 1775, ibid.; Love, *Vestiges of Old Madras*, vol. 3, 368.

41. Cf. Patrick Ross to Colin Mackenzie, 6 July 1787; Chief Engineer's Books, BL/OIOC/Mss Eur/Mack Gen/69; also 22 September 1787, ibid.

42. CD to B (FW), 20 November 1767, *FWIHC*, vol. 5 (Public Series 1767–1769), edited by Narenda Krishna Sinha (Delhi, 1949), 33–63, here 60, para. 112.

43. Regulation Act para. XXIII and para. XXVII, in P.J. Marshall (ed.), *Problems of Empire: Britain and India 1757–1813* (London, 1968), 152f.

44. Cf. Marshall, *East Indian Fortunes*, 141–47.

45. Cf. Irschick, *Dialogue and History*, 18.

46. For Archibald Campbell's attempts to curb former practices in Madras in the 1780s see Furber, 'Trade and Politics', 68–81; for Dundas' influence on the new policy see id., *Henry Dundas: First Viscount Melville 1742–1811: Political Manager of Scotland, Statesman, Administrator of British India* (London, 1931), 55–62.

47. Colin Mackenzie to Francis Humberston Mackenzie, 31 January 1792, NAS/GD/46/17/4, 316–28, here 318–20. Mackenzie orientated himself to the official policy of Governor General Cornwallis, who explained to the Court of Directors: 'the only mode that can be successful to prevent peculation and other abuses, will be, by annexing liberal allowances … and give … gentlemen a prospect of acquiring by oeconomy a moderate fortune from the fair savings of their salaries'. Cornwallis to CD, 18 August 1787, *FWIHC*, vol. 10 (Public Series 1786–1788), edited by Raghubir Sinh (Delhi, 1972), 510–14, here 511, para. 5.

48. Colin Mackenzie to William Bentinck, 23 June 1805, BL/OIOC/Mss Eur/F/228/39.

49. Patrick Ross to Lord Macartney, 17 October 1783, Chief Engineer's Books, BL/OIOC/Mss Eur/Mack Gen/68.

50. CD to B (FSG), 9 December 1784, Chief Engineer's Books, BL/OIOC/Mss Eur/Mack Gen/68.

51. Charles Freeman to Patrick Ross, 1 November 1783, Chief Engineer's Books, BL/OIOC/Mss Eur/Mack Gen/68.

52. Colin Mackenzie to Sec. Gov., Mil. Dep. (FSG), 19 January 1811, BL/IOR/P/257/15, 1666–78, here 1675f.

53. Patrick Ross to Colin Mackenzie, 6 July 1787, Chief Engineer's Books, BL/OIOC/Mss Eur/Mack Gen/69; Phillimore, *Historical Records*, vol. 1, 111.

54. Cf. J. Black, *British Foreign Policy in an Age of Revolutions, 1783–1793* (Cambridge, 1994), 164f; Frykenberg, *Guntur*, 29–31; Vibart, *Military History of the Madras Engineers*, vol. 1, 210.

55. Patrick Ross to Colin Mackenzie, 29 August 1788; Patrick Ross to Johnstone, 15 September 1788 and 24 October 1788, Chief Engineer's Books, BL/OIOC/Mss Eur/Mack Gen/69. See also Mackenzie to Chief Sec. Gov. FSG, 2 January 1817, BL/IOR/P/259/56, 4845–56.

56. C. Mackenzie, 'Account of the Construction of the Plan of the Roads from Nellore to the Western Passes, and to Ongole, &c., Measured in 1788 by Colin Mackenzie Practitioner-Engineer', in A. Dalrymple (ed.), *Oriental Repertory* 1(1) (London, [1791?]), 57–64. One of the original maps is in the National Archives of India (NAI/F/150/46). Cf. S.N. Prasad, *Catalogue of Historical Maps of the Survey of India* (New Delhi, 1975).

57. Patrick Ross to Colin Mackenzie, 14 March 1789, Chief Engineer's Books, BL/OIOC/Mss Eur/Mack Gen/69.

58. Patrick Ross to John Holland, 20 July 1789, Chief Engineer's Books, BL/OIOC/Mss Eur/Mack Gen/69.

59. Patrick Ross to Colin Mackenzie, 15 January 1790, Chief Engineer's Books, BL/OIOC/Mss Eur/Mack Gen/69.

60. It was not until twenty years later that, at Mackenzie's instigation and under his leadership, a complete survey of the Northern Circars was carried out. Cf. Mackenzie to Chief Sec. Gov., 20 November 1815, BL/IOR/F/4/554 (13476), 127–39; Public Letter from FSG, 29 February 1816, ibid., 7–9.

61. Colin Mackenzie to Chief Sec. Gov. FSG, 2 January 1817, BL/IOR/P/259/56, 4845–56.

62. Cf. Callahan, *East India Company and Army Reform*, 21.

63. General Letter from CD, 23 March 1770, Chief Engineer's Books, BL/OIOC/Mss Eur/Mack Gen 68.

64. The two of them intervened with Henry Dundas, seeking to improve the promotion prospects for the higher grades and to increase the strength of the corps: Lt. Col. Patrick Ross, Chief Engineer, Madras, and Lt. Col Mark Wood, Chief Engineer, Bengal, to Henry Dundas, President of the Board of Commissioners for India Affairs, 4 December 1794, BL/IOR/H/91, 171–73. From 1782 at the latest Ross regularly corresponded with Dundas. Cf. Furber, *Dundas*, 18, 63; and Callahan, *East-India Company and Army Reform*, 38.

65. Mackenzie, who by now had come to terms with the idea of a long career India, assessed this explicitly as a great advantage. Cf. Colin Mackenzie to Francis Humberston Mackenzie, 9 August 1796, NAS/GD/46/17/4, 485–95, here 494.

66. *General Orders by Government, Fort St. George, Twelfth July M.DCC.XCVI* (Madras, 1796), 4.

67. Of the fifty-eight engineers under Ross's command between 1770 and 1794, seven died in military service, twenty-three of various illnesses in India and another three in Europe of illnesses contracted in India. Only four retired and received a pension. Cf. 'List of Engineers in the Madras Establishment from their Formation on a Military Plan in March 1770 to the last Return from India in 1794', BL/IOR/H/91, 175–77.

68. *Bengal Calendar for the Year 1789*, 153f; *The East India Kalendar, or, Asiatic Register for Bengal Madras, Bombay, Fort Marlborough, China and St. Helena for the Year 1791: On a More Extensive Plan than Any Hitherto Offered to the Public* (London, 1791), 110; *The East India Kalendar, or, Asiatic Register for Bengal Madras, Bombay, Fort Marlborough, China and St. Helena for the Year 1793: On a More Extensive Plan than any Hitherto Offered to the Public* (London, 1793), 124; *The East India Kalendar, or, Asiatic Register for Bengal Madras, Bombay, Fort Marlborough, China and St. Helena for the Year 1794: On a More Extensive Plan than Any Hitherto Offered to the Public*, A New Edition (London, 1794), 124f; *The Bengal or East-India Calendar, for the Year MDCCXCV: Including a List of the Hon. and United East-India Company's Civil and Military Servants on the Bengal Establishment, &c.: Also Those at*

Madras, Bombay, Fort Marlborough, China, and St. Helena (London, 1795), 155f. *The East India Kalendar, or, Asiatic Register for Bengal Madras, Bombay, Fort Marlborough, China and St. Helena for the Year 1796: On a More Extensive Plan than Any Hitherto Offered to the Public*, A New Edition (London, 1796), 127f; *The East India Kalendar, or, Asiatic Register for Bengal Madras, Bombay, Fort Marlborough, China and St. Helena for the Year 1797: On a More Extensive Plan than Any Hitherto Offered to the Public*, A New Edition (London, 1797), 127f; *The East India Kalendar, or, Asiatic Register for Bengal Madras, Bombay, Fort Marlborough, China and St. Helena for the Year 1798: On a More Extensive Plan than Any Hitherto Offered to the Public*, A New Edition (London, 1798), 128; *The East India Kalendar, or, Asiatic Register for Bengal Madras, Bombay, Fort Marlborough, China and St. Helena for the Year 1800: On a More Extensive Plan than any Hitherto Offered to the Public*, A New Edition (London, 1800), 128f.

69. On average they seem to have been in a worse position than other army units (for example infantry, artillery or cavalry) where the time needed to reach the rank of colonel was little more than thirty years in the 1780s. Cf. Callahan, *East India Company and Army Reform*, 21–23.

70. Cf. Robb, *Mackenzie, ODNB*.

71. The orders of 1796, which largely brought the engineers' wages into line with those of the infantry, envisaged a sixty-nine per cent monthly increase on promotion from lieutenant to captain, and a further increase of about sixty-six per cent on subsequent promotion to major. If, as was often the case with the engineers, the officers were not serving in a garrison or military quarters and were receiving extra funds originally intended for general living costs (*batta*), horse and tent, then the rate of increase was still fifty-nine per cent for a captain and a handsome eighty-three per cent for a major. For details see 'Table of Pay and Allowances for a Month of Thirty Days, to the Officers in the Madras Establishment', *General Orders by Government, Fort St. George, Twelfth July, M.DCC.XCVI*, 13. For the payment of *batta*, which was originally intended as general compensation for additional expenses in the field, but which later became one of the most important components of an officer's pay, see D.M. Peers, 'Between Mars and Mammon. The East India Company and Efforts to Reform its Army, 1796–1832', *Historical Journal* 33(2) (1990), 385–92.

72. Colin Mackenzie to Francis Humberston Mackenzie, 2 March 1793, NAS/GD/46/17/4, 434–438, here 435.

73. Colin Mackenzie to Francis Humberston Mackenzie, 9 August 1796, NAS/GD/46/17/4, 485–95, here 485.

74. Mackenzie had taken part as Chief Engineer and commanded a small corps. Cf. William Gent, Chief Engineer, to Colin Mackenzie, 13 December 1795, Chief Engineer's Books, BL/OIOC/Mss Eur/Mack Gen/68; Gent to Mackenzie, 29 December 1795, ibid.; Mackenzie, 'Memorandum abstracted from the Journal of Captain Mackenzie', 22 January 1809, BL/OIOC/Mss Eur/Mack Misc/136. For the course and background to the conquest see A. Schrikker, *Dutch and British Colonial Intervention in Sri Lanka, 1780–1815: Expansion and Reform* (Leiden and Boston, 2007), 131–34; and L.A. Mills, *Ceylon under British Rule 1795–1932: With an Account of the East India Company's Embassies to Kandy 1762–1795* (London, 1964), 9–15.

75. The expedition was interrupted at short notice after part of the Bengali fleet had sunk in a storm. Cf. Colin Mackenzie to Seaforth, 27 August 1797, NAS/GD/46/17/4, 509f; also 4 September 1797, ibid., 512–18; 'Memorandum on the Duties Colin Mackenzie has been employed since 1790' (copy of a Paper given to General Harris, 14 August 1798), NAS/GD/46/17/4, 538–40.

76. See Colin Mackenzie, 'Journal on the March from Hydrabad to Seringapatam during the Mysore Campaign, 1798/99, Part II: From the Junction of the Nizam's Forces with the

Grand Army near Ambore in February to the Storm & Capture of Seringapatam on 4 May 1799', BL/Mss Add/13663, 1–95.

77. Colin Mackenzie, 'Report of Proceedings on the North Coast of Java agreeable to the Instructions of His Excellency Sir J. Auchmutty CinC &c. Dated at Malacca of 6 June 1811', BL/OIOC/Mss Eur/Mack Priv/14, 57–69.

78. Colin Mackenzie, 'Report and Journal of the Proceedings of Lieut. Colonel Colin Mackenzie Chief Engineer on the Expedition to Batavia on the Island of Java from October 1811 to June 1813', 14 December 1813, BL/OIOC/Mss Eur/Mack Priv/14, 215–62.

79. See for example, for reconnaissance of landing sites on Java under his leadership [J. Blakiston], *Twelve Years' Military Adventure in Three Quarters of the Globe: Or, Memoirs of an Officer who Served in the Armies of His Majesty and of the East India Company, Between the Years 1802 and 1814, in Which Are Contained the Campaigns of the Duke of Wellington in India, and His Last in Spain and the South of France*, 2 vols (London, 1829), vol. 2, 9–29.

80. See for example Vibart, *Military History of the Madras Engineers*, vol. 1, 306–9, 313; and J. Martin, 'An Engineer in the Mysore War of 1791–1792', *Journal of the Society for Army Historical Research* 22(90) (1944), 324–38.

81. In 1811, under his command, bridges before Batavia destroyed by the Dutch were replaced by temporary structures. A year later he supervised the construction of ladders for storming Yogyakarta. Cf. A. Harfield, *British and Indian Armies in the East Indies 1685–1935* (Chippenham, 1984), 91; P. Carey, 'Changing Javanese Perceptions of the Chinese Communities in Central Java, 1755–1825', *Indonesia* 37 (1984), 22f.

82. Mackenzie, *Colonel Colin Mackenzie*, for example 33–47, 49–51, 62–76, 109–22, 152–56.

83. See for example 'General After Orders, 19 October', printed in M. Dirom, *A Narrative of the Campaign in India Which Terminated the War with Tippoo Sultan in 1792* (London, 1793), 47–49, here 49; R. Mackenzie, *Sketch of the War with Tippoo Sultaun*, vol. 2, 149; 'General Orders, by the Commander of the Forces Major-General Gillespie, 21 June 1812' and 'General Orders, by the Commander in Chief in India, 30 September 1812', both printed in W. Thorn, *The Conquest of Java: Nineteenth-century Java seen through the Eyes of a Soldier of the British Empire* (1815), edited by John Bastin (Hong Kong, 2004), 192–97 and 197–200.

84. Shore, *Reminiscences of Many Years*, vol. 2, 349.

85. After the victorious war of 1790–1792 Cornwallis gave the army about 22,000 pounds; and after the final victory over Tipu seven years later Wellesley gave as much as around 93,000 pounds. Cf. Mornington, Clive, E.W. Petrie and E.F. Fallofield to CD, 4 August 1799, in East India Company (ed.), *Copies and Extracts of Advices to and from India, Relative to the Cause, Progress, and Successful Termination of the War with the Late Tippoo Sultaun, Chief of Mysore, the Partition of his Dominions in Consequence Thereof; and the Distribution of the Captured Property found in Seringapatam* ([London],1800), 247–50, here 248, para. 10; Cornwallis to CD, 4 March 1792, in C. Ross (ed.), *Correspondence of Charles, first Marquis Cornwallis*, 3 vols. (London, 1859), vol. 2, 524–33, here 532; and Cornwallis to CD, 7 March 1793, ibid., 215f.

86. Colin Mackenzie to Francis Humberston Mackenzie, 9 August 1796, NAS/GS/46/17/4, 485–95, here 487f.

87. If royal troops were involved, which was quite common, the monarch himself was originally supposed to have this prerogative, but in reality it was rarely the case, partly due to the long communication distance between India and Britain. For instance, after the conquest of Seringapatam and Tipu Sultan's immense treasures in 1799 Wellesley argued that dividing up the prize money could no longer be delayed as this was a threat to army discipline; he also argued that if it were done later complications could be expected because large sections of the troops would have left. So he simply commissioned the Comander-in-Chief, General Harris, to divide up the money – 'proportioned to the magnitude and importance of ...

services'. Cf. CD to B (FW), 3 March 1758, *FWIHC*, vol. 2 (Public Series 1757–1759), ed. by H.N. Sinha (Delhi, 1957), 55–98, here: 96–98, para. 186–88; Mornington, Clive, E.W. Petrie and E.F. Fallofield to CD, 4 August 1799, in East India Company, *Copies and Extracts of Advices*, 247–50, quote 249, para.14. For general information on the practice of handing out prize money in the British army from the time of William IV see H.L. Scott, *Military Dictionary: Comprising Technical Definitions; Information on Raising and Keeping Troops; Actual Service, including Makeshifts and Improved Materiél; and Law, Government, Regulation, and Administration relating to Land Forces* (1861; reprinted New York, 1968), 97–109.

88. In 1792 Cornwallis had decided that every officer involved should receive a sum that was at least six times as high as his monthly *batta*. Cornwallis to CD, 4 March 1792, in Ross, *Correspondence of Cornwallis*, vol. 2, 524–33, here 532. In 1799 Wellesley also followed this model in principle.

89. Colin Mackenzie to Francis Humberston Mackenzie, 21 July 1794, NAS/GD/46/17/4, 440–47, here 441. See also 2 March1793, ibid., 434–39.

90. Colin Mackenzie to Alexander Walker, 14 March 1800, NLS/Ms 13602, 5–7; Phillimore, *Historical Records*, vol. 1, 350; vol. 2, 427.

91. Colin Mackenzie to George Barlow, 26 April 1808, BL/IOR/P/256/29, 4243–55.

92. For instance for the Fourth Mysore War: Barry Close to Colin Mackenzie, 30 March 1808, BL/IOR/P/256/29, 4269f; Macauley to Colin Mackenzie, 29 March 1808, ibid., 4270–72; and John Malcolm to Colin Mackenzie, 29 February 1808, ibid., 4273.

93. Colin Mackenzie to Francis Humberston Mackenzie, 21 July 1794, NAS/GD/46/17/4, 440–47, here 442.

94. Colin Mackenzie to Francis Humberston Mackenzie, 14 September 1796, NAS/GD/46/17/4, 497–500, here 498.

95. The alternatives for experienced officers were highly paid secondments to army divisions financed by the Company's Indian allies, or appointments to political positions. See Peers, *Mars and Mammon*, 76; and Callahan, *East India Company and Army Reform*, 33.

96. McLaren, *British India and British Scotland*, 30.

97. Cf. 'Memorandum on the Duties Colin Mackenzie has been employed since 1790', NAS/GD/46/17/4, 538–40.

98. George Abercrombie Robinson to Colin Mackenzie, 22 August 1805, BL/OIOC/Mss Eur/F/228/39. During the war Mackenzie personally took part in Cornwallis's discussions with his generals: Colin Mackenzie to Francis Humberston Mackenzie, 31 January 1792, NAS/GD/46/17/4, 316–23, here. 320f.

99. Colin Mackenzie to Francis Humberston Mackenzie, 31 January 1792, NAS/GD/46/17/4, 316–23, here 320f. For the 74th Highland Regiment, which supported the Madras Presidency's army until 1803, see J. Browne, *A History of the Highlands and of the Highland Clans*, 4 vols (Glasgow, 1835–1838), vol. 4, 317–19.

100. Colin Mackenzie to Francis Humberston Mackenzie, 2 March 1793, NAS/GD/46/17/4, 434–38, here 438.

101. Alexander Mackenzie had personally introduced Colin Mackenzie to Madan: Colin Mackenzie to Francis Humberston Mackenzie, 21 July 1794, NAS/GD/46/17/4, 440–47, here 441.

102. For the relationship between the Mackenzies of Coul and the Seaforths see Mackenzie, *History of the Mackenzies*, 606f.

103. For the Maxwells of Monreith cf. Anderson, *Scottish Nation*, vol. 3, 130.

104. For William James Madan see the obituary. 'Colonel Madan', *Gentleman's Magazine* 100(1) (May 1830), 470f; F. Madan and W. Gibson, 'Spencer Madan, Bishop of Peterborough, 1728–1813', *ODNB*.

105. Cf. Colin Mackenzie to Francis Humberston Mackenzie, 9 August 1796, NAS/GD/46/17/4, 485–95, here 495.

106. The relationship between the two young women was so close that they even kept a joint 'commonplace book': 'Commonplace book of verse, mostly anonymous, kept by Mary Proby [later countess of Seaforth] and Charlotte Madan', NAS/GD/46/15/269. Details from the online catalogue of the National Archives of Scotland.

107. Mackenzie considered Madan to be one of the people to whom he owed this appointment. Colin Mackenzie to Francis Humberston Mackenzie, 21 July 1794, NAS/GD/46/17/4, 440–47, here 442.

108. See A. Mackillop, 'Europeans, Britons and Scots: Scottish Sojourning Networks and Identities in India, c.1700–1815', in A. McCarthy (ed.), *A Global Clan: Scottish Migrant Networks and Identities since the Eighteenth Century* (London, 2006), 19–47, esp. 24.

109. Since 1786, at the initiative of Cornwallis, who was appointed at this time, the Governor General could also hold the office of Commander-in-Chief. This became quite usual, especially when there was a war. Cf. Furber, *Dundas*, 55.

110. For the civil administration see Bowen, *Business of Empire*, esp. 53–83, 182–218; and B.B. Misra, *The Central Administration of the East India Company 1773–1834* (Manchester, 1959); for the complicated hierarchy of the military, which at this time actually consisted of three different armies – those of Bengal, of Madras and of Bombay – see Peers, *Mars and Mammon*, 46–48; and Callahan, *East India Company and Army Reform*, 41f.

111. The Brodies were so closely connected to Seaforth that at times he corresponded with Mackenzie via James Brodie. Cf. Colin Mackenzie to Francis Humberston Mackenzie, 21 July 1794, NAS/GD/46/17/4, 440–47, here 440. For Brodie's positions in Madras see *East India Kalendar for the Year 1791*, 93; *East-India Kalendar for the Year 1794*, 104; *East India Kalendar for the Year 1800*, 106. See also Colin Mackenzie to John Warren, 17 June 1800, NAI/SIR/M/6, 124–26.

112. Colin Mackenzie to Francis Humberston Mackenzie, 31 January 1792, NAS/GD/46/17/4, 316–323, here 321f.

113. Colin Mackenzie to Francis Humberston Mackenzie, 9 August 1796, NAS/GD/46/17/4, 485–95, here 485.

114. Ibid., 492. Mackenzie was referring here to a possible stay in Britain.

115. Cf. Colin Mackenzie to Francis Humberston Mackenzie, 27 August 1797, NAS/GD/46/17/4, 509f; John and Alexander Anderson to Francis Humberston Mackenzie, 27 December 1797, ibid., 520.

116. Colin Mackenzie [to John Mackenzie?], 18 February 1798, NAS/GD/46/17/4, 530f.

117. John and Alexander Anderson to Francis Humberston Mackenzie of Seaforth, 15 March 1797, NAS/GD/46/17/4, 505–8; Colin Mackenzie to John Mackenzie, 14 February 1798, ibid., 528f; John and Alexander Anderson to Francis Humberston Mackenzie, Lord Seaforth, 7 August 1798, ibid., 532f; John Mackenzie to Francis Humberston Mackenzie, Lord Seaforth, 10 August 1798, ibid., 534–37.

118. Colin Mackenzie to Francis Humberston Mackenzie, 21 July 1794, NAS/GD/46/17/4, 440–47, here 443.

119. These were John MacPherson (1785–1786), Cornwallis (1786–1793), John Shore, Lord Teighnmouth (1793–1798), Alured Clarke (1798) and Richard Wellesley (1798–1805). For a complete list with brief descriptions of the most important characters see V. Mersey, *The Viceroys and Governors-General of India, 1757–1947* (London, 1949). See also H. Morris, *The Governors-General of British India*, 2 vols (1907; reprint, New Delhi, 1984).

120. Cf. Colin Mackenzie to Henry Trail, 2 August 1805, BL/OIOC/Mss Eur/F/228/39.

121. For William Medows (1738–1813), Governor of Bombay and for a time Commander-in-Chief of the army, see A.W. Massie, 'Sir William Medows', *ODNB*.

122. Probably William Adam of Woodstone, Kincardine and Blair-Adam (1751–1839). See Brooke and Namier, *House of Commons 1754–1790*, vol. 2, 8–10.
123. Colin Mackenzie to [Mary] Stewart Mackenzie, 24 March 1819, NAS/GD/46/17/51. See also Colin Mackenzie to Alexander Gillanders, 25 July 1794, NAS/GD/46/17/4, 448–55, here 452.
124. Reference to the year 1786 – Mackenzie had already joined the East India Company three years earlier – is probably explained by the fact that Cornwallis was appointed as Governor in that year.
125. Colin Mackenzie to John Leyden, 13 November 1809, NLS/Ms 3380, 115–19, emphases in the original. Mackenzie clearly quotes freely from the Acts of the Apostles 7:18. The original text from the King James Bible, used almost exclusively in the eighteenth century, is as follows: 'Till another King arose who knew not Joseph'. Religious considerations obviously did not play any great role for Mackenzie, if at all. The fact that he was buried in the Park Street Cemetery in Calcutta suggests that he was a Protestant as there was also a Catholic cemetery in Calcutta at this time. Cf. *Bengal Obituary*, 135; and R. Travers, 'Death and the Nabob: Imperialism and Commemoration in Eighteenth-Century India', *Past and Present* 196(1) (2007), 111–13.
126. He particularly sought to attract the attention of the influential Alexander Brodie of Brodie. Cf. Colin Mackenzie to Francis Humberston Mackenzie, 21 July 1794, NAS/GD/46/17/4, 440–47, here 443; also 9 August 1796, ibid., 485–95, here 491.
127. Cf. Vibart, *Military History of the Madras Engineers*, vol. 1, 285; 'Extract of a Military Letter from Fort St. George [to CD]', 16 October 1804, BL/IOR/F/4/183 (3692), 1–3; and Arthur Wellesley to Henry Wellesley, 2 August 1799, *Supplementary Despatches and Memoranda of Arthur, Duke of Wellington,* 15 vols (London, 1858–1872), vol. 1, 287.
128. 'Memorandum from Lord Seaforth to Mr Charles Grant relative to the Claims of Captain Colin Mackenzie of the Madras Engineers to be appointed Military Surveyor General on the Coast of Coromandel should such Appointment take place', July 1799, NAS/GD/46/17/4, 541f; Seaforth's memorandum followed the 'Memorandum of Captain Mackenzie of the Madras Engineers', 13 February 1798, ibid., 524–26. See also Colin Mackenzie to Francis Humberston Mackenzie, 9 August 1796, ibid., 485–95; also 14 September 1796, ibid., 497–500 and 13 February 1798, 521f. For Charles Grant see B.R. Garg, *Charles Grant: The Forerunner of Macauley's Educational Policy* (Ambala, Cantt, 2003), esp. 33–65.
129. Colin Mackenzie, 'Memorandum', 28 February 1805, BL/OIOC/Mss Eur/F/228/39, 7, no. 8. Mackenzie had obviously expected this rejection. See the version of the recommendation with commentary by Mackenzie: 'Extract of a General Letter to the Honble Court of Directors in the Military Department. Dated 16 October 1804', ibid., 17f, no. 12.
130. For Helena Oakeley, née Beatson, a talented painter, see A.F. Steuart, 'Miss Katherine Read, Court Paintress', *Scottish Historical Review* 2 (1904), 44–46.
131. He does, however, appear to have had certain qualifications as an engineer, as evidenced by his appointment as 'Acting Engineer at Masulipatam' in 1778. Cf. Vibart, *Military History of the Madras Engineers*, vol. 1, 135.
132. CD to FSG (Public), 9 May 1797, BL/IOR/F/4/17 (754), 3–5; 'Memorandum of Captain Mackenzie of the Madras Engineers', 13 February 1798, NAS/GD/46/17/4, 524–26.
133. See R.H. Grove, *Green Imperialism: Colonial Expansion, Tropical Island Edens and the Origins of Environmentalism, 1600–1860* (Cambridge, 1995), 345–47, 356–60; S. Hotts, 'Alexander Beatson', in A.W. Skempton, *A Biographical Dictionary of Civil Engineers in Great Britain and Ireland, vol. 1: 1500–1830* (London, 2002), 47f; Phillimore, *Historical Records*, vol. 1, 11f.
134. See L. Shaw, 'The Family of Brodie', in id., *The History of the Province of Moray … By the Reverend Mr Lachlan Shaw, Minister of the Gospel at Elgin* (Edinburgh, 1775), 105–107; B. Burke, *A Genealogical and Heraldic Dictionary of the Landed Gentry of Great Britain*

and Ireland, 2 vols, 4th edn. (London, 1862f), vol. 1, 156; and C. Kearsley, *Kearsley's Complete Peerage, of England, Scotland and Ireland; Together with an Extinct Peerage of the Three Kingdoms* (London, 1794), 344f.

135. Cf. Brooke and Namier, *House of Commons,* vol. 2, 119f. See also Furber, *Dundas,* 208–14, 229, 242; and Love, *Vestiges of Old Madras,* vol. 3, 138, 164, 174, 240.

136. Cf. H. Furber, 'The United Company of Merchants of England Trading to the East Indies, 1783–96', in id., *Private Fortunes and Company Profits in the India Trade,* edited by Rosane Rocher (Aldershot, 1997), 144.

137. In 1800 James Brodie was officially ordered either to give up his private trading or to quit his job. Cf. Love, *Vestiges of Old Madras,* vol. 3, 539.

138. Cf. M.D. Raghavan, 'Some old Madras Houses', in *Madras Tercentenary Commemoration Volume,* 116f. Today the Tamil Nadu College of Music is housed in Brodie Castle.

139. Cf. Love, *Vestiges of Old Madras,* vol. 3, 420, 562.

140. Robb, 'Completing "Our Stock of Geography"', 182.

141. D. Kumar, *Science and the Raj, 1857–1905* (Delhi, 1995), 229. In Britain a ministry of science was not set up until 1916. Cf. Gascoigne, 'Royal Society and the Emergence of Science', 183.

142. Arnold, *Science, Technology and Medicine,* 25. Sangwan, 'Natural History in Colonial Context', 294, comes to similar conclusions.

143. D. Arnold, *The Tropics and the Travelling Gaze: India, Landscape and Science 1800–1856* (Delhi, 2005), 17.

144. In today's Kilpauk. Cf. Love, *Vestiges of Old Madras,* vol. 3, 566; and 'Plan of Col. Mackenzie's Garden House at Madras 1817. Upper Story. Lower or Ground Story', BL/OIOC/WD/856. During longer absences he seems to have let out his accommodation. Cf. Colin Mackenzie to Thomas Arthur, 16 May 1801, NAI/SIR/SGO/90, 248; also 20 May 1801, ibid., 249–51.

145. Even Frykenberg, who certainly emphasizes the cooperation between the various groups most clearly, talks of them as 'small hard pieces' of a segmented society each organized according to their own cultural rules. See Frykenberg, 'Social Morphology of Madras', 21.

146. Due to lack of sources one can only speculate about Mackenzie's relationship with the Freemasons, who were virtually ubiquitous in India. In any case, for men with orientalist interests the lodges in Madras played an important role and many of his close friends and supporters could be identified as members. The same can be said of his acquaintances in Stornaway: these also included a large number of Freemasons, amongst them the teacher Alexander Anderson, often regarded as particularly important for his mathematical education. Cf. (esp. for Ellis und Erskine) Trautmann, *Languages and Nations,* 83; for Stornoway see J.C. Smith, *Annals of Lodge Fortrose A.F. & A.M. No. 108: Compiled from the Lodge Records* (Toronto, 1905), 30–33.

147. Cf. Marshall, 'British Society in India', 101f.

148. Colin Mackenzie to Francis Humberston Mackenzie, 2 March 1793, NAS/GD/46/17/4, 434–38, here 437.

149. Cf. E.C. Mossner and I.S. Ross (eds), *The Correspondence of Adam Smith* (The Glasgow Edition of the Works and Correspondence of Adam Smith, vol. 6) 2nd edn (Oxford, 1987), 299, fn 1. Due to his contacts with India and in London, Smith can be regarded as one of Ross's important supporters.

150. Cf. Mackillop, 'Fashioning a "British Empire"', 255.

151. Cf. Love, *Vestiges of Old Madras,* vol. 3, 369.

152. Colin Mackenzie to Francis Humberston Mackenzie, 21 July 1794, NAS/GD/46/17/4, 440–47, here 444.

153. For Anderson see R. Desmond, 'James Anderson (1738–1809)', *ODNB*; J.M. Sweet, 'Instructions to Collectors: John Walker (1973) and Robert Jameson (1817); with

Biographical Notes on James Anderson (LL.D.) and James Anderson (M.D.)', *Annals of Science* 29(4) (1972), 397–414, esp. 411–13.

154. Cf. Desmond, *European Discovery of the Indian Flora*, 39f, 47–70; Thomas, 'Establishment of Calcutta Botanic Garden'.

155. Cf. A. Grout, *Geology and India, 1770–1851: A Study in the Methods and Motivations of Colonial Science* (Ph.D. dissertation School of Oriental and African Studies London, 1995), 70–72; D.P. Miller, 'Joseph Banks, Empire and "Centers of Calculation" in late Hanoverian London', in D.P. Miller and P.H. Reill (eds), *Visions of Empire: Voyages, Botany, and Representations of Nature* (Cambridge, 1996), 21–37; and Grove, *Green Imperialism*, 339.

156. Colin Mackenzie to William Bentinck, 23 June 1805, BL/OIOC/Mss Eur/F/228/39.

157. Patrick Ross to Colin Mackenzie, 1 August 1792, Chief Engineer's Books, BL/OIOC/Mss Eur/Mack Gen/68.

158. Colin Mackenzie to Francis Humberston Mackenzie, 21 July 1794, NAS/GD/46/17/4, 440–47, here 444. For the role of geology under the EIC see Grout, *Geology and India 1770–1851*; id., 'Geology and India, 1775–1805', 1–18; and S. Sangwan, 'Reordering the Earth: The Emergence of Geology as a Scientific Discipline in Colonial India', *Indian Economic and Social History Review* 31(3) (1994), 291–310.

159. Cf. Love, *Vestiges of Old Madras*, 443f; D. Kincaid, *British Social Life in India 1608–1937* (Port Washington and London, 1971), 69.

160. See for example Colin Mackenzie to Alexander Gillanders, 25 July 1794, NAS/GD/46/17/4, 448–55; id. to John Leyden, 3 August 1805, NLS/Mss 3380, 66.

161. See for example Colin Mackenzie to John Leyden, 13 November 1809, NLS/Mss 3380, 115–19.

162. Colin Mackenzie to John Leyden, 10 February 1805, NLS/Mss 3380, 61–63.

163. Colin Mackenzie to Thomas Arthur, 7 June 1801 and 26 June 1801, NAI/SIR/SGO/90, 252–55, 260f; id. to Benjamin Heyne, 25 May 1801, NAI/SIR/M/6, 265f; id. to John Leyden, 9 October 1810, NLS/Mss 3380, 140–43.

164. 'List of Books purchased from Colonel Mackenzie to be retained in the College', D. Hill, Sec. Gov. FSG, to Board of Superintendance to the College of FSG, 14 August 1816, BL/IOR/F/4/541 (12148), 23–26.

165. Richard Heber to Colin Mackenzie, 8 October 1816, BL/OIOC/Mss Eur/Mack Misc/171; John Leyden to Colin Mackenzie, 21 August 1805, NLS/Ms 3383, 239–45.

166. Homer, *The Iliad and Odyssey of Homer, translated into English blank verse, by W. Cowper*, 2 vols (London, 1791). For Mackenzie's reading cf. 'Memoir on the Various Modes of Watering Land practised by the Natives of India: More particularly in the Provinces anciently designed under the names of Carnatic and Tallangana, wrote in April 1793 by C. Mackenzie Lieutt. Of Engineers at the service of, & comments to Andrew Ross Esqu.', BL/OIOC/Mss Eur/Mack Gen/59.

167. Mackenzie cites these and other authors in his 'Memorandum on the Ancient Hindoo System of Government and its Vestiges in the South of the Peninsula', BL/OIOC/Mss Eur/Mack Gen/45, 1–11. For the available translations see L.W. Brüggemann, *A View of the English Editions, Translations and Illustrations of the Ancient Greek and Latin Authors, with Remarks* (Stettin, 1797).

168. Colin Mackenzie to John Leyden, 9 October 1810, NLS/Mss 3380, 140–43, here 141.

169. Herodot, *Histoire d'Hérodote traduite du Grec, avec des Remarques historiques et critiques, un Essai sur la Chronologie d'Hérodote, et une Table géographique par M. Larcher*, 7 vols. (Paris, 1786); Colin Mackenzie to John Leyden, 10 February 1805 and 9 October 1810, NLS/Mss 3380, 61–63 and 140–43.

170. Colin Mackenzie, 'Memoir on the Various Modes of Watering Land', 1793, BL/OIOC/Mss Eur/Mack Gen/59. He quotes from Homer, *Iliad and Odyssey*, trans. W. Cowper, vol. 1, 481.

171. Colin Mackenzie to Francis Humberston Mackenzie, 21 July 1794, NAS/GD/46/17/4, 440–47, here 445.

172. Anderson's nephew Dr Berry was mainly involved in setting up the garden and in later years at least was also a good friend of Mackenzie. After Anderson's death he set up a memorial with Mackenzie. Cf. CD to B (FSG), 19 March 1793, BL/IOR/F/4/78 (1750), 5f; Colin Mackenzie to John Leyden, 10 May 1808, NLS/Ms 3380, 98–100; id. to Benjamin Swain Ward, 1 March 1810, NAI/SIR/SGO/90A, 17f.

173. Cf. D. Kumar, 'The Evolution of Colonial Science in India: Natural History and the East India Company', in J.M. MacKenzie (ed.), *Imperialism and the Natural World* (Manchester, 1990), 51; Desmond, 'Anderson' *ODNB*.

174. See for example J. Anderson, *Five Letters to Sir Joseph Banks ... on the Subject of Cochineal Insects, Discovered at Madras* (Madras, 1787); id., *A Sixth Letter to Sir Joseph Banks* (Madras, 1787); id., *A Seventh, Eighth and Ninth Letter to Sir Joseph Banks* (Madras, 1787); id., *A Tenth Letter to Sir Joseph Banks* (Madras, 1787); id., *An Eleventh Letter to Sir Joseph Banks* (Madras, 1787); id., *The Continuation of Letters on the Progress and Establishment of the Culture of Silk, on the Coast of Coromandel* (Madras, 1792); id., *The Conclusion of Letters on the Culture of Silk, with Additional Accounts of both Kinds of Bread Fruit Trees and the Distribution of Nopal* (Madras, 1792); id., *Miscellaneous Communications* (Madras, [1795]); id., *Letters, &c.* (Madras, 1796).

175. James Anderson to Lord Hobart, 5 September 1795, in Anderson, *Miscellaneous Communications*, 79f.

176. 'Extract of a General Letter from England, 21 May 1794', in Anderson, *Miscellaneous Communications*, 26f.

177. The Company's support for natural history was often seen simply as part of its economic interests. See for example Kumar, 'Evolution of Colonial Science in India'; Sangwan, 'Natural History in Colonial Context'. Sangwan later admitted that there might also be a certain enthusiasm for science. This view is also shared by Grout and Desmond: Sangwan, 'Reordering the Earth'; Grout, 'Geology and India, 1775–1805'; Desmond, *European Discovery of the Indian Flora*, v.

178. Cf. Teroovercadoo Mootiah, 'A Historical and Chronological Journal, of the Life of Teroovercadoo Mootiah, Together with Notes to the Terms therein Occured, and Also with a Letter to Mr Ross Thereunto Prefixed, 24. Jan., 1795', in A. Dalrymple (ed.), *Oriental Repertory* 2(4) (London, [1797]), 559–76; id. to James Anderson, 27 July 1796, in J. Anderson, *Letters &c.*, 6f; Anderson to Vea Permall Pilly, 2 November 1794, in id., *Miscellaneous Communications*, 26.

179. For the fluid boundaries between 'useful knowledge' and 'science' in the eighteenth century see Gascoigne, *Science in the Service of Empire*, 3. For Banks's conviction about the usefulness of the sciences see also id., *Sir Joseph Banks and the English Enlightenment: Useful Knowledge and Polite Culture* (Cambridge, 1994).

180. Colin Mackenzie to Francis Humberston Mackenzie, 21 July 1794, NAS/GD/46/17/4, 440–47, here 444.

181. Colin Mackenzie to George Buchan, 10 September 1806, NAI/SIR/M/18, 190–96, here 194.

182. Mackenzie, 'Statement of the Literary Labours', 242.

Chapter 3

ON THE ROUTE
FROM MILITARY IMPERATIVES TO THE TASKS OF GOVERNMENT

Military Objectives

Mackenzie's career as a surveyor began at a time when the military's interest in cartography played a key role. This is hardly surprising given that for a long time the EIC's rule had all the characteristics of a garrison state.[1] In the last decades of the eighteenth century it not only maintained one of the largest standing armies in the world on the subcontinent,[2] but its entire system of rule can appropriately be described as military fiscalism.[3] The interests of the military generally had priority, while at the same time an aggressive revenue policy ensured it could be maintained, swallowing up most of government spending. The fact that government policy was geared towards military interests also manifested itself clearly in the sphere of cartography. As the Company rose to become a territorial power, those responsible had quickly realized that the few maps they had of the country's interior were of little practical use as they were either unreliable or drawn to an extremely small scale.[4] So they had started their own surveying work at an early stage.[5] The standard was set by the officer James Rennell, who after two decades of mapping in Bengal was able to publish the results in his *Bengal Atlas* in 1781.[6] In the Madras presidency, however, whose territory did not start its rapid growth until the 1790s, hardly any major cartographical work had been carried out until then, except for a survey of the Jaghire.[7]

Mackenzie was one of the first in the Madras presidency to specialize as a surveyor. As far as methods were concerned he could, of course, refer to the models from Bengal. Rennell and his successors had mainly carried out route surveys, which Matthew Edney has described in detail. The surveyors usually travelled on roads or rivers, their most important task being to measure the distances between the places on their route. On water the estimated travelling speed was calculated by measuring the length of time taken using a clock; while on roads perambulators were used (large measuring wheels calibrated to a certain scale with a mechanism for counting the number of rotations, which were pushed or pulled by soldiers or bearers). Changes in direction were established by using a compass, though this depended on the accuracy of the instrument and the surveyor's assessment. Differences in height, which substantially increased the length of a route, could not be taken into account at all.[8]

The typical route maps constructed from these surveys were basically restricted to the course of the road itself and the objects the surveyor could observe by travelling these routes, including elevations sometimes ascertained by simple triangulation, chains of mountains and villages and towns that lay on the way. This meant that large parts of the sheets they were drawn on remained blank. Usually they were accompanied by journals giving distances between localities passed, water supply and possible daily stages as well as further information about rivers crossed, side roads and the landscape observed on either side of the route.[9]

Despite its obvious shortcomings, route surveying offered a number of practical advantages. For one thing, it was a method that could be easily learned, which was very important given the lack of trained experts. Even the celebrated James Rennell was self-taught when it came to cartography, initially by reading two military introductions to geometry geared entirely to practical application and whose aim it was 'to reduce the principal parts of the extensive science of Mathematics into so narrow a compass as to contain no more than what is absolutely necessary to be known ... and hereby save both time and expense, as well as prevent that disgust occasioned to many students, from a tedious round of intricate, and at the same time useless, speculations ...'.[10] Secondly, a route survey could be carried out relatively quickly and cheaply by commissioning an officer marching with a unit who had to provide most of the necessary instruments.[11]

Finally, the information acquired by this method satisfied the needs of the Company. By combining several plans of this sort, maps of entire provinces could be produced; the large scale generally used may have disguised many inaccuracies and omissions, but the maps gave a rough overview. For much of the eighteenth century this, and the ability to move goods and troops quickly along the routes of which knowledge was acquired, seem to have been enough for those responsible in India. If we use the Company's cartographical activities as a yardstick for the character of its rule in India, it seems to have been extremely superficial at this time. Knowledge of routes and the location of strategically important places was enough to maintain rule by military means, while exact knowledge about areas beyond the main roads – the white patches on the route surveyor's map – seems to have been of little interest. At the same time as largely ignoring details of the interior of the areas they had conquered, however, those responsible in the Company – at least if their cartographical activities are anything to go by – set their sights on further expansion. The surveying of more and more new routes, increasingly in areas belonging to allies or competing powers and sometimes in secret missions, also prepared the way for further military movements.[12]

Mackenzie's early surveys, as pure route surveys, were also clearly geared towards these interests, as were those he conducted after the Third Mysore War in 1792 as official Surveyor to the Nizam's Detachment, where his task was explicitly to survey passes and roads.[13] In so doing he only spent a small amount of time with his unit (the small British military corps stationed near Hyderabad town), and was mostly in far-off provinces, only occasionally accompanied by other European officers or even the Resident.[14]

Although the Nizam had entered a binding alliance with the British after the war, manifested by the presence of the corps and also that of the influential British Resident near the capital, their relationship was still somehow ambiguous during the 1790s.[15] While peace in South India seemed less and less secure, the situation in Hyderabad was seen as even more complicated given the fact that there was a French corps stationed there along with the British one until 1798; and it was not entirely clear if the Nizam would side with the British in the event of a conflict. Knowledge of his territory could thus not only be crucial in a regional war but also against the background of the global conflict with France that was to influence Mackenzie's career in India for many years. Mackenzie himself was not entirely uncritical of these wars: for instance, as he wrote to Seaforth about the first Coalition War:

> it is hoped ... that you will at last come to your senses at home, & dropping these fake ideas of aggrandizing yourselves by the ruin of your neighbours conceding peace as the best policy of an enlightened & commercial nation ... did not a desire ... to add to our dominion, our commerce, or our influence, prompt us to enter too rashly in a quarrel in which we have been left one by one by our profligate, ambitious allies, to call them by no worse appellation?[16]

But his critique should not be misunderstood as a general statement of doubt about the legitimacy of expanding the Empire, as becomes clear in the same letter when he states that for geostrategical reasons it would be impossible to give up the recent acquisitions of Ceylon and the Cape Colony. He himself always carried out his work for the military with great diligence and indeed his work in Hyderabad can be seen as conclusive evidence of how valuable surveying could be for the British army. Mackenzie's task there was quite tricky because he was bordering on espionage in the territory of an ally, where British surveying was regarded with great mistrust by both officials and the general population. Mackenzie's Bengal colleague Blunt, for instance, who when surveying a road accidentally ended up in the Nizam's territories, was prevented from carrying on with his work and could only do so after he had made the local Rajah the gift of a horse.[17] Unlike Blunt, Mackenzie usually had one of the Nizam's passes with him, which made it easier to get on,[18] but even he had been officially instructed to avoid attracting any attention and if possible to keep his instruments hidden. As he later wrote, in Hyderabad he had never felt able to carry out his surveying in complete freedom.[19]

In addition to these difficulties Mackenzie's surveys in Hyderabad were regularly interrupted by long illnesses and war deployment but, nevertheless, by 1796 he had managed to survey three thousand miles in the Nizam's territory,[20] the results of which can be seen in the many route maps he drew during that period.[21] While Mackenzie's methodology in these years can hardly be regarded as innovative, his Hyderabad maps are generally of a very high quality. Giving unusually rich information and topographical detail, they may be seen as some of the finest results of route surveying in India, which, under his own influence, came increasingly to be replaced by triangulation in the early nineteenth century. A very good example of how single surveys could be combined to give a clearer picture of a whole region is a map of the roads to the north of Hyderabad town (Figure 3.1) which Mackenzie drew in 1797 to summarize the results of two of his previous surveys.[22]

Mackenzie usually started his surveys, as the journal for the second of these surveys details, from the Hyderabad Resident's garden, and tried to organize them in the form of round trips, wherever possible using different roads for return.[23] Both map and journal clearly demonstrate that Mackenzie followed the usual methods, observing mainly topographical details about the roads he travelled on as well as the surrounding area. The positions of objects that could be seen from a distance were ascertained by bearings from the route, and the features of the landscape described in more detail in the journal were represented graphically on the map. However, the limitations of the method become clear from the fact that large parts of it remain blank, even though Mackenzie gives short written descriptions of the landscape including, for example, topography, crops cultivated and some hints about irrigation systems and the course of rivers. Mackenzie's clear distinction between information derived from actual survey, and enquiry, reinforces the impression of precision which the map gives. Roads actually measured, for example, are marked in red while courses of rivers known from secondary information only are symbolized by dotted lines or question marks. In addition, the stations used for triangulation are inserted in the map to clarify the ways in which the two surveys were combined. For instance, the position of hills that could be seen from the west or east side only during each of the surveys, and whose distance could be calculated through triangulation, made it possible (as Mackenzie noted on the map), not only to combine but also 'to verify and correct both surveys'.

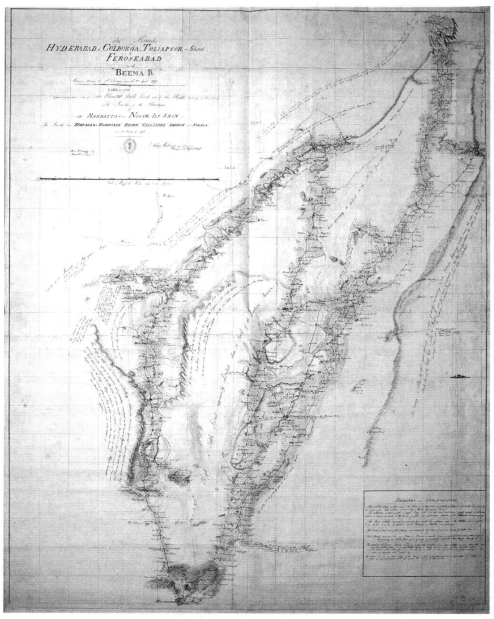

Figure 3.1 Colin Mackenzie, 'The Roads from Hyderabad to Culboorga, Toljapor-Ghaat & Feroseabad on the Beema River, Fort St. George', 10 December 1797.
Source: © The British Library Board BL/IOR/X/2066.

On closer inspection both the journal and the map reveal the priority of military objectives. The journal in particular gives many details relevant for marching troops, such as possibilities for supply and encampment; on the map it seems that, wherever possible, passes that could be used to reach Hyderabad from the east coast are sketched in, even though no exact information about the roads connecting them with the interior could be provided. Special attention is given to fortified places, even though Mackenzie remarks that they were 'sketched in from observations but not from actual plans, as no opportunity offered for taking measurements of their complete extents; it has however been attempted to give as accurate an idea of them, and of the face of the country, as the nature of the situation could admit of'. This becomes particularly clear if one looks at the area surrounding Hyderabad town and Golconda, which were supposed to be the Nizam's strongholds (Figure 3.2).

While Mackenzie's surviving journals all demonstrate the military objectives of his assignment,[24] this background to his work is certainly manifested most clearly in a piece he wrote for Governor Lord Hobart in 1796. Here he summarized diverse observations from his surveys of the eight previous years under the title 'Remarks on the Frontier Roads & Military Posts between the Kistna & Hyderabad'.[25] The piece represents nothing other than a plan for a military invasion, as Mackenzie later confirmed in a letter to Arthur Wellesley.[26] It begins with a fairly lengthy discussion of the various possibilities for invasion. To start with, suitable places for British troops to land on the coast of the Northern Circars are put forward as favourable points of departure; then Mackenzie turns to the strategically important points in the Nizam's territory. In particular he gives a good overview of the weir systems in the town of Hyderabad, not only describing the weak spots in the defences and walls, but also the position of the arsenals and important buildings inside the city. This suggests that he was also working with informants since the fortifications could normally only be visited with express permission;[27] he himself had only ridden through the town once and had otherwise only seen it from outside. It must have been due to the Nizam's justifiable mistrust that his unit was stationed several miles outside the capital.[28] However, of far greater strategic significance than storming Hyderabad, he wrote, was to conquer the nearby fortress of Golconda, which he had visited himself[29] and where most of the weapons and ammunition as well as the state treasures were stored. In the second part of the paper he gives a tabular overview of various alternative routes for marching towards Hyderabad. This section contains extremely detailed information about military posts, rivers and passes to be crossed, and also places where water and food could be acquired.[30]

None of Mackenzie's writing shows more clearly than this memorandum the extent to which his tasks in Hyderabad were geared towards military objectives. As officer and engineer he had to take on similar tasks quite often during his long career, and similar invasion plans, devised of course less from personal observation than from the compilation of the available material, meant that he made a major contribution to the conquest of Ceylon in 1796[31] and Java in 1811.[32] But this did not mean that Mackenzie saw surveying mainly as an activity geared solely towards military objectives – on the contrary, it was exactly during his years in Hyderabad that he started to formulate ideas about surveying that went far beyond these objectives. In part this was initiated by the increasing interest in Indian culture and history he developed during these years of travel.

New Perspectives

Equipped with few more comforts than a tent, camping bed, table and chair, route surveyors were often on the road for weeks on end. This usually involved getting up very early and, apart from a break at midday, marching all day long. Most of the time during the breaks was taken up with astronomical observations or writing journals. On the Deccan, Mackenzie also had to put up with intense heat. In the very year of his appointment he became so ill that probably due to a long fever he was unable to move one of his legs for quite some time and was granted several months' leave at the coast to recover.[33] Shortly

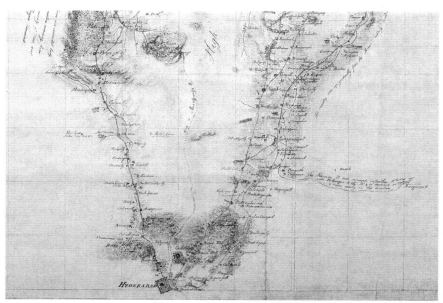

Figure 3.2 Detail from Mackenzie, 'The Roads from Hyderabad'.
Source: © The British Library Board BL/IOR/X/2066.

after returning to his duties he was again afflicted by fever, this time so severely that he required the help of the local Rajah in order to get back to his unit's encampment, where he needed several more months' recovery.[34] But despite many interruptions he spent about half his time between 1792 and 1797 doing surveying, so the remark he made during this period that he was forced to live a 'wandering life' certainly does not seem like an exaggeration.[35]

His tasks were demanding and considering the size of the country hardly possible for one man alone to carry out. Years later, somewhat disillusioned, he described the practice of allocating such huge areas to one surveyor as follows: 'It is in fact a never ending & heartbreaking undertaking to employ one Man in such a situation & if health is preserved it must take many years or be a very imperfect work'.[36] Nevertheless, as he pointed out to Seaforth, although his surveys were very strenuous they had also given him great pleasure: 'you will observe how little time I have had on my hands for some years to spare for amusement or pleasure, (tho' in fact I derived much of both from this disposal of my time) I can safely assure that since my recovery from my last great illness in October 1794 I have not been a single day without being fully occupied either with the duties of the Survey or those of the Engineer Department from the Latitudes of 8° to 17° North'.[37]

Given his intellectual openness and firm belief in the value of knowledge it is hardly surprising that in these years Mackenzie started to take an intense interest in the culture and history of the regions through which he travelled. His work took him to routes hitherto barely touched by any Europeans and brought him to remote places of historical relevance, whose commemorative buildings, pagodas or ruins understandably aroused his interest. It was also in Hyderabad that he started to work closely with Indians. Mackenzie was largely isolated from his European friends here, 'secluded from any relief of social intercourse',[38] meaning the social life in Madras and the British garrison towns. On the other hand, during his surveys he lived, of necessity, with his retinue of Indian co-workers – apart from bearers, personal servants and sepoys for protection, there were two *harkaras* and a translator.[39] In addition he was constantly making the acquaintance of representatives of the local elites. Years later Mackenzie was still mentioning some of these acquaintances with great respect in his letters. And eighteen years later he still had presents sent via one of his assistants to the Nabob of Curnoul, who had helped him during his illness in 1792.[40]

Much of the communication, of course, had to be conducted via translators. Mackenzie regarded the fact that during his early years with the Company he had not learned a single local idiom as a great failing – though his strenuous duties that involved constantly changing location, and therefore also regional language, would have made any intensive language studies impossible at that time. Furthermore, he went on, there was as yet no official support for learning

Indian languages.[41] He may perhaps have made rather too much of this point since other officers, such as Munro and Elphinstone, managed to gain knowledge of languages during the same period, which became a basis for their brilliant careers.[42] Even after his death Mackenzie was sometimes put forward as a poor role model in this respect,[43] but his lack of linguistic knowledge also meant that his Indian co-workers had a great influence on formulating his ideas about Indian culture and history. This applies in particular to the time after 1796 when, on the way back from Ceylon, he got to know Kavali Venkata Borayya, who had previously been employed by the EIC as scribe and translator in the Northern Circars.[44]

Even before he met Borayya, Mackenzie had recognized the value of involving Indians in his work. Not only had friends in Madras, such as James Anderson, employed Indian co-workers, but in Hyderabad the value of collaboration was particularly obvious. The British Resident was intimately involved in the life of the Nizam's court, so for him, as for other high-ranking figures in the political system there, it was a matter of course to act as patrons for a number of artists, poets and intellectuals.[45] The two Residents John Kennaway and William Kirkpatrick, under whom Mackenzie served, also had good contacts within the Nizam's administration and Kirkpatrick in particular was known for having a network of Indian co-workers, which meant that he was always exceptionally well informed. His Indian scribes not only copied files from the Nizam's archives but also helped him to compile geographical information.[46]

The most important thing for Mackenzie's professional activities was working with the *harkaras*, without whose cooperation much of the British surveying would probably have been impossible.[47] The *harkaras* represented a group of professional guides and agents whose local knowledge was virtually indispensable for route planning and acquiring provisions.[48] As early as 1776 it had been decided that every survey should be supported by two *harkaras*[49] and in the following decade their own corps was set up in Madras to support both the military and civil employees.[50] Support from *harkaras* was not unique to Mackenzie's surveys but unlike many other cartographers, who tried to underplay, or indeed keep quiet about their Indian sources,[51] he expressly mentioned how important they were and stressed 'the advantages of attending to the notices, which may be procured in the Country, from the People early habituated by Profession to act as Conductors on the great roads ... who tho' they may not with geometrical accuracy give the distances and directions, are yet very usefull in giving very important information'.[52] What seems interesting in this context, as Jennifer Howes has shown, is that at the time of his survey in Guntoor, Mackenzie was already collecting maps drawn by *harkaras*.[53]

Nevertheless, Mackenzie later described the first thirteen years of his stay in India, until he met Borayya, as 'of little moment with regard to the objects pursued latterly, as collecting observations and notices of Hindu manners, of geography and history'.[54] But even if he did not start collecting until he was nearing the end of his time in Hyderabad his broad interest in South Indian culture and history that was to form the basis of his subsequent project to research them systematically developed during these years. This is demonstrated firstly, as Jennifer Howes has pointed out, by the illustrations Mackenzie drew at this time. During his early years in India he had already started to make sketches and watercolours of places he had travelled to – not unlike many other Britons who regarded dabbling in watercolours as a hobby worthy of a gentleman. He also carried on with this during his time in Hyderabad – though along with the usual topographical views he now included detailed illustrations of objects such as sculptures, which suggests a deeper interest in the objects depicted.[55] Secondly, this interest is also manifest in various publications from this period, some of which were closely connected with these illustrations.

In the early 1790s, for instance, along with two smaller geographical pieces, he published in hydrographer Alexander Dalrymple's *Oriental Repertory* an account of a reservoir in today's Andhra Pradesh, based in essence on a local legend about its origins.[56] Around the middle of the decade Mackenzie began to publish longer pieces. At this time he also became a member of the Asiatic Society of Bengal, in Calcutta, then the only British scientific society in India, to which many people from the Madras presidency also belonged.[57] His membership can possibly be attributed to the initiative of the Resident of Hyderabad William Kirkpatrick since he is the one who sent Mackenzie's first piece published in the *Asiatic Researches*, the society's journal, to Calcutta. This was a detailed description of a pagoda on the southern bank of the Kistna that Mackenzie had produced in 1794 and which, because part of it is in the form of a personal account, shows very well the way in which a visit to such edifices took place.[58]

What is certainly his most important publication from this period appeared in the next volume of *Asiatic Researches*. This dealt with the geography and antiquities of Ceylon and was based on a journal he had kept during the British conquest of the island between January and April 1796.[59] In the usual style of contemporary travelogues Mackenzie gives a chronological account of the individual stages of his journey, devoting a good deal of space to the ruins, monuments and holy sites he visited. He also describes local customs, the population, or quite generally the topography of the regions. Theoretical speculations can also be found, for instance about the former course of the coasts based on fossils found there and geological characteristics. The article is significant above all because of the passages containing methodological ideas about researching the history of South Asia, which anticipate much of what Mackenzie was later to practise. This applies, firstly, to his insistence on combining various types of source: architectural evidence must, he said, be brought into line with inscriptions and literary evidence in order to maintain a chronological order that was as accurate as possible. Secondly, he stresses the opportunity to acquire knowledge by multiregional comparison. So a system of classifying the age of buildings according to style could also be applied to South India and Ceylon. For example, a certain plainness in religious buildings could often be a sign of great age. What is more, by observing the languages formerly used in a region, for instance as they appeared in place names, conclusions could also be drawn about the earlier distribution of certain population groups.[60]

Despite Mackenzie's broad interests, during these years the official objects of his surveys necessarily remained limited – in his two articles for *Asiatic Researches* he stresses that he was only able to carry out his studies on the side and under time pressure because in his official duties he was dealing with 'objects of a very different nature'.[61] At this time he could still distinguish between his official duties, mainly military, and his private interests. He later wrote that his career also showed 'that science may derive helps, and knowledge be diffused, in the leisure moments of camps and voyages'.[62] But it is also clear that during these years, and especially after meeting Borayya, he was developing plans for a more comprehensive survey that would not be restricted to cartography for military purposes but bring together his broad spectrum of interests in South India. In his Hyderabad years, however, his own prospects for a successful career still seemed to be more important to him than the ideas that anticipated his later emphasis on the usefulness of surveys for civil purposes.

Cartography and Career

The position Cornwallis had given Mackenzie as Surveyor to the Nizam's Detachment had been intended as a personal reward. However, this turned out to be far less lucrative than Mackenzie had originally thought because the Governor had not concerned himself with details such as remuneration,[63] and in the official orders his appointment had initially been overlooked.[64] So it was that after a period of uncertainty as to who should actually pay him, Mackenzie's salary was set up in such a way that he soon came to regard his appointment as financially useless.[65] 'Many in this case would have contented themselves with Surveying a little to keep up appearances', he wrote to Seaforth, 'but my views extended further, & this was not the intention of the friends who suggested my nomination'.[66]

Mackenzie also expected that the conscientious fulfilment of his duties and the considerable results he could present to his superiors would serve to advance his career further. In the mid 1790s he expected to be appointed as Surveyor General of Madras, probably because his long-time superior Patrick Ross had suggested this as a medium-term prospect. If rewarded with this post, he hoped he would be able to return to Britain at least for a while after more than twelve years in India:

This appointment now solicited by me will not stand in the way of my going to Europe when occasion calls, & my rank still going on in the Army (for now the Engineers can raise thro' all the gradations) leaves me at liberty to return within a certain period, or avail myself of any other opportunity of rising; I shall be able to embrace any favourable opportunity with effect if I could master for Ten thousand Pounds to Fifteen Thousand (tho' far distant yet from this amount).[67]

Setting up the position of Surveyor General in Madras had already been discussed for a long time; Bengal in particular was the model,[68] where James Rennell had already been appointed to this office in 1767. However, the importance of the post there remained very limited until well into the nineteenth century. Given their responsibilities as engineers, Rennell's successors – John Call, Thomas Wood and Alexander Kyd – regarded the position largely as a sideline designed to increase their income, and did not even keep any separate files on their activities as Surveyor General.[69] Call and Wood had voluntarily given up the post when they were offered the chance to become chief engineers and Kyd had largely left the running of the department to his assistant, Robert Hyde Colebrooke.[70] It was not until Colebrooke was officially appointed as Surveyor General, in 1794,[71] that the situation began to change to some extent. Colebrooke made it his aim, in his fourteen-plus years in office, to turn what was previously regarded as a sinecure into an efficient office that would direct all cartographical activity in the presidency. All in all, however, despite certain reforms, even his period in office should be regarded as being fairly unsuccessful.

Even though the model used was somewhat dubious, due to lack of knowledge of the actual situation in Bengal, by the 1780s the idea of setting up a position to organize surveying work and to administer cartographical material in the ever-expanding presidency of Madras was already regarded as by no means improbable. Mackenzie had prepared his strategy well and in 1795 was already holding conversations with Governor Lord Hobart about his future prospects.[72] Above all, his map of Hyderabad with the accompanying memoir, which he started working on in the same year[73] and completed in the next, was supposed to underpin his claims.[74] The strategy of attracting the decision makers' attention by making a general map had been widespread amongst British surveyors in India since Rennell's time. The attempts by Call and Colebrooke to produce up-to-date maps of India in the 1780s and 1790s had failed due to their premature deaths, but the Bombay Surveyor General Charles Reynolds had produced a map thirty-seven square metres in size that had undoubtedly provided proof of his diligence and was given a special room of its own in India House in London.[75]

Mackenzie's map was also received with great acclaim. The Directors promised him a relatively high remuneration of 2,400 pagodas or about 900 pounds,[76] and after he had written another memo his salary more than doubled.[77] However, his appointment as Surveyor General, which was supported by the government in Madras and which Mackenzie was still convinced would happen in 1797,[78] soon seemed to be called into question. Mackenzie himself regarded the competing interests and intrigues of his colleague Alexander Beatson as the main obstacle[79] but also apparently the numerous offices in the presidency already dealing with cartographical tasks, for instance the astronomer, the Marine Surveyor, the Chief Engineer and the Superintendent of Waterworks, Tanks, Embankments or Canals. So he made another attempt to improve his prospects by asking for a clear distinction to be made between the various tasks. What he wanted, he now made clear, was the office of Military Surveyor General, who should be solely responsible for military geography.[80] However, London firmly rejected his appointment.[81]

There are good reasons to assume that for application to an explicitly military post strategic considerations were crucial – the advancement of his own career still seemed more important to him than the ideas of a much broader approach to the production of knowledge through surveying that he developed during the same years. Although Mackenzie constantly emphasized the value of his work to the army, he himself had long since become interested in investigating objects that went far beyond military use. This is also apparent in the memoir accompanying his map of Hyderabad, which generally followed the usual rules of an eighteenth-century cartographical memoir. Using known geographical locations, this meant combining his own measurements with geographical information derived from other sources and providing as detailed information as possible about the material used.[82] For instance, Mackenzie referred to the work of Tavernier and Thévenot, the map by a Jesuit from Goa, the road-book of an Indian government employee or even the geographical manuscripts from the Mughal period.[83] With the aid of the Resident, Mackenzie had already tried to get hold of more recent British surveys of the bordering regions,[84] a difficult undertaking because at a time of global conflict the Directors had decreed that militarily sensitive cartographical information could only be passed on by the government of the presidency in question.[85] But still, mainly with the help of the Surveyor General of Bengal, who constantly praised Mackenzie's achievements, he managed over the years to acquire a considerable amount of additional material[86] that he was able to work into the second version of his map of 1800.[87]

All this was fully in keeping with what would be expected for making a general map. Other aspects mentioned in his memoir, however, went far beyond this. This applies, firstly, to the way Mackenzie dealt with place names, a method he was to retain in his future work. In both European and Indian sources place names were equally difficult to identify. This arose from the fact that different places could have similar or even the same names, but also, and this was the main problem, from lack of clarity in transcribing the diverse scripts used in India. Indeed, until well into the nineteenth century there was no unified system for this.[88] There were basically two opposing schools: on the one hand the representatives of the phonetic approach, who tried to render the words in Latin purely according to how they sounded, and on the other the supporters of the system invented by William Jones. In the first volume of his *Asiatic Researches* Jones had already called for a system of transcription based on rendering the individual letters, with less attention to phonetics.[89] One of his reasons for this was that it was the only way to produce a unified transcription for all European languages – indeed the differences produced by phonetic transcription were a problem that sometimes made French sources virtually useless to British cartographers.[90]

However, for pragmatic reasons and often because they did not have adequate command of the Indian scripts, most British cartographers continued to use the phonetic method, which understandably led to a certain anarchy in the transcription of Indian words.[91] Mackenzie became aware of this problem at an early stage, even though his own work often contains imprecisions. So he only allowed the transcriptions for his map of Hyderabad to be done by Indian experts who knew the places and languages.[92] Years later he still insisted that in the Surveying Department translators be employed to ensure the correct spelling of place names,[93] and in official correspondence he did not hold back in his criticism of other surveyors' lack of precision.[94]

Secondly, parts of Mackenzie's memoir can be read as an appeal for his survey to be extended to objects that were by no means solely of military significance – which may be seen as highly consequential since instead of Military Surveyor General, he was soon to become the strongest proponent of surveying for civil purposes in the Madras presidency. He considered it important, for instance, to go beyond information about roads and to examine the forms of administrative territorial organization, in their historical dimension as well, because in political negotiations reference was constantly made to the old territorial units.[95] What is more, as he had stated in his letter to Seaforth, he also wanted to supplement his map with an 'account of the productions & state of these interesting provinces' but had abandoned this idea due to the prospect of rapid career advancement; nonetheless he had already collected a large amount of material that could be used for it.[96] In his memoir on the construction of the map he also makes these ideas clear officially: it would do honour, he wrote, to the British as 'commercial people' if maps such as his were supplemented by descriptions of the 'Revenues, Resources, Population, Natural Productions and Manufactures'.[97]

Surveying and the Tasks of Government

The plans for a comprehensive survey that Mackenzie had been developing since the mid 1790s were partly based on his increasing interest in culture and history. Due to his contacts with the Nizam's administration, but above all his acquaintance with Borayya, he became convinced that such research could be carried out systematically if only consistent use were made of the information available at the various levels of the Indian administration. However, in order to understand the wider significance of his plans it is not enough to interpret them simply against the background of his individual experiences on the Deccan – they can be only understood in the context of the discussions about the legitimate forms of British rule in India conducted in the Madras presidency from the 1780s. If British rule beyond the city boundaries of Madras had so far been fairly nominal,[98] new forms of control over the area of British rule now started to be sought. In particular, the territories gained after victory in the Third Mysore War, when part of Tipu Sultan's territory was annexed, provided an important incentive for developing a regular administration.

It was characteristic of Madras that the model of Bengal, where similar processes had already set in some twenty years earlier, was not simply followed without exception. Here, as there, a 'historicist' argument was made, in analogy with the English political discourse with its emphasis on ancient rights, custom and precedence; if possible the new regime in India should connect with its predecessors and respect customary rights. On the other hand – this was the widespread view of the British in Madras – the south was different from Bengal, so other yardsticks had to be applied here, an attitude that gave 'historicism' even greater significance than in the other presidencies. As David Washbrook has shown, the reasons behind this attitude, apart from seeking a certain political autonomy, were: the economic connections between Indians and Europeans at a local level, often spanning generations; the relatively endangered position of the small British minority; competition with regional powers such as Hyderabad or Mysore; and the cultural pluralism rooted for centuries in South India.[99]

In the 1790s emphasis on the specific conditions in South India was most obvious in the matter of revenue, which at this time was one of the administration's key issues. In Bengal, after a long period of experimentation, the Permanent Settlement had been agreed upon, a system whereby, in principle, tax should be collected by the *zamindars*. These were regarded as major landowners who had previously had a certain function in collecting revenue and jurisdiction, and this was a way of restoring their 'original' property rights.[100] However, in the Madras presidency, where Governor General Cornwallis wanted to adopt the Permanent Settlement, the attitude towards this system was fairly critical. Sullivan, for instance, a long-time civilian employee of the Company in Madras, expressed the opinion of many people when he said that 'no man will be found so sanguine as to maintain that such a resolution could, with prudence, or any reasonable hope of success, be acted upon in our other possessions'.[101] As a result of such reservations a long phase of experimenting with systems of raising revenue began in South India. Along with the *zamindari* system, revenue systems based on village communities or even individual peasants were tried out.[102]

None of these systems was supposed to represent a fundamental innovation, but was to be adjusted to each local context and the 'ancient' practices for collecting revenue. However, in contrast to the *zamindari* system, direct contact with peasants meant that detailed information had to be acquired, for instance about the size and yield of individual fields, cultivation methods and crops grown.[103] So beginning with the work by Alexander Read, Thomas Munro and John Mather in the district of Salem and Barramahal the revenue surveys typical of Madras were introduced,[104] generally carried out by civil assistants trained in the basic concepts of surveying under the leadership of each region's collector. From 1798 onwards these assistants were responsible to the Inspector of Revenue Surveys based in Madras.[105]

In the discussion that accompanied the imposition of direct territorial control in South India the question was raised as to what consequences this new policy would have for the relationship between the EIC and its Indian subjects. Two texts that Burton Stein sees as crucial for the debates of the 1790s explicitly stress the responsibility that accrued to the government of Madras through collecting revenue, namely John Sullivan's *Tracts upon India* and the three-volume work *British India Analyzed* by the British MP, natural historian and friend of Seaforth, Francis Greville.[106] Sullivan, whose work is a commentated edition of letters he wrote himself, referred to his own experiences in the Madras presidency in the preceding decade, while Greville, who had never been in India, argues on the basis of an extensive collection of relevant material. Both authors basically agreed that a British government in India must assume certain responsibilities towards its subjects, particularly the simple farmers, and contribute to the economic development of the conquered territories. Sullivan, for instance, developed a complete programme of 'improvement' for the Northern Circars which included the promotion of manufacturing, forestry and mining as well as setting up storehouses for grain in times of need, the reduction of customs duties to promote trade, and road building. In this way a 'strong cement of union between the native subjects and the British power' should be created, underpinned by government-funded establishments for Indians to learn English and for the British to learn the South Indian languages.[107] Similar ideas can also be detected behind Greville's often programmatic statements, for instance when he stresses that 'Government cannot longer avoid a *direct* and *minute* attention to the circumstances of the country and its inhabitants'.[108]

One of the most important points in both authors' critique was the Company's responsibility for maintaining the irrigation systems of South India given that their efficient functioning was one of the keystones of the agricultural economy there. The discussion about financing the maintenance of tanks was by no means new. Alexander Dalrymple, for instance, a Scot, hydrographer with the Company in London, and former civilian employee in Madras,[109] had already pointed out in the 1780s that the Company should be responsible for maintaining tanks and that part of the revenue had traditionally been reserved for this purpose. The fact that under the rule of the Company, which had delegated the maintenance to tenants, the state of irrigation systems in the Jaghire had substantially deteriorated was sufficient evidence for him to suggest that the government in Madras should take direct responsibility.[110] Ten years later Greville and Sullivan not only agreed with this view[111] but also, like many other people, wanted the Company to build new irrigation facilities as they regarded the traditional system, based mainly on local tanks of various sizes without any external inflow, as inadequate. In the 1770s Sullivan had already proposed for the Northern Circars that some of the water from the region's two great rivers, the Kistna und the Godavery, be diverted into canals for use in agriculture,[112] and twenty years later this idea was taken up again by various Company employees in India – such as the doctors and natural historians James Anderson and William Roxburgh, as well as private individuals such as the Scottish merchant Andrew Ross. Alexander Dalrymple published their proposals,[113] and Greville and Sullivan also made reference to them in their work.[114]

It was precisely in the matter of irrigation that the Company's inconsistent attitude was most apparent; on occasion it was prepared to promote major prestigious projects,[115] but at the same time it neglected essential necessities in the regions it was administering. So Sullivan's proposal for building canals did lead to some preparatory surveying work, but this was never completed. The project initially disappeared into oblivion until in 1792/1793 a famine broke out in the Northern Circars due to a disastrous drought; contemporaries estimated that it cost the lives of a good part of the population of this region.[116] Once again the inefficiency of the existing irrigation systems was held responsible and, based on the proposals already known, the surveyor Michael Topping now developed a plan whereby the land between the Kistna and the Godavery should be irrigated by a system of canals, sluices and dams.[117] Topping was then officially commissioned, along with his assistants, to carry out the necessary surveying work.[118] But although he, and after his death Alexander Beatson, worked on this for years,[119] once the Fourth Mysore War started those responsible in the EIC again lost sight of the project. It was not until the 1850s that a similar project was finally carried out, after a completely new start.[120]

For those affected by the famine of the 1790s this surveying work was initially of no consequence. As one official from Ganjam reported to Madras in 1795: 'populous and once flourishing Villages are now desolated and overgrown with Jungle, the Inhabitants wretchedly poor'.[121] In this and the following year the situation again became critical when massive rainfall caused floods in the Chicacole district, leading to many deaths and the destruction of crops and cattle.[122] It was quite clear that the catastrophic floods were due to the poor condition of the irrigation systems – particularly the tanks, whose dams were incapable of holding back such a mass of water.[123] The EIC was held at least partly responsible since even though it had planned a major new project it had grossly neglected its traditional responsibility as recipient of revenue, namely the maintenance of the existing irrigation systems.[124]

Some of those responsible on the ground now felt obliged to find some sort of quick remedy. These include Michael Keating, Collector in Chicacole, who made a tour of the devastated district shortly after the flood[125] and was clearly so affected by the extent of the destruction that without consulting his superiors in Fort St George he made funds available to the inhabitants for rebuilding their houses and for carrying out the necessary repairs to the tanks.[126] Keating's alarming reports and his quick response made a rapid reaction by the Board of Revenue in Madras inevitable, so Topping, who was already working in the Circars, was summarily commissioned to write a report on the state of the tanks in Chicacole and Vizagapatam,[127] and was subsequently appointed Superintendent of Tank Repairs in the Madras presidency.[128]

From personal observations and questionnaires given to the inhabitants Topping tried to convey the extent of the devastation and the repairs needed.[129] It seems that the Board of Revenue, keen on saving money, was not prepared to take any measures until it received his report, but once again it was Keating who insisted on rapid action. At Topping's suggestion he allocated large up-front sums of money to the villages affected – they were supposed to carry out the repairs themselves with full financial compensation from the Company – without paying any attention to his superior's instructions, which in this respect were far from unambiguous.[130] Keating attracted a great deal of criticism for this,[131] and was even accused of dereliction of duty,[132] but he had caused the government a dilemma that did not permit any further delay. On the one hand it said that the repairs were too expensive and wanted only the most important tanks to be restored,[133] but on the other hand the investments granted by Keating and already activated would be lost for ever if the work were interrupted. A petition signed by the inhabitants and forwarded by Keating applied even more pressure,[134] to which Governor Hobart eventually succumbed: 'In this dilemma the necessity of incurring the further charges for the repairs of tanks leaves the President in Council no choice' – this is how he justified his decision to allow the work to continue even after Topping's death in March 1796, under the supervision of the engineer Pittman.[135]

In the same year a separate Tank Department was set up in the revenue administration,[136] and in the following years the post of Superintendent of Tank Repairs was gradually extended and eventually allocated six assistants.[137] The efficiency of the new department in its early years should certainly not be overstated – years later the repairs in the Northern Circars had still not been completed.[138] But the fact that it was set up at all illustrates very clearly a trend in the Company in South India to redefine its role as a territorial power in internal affairs as well. The basis for this was growing criticism amongst the British public about the poor state of the provinces under the Company's rule made obvious in the publications by Greville, Sullivan and Dalrymple, the pressure arising from the situation on the ground, the petitions submitted by the population, and finally the personal initiatives by individual British inhabitants of the presidency. By creating the Tank Department the EIC recognized that there was a sphere of public work for which the government must show itself to be responsible. However, at the same time it became obvious that without exact knowledge of the local conditions it would be impossible to get on top of these tasks or to find a suitable solution to the question of revenue. So during these years the first, generally not very systematic, surveys for civil purposes were started.

Although Colin Mackenzie was at the time primarily involved in surveying routes for military purposes, he also took part, at least indirectly, in the discussion about irrigation.[139] For Andrew Ross, the merchant, he prepared a paper in 1793 entitled 'Memoir on the Various Modes of Watering Land practised by the Natives of India',[140] in which, during the first devastating famine, he summarized his observations on this topic made during his surveys. Andrew Ross was one of the most important independent traders in the Madras presidency[141] and along with James Anderson and William Roxburgh one of those who initiated the public discussion about irrigation in the Northern Circars. Ross's motives for this initiative are rather unclear, but Alexander Dalrymple's explanation may be right, namely that Ross was a man, 'whose zeal for the public welfare has on every occasion been suspicious',[142] since the merchant pursued a number of projects not directly connected with his business interests. For instance, he employed Teroovercadoo Mootiah, one of James Anderson's co-workers, to translate historical documents from Malayalam,[143] or had ideas about extending cultivated areas in South India, and suggested that soldiers should not be recruited from the population there.[144] It is hardly surprising that Mackenzie was in contact with him because for many young Scots Ross was the first point of contact for sorting out financial affairs.[145] Since Mackenzie had already served in the Northern Circars in the 1780s, Ross, who turned to various correspondents with queries of this sort,[146] probably contacted him with a request for more detailed information.

As Mackenzie says himself at the beginning of his memoir, it should also been seen as a direct reaction to the famine in the Northern Circars. However, his observations also included large sections of South India between Madura in the south, the Kistna in the north, and Seringapatam and Gooty in the west, so that he gave an overview of virtually the whole presidency, and some of the bordering areas, for which he described the various forms of irrigation, namely tanks, wells, canals and sluices. But he did not confine his presentation to the technical side of these installations; he also stressed the physical features that explained regional differences and had consequences for cultivating certain crops, for nutritional practices and also for the patterns of trade. For instance, he described the particularities of the dry plain at the headwaters of the Pennar above the Ghauts that he had visited two years earlier.[147] Due to the lack of precipitation and consequent aridity the river remained almost dry for part of the year, and topography led to huge differences in the forms of irrigation and consequently cultivation of crops between the upper plain and the lower areas where the lands could be watered by using canals:

> In this tract, very little Paddy is cultivated which can be only owing to the fall from the level being too small to admit of Conduits being carried off from the bottom of the River to any Reservoir, on following the course of the River into the Carnatic, the mode of cultivation immediately changes with the aspect of the country and the attention of the natives to the management of water confirms an opinion that the want of a proper level and the height of the sand banks is the reason that the Cultivation of Paddy or Rice does not take place so generally above the Gaats, as below, along the course of this River. The Principal subsistence of the great body of People in these upper countries is dry Grain. Indigo and Cotton are produced in considerable quantities, which are sent into the Carnatic and exchanged for Salt and Tobacco.[148]

Based on such observations made in the various regions Mackenzie came to the conclusion that the 'various modes of providing and preserving water for the melioration of the ground' were 'suited to the peculiar habits of the natives'.[149] This assessment was clearly quite different from that of Topping, who described the irrigation techniques in the Northern Circars in quite general terms as 'deficient, of course'.[150] Mackenzie did not oppose building new irrigation in principle, but to start with the existing facilities should be extended; and he complained about their poor condition. He also gently criticized the EIC's policy when he suggested 'proper application of the funds destined for these purposes and frequent inspections and reports'. This, he went on, was not being proposed only for humanitarian reasons, but because it would also be in the Company's interests. The prosperity of the country and the revenues depended on expansion of agriculture to guarantee further population growth. So now it was necessary to turn to the 'comforts of the useful Class of the cultivators of the soil'.[151]

Mackenzie also gave 'historicist' backing to the Company's responsibility, for instance when reporting about maintenance of the irrigation systems: 'the care of making and keeping them in constant repair has been always a peculiar object of the Police of the Hindoo Governments, and after them of such of the Mahommedan Chiefs as were most distinguished for a regard to the welfare of their subjects'.[152] He also referred here to the great age of some of the irrigation facilities and the great respect still accorded in contemporary narratives to those who introduced reservoirs or dams. Also of interest in this context is his publication concerning the Cummum tank, which at Andrew Ross's suggestion was published in Dalrymple's *Oriental Repertory*.[153] (He had visited and surveyed it in October 1792.[154]) The publication does not, however, give any technical description of the reservoir and is basically confined to recounting a local legend of the tank's origin. A brief commentary by Mackenzie points to the real core of the story – a statue of the legendary founder stands at the edge of the tank – and dates these events on the basis of Jonathan Scott's *Historical and Political View of the Decan* published two years earlier.[155] Although the text says nothing more about the problem of water supply, it too can be seen as a strong argument praising the longevity of Indian irrigation systems (in this case seven hundred years), and thus for the functionality of the traditional methods of maintaining them.

Above all, however, the 'Memoir on the Various Modes of Watering the Lands' contains a whole series of arguments that were later to form the basis of his concept of a comprehensive survey: firstly, the need for more precise knowledge of local conditions if the government were to take sensible measures. Secondly, emphasis on the notion that local conditions should also be perceived in their historical dimension so that the role of the EIC could be appropriately adapted. And finally, connected with this, an idea of 'improvement' geared less towards a radical transformation of the land and its people than towards gradual change in harmony with social, cultural and natural conditions. The basis for this argumentation lay in the concept of the EIC's responsibility for the welfare of its subjects: the form of rule envisaged by Mackenzie and many others should by no means be orientated only to military or fiscal interests, but should also include many spheres associated with a civil administration. The production of knowledge through surveying, seen in such a way, was to facilitate the tasks of Government – at the same time, however, it was also to define these tasks as they necessarily had to be based on familiarity with local conditions. And what is more, an important consequence of this perspective was that comprehensive surveying itself had to be seen as a task of government as it was the sole secure foundation on which responsible policies could be based.

As the Memoir makes clear, Mackenzie had already developed these views in the early 1790s. It took his years in Hyderabad, however, gradually to elaborate them into a comprehensive project of surveying that was to fill a gap left by the two types of surveying usual in Madras, which can be seen as a direct product of military fiscalism – route surveying and revenue surveys. The ties with Indian experts that he established during that period convinced him of the practical feasibility of such a project, while from this perspective his interest in South Indian culture and history seems to be of far more significance than the favourite pastimes of an antiquarian. However, it was not until after the Fourth

Mysore War that he had the opportunity to put his project into practice, and indeed on a far greater scale than he would ever have dared to hope for just a few years earlier.

Notes

1. Cf. Peers, *Mars and Mammon*.
2. Between 1789 and 1805 the number of troops rose from 115,000 to 155,000. Cf. Bayly, *Indian Society*, 85.
3. See for example Peers, 'State, Power, and Colonialism', 16–43.
4. For an overview of the early European cartography of India see P.L. Madan, *Indian Cartography: A Historical Perspective* (Delhi, 2001), esp. 47–56; S. Gole, *India within the Ganghes* (Delhi, 1983), 103–227; and ead., *Early Maps of India* (New Delhi, 1976), 91–119. Facsimiles of some of these maps can be found in S. Gole, *A Series of Early Printed Maps of India in Facsimile*, 2nd edn. (Delhi, 1984).
5. As early as 1758 William Frankland, member of the Board of Calcutta, was commissioned to carry out a survey of the twenty-four *parganas* and three years later Hugh Cameron was officially appointed Surveyor of the New Lands. Cf. B to Secret Committee of Affairs, 13 January 1758, *FWIHC*, vol. 2 (Public Series 1757–1759), edited by H.N. Sinha (Delhi, 1957); 299; also 23 January 1758, ibid., vol. 2, 307; B to CD, 12 November 1761, ibid., vol. 3, 372; also 8 April 1762, ibid., 417.
6. J. Rennell, *A Bengal Atlas: Containing Maps of the Theatre of War and Commerce on That Side of Hindoostan. Compiled from the Original Surveys; and Published by Order of the Honourable the Court of Directors for the Affairs of the East India Company* ([London], 1781).
7. In 1815, after a review of the Surveying Department, in an official report Mackenzie mentioned only two surveys carried out in the Madras presidency before 1790: Thomas Barnard's survey of the Jaghire and a military survey of Palnaud from 1787. Cf. Colin Mackenzie to Chief Sec. Gov., 14 December 1815, BL/IOR/F/4/554 (13476), 147–245, here 199.
8. Cf. Edney, *Mapping an Empire*, 91–96. For a detailed description of the use of this method by Mackenzie himself during his early surveys see Mackenzie, 'Account of the Construction of the Plan of the Roads from Nellore', 57f.
9. Even after decades of route surveying, in 1802 the Surveyor General of Bengal, Robert Hyde Colebrooke, was asking for general rules for what should be entered in such a field book. Cf. Robert Hyde Colebrooke to Captain Hook, Sec. Gov. Mil. Dep. FW, 4 September 1802, NAI/SIR/SGO/54B, 122–24.
10. J. Muller, *A New System of Mathematics Containing Plane Geometry; General Investigation of Areas, Surfaces, and Solids; Greatest and Least Quantities; Trigonometry; Logarithms; Motion, Uniform, Compound, Accelerated, Retarded, Projectiles, Application: To Which is Prefixed the First Principles of Algebra, by Way of Introduction* (London, 1769), i; id., *The Attack and Defence of Fortified Places: In Three Parts: Illustrated with Twenty-five Large Copper-Plates*, 2nd edn., (London, 1757). For Rennell's reading see James Rennell to Reverend Gilbert Burington, 21 December 1759, BL/OIOC/MSS Eur/D/1073.
11. From 1788 this was made compulsory by a general order that was repeated at the beginning of the nineteenth century. See 'Fort William General Order', 12 January 1804, BL/IOR/F/4/183 (3692), 21–26; and Robert Hyde Colebrooke to L. Hook, Sec. Gov. Mil. Dep., 4 September 1802, NAI/SIR/SGO/54B, 122–24. See also Phillimore, *Historical Records*, vol. 1, 43, 184–89, 198f.

12. For instance Reynolds, a Bombay surveyor, travelled around the subcontinent on various occasions in the 1780s and early 1790s and in those areas where the rulers mistrusted the British he used diverse ruses to conceal the true purpose of his journey. Cf. Phillimore, *Historical Records*, vol. 1, 125–28.

13. Patrick Ross to Alexander Ross, 16 July 1792, Chief Engineer's Books, BL/OIOC/Mss Eur/ Mack Gen/69; Colin Mackenzie to Charles Oakeley, 13 February 1793, ibid.

14. For instance in 1795, when he accompanied the Nizam's expedition against the Marathas along with Kirkpatrick. Cf. William Kirkpatrick to Charles Warren Malet, 3 May 1795, BL/ IOR/H/446/1, 13–19; and Colin Mackenzie to William Kirkpatrick, 30 April 1795, ibid., 20–23.

15. For British influence in Hyderabad cf. M.H. Fisher, 'Indirect Rule in the British Empire: The Foundations of the Residency System in India (1764–1858)', *Modern Asian Studies* 18(3) (1984), 393–428; and id., *Indirect Rule in India*, esp. 43–56.

16. Colin Mackenzie to Francis Humberston Mackenzie, 4 September 1797, NAS/GD/46/17/4, 512–18, here, 514f.

17. Cf. Robert Hyde Colebrooke to J.H. Harrington, 26 February 1796, NAI/SIR/SGO/52, 113–16.

18. Cf. Colin Mackenzie to Barry Close, 20 March 1800, NAI/SIR/M/6, 89–92, here 92; Colin Mackenzie to Arthur Wellesley, 28 July 1800, ibid, 157–59.

19. Colin Mackenzie to Barry Close, 10 December 1799, NAI/SIR/M/6, 35–37, here 35f.

20. For details see Colin Mackenzie, 'Memorandum on the Duties Colin Mackenzie has been employed since 1790' (Copy of a Paper given to General Harris, 14 August 1798), NAS/ GD/46/17/4, 538–40.

21. Many of these maps are today in the British Library (BL/IOR/X/2298; BL/IOR/X/2297/2; BL/IOR/X/2302; BL/IOR/X/2066) and in the National Archives of India (NAI/ F/64/C/1–33); cf. Prasad, *Catalogue of Historical Maps*.

22. Colin Mackenzie, 'The Roads from Hyderabad to Culboorga, Toljapor-Ghaat & Feroseabad on the Beema River Surveyed between the 15th February and the 3rd April 1797 to which are added (to give a more distinct idea of the Elevated Table Land, and of the Ghaats, bordering at that part of The Frontier of the Dominions of the Dominions of the Marhattas and Nizam Aly Khan) The Roads from Hydrabad to Hoomnabad, Beder, Callianee, Dharoor and Kurdla from the Survey of 1795 by Colin Mackenzie Capt. of Engineers Surveyor to the Nizam's Detachment', Fort St George, 10 December 1797, BL/IOR/X/2066.

23. Colin Mackenzie, 'Remarks and Observations made on the Survey in the Nizam's Dominions in 1797 by Colin Mackenzie, Capt. of Engineers, Surveyor to the Nizam's Dept', 5 February 1798, BL/Mss Add/13582, 1–32,

24. See in particular his extensive journal from the Fourth Mysore War. Colin Mackenzie, 'Journal on the March from Hydrabad to Seringapatam during the Mysore Campaign, 1798/99, Part II: From the Junction of the Nizam's Forces with the Grand Army near Ambore in February to the Storm & Capture of Seringapatam on the 4th May 1799', BL/ Mss Add/13663, 1–95.

25. Colin Mackenzie, 'Remarks on the Frontier Roads & Military Posts between the Kistna & Hyderabad 1796 (September)', SUL/WP/1/58. In 1800 Mackenzie sent a copy to Arthur Wellesley, who was commander in Mysore at the time. The probable draft with the same title is in BL/OIOC/Mss Eur/Mack Gen/60, 303–17.

26. Colin Mackenzie to Arthur Wellesley, 8 November 1800, SUL/WP/1/58.

27. Cf. Colin Mackenzie to Barry Close, 10 December 1799, NAI/SIR/M/6, 35–37, here 36.

28. Cf. Benjamin Heyne's report of his visit to Mackenzie in Benjamin Heyne, 'Cursory Remarks on a Tour to Hyderabad in 1798', NAI/SIR/M/3, 1–48, here 18–20. Heyne later published his journal with the title 'Observations made on a Tour from Samulcottah to Hydrabad' in

id., *Tracts, Historical and Statistical, on India; with Journals of Several Tours through Various Parts of the Peninsula: also, An Account of Sumatra in a Series of Letters, by Benjamin Heyne, M.D., F.L.S, Member of the Asiatick Society of Calcutta, and the learned Societies of Bombay, Berlin, &c., and Surgeon and Naturalist on the Establishment of Fort St. George* (London, 1814), Tract XVII, here 263.

29. Mackenzie had visited Golconda in 1793/1794. Cf. Colin Mackenzie to Francis Humberston Mackenzie, 21 July 1794, NAS/GD/46/17/4, 440–47, here 447.

30. Cf. Mackenzie, 'Remarks on the Frontier Roads', SUL/WP/1/58.

31. His main task here was preparation for the siege of Colombo, which also involved compiling topographical material. Cf. Colin Mackenzie, 'Memorandum abstracted from the Journal of Captain Mackenzie', Madras, 22.1. 1809, BL/OIOC/Mss Eur/Mack Misc 136.

32. Colin Mackenzie, 'Memoir of the Present State of the Fortresses, Fortifications, Roads & Landing Places in Java. Compiled from different authorities May 29th 1811. With a Military Map of Java exhibiting the different Roads, Posts, and other Relative Positions. Presented to the Commander in Chief on his arrival at Malacca June 1811', BL/OIOC/Mss Eur/Mack Priv/14, 19–35; id., 'Report of Proceedings on the North Coast of Java agreeable to the Instructions of His Excellency Sir J. Auchmutty Cin C &c. dated at Malacca of the 6th June 1811', ibid., 57–69.

33. Colin Mackenzie to Francis Humberston Mackenzie, 2 March 1793, NAS/GD/46/17/4, 434–38, here 434; id. to Alexander Gillanders, 25 July 1794, ibid., 448–55, here 450.

34. Cf. Colin Mackenzie to Benjamin Swain Ward, 27 January 1810, NAI/SIR/SGO/90A, 13f. For the stay in Hyderabad see id. to Francis Humberston Mackenzie, 21 July 1794, NAS/GD/46/17/4, 440–47, here 440.

35. Colin Mackenzie to Alexander Gillanders, 25 July 1794, NAS/GD/46/17/4, 448–55, here 451. For Mackenzie's absences see also Howes, *Illustrating India*, 22–24.

36. Colin Mackenzie to W.B. Bayly, 7 September 1818, NAI/SIR/SGO/435D, 5–7, here 6.

37. Colin Mackenzie to Francis Humberston Mackenzie, 9 August 1796, NAS/GD/46/17/4, 485–95, here 490.

38. Colin Mackenzie to George Buchan, 10 September 1806, NAI/SIR/M/18, 190–96, here 192.

39. 'Extracts from the Minutes of Consultation dated 1 Nov 1776', Chief Engineer's Books, BL/OIOC/Mss Eur/Mack Gen/68. For the sepoys who accompanied Mackenzie in Hyderabad see Colin Mackenzie to John Warren, 15 September 1800, NAI/SIR/M/6, 182f.

40. Cf. Colin Mackenzie to Benjamin Swain Ward, 27 January 1810, NAI/SIR/SGO/90A, 13f.

41. Mackenzie, 'Statement of the Literary Labours', 242f.

42. Cf. McLaren, *British India and British Scotland*, 31, 36, 38.

43. When there were discussions about making language lessons compulsory for higher Company employees. Cf. 'Debate at the India House, 28 September 1825', *Oriental Herald and Journal of General Literature* 7 (October–December 1825), 382f.

44. Kavali Venkata Ramaswami, *Biographical Sketches of Dekkan Poets, being Memoirs of the Lives of Several Eminent Bards, both Ancient and Modern, Who Have Flourished in Different Provinces of the Indian Peninsula* (Calcutta, 1829), 154f. See also N.V. Rao, 'Pioneers of English Writing in India: The Cavally Telugu Family', *Annals of Oriental Research* 18(2) (1963), 3–5.

45. Cf. M.H. Fisher, 'The Resident in Court Ritual, 1764–1858', *Modern Asian Studies* 24(3) (1990), 419–58; K. Leonard, 'The Hyderabad Political System and its Participants', *Journal of Asian Studies* 30(3) (1971), 571–73.

46. See S. Förster, *Die mächtigen Diener der East India Company: Ursachen und Hintergründe der britischen Expansionspolitik in Südasien, 1793–1819* (Stuttgart, 1992), 105–7; and B. Carnduff, 'William Kirkpatrick (1754–1812)', *ODNB*.

47. This is particularly emphasized by K. Raj, 'Colonial Encounters and the Forging of New Knowledge and National Identities: Great Britain and India, 1760–1850', *Osiris* 15 (2000), 127–33. See also id., 'When Human Travellers become Instruments: The Indo-British Exploration of Central Asia in the Nineteenth Century', in M.-N. Bourguet, C. Licoppe and H.O. Sibum (eds), *Instruments, Travel and Science: Itineraries of Precision from the Seventeenth to the Twentieth Century,* (London and New York, 2002), 156–88.

48. Cf. Bayly, *Empire and Information*, 58–66.

49. 'Extracts from the Minutes of Consultation dated 1 Nov 1776', Chief Engineer's Books, BL/OIOC/Mss Eur/Mack Gen/68.

50. Cf. Phillimore, *Historical Records*, vol. 1, 95–97; and Bayly, *Empire and Information*, 66–69.

51. This applies to James Rennell, for instance, who constantly raised doubts about the *harkaras'* reliability and made it the aim of his work to make the British independent of them. However, his journals show that he regularly required their help. Cf. J. Rennell, *Description of the Roads in Bengal and Bahar* (London, 1778), i; id., 'The Journals of James Rennell, First Surveyor General of India', edited by T.H.D. LaTouche, *Memoirs of the Asiatic Society of Bengal* 3 (1914), see for example 111f, 115, 125, 146, 148, 189, 190.

52. Colin Mackenzie, 'Memoir of a Map of the Dominions of Nizam Ally Khan', 1795, BL/OIOC/Mss Eur/Mack Gen/60, 61–96, here 62.

53. Howes, *Illustrating India*, 9f. For the possible use of Indian maps in Mackenzie's surveys see P.P. Gogate and B. Arunchalam, 'Area Maps in Maratha Cartography: A Study in Native Maps of Western India', *Imago Mundi* 50 (1998), 139.

54. Mackenzie, 'Statement of the Literary Labours', 242.

55. Cf. Howes, *Illustrating India*, 50.

56. C. Mackenzie, 'The History of the Cummum Tank from Relation of Senabella Fackier', in A. Dalrymple (ed.), *Oriental Repertory*, vol. 2(2), London [1794?], 333f; id., 'Source of the Pennar River', ibid., 335f; id., 'Account of the Construction of the Plan of the Roads from Nellore'.

57. He was included in the official published list of members for the first time in 1797. Cf. 'Members of the Asiatic Society, 1797', *Asiatic Researches* 5 (1799), 428. For the Asiatic Society see O.P. Kejariwal, *The Asiatic Society of Bengal and the Discovery of India's Past 1784–1838* (Delhi, 1988); and J.M Steadman, 'The Asiatick Society of Bengal', *Eighteenth-Century Studies* 10(4) (1977), 464–83.

58. C. Mackenzie, 'Account of the Pagoda at Perwuttum: Extract of a Journal by Captain Colin Mackenzie. Communicated by Major Kirkpatrick', *Asiatic Researches* 5 (1799), 303–14; reprinted in *New Annual Register, or General Repository of History, Politics and Literature for the Year 1799* (London, 1800), 144–50. See also the detailed summary in Howes, *Illustrating India*, 28–32.

59. C. Mackenzie, 'Remarks on some Antiquities on the West and South Coasts of Ceylon. Written in the Year 1796', *Asiatic Researches* 6 (1801), 425–54.

60. Ibid., 441–44.

61. Ibid., 425; Mackenzie, 'Account of the Pagoda', 306.

62. Mackenzie, 'Statement of the Literary Labours', 242.

63. Mackenzie tried to attract Cornwallis' attention for his case via Patrick Ross and Colonel Alexander Ross. A personal letter from Mackenzie to Cornwallis was useless because the latter had already left. Cf. Patrick Ross to Colin Mackenzie, 4 September 1792, Chief Engineer's Books, BL/OIOC/Mss Eur/Mack Gen/69; also 15 September 1792, ibid.

64. Minute, B (FSG), 12 March 1793, BL/IOR/P/253/11, 1350f.

65. Cf. Colin Mackenzie to Francis Humberston Mackenzie, 21 July 1794, NAS/GD/46/17/4, 440–47, here 441.

66. Colin Mackenzie to Francis Humberston Mackenzie, 9 August 1796, NAS/GD/46/17/4, 485–95, here 486.

67. Ibid., 492. Mackenzie's hope of taking over the post of Chief Engineer and Surveyor General of Ceylon had meanwhile been dashed because the island had been handed over to the Crown. Cf. ibid., 485. For the background to the handover see Schrikker, *Dutch and British Colonial Intervention*, 142–59.

68. In his attempts to get a Surveyor General appointed (in 1773 and 1783) Patrick Ross had explicitly referred to the Bengal model. Cf. Patrick Ross to Wynch, 29 May 1775, Chief Engineer's Books, BL/OIOC/Mss Eur/Mack Gen/68; and Patrick Ross to Lord Macartney, 17 October 1783, ibid.

69. In the *Survey of India Records* there are no files of this sort apart from a few letters and reports by Thomas Wood, and at the start of his time in office Colebrooke was already complaining that he could find no instructions relating to the surveys carried out by his predecessors. Robert Hyde Colebrooke to John Murray, Mil. Aud. 24 June 1795, NAI/SIR/SGO/52, 87. For an exception see [Thomas Wood], 'Report of Work under the Direction of the Surveyor General', 5 April 1788, ibid., 9–15.

70. The fact that the Directors wanted this is, at least in part, evidenced by their detailed description of the duties of the assistant who should be mainly responsible for administering the geographical material and copies. Cf. 'Extract of a General Letter from the Honourable Court of Directors dated 20. August 1788', NAI/SIR/SGO/574, 11; E. May to Robert Hyde Colebrooke, 25 February 1789, ibid., 12.

71. In the previous year he had already taken responsibility for running the office, but had had to be content with an assistant's wages since Kyd, though absent, continued to be paid. Cf. Robert Hyde Colebrooke to G. Elliot, 30 August 1793, NAI/SIR/SGO/52, 37f.

72. Colin Mackenzie to Francis Humberston Mackenzie, 9 August 1796, NAS/GD/46/17/4, 485–95, here 488.

73. This is when Mackenzie mentioned this plan for the first time to the Resident of Hyderabad. See Colin Mackenzie to William Kirkpatrick, 30 April 1795, BL/IOR/H/446(1), 20–23. See also Colin Mackenzie, 'Memorandum on the Duties Colin Mackenzie has been employed since 1790' (Copy of a paper given to General Harris, 14 August 1798), NAS/GD/46/17/4, 538–40.

74. Colin Mackenzie, 'Memoir of a Map of the Dominions of Nizam Ally Khan', 1795, BL/OIOC/Mss Eur/Mack Gen/60, 61–96; id., 'A Map of the Dominions of Nizam Aly Khan comprehending the most considerable part of the Six Soubahs of the Dekan (including the Cessions made to Mahrattas; & the Frontiers of the neighbouring powers in 1795) & divided into Circars according to the provincial divisions of the Assufiah Register, constructed chiefly from Surveys made, and various authentick Materials collected since 1790 designed to illustrate the History, Geography & Territorial arrangement of these provinces Respectfully inscribed to The Right Honourable Lord Hobart, President & Governor of FSG', 30 July 1796, BL/IOR/X/2065.

75. Cf. Edney, *Mapping an Empire*, 202f.

76. Cf. 'General Orders by Government, Fort St George, 24 December 1800', in *Asiatic Annual Register, or a View of the History of Hindustan and of the Politics, Commerce and Literature of Asia for the Year 1801* (London, 1802), 55; and Edney, *Mapping an Empire*, 149.

77. Cf. Colin Mackenzie, 'Memorandum', February 1798, BL/OIOC/Mss Eur/Mack Misc/171; Colin Mackenzie to Lord Bentinck, 16 July 1806, NAI/SIR/M/18, 182–84.

78. 'I had the satisfaction of delivering it [the general Map] to Lord Hobbart, who expressed himself much satisfied with it, & has promised to forward it by the next dispatch ... next month, with a strong recommendation of my being appointed Surveyor General on this Establishment', Colin Mackenzie to Francis Humberston Mackenzie, 9 August 1796,

NAS/GD/46/17/4, 485–95, here 489. See also Colin Mackenzie to Francis Humberston Mackenzie, 4 September 1797, NAS/GD/46/17, 512–18, here 518; Vibart, *Military History of the Madras Engineers*, vol. 1, 285.

79. Cf. Colin Mackenzie to John Mackenzie, 14 February 1798, NAS/GD/46/17/4, 528f; Alexander Beatson to CD, 14 April 1797, BL/IOR/F/4/17 (754).

80. 'Memorandum of Captain Mackenzie of the Madras Engineers', 13 February 1798, NAS/GD/46/17/4, 524–26, here 524. See also 'Memorandum from Lord Seaforth to Mr Charles Grant relative to the Claims of Captain Colin Mackenzie of the Madras Engineers to be appointed Military Surveyor General on the Coast of Coromandel should such Appointment take place', July 1799, NAS/GD/46/17/4, 541f.

81. 23 May 1798. Cf. Edney, *Mapping an Empire*, 187.

82. See Edney, *Mapping an Empire*, Chapter 3: 'Surveying and Mapmaking', 77–118, esp. 94–98.

83. Cf. Mackenzie, 'Memoir of a Map of the Dominions of Nizam Ally Khan', BL/OIOC/Mss Eur/Mack Gen/60, 65–72. The works by the two French travellers from the seventeenth century had long been available in English translation. See J. de Thévenot, *The Travels of Monsieur de Thevenot into the Levant: In Three Parts. Viz. into I. Turkey. II. Persia. III. The East-Indies. Newly Done out of French* (London, 1687); J.B. Tavernier, *The Six Voyages of John Baptiste Tavernier, Baron of Aubonne, through Turkey, into Persia and the East-Indies, for the Space of Forty Years Giving an Account of the Present State of those Countries …: to Which is Added, a New Description of the Seraglio made English by J.P.; Added Likewise, A Voyage into the Indies, &c. by an English Traveller, Never Before Printed, Publish'd by Dr Daniel Cox.* (London, 1677); for the Indian sources see Chapter 5, this volume, 'Mapping History, Producing Territory'.

84. Cf. William Kirkpatrick to Charles Warren Malet, Resident of Poonah, 3 May 1795, BL/IOR/H/446(1), 13–23.

85. Even the Surveyor General of Bombay had to ask the government for permission to copy the maps of his colleague in Bengal. [Alexander Kyd] to Edward Hay, Sec. Gov., 26 September 1793, NAI/SIR/SGO/52, 39f. See also CD to Gov. Gen. (Mil. Dep.), 7 May 1800, NAI/SIR/SGO/574, 74f.

86. Cf. Robert Hyde Colebrooke to Colin Mackenzie, 7 December 1797, NAI/SIR/SGO/361, 63f; id. to J. Stracey, Sub. Sec. Gov. (FW), 13 December 1797, ibid., 65f; id. to Mackenzie, 23 March 1798, ibid., 77–79; id. to Stracey, 23 April 1798, ibid., 82; also, 28 May 1798, ibid., 84; 12 July 1798, ibid., 89f; and 14 July 1798, ibid., 99; id. to Lieutenant J. Hooke, 18 June 1799, ibid., 129; Stracey to Colebrooke, 15 December 1797, NAI/SIR/SGO/574, 53; also 20 March 1798, ibid., 55; Mackenzie to Lieutenant General Harris, 24 February 1798, ibid., 55f.

87. Cf. Colin Mackenzie to James Achilles Kirkpatrick, 28 February 1800, NAI/SIR/M/6, 81.

88. Cf. Markham, *Memoir on Indian Surveys*, 384–89.

89. W. Jones, 'A Dissertation on the Orthography of Asiatic Words', *Asiatic Researches* 1 (1788), 1–56.

90. The Surveyor General of Bengal, Colebrooke, considered maps he was sent to be largely useless due to the difficulty in understanding place names written according to 'French orthography'. See Robert Hyde Colebrooke to N.B. Edmonston, 16 June 1802, NAI/SIR/SGO/54B, 108–10.

91. The problem of writing place names in various different ways was not solved until the 1870s, with Hunter's Gazetteers. See Markham, *Memoir on Indian Surveys*, 396; and F. Skrine, *Life of Sir William Wilson Hunter, K.C.S.I., M.A. LL.D., Vice-President of the Royal Asiatic Society, etc.* (London, New York and Bombay, 1901), 165–73.

92. Colin Mackenzie, 'Memoir of a Map of the Dominions of Nizam Ally Khan in 1795', BL/ OIOC/Mss Eur/Mack Gen/60, 61–96, here 68f.

93. Colin Mackenzie to John Riddell, 17 April 1818, NAI/SIR/SGO/573, 318–24, here 322.

94. Cf. Colin Mackenzie to Chief Sec. Gov., 2 January 1817, BL/IOR/P/259/56, 4845–56.

95. Colin Mackenzie, 'Memoir of a Map of the Dominions of Nizam Ally Khan in 1795', BL/ OIOC/Mss Eur/Mack Gen/60, 61–96, here 68f.

96. Colin Mackenzie to Francis Humberston Mackenzie, 9 August 1796, NAS/GD/46/17/4, 485–95, here 490.

97. Colin Mackenzie, 'Memoir of a Map of the Dominions of Nizam Ally Khan in 1795', BL/ OIOC/Mss Eur/Mack Gen/60, 61–96, here 61.

98. It was not until 1782 that the Company took direct control of the Jaghire. Cf. Irschick, *Dialogue and History*, 20.

99. Cf. Washbrook, 'Colonial Transition', 487–95.

100. Cf. J.E. Wilson, 'Anxieties of Distance: Codification in Early Colonial Bengal', *Modern Intellectual History* 4(1) (2007), 12f; R. Travers, '"The Real Value of the Lands": The Nawabs, the British and the Land Tax in Eighteenth-Century Bengal', *Modern Asian Studies* 38(3) (2004), 536f. For the classical interpretation of the Permanent Settlement as an attempt to create new property rights see R. Guha, *A Rule of Property for Bengal: An Essay on the Idea of the Permanent Settlement* (Paris, 1963).

101. J. Sullivan, *Tracts upon India; Written in the Years, 1779, 1780, and 1788... With Subsequent Observations* (London, 1794), vi.

102. See for example M. Mustafa, 'The Shaping of Land Revenue Policy in Madras Presidency: Revenue Experiments – the Case of Chittoor District', *Indian Economic and Social History Review* 44(2) (2007), 213–36; and D.S. Reddy, 'The Ryotwari Land Revenue Settlements and Peasant Resistance in the "Northern Division of Arcot" of the Madras Presidency during Early British Rule', *Social Scientist* 16(6/7) (1988), 35–50.

103. Here too the projects in South India were to some extent at odds with those in Bengal, where the Permanent Settlement made the production of cadasters unnecessary until well into the nineteenth century. Cf. R.J.P. Cain, *The Cadastral Map in the Service of the State: A History of Property Making* (Chicago and London, 1984), 325–30.

104. See B. Stein, *Thomas Munro: The Origin of the Colonial State and his Vision of Empire* (Delhi, 1989), 57–63; T.H. Beaglehole, *Thomas Munro and the Development of Administrative Policy in Madras, 1792–1818* (Cambridge, 1966), 16–34; N. Mukherjee, *The Ryotwari System in Madras, 1792–1827* (Calcutta, 1962), 125–32. There are also copies of much of the material worked on by Read and Munro in Mackenzie's Collection. See BL/OIOC/Mss Eur/Mack Gen/46, 171–385.

105. John Goldingham was appointed as the first Inspector of Revenue Surveys in 1798. Cf. CD to B (FSG), 15 May 1799, BL/IOR/F/4/165 (2829), 1–3.

106. Stein, *Munro*, 24–37; Sullivan, *Tracts upon India*; [C.F. Greville], *British India Analyzed: The Provincial and Revenue Establishments of Tippoo Sultaun and of Mahomedan and British Conquerors in Hindostan, Stated and Considered*, 3 vols (London, 1793).

107. Sullivan, *Tracts upon India*, 237–45, 263f, 277f, 298–305, quote 300.

108. [Greville], *British India Analyzed*, vol. 2, 511. Emphases in the original.

109. For Dalrymple see H.T. Fry, *Alexander Dalrymple (1737–1808) and the Expansion of British Trade* (London, 1970), for his role as hydrographer esp. 222–66; and A.S. Cook, 'Establishing the Sea Routes to India and China: Stages in the Development of Hydrographical Knowledge', in H.V. Bowen, M. Lincoln and N. Rigby (eds), *The Worlds of the East India Company* (Woodbridge, Suffolk, 2002), 123–35.

110. [A. Dalrymple], *A Short Account of the Gentoo Mode of Collecting the Revenues, on the Coast of Choromandel* (London, 1783), 2, 10–13.

111. [Greville], *British India Analyzed,* vol. 2, 498–502; Sullivan, *Tracts upon India,* 265.

112. Sullivan, *Tracts upon India,* 226–35.

113. A. Dalrymple, 'On Watering the Northern Circars', in id. (ed.), *Oriental Repertory,* vol. 2(3) (London, [1795?]), 34.

114. [Greville], *British India Analyzed,* vol. 2, 502–11; Sullivan, *Tracts upon India,* xif.

115. For a discussion of this attitude see D. Ludden, *Peasant History in South India* (Princeton, 1985), 144–47.

116. James Anderson to Colonel Kyd, 9 August 1792, cited in Dalrymple, 'On Watering the Northern Circars', 34.

117. See Topping's plan: Michael Topping to Charles Oakeley and B (FSG), 14 February 1794, BL/IOR/X/3948; CD to B (FSG), 21 May 1794, BL/IOR/E/4/880, 631–34.

118. Cf. CD to B (FSG), 10 June 1795, BL/IOR/E/4/881, 357; B Rev. (FSG) to CD, 2 October 1795, BL/IOR/F/4/17 (754), 2; James Lillyman Caldwell to Michael Topping, (n.d: [before May 1794]), BL/OIOC/Mss Eur/D/1058a, 1; id. to Allan, (n.d. [May–July 1794]), ibid., 14f.

119. Cf. Topping's detailed maps of the region of 1793/1794: BL/IOR/X/595/1; X/595/2; X/596/1–3; X/597; X/598; X/599; X/600; X/601/1–2; X/602/1–2, and his reports in BL/IOR/X/3948 and X/3949. See also Alexander Beatson to CD, 14 April 1797, BL/IOR/F/4/17 (754), 6; CD to B (FSG), 9 May 1797, BL/IOR/E/4/883, 283–94; and id., 'Surveys in the Circars by Mr Topping, Captain Caldwell & Major Beatson inscribed to William Petrie Esqur. President and Charles White, Thomas Cockburne & William Harrington Esqurs. Members of the Board of Revenue by their most faithful and Obedient Humble Servant, A. Beatson, Major, Fort St. George' January 1799, BL/IOR/X/2315/1.

120. See B. Wallach, 'British Irrigation Works in India's Krishna Basin', *Journal of Historical Geography* 11(2) (1985), 160–62; G.T. Walch, *The Engineering Works of the Gódávari Delta: A Descriptive and Historical Account. Compiled for the Madras Government,* 2 vols (Madras, 1896); and F.R. Hemingway, *Gódávari* (Madras District Gazetteers) (Madras, 1907), 79–84.

121. Balfour to Edward Saunders, 2 November 1795, BL/IOR/F/4/18 (757), 33–51.

122. Cf. Balfour to B Rev. (FSG), 2 November 1795, BL/IOR/F/4/18 (757), 27f; B (FSG) to CD (Rev) 23 February 1796, BL/IOR/F/4/18 (758), 1f.

123. Michael Keating to Edward Saunders, 22 October 1795, BL/IOR/F/4/18 (758), 40–55; B Rev. (FSG) to CD, 6 August 1796, F/4/18 (757), 9–11.

124. Cf. Michael Keating to Edward Saunders, 22 October 1795, BL/IOR/F/4/18 (758), 40–55. For the various forms of financing irrigation in precolonial South India see D. Mosse, *The Rule of Water: Statecraft, Ecology, and Collective Action in South India* (New Delhi, 2003), 53–91; and D. Ludden, 'Patronage and Irrigation in Tamil Nadu: A Long-term View', *Indian Economic Social History Review* 16(3) (1979), 347–65.

125. See Michael Keating's 'Journal', October/November 1795, BL/IOR/F/4/18 (758), 83–110.

126. Cf. Michael Keating to Josiah Webbe, 4 November 1795, BL/IOR/F/4/18 (758), 63f; Michael Keating to B Rev. (FSG), 27 November 1795, ibid., 75–77. See also 'Lists of Tanks that have suffered from the late Heavy Rains in the Chicacole Havelly', 29 September 1795, ibid., 33f; and 'Lists of Tanks that have suffered from the Rains since the 20th Ultimo in the Chicacole Havelly', 7 October 1795, ibid., 37–39.

127. Cf. Josiah Webbe to Michael Topping, 7 November 1795, BL/IOR/F/4/18 (758), 60f; Michael Topping to Edward Saunders, 13 November 1795, ibid., 68f, and 'Report of B Rev (FSG)', ibid., 10 January 1796, 9–12.

128. Although the Directors in London rejected Topping's appointment of 14 February 1795, on the grounds that he already had enough to do, they accepted in principle that the post should be set up. See CD to B Rev. (FSG), 5 August 1796, BL/IOR/E/4/882, 705–36, here 718.

129. Cf. Michael Topping to B Rev. (FSG), 7 January 1796, BL/IOR/F/4/18 (758), 111–20; Michael Topping, 'Sketch for the Repair of the Tanks in the Honble. Company's Districts', ibid., 139–46.

130. Cf. Michael Topping to Michael Keating, 17 December 1795, BL/IOR/F/4/18 (758), 129; and Keating to Stephen Lushington, Sec. B Rev. (FSG), 16 March 1796, ibid., 161–65.

131. B Rev. (FSG) to B (FSG), 25 February 1796, BL/IOR/F/4/18 (758), 149–57; B Rev. (FSG) to Keating, 25 February 1796, ibid., 158–60; 'Proceedings' B Rev, 23 June 1796, ibid., 242; FSG (Rev.) to CD, February 1796, ibid., 3–7.

132. B Rev. (FSG) to Lord Hobart, 17 March 1796, BL/IOR/F/4/18 (758), 172–77.

133. 'FSG Rev Consultation', 12 February 1796, BL/IOR/F/4/18 (758), 146.

134. 'A Representation from the Chicacole Havelly Renters to Michl. Keating Collector dated February 1796', BL/IOR/F/4/18 (758), 167f. See also Michael Keating to Edward Saunders, 17 March 1796, ibid., 166f.

135. Josiah Webbe to Michael Keating, 10 March 1796, BL/IOR/F/4/18 (758), 181–85, here 182; also 22 March 1796, ibid., 192f.

136. Cf. Edney, *Mapping an Empire*, 172; Phillimore, *Historical Records*, vol. 1, 108.

137. Thomas Gahagan, Dep. Sec. B Rev. (FSG) to Chief Sec. Gov. (FSG), 10 December 1810, BL/IOR/F/4/362 (9021), 73–97, here Enclosure 2, 95–97; id. to B Rev. (FSG), 29 November 1811, ibid., 115–30, here 122–24; William Oliver, Sec. B Rev. (FSG) to William Morrison, Act. SG, 29 July 1811, NAI/SIR/SGO/319, 83f.

138. Cf. CD to B Rev. (FSG), 23 May 1798, BL/IOR/E/4/884, 479–502, here 492.

139. His interest in irrigation during these years is also reflected in his drawings. Cf. Howes, *Illustrating India*, 33.

140. Colin Mackenzie, 'Memoir on the Various Modes of Watering Land practised by the Natives of India. More particularly in the Provinces anciently designed under the names of Carnatic and Tallangana wrote in April 1793 by C Mackenzie Lieutt. of Engineers at the service of, & comments to Andrew Ross Esqu.', April 1793, BL/OIOC/Mss Eur/Mack Gen/59, 63–81.

141. For Andrew Ross see the brief reference in Mackillop, 'Fashioning a "British" Empire', 219, 225; Furber, 'Trade and Politics', 76.

142. Dalrymple, 'On Watering the Northern Circars', 33.

143. Cf. Teroovercadoo Mootiah, 'A Historical and Chronological Journal of the Life', 569.

144. Cf. Fry, *Alexander Dalrymple*, 160.

145. This applies, for instance, to Thomas Munro. Cf. Stein, *Munro*, 136.

146. 'Correspondence between Andrew Ross Esqr. at Madrass and George Andrew Ram Esqr. at Tanjore, on the Subject of Furnishing Water to the Northern Circars', in A. Dalrymple (ed.), *Oriental Repertory*, vol. 2(3) (London, [1795?]), 457–63.

147. Cf. Mackenzie, 'Source of the Pennar River'.

148. Mackenzie, 'Memoir on the Various Modes of Watering Land', BL/OIOC/Mss Eur/Mack Gen/59, 69f.

149. Ibid., 67.

150. Michael Topping to Charles Oakeley and B (FSG), 14 February 1794, BL/IOR/X/3948.

151. Mackenzie, 'Memoir on the Various Modes of Watering Land', BL/OIOC/Mss Eur/Mack Gen/59, 79.

152. Ibid., 68.

153. Mackenzie, 'History of the Cummum Tank'. Andrew Ross had sent the paper to Dalrymple, the publisher, along with another essay by Mackenzie written in 1792. Cf. A. Dalrymple, 'Introduction to the Second Number', id. (ed.), *Oriental Repertory* vol. 2(2) (London, [1794?]), iv. The second paper was Mackenzie, 'Source of the Pennar River'.

154. In Mackenzie's collection there is also a plan of the embankment of 1792: Colin Mackenzie, 'Plan of the Embankment of the Great Tank, Cumbum 1792', BL/OIOC/WD/2709,

likewise an illustration of the tank of 1794: 'View of the Great Tank of CUMMUN & of the Celebrated Embankment across the Culacummum River', March 1794, BL/OIOC/WD/600. The plan, which is not attributed in the BL catalogue, is by Mackenzie. See 'List of Maps, Plans and other Documents resulting from the Operations & Investigations of the Mysore Survey. Constructed or copied off & communicated by the Superintendent of the Survey since January 1802', 3 July 1803, NAI/SIR/M/6, 59–62, 59.

155. Mackenzie, 'History of the Cummum Tank', 334; [J. Scott], *An historical and political View of the Decan, South of the Kistnah; including a Sketch of the Extent and Revenue of the Mysorean Dominions, as possessed by Tippoo Sultaun, to the Period of his latest Acquisitions of Territory* (London, 1791), 14. Mackenzie falsely attributed this piece, published anonymously, to (James?) Grant. For the authorship see Scott's obituary: 'Jonathan Scott Esq. LLD', in *Gentleman's Magazine* 99(1) (May 1829), 470f.

Chapter 4

MACKENZIE'S SURVEY

Restructuring the Political Landscape

With the defeat of Tipu Sultan in the Fourth Mysore War, in 1799, the British had removed for good one of the three rival Great Powers on the Deccan Plateau. This led to a dramatic restructuring of the political landscape of South India that fundamentally changed the power constellation on the Deccan. Despite his territorial losses in 1792 Tipu had continued to rule over the largest part of the Deccan south of the Tungha Badra and the Kistna, as well as Canara, the coast of today's Karnataka from Carwar in the north to south of Mangalore on the Arabian Sea. Even before the war had started, Wellesley[1] had considered it a fait accompli that neither Tipu nor his heirs would ever regain possession of these regions.[2] Thus, after the war Britain's only remaining rival powers in South India were the Marathas in the west, and the Nizam, though the latter was bound tightly to the EIC by various subsidiary treaties. Of course, from the British point of view the war and the subsequent expansion of the area should never give the Nizam the chance to regain his independent position, and this is what, in the summer of 1800, dominated British discussions about the restructuring of the political landscape.

Wellesley appointed a commission of experienced officers who should take responsibility for the further division and internal restructuring of Mysore. Along with military commanders such as Commander-in-Chief George Harris and Wellesley's brothers Henry and Arthur (later Wellington), it was also made up of people such as the former Resident of Hyderabad, Kirkpatrick, and Lieutenant Colonel Barry Close, who were well versed in the languages and political customs of South India; John Malcolm and Thomas Munro were also appointed as secretaries.[3] Colin Mackenzie was summoned to Mysore as the commission's geographical advisor.[4] His job was to provide the commission with topographical information and cartographical material that was to be used as a basis for determining where the border should run, such that it could be most easily defended militarily and was fiscally most lucrative.[5] So he drew up maps for a memorandum to the Directors in London showing the various possibilities for the division of Mysore that the commission was considering.[6] Quite probably it was, among other factors, Mackenzie's influence here that guaranteed the orientation of the partition treaty to older forms of territorial organization.

As victors in the war the British felt justified, along with the Nizam, in annexing the whole of Tipu's territory. However, to do so, even though it would undoubtedly have brought the Company the greatest territorial gains, did not seem at all advisable in political terms. Since half of the conquered territory would have belonged to the Nizam under the terms of an older treaty,[7] and also because the British wanted to avoid irritating the Marathas, the most sensible course seemed to be to reinstate the family of the Rajah of Mysore, who had been de facto deposed by Tipu's father, Haidar Ali around 1760, in a much smaller Mysore state under British military control.[8] While the Marathas were offered areas in the northwest, the Nizam was given the provinces bordering his sphere of power to the south. The Company was given the whole of Canara in the west, Wynaad and Coimbatoor in the south, and the regions below the Ghauts in southeast Mysore, which created a territorial link between the west and east coasts.[9]

The newly created landlocked state of Mysore was certainly not, however, intended to be a fully independent state, as Wellesley made clear in a letter to the Directors in London:

> I resolved to reserve to the Company the most extensive and indisputable powers of interposition in the internal affairs of Mysore, as well as an unlimited right of assuming the direct management of the country (whenever such a step might appear necessary for the security of the funds designed to the subsidy), and of requiring extraordinary aid beyond the amount of the fixed subsidy, either in time of war, or of preparations for hostility.[10]

This objective was achieved when the subsidiary treaty was concluded with representatives of the new, three-year-old Rajah of Mysore. It went beyond all earlier subsidiary treaties in India by determining that the EIC should not only take over foreign-political and military representation of the only nominally independent state, but also had the right to intervene in its internal affairs.[11] This stipulation did indeed create a powerful instrument of indirect rule that could be transformed at any time into direct rule: while the Company initially governed through Minister Purnaiya, who felt more obliged to fulfil the wishes of the British Resident than those of the Rajah, in 1813 Mysore was formally placed under temporary British rule.[12]

The fact that Britain's external boundaries were pushed ever deeper into the subcontinent is generally regarded as the most significant legacy of Wellesley's time in office. His deliberately aggressive foreign policy, the unscrupulous annexations and the system of indirect rule perfected under him guarantee him a secure place amongst the imperially minded *men on the spot* so typical of British expansion in India. They blithely pursued the goal of British rule over the sub-continent, ignoring the reservations of Parliament and the Directors in London, in order to fulfil their own ambitions.[13] But even men like Wellesley were aware that British rule over India could not be based purely on the power of weapons; a certain degree of assent on the part of the subjects was also required.[14]

It was not so much Wellesley's attempt to transfer Cornwallis's principles to South India that proved consequential as the fact that he promoted officers like Barry Close, Thomas Munro and John Malcolm to important positions in the civil administration after the Fourth Mysore War. They all had the distinction of being able to master South Indian languages and of being well acquainted with local conditions. Just how well aware Wellesley was that the British administration needed employees with a fundamental knowledge of Indian affairs is illustrated by the fact that in early 1800 he founded the College of Fort William, where in future everyone destined for administrative posts should be trained for their job.[15]

As early as summer 1799 Wellesley was already planning to raise all sorts of data in the conquered territories.[16] So in November Mackenzie, who had recently attracted the Governor General's attention with his work for the commission, was finally appointed personally by Wellesley as superintendent of a survey of Mysore which should also, though not exclusively, serve military purposes. The first important aim, fully in line with the commission's work, was an 'accurate settlement of our frontier'.[17] It was assumed here that the territory formally under the Rajah's control would be regarded as part of the British conquest, as illustrated by the fact that Mackenzie described the borders of Mysore, which was nominally independent, as a 'British Frontier'.[18] Clearly it seemed to him to be only a matter of time before Mysore was officially incorporated into the British sphere of rule, and so the aims and objectives of his survey of Mysore were just the same as those in regions under direct British control; the survey, fully in keeping with Mackenzie's ideas, should also accommodate the needs of a civil administration. 'As it ... will also tend', to quote his official order,

> ... to augment our knowledge of Indian Geography and to produce immediate and important benefits, in conducting the government to be established in the con-quered provinces ... attention is not only to be paid to mere military or geographical

information; but ... your enquiries are also to be extended to a statistical account of the whole country.[19]

Wellesley was convinced by the idea of such a statistical account of the country for the government's use, as demonstrated by the fact that he was not prepared to sacrifice a systematic, detailed and above all time-consuming process to short-term propagandist interests. As Marika Vicziany has shown, from the summer at the latest he realized that his conquest of Mysore was not without its critics amongst Britain's decision makers and that if he wanted to earn a reputation as a great conqueror he would have to convince the public of the significance of his military success; a rapidly produced description of Mysore's riches could certainly be of great help in this.[20] By the time Mackenzie had presented his 'Plan of the Mysore Survey and the Manner on which it is proposed to be executed', to the government in January 1800, however, it had become clear that this was a project that was likely to take many years to complete.[21]

Wellesley's reaction was not to reject Mackenzie's plan out of hand or to insist that it be carried out more quickly; he simply ordered another research trip that was to be undertaken rapidly and with far more superficial aims. In February 1800 he commissioned the Scottish doctor, Francis Buchanan, who sympathized with his policy of conquest,[22] to examine 'the state of agriculture, arts, and commerce, in the fertile and valuable Dominions acquired in the recent and former War from the late Sultaun of Mysoor'.[23] Mackenzie was required to support Buchanan in all aspects of his work and was also officially informed that the two projects should not be in competition with one another.[24] It says much for Mackenzie's concept of loyalty and duty that he not only gave Buchanan every possible support[25] but in the years to come freely shared with him the results of his own research.[26]

Buchanan did not disappoint Wellesley's expectations. His concluding report, later published, stressed not only Mysore's botanical and geological treasures, but also its potential for revenue, which in his view had so far not been sufficiently appreciated. In this account Wellesley's campaign became a just war against a despotic enemy, while the clever way in which the administrators appointed by him dealt with the matter pointed the country towards a better future.[27]

Building the Machinery

If it can be said that in Buchanan Wellesley found exactly the right man for the task, the same can certainly be said of Mackenzie. As soon as he heard about the project he was to undertake he started planning, something that was to take him several months. It was clear right from the start that this was a project on a far greater scale than any surveys conducted in India so far.[28] Even in the first year there were probably over a hundred official staff working on the survey. Europeans, albeit in the senior positions, were only a small minority. The size of the project also meant that there were no models for its logistical and administrative organization. So it was no mean achievement that Mackenzie managed, within a really short space of time, to put together a functioning 'machinery' for the Mysore Survey, as he later liked to call his team of co-workers.[29]

By January 1800 Mackenzie had worked out his 'Plan of the Mysore Survey', in which he requested the support of at least four experienced European assistants initially to play a leading role.[30] The plan was that each of them should independently lead the surveying of one part of the territory, so to start with Mackenzie had to collect and arrange all available geographical material in such a way that coordination of work in a region largely unknown to the British would be at all possible in the first place.[31] Equipment needed by each independent team had to be organized. Even if the surveyors provided most of their instruments themselves, repairs would have to be carried out as required, and equipment that was large or difficult to acquire, such as measuring wheels or thermometers, as well as suitable tents and means of transport had to be acquired from military supplies.[32]

Mackenzie had considerable influence on the selection of his European assistants. It is surely no coincidence that most of these turned out to be Scottish compatriots, or that Mackenzie knew personally three or four European assistants who were initially appointed. The only exception here was John Mather, though in the years to come he was to be his most important colleague. Mather, who had taken part in the survey of Salem and Barramahal under Read and Munro, was personally recommended to the Mysore commission by Alexander Read in summer 1799,[33] and after Mackenzie had assessed material from this survey sent to him by Arthur Wellesley, he also supported Mather's appointment.[34] In the following years a very close relationship developed between the two men, roughly the same age, who met in the summer or autumn of 1799 in Madras. Their relationship was defined primarily by the work they had in common, but the familiarity revealed in their later correspondence was obviously generated by their shared origins in Scotland. Like Mackenzie, Mather seems to have grown up in a simple household, near Aberdeen.[35] However, he had the opportunity to enrol in Aberdeen university before going to Madras in the early 1790s, where, 'to shield me from the fear of want',[36] he had decided to become a surveyor. From August 1794 he had worked under Read and Munro, who employed him as a professional surveyor even though he did not officially work for the EIC.[37] Right from the start Mackenzie had placed such faith in Mather that he allowed him considerable influence on the survey planning. He often consulted him, for instance on the best way to proceed with the mapping, and eventually adopted methods similar to those Mather had used in Barramahal.[38]

Mather also had a certain influence on working out the plan for the statistical studies[39] and it must be due to him that part of the survey of Mysore – even though it did not extend to a detailed examination of revenue issues[40] – can in some respects be regarded as a continuation of his previous project.[41]

Mackenzie had a less close relationship with his other co-workers, even though he already knew them all before he was appointed. He actively supported the application of Lieutenant John Warren,[42] the son of a Jacobite émigré who had come to India as a businessman, had bought a commission in the Royal Army, and had already served as Mackenzie's assistant in the siege of Seringapatam.[43] Warren was eventually appointed in December 1799.[44] In April 1800 – again with Mackenzie's support – he was joined by the young Scottish engineer and officer Thomas Arthur,[45] whom Mackenzie likewise knew from the war.[46] In response to a personal recommendation in 1801 he also sought to appoint William Morison, a Scot who had trained in Britain as a surveyor,[47] but this was not approved until Warren left the project in 1802.[48]

Amongst the European assistants, special status was held by the German doctor and natural historian Benjamin Heyne. In his plan of the survey Mackenzie distinguished between a 'mathematical' and a 'physical' part, the first to include all cartographic work, while the second would involve not only irrigation techniques and cultivation methods, social and cultural composition and the population's general customs and practices, but also flora and fauna, minerals and climate.[49] It was obvious that an expert was needed for this and Benjamin Heyne, who not only knew Mackenzie personally from his time in Hyderabad[50] but also had some experience with natural-historical studies in South India,[51] seemed the perfect choice: 'he enters fully into the spirit of it much to my satisfaction', Mackenzie wrote to Kirkpatrick and Wellesley,

'as it is not easy always to meet with people possessed of the same talents, ardour and wish to pursue these investigations, at the [cost?] of health, comfort, and perhaps more flattering prospects: care should ... be taken to encourage this spirit by [showing?] the world, it is the way to distinction and favour'.[52]

This was more than a standard recommendation for a co-worker who, as it turned out, was to prove the greatest disappointment.

Most of the personnel involved in the survey, however, were Indian. Each surveyor was allocated his own staff. The number of *lascars*, *puckallies*, *tindals* and *peons* – tent-pitchers, water carriers, servants and messengers – as well as *harkaras*, interpreters, draftsmen, scribes, craftsmen and, in Heyne's case, plant collectors, ranged from ten for Mather, to nineteen for Heyne, right up to thirty-six for Mackenzie, so that they clearly constituted the majority of those involved in the survey.[53] In addition there were extra bearers and guides, employed locally, sepoys to protect people and materials and, at least in Mackenzie's case, a number of private employees. Some of the Indian co-workers also took their families with them, which must have increased the size of the individual groups considerably.[54]

Mackenzie himself not only took on some of the work on the ground but was also responsible for supervising and coordinating the project, and writing regular reports to government; given the numerous tasks involved, his successful superintendence was a not inconsiderable administrative achievement. A major practical problem, temporarily solved by advancing money[55] but in need of a more permanent solution in the medium term, was how to make regular payments to the teams working far away from the presidency. Initially Mackenzie, against his express wishes,[56] was supposed to take responsibility for his co-workers' accounts, which inevitably led to a series of delays.[57] The situation was further complicated by the fact that although the survey was primarily a project with civil objectives and was not supposed to be funded by the military, in Mysore the only pay stations available were military, and they initially refused to take responsibility.[58] It was only as a result of extensive correspondence involving various military and civil authorities that in summer 1800 a solution was finally reached, whereby the assistants were allowed to submit their own accounts. Although payments were to be made via military posts, they were to be drawn from the civil budget.[59] The only exception was the payment of *tindals* and *lascars*, who along with tents, means of transport and other materials were regarded as equipment and as such continued to be administered via the authorities in Madras.[60]

Apart from the accounts, however, as superintendent Mackenzie sought to exert far-reaching control over his co-workers' activities. He established a strict hierarchy and centralization in the lines of communication which meant that all his assistants' official correspondence had to pass via him as their direct superior. Correspondence with officials not directly connected with the survey he generally forwarded via the Resident in Mysore, who had been designated as his direct superior at the beginning of the survey,[61] while requests for equipment or consumables such as ink and paper were passed to the relevant offices in the military[62] and civil administration.[63] Given the difficulties in conducting correspondence over long distances and the fact that the surveyors were constantly changing their location, the disadvantages of this system are obvious. This complicated line of communication constantly led to awkward delays. At the end of 1800, for instance, John Mather had to manage for almost two months without any military protection, which, as experience had shown, meant that his instruments and other equipment were in danger of being stolen, even in a peaceful area.[64]

The major advantage, however, was that in this way Mackenzie not only had greater control over his co-workers, but was also able to document all administrative procedures. The sheer volume of files from the Mysore Survey, which far exceeded all the documents in the Bengal Surveyor General's Department – up to 1800 put together –, shows very clearly the determination with which Mackenzie approached this task. As former comptroller at the Scottish customs, for whom correctness and a clear system in bookkeeping and correspondence were particularly important, he had plenty of experience in all this. He kept various differènt files now bound into letter-books, for instance one for his own official correspondence, which contained not only copies and drafts of letters to his superiors, but also instructions given to his assistants.[65] Correspondence relating to the survey, but which also touched on private matters, was filed separately,[66] as were all official orders from the government, so that he could easily refer to them in case of doubt.[67] What is more, he archived copies of his co-workers' journals and other materials, all official reports to superiors, as well as the completed maps and statistical reports. Documents not needed immediately were taken to Madras, where he initially stored them in a room at the Fort, then at a house he had rented.[68]

Even if such organizational details seem fairly incidental and obvious from today's point of view, at the time they represented significant innovations within the British Surveying Department in India. The Survey of Mysore, which was, after all, supposed to extend over a territory of some fifty-two thousand square miles – about five-eighths of the size of Great Britain and slightly larger than that of England[69] – provided for the first time in British India a model of logistics, coordination and documentation that could be followed by similar projects in the course of the nineteenth century.

The Survey in Practice

In the late spring of 1800 all the teams had reached the regions in the various parts of Mysore assigned to them. The Europeans' means of transport were horses, palanquins and, particularly when surveying was to be carried out, their own two feet.[70] Equipment and luggage were transported by ox-carts and bearers, while the lower-ranking Indian co-workers apparently walked most of the way.[71] Mackenzie's writers had to arrange their own transport 'as I have so many that it would require a troop to mount them and therefore I stipulate that each provide their own carriage'.[72] A larger camp was usually set up in a central location, from which smaller excursions with light luggage could be undertaken, while tents and bearers were always sent in advance so that when the teams arrived at the agreed place they found a camp prepared for them.[73] Apart from tents, overnight accommodation was occasionally private houses provided by local officials, or local pagodas.[74]

Mackenzie was a loyal superior to his assistants and did not fail to stress their achievements to the government on a regular basis. At the same time, however, he insisted that duties be carried out diligently and, when necessary, underlined that his assistants must obey his instructions[75] – though he did give them a certain amount of leeway, telling Heyne, for instance, that 'making my will your rule ... is certainly more than I expect in its literate sense from any person'.[76] So his instructions were mainly geared towards coordinating the project and methodological issues, while the assistants on the ground could decide for themselves about the details of how their survey was to be carried out. Each of them had the power to give orders to his staff and could hand out punishments if they failed to do things properly. Mackenzie himself tended to pay his Indian team at the end of the month 'to keep [them] in austerity to prevent any possible disorder'.[77] Occasional desertions were inevitable,[78] but all in all problems were an exception.

More problematic was how to deal with local officials and the population, if only because this had to be worked out by the *tindals* as the European surveyors did not speak the local languages. The individual teams were always dependent on local support. This applied not only to the surveying work, for which cooperation with the local guides who knew the area was essential, but especially to the provision of food and drink, as well as means of transport and bearers, which were always needed for special tasks. Although the local revenue officials (called *amildars*) were generally informed that the teams were coming before they arrived and were commanded to provide them with every assistance, this did not always mean that things ran smoothly. Great potential for conflict arose from the fact that in Mysore all costs while on site, apart from animals' fodder,[79] had to be paid from the budgets – in other words the salaries – of the individual surveyors. This made it very tempting to reduce costs by means that were sometimes rather dubious, even though the assistants were obliged, in principle, to pay the going local rates. Thomas Arthur, for instance, constantly complained about inflated prices and incompetent guides; but he himself was repeatedly accused of suppressing prices and of acquiring foodstuffs illegally.[80]

Mackenzie was to experience the unpleasant consequences of such complaints at first hand when, at the turn of the year 1800/1801, he was surveying the frontier between Mysore and the Ceded Districts, an area formerly belonging to the Nizam and now under the Company's administration, where Thomas Munro was responsible as Collector.[81] Munro was an acquaintance of Mackenzie[82] and had the reputation of taking complaints by the locals against Company officials very seriously.[83] In the previous weeks there had already been problems because Mackenzie's co-worker, Kavali Venkata Borayya, had allegedly been in possession of a stolen horse;[84] in January 1801 the situation became critical after Mackenzie complained to Munro about the *amildar* of Raidroog's lack of willingness to cooperate.[85] When Munro called the *amildar* to account the latter, for his part, made serious accusations against Mackenzie's co-workers: they had not, he reported, wanted to pay for their horses' feed.

Furthermore, Mackenzie's commissionaire (or *dubash*), Venkat Row, had insulted the *amildar*; Mackenzie's sepoys had temporarily detained him and forced his man, Narsing Row, to stand in the sun for a whole day because he had not been able to provide them with any milk.[86]

The fact that Munro wanted to pursue these complaints enraged Mackenzie beyond measure, even though Munro had made it clear from the start that in his opinion this was a dispute between servants. Mackenzie declared that he had 'been very scrupulous regarding the Natives of the Country; ... if any severity of mine can be hinted at it could be only from our own party who I thought at right to keep in awe to prevent any possible disorder'.[87] He insisted that never in his life had he been confronted by such complaints, immediately sent a number of his staff to Munro to clarify the case, offering to have himself and his whole team interrogated, and demanded a statement to refute the accusations from Arthur and the doctor, Sauters, who had also been in Raidroog. Although Mackenzie himself had not been accused, he was not prepared for his co-workers to be connected with dubious practices.[88]

Munro subsequently settled the matter in Mackenzie's favour and as a consequence the *amildar* even lost half of his district. Although Mackenzie now tried to present the affair to his superiors in a favourable light, he was very concerned that the accusations had been entered in the EIC's official files because this could, he thought, create a bad impression of the survey in London.[89] From now on caution was called for at all times: 'This however shews the necessity of being always vigilant', he wrote to Arthur, 'for had any incorrectness appeared in my conduct there is little doubt but it would be eagerly grasped at'.[90] As a consequence he also constantly exhorted his other assistants to avoid any conflict with the local population,[91] and requested the government give even more precise instructions regarding the prices to be paid for foodstuffs and animal fodder.[92] Yet as the following years were to show, even these measures did not make conflicts with the local officials and population completely unavoidable.

What was undoubtedly the greatest problem in the early years of the survey were the permanent delays caused by co-workers dropping out. Illnesses played a major role here; the surveyors were often afflicted due to carrying out arduous work in an unfamiliar climate. The poor state of health of Mackenzie and Mather, both of whom were, after all, over forty years old and had served as surveyors for many years, had caused a delay in beginning the survey in early 1800,[93] and subsequently their work and that of their assistants was constantly interrupted. Just a few months after he set off, Mather was again so seriously ill that he was given a medical certificate advising that he spend several months at the coast.[94] This was just the start of a series of delays caused by illness. For instance, for three-and-a-half months from December 1800 and again from July to September 1800 work came to an unexpected halt due to an outbreak of fever that raged amongst the Mysore population and affected most of

Mackenzie's team. Two years later John Mather had to take another break of eight months in Madras; likewise Thomas Arthur left the survey in early 1802 and could only return to his team almost a year later after a period of recuperation on Prince of Wales Island (now Penang Island).[95]

Nevertheless, Mackenzie did not have to restrict the broad scope of his survey, apart from the researches in natural history that failed due to the fact that he did not see eye to eye with Benjamin Heyne, who was not prepared at all to fit into Mackenzie's 'machinery' and pursued his own interests virtually all the time. It seems Mackenzie had originally envisaged that parallel to the surveying work and statistical studies a natural-historical stocktaking of the individual districts should be carried out which, unlike a simple collection and classification of plants, should also examine their geographical distribution. Heyne of course showed little interest in accompanying the surveyors and right at the start of the survey left for Bangalore with his people in order to move on from there to study copper mines outside the territory of Mysore – a project he constantly pursued in the coming years despite Mackenzie's objections.[96] Above all, however, Heyne planned to convert part of the Rajah's garden in Bangalore into a botanical garden, where he wanted to cultivate both imported and local crops.[97]

Mackenzie does not appear to have rejected this idea out of hand but insisted that Heyne should still carry out the tasks assigned to him. In the first half of 1800 he frequently summoned Heyne at short notice,[98] but it soon became clear that he had such good connections in Madras[99] that he could ignore such orders. In particular, by avoiding the lines of communication prescribed by Mackenzie, he was able to receive his orders directly from the government, which tied Mackenzie's hands.[100] At his own initiative Heyne had been commissioned by Governor Lord Clive to find a suitable location for a botanical garden in Mysore,[101] and before that it had already been decided that a temporary 'depository of plants from different parts of the country' should be set up in Bangalore.[102]

Although Mackenzie asked the government for a clear ruling on his relationship with Heyne[103] and although the latter had been informed at an early stage that his duties in Bangalore should not, under any circumstances, distract him from his tasks with the survey,[104] this conflict meant that the natural-historical research Mackenzie was so keen on was never systematically carried out. After numerous complaints by Mackenzie the botanist was eventually suspended for the 'injuries which Dr Heyne's health has sustained' without further pay in March 1802,[105] but was allowed to continue running the botanical garden in Bangalore – now paid independently of Mackenzie – until it was closed down five years later.[106] His Scottish successor with the survey, Dr John Leyden, who was appointed as its naturalist in early 1804,[107] was not able to make much progress either since he became seriously ill after just a few months, went to the west coast to recuperate after a long stay in Seringapatam, and was eventually withdrawn from the project altogether at the end of the following year.[108]

Support and Opposition

Heyne's withdrawal was by no means the only problem Mackenzie was confronted with in summer 1802 because at this time the survey came to an almost complete standstill. Mather and Arthur had to leave for the coast due to ill health, Warren left the survey, and Mackenzie himself was busy in Madras compiling the material that had been collected and constructing maps; not a single surveyor was working in the field any longer. In addition, Mackenzie's allowance of four hundred pagodas per month, generously provided by Wellesley, was, according to an order by the Court of Directors, to be cut in half and his European assistants' salaries also revised downwards.[109] The Madras government imposed these cuts in the same year.[110] Indeed this crisis, as various historians have pointed out, was the low point of Mackenzie's survey;[111] but unlike what is sometimes assumed, the reduction of the allowances should not be seen as proof that the project met with a general lack of interest or that there was unwillingness to support Mackenzie's enquiries further.

Indeed, London expressly recognized the general usefulness of the project, while only the high sums paid out as allowances had been criticized. Given the fact that most surveyors drew officers' salaries in addition to their generous pay as surveyors, the Directors regarded their total income as excessive. Even Mackenzie himself, who with some justification never tired of complaining about the reduction, was still convinced that work on the survey was attractive enough to arouse the interest of many young officers.[112] Due to the pay cuts, work on the project had become far less lucrative for European officers, but given that their allowances included their staff's pay it was still possible for them to increase their own earnings by reducing the number of staff.[113] Mackenzie himself managed to retain a relatively generous salary in a way that was barely discernible in London;[114] this was largely due to the fact that in addition to his salary in Mysore he was able to secure another income from Hyderabad – because he officially kept his position there, despite his absence.[115] It was only in 1805, when at the initiative of the Military Department the position of surveyor in Hyderabad was re-awarded and the continued payment of this salary made public, that he had to dispense with these allowances.[116] Now, however, instead of this salary Mackenzie was granted a 'gratuitous allowance' of around 160 pagodas per month by the government in Madras.[117] Furthermore, in 1803 William Bentinck had already guaranteed a further hundred pagodas 'on honor', in other words without exact accounting, for his establishment, and indeed backdated to the time of his pay cut.[118] These were funds that

Mackenzie could use specifically for the statistical and historical studies, which at this time were not curtailed at all.[119]

Clearly, after the reduction of his allowances decided upon in London, Mackenzie had a number of supporters in the presidency who were keen to minimize its effects on the survey. Particularly in Chief Secretary Josiah Webbe, Wellesley's man in Madras, he did have an important ally at the presidency's power centre,[120] but he was well aware that his ideas also met with opposition in government circles: 'some people in Office here', he wrote to a friend, 'were never looked on as warm friends of mine'.[121] And he was fully aware that London's failure to understand his project could also have consequences for its acceptance in India: 'the embarrassment arising from the evident misapprehension of the design at home', he assessed the situation in early 1804, 'has not been more prejudicial to my hopes on principles generally recognized than prejudicial to the earlier completion of the work & in weakening in the depending branches the confidence so necessary for every arduous undertaking'.[122]

Indeed, Mackenzie had every reason to assume that in London his survey had been misunderstood. Just a few months after the pay cut he was sent a memorandum by James Rennell, who had meanwhile become the Company's geographical advisor.[123] Rennell obviously regarded Mackenzie's survey and William Lambton's geodetic project in South India, both supported by Wellesley's patronage, as one and the same thing. The false assumption that Lambton's project simply served to determine astrological positions in support of Mackenzie was, as Matthew Edney has shown, by no means uncommon in the early years of the two surveys (though surprising for a geographical expert) and must have been difficult for Lambton in particular;[124] but it also put indirect financial pressure on Mackenzie[125] since Rennell recommended, instead of Lambton's 'additional and separate Establishment', employing an astronomer, thus giving the impression of further potential savings to be made.[126]

So, as Peter Robb has shown, Mackenzie considered better information about his project as essential for its continuation and started an intensive lobbying campaign[127] While his first report of 1800 on the state of the survey had been fairly brief,[128] he now set about describing detailed aims, operations and results in a flood of reports to government. From late 1802 to summer 1803 he delivered to various military officers, the Resident of Mysore and the Board in Madras, maps, statistical memoirs, road books and other information, some of which was obviously designed to address military interests.[129] The most important document, however, was the lengthy 'Second General Report on the Mysore Survey' of summer 1803, to which an extensive appendix was attached[130] and which expressly emphasized the difficulties obstructing his project, in order to justify its rather slow progress.[131] Governor General Wellesley was treated in addition to several extensive discourses on the state of affairs until his departure from India,[132] and in October 1803, when Lord Bentinck came to Madras as the new

Governor, he was given the delight – not for the last time – of a detailed report on the survey. A few years later Lord Minto, Wellesley's successor, was likewise sent a lengthy report as soon as he arrived in India.[133]

In his lobbying Mackenzie did not, of course, confine himself to official channels but sought allies everywhere, trying to stress common interests. To Wellesley's confidant Kirkpatrick, for instance, he hinted that an intrigue against the Governor General was behind the pay cut: 'I apprehend it forms … part of a more extensive plan, hostile to interests of much greater importance'. But he himself, he said, remained loyal to Wellesley, and would therefore continue with the survey: 'I owe it in justice however to the Nobleman who originally instituted this work to wind it up in a manner to reflect no discredit on his suggestions so far as lays with me; and I owe it to myself'.[134] Of course, this did not prevent him from focussing on other loyalties in his official correspondence: 'The Survey however must be carried on further as they [the Court of Directors] approve of it' as he wrote, for example, to a government secretary.[135]

However, providing information for the Directors proved to be difficult since Mackenzie did not have much luck in sending material over. Although his 'Second General Report' did arrive in London, numerous bound manuscripts and maps that he sent, in April 1804, to the Directors, the former Governor Lord Hobart, and the India expert and confidant of Seaforth's, Greville, went down with the shipwrecked *Prince of Wales*. This was all the more disastrous since by the time Mackenzie was informed of it he was again busy surveying and was unable to provide replacements quickly due to lack of time and the fact that the material was stored in Madras.[136]

More successful, it seems, were his attempts to use private channels for lobbying in London. Thus he regularly informed Kirkpatrick, who returned to England in 1802, about the survey's progress.[137] He sent his friend Henry Trail, an influential India trader in London[138] whom Mackenzie seems to have got to know in Portsmouth before his departure, copies of virtually all reports and many extracts from his correspondence. Both Bentinck and Wellesley had pointed out Mackenzie's achievement to London,[139] but in Mackenzie's view official approval from India in reaction to his endless reports was clearly not enough: 'these official approvals will never do without something more substantial'.[140] Trail did indeed attempt to support Mackenzie by turning to the influential Director Charles Grant: 'I have … to thank you sincerely for at once going to the Fountainhead by speaking to Mr Grant', was Mackenzie's response[141] but the results of this intervention only became apparent years later since the administration in London worked slowly and communication with India took a long time.

Mackenzie's desperate attempts to gain more support were, however, clearly not caused by the position taken in London alone as it was in Madras that the opposition to his project became ever clearer. Initially Mackenzie particularly identified it in his private letters with the Commander-in-Chief in Madras James Stuart,[142] who since 1804 had been officially referring to perceived short-comings in Mackenzie's survey in the military sphere.[143] It soon became apparent, however, that despite Mackenzie's attempts to get the military machine behind him by sending over material there were also other military decision makers who had little interest in his survey, geared as it was towards civil interest, and who had started their own surveying in the presidency at the Madras Military Institution set up in 1805.[144] So during the Mysore Survey a conflict with the military authorities had already begun that was to drag on beyond Mackenzie's appointment as Surveyor General in 1810.

In 1802 Mackenzie had already been complaining that the military was denying him access to valuable geographical material.[145] Now he got the impression that his project was being deliberately sabotaged, since material was removed from his storeroom without his permission,[146] or cumbersome copies of certain documents were asked for which would have taken a long time to produce and which once again would have considerably delayed the survey. Given that the government wanted him to finish the project as quickly as possible the situation, as he wrote in 1805, 'in the most moderate language, can be safely called by no other name than oppression'. He estimated that the endless obstacles put in his way by the military had so far cost him at least a year.[147]

By far the greatest problem, however, was the fact that the military leaders had the right to commandeer individual surveyors for deployment elsewhere and the survey's progress was impeded more and more frequently by the withdrawal of assistants. John Warren had left in 1802 of his own accord, because he thought he would get a higher salary by changing to Lambton,[148] but early in the next year his successor Morison was withdrawn, and despite plans to return in the autumn was ordered to rejoin his corps permanently;[149] Arthur also had to leave the survey under pressure from the Mysore Resident after there had been constant complaints from the population about him and his team; Thomas de Havillard, an acquaintance of Mackenzie who was supposed to succeed him,[150] was instead appointed to replace Mackenzie himself as Surveyor of the Nizam's Detachment, clearly at the instigation of the military;[151] and during the Maratha War of 1803 even Mackenzie himself had been ordered back to his corps and it was only thanks to intervention by the Resident of Mysore that he was excused from this until the survey was finished.[152]

Reorganization and Demilitarization

By the summer of 1805 John Mather was the only assistant Mackenzie had left. At the same time the government had long since been demanding that the work soon be finished,[153] even though so far only about sixty per cent of the territory had been surveyed.[154] Mather was Mackenzie's most important man – he and his team had surveyed an area more than twice the size of that of all the other assistants put together – so it was a particularly harsh blow when Mather wanted to leave in mid 1806 due to serious illness. Mackenzie tried to persuade him to stay until the survey was finished,[155] but Mather refused: 'I am well aware', he wrote to Mackenzie, 'that a longer perseverance in this struggle will end fatally, which no consideration on Earth shall induce me any further to run the risk of'.[156] Although Mackenzie was bitter about Mather's leaving – to some extent he felt betrayed since he had helped to get Mather a small pension and a much better salary, expecting in return that he would stay until the end of the survey[157] – he had no option but to forward Mather's request to the government.[158]

In previous years Mackenzie had toyed with the idea of not appointing any more engineers or members of the military because of the permanent threat that they would be withdrawn – but had avoided taking this decision for lack of any alternative.[159] Now that his sole civil co-worker had left he did not want to employ any more European assistants at all. The official reason he gave was the length of time it took to train them, which could further delay the survey that was now nearing completion;[160] but in private letters what he expressed above all was disappointment. He wanted to save the money, he wrote to Munro for instance, that 'an European assistant gets for doing nothing at all or worse than nothing sometimes as I have experienced to my great annoyance & delay'.[161] So a reorganization of the survey came about that pointed the way to the future and ultimately guaranteed that in the years to come surveys based on Mackenzie's system could be extended to the whole of South India. The keystone of this reorganization had already been laid in the early years of the survey when Mackenzie, with John Mather's support, had started to instruct a number of Anglo-Indian boys from the school for orphans in Madras in the skills necessary for surveying work.

The Madras Male Asylum, as it was officially called, was founded in 1789 for illegitimate sons of European fathers and Indian mothers, with the aim of giving them basic instruction in reading, writing, arithmetic and the Protestant faith.[162] By 1794 Michael Topping had already had the idea of training some of the boys for his tank survey in the Northern Circars, and subsequently a surveying school had been set up under his assistant, John Goldingham, for boys over the age of ten.[163] Once trained and given a rudimentary knowledge of land surveying the boys were much sought after in the various branches of the administration, but in early 1798, in Hyderabad, Mackenzie managed to acquire one of these boys, James Ross, as an apprentice.[164]

When he requested more boys for the Mysore Survey the reason he gave was the educational value of further training with him: 'as I have had frequent occasion to observe ... that many instances occur of boys manifesting talents and genius that under proper culture might be improved ... to qualify them to be useful members of society'.[165] Possibly due to this philanthropic argument two more boys were made available to him at an early stage, probably his long-time writer Lucius Rawdon Burke and the future surveyor William Lantwar.[166] Mackenzie subsequently made repeated attempts to employ more boys[167] until by early 1803 there were six of them.[168] Although they travelled with the individual surveying teams, after the pay cuts of 1801 Mackenzie made sure that they were paid separately from the European assistants so that, unlike many other co-workers, they were not affected when the Europeans left.[169]

Right from the start Mackenzie regarded employing the boys as a 'kind of Seminary of Practical Survey' that should complement the theoretical knowledge acquired at the school. What is more, by doing practical work in their early years they should get used to the climate and thus become less susceptible to illnesses.[170] The boys' training was as pragmatic as it was efficient: to start with they were mainly given writing and minor drawing tasks; after that they were directly involved in the surveying work, and eventually they were allowed to carry out their own surveying, under supervision, and to copy maps and plans.[171] In order to increase their future usefulness Mackenzie himself paid for some of the boys to learn South Indian languages – especially Marathi and Canara – and provided rewards such as books or small sums of money for the most successful pupils.[172]

Mackenzie proved to be a responsible superior to the boys. He regularly asked his assistants how they were getting along, made sure that on their trips to the various teams they were accompanied by reliable people, and also provided them with clothes and equipment.[173] What is more, a regular pay structure with the possibility of promotion to subassistant surveyor was set up for the boys, soon known as apprentices. As the oldest of the boys, James Ross became the model case: while the working boys from the surveying school were generally paid a small wage,[174] Mackenzie saw to it that this was increased on their eighteenth birthday.[175] When their training was complete they were appointed as subassistant surveyor and then received a regular salary plus additional funds for teams and equipment, which was roughly equivalent to the salary of an ensign in a garrison.[176] The regulations Mackenzie managed to bring about for James Ross were eventually introduced, with slight changes, for all apprentices in 1807.[177] Above all, however, just as Patrick Ross had done with him, Mackenzie offered the prospect of early rewards for a job well done, as shown by his letter to James Ross, the first boy who went on survey by himself:

As I hope the experience derived in the course of you being attached to me will enable you to proceed in this Survey with advantage to the service & credit to yourself as it will be gratifying to me from the report I receive from your zeal & Progress to have the means of recommending such further measures as may be approved of for your comfort & encouragement.[178]

Two years later James Ross was taken back to the presidency by a troop of soldiers after various complaints were made about him – hunting instead of working, mistreatment of staff and finally seduction of a young temple dancer.[179] Nonetheless, when Mather resigned in 1806 Mackenzie still had three well-trained subassistants (Michael Dunigan, Henry Hamilton and Benjamin Swain Ward), and two apprentices (James Summers and William Howell), whose training was nearing completion. He also had William Lantwar, who although he had not officially been at the surveying school, had been trained by Mackenzie himself along the same lines.[180] Mackenzie now considered the young men to be sufficiently experienced to carry out surveying work on their own and in early 1807 sent the first of them – as a rule two of the young men were supposed to work together – to the areas that had not yet been surveyed.[181] He himself, having been occupied with surveying without much of a break since 1804, now planned to return to Madras to compile the material, construct maps, and thus bring the survey to a speedier conclusion.[182]

There is no question that the decision to do without European surveyors made the survey cheaper, which gave Mackenzie further justification for carrying on with it.[183] In a system in which people were paid according to ethnic criteria Anglo-Indians, mostly illegitimate sons of British men and Indian women, were far less expensive employees. Generally not regarded as full members of either the European or the Indian community, yet familiar with both cultures, for the EIC they represented an interesting potential as employees in the lower ranks – though due to their origins they usually remained barred from higher positions.[184] So Mackenzie had no hesitation in justifying their employment in economic terms too – though on the other hand he made sure that the boys were given a regular pay structure with opportunities for promotion. Given his ongoing conflict with the Military Department, another principal consideration may also have been crucial for Mackenzie: employing them meant de facto that his survey had become even more demilitarized, since civilians now took the place of European officers, thus creating greater independence from the military.[185]

No End in Sight

In July 1807 Mackenzie returned to Madras. Although he once went back to Mysore briefly in the following year to check on his assistants' work,[186] preparation of the final documents and maps progressed quickly, and in summer 1808 Mackenzie announced that the survey would be completed by the end of the year, at which point his salary as superintendent would cease.[187] The results of nine years' work that he sent to London were undoubtedly impressive enough on their own: a general map of Mysore was supplemented by eight detailed maps of the individual parts of the country;[188] then came statistical and historical memoirs of some of the 120 districts examined, collated in six or seven folio volumes.[189] As a partial result of his historical work he sent an index of collected inscriptions with more than eleven hundred entries, and in addition the Directors were treated to a statue, which he had taken with him from a Jain temple in Canara and transported over five hundred miles through South India.[190]

Mackenzie's results were praised throughout the civil administration, in the final phase of the survey by the former Residents in Mysore John Malcolm and Mark Wilks, right up to Governor Bentinck, and once it had been completed also by the Court of Directors.[191] His rewards were correspondingly generous; in October 1808 he was appointed Barrack Master of Mysore – a lucrative sinecure that Mackenzie had already coveted for several years but which Bentinck, as he freely admitted, had given to someone else, in 1805, due to personal obligation.[192] The Directors not only confirmed this appointment, which they hoped would allow Mackenzie sufficient time to collate his statistical and historical material, but also granted him an additional payment of nine thousand pagodas (or about 3,350 pounds) for his cartographical work: this may well have been influenced by Mackenzie's indirect contacts with Charles Grant.[193]

Although Mackenzie calculated that this was only a fraction of what he would have earned without the pay cut, this largely put an end to what David M. Blake describes as, 'grumbles about his pay and allowances', which hitherto had represented a 'constant, and unattractive feature of Mackenzie's correspondence'.[194] The constant reports, memoranda and other missives had clearly beleaguered poor William Bentinck to such a degree that he could not resist spicing up his letter with an ironic characterization of the man he was recommending. 'He considers himself I know', wrote Bentinck,

> most hardly used by myself & others. I say not this to his prejudice, but rather for the purpose of making himself exactly known. He has at the expense of his constitution & with the sacrifice of all his own private fortune prosecuted with the most indefatigable zeal the public work upon which he has been employed. He has attached to his pursuit the greatest importance. He has known his own labours, & the successful results of them. He fancies to have found no person a corresponding interest. Worn out in the Service he finds himself in Poverty. Far advanced in Military Rank, he perceives his inferiors who have toiled less in greater affluence & consideration. There is I must allow just cause for these feelings. The Orders however from the Court of Directors have precluded us from giving him the aid which would be well bestowed on him. ... It has been impossible for me or the Commander in Chief to improve his Military Situation.[195]

Mackenzie's self-depiction, which Bentinck reproduces here in exaggerated form, was not, of course, completely justified. There could, for instance, be no question of poverty and using up all his private means; after all, in 1805 he had been able to transfer to his brother the not inconsiderable sum of five thousand pounds.[196] Nonetheless he had, of course, made a number of sacrifices, not least the fact that at the age of almost fifty he was subjecting himself to the exertions involved in carrying out surveying work, and there can be no doubt that Mackenzie's health was permanently affected. In particular, eye strain caused by constant reading, writing and drawing, often in poor light, led to problems that were to endure for the rest of his life.[197]

The more Mackenzie sought to overcome opposition to his survey, the more his future career chances became dependent on its completion. The reason for the determination with which he always overcame new frustrations and obstacles is not, however, solely connected with his personal ambitions: 'It is indeed time', he had, for instance, written to Trail in 1805,

> I should retire ...; but one should retire with decency if not credit, nor forget what is due to justice & propriety – having suggested a plan which would have done honour to any administration, it is my business to shew that I could complete it; ... prudential considerations too require that I should not prematurely abandon myself or my relations, by hastily relinquishing the only chance left me.[198]

Mackenzie was so convinced of his project's usefulness that continuing it really did become a sort of obsession. There is no better proof of this than the fact that despite all difficulties he continued to push for the survey to be extended to other provinces.[199] After various failed attempts to have Canara on the east coast and initially belonging to the Bombay presidency surveyed by Bombay engineers,[200] in 1806, in a '*coup de main*' it was made the Mysore Survey subassistants' responsibility.[201] Since Canara was part of Mackenzie's original plan to include all regions allocated to the Company and the Rajah after the Fourth Mysore War, this was perfectly justifiable.[202] What were not included in the original order, however, were the so-called 'Ceded Districts', the part of Mysore originally allocated to the Nizam after it was split up in 1799, and then transferred to the Company's direct control in 1801, allegedly to pay the British troops in Hyderabad. When surveying the border there Mackenzie had already included parts of these districts in his work and repeatedly mentioned this in official reports; and in 1805 he approached Bentick for the first time, suggesting that the survey be extended.[203] In the following years, too, he sought supporters for this proposal in the administration, but it soon became clear that no decision would be reached until the Mysore Survey was finished as originally planned.[204]

Mackenzie used similar arguments in all these writings. Firstly he stated that right from the start the survey had been a continuation of research he had started in Hyderabad – as part of a general survey of South India. This, he said, was also demonstrated by the fact that he had retained his post in Hyderabad for so long. A second line of argumentation, which became more prominent as the Mysore Survey neared its conclusion, was based on the justified assertion that those responsible on the ground wanted an exact survey of the Ceded Districts, and that all attempts to achieve this had so far proved to be totally inadequate.[205] His work on the other hand – he went on – was regarded as useful by all concerned: all that had so far prevented its extension was fear of inflated costs. But now he had a cheap team of trained subassistants who could be usefully employed once the Mysore Survey was finished. He himself, he said, would gain absolutely no advantage from it and as superintendent would forego any salary. He showed that the costs would be low by producing a detailed account of the reduced expenditure since 1803.[206]

In February 1809 Mackenzie received the order to coordinate a survey of the Ceded Districts to be carried out by his subassistants – some of whom had now been promoted to assistants,[207] but for him this represented little more than a partial victory. He was convinced that his surveys would be so advantageous to 'Government & to Science in General' that they must continue at all costs. 'It may be unnecessary', he wrote, 'to urge the *utility of combining an extensive investigation with a Geographical Survey*; the principle I believe is generally approved of & its application to British India in general estimated useful; & what has already been effected may remove any early doubts of its practicability.[208] So extension of his studies became his life's goal and years later, when he was Surveyor General of India and it seemed at least possible that his system would be applied to the entire subcontinent (and potentially beyond), the prospect made him positively ecstatic: 'And what a noble work would result? What a clear view of British India?'[209]

Notes

1. Lord Richard Mornington was not appointed as Marquess Wellesley in the Peerage of Ireland until April 1800. For simplicity's sake he is referred to by this name before this time.
2. Before the war Wellesley had already announced the 'entire destruction of his power', the (unacceptable) conditions for peace explicitly included the exclusion from power of his family and descendants. Cf. R. Wellesley, 'Minute, 12. August 1798', in R.M. Martin (ed.), *The Despatches, Minutes and Correspondence of the Marquess Wellesley, K.G., during his Administration in India*, 5 vols (1836/1837; reprinted Delhi, 1984), vol. 1, 159–208, here 206f.
3. Richard Wellesley to Commissioners for the Affairs of Mysore, 4 June 1799, BL/IOR/H/255, 377-387, here 377.
4. Josiah Webbe, Sec. Gov. (FSG), to Colin Mackenzie, 13 June 1799, NAI/SIR/SGO/3, 7f.
5. Colin Mackenzie to Thomas Munro, 8 July 1799, NAI/SIR/SGO/3, 441 and NAI/SIR/M/6, 17. See also Colin Mackenzie, 'Memoir of the Construction of the Map of the Partition of Mysore at Seringapatam', June 1799, BL/OIOC/Mss Eur/Mack Gen/60, 135–38.
6. [Richard Wellesley], 'Memorandum on the Partition of Mysore', [1799], BL/IOR/H/255, 539–77. There are six maps in all in the memorandum. The five maps showing the

possibilities for partition are surely by Mackenzie even though only one bears his signature. A sixth, based on Rennell's work, is probably by Lieutenant Colonel Richardson, then Quarter Master General. The map of the actual partition was later published: 'Map of the Dominions of the late Tippoo Sultaun exhibiting their Partition among the Allied Parties and the Rajah of Mysore, according to the Partition Treaty of Mysore concluded the 22nd June 1799, by Captain Colin Mackenzie of the Engineers', in: A. Beatson, *A View of the Origin and Conduct of the War with Tippoo Sultaun; Comprising a Narrative of the Operations of the Army under the Command of Lieutenant-General George Harris, and of the Siege of Seringapatam* (London, 1800), 248–49.

7. The treaty had been concluded before the 1791/1792 campaign. See 'Treaty of Offensive and Defensive Alliance between the Honourable United English East India Company, the Nawab Ausuph Jah Bahadoor, Soubadar of the Deccan, and the Peishwa, Sewoy Madho Rao Narain Pundit Prudhan Bahadoor against Futti Alhi Khan, Known by the Denomination of Tippoo Sultan, Settled by Captain John Kennaway on the Part of the Said Honourable Company, with the Said Nawab Asuph Jah, by Virtue of the Powers Delegated to Him by the Right Honourable Charles Earl Cornwallis, K.G., Governor-General in Council, Appointed by the Honourable the Court of Directors of the Said Honourable Company to Direct and Control All Their Affairs in the East Indies, 4 July 1790', in C.U. Aitchison (ed.), *A Collection of Treaties, Engagements and Sanads relating to India and Neighbouring Countries*, 14 vols (Calcutta, 1929–1933), vol. 9, 44–47, 45, para. 6.

8. In fact Tipu officially ruled until 1795 in the name of the Rajah. Cf. Fisher, *Indirect Rule in India*, 403.

9. See 'Treaty for Strengthening the Alliance and Friendship Subsisting Between the English East India Company Bahadoor, His Highness the Nawab Nizam-ood-Dowlah Ausuph Jah Bahadoor, and the Peishwa Rao Pundit Prudhan Bahadoor and for Effecting a Settlement of the Dominions of the late Tipoo Sultan, 22 June 1799', in Aitchison, *Collection of Treaties*, vol. 9, 53–61.

10. Richard Wellesley to CD, 3 August 1799, in Martin, *Despatches, Minutes and Correspondence*, vol. 2, 72–101, here 85. See also the official orders to the Resident of Mysore: William Kirkpatrick to Barry Close, 4 September 1799, BL/OIOC/Mss Eur/F/88/402.

11. 'A Treaty of Perpetual Friendship and Alliance Concluded on the One Part by his Excellency Lieutenant-General George Harris, Commander-in-Chief of the Forces of His Britannic Majesty and of the English East India Company Bahadoor in the Carnatic and on the Coast of Malabar, the Honourable Colonel Arthur Wellesley, the Honourable Henry Wellesley, Lieutenant-Colonel William Kirkpatrick, and Lieutenant-Colonel Barry Close, on behalf and in the Name of the Right Honourable Richard, Earl of Mornington, K.P., Governor-General for all Affairs, Civil and Military, of the British nation in India by Virtue of Full Powers Vested in Them for this Purpose by the Said Richard, Earl of Mornington, Governor-General; and on the Other Part by Maharajah Mysore Kishna Rajah Oodiaver Bahadoor, Rajah of Mysore, 8 July 1799', in Aitchison, *Collection of Treaties*, vol. 9, 240–45.

12. Cf. Fisher, *Indirect Rule in India*, 408–21.

13. See Förster, *Die mächtigen Diener der East India Company*. For Wellesley's ambitions see also E. Ingram, 'Empire Building as Career-building: The Wellesleys in India', *Consortium on Revolutionary Europe: Selected Papers* (1998), 453–61; id., *Commitment to Empire: Prophecies of the Great Game in Asia, 1797–1800* (Oxford, 1981), 115–91.

14. See his statements, later published, on the transfer of Cornwallis's principles to South India: R. Wellesley, 'Copy of the Letter, Dated the 19th of July 1804, from the Governor General in Council of Bengal, to the Government of Fort St. George, Relative to the Interior Government of the Country, and the Provision of Goods for the Company's Investment', in

Papers relating to East India Affairs, ordered, by the House of Commons, to be printed, 12 May 1813, [London 1813], 91–103.

15. Cf. R. Wellesley, 'Governor-General's Notes with Respect to the Foundation of a College at Fort Wiliam'; in Martin, *Despatches, Minutes and Correspondence*, vol. 2, 325–55. See also S.K. Das, *Sahibs and Munshis: An Account of the College of Fort William* (Calcutta, Allahabad, Bombay and Delhi, 1978).

16. Cf. Josiah Webbe, Sec. Gov. (FSG), to Colin Mackenzie, 13 June 1799, NAI/SIR/SGO/3, 7f.

17. Josiah Webbe to Colin Mackenzie, 4 November 1799, NAI/SIR/SGO/3, 9–12, here 9f. See also 'Minute', 4 November 1799, BL/IOR/P/254/41, 6058–62; B (FSG) to CD, 19 October 1799, BL/IOR/F/4/280 (6426), 13A–14A.

18. See for example Colin Mackenzie, 'Second General Report on the Mysore Survey', 1803, NAI/SIR/REP/2, 17–35, here 19 and passim.

19. Josiah Webbe to Colin Mackenzie, 4 November 1799, NAI/SIR/SGO/3, 9–12, 9f. See also 'Minute', 4 November 1799, BL/IOR/P/254/41, 6058–62; B (FSG) to CD, 19 October 1799, BL/IOR/F/4/280 (6426), 13A–14A.

20. Cf. M. Vicziany, 'Imperialism, Botany and Statistics in Early-Nineteenth Century India: The Surveys of Francis Buchanan 1762–1829', *Modern Asian Studies* 20(4) (1986), 627–29.

21. Colin Mackenzie, 'Plan of the Mysore Survey and the Manner on which it is proposed to be executed by C. Mackenzie Capt. Engineers', 28 January 1800, BL/IOR/P/254/52, 729–45.

22. Buchanan was not only close to Wellesley, but was always a committed supporter of an aggressive British policy of expansion. In 1803, for instance, in the context of a study on the possibilities of shipbuilding in India, he suggested to the government amongst other things that the Portuguese and Dutch strongholds of Goa and Kochi should simply be annexed because there was an opportunity to set up wharfs there. See his report in BL/Mss Add/37275, 361–77, here 376; for the background see M. Mann, *Flottenbau und Forstbetrieb in Indien 1794–1823* (Stuttgart, 1996). For Buchanan in general see Desmond, *European Discovery of the Indian Flora*, 71–79; W. van Schendel, 'Introduction' in id. (ed.), *Francis Buchanan in Southeast Bengal (1798): His Journey to Chittagong, the Chittagong Hill Tracts, Noakhali and Comilla* (Dhaka, 1992), ix–xxv.

23. Crommelin to Francis Buchanan, 24 February 1800, BL/IOR/F/4/260 (5707), 13–26, here 13. See also Minute by Mornington (Wellesley), 24 February 1800, ibid., 10f. Further copies in BL/IOR/H/256/1, 8–13.

24. Josiah Webbe to Colin Mackenzie, 5 April 1800, NAI/SIR/SGO/3, 45f.

25. Colin Mackenzie to Francis Buchanan, 25 May 1800, NAI/SIR/M/6, 113–15. Another copy in NAI/SIR/SGO/90, 455f.

26. Colin Mackenzie to Francis Buchanan, 5 June 1800, NAI/SIR/M/6, 119–21; also 5 July 1800, ibid., 146f; and 14 November 1800, NAI/SIR/SGO/90, 458f. Mackenzie, to whom Buchanan was also personally recommended by his former superior Kirkpatrick and whose work in the *Asiatic Researches* he knew, particularly drew his attention to the Jains' religion and certain South Indian manuscripts he knew.

27. F. Buchanan, *A Journey from Madras through the Countries of Mysore, Canara, and Malabar, Performed under the Most Noble Marquis Wellesley, Governor General of India, for the Express Purpose of Investigating the State of Agriculture, Arts and Commerce; the Religion, Manners, and Customs; the History Natural and Civil, and Antiquities, in the Dominions of the Rajah of Mysore, and the Countries Acquired by the Honourable East India Company, in the Late and Former Wars, from Tippoo Sultaun*, 3 vols (London, 1807). For a brief analysis of the contents see Vicziany, 'Imperialism, Botany and Statistics', 632–35.

28. Although for his survey of Bengal in the 1760s and 1770s Rennell (as Surveyor General) likewise had four European assistants at his disposal, he had little influence on their practical work. Apart from his own surveying, his role was mainly confined to compiling diverse

material. Furthermore, his assistants (such as de Gloss) were generally under the command of local officers. Lack of any systematic documentation can be regarded as a further indication that the survey was fairly uncoordinated. Cf. Rennell, 'Journals', 186; Lewis de Glosse, 'Abstract of the Journal Containing the Proceedings of Lewis Felix Degloss Captain of Engineers and Surveyor, in Coarse of Survey in the Province of Subah Bahar. Commencing Nov. 29 1766', BL/OIOC/Mss Eur/Orme/OV/6, 3.

29. See for instance Colin Mackenzie, 'Plan of Arranging the Surveyor General's Department & Generally all Surveys under the Presidency of Fort St. George', 29 November 1810, NAI/SIR/SGO/60. 4–7; Colin Mackenzie to W.B. Bayly, 7 September 1818, SGO/435D, 5–7, here 6.

30. See Colin Mackenzie, 'Plan of the Mysore Survey', 28 January 1800, BL/IOR/P/254/52, 729–45, here 740f.

31. Colin Mackenzie to Barry Close, 5 December 1799, NAI/SIR/M/6, 32–34; also 28 December 1799, ibid., 39f.

32. It was not until 1802 that Mackenzie was given permission to buy instruments from public funds. At the same time tents hitherto requisitioned from the Military Stores in Madras were replaced by means of an additional payment. Colin Mackenzie to Josiah Webbe, 13 September 1802, BL/IOR/F/4/152 (2598), 67–79; B (FSG) to Webbe, 20 September 1802, ibid., 79f; B (FSG) to CD, 4 October 1802, ibid. 1–4.

33. Alexander Read to Lieutenant General Harris & Commissioners for the Affairs of Mysore, 9 July 1799, NAI/SIR/M/6, 21f.

34. Colin Mackenzie to Arthur Wellesley, 18 July 1799, NAI/SIR/M/6, 17f. The material sent over was probably John Mather, 'Records of the Barramahl & Salem &c. Districts - Section IInd, Geography', 1794–1798, NAI/SIR/M/1. There is an abridged copy in BL/OIOC/Mss Eur/Mack Gen/46, 171–232.

35. For Mather see Phillimore, *Historical Records*, vol. 1, 354f; vol. 2, 428f.

36. John Mather to Colin Mackenzie, 11 November 1802, NAI/SIR/M/6, 352f.

37. Cf. Mather, 'Records of the Barramahl and Salem Districts', NAI/SIR/M/1, 7.

38. See for instance Colin Mackenzie to John Mather, 2. April 1800, NAI/SIR/M/6, 103; id. to Barry Close, 26 May 1801, ibid., 266–68; id. to John Warren, 17 June 1800, ibid., 124–26.

39. Cf. Colin Mackenzie to Josiah Webbe, 21 November 1802, NAI/SIR/M/6, 354f.

40. Cf. Mackenzie, 'Plan of the Mysore Survey', BL/IOR/P/254/52, 729–45, here 736f, 739; see also Colin Mackenzie to Barry Close, 9 November 1799, NAI/SIR/M/6, 27–32; Colin Mackenzie to John Warren, 5 September 1800, ibid., 176–79.

41. This is manifested by the obvious similarities between Mather's geographical memoir of Salem and Barramahl and the memoirs written during the Mysore Survey. See for instance [Colin Mackenzie], 'Memoirs of a Geographical, Statistical and Historical Survey of the Mysore Dominions commenced on the Partition of Mysore 1799, The Company's Territories, Canara' [1806/7], NAI/SIR/M/22 and Mather, 'Records of the Barramahl and Salem Districts', NAI/SIR/M/1.

42. Mackenzie to Barry Close, 14 September 1799, NAI/SIR/M/6, 27; Mackenzie to Close, 5 December 1799, ibid., 32–34, here 32.

43. Cf. W. Gent to Mackenzie, 17 April 1799, BL/Mss Add/13663, 148. For Warren see Phillimore, *Historical Records*, vol. 2, 449–53.

44. Josiah Webbe to Colin Mackenzie, 18 December 1799, NAI/SIR/SGO/3, 15. There is another copy in NAI/SIR/M/6, 39. See also Colin Mackenzie to Warren, 21 December 1799, ibid., 39. Warren was to replace Thomas Sydenham, the original appointee, who had become seriously ill. Cf. Mackenzie to Barry Close, 9 November 1799, ibid., 27–32, here 30. See also Sydenham [to Close], n.p., n.d. [Seringapatam, 1799], NAI/SIR/SGO/3, 29–40.

45. Cf. Josiah Webbe to Mackenzie, 23 April 1800, NAI/SIR/M/6, 151. See also Mackenzie to Barry Close, 24 March 1800, ibid., 96f; Mackenzie to Close, 22 May 1800, ibid., 107f.

46. Cf. Norris [to Colin Mackenzie], 24 April 1799, BL/Mss Add/13663, 159. For Arthur see Phillimore, *Historical Records*, vol. 2, 376–80.

47. Colin Mackenzie to Barry Close, 14 October 1801, NAI/SIR/M/6, 295–97; William Morison to Mackenzie, 16 June 1802, BL/IOR/F/4/152 (2598), 17; for Morison see Phillimore, *Historical Records*, vol. 2, 431.

48. Cf. Colin Mackenzie to William Morison, 5 June 1802, NAI/SIR/SGO/90, 207; John Chamier to Colin Mackenzie, 24 June 1802, NAI/SIR/SGO/3, 81 (=BL/IOR/F/4/152 (2598), 15); Mackenzie to Morison, 2 June 1802, NAI/SIR/M/6, 337; Mackenzie to Chamier, 10 June 1802, ibid., 335f; id. to Josiah Webbe, 15 September 1802, ibid., 342f; id. to Morison, 7 October 1802, ibid., 345–47; B (FSG) to CD, 4 October 1802, BL/IOR/F/4/152 (2598), 1–4.

49. Cf. Colin Mackenzie, 'Plan of the Mysore Survey', 28 January 1800, BL/IOR/P/254/52, 729–45, here 730–39.

50. Heyne himself reported on a visit to Mackenzie in Hyderabad in 1798: Benjamin Heyne, 'Cursory Remarks on a Tour to Hyderabad in 1798', NAI/SIR/M/3, 1–48, here 18–20.

51. Heyne (in German, 'Heine'), a German doctor who had come to the Danish stronghold of Tranquebar in 1790, at this time held the post of the Company's botanist. His duties included supervising the import and cultivation of useful plants. See Desmond, *European Discovery of the Indian Flora*, 41–44.

52. Colin Mackenzie to William Kirkpatrick, 31 December 1799, NAI/SIR/M/6, 40–43, here 41.

53. Cf. Colin Mackenzie to Josiah Webbe, 5 November 1799, NAI/SIR/M/6, 24–26; id. to Barry Close, 4 February 1800, ibid., 68–70; Webbe to Mackenzie, 22 November 1799, NAI/SIR/SGO/3, 13f; 'Establishment for Capt. Mackenzie Superintending the Mysore Survey for a Month of 30 Days', 4 February 1800, NAI/SIR/M/6, 69; Colin Mackenzie to Josiah Webbe, 4 February 1800, ibid., 68–70; Webbe to Mackenzie, 6 January 1800, NAI/SIR/SGO/3, 19–24, here 19. Translation of some of the Anglo-Indian professional descriptions is given in J.H. Stocqueler, *The Oriental Interpreter and Treasury of East India Knowledge: A Companion to the Handbook of British India* (London, 1848), for example 137, 184, 192.

54. The widespread practice of taking families along was apparently, however, to be curbed. In March 1800 it was decided that so-called 'family allowances' – support for families of Indian co-workers working outside the presidency – should henceforth only be paid in Madras. Cf. Colin Mackenzie to John Mather, 5 March 1800, NAI/SIR/M/6, 81f; id. to John Warren, 6 March 1800, ibid., 82f; id. to Major Clarke, Commissary of Stores, Madras, 17 April 1800, ibid., 99f; id. to Mather, 1 July 1800, ibid., 130f; id. to John Mather, 7 July 1800, ibid., 137f; id. to Warren, 7 July 1800, ibid., 138–40.

55. Cf. Colin Mackenzie, Memorandum for Barry Close, 20 March 1800, NAI/SIR/M/6, 91f; Colin Mackenzie to Barry Close, 19 April 1800, ibid., 97.

56. Colin Mackenzie to Barry Close, 17 May 1800, NAI/SIR/M/6, 106.

57. Cf. Mr Cochrane, Asst. Res. Mys, to Colin Mackenzie, 6 May 1800, NAI/SIR/SGO/3, 273–79; Colin Mackenzie to Gordon, Paymaster of Mysore, 7 July 1800, NAI/SIR/M/6, 140f; id. to Barry Close, 9 July 1800, ibid., 144–46; id. to Cecil Smith, Esqu., Civil Auditor, Fort St George, 15 July 1800, ibid., 151f.

58. Cf. Colin Mackenzie to Barry Close, 21 February 1800, NAI/SIR/M/6, 79; also 28 February 1800, ibid., 80.

59. Cf. Colin Mackenzie to Gordon, 7 August 1800, NAI/SIR/M/6, 165f; id. to John Warren, 14 August 1800, ibid., 167. For repercussions in Bangalore and Chittledroog see also Mackenzie to Gordon, 7 July 1800, ibid., 140f.

60. Colin Mackenzie to Major Clarke, Commissary of Stores, 13 June 1800, NAI/SIR/SGO/90, 429; also 16 August 1800, NAI/SIR/M/6, 169.
61. Cf. Josiah Webbe to Colin Mackenzie, 4 November 1799, NAI/SIR/SGO/3, 9–12, here 12; also 22 November 1799, ibid., 13f.
62. Cf. Colin Mackenzie to Captain MacLean, Sec. B Mil. (FSG), 21 March 1800, NAI/SIR/M/6, 92; id. to Major Clarke, Commissary of Stores (FSG), 16 August 1800, ibid., 169; id. to Captain Fowler, Commissary of Store (Vellore), 23 October 1802, ibid., 349.
63. Cf. Josiah Webbe to Colin Mackenzie, 22 November 1799, NAI/SIR/SGO/3, 13f; Colin Mackenzie, 'Indent on Mungo Dick Esqu. Superintendant Import Department for the Delivery of the following Stationary required for the use of the Survey in Mysore', 10 December 1800, NAI/SIR/M/6, 228f and the explanatory letter to Close of the same date, ibid., 228.
64. Cf. Colin Mackenzie to Colonel Stevenson or the Officer Commanding in Mysore, 27 December 1800, NAI/SIR/M/6, 237f; id to Captain Barclay, Deputy Adjutant General in Mysore, 27 December 1800, ibid., 238; id. to John Mather, 18 January 1801, ibid., 243. It was obviously not enough to have the equipment guarded by *lascars*. For instance, in early 1808, despite this measure, Lantwar and Hamilton were robbed at night of all their money and some of their instruments. Those regarded by the thieves as useless or too heavy to transport – but not their vital theodolites – they found strewn over the whole area in the following days. See Henry Hamilton, 'Field Book containing the Survey of Conjeveram &c. commencing May 1808', NAI/SIR/FB/38, 59–141, here 126f.
65. 'Public and Official Letterbook of the Superintendent of the Mysore Survey, from the Partition of Mysore to July 13th 1803', NAI/SIR/M/6; 'Mysore Survey Official Public Letter Book commencing 13. April 1803', NAI/SIR/M/18.
66. 'Letters Public and Private (connected with the Mysore Survey, 1799-August 1806', NAI/SIR/SGO/90.
67. 'Official Letters & Public Orders from Government and from other Public Authorities relating to the Surveys and more particularly to the Survey of Mysore addressed to C. Mackenzie, 1799–1807', NAI/SIR/SGO/3.
68. Colin Mackenzie, Memorandum for Josiah Webbe, 8 March 1800, NAI/SIR/M/6, 86f; id. to George Buchan, 13 July 1803, ibid. 372f.
69. Colin Mackenzie, 'View of the State of the Mysore Survey on 1st October 1803', NAI/SIR/REP/2, 239–53, here 252. There is a copy in BL/OIOC/Mss Eur/F/228/39.
70. Mackenzie preferred to go on horseback or on foot since this enabled him to make observations on the way. See Colin Mackenzie to William Lambton, 14 September 1800, NAI/SIR/SGO/90, 337–39.
71. Cf. for instance Colin Mackenzie to John Warren, 6 March 1800, NAI/SIR/M/6, 82f; also 17 June 1800, ibid., 124–26.
72. Colin Mackenzie to William Lambton, 14 September 1800, NAI/SIR/SGO/90, 337–39.
73. Cf. for example Colin Mackenzie to Thomas Arthur, 20 May 1801, NAI/SIR/SGO/90, 249–51, here 250; John Mather, 'Journal of the Proceedings of the Survey in Mysore with an account of the Weather during 1804', NAI/SIR/M/12, 291–320, here 295, 313.
74. Cf. for example Thomas Arthur, 'Journal', 14 July 1801–28 June 1803, NAI/SIR/M/12, 45–94, here 60 and passim; 'Journal kept by Benjamin Heyne, Assistant, on the Mysore Survey 1800–1802', NAI/SIR/J/8, 17–182, here 140 and passim.
75. To Warren, for instance, he explicitly stressed that his role as an 'assistant surveyor' was below his – that of 'general superintendancy' – and that he should therefore adhere strictly to the prescribed communication paths. (Colin Mackenzie to John Warren, 6 March 1800, NAI/SIR/M/6, 82f.)
76. Colin Mackenzie to Benjamin Heyne, 13 December 1800, NAI/SIR/SGO/90, 17–20.

77. 'Extract of the Letter from Major Munro, Dated Callindroog 2 May 1801', NAI/SIR/SGO/90, 246f, note by Mackenzie, 247.
78. Cf. Colin Mackenzie to Barry Close, 12 June 1800, NAI/SIR/M/6, 121f; id. to Major Clarke, 6 July 1800, ibid., 147–49; id. to John MacLeane, 18 November 1800, ibid., 222; id. to William Lambton, 14 September 1800, NAI/SIR/SGO/90, 337–39; id. to Thomas Arthur, 13 March 1803, ibid., 300f.
79. Cf. Colin Mackenzie to Thomas Arthur, NAI/SIR/SGO/90, 243.
80. Cf. Thomas Arthur, 'Journal', 14 July 1801 – 28 June 1802, NAI/SIR/M/12, 45–94, here 60, 72f; and 'Translation of an Extract of a Letter from the Aumildar of Narsipoor addressed to the Dewan of Mysore', 15 June 1804, NAI/SIR/SGO/3, 469–71.
81. Cf. Stein, *Munro*, 74–138; Beaglehole, *Munro*, 55–86.
82. The two of them had met for the first time in 1787 in Vellore. Cf. Colin Mackenzie to Thomas Munro, 1 January 1819, BL/OIOC/Mss Eur/F/151/39, 268–73, here 273.
83. Cf. Colin Mackenzie to Thomas Arthur, 7 June 1801, NAI/SIR/SGO/90, 252–55, here 252.
84. Here too Munro instigated an investigation. However, it is unclear whether the horse, initially confiscated, was ever returned to Borayya. See Colin Mackenzie to Thomas Munro, 28 December 1800, NAI/SIR/SGO/90, 381f; also 4 January 1801, ibid., 383–85; and 22 January 1801, ibid., 385f; id. to Thomas Arthur, 5 May 1801, ibid., 243.
85. Colin Mackenzie to Thomas Munro, 4 March 1801, NAI/SIR/SGO/90, 386–89.
86. 'Extract of the Letter from Major Munro, Dated Callindroog, 2 May 1801', NAI/SIR/SGO/90, 246f.
87. Ibid., fn 9.
88. Colin Mackenzie to Thomas Munro, 3 May 1801, NAI/SIR/SGO/90, 392; also 3 May 1801, ibid., 393. The second letter was brought to Munro by Mackenzie's co-workers in person. See also Mackenzie to Thomas Arthur, 5 May 1801, ibid., 244–46, here 245.
89. Colin Mackenzie to Thomas Arthur, 7 June 1801, NAI/SIR/SGO/90, 252–55, here 253; id. to J.H. Peile, 29 May 1801, ibid., 401–3.
90. Colin Mackenzie to Thomas Arthur, 18 June 1801, NAI/SIR/SGO/90, 256–60, here 259.
91. See for example Colin Mackenzie to John Mather, 26 June 1801, NAI/SIR/M/6, 274f; also 26 July 1801, NAI/SIR/SGO/90, 60–62, here 61.
92. Colin Mackenzie to J.H. Peile, 29 May 1801, NAI/SIR/M/6, 268–70.
93. In summer 1799 Mackenzie's health was so bad that his doctors had recommended a sea voyage. However, in order to do his duty as superintendent he had remained in Madras. Here his condition improved so dramatically that he was able to leave in March 1800. Mather's departure was also delayed to February 1800 due to illness. Cf. Colin Mackenzie to Barry Close, 9 November 1799, NAI/SIR/M/6, 27–32; also 28 December 1799, ibid., 39f; Colin Mackenzie to William Kirkpatrick, 31 December 1799, ibid., 40–43; id. to Barry Close, 30 January 1800, ibid., 64f; id. to John Mather, 30 January 1800, ibid., 65f; id. to Josiah Webbe, 10[?] March 1800, ibid., 86f.
94. Cf. Colin Mackenzie to Thomas Munro, 23 May 1800, NAI/SIR/M/6, 110f; id. to John Mather, 17 June 1800, ibid., 122f; id. to Barry Close, 1 July 1800, ibid., 127–30; id. to Mather, 1 July 1800, ibid., 130f; also 15 July 1800, ibid., 150f; and 15 October 1800, ibid., 195.
95. Cf. Colin Mackenzie, 'Second General Report on the Mysore Survey', 12 July 1803, NAI/SIR/REP/2, 17–35, here 19–25, 29f; id., 'Present State of the Distribution of the Surveyors on the Establishment of the Mysore Survey', 1 September 1802, NAI/SIR/M/6, 340–42; Thomas Arthur, 'Journal', 14 July 1801 – 28, June 1802, NAI/SIR/M/12, 45–94, here 94.
96. Cf. Benjamin Heyne to Colin Mackenzie, 23 May 1800, NAI/SIR/M/6, 113; Colin Mackenzie to Barry Close, 3 June 1800, ibid., 116. See also Benjamin Heyne, 'Memoir on the Copper Mines in the Callastry & Venketgherry District in the Latitude of Ongole', NAI/

SIR/J/8, 183–209. Mackenzie later refused to present Heyne's report as a product of the Survey: see Colin Mackenzie to Benjamin Heyne, 13 February 1802, NAI/SIR/M/6, 327f.

97. Cf. Benjamin Heyne to Lord Clive, 2 May 1800, BL/IOR/F/4/78 (1750), 53; id., 'Sketch of a Plan for a Botanical Garden at the Madras Establishment', ibid., 54–72.

98. Cf. 'Journal kept by Benjamin Heyne, Assistant, on the Mysore Survey 1800–1802', NAI/SIR/J/8, 17–182, here 42.

99. Cf. Colin Mackenzie to Thomas Arthur, 7 June 1801, NAI/SIR/SGO/90, 252–55, here 252; also 18 June 1801, 256–60, here 258.

100. Cf. Colin Mackenzie to Barry Close, 23 December 1800, NAI/SIR/M/6, 233f; id. to Benjamin Heyne, 23 December 1800, ibid., 234; also 16 January 1800, ibid., 241f; 16 March 1801, ibid., 254; 27 March 1801, ibid., 256; and 24 April 1801, ibid., 262; id. to Barry Close, 27 June 1801, ibid., 276–78; id. to Heyne, 15 July 1801, ibid, 281; also 23 December 1800, NAI/SIR/SGO/90, 21f; and 25 June 1801, ibid., 26f.

101. Minute by Lord Clive, 18 March 1800, BL/IOR/F/4/78 (1750), 18f.

102. Josiah Webbe to Colin Mackenzie, 6 November 1800, NAI/SIR/SGO/3, 19–24, here 22f; Benjamin Heyne to Josiah Webbe, 20 May 1800, NAI/SIR/M/6, 116f.

103. Colin Mackenzie to Barry Close, 24 December 1800, NAI/SIR/M/6, 235–37. See also Mackenzie's clear criticism of Heyne in his first Report: Colin Mackenzie to Lord Clive, 24 October 1800, ibid., 199–210, here 207.

104. Robert Alexander to Benjamin Heyne, 17 May 1800, NAI/SIR/M/6, 117f.

105. George Keble to Colin Mackenzie, 19 June 1802, NAI/SIR/SGO/3, 79. See also Heyne's (unsuccessful) justification which he in turn sent directly to the Governor: Benjamin Heyne to Lord Clive, 23 April 1802, BL/IOR/F/4/78 (1750), 25–39.

106. Cf. B (FSG) to CD, 20 October 1802, BL/IOR/F/4/275 (6129), 17f; Benjamin Heyne to William Bentinck, 26 March1807, ibid., 69f.

107. George Buchan to Colin Mackenzie, 14 January 1804, NAI/SIR/SGO/3, 95–97; B (FSG) to CD, 29 March 1804, BL/IOR/F/4/280 (6426), 21–27; CD to B FSG, 23 October 1805, ibid., 39–41; Mackenzie to John Leyden, 13 July 1804, NAI/SIR/M/18, 69.

108. Cf. John Leyden to Colin Mackenzie, 12 April 1805, NLS/Ms 3383, 218f; also 21 August 1805, ibid., 239–45; id. to William Bentinck, 17 June 1805, ibid.; Mackenzie to Leyden, 10 February 1805, NLS/Ms 3380, 61–63; John Leyden to his father, 20 November 1805, ibid., 72; Colin Mackenzie, 'Memorandum of the Origin, Progress and Present State of the Geometrical and Statistic Survey of Mysore, to July 1st 1807', BL/Mss Add/14380, 24, 30f. Leyden's only direct contribution to the survey seems to be a journal of 1804: John Leyden, 'Journal from Madras to Seringapatam', June 1804, NLS/Ms 3383, 176–79.

109. Josiah Webbe to Colin Mackenzie, 4 November 1799, NAI/SIR/SGO/3, 9–12, here 10f; B (FSG) to CD, 19 October 1799, BL/IOR/F/4/280 (6426), 13A–14A; CD to B (FSG), 10 June 1801, NAI/SIR/SGO/3, 57f.

110. John Chamier to Colin Mackenzie, 10 November 1801, NAI/SIR/SGO/3, 55. Subsequently Mackenzie was only to receive 420 pagodas *including* establishment, Mather 116, Heyne 110 and Warren and Arthur 100 pagodas.

111. Cf. Robb, 'Completing "Our Stock of Geography"', 188f; Dirks, 'Colonial Histories and Native Informants', 285.

112. Cf. Mackenzie to J.H. Peile, 26 November 1803, NAI/SIR/SGO/90, 425–27, here 426.

113. In 1802 Mather was also given permission to draw the, 'Surveyor's Allowance from the first day of his appointment to be an assistant to the Mysore Survey'. This represented a considerable salary increase. See George Keble to Colin Mackenzie, 15 December 1802, NAI/SIR/SGO/3, 83f; B (FSG) to CD, 22 February 1802, BL/IOR/F/4/152 (2598), 5–7.

114. In 1808 the Directors expressed their displeasure as follows: 'We consider the continuance of a Salary to any Officer granted originally for Duties which from whatever cause he can

no longer perform as a gross impropriety and we are much surprised to observe that Major Mackenzie who held the Appointment of Engineer to the Hyderabad Detachment, was permitted to draw the Allowances annexed to that Station for three Years subsequent to his being appointed to the Mysore Survey the Duties of which effectually prevented his attending to those of the former employ', CD to B (FSG), 7 September 1808, BL/IOR/F/4/280 (6426), 53–56, here 53.

115. Mackenzie apparently drew this salary again from 1802, though not the additional sum of 200 pagodas granted him in 1798. Before 1805 he himself was somewhat ambiguous about it. He wrote to Kirkpatrick, for instance, that he wanted to use his position in Hyderabad, though in which way he was not prepared to commit to paper ('more at meeting'). Later correspondence however, indicated that he drew it for three years from 1802. The Directors' position, and indeed Mackenzie's own statements suggest against Blake's view that Mackenzie had not drawn this salary continuously from 1799. Cf. Colin Mackenzie to William Kirkpatrick, 16 November 1801, BL/OIOC/Mss Eur/F/228/19; id. to William Bentinck, 16 July 1806, NAI/SIR/M/18, 182–84. See also Blake, 'Colin Mackenzie: Collector Extraordinary', 142. For the additional 200 pagodas paid to Mackenzie in 1798/1799 cf.: Colin Mackenzie to Barry Close, 19 March 1800, NAI/SIR/M/6, 88f; and Colin Mackenzie to Barlow, 26 April 1808, BL/IOR/P/256/29, 4243–255, here 4243.

116. Minute by Cradock, 9 April 1805, BL/OIOC/Mss Eur/F/228/39, No. 13, 19.

117. 'Extract Minute of Council', 15 April 1805, ibid., No. 14, 19f; George Buchan to Colin Mackenzie, 18 April 1805, NAI/SIR/SGO/3, 131–26; B (FSG) to CD, 8 September 1805, BL/IOR/F/4/280 (6426), 35–39.

118. George Buchan to Colin Mackenzie, 19 November 1803, NAI/SIR/SGO/3, 91–93, here 92. See also Colin Mackenzie, 'Statement of the Establishment proposed for Major Mackenzie Superintendant of the Mysore Survey to commence from 1st October 1803 for a Month of 30 days', 21 December 1803, BL/IOR/F/4/280 (6426), 71f; B (FSG) to CD, 29 March 1804, ibid., 21–27. There is a copy of the statement in NAI/SIR/M/18, 40.

119. Cf. Colin Mackenzie to William Bentinck, 23 June 1805, BL/OIOC/Mss Eur/F/228/39, No. 11, 15.

120. Cf. Stein, *Munro*, 93–98; M.H. Fisher, 'Indirect Rule in the British Empire', 413, fn 42. For Webbe's support see Colin Mackenzie to William Kirkpatrick, 12 July 1801, BL/OIOC/Mss Eur/228/19; also 4 October 1801, ibid.

121. Colin Mackenzie to Henry Trail, 2 August 1805, BL/OIOC/Mss Eur/F/228/39.

122. Colin Mackenzie to Major Merrick Shawe, Priv. Sec. GG, 1 May 1804, NAI/SIR/M/18, 57–60, here 58.

123. 'Major Rennells Observations on the Plans proposed by Captain Mackenzie & Brigade Major Lambton for a Survey of Mysore', n.d [1801], NAI/SIR/SGO/3, 49f. Mackenzie received this report in March 1802. See George Keble to Colin Mackenzie, 16 March 1802, ibid., 65.

124. Edney, *Mapping an Empire*, 157f, 179–84. Probably as a reaction to this misunderstanding Lambton also wrote a detailed interim report: William Lambton, 'A Memoir containing an account of the principal operations of the Survey carried on in Mysore in the Year 1801 and explaining the general principles on which it has been conducted', n.d. [February/March 1802], NAI/SIR/M/14, 13–103.

125. Clearly the Directors had indeed included the expenses for Lambton's survey in Mackenzie's, and Mackenzie had immediately protested. See CD to B (FSG), 10 June 1801, NAI/SIR/SGO/3, 57f; and Colin Mackenzie to J.H. Peile, 23 November 1801, NAI/SIR/M/6, 312f.

126. In addition Rennell recommended the abolition of the botanical gardens in Bangalore - Mackenzie had never regarded this as an important component of his survey. See 'Major Rennells Observations on the Plans proposed by Captain Mackenzie & Brigade Major

Lambton for a Survey of Mysore', n.d [1801], NAI/SIR/SGO/3, 49f; and George Keble to Colin Mackenzie, 16 March 1802, ibid., 65.

127. Cf. Robb, 'Completing "Our Stock of Geography"', 189.

128. In the form of a letter to the Governor of Madras: Colin Mackenzie to Lord Clive, 24 October 1800, NAI/SIR/M/6, 199–210, here 207.

129. Partly this material was also produced by Mather. See John Mather to Colin Mackenzie, 11 November 1802, NAI/SIR/M/6, 354; Mackenzie to Josiah Webb, 21 November 1802, ibid., 354f; and Colin Mackenzie, 'Statement of the Work now in preparation to accompany a General Report of the Survey carried on in Mysore for the Information of Government & of The Court of Directors', 21 November 1802, ibid., 363–65; id., 'List of Maps, Plans and other Documents resulting from the Operations & Investigations of the Mysore Survey: Constructed or copied off & communicated by the Superintendant of the Survey since January 1802', 3 July 1803, NAI/SIR/M/6, 59–62.

130. Colin Mackenzie, 'Second General Report on the Mysore Survey', 12 July 1803, NAI/SIR/REP/2, 17–35. This report was supplemented by a map of the surveyed area, a plan of the trigonometrical operations and, amongst other things, the following scripts: id., 'Memoir of the Survey of the Boundary & Northern Districts of Mysore in 1801/1802', 15 May 1803, 45–70; id., 'Remarks on Forts along the Northern Frontier of Mysore in 1800 & 1801. Extracted from the Papers of the Mysore Survey', ibid., 169–219; id., 'General Heads of Instructions for the Geometrical & Geographical Survey of a Purgunnah or Hobely in Mysore', ibid. 83–85; id., 'Comparative View of the Forts of Ghooty and Ballary from a cursory Inspection in February 1801', ibid., 222–35; Kavali Venkata Borayya, 'Memoir of the Civil Administration Police, Commerce & Revenue Management of the Balla Ghaat Carnatic form Enquiries Instituted in 1800 and 1801 & Information collected for Colin Mackenzie on the Mysor Survey by Cavelly Venkata Boria Interpreter of the Survey', ibid., 103–42; and Thomas Arthur, 'Abstract of a Set of Astronomical Observations made on a journey in the Northern Parts of Mysore in 1800–1801', ibid., 143–67.

131. Cf. Colin Mackenzie to Arthur Wellesley, 3 September 1802, SUL/WP/1/124.

132. Colin Mackenzie to Major Merrick Shawe, Priv Secr GG, 1 May 1804, BL/OIOC/Mss Eur/F/228/39, No. 1, 1–3; also 25 June 1805, ibid., No. 19, 23–26; draft or copy in NAI/SIR/M/18, 57–60, 121–24; id., 'Memorandum', 2 August 1805, BL/OIOC/Mss Eur/F/228/39, 39.

133. Colin Mackenzie, 'View of the State of the Mysore Survey on 1st October 1803', NAI/SIR/REP/2, 239–53; Colin Mackenzie to Lord Bentinck, 23 June 1805, No. 11, 13–16; id., 'Memorandum of the Origin, Progress and Present State of the Geometrical and Statistic Survey of Mysore, to July 1st 1807', NLS/Ms 11722,(i) 1–8. Obviously Wellesley also received a copy. Today it is held in his papers: BL/Mss Add/14380.

134. Colin Mackenzie to William Kirkpatrick, 16/19 November 1801, BL/OIOC/Mss Eur/F/228/19.

135. Colin Mackenzie to J.H. Peile, 26 November 1803, NAI/SIR/SGO/90, 425–27, here 425.

136. Cf. Colin Mackenzie to Henry Trail, John and Alexander Anderson, Alexander Mackenzie, 30 July 1805 BL/OIOC/Mss Eur/F/228/39; id. to Henry Trail, 2 April 1805, ibid.; id., 'Memorandum of the Origin, Progress and Present State of the Geometrical and Statistic Survey of Mysore, to July 1st 1807', BL/Mss Add/14380, 26.

137. See the reports for 1802, 1804 and 1805 in BL/OIOC/Mss Eur/F/228/39.

138. Like Mackenzie, Henry Trail had come to India in 1783, had settled in Calcutta and had initially run an insurance business there, before co-founding an Agency House. As treasurer of the Asiatic Society in the late 1790s he was a highly respected member of Calcutta society before returning to London, where he carried on successfully with his businesses. Cf. *The Bengal Calendar & Register, for the Year One Thousand Seven Hundred & Ninety; Containing*

Complete and Accurate Lists of the Honorable East India Company's Servants, on the Bengal Establishment, Upon a New and More Extensive Plan than Any Ever Before (London, 1790), 136; and 'Members of the Asiatic Society, 1797', 427. For the influence of the important London Agency House, Cockerell and Trail, see A. Webster, 'The Strategies and Limits of Gentlemanly Capitalism: The London East India Agency Houses, Provincial Commercial Interests, and the Evolution of British Economic Policy in South and South East Asia 1800–50', *Economic History Review* 59(4) (2006), 746–49; for its activities in Bengal and Sri Lanka see S.B. Singh, *European Agency Houses in Bengal (1783–1833)* (Calcutta, 1966), 107f; 171, 185.

139. Cf. Merrick Shawe to Colin Mackenzie, 6 July 1804, BL/OIOC/Mss Eur/F/228/39, No. 6, 6; Lord Bentinck to Mackenzie, 4 April 1805, ibid., No. 10, 9.

140. Colin Mackenzie to Henry Trail, 2 August 1805, BL/OIOC/Mss Eur/F/228/39.

141. Ibid.

142. Ibid.; and Mackenzie's annotations on William Bentinck to Colin Mackenzie, 4 April 1805, ibid., No. 10, 9; 'Extract of a General Letter to the Honble Court of Directors in the Military Department' 16 October 1804, ibid., No. 12, 17f. For James Stewart see M. Fry, 'Stuart, James (1741–1815)', *ODNB*.

143. James Stewart, Minute, 12 January 1804, BL/IOR/F/4/183 (3692), 5–21, here 20f.

144. Cf. Edney, *Mapping an Empire*, 165–69, esp. 166, Fig. 5.1; id., 'British Military Education, Mapmaking, and Military "Map Mindedness" in the later Enlightenment', *Cartographic Journal* 31(1) (1994), 14–20.

145. Colin Mackenzie to Arthur Wellesley, 3 September 1802, SUL/WP/1/124.

146. Cf. the version commentated by Mackenzie of an official letter recommending the office of the Quarter Master General as the cartographical archive: 'Extract of a General Letter to the Honble Court of Directors in the Military Department' 16 October 1804, BL/OIOC/Mss Eur/F 228/39, No. 12, 17f.

147. Colin Mackenzie, 'Memorandum', 2 August 1805, BL/OIOC/Mss Eur/F/228/39, 39.

148. Cf. Colin Mackenzie to John Warren, 11 December 1801, NAI/SIR/SGO/90, 190f.

149. Cf. Colin Mackenzie to J.H. Peile, 24 February 1803, NAI/SIR/M/6, 365; id. to William Morison, 12 March 1803, ibid., 366; also 16 January 1803, NAI/SIR/SGO/90, 213f; Colin Mackenzie, 'Second General Report on the Mysore Survey', 12 July 1803, NAI/SIR/REP/2, 17–35, here 30; id. to Morison, 10 September 1803, NAI/SIR/SGO/90, 366; Colin Mackenzie, 'View of the State of the Mysore Survey on 1st October 1803', NAI/SIR/REP/2, 239–53, here 247.

150. Mackenzie knew him from the Ceylon expedition. See William Gent to Colin Mackenzie, 29 December 1795, Chief Engineers Books, BL/OIOC/Mss Eur/Mack Gen/68.

151. Cf. Colin Mackenzie to William Bentinck, 23 June 1805, BL/OIOC/Mss Eur/F/228/39, 15; Colin Mackenzie to Henry Trail, 2 August 1805, ibid.

152. Cf. Colin Mackenzie to Josiah Webbe, 22 February 1803, NAI/SIR/M/6, 362; George Buchan to Webbe, 25 February 1803, NAI/SIR/SGO/3, 429f; Mackenzie to Thomas Arthur, 17 April 1803, NAI/SIR/SGO/90, 298f; id. to J.H. Peile, 25 October 1803, ibid., 422f. For the background and course of this campaign see R.G.S. Cooper, *The Anglo-Maratha Campaign and the Contest for India: The Struggle for Control of the South Asian Military Economy* (Cambridge, 2003).

153. 'Extract of a General Letter from England in the Public Department', 27 June 1804, BL/OIOC/Mss Eur/F/228/39, No. 16, 21; John Malcolm to Colin Mackenzie, 2 March 1805, NAI/SIR/SGO/3, 497–503.

154. Cf. Colin Mackenzie, 'General Abstract of the Result of the Geometrical Survey of Mysore according to the Partition of 1799 – from September 1799 to September 1805', BL/OIOC/Mss Eur/F/228/39.

155. He had already successfully encouraged Mather on several occasions to carry on with the survey, for instance in 1801: 'Health is a valuable blessing too often sacrificed in our Indian pursuits; but you ought to consider that you are not the only person whose vocations call them into situations detrimental to health and that particularly every Military person in the Company's Service has no choice where their duty calls them', Colin Mackenzie to John Mather, 25 April 1801, NAI/SIR/SGO/90, 54–57, here 55. See details of Mackenzie's attitude in Robb, 'Completing "Our Stock of Geography"', 193f.

156. John Mather to Colin Mackenzie, 22 June 1806, BL/IOR/P/243/9, 5207–211, here 5208. It is one of history's bitter ironies that soon after coming home Mather was shipwrecked off the British coast and drowned. He left a part of his fortune to the magistrate in his hometown, who was meant to give scholarships to needy pupils at Marischal College. See Mather's will: BL/IOR/L/AG/34/23/209, 1–5; Phillimore, *Historical Records*, vol. 2, 429.

157. Cf. Colin Mackenzie to Thomas Munro, 25 August 1806, BL/OIOC/Mss Eur/F/151/9, 80f; also 28 January 1807, ibid., 142–45; George Keble to Colin Mackenzie, 15 December 1802, NAI/SIR/SGO/3, 83f; John Malcolm to Colin Mackenzie, 2 March 1805, ibid., 497–503.

158. Cf. the correspondence between Mackenzie and Mather from the spring and summer of 1806, which the Board of Madras sent on to London: BL/IOR/P/243/9, 5186–211. See also Colin Mackenzie to John Mather, 30 August 1806, NAI/SIR/M/18, 192; also 11 September 1806, ibid., 197.

159. Colin Mackenzie to Barry Close, 14 October 1801, NAI/SIR/M/6, 295–97; id. to J.H. Peel, 25 October 1803, NAI/SIR/SGO/90, 422f; also 26 November 1803, ibid., 425–27.

160. Colin Mackenzie to Major Shawe, 25 June 1805, NAI/SIR/M/18, 121–24, here 122f.

161. Colin Mackenzie to Thomas Munro, 25 August 1806, BL/OIOC/Mss Eur/F/151/9, 80f, here 81.

162. For details see A. Bell, *The Madras School or Elements of Tuition, Comprising the Analysis of an Experiment in Education, Made in the Male Asylum, Madras, with is Facts, Proofs and Illustration* (London, 1808).

163. Cf. CD to B (Rev.), 5 August 1796, BL/IOR/E/4/882, 718–26; John Goldingham to Travers, 24 April 1800, BL/IOR/F/4/165 (2829), 19–29 with a list of all current and former pupils.

164. Cf. Colin Mackenzie, 'Establishment for Capt. Mackenzie Superintending the Mysore Survey for a Month of 30 Days', 4 February 1800, NAI/SIR/M/6, 69.

165. Colin Mackenzie to Reverend Mr Herr, Male Asylum, 14 December 1799, NAI/SIR/M/6, 38f; see also id. to Josiah Webbe, 5 November 1799, ibid., 24.

166. Both Burke and Lantwar are included in the asylum's list of pupils from 1789/1790. Cf. Bell, *Madras School*, 220–23.

167. Cf. Barry Close to Colin Mackenzie 7 January 1800, NAI/SIR/SGO/3, 329–36; George Buchan to Mackenzie, 9 February 1801, ibid., 47–49; Mackenzie to John Goldingham, 11 March 1801, NAI/SIR/SGO/90, 395.

168. Cf. John Goldingham to George Buchan, 19 February 1801, NAI/SIR/SGO/3, 53; Colin Mackenzie, 'Second General Report', NAI/SIR/REP/2, 243f, 348; id., 'List of Apprentices now with the Mysore Survey attached from the Company's School', 13 June 1805 and 'Return of the Apprentices from the Surveying School attached to the Mysore Survey attached since its Commencement in 1799', 15 June 1805, NAI/SIR/M/18, 115f.

169. Cf. Colin Mackenzie to J.H. Peile, 10 December 1801, NAI/SIR/SGO/90, 410f; George Keble to Colin Mackenzie, 16 January 1802, NAI/SIR/SGO/3, 59–61; Mackenzie to John Chamier, 27 December 1801, NAI/SIR/M/6, 321f; id. to J.H. Peile, 27 December 1801, ibid., 322f; id. to John Warren and John Mather, 12 February 1802, ibid., 327.

170. Colin Mackenzie to Lord Clive, 24 October 1800, NAI/SIR/M/6, 199–210, here 206f. See also id. to John Goldingham, 11 March 1801, NAI/SIR/SGO/90, 395.

171. Cf. Colin Mackenzie, 'Second General Report on the Mysore Survey', 12 July 1803, NAI/SIR/REP/2, 17–35, here 32; John Mather, 'Journal of the Proceedings of the Survey in Mysore with an account of the Weather during 1804', NAI/SIR/M/12, 291–320, here 299f.
172. Cf. Colin Mackenzie to John Mather, 19 April 1802, NAI/SIR/SGO/90, 84f; also 13 January 1804, ibid., 115f; Mackenzie to William Bentinck, 23 June 1805, BL/OIOC/Mss Eur/F/228/39, No. 11, 13–16, here 14.
173. Cf. Colin Mackenzie to John Warren, 15 March 1801, NAI/SIR/M/6, 253; id. to John Goldingham, 15 March 1803, ibid., 254; Colin Mackenzie to John Chamier, 21 January 1803, ibid., 358 (=BL/IOR/F/4/152 (2598), 107–9); Lucius R. Burke to John Mather, 18 January 1801, NAI/SIR/SGO/90, 139.
174. Cf. Colin Mackenzie, 'Estimate of the Salary and Establishment for Mr Mather Assistant on the Mysore Survey (for 1 Month of 30 Days)' and 'Establishment for Capt. Mackenzie Superintending the Mysore Survey for a Month of 30 Days', 4 February 1800, NAI/SIR/M/6, 69; Mackenzie to George Buchan, 21 May 1801, ibid., 265.
175. Although Ross had already celebrated his birthday, on 17 May 1801, this regulation did not become effective retrospectively until 1802. See Colin Mackenzie to J.H. Peile, 25 March 1802, NAI/SIR/M/6, 331; id. to William Jones, 25 March 1802, ibid.; id. to John Chamier, 12 May 1802, ibid., 332.
176. Cf. Colin Mackenzie to George Buchan, 21 December 1803, BL/IOR/F/4/280 (6426), 65–67; George Keble to Mackenzie, 2 November 1803, NAI/SIR/SGO/3, 87–89; Buchan to Mackenzie, 14 January 1804, ibid., 95–97. See also 'Table of Pay and Allowances'.
177. 'Regulations for determing the System of Education to be followed at the Government Surveying School. Also fixing the Salary, Allowances, and Establishment of Revenue Surveyors employed under Collectors and Civil or Military Surveys and for defining the duties of the Office of Inspector of Revenue Surveys', 17 January 1807, NAI/SIR/SGO/8, 302–20. See also Colin Mackenzie, 'Statement of Expences incurred in Account of Boys of the Surveying School attached to different persons on the Mysore Survey since its Commencement under the Superintendance of Major Mackenzie in 1799', 13 June 1808, NAI/SIR/SGO/90A, 227; Thomas Gahagan, Dep. Sec. B Rev. (FSG) to Chief Sec. Gov. (FSG), 10 December 1810, BL/IOR/F/4/362 (9021), 73–82.
178. Colin Mackenzie to James Ross, 26 August 1803, NAI/SIR/M/18, 3f.
179. Cf. in detail Robb, 'Completing "Our Stock of Geography"', 191. See also John Mather, 'Journal of the Proceedings of the Survey in Mysore with an account of the Weather during 1804', NAI/SIR/M/12, 291–320, here 312.
180. Cf. Colin Mackenzie to George Buchan, 13 July 1807, NAI/SIR/SGO/90A, 39; George Keble to Colin Mackenzie, 18 July 1807, ibid.
181. Cf. Colin Mackenzie to Alexander Read, Superintending Collector of Canara, 19 January 1807, NAI/SIR/M/18, 208–10; id. to H.J. Grome, 19 January 1807, ibid., 210; id. to Benjamin Swain Ward, 22 January 1807, ibid., 211f; id. to James Summers, 23 January 1807, ibid., 121; Michael Dunigan, 'Journal of the Progress of a Survey through South Canara & Nuggur from March to June 1807', NAI/SIR/J/3, 109–142, esp. 111–13.
182. Cf. Colin Mackenzie to George Buchan, 10 September 1806, NAI/SIR/M/16, 190–96. Apparently the return was not immediately approved but Mackenzie was initially permitted to lodge with the Resident, Mark Wilks. See Colin Mackenzie to John Leyden, 30 April 1807, NLS/Ms 3380, 81–85.
183. Cf. Robb, 'Completing "Our Stock of Geography"', 190–92; Edney, *Mapping an Empire*, 176.
184. Cf. C.J. Hawes, *Poor Relations: The Making of a Eurasian Community in British India 1773–1833* (Richmond, 1996), 36–54; D. Arnold, 'European Orphans and Vagrants in India in the Nineteenth Century', *Journal of Imperial and Commonwealth History* 7 (1979), 104–27; D. Gosh, *Sex and the Family in Colonial India* (Cambridge, 2006), 35–68; 224–41. The

fathers' social status largely determined the sons' career chances, but among the three boys working on the Mysore Survey whose fathers can be identified there was one William Scott, son of a ordinary soldier. William Lantwar was a captain's son; Benjamin Swain Ward's father was a colonel. For Ward cf. Colin Mackenzie to Thomas Gahagan, 16 March 1809, NAI/SIR/SGO/90A, 53–55; for Lantwar cf. 'Asiatic Intelligence: Madras: Deaths', *Asiatic Journal and Monthly Register for British India and its Dependencies* 5(25) (January 1818), 89; for Scott cf. Edney, *Mapping an Empire*, 306.

185. The fact that Benjamin Swain Ward, son of an officer, later joined the army with Mackenzie's support, because it promised better remuneration and career opportunities, was an exception that proved the rule. Of the twenty-one Anglo-Indian surveyors at Mackenzie's disposal in 1815 in Madras he was the only one who had joined the army. Cf. Colin Mackenzie to Chief Sec. Gov., 14 December 1815, BL/IOR/F/4/554 (13476), 147–245, here 158, 237f. Mackenzie had supported Ward via Dr Berry, the nephew of Mackenzie's former mentor Dr James Anderson. Cf. Colin Mackenzie to Benjamin Swain Ward, 1 March 1810, NAI/SIR/SGO/90,17f; also 31 March 1810, ibid., 19f; 17 July 1810, ibid., 26–28; and 8 August 1810, ibid., 30.

186. Cf. Colin Mackenzie to George Buchan, 3 March 1808, NAI/SIR/M/18, 218–20.

187. Colin Mackenzie to George Buchan, 29 July 1808, NAI/SIR/M/18, 250–55; see also George Keble to Colin Mackenzie, 26 March 1808, NAI/SIR/SGO/3, 181–83; George Buchan to Mackenzie, 17 August 1808, ibid., 189; B (FSG) to CD (Public), 24 October 1808, BL/IOR/F/4/280 (6426), 11–15.

188. Colin Mackenzie, 'A General Map of Mysore comprehending the Territories ceded to the Rajah of Mysore, the Provinces ceded to the Honorable East India Company in Lower Canara and Soonda, and in the Eastern Districts extending from Ponganoor to the Cauvery River', drawn by Henry Hamilton, 27 February 1808, BL/IOR/X/9599 and seven provincial maps in BL/IOR/X/2108, 1–7 (with Index) of 1–17 October 1808.

189. Cf. Colin Mackenzie to George Buchan, 29 July 1808, NAI/SIR/M/18, 250–55, here 252; George Buchan to William Ramsey, 24 October 1808, BL/IOR/F/4/280 (6426), 17f; Colin Mackenzie, 'Brief View of the Collection of notes observations and Journals of 31 years and of Collections of Manuscripts, Inscriptions, drawings &ca. for the last 19 years made by Colonel Mackenzie in India, exclusive of a considerable collection of Native Manuscripts in all Languages of India', [1813/14], BL/IOR/F/4/867 (22924), 60–139, here 66.

190. Cf. Colin Mackenzie to Charles Wilkins, 25 October 1808, BL/OIOC/Mss Eur/Mack Gen/18, 275–78; id. to Acting Chief Sec. B (FSG), 29 February 1808, BL/IOR/F/4/280 (6426), 147–49; George Keble to William Ramsey, 29 February 1808, ibid., 7–9; Colin Mackenzie, 'Register of a Collection of Ancient Sassanums or Grants and Inscriptions, on Public Monuments, Pillars & Temples; or on Grants preserved in private hands (under the two Descriptions of Silla or Stone and Tambra or Copper) issued by the several Governments that have prevailed in Balla-Ghaat. Collected in the Course of several Journeys through Mysore, Bednore & Canara from 1804 to 1807 with an Appendix containing Copies of FacSimilies, Translations & Drawings of some of the Inscriptions registered, as Specimens of the Manner in which they may illustrate the Ancient History, Government, Institutions, Laws, Civil & Religious Tenures & the State of Property in the Country', Madras, 12 October 1807, BL/OIOC/Mss Eur/Mack Gen/18A. For the statue now in the Victoria and Albert Museum see Howes, *Illustrating India*, 72–74.

191. Mark Wilks to George Buchan, 4 March 1807, NAI/SIR/SGO/3, 565–71; John Malcolm to William Bentinck, 5 March 1807, ibid., 553–55; Minute in Council by Lord William Bentinck, n.d. [March 1807], ibid. 557–60; see also 'Extract of a General Letter from England in the General Department dated February 9 1809 to the Government of Fort St George', *Madras Journal of Literature and Science* 2(9) (1835), 364–69.

192. Cf. B (FSG) to CD, 24 October 1808, BL/IOR/F/4/280 (6426), 11–15; Colin Mackenzie to William Bentinck, 4 August 1804, BL/OIOC/Mss Eur/F/228/39, 4, No. 2; Bentinck to Mackenzie, 4 May 1804, ibid., No. 3. Mackenzie had aspired to this position from no later than 1801. Cf. Colin Mackenzie to William Kirkpatrick, 16/19 November 1801, BL/OIOC/Mss Eur/F/228/19.

193. Cf. Colin Mackenzie to John Leyden, 9 October 1810, NLS/Ms 3380, 136–39. Mackenzie explicitly mentions here Charles Grant's influence. See also 'Extract of a General Letter from England', 364–69.

194. Blake, 'Colin Mackenzie: Collector Extraordinary', 131.

195. Minute in Council by Lord William Bentinck, n.d. [March 1807?], NAI/SIR/M/18, 557–60; see also Mark Wilks to George Buchan, 4 March 1807, ibid., 565–71; John Malcolm to William Bentinck, 5 March 1807, ibid., 553–55.

196. In 1809, while still waiting for his remuneration, he stressed that he was not absolutely dependent upon it: 'Indeed I feel little obliged by them & if they & their System go to pot, I am not bound to bewail either their Justice or their Indulgence'. See Colin Mackenzie to Henry Trail, 2 August 1805, BL/OIOC/Mss Eur/F/228/39; id. to John Leyden, 13 November 1809, NLS/Ms/3380, 115–19, here 117.

197. By 1801 he could no longer write his own letters due to problems with his eyesight and in 1809 he wrote to Leyden that his sight was 'discouraging ' and was not really improving. Cf. Lucius Rawdon Burke to Thomas Arthur, 20 October 1801, NAI/SIR/SGO/90, 283; and Colin Mackenzie to John Leyden, 13 November 1809, NLS/Ms 3380, 115–19, here 116.

198. Colin Mackenzie to Henry Trail, 2 August 1805, BL/OIOC/Mss Eur/F/228/39.

199. Mackenzie had already been pursuing this idea since his time in Hyderabad. See Colin Mackenzie to William Kirkpatrick, 31 December 1799, NAI/SIR/M/6, 40–43.

200. For instance Captain Johnston of the Bombay Engineers, who from January 1801 was supposed to support the survey by carrying out surveying in Canara, became ill after just a few days and was recalled to his corps in the same year without ever being able to carry out the task he had been given. Cf. Colin Mackenzie to Captain Johnston, 8 October 1800, NAI/SIR/M/6, 193; also 16 November 1800, ibid., 217–19, id. to Barry Close, 4 January 1801, ibid., 239; id. to Johnston, 6 January 1801, ibid., 240f; Close to Mackenzie, 23 August 1800; NAI/SIR/SGO/3, 311–16; also 31 January 1801, ibid., 345–48; Colin Mackenzie, 'View of the State of the Mysore Survey on 1st October 1803', NAI/SIR/REP/2, 239–53, here 242.

201. Colin Mackenzie to Thomas Munro, 25 August 1806, BL/OIOC/Mss Eur/F/151/9, 80f, here 80.

202. Canara had always been mentioned as possibly part of the survey. But in 1801 Mackenzie was still emphasizing the view he had always held, that Canara should be surveyed by the 'Bombay Surveyors'. Colin Mackenzie to Captain Johnston, 7 July 1800, NAI/SIR/M/6, pp.141–44; id., 'Plan of the Mysore Survey and the Manner on which it is proposed to be executed', 28 January 1800, BL/IOR/P/254/52, 729–45, here 734f; Josiah Webbe to Colin Mackenzie, 4 November 1799, NAI/SIR/SGO/3, 9–12.

203. Colin Mackenzie to William Bentinck, 23 June 1805, BL/OIOC/Mss Eur/F/228/39, 15.

204. Colin Mackenzie to Thomas Munro, 25 August 1806, BL/OIOC/Mss Eur/F/151/9, 80f; also 28 January 1807, ibid., 142–45; and 1 May 1807, ibid., 161–63; id. to John Leyden, 30 April 1807, NLS/Ms/3380, 81–85; id. to George Buchan, 10 September 1806, NAI/SIR/M/18, 190–96; also 29 July 1808, ibid., 250–55.

205. See the Collector of Bellary's opinion: Frederick Gahagan to B Rev. (FSG), 5 December 1808, NAI/SIR/SGO/3, 200–4.

206. Colin Mackenzie, 'Statement of the present Expence & Establishment of the Mysore Survey with its probable Period by a Gradual Reduction on 1st May 1808', NAI/SIR/M/18,

253–55; id., 'Memorandum showing the Reduction of the Expence of the Mysore Survey to 1st February 1809', ibid., 265f.

207. Cf. George Keble to Colin Mackenzie, 18 February 1809, NAI/SIR/SGO/90A, 41f.
208. Colin Mackenzie to George Buchan, 10 September 1806, NAI/SIR/M/18, 190–96, here 193; also 29 July 1808, ibid., 250–55, here 250. Emphasis in the original.
209. Colin Mackenzie to W.B. Bayly, 7 September 1818, NAI/SIR/SGO/435D, 5–7, here 6.

Chapter 5

MAPPING HISTORY, PRODUCING TERRITORY

Cartographical Appropriation

From the early summer of 1799 onwards the population in various parts of Mysore was presented with a strange spectacle. It started with the arrival of thirty- to forty-strong groups of men, some of them soldiers, led by a European officer. Some were travelling on horseback, others on palanquins or on foot, bringing with them a huge amount of equipment on carts or carried by bearers. First of all, at an appropriate place, they set up a large central camp consisting of various tents, fire pits, and stalls for the animals they had brought along. In the days that followed, after talking to the local officials, the teams started work. Between two places that could be seen from a distance – mountain tops, protruding trees or pagoda towers – they cleared as straight a stretch as possible of natural impediments such as copses or bushes and then measured it using huge measuring wheels, iron chains or rods. They marked the end point of what they had measured with large, striking flags; all the region's higher elevations were likewise dotted with flags. For several weeks afterwards they travelled around the area using complicated instruments to measure the angles between the flags from various points, being shown boundary stones, villages and reservoirs, and recording all their observations in the form of sketches or notes in their field books. At the end of all this they gathered up their flags, dismantled their camp and left the region.

The surveying of the Indian landscapes, which generally took place directly after they had been conquered, had, either intentionally or otherwise, a clearly recognisable symbolic quality for the local population as well. It can easily be regarded as a variation of older rituals of imperial land-seizure, even though in India it was not so much a question of possession as a claim to rule.[1] The EIC's presence as a new power was made visible for the first time in many areas by the surveyors, and covering entire regions with flags signalled very clearly to the inhabitants what opportunities this new power had for seizing land. This staging of power was clearly understood by the local population, which led to a certain cautiousness on the part of the surveyors. A curious example of the turmoil that could be created by surveying procedures is the case of the surveyor Turnbull, who caused much irritation when, due to his myopia, he erected many more flags than was usually necessary.[2] Colin Mackenzie, of course, rejected a symbolic interpretation of his operations and attributed the disquiet they caused simply to the population's ignorance of scientific matters. He was, however, fully aware that precisely for this reason his project could only extend to areas under the Company's control: 'What speculations and suggestions it could give rise to among people who can scarcely separate the idea of taking possession of a Country from that of surveying it?', he asked himself, and was by no means sure 'whether the time is yet arrived when important considerations should be risked, and popular prejudices hazarded for an improvement of Science which however grand, is not there [in the non-British Territories] immediately necessary for use, as on the Sea Coast, and in our own Provinces'.[3]

The entanglement between cartography and imperialism is of course not only to be found in the symbolic practice of surveying. In both a practical and a propagandistic sense maps were useful and powerful instruments of Empire. They facilitated conquest and made territorial control possible.[4] From as early as the eighteenth century, they were laboriously reproduced in periodicals such as the *Gentleman's Magazine*, which popularized the idea of Empire amongst a public in Britain that was becoming increasingly familiar with maps.[5] What is more, as cartographic historians following John Brian Harley have argued, maps always comprise an ideological component: although they seem to be 'innocently' mathematized images of a physical reality and claim great authority as a representational form, they should also always be seen as an expression of ideas and ideologies buried beneath the 'mask of a seemingly objective science'.[6] Or, in the words of the literary scholar Graham Huggan: 'maps are ultimately neither copies nor semblances of reality but modes of discourse which reflect and articulate the ideologies of their makers'.[7]

As recent research has shown, this connection between mapping and power is not only true for imperial mapping but also, from a more general perspective, for the genesis of the modern state and its territory. Some studies demonstrate how early modern and modern states instrumentalized cartography, for instance for imposing taxes, tariffs and road charges[8] but in general there is a perceptible tendency to concentrate on examining the connection between cartographical practices and modern notions of territoriality – frequently in connection with the question of the formation of nations.[9] So maps are no longer regarded merely as instruments of the modern state; cartography and modern territorial state are seen as mutually constituting elements. On the one hand, from the early modern period onwards cartographical activities often served various sovereigns' attempts at centralization; on the other, the notion of a clearly defined territory, rationally divided into spatial units and subunits, is barely conceivable as the basis of administration without maps.[10] The idea that boundaries should be linear and that different spheres of rule should be clearly separated from one another, which supplanted an older acceptance of boundary regions as spaces where different claims to rule were intermingled, is also a result of visualization techniques used by modern cartography.[11]

These perspectives on the history of cartography are clearly also relevant for the South Asian context. In his influential work on the Great Trigonometrical Survey, the famous British geodetic surveying project of the nineteenth century, Matthew Edney demonstrates the extent to which the fundamental 'cartographical ideal' of precision and objective depiction could serve as an ideological crutch for British rule that was seen as rational and progressive. In this way the results of this surveying were indeed useful for the Empire, but of limited value to the administration on the ground.[12] Ian Barrow, whose book inspired the title of this chapter, stresses like Edney that map drawing served the production of 'territory'. Without going into the specific structures of territorial organization in any more detail, however, he contents himself with the fairly general conclusion that cartographical representations wrote a 'history of possession', promoted control over India, and ultimately were to allow British rule to appear legitimate and stable.[13]

The actual processes here, within which the British defined and arranged territory, can say a good deal about the character of British rule on the subcontinent. If route surveys reflected the overriding interest of the EIC in the movement of troops and goods, then Mackenzie's surveys can be seen as the first great project of surveying in India that went far beyond that interest by systematically collecting data needed for an effective administration. Combined with statistical and historical material, maps were to help solve a dilemma in the British administration that Bernardo Ammedeus Michael has described as the phenomenon of 'territorial illegibility'. This illegibility, according to Michael, was founded not only in the lack of precise maps, but also in a failure to understand political, social and cultural forms of organization that were different from contemporary European concepts.[14] In any case, as he later stated more specifically, maps that included precolonial forms of territorial organization were an essential prerequisite for creating a colonial territory in which certain principles of the modern state could be applied – one only has to think of the fact that the responsibility of certain legal or fiscal authorities is often organized along territorial lines.[15]

As the survey of Mysore was intended to promote administrative rather than military governability, the maps produced contained many details, for instance about the territory's internal organization, that were at best of secondary importance in military terms.[16] Of course this does not mean that the interests of the army were not considered at all, especially in the years immediately after conquest. It was impressed upon Mackenzie that surveying the external boundaries was his most urgent task.[17] The role played by concrete military considerations is demonstrated by the fact that he had to give up his original plan to start with the boundary between Mysore and the Nizam's sphere of rule in order to connect with his work from Hyderabad.[18] First of all he was sent to the northwest boundary with the Marathas, a particularly hot political potato, where there had already been further conflicts in 1800.[19] It was not until he had finished surveying this boundary – Mysore's only genuinely external one; otherwise it bordered territory either directly under British control or that of the Nizam and the Rajah of Coorg, who was largely powerless against the British – and had produced a detailed description of the fortifications there[20] that Mackenzie could start work on Mysore's interior. Here, of course, as was the case with later surveys led by him, military interests hardly played any further role.[21]

Systems of Reference

Mackenzie's abandonment of cartography for purely military objectives becomes clear from the fact that he turned away from the route surveys he had himself practised in Hyderabad. Although when covering long distances he and his assistants did continue to measure roads as well, sometimes producing detailed journals as they went along, this was mainly in order to be able to provide material quickly for military purposes.[22] The 'proper' survey however was based on triangulation, and therefore it seems rather misleading to regard it as a variant of transition between trigonometrical procedures and the older forms of topographical surveying.[23]

Unlike many earlier mappings that had relied on heterogeneous materials, uniformity of method was fundamental for Mackenzie's project. Given that the survey was conducted with a number of assistants that would change over time, he saw it as crucial to guarantee the coherence of the project and he did so by formulating a 'general plan'.[24] This seemed to be all the more important since the teams were allocated to individual regions that they were supposed to survey independently of one another. So he put together a 'General Heads of Instruction', a detailed series of instructions on how the work was to be carried out, which each of his assistants had to follow. He was convinced 'if that is adhered to, that the detailed surveys in several parts may be brought to coalesce and form one General Uniform Work'.[25] Largely in accordance with the partition treaty of 1799, he divided the area to be surveyed into a total of seven large regions, which were again subdivided into 174 *parganas* or subdistricts.[26] Each of the surveyors was to start by measuring an individual *pargana* in one of the regions, only moving on to neighbouring areas once work there was complete.

The methodological model for the cartographical part of the survey were the maps drawn by John Mather in Barramahal, based on what were then the most detailed trigonometrical measurements taken in India.[27] The many preserved reports on method show how fastidiously the survey of Mysore was executed. Base lines were frequently re-measured and difference in height was calculated in complicated and time-consuming procedures.[28] Mackenzie tried to make sure that his assistants worked with the most modern instruments available.[29] Each *pargana* should be measured according to the same procedure: using the highly visible endpoints of the base line measured on the ground the relative positions of similarly marked secondary stations should be calculated. On this basis, in a third step further triangulation was used to determine the relative positions of all features to be included in the map such as villages, tanks or forts. It was only for pragmatic reasons that some details such as the courses of rivers and roads between the established positions were investigated through other means. Triangulation thus clearly stood in the foreground of the survey. Nevertheless, the survey pursued goals that were different from those of other trigonometrical projects, especially that of William Lambton which came to be known as the Great Trigonometrical Survey and had completely different objectives.

Lambtons survey, still called 'astronomical' in early 1801, was initially planned to come in support of Mackenzie.[30] Its focus, however, was neither astronomical observation nor topographical detail. Lambton, through trigonometrical calculation, wanted to establish a general system of reference for determining positions according to latitude and longitude which could then be used by all other surveying projects in South India and would connect the East and the West coasts through a system of large-scale triangles. The high scientific content of this project is illustrated by the fact that the curvature of the earth was also supposed to be taken into account – in contrast to Mackenzie's work although he, unlike many of those responsible in Madras and London, did at least understand Lambton's approach.[31] The major achievement of the Great Trigonometrical Survey in the decades to follow was that the system of triangles initiated by Lambton was eventually extended to the entire subcontinent. Although this form of surveying was virtually useless for administrative purposes, the Great Trigonometrical Survey still became one of the most celebrated scientific projects carried out by the British in India because, combined with similar work from other parts of the world, it allowed deductions to be made about the size and shape of the globe.[32]

In this light it is quite understandable that Edney makes the following judgement of Mackenzie's survey, that 'there was little sense that the different triangulations would form some larger whole',[33] even though Mackenzie himself, of course, was keen to connect the individual parts of the survey with one another.[34] In particular the base lines should be set in relation to one another, which could, for instance, be achieved by a chain of stations and would allow corrections in the whole system.[35] So when measuring boundaries in 1801/1802 Mackenzie, with Arthur's support, developed a system of 212 triangles in all that linked the Tungha Badra in the northwest of Mysore with the Cavery in the southeast and was founded on two base lines roughly 140 miles apart.[36] Despite these efforts, however, the main initial aim was to render each *pargana* individually in a correct and self-contained system. That a 'larger whole' in the sense of the global system of reference aspired to by Lambton was of secondary significance is also illustrated by the fact that determining the positions of individual places according to longitude and latitude was only carried out for supplementary purposes, and in the course of the survey was increasingly replaced by Lambton's reference system.[37]

Largely forgoing establishing positions astronomically can be seen as a means of increasing efficiency; and, in fact, Lambton's triangulations made it more or less unnecessary to observe heavenly bodies. Neither Mackenzie nor Mather was an expert in astronomical measurement and in his original plan Mackenzie had already pointed out the need to employ an astronomer.[38] The decision to measure each *pargana* individually was also partly based on pragmatic considerations. Given the constant uncertainty as to whether the assistants could really be retained on a sustained basis, it was virtually inevitable that they should be given spatial units to deal with that were as small as possible and could be measured within an acceptable period of time. In particular, this should avoid surveyors being confronted with the almost impossible task of carrying on with a colleague's complex measurements and calculations, which in practice would have meant starting all over again.[39] In a largely unknown region, the *parganas* introduced in the partition treaty offered a useful principle for subdivision since their approximate position had already been established with the support of staff from Tipu's former administration.[40]

This method undoubtedly offered a number of practical advantages but, at the same time, it should be seen as part of a more comprehensive research aim. Mackenzie argued, for instance, that Mysore should only be regarded as part of the political landscape of the Deccan that had evolved historically, and that his research should facilitate a detailed understanding of it: 'in fact', he wrote as early as March 1800, 'these Surveys ... may be considered as forming a part of one *Great Work*, a *General Survey of the whole Deckan*, which is so intimately blended in its Divisions as well as Political Relations, that to be generally useful, as much as can be conveniently effected of the several Provinces should be embraced within its Compass'.[41] So he, too, had a concept of a 'larger whole'; it was just that his system of reference was not based on a mathematized observation of the globe, but on the historical geography of a cultural region. Bearing in mind his interest in 'Political arrangements, [and] Provincial Divisions of the

Deckan ... from the earliest time till the arrangement made by Asoph Jah',[42] his decision to make precolonial territorial organization in the form of *parganas* the basis of his surveying work points to far more than mere pragmatism: he had already started to show an interest in this territorial organization during his time in Hyderabad.

Exploring Precolonial Territorial Organization

In the 1790s British geographers and administrators had known for a long time that many of the successor states to the Mughal Empire had adopted its territorial organization. Despite considerable differences from region to region, some of which already existed during Mughal rule, and a certain ambiguity of terms, the hierarchical subdivision of the Mughal Empire into *subas* (provinces), *sarkars* (districts) and *parganas* (subdistricts) continued after it disintegrated.[43] In the course of the eighteenth century individual *subas*, like Bengal or Hyderabad, had largely emancipated themselves from the rulers in Delhi,[44] but from the start of their expansion the British were still faced with the other two subordinate territorial units. The need to make new boundaries binding after annexations and peace treaties was often enough in itself to make recourse to recognized territorial units unavoidable. Designations such as 'Northern Circars' (*sarkars*) or 'twenty-four parganas', as the first major British territorial possession since 1757 was called, are sufficient evidence of this.

The internal structures of the Mughal Empire had also aroused the interest of British orientalists. In the 1780s Francis Gladwin's translation of the *Ain-i Akbari* marked a milestone in their research. In the sixteenth century, during the rule of Akbar, its author, courtier Abul al-Fazl ibn Mubarak, had written a detailed description of the empire that also contained a list of all the *subas* and the *sarkars* and *parganas* under them.[45] But although this was a valuable source describing the territorial organization of the Mughal Empire and its successor states in northern India, and formed the basis of several relevant publications,[46] the south remained largely unknown: 'we have a standard for Hindoostan proper [northern India] in the time of Akbar', James Rennell still stated in the second edition of his *Memoir of a Map of Hindoostan* in 1792, 'but for the Deccan in general, no authority has ever come to my knowledge'.[47] In fact the Mughal Empire had not extended into the Deccan until about a hundred years after Akbar, under his successor Aurangzeb.

Even in northern India, knowledge of *parganas* was confined to names and approximate positions. In the medium term, lack of knowledge – and often lack of understanding – led to huge administrative problems. Even in negotiations about cession of territory by Indian states that were so characteristic of British expansion, the EIC was already faced with a dilemma: in general these agreements referred to unfamiliar territorial units so the British delegations often had no idea exactly which areas they were annexing.[48] For instance, the peace negotiations with Tipu Sultan after the victorious war of 1792 could only be successfully conducted with the help of the Marathas' and the Nizam's delegations, who were clearly far more familiar with the Mysore territory than the British. Although Tipu was playing for time and initially refused to make documents from his administration available, experts from these allies managed to compile a complete list of his administrative units which formed the basis of the territorial cessions of 1792 and the future partition treaty of 1799.[49]

It is certainly no coincidence that Mackenzie's papers include a copy of these negotiations[50] – the British lead negotiator, John Kennaway, was the first Resident under whom Mackenzie had served in Hyderabad.[51] Certainly by the time he was working for the Mysore commission these papers had become indispensable to Mackenzie, but his interest in the territorial organization of South India had already begun much earlier, as demonstrated by a list of further research desiderata contained in the memoir on his map of Hyderabad. 'In order to understand the frequent negotiations, and contests relative to territory and claims under various appellations', he wrote here,

> ... a clear idea of the Provincial Divisions of the Dekan, as it was arranged under the government of the descendants of Timur [the Mughals], is necessary, for tho' these Provinces are no longer subject to this race of Souvereigns, which formed and divided the ancient Kingdoms into Soubahs and Circars, gradually, in the order they were conquered, yet the Cessions and Transfers which have repeatedly taken place of late years, have constantly a reference to these principal arrangements.[52]

Along with Kennaway's successor, William Kirkpatrick, Mackenzie attempted to fill these gaps in knowledge. Kirkpatrick's networks afforded him certain access to the Nizam's archives and as a result of his many years' experience in the EIC's political line he also had excellent knowledge of Persian, which made dealing with these sources much easier.[53] So in the mid 1790s, when Mackenzie was drawing his general map of the Nizam's territory, Kirkpatrick was able to provide him with useful material. One of the most important manuscripts was the *Daftar Asufiah*, a tax register of 1668, written in Persian, containing a complete list of the Deccan's six *subas*, divided according to *sarkars* and *parganas*. Kirkpatrick had given Mackenzie extracts from the register;[54] until he managed to acquire his own copy of the *Daftar* via a middleman in Aurungabad in 1795,[55] which he had in part translated by his Indian co-workers.[56]

The way in which the EIC employees used their contacts with the local administration is illustrated above all by the emergence of another Persian-language register, called *Haqiqatha-i-Hindustan*, which Mackenzie received directly from its author Lachmi Narayan Shafiq in 1798. Similar in style to the *Daftar,* it represents a compilation of various administrative documents, which gives further details of the Deccan's territorial organization and documents the state of the provinces until 1789.[57] At this time Lachmi Narayan was one of the most important intellectuals at the Nizam's court.[58] He came from a family that for generations had gained experience in the administration. His father, Rai Mansaram, held one of the Nizam's highest administrative positions in Aurungabad and thus had access to the holdings in the archives of this ancient administrative centre that stretched back to the Mughal period. From here he sent the sources which his son used to compile the *Haqiqatha-i-Hindustan* at the request of William Kirkpatrick, to whom the copy retained in the British Library is dedicated.[59]

With the *Daftar Asufiah*, the *Haqiqatha-i-Hindustan* and the documents on the treaties of 1792 and 1799, when he started his Mysore Survey Mackenzie had access to materials giving detailed information about the precolonial territorial organization of large sections of South India. What was striking was that the subdivision into *parganas* – often called *taluks* in Mysore – could also be observed in those areas which, as border regions, were far less influenced by the administration of the Mughal Empire.[60] For this reason too it seemed clear to Mackenzie that the territorial organization of the Mughal Empire was, for its part, fundamentally influenced by older models. Although there could be no doubt, as generally assumed, that Akbar introduced this subdivision of the empire, there were, he maintained, more than just hints that it was primarily a pragmatic continuation of the organization in the states that preceded it. As he said, a fundamental principle of the Mughal Empire was 'to adopt such of the Ancient Institutions of the Countries subdued, as were not directly hostile to the Security & Supremacy of the New Government'.[61] The origins of this sort of territorial organization lay in the centuries before the birth of Christ, when the first states were formed and, because of their size, could no longer be governed by one single person.[62]

Mackenzie's decision to retain this historical continuity in his surveying work by taking the *pargana* system as the 'foundation of the Survey'[63] should be seen as part of his far-reaching 'historicist' agenda. Even the cartographical work was designed not to represent any break with the precolonial past but rather to do justice to the historical dimension of territorial organization that had developed over centuries. Mackenzie considered that this would be of great advantage to the British administration since it allowed them to use the administrative structures organized on the basis of the territorial subdivisions. This applied in particular to the precolonial tax administration, whose files could be used, he argued:

> in the Present Political System of the South the Standard thus formed of the relative value & Importance of the Territories of each State may be applied with considerable advantage in the existing circumstances at least until a more regular Permanent Adjustment can be formed both of the Territories occupied by the Native States & of those under the immediate Management of the British Government.[64]

This idea formed a key element in Mackenzie's 'historicist' conception of state organization under the EIC. Existing administrative practices should be adopted because they were better suited than any hasty innovation, whatever rational principles it were based on, to do justice to the social, cultural and economic structures that had evolved historically. Although he did not rule out changes and, at the request of his superiors for instance, made suggestions for adjusting the British sphere of rule by exchanging certain areas, this also applied to the forms of precolonial territorial organization which he deliberately wanted to adopt for his surveying work.

Cultural Sensitivity and Cartographical Logic

If Mackenzie was a pioneer in his theoretical preoccupation with South India's precolonial territorial organization, then the same can be said to an even greater degree of the fact that he was not content with theoretical knowledge but also wanted to measure the size and location of each individual *pargana* in the field. In the north of India, where the registers of the Mughal Empire had been available for quite some time, information about the approximate position had generally been deemed sufficient. The main reason for this must have been that in Bengal until the first decade of the nineteenth century it was more or less only routes that were surveyed and this method made it virtually impossible to measure boundaries, which of course were not visible from the roads. In 1801, for instance, the surveyor Fleming was instructed, when he arrived at a place, to enquire which particular *pargana* it belonged to and to ask a local official for the 'distance to which his Purgunnah extends in every directions, and whether any of the places within sight belong to any other Purgannah'.[65] If the outlines of *parganas* were mapped in this way, it only concealed lack of actual knowledge, since in administrative practice such maps were, of course, more or less useless.[66]

Michael has demonstrated the complications this caused for the British administration and stressed that they gave rise to an even greater desire for more accurate maps.[67] Presumably because his study concentrates on northern India, Michael dates the start of the systematic surveying of *parganas* to the 1820s and 1830s, ignoring Mackenzie's work on the Deccan. Colebrooke, however, Surveyor General of Bengal, had already assessed Mackenzie's map of Hyderabad: 'with regard to the Boundaries and Divisions of the Country … infinitely superior to any I have yet seen'.[68] Given the difficult conditions Mackenzie had worked under in the Nizam's territory, and his use of a much more sophisticated method, it is safe to assume that here his later surveys achieved even greater accuracy.

Unlike surveying roads, river courses or mountain ranges, mapping boundaries, unless they coincided with natural features, was totally impossible without local support. The entries in the registers could only be verified with the help of people with local knowledge: 'Tho' the accounts procured ... are at a distance frequently found obscure and apparently contradictory', Mackenzie reported, for example, in connection with his map of Hyderabad, 'yet upon the spot, the opportunity of discriminating and selecting, and of reconciling these seeming inconsistencies, by the aid of local knowledge, obviated these inconveniences, and rendered the information of real use, at least by facilitating further enquiry'.[69] While Mackenzie was able to take advantage of his superior's good contacts with the Nizam's administration here, which regularly assured him of support from local officials,[70] in the regions directly administered by the Company and in Mysore (where the boy Rajah's regent Purnaiya was controlled by the British Resident), there was an even better opportunity to secure local support, through official instructions.

At the start of the survey Mackenzie requested, via Resident Close, 'Orders from Purneah to the Amuldars or Managers of the Purgannas and Districts .... to furnish guides, information of the Boundaries and Landmarks, Lists & Names of the Villages & such other assistance or information as may be requisite ... for the purposes of the Survey to Capt. Mackenzie or those employed by him'.[71] The authority of the *dustucks* (passes) issued in Purnaiya's name was underscored by being accompanied by some of his *harkaras*.[72] Thus, support from local officials could generally be expected, including the provision of revenue documents giving details about district boundaries. On this basis it should, in theory, have been easy enough for Mackenzie to carry out the survey as he wanted. Once the stations had been flagged, all that had to be done was to establish the positions of the features to be included in the maps; in the case of villages, using lists, called *dehazadas*[73] that had been provided. Local staff could then show them the course of the boundary without further difficulty.[74]

In practice, however, things turned out to be much more complicated, and not only in cases of conflict with the local officials. While *dehazadas* were regularly consulted, they caused a certain amount of confusion because as far as the surveyors could see they did not correspond to the actual reality.[75] Some of the villages found were not listed in the documents, while others listed lay in ruins. The situation was further complicated by the fact that in the registers the villages were listed hierarchically as *asali* and *dakhali* villages[76], a distinction the surveyors interpreted as a division between 'large' and 'small' or 'original' and 'detached' villages, although they were unable to discern any generally valid system behind this.[77]

Despite these difficulties, Mackenzie thought the use of the registers to be indispensable, partly because of their potential value for revenue administration. However, at the same time, he regarded them as testimonies of a territorial organization that had lasted for centuries almost unchanged.[78] This was predicated on the idea that villages and their surroundings had to be seen as the smallest territorial unit in India and formed the basis of all larger territorial entities. This way of structuring territory had, in Mackenzie's eyes, hardly been touched by Muslim rulers:

> we find a Soobah or Province formed of what constituted a Dasum in the Ancient registers & sometimes Naads; comprehending nearly the same Purgunnahs or Subdivisions under the Names of Mahals & these composed again of the former Number of Villages or Mouzas & under arrangement which appears to have been general in the Deckan, if not throughout Hindostan, of Asselee & Dakelee or Original & Detached Villages – An Arrangement which it is apprehended originated in the Ancient System peculiar to India; of settling a Country by little communities in Groups of Villages instead of the European Mode of subdividing the Land into Estates & Farms occupied by single Families; a trail which seems to form a marked distinction in the Agricultural Oeconomy of India.[79]

Therefore, for Mackenzie village boundaries played a central role in the measurement of any boundaries, even if he considered it a practical impossibility to establish the boundaries of every village.[80] The only sections of village boundaries that should be surveyed were those that coincided with the external boundaries of a *pargana*. Given the modalities of partition in 1799, this by necessity included all external boundaries.[81]

When surveying boundaries the surveyors, with the support of local guides, could usually orientate themselves to generally recognized natural features such as isolated trees or, alternatively, landmarks which in Mackenzie's view were very old and had survived for centuries under various rulers: 'a religious observance of established Landmarks is firmly established in the superstitious prejudices of the Natives', he stated, 'for every village has its distinct landmarks & the destruction of the Country seldom affects these established Symbols even where a spirit of animosity has been long kept up'.[82] Although the surveyors could generally use these landmarks for orientation, there were indeed many cases where they were confronted with difficulties.

Mackenzie himself, for instance, reported on the boundary with the Ceded Districts that 'in several instances the Boundary passes through Corn fields where the limits are at least doubtful, and are frequent subjects of contention'.[83] In 1804 John Mather had to concede that his survey of part of the boundary of a *pargana* was useless because he had been shown an actual boundary that did not tally with the one mentioned in the partition treaty.[84] In the following year he not only had to admit that boundary stones placed by the British years earlier had since been moved, but also that the people of one *pargana* supposedly knew nothing about a fixed boundary with their neighbours.[85] So the surveyors, actually looking for the 'real boundaries',[86] were constantly forced into the role of referee in local conflicts. Arthur, for instance, declared that 'it was not ... [his] business to settle Boundaries but to survey such as ... [he] thought the right ones',[87] but often enough this turned out to be one and the same thing. In the Chittledroog district, for example, where there seem to have been regular boundary disputes between neighbouring *parganas,* the Resident stipulated explicitly that Mackenzie's surveying work should put a definitive end to these conflicts.[88] In such cases the surveyors tried, where possible, to reach a compromise by working together with those responsible on both sides. In 1804/1805, for instance, when Mackenzie was supposed to survey the boundary between Mysore and Coorg, which was not clearly defined in some places, he consulted with official delegations on both sides before establishing points where boundary stones should be laid. Other sections of the boundary were clearly marked by a sort of fence.[89]

The most important prerequisite for settling boundary conflicts harmoniously was both parties' willingness to cooperate, but this was certainly not always a given. When surveying the boundary with the Ceded Districts, for example, Mackenzie was only given support by officials from Purnaiya's administration; the *amildars* in the Ceded Districts, however, refused any sort of cooperation. The situation was further complicated by the fact that trees recognized as marking the boundary had obviously been felled recently and the boundary stones moved.[90] Pressure from Collector Munro and help from Mysore meant that Mackenzie was still able to map the dubious boundary, but years later he was still complaining about how difficult this work had been, implying that in this area his map did not really come up to his own standards.[91] Thomas Arthur had a similar experience in 1805. The background to all this seems to be that a section of the boundary had not been fixed until Tipu Sultan's time and was not accepted by a number of villages.[92]

The fact that surveyors were being used as referees for local conflict clearly suggests that an awareness of these boundaries existed among villagers, even if their exact position was often contentious.[93] At the same time, the course of action taken by the surveyors proves their unwillingness to change boundaries arbitrarily. It is true that Mackenzie made a number of suggestions for rearrangement during his survey, but this did not signify the wish for any fundamental restructuring of territory – on the contrary, exact surveying of the internal boundaries was to facilitate an exchange of territorial units on the lines of the structures detailed in the precolonial files.[94] And even where he suggested that exclaves should be integrated into the surrounding *parganas,* this can be interpreted as aiming at the restoration of an earlier situation, as these exclaves in a sense formed an aberration from the principles of the 'ancient proprietors': 'this intermixture of districts arising from causes long ceased ... might now without inconvenience give way to a more simple system of Internal Arrangement'.[95]

Mackenzie's approach to mapping, whatever its results, did certainly not simply aim at reducing India to a mathematized space that could be known 'without having to worry about the particulars'.[96] The pains he took to understand and preserve the precolonial systems of organizing territory in a way seems to qualify Robb's argument that Mackenzie followed 'objective' rather than 'men-made' criteria in his surveys.[97] Mackenzie, for example, advised his surveyors to map villages listed in the *dehazadas* separately, even where they merged[98] – this indicates that in at least some instances he privileged cultural and political history over observable criteria. Certainly such an approach also served to facilitate the use of precolonial archives for the administration of revenue – however, given Mackenzie's interest in Indian geography that went far beyond pure measurement, it might also be understood as part of a greater vision of connecting British rule to institutions that were of ancient origin and survived all kinds of rulers through the centuries.

Nevertheless, it is true that Mackenzie's maps followed a seemingly 'objective' and 'universal' understanding of space in which it was reduced to 'a matter of physical location'.[99] This points to the paradox of his cartographical work that he himself might have been only partially aware of: the cultural sensitivity that characterized his surveys, and the logic of European cartography stood in insurmountable tension with each other. As a matter of necessity, European mappings were based on the idea of an abstract, mathematized space in which place was defined through geographical coordinates and which offered only very limited opportunity to integrate differing cultural perspectives. Mackenzie attempted to balance this problem through certain procedures, for instance when he insisted on the transcription of place names according to the Jonesian system, not only to avoid confusion but also to be able to decode their cultural and historical meanings through etymological analysis.[100] But of course this did not relieve him of the need to follow cartographic logic, such as in cases where 'new' villages not mentioned in the registers had indeed to be mapped on the sole basis of their physical location. In many instances cultural sensitivity had to be replaced by the logic of the European map. While Mackenzie and his assistants tried, on the one hand, to understand a historically grown administrative space according to its own logic, on the other hand they continuously redefined it according to the rules of European cartography.

Producing Territory

Since Mackenzie used the representational form of European cartography he was forced to bow to its implicit logic.[101] The maps produced by Mackenzie and his co-workers reveal little of the uncertainties and ambiguities that accompanied the surveying project. In their wealth of detail and efforts to reproduce the precolonial territorial organization in the form of *parganas* as authentically as possible, they set standards that were to prevail for most of the nineteenth century. Looking at a page from the atlas of the Ceded Districts (Figure 5.1) the characteristics typical of maps produced following his system can easily be seen: it shows several *parganas* put together in groups that are distinguished from one another by clear boundaries. Equally clearly distinguished are areas that were isolated within the boundaries of another *pargana*.

However, the most telling sign that *parganas* were regarded as the fundamental territorial units is the fact that the edges of the page beyond the boundaries are shown on the map as a white area – only mountains and towers that served as stations for the surveying and small areas beyond the boundaries are

Figure 5.1 'Plan of the Districts of Hunda-Annantapur, Durmawaram, Taudamurry & Taudaputree. Surveyed in 1810–11', sheet 9 of the *Atlas of the Provinces ceded by the Nizam in 1800 to the Honble East India Company from Surveys executed from 1809 to 1815'. Source:* © The British Library Board BL/IOR/X/2314/9.

included. And obviously it is not designed to give much information about geographical position according to degrees of longitude and latitude, even if cardinal directions are inserted.

The map shows the topography of the respective *parganas* in great detail (see Figure 5.2). Mackenzie had given his co-workers detailed instructions about which objects should be drawn on the maps. These included forts and villages, which should be identified by various typefaces and symbols according to their significance and condition; likewise roads, water courses and boundaries. Lakes and irrigation sites should also be included but not measured exactly because the water level and the surface area changed with the seasons. An exact distinction was to be made between cultivated land, wasteland, jungles, swamps or mountains, thus anticipating British interests in the country's revenues.[102] In the Ceded Districts, where Mackenzie's assistants were supposed to take account of the British Collector's interests, *inam* villages, which were exempt from regular taxation, were given a special colour code. One characteristic of virtually all maps produced under Mackenzie is their high degree of uniformity and compatibility. Particularly striking is the scale used, which, after a period of experimentation during the survey of Mysore, was fixed at one inch to two miles.[103]

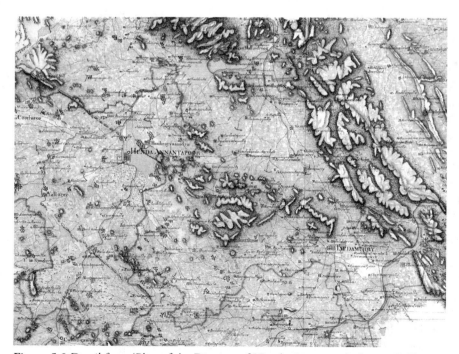

Figure 5.2 Detail from 'Plan of the Districts of Hunda-Anantapur'. *Source:* © The British Library Board BL/IOR/X/2314/9.

Individual pages that conformed to strongly defined criteria could, as in the case of Mysore and the Ceded Districts, be compiled into regional atlases, typically accompanied by maps covering a larger area on a smaller scale.[104]

Although hardly any map actually drawn by Mackenzie was published during his lifetime[105] a considerable amount of material now generally accessible is based on his work. His idea of an atlas that allowed more stretches of land to be added in depending on the progress of the surveying work and the state of British conquest proved to be particularly influential.[106] From the late 1820s successive versions of the *Atlas of India* were published and this was to continue for almost a hundred years; it not only adopted Mackenzie's idea of continuous updating, but its first pages were essentially based on his work. Due to the expected size of this atlas, however, a much smaller scale of one inch to four miles was used.[107]

Both the numerous hand-drawn maps produced under Mackenzie's aegis and the *Atlas of India* – intended by Mackenzie to avoid the time-consuming process of copying maps requested by different government departments by hand in future – were primarily meant for practical use and to make administrative work easier. At the same time, of course, by presenting a picture of an ordered, intelligible and thus governable landscape they should also be seen as part of the cultural production of modern territory: every settlement, every mountain, every fortification and every jungle in its place determined by objective criteria, marked with a geometric symbol; clear and consistent subdivisions in the form of boundaries that could be reproduced without any doubt. The maps indeed transported an illusion of 'territorial legibility' that could form a basis for the idea of an ordered and delimited territory.

So the maps also represented part of a process in which alternative notions of space were increasingly dominated by those of the modern state. It is not that they reproduced space incorrectly, according to their own logic: the American archaeologist Barry Lewis, for instance, has compared the original survey maps with his own studies and discovered that the places drawn in generally correspond so well with the buildings, ruins and other remnants that still exist today that he sees them as a suitable basis for a spatial analysis of Mysore's cultural geography at the time of the British conquest.[108] What is more, through computer analysis of the maps he has established that *parganas* can often be regarded as the sphere of influence of one single large town, which has been confirmed by social historians using a quite different methodological approach. Indeed it seems that the boundary drawn by the surveyors on their maps actually did correspond – roughly – to territorial units that had evolved historically.[109]

Nonetheless, as Peter Robb has noted, greater changes can perhaps be attributed to Mackenzie's project than just the fixing and locating of what was previously rather vague.[110] If one accepts the idea that conceptions of space among the population of South India were moulded by a number of coexisting systems of meaning bequeathed by different rulers, religions and social groups through the centuries, it becomes clear that the surveyors' decision to use precolonial official documents had been highly consequential, as it privileged understandings of space closely linked to the interest of rulers. Through this perspective and in following the rules of European cartography, the surveyors necessarily marginalized alternative forms of conceptualizing space. In this sense, the maps resulting from Mackenzie's surveys may indeed be seen as 'colonial text' in which alternative conceptions of topography can only be found by reading 'between the lines' – if at all.[111]

The interest in historically grown territorial structures that characterized Mackenzie's surveys means, however, that his project – arguably in much greater measure than the Great Trigonometrical Survey, for instance – would have been impossible without the active cooperation of Indian intellectuals and administrators. The fact that they not only provided vital documents, but also sought to influence the cartographical activities, may illustrate that this was not the case where active agents of colonial rule opposed a passive population whose indigenous knowledge formations were uncompromisingly replaced by European notions. Thus, this cartographical production of territory should not be seen primarily as a radical break with a precolonial past that was fundamentally different. It might well be, for instance, that the *parganas* as territorial subdivisions mattered most to rulers, but they were certainly also of some local significance.[112] Accepted landmarks did exist in many cases, and the delimitations of the *parganas*, even where not as clearly defined as the surveyors' records would later suggest, formed part of local populations' understanding of space, beyond the circles of administrative officials. Thus, the possibility of adopting the *parganas'* boundaries, but also attempts on the part of the population to manipulate these boundaries for their own ends, show that it was not a question here of two diametrically opposed concepts of space, irreconcilable in principle.

It should also be noted that the replacement and transformation of traditional concepts of space brought about by the EIC surveyors' mapping of India was by no means a unique colonial process; very similar processes can be observed all over the world where the modern territorial state was gaining ascendency. Whether in early modern Venice, eighteenth-century France or postcolonial Mexico, boundaries were sought and fixed everywhere, places defined and clearly named, and ultimately, by taking up a multitude of further information, images produced of ordered territories. The fact that alternative conceptions of space were increasingly marginalized, and in some cases lost sight of altogether, was an inevitable result of this process. In any case, at the end of it stands a phenomenon which to modern people seems as obvious as it is banal: the fact that on our mental maps we automatically associate the notion of a state with that of a clearly defined and integrated territory.

Notes

1. For older rituals in the American context see J.H. Elliott, *Empires of the Atlantic World: Britain and Spain in America 1492–1830* (New Haven and London 2006), 30–32. For the symbolic quality of British surveys in India see also Edney, *Mapping an Empire*.
2. Cf. B. Ward to Colin Mackenzie, 28 November 1816, NAI/SIR/SGO/573, 246–52, also 28 March 1817, ibid., 263–66.
3. Colin Mackenzie to Barry Close, 10 December 1799, NAI/SIR/M/6, 35–37, here 36.
4. Highly influential in putting this argument forward: J.B. Harley, 'Maps, Knowledge, and Power', in D. Cosgrove and S. Daniels (eds), *The Iconography of Landscape: Essays on the Symbolic Representation, Design and Use of Past Environments* (Cambridge Studies in Historical Geography vol. 9) (Cambridge, 1988), 282.
5. Cf. E.A Reitan, 'Popular Cartography and British Imperialism: The Gentleman's Magazine, 1739–1763', *Journal of Newspaper and Periodical History* 2(3) (1986), 2–13; and K. Wilson, *The Island Race: Englishness, Empire and Gender in the Eighteenth Century* (London and New York, 2003), 32f.
6. J.B. Harley, 'Deconstructing the Map', *Cartographica* 26(2) (1989), 3, 7.
7. G. Huggan, *Territorial Disputes: Maps and Mapping Strategies in Contemporary Canadian Fiction* (Toronto, Buffalo and London, 1994), 11.
8. See for example D. Schlögl, *Der planvolle Staat: Raumerfassung und Reformen in Bayern, 1750–1800* (Munich, 2002); R.J.P. Kain and E. Baigent, *The Cadastral Map in the Service of the State: A History of Property Mapping* (Chicago, 1992); and D. Buisseret (ed.), *Monarchs, Ministers, and Maps: The Emergence of Cartography as a Tool of Government in Early Modern Europe* (Chicago, 1992).
9. See for example A. Landwehr, *Die Erschaffung Venedigs: Raum, Bevölkerung und Mythos 1570–1750* (Paderborn and Munich, 2007), 20–192; R.B. Craib, *Cartographic Mexico: A History of State Fixations and Fugitive Landscapes* (Durham and London, 2004); and M.G. Hannah, *Governmentality and the Mastery of Territory in Nineteenth-Century America* (Cambridge, 2000), 113–49. J.W. Konvitz's work on France is pioneering: J.W. Konvitz, 'The Nation-State, Paris and Cartography in Eighteenth- and Nineteenth-Century France', *Journal of Historical Geography* 16(1) (1990), 3–16; id., *Cartography in France 1660–1848: Science, Engineering, and Statecraft* (Chicago and London, 1987). For cartography and nation building see of course B. Anderson, *Imagined Communities: Reflections on the Origin and Spread of Nationalism*, revised edn. (London and New York, 2006) and, for example, D. Guggerli and D. Speich, *Topografien der Nation: Politik, kartografische Ordnung und Landschaft im 19. Jahrhundert* (Zurich, 2002); and W. Kivelson, *Cartographies of Tsardom: The Land and its Meanings in Seventeenth Century Russia* (Ithaca and London, 2006).
10. Cf. R.B. Craib, 'A National Metaphysics: State Fixations, National Maps, and the Geo-Historical Imagination in Nineteenth-Century Mexico', *Hispanic American Historical Review* 82(1) (2002), 67f; M. Biggs, 'Putting the State on the Map: Cartography, Territory and European State Formation', *Comparative Studies in Society and History* 41(2) (1999), 398; and M. Escolar, 'Exploration, Cartography and the Modernization of State Power', *International Social Science Journal* 151 (1997), 73f.
11. Cf. Biggs, 'Putting the State on the Map', 385–87.
12. Cf. Edney, *Mapping an Empire*, 336.
13. Cf. Barrow, *Making History, Drawing Territory*, 183–85.
14. B.A. Michael, 'Separating the Yam from the Boulder: Statemaking, Space, and the Causes of the Anglo-Gorkha War of 1814–1816' (Ph.D. dissertation, University of Hawaii, 2001).

15. B.A. Michael, 'Making Territory Visible: The Revenue Surveys of Colonial South Asia', *Imago Mundi* 59(1) (2007), 78–95.

16. Contrary to Michael Mann's view that in the colonial context cartography, following James Rennell's model but especially after 1804, was confined to military objectives, Mackenzie's project certainly aimed to gain, 'insight into the indigenous local economic structures and communication systems'. See M. Mann, 'Mapping the Country: European Geography and the Cartographical Construction of India, 1760–90', *Science, Technology and Society* 8 (2003), 38f.

17. Cf. Colin Mackenzie, 'View of the State of the Mysore Survey on 1st October 1803', NAI/SIR/REP/2, 239–53, here 239. The first surveying work in the conquered areas in Bengal had already followed this scheme of privileging external boundaries, as demonstrated by the procedures used by the Company's first official surveyor after Plassey, Hugh Cameron. Cf. B (FW) to CD, 8 April 1762, *FWIHC*, vol. 3, 417.

18. For this plan see Colin Mackenzie to Arthur Wellesley, 7 March 1800, NAI/SIR/M/6, 85; Colin Mackenzie to Lord Clive, 24 October 1800, ibid., 199–210.

19. Josiah Webbe to Colin Mackenzie, 5 March 1800, NAI/SIR/SGO/3, 41; see also Richard Wellesley to Lord Clive, 4 February 1800, ibid., 43. In particular there was open conflict with the rebel Dundia Wagh, who was fought by Arthur Wellesley. Cf. Beaglehole, *Munro*, 40–42.

20. Colin Mackenzie, 'Remarks on Forts along the Northern Frontier of Mysore in 1800 & 1801. Extracted from the Papers of the Mysore Survey', NAI/SIR/REP/2, 169–219; id., 'Comparative View of the Forts of Ghooty and Ballary from a cursory Inspection in February 1801', ibid., 222–35.

21. Cf. Colin Mackenzie, 'On the State of the Mysore Survey', 25 June 1805, NAI/SIR/M/18, 121–24, here 123.

22. On the way from Vellore to Bangalore, for instance, Mackenzie also surveyed roads, but only 'as far as they will not delay my Journey'. He apologized to Arthur Wellesley for only having been able to collect a small amount of military information because his project had other priorities: Colin Mackenzie to Barry Close, 24 March 1800, NAI/SIR/M/6, 96f. See also 20 March 1800, ibid., 89–92, here 92; id. to Arthur Wellesley, 31 July 1804, SUL/WP/3/3/100; and id., 'View of the State of the Mysore Survey on 1st October 1803', NAI/SIR/REP/2, 239–53, here 248. See also the maps in Thomas Arthur and Colin Mackenzie, 'The Roads from No. I Bangalore to Needgul; II Needghul to Shullor; III. Shullor to Sera; IV u. V Chittledroog by Myconda to Hurryhurr. On a Scale of two British Miles to one Inch', 30 June 1800, BL/IOR/X/2110/1–5. Hamilton wrote a detailed journal of a route survey in the context of the Mysore Survey: Henry Hamilton, 'Field Book containing the Survey of Conjeveram &c. commencing May 1808', NAI/SIR/FB/38, 59–141, here 65–107.

23. For this perspective cf. Edney, *Mapping an Empire*, 177; and Barrow, *Making History, Drawing Territory*, 77–79.

24. Colin Mackenzie to Barry Close, 31 October 1800, NAI/SIR/M/6, 197f. Statements by John Mather on this subject show that at this time triangulations were also by no means all based on the same method: 'from the yet infant state of surveying, no one general & decisive plan of operation has been determined upon; one carries on the process, by a continued mensuration of sides & angles, or by a continued chain of triangles; some measure their distances with the Wheel, some with the Chain, & other with Rods ... One takes his angles with the needle, one with Theodolite or Sextant, & a third with a common compass; the way in which one proceeds in a Survey necessarily restricts his performance; another takes a method by which he surveys more in a year, than the other could in three, & even after the materials are collected, no two surveyors probably arrange or construct their Maps by them, or even keep their field notes the same way; though all to the same purpose', John Mather,

'Memoirs and Documents of a Survey of Akosgury, Sologury, Bauglore, Oussoor, Rulnagury, & Denkanikota in Mysore. Executed in 1800–01', NAI/SIR/M/10, 6.

25. Colin Mackenzie, 'View of the Progress of the Survey of Mysore and the Present State in January 1802', BL/OIOC/Mss Eur/F/228/39; see also id., 'General Heads of Instructions for the Geometrical and Geographical Survey of a Purgunna (a Hobely in Mysore)', ibid.; another copy in NAI/SIR/REP/2, 83f.

26. Colin Mackenzie, 'Plan of the Mysore Survey and the Manner on which it is proposed to be executed', BL/IOR/P/254/52, 28 January 1800, 729–45, here 734f. See also 'Treaty for strengthening the Alliance and Friendship subsisting between the English East India Company Bahadoor, His Highness the Nawab Nizam-ood- Dowlah Ausuph Jah Bahadoor, and the Peishwa Rao Pundit Prudhan Bahadoor and for effecting a settlement of the dominions of the late Tipoo Sultan, 22 June 1799', in Aitchison, *Collection of Treaties*, vol. 9, 53–61; see also Colin Mackenzie, 'Second General Report on the Mysore Survey', 12 July 1803, NAI/SIR/REP/2, 17–35, here 17.

27. The similarities are clearly manifested in Mather's presentation of his method in the introduction to his memoir on surveying in Salem and Barramahal. See John Mather, 'Records of the Barramahl & Salem &c. Districts – Section IInd, Geography', NAI/SIR/M/1, esp. 7–15; see abridged version as 'Memoir of a Map & Records of the Baramahal & Salem Districts', BL/OIOC/Mss Eur/Mack Gen/46 (14), 171–232.

28. John Mather, 'Journal of the Proceedings of the Survey in Mysore with an account of the Weather during 1804', NAI/SIR/M/12, 291–320, here 297–300; id., 'Memoirs and Documents of a Survey of Akosgury, Sologury, Bauglore, Oussoor, Rulnagury, & Denkanikota in Mysore. Executed in 1800–01', NAI/SIR/M/10, 7–9; id., 'Journal of the Proceedings of the Survey in Mysore with an account of the Weather during 1805', NAI/SIR/M/12, 323–43; Thomas Arthur, 'An Account of the Measurement of a Base Line near Hurryhur in August 1800, under the direction of Capt. C. McKenzie, Superintendant Mysore Survey', ibid., 21–40; id., 'Account the Measurement of a Base Line near Ballapoor in December 1801', NAI/SIR/REP/2, 89–95.

29. Mackenzie warned Mather, for example, who was still measuring angles with his compass in Barramahal, not to rely on this alone. He made sure that all the boys from the surveying school were equipped with theodolites. Cf. Colin Mackenzie to John Mather, 10 March 1801, NAI/SIR/M/6, 249f; John Mather, 'Records of the Barramahl & Salem &c. Districts - Section IInd, Geography', NAI/SIR/M/1, 16; Colin Mackenzie to John Chamier, 21 January 1803, NAI/SIR/M/6, 358; Mackenzie to James Ross, 26 August 1803, NAI/SIR/M/18, 3f.

30. Cf. Josiah Webbe to William Lambton, 6 February 1800, NAI/SIR/SGO/3, 25–29; id. to Colin Mackenzie, 6 January 1800; ibid., 19–24; Colin Mackenzie to Barry Close, 10 December 1799, NAI/SIR/M/6, 35–37; also 5 January 1800, ibid., 43–45. The government order that Lambton and Mackenzie should work closely together is the basis of Rennell's later confusion of the two projects.

31. At an early stage he was already describing this survey as 'spherical'. Cf. Colin Mackenzie to Barry Close, 10 December 1799, NAI/SIR/M/6, 35–37, here 35; and id., 'View of the State of the Mysore Survey on 1st October 1803', NAI/SIR/REP/2, 239–53, here 241. For details of Lambton's method, aims and models see William Lambton, 'A Memoir containing an account of the principal operations of the Survey carried on in Mysore in the Year 1801 and explaining the general principles on which it has been conducted', NAI/SIR/M/12, 14–104; id., 'An Account of a Method for extending a Geographical Survey across the Peninsula of India', *Asiatic Researches* 7 (1801), 312–35.

32. For the broader scientific context of the project see M.R. Hoare, *The Quest for the True Figure of the Earth: Ideas and Expeditions in Four Centuries of Geodesy* (Aldershot and Burlington, Vermont, 2005).

33. Edney, *Mapping an Empire*, 177.

34. Beyond Mysore's borders as well. For instance he initially sent John Mather to the border region between Mysore and the Barramahal so that he could link up with the measurements he took there. Cf. Colin Mackenzie to Josiah Webbe, 5 November 1799, NAI/SIR/M/6, 24; id. to Barry Close, 9 November 1799, ibid., 27–33.

35. Cf. for example Colin Mackenzie to John Warren, 21 January 1800, NAI/SIR/M/6, 63f; id. to John Mather, 8 May 1800, ibid., 104f; also 18 January 1801, ibid., 243; id. to William Morison, 7 October 1802, ibid., 345–47, here 346.

36. Cf. Colin Mackenzie, 'Memoir of the Method followed in carrying on the Survey of the Boundary & Northern Provinces of the Mysore Dominions & of the Series of Triangles carried on for that purpose on which is founded the Geometrical Construction of the Charts of the Survey executed in 1800 and 1801', NAI/SIR/REP/2, 49–70, here 68.

37. The material Mackenzie collected for determining positions suggests that at first it was mainly Thomas Arthur who took the astronomical measurements, while in the later years of the survey this was largely taken over by Lambton. See Thomas Arthur, 'Abstract of a Set of Astronomical Observations made on a journey in the Northern parts of Mysore in 1800 and 1801', BL/OIOC/Mss Eur/Mack Gen/60, 251–77 (copy NAI/SIR/REP/2, 143–67); 'Latitudes and Longitudes of Places in India from various Authorities communicated by Mr Goldingham Astronomer to Govt. in 1803', ibid., 211–22; and 'Positions of the Principal Points of the Trigonometrical Survey of the Upper & Lower Carnatic & Mysore by Major Lambton from 1800 to 1807. Communicated by Major Lambton', ibid., 281–99.

38. Colin Mackenzie, 'Plan of the Mysore Survey and the Manner on which it is proposed to be executed', BL/IOR/P/254/52, 28 January 1800, 729–45, here 734. Mather's surveying of the Barramahal was planned to be supplemented by astronomical measurements taken by someone else later: cf. John Mather, 'Records of the Barramahl & Salem &c. Districts - Section IInd, Geography', NAI/SIR/M/1, 7.

39. Cf. Colin Mackenzie to Barry Close, 9 November 1799, NAI/SIR/M/6, 27–32, here 29.

40. Cf. Colin Mackenzie, 'Memoir of the Construction of the Map of the Partition of Mysore at Seringapatam', June 1799, BL/OIOC/Mss Eur/Mack Gen/60, 135–38, here 137.

41. Colin Mackenzie to Josiah Webbe, 10 March 1800, NAI/SIR/M/6, 86f. Emphases in the original.

42. Colin Mackenzie, 'Brief View of the Collection of notes observations and Journals of 31 years and of Collections of Manuscripts, Inscriptions, drawings &ca. for the last 19 years made by Colonel Mackenzie in India, exclusive of a considerable collection of Native Manuscripts in all Languages of India', [1813/14] BL/IOR/F/4/867 (22924), 60–139, here 74.

43. Cf. Michael, 'Separating the Yam from the Boulder', 273–75; I. Habib, 'An Atlas of the Mughal Empire: Political and Economic Maps with detailed Notes, Bibliography and Index (Delhi, Oxford and New York, 1982); and A. Hintze, *The Mughal Empire and its Decline: An Interpretation of the Sources of Social Powe*r (Aldershot, Hampshire, and Brookfield, Vermont, 1997), 68–70.

44. Mysore, not formally integrated into the Mughal Empire until about 1700, emancipated itself in particular from 1782 onwards, under Tipu Sultan. Cf. K. Brittlebank, *Tipu Sultan's Search for Legitimacy: Islam and Kingship in a Hindu Domain* (Oxford, 1997), 65–78; Habib, 'Introduction: Essay on Haidar Ali and Tipu Sultan', xxivf.

45. Abu al-Fazl ibn Mubarak, *Ayeen Akkbery or Institutes of the Emperor Akber*, translated by Francis Gladwin, 3 vols (Calcutta, 1783–1786), esp. vol. 2.

46. See for example J. Rennell, *Memoir of a Map of Hindoostan; or the Mogul's Empire: with an Examination of Some Positions in the Former System of Indian Geography; and Some Illustrations of the Present One: and a Complete Index of Names to the Map* (London, 1783); and T. Maurice, *Indian Antiquities: or, Dissertations, relative to the Ancient Geographical Divisions, the Pure System of Primeval Theology, the Grand Code of Civil Laws, the Original Form of Government, and the Various and Profound Literature, of Hindostan. Compared, throughout, with the Religion, Laws, Government, and Literature, of Persia, Egypt, and Greece. The Whole Intended as Introductory to, and Illustrative of, the History of Hindostan*, 5 vols (London, 1793f), vol. 2.

47. J. Rennell, *Memoir of a Map of Hindoostan; or the Mogul Empire: with an Introduction, Illustrative of the Geography and Present Division of that Country; and a Map of the Countries Situated between the Heads of the Indian Rivers, and the Caspian Sea. ... To Which Is Added, an Appendix ... The Second Edition. With Very Considerable Additions, and many Corrections: and a Supplementary Map* (London, 1792), cxi.

48. As an example from northern India, after a treaty on territory to be ceded by the Nawab of Oudh in 1801 the Surveyor General Colebrooke gave his assistant the following instruction: 'You will be pleased to ascertain, either by Survey should it lie in your way, or from the reports of the Natives, the situation of the Town and Districts of Asophabad, which is mentioned in the Treaty with the Nabob, but which has not even been inserted in any of our Maps': Robert Hyde Colebrooke to Thomas Wood, 10 February 1802, NAI/SIR/SGO/54B, 72–74, here 74.

49. 'A Statement of the different Talooks in Tippoo's Dominion with the amount of their revenue', BL/OIOC/Mss Eur/Mack Gen/61, Appendix 12, 287–320; Colin Mackenzie, 'Memoir of the Construction of the Map of the Partition of Mysore at Seringapatam', June 1799, BL/OIOC/Mack Gen/60, 135–38.

50. John Kennaway, 'Statement of what passed at the different Conferences held with Tippoo's Vakeels from the 14th to the 19th February', 20 February 1792 and 'Continuation, 22 Feb 1792', BL/OIOC/Mss Eur/Mack Gen/61, 3–35, 39–52.

51. The way Kennaway conducted the negotiations at his time was generally regarded as very successful and even earned him a baronetcy. For Kennaway see B. Carnduff, 'Kennaway, Sir John, First baronet (1758–1836)', *ODNB*; for his diplomatic activity in Hyderabad, see Black, *British Foreign Policy*, 164f.

52. Colin Mackenzie, 'Memoir of a Map of the Dominions of Nizam Ally Khan in 1795', BL/OIOC/Mss Eur/Mack Gen/60, 61–96, here 61.

53. As early as 1785, when he was working as Persian Secretary to the military commander-in-chief in Bengal, he had published a dictionary: W. Kirkpatrick, *A Vocabulary, Persian, Arabic and English; Containing Such Words as Have Been Adopted from the Two Former of Those Languages, and Incorporated into the Hindvi* (London, 1785).

54. Cf. Colin Mackenzie, 'Memoir of a Map of the Dominions of Nizam Ally Khan in 1795', BL/OIOC/Mss Eur/Mack Gen/60, 61–96, here 68f, 91–94. Kirkpatrick had obviously sent the same extracts to James Rennell in London in advance. Cf. J. Rennell, *Memoir of a Map of the Peninsula of India; from the Latest Authorities Exhibiting its Natural and Political Divisions ... the Latter, Conformable to the Treaty of Seringapatam, in March 1792* (London, 1793), 14 and passim.

55. Cf. H. Ethé, *Catalogue of Persian Manuscripts in the Library of the India Office*, 2 vols (Oxford, 1903–37), vol. 1, No. 2837.

56. 'Translation of the Dafter Asuphia or Register of the Six Soobahs of Deckan as Registered Provincially under the Moghul Government from an Original Persian Mss ... translated from the Original ... by Moonshees under the Direction of Major Mackenzie', BL/OIOC/Mss Eur/Mack Gen/43, 93–152. The translation was probably done in 1805. Cf. Mackenzie

to Major Merrick Shawe, Priv. Sec. GG, 1 May 1804, BL/OIOC/Mss Eur/F/228/39/No. 1, 1–3, here 3.

57. Mackenzie had part of this index translated: 'Haakekut Hindoostan Part III & IV containing an Account of the Modern Provinces, Divisions, Revenues, Limits, Extent, Rivers & Mountains with a succinct view of The History and Gradual Reduction by the Mogul Government of the Six Soobahs of the Deckan. From a Persian MS compiled from the Ancient Dafters & Records of the Government down to 1789. With Notes, Explanations & Maps', BL/OIOC/Mss Eur/Mack Gen/44.

58. He wrote several historical pieces and published three anthologies of Indian poets. Cf. T.G. Baily, 'Review: Camanistan i Shu'arā by Lachmi Narayan Shafiq, Edited by Abdul Haq, Aurungabad 1928', *Bulletin of the School of Oriental Studies* 5(4) (1930), 927f.

59. Cf. C. Rieu, *Catalogue of Persian Manuscripts in the British Museum*, 3 vols (London, 1879–1883), vol. 1, 238a and vol. 3, 1038a; Ethé, *Catalogue of Persian Manuscripts*, vol. 1, No. 426.

60. Towards the end of the seventeenth century Chikkadevaraja Wodeyar, Rajah of Mysore, had introduced a system that divided the country into *taluks* (or *gadis*) which in turn consisted of several *hobelies*. This was in line with earlier models. From the mid eighteenth century, Haidar Ali had reformed the administrative system following the model of the Mughal Empire. Different designations in different languages, reforms that were not implemented everywhere to the same extent, and obvious misunderstandings subsequently led to ambivalent usage of the terms. Mackenzie, for instance, sometimes used *pargana*, *taluk* and *hobeli* as synonyms. Cf. A. Satyanarna, *History of the Wodeyars of Mysore (1610–1748)* (Mysore, 1996), 136f; Habib, 'Introduction: Essay on Haidar Ali and Tipu Sultan', xix–xxii.

61. Colin Mackenzie, 'Memorandum of the Financial Records of the Deckan', 12 June 1809, BL/OIOC/Mss Eur/Mack Gen/44, 1–3, here 2.

62. Cf. Colin Mackenzie, 'Memorandum on the Ancient Hindoo System of Government and its Vestiges in the South of the Peninsula', n.d., BL/OIOC/Mss Eur/Mack Gen/45, 1–11, here 1.

63. Colin Mackenzie, 'General Heads of Instructions for the Geometrical and Geographical Survey of a Purgunna (a Hobely in Mysore)', BL/OIOC/Mss Eur/F/228/39, para. 1.

64. Colin Mackenzie, 'Memorandum of the Financial Records of the Deckan', 12 June 1809, BL/OIOC/Mss Eur/Mack Gen/44, 1–3, here 3.

65. Robert Hyde Colebrooke to Captain G. Fleming, 24 April 1801, NAI/SIR/SGO/54B, 37–40, here 38.

66. In particular the *Bengal Atlas*, welcomed with such enthusiasm in London, was renowned for its inaccuracy in details. This was also noted by Francis Buchanan when he travelled through Bengal in the early nineteenth century. Not only was he unable to follow the district boundaries given on the map but some mountains, villages and forts were either non-existent or located in completely different places. Cf. F. Buchanan, *Journal … Kept during the Survey of the Districts of Patna and Gaya in 1811–1812*, edited and introduced by V.H. Jackson (Patna, 1925), 4f, 8, 70, 78, 154, 165; id., *Journal … Kept during the Survey of the District of Shahabad* in 1812–13, edited and introduced by C.E.A.W. Oldham (Patna, 1926), 75. For Buchanan's use of the atlas see also Francis Buchanan to Gov. FW, 13 September 1807, NAI/SIR/SGO/364, 13f.

67. Cf. Michael, 'Making Territory Visible', 83.

68. Robert Hyde Colebrooke to Colin Mackenzie, 7 December 1807, NAI/SIR/SGO/361, 63f, here 64.

69. Colin Mackenzie, 'Memoir of a Map of the Dominions of Nizam Ally Khan in 1795', BL/OIOC/Mss Eur/Mack Gen/60, 61- 96, here 62.

70. He had carried *dustucks* issued by the Nizam. Cf. Colin Mackenzie to Arthur Wellesley, 28 July 1800, NAI/SIR/M/6, 157–59, here 158.

71. Colin Mackenzie to Barry Close, 19 March 1800, NAI/SIR/M/6, 89–92, here 91. See also Colin Mackenzie to John Warren, 21 January 1800, NAI/SIR/M/6, 45 and 63f; id. to Barry Close, 21 January 1800, ibid., 45f; id. to Alexander Read, Colonel Canary and Mangalore, 19 January 1807, NAI/SIR/M/18, 208–10; for similar requests regarding the Ceded Districts see id., 'Memorandum for Josiah Webbe', 8 March 1800, NAI/SIR/M/6, 87; id. to Thomas Gahagan, Colonel Ballary, 16 March 1809, NAI/SIR/SGO/90A, 53–55; and id. to R.C. Ross, Colonel Cuddapa, 31 January 1810, ibid., 90f.

72. Mackenzie regularly complained about the *harkaras'* insubordination, but at the same time stressed their usefulness. Cf. Colin Mackenzie to John Cockrane, 29 April 1800, NAI/SIR/M/6, 102f; id. to Barry Close, 11 March 1801, ibid., 250–52; also 27 March 1801, ibid., 255f; id. to J.H. Peile, 29 May 1801, ibid., 268–70; also 12 July 1801, ibid., 280f.

73. Mackenzie himself described the *dehazada* as a 'Register of Villages furnished in the several Districts of Mysore for the use of the Survey': Colin Mackenzie to Mountstuart Elphinstone, 7 September 1818, NAI/SIR/SGO/435D, 9–14, here 14. *Dehazadas* seem to have been kept far beyond Mysore and the Ceded Districts. Cf. for example S. Bayly, *Saints, Goddesses and Kings: Muslims and Christians in South Indian Society, 1700–1900* (Cambridge, 1989), 81f (fn 16), 88; D. Ludden, 'Agrarian Commercialism in Eighteenth Century South India: Evidence from the 1823 Tirunelveli Census', *Indian Economic Social History Review* 25(4) (1988), 493–519; and A.R. Kulkarni, 'Source Material for the Study of Village Communities in Maharashtra', *Indian Economic Social History Review* 13(4) (1976), 513–23.

74. For this approach see 'General Heads of Instructions for the Geometrical and Geographical Survey of a Purgunna (a Hobely in Mysore)', NAI/SIR/REP/2, 83f; Colin Mackenzie to John Warren, 24 April 1801, NAI/SIR/M/6, 258.

75. Cf. also Robb, 'Completing "Our Stock of Geography"', 202–4.

76. This distinction between *asali* and *dakhali* or 'primary' and 'secondary villages or hamlets', apparently customary in the region, also occurs in the later gazetteer for Mysore by the archaeologist Benjamin L. Rice, though without further details about the origin and legal significance of these terms. Cf. B.L. Rice, *Mysore: A Gazetteer compiled for Government*, revised edn., 2 vols (London, 1887; reprinted New Delhi, 2001), vol. 2, for example 29 (quote), 169, 230, 336, 383, 508.

77. John Mather, 'Records of the Barramahl & Salem &c. Districts – Section IInd, Geography', NAI/SIR/M/1, 34.

78. Indeed the number of villages entered in lists of this sort hardly changed for centuries. In the case of Indapur, northwest of Mysore, for instance, comparison of a document of 1684 with a *dehazada* of 1818 reveals an extremely small difference – eighty-five villages listed identically and only one single 'new' village. Cf. Kulkarni, 'Source Material', 515.

79. Colin Mackenzie, 'Memorandum of the Financial Records of the Deccan', 12 June 1809, BL/OIOC/Mss Eur/Mack Gen/44, 1–3, here 3.

80. Mackenzie understood his method as a 'medium between the endless method of separate village Surveys & the loose Method of General Topographical Maps which never complete anything & for ever require corrections': Colin Mackenzie to Mountstuart Elphinstone, 7 September 1818, NAI/SIR/SGO/435D, 9–14, here 12. In this sense the survey was also not supposed to be an 'agricultural survey' based, amongst other things, on producing cadastre maps. See Mackenzie to Barry Close, 9 November 1799, NAI/SIR/M/6, 27–32, here 28; id. to John Warren, 5 September 1800, ibid., 176–79. See also id. to Lieutenant Sims, 13 May 1816, NAI/SIR/SGO/573, 50–52.

81. For instance, this explains a list by Alexander Read retained amongst the survey's documents: A. Read, 'An Account of the Villages whose lands terminate the Collectorate of Canara and Soonda with some Description of the Principal Landmarks which define the Boundary at several Places in the said Collectorate', NAI/SIR/M/12, 103–78.

82. Colin Mackenzie, 'Memoirs (Account) of the Process & Method observed in the Survey of the Boundary of Mysore & Koorg and of the Construction of the Map accompanying in February & March 1805, with a Map of the Frontier Surveyed', NAI/SIR/M/12, 243–50, here 248. Thomas Munro made similar observations in Canara and came to the conclusion that the boundary stones marked land in communal ownership. Cf. Stein, *Munro*, 67.

83. Colin Mackenzie to Barry Close, 21 October 1800, NAI/SIR/M/6, 195f, here 196.

84. John Mather, 'Journal of the Proceedings of the Survey in Mysore with an account of the Weather during 1804', NAI/SIR/M/12, 291–320, here 295.

85. John Mather, 'Journal of the Proceedings of the Survey in Mysore with an account of the Weather during 1805', NAI/SIR/M/12, 323–43, here 329, 339. Mathers was probably referring here to surveying boundaries in Coorg in 1792/1793. Cf. Phillimore, *Historical Records*, vol. 1, 131.

86. Colin Mackenzie to John Warren, 24 April 1801, NAI/SIR/M/6, 258f.

87. Thomas Arthur to Thomas Munro, 14 July 1805, BL/OIOC/Mss Eur/F 151/8, 112f, here 112.

88. Barry Close to Colin Mackenzie, 28 October 1800, NAI/SIR/M/6, 317–21, here 319.

89. Cf. Colin Mackenzie, 'Memoirs (Account) of the Process & Method observed in the Survey of the Boundary of Mysore & Koorg and of the Construction of the Map accompanying in February & March 1805, with a Map of the Frontier Surveyed', NAI/SIR/M/12, 243–50, here 244f, 248f.

90. Cf. Colin Mackenzie to Thomas Munro, 29 April 1801, NAI/SIR/SGO/90, 390–92.

91. Colin Mackenzie to James Gahagan, 9 May 1809, NAI/SIR/SGO/90A, 58–60.

92. Cf. Thomas Arthur to Thomas Munro, 14 July 1805, BL/OIOC/Mss Eur/F/151/8, 112f.

93. For this observation see also M. Katten, 'Manufacturing Village Identity and its Village: The View from Nineteenth-Century Andhra', *Modern Asian Studies* 33(1) (1999), 87–120.

94. Cf. Colin Mackenzie, 'View of the State of the Mysore Survey on 1st October 1803', NAI/SIR/REP/2, 239–53, here 245f.

95. Colin Mackenzie, 'Second General Report on the Mysore Survey, 12 July 1803', NAI/SIR/REP/2, 17–35, here 21.

96. Cf. Edney, *Mapping an Empire*, 115, 324. Indeed, Mackenzie once suggested replacing village names by geographical coordinates, but this was – far from being a general suggestion – just a makeshift solution in a situation in which *dehazadas* had not been consulted before surveying. Cf. Colin Mackenzie to George Strachey, 1 June 1817, BL/IOR/F/4/636 (17424), 239–49, here 242f.

97. Robb, 'Completing "Our Stock of Geography"', 205.

98. Colin Mackenzie to John Warren, 5 September 1800, NAI/SIR/M/6, 176–79, here 178.

99. Robb, 'Completing "Our Stock of Geography"', 203.

100. Colin Mackenzie, 'Hints or Heads of Enquiry for facilitating our knowledge of the more Southern parts of Deckan', 1800, BL/OIOC/Mss Eur/F/128/213. For a later example see id., 'Heads of Memoir of the Regentship or District of – in Java intended for obtaining a complete Geographical & Statistical view of the Island. Communicated for Circulation, [1811]', BL/OIOC/Mss Eur/Mack Priv/14, 303–9.

101. 'To be a practising cartographer,' Matthew Edney sums this up, 'one had to accept the intellectual order and structure imposed on the map by both the Enlightenment's scientism and the existing social order', Mackenzie, whose social advancement was essentially based on his professional qualifications, had no alternative but to adapt to the norms of scientism, borne in the eighteenth century initially by social elites. See M. Edney, 'Mathematical Cosmography and the Social Ideology of British Cartography, 1780–1820', *Imago Mundi* 46 (1994), 112.

102. Colin Mackenzie to John Warren, 5 September 1800, NAI/SIR/M/6, 176–79.

103. In his experience this was enough to establish all the information with suitable accuracy. To start with, following Mather's model, the scale was set at one inch to one mile but from the end of 1803 onwards, in order to speed up the work, it was increased to one inch to two miles. Cf. Colin Mackenzie to John Warren, 6 March 1800, NAI/SIR/M/6, 82f; id. to John Mather, 26 April 1800, ibid., 103; also 8 May 1800, ibid., 104f; id. to Warren, 5 September 1800, ibid., 176–79; id. to Mather, 12 March 1803, ibid., 366; id. to Thomas Arthur, 12 March 1803, ibid.; also 13 March 1803, NAI/SIR/SGO/90, 298; and 17 March 1803, ibid., 206f.

104. Colin Mackenzie, 'Series of Maps constructed from the Results of the Survey of Mysore and Canara, designed as the Foundation of an Atlas of the Provinces dependent on the Presidency of Fort St. George' (with Index), July–October 1808, BL/IOR/X/2108, 1–7; id., 'Atlas of the Provinces ceded to by The Nizam in 1800 to the Honble East India Company from Surveys executed from 1809 to 1815. Compiled from the Original Surveys under the Direction & on the Proposition of Colin Mackenzie, Surveyor General in India', 1 January 1819, BL/IOR/X/2314/1–20.

105. Exceptions are a route survey of 1788 and his map of the partition of Mysore: Mackenzie, 'Account of the Construction of the Plan of the Roads from Nellore'; id., 'Map of the Dominions of the late Tippoo Sultaun' and a number of maps published in Wilks, *Historical Sketches*, vol. 1.

106. From 1818 onwards Mackenzie had been trying to get the government in Calcutta to accept this idea. Cf. Colin Mackenzie to Stephen Lushington, 7 March 1820, BL/Mss Add/14380, 39–52, here 49f.

107. Mackenzie himself proposed a publication using this scale. Cf. 'Surveys in India', *Asiatic Journal and Monthly Register for British India and its Dependencies* 27(157) (January 1829), 56. For the origins and Mackenzie's contribution see also 'The Atlas of India. Published by the East India Company', *Asiatic Journal and Register for British India and its Dependencies* 27(162) (June 1829), 723f; M. Edney, 'The Atlas of India 1823–1947: The Natural History of a Topographic Map Series', *Cartographica* 28(4) (1991), 59–91.

108. B. Lewis, 'The Mysore Kingdom at AD 1800: Archaeological Applications of the Mysore Survey of Colin Mackenzie', in C. Jarrige and V. Lefèvre (eds), *South Asian Archaeology 2001: Proceedings of the Sixteenth International Conference of the European Association of South Asian Archaeologists, held in Collège de France, Paris, 2–6 July 2001*, 2 vols (Paris, 2005), vol. 2, 558f.

109. B. Lewis and C.S. Patil, 'Chitradrurga: Spatial Patterns of a Nayaka Period Successor State in India', *Asian Perspectives* 42(2) (2003), 273–75; S. Gordon and J.F. Richards, 'Kinship and *pargana* in Eighteenth Century Kandesh', *Indian Economic and Social History Review* 22(4) (1985), 371–98, esp. 396.

110. Robb, 'Completing "Our Stock of Geography"', 203.

111. A. Tickell, 'Negotiating the Landscape: Travel, Transaction, and the Mapping of Colonial India', *Yearbook of English Studies* 34 (2004), 27. Tickell refers to George Everest's cartographic reports here.

112. See the argument put forward in relation to Kandesh by Gordon and Richards, 'Kinship and *pargana*'.

Chapter 6

KNOWLEDGE FOR THE FUTURE

Statistical Knowledge in Scotland and India

When the third volume of the *Transactions of the Literary Society of Bombay* was published, in 1805,[1] its reviewers in the *Gentleman's Magazine* were full of praise. If India were ever to remain an integral part of the British Empire, they wrote, articles such as these were indispensable. Typical of periodicals by Anglo-Indian learned societies the volume contains a mixture of natural-historical observations, archaeological and historical descriptions and translations of original documents. Two of the articles, however, both statistical descriptions of small regions in western India, attracted the reviewers' criticism. This, of course, was directed less at their content than at their place of publication. Nothing, they declared, was a 'more plain want of policy, than the neglect of having any country intended for a permanent possession regularly mapped and statistically investigated'. So it was regrettable that the two statistical articles were not published in an official government publication but in a learned periodical. Certain pieces of knowledge, they went on, including statistical and topographical information, undoubtedly belonged in the government's sphere and should therefore be described as 'governmental'.[2]

What they overlooked in their criticism, of course, was that statistical studies of this sort had already been under way in India for about twenty-five years, in fact, since the survey of Mysore. Even at that time the idea of combining cartographical material with a description of a region's natural and cultural features was by no means new, but to some extent followed a tradition of geographical work embodied in the eighteenth century, for example by Anton Friedrich Büsching's influential *Neue Erdbschreibung*.[3] It is perhaps no coincidence that Mackenzie's plan for his survey of 1800 reflected Büsching's distinction between the earth's 'mathematical' and 'physical' properties, whereby the 'mathematical' part contained all cartographical work while the 'physical' included not only irrigation techniques and cultivation methods, social and cultural composition, and the population's general customs and practices, but also flora and fauna as well as minerals and climate.[4]

In the eighteenth century the boundary between statistics and geography was fluid and in his scientific work Büsching often moved in the border areas between branches of science that were becoming differentiated only slowly.[5] Büsching himself, however, had hardly carried out any empirical research, largely confining himself to comparing and compiling work already done. Another model was far more important for the early British statistical studies in India, namely John Sinclair's *Statistical Account of Scotland* published between 1791 and 1799.[6] Wellesley obviously had this work in mind when he explicitly asked for a 'statistical account of the whole country'[7] since the concept of 'Statistik', developed, amongst others, by the Göttingen university professor Achenwall,[8] had only become current in the English-speaking world in the 1790s, under Sinclair's influence.[9] Sinclair, a Scottish MP, had got to know about the German discipline of statistics in the mid 1780s during a trip to Prussia and Hanover and had transferred the term to English in the belief that it might attract greater attention to his Scottish project.[10]

In Sinclair's sense, 'statistical' referred less to the systematic application of numerical processes than to a detailed description of individual regions.[11] On the one hand he was applying the tradition of descriptive German 'university statistics', which was by no means confined to interpreting quantitative data but was concerned with the historical description of constitution, legal system and economy,[12] and was thus very different from mathematical statistics that was becoming increasingly influential in the nineteenth century.[13] On the other hand Sinclair had recourse to models from Scotland, especially the tradition of land description. Starting around the time of the royal geographer, Sir Robert Sibbald, at the turn of the eighteenth century there had been various similar initiatives in Scotland, such as Walter Macfarlane's geographical collection from the first half of the century or the largely unsuccessful attempts by the Society of Antiquaries of Scotland in the 1780s, whose meagre results were not published until 1792.[14]

What was new about Sinclair's approach in the Scottish context, however, was the extensive scope of the data raised and the extremely systematic way in which he carried out his project. In the introduction to the *Statistical Account* he lists fifty-seven rubrics under which the information is arranged. The list ranged from topographical details about the climate to periods of sewing and harvesting, from cultivation methods to predominant illnesses and wages paid in particular places, from prices and sizes of farms to details of local production and consumption. Also included, of course, was a description of local customs and practices and of the antiquities and history of each of the parishes.[15]

A project with such broad scope must, of necessity, be based on local knowledge that had to be acquired in the field. At the same time, of course, it needed centralized organization that could coordinate the project and establish unified criteria for collecting information. Sinclair solved this problem by bringing his influence to bear on the General Assembly of the Kirk in order to gain the necessary support for his statistical studies. From 1790 onwards he had comprehensive questionnaires circulated in the Scottish parishes, which each minister was supposed to answer. Once he had received the first satisfactory answers he sent these out as templates and also sent out 'statistical missionaries', who were supposed to convince hesitant ministers of the project's usefulness.[16] In the years that followed Sinclair corresponded with almost a thousand Scottish clerics.[17] His efforts were rewarded and in 1799 the last of the twenty-one volumes of *Statistical Accounts* could finally be published, containing detailed descriptions of all 936 Scottish parishes.

Sinclair's *Statistical Account* was the project of an enthusiast who could rely on the 'Enlightenment idealism' of the Presbyterian ministers.[18] State support for his work was confined to free postage, usual for MPs, and a one-off payment of two thousand pounds to the Society for the Benefit of the Sons of the Clergy, which was also given the publication rights. Sinclair hoped that with the government's support he would soon be able to extend his projects to other parts of Britain: however, his parochial survey in England, conceived when he was President of the Board of Agriculture, failed after just a few years due to lack of funds and support.[19] Mackenzie's enterprise, on the other hand, was a state project right from the start. Unlike in Britain, in the newly conquered regions even the most rudimentary knowledge for building up an efficient administration on the ground was lacking. Even if Dundas in London showed no interest in Sinclair's suggestion that a statistical account of India be prepared,[20] the pressure to invest in new processes of knowledge production was considerably greater here. What is more, the EIC could expect to gain prestige from a statistical project regarded by contemporaries as 'scientific' – certainly a reason why under Wellesley the Company supported more scientific projects than the administration in Britain.[21]

Although in the beginning Mackenzie clearly had only a superficial knowledge of the concept of 'statistics' – it was, he wrote, an 'interesting (tho' to me ... new) subject of occupation' – he always regarded statistical studies as a 'material part of the Survey'.[22] In the flood of reports and material with which he tried to convince his superiors of his project's usefulness in the following years, he always devoted a good deal of space to this part of his work, and this was certainly appreciated. The government of Madras, for instance, once they had been able to assess the first results, expressly praised the valuable material he had collected and the usefulness of the information derived from his 'enquiry into the resources of the territories of Mysore'.[23] Like Sinclair in

Britain, in India he was not required to pay for any postage.[24] Once the survey was complete the Directors in London also expressly praised Mackenzie's pioneering achievement.[25]

In the first years Mackenzie, who had only listed the research goals of his survey in very general terms in his plan of 1800, worked out a dedicated programme setting out both the information to be collected and its practical realization. As was the case with his surveying work, here too he propagated the absolute necessity of a 'generally uniform system' that all the research should follow, and as with the surveying work he designed this in such a way that it could potentially be applied to any other region of India without any great adjustments. So during the survey of Mysore he also developed a system for acquiring statistical information, which he consistently adhered to in his later capacity as Surveyor General and which was also to remain a model for similar enterprises well after his death.

The Limits of Observation

John Sinclair defined 'statistics' as empirical science based only on inductive processes. According to his theory, statistical knowledge must be based on exact local studies and the statistician, like the natural scientist, must pay attention to 'anatomical minuteness' when collecting information. '[The] minute and extensive investigation of local facts', he wrote, 'is following the example of Bacon, who tested the basis of natural philosophy on minute enquiries, accurate experiments, and inferences deduced from them'.[26] So statistics should be a sort of 'natural history' of the socioeconomic, political, historical, cultural and topographical conditions in a country and should, where possible, copy the three-step methodology of this knowledge collection – observation, classification, documentation. In this way geographical units, in Scotland's case the Presbyterian parishes, should be inventorized as completely as possible. Once comparable sets of data had been created, these could be combined and examined further. At an early stage Sinclair had already planned to condense the results of the individual parishes into descriptions of entire constituencies, and in the 1820s he finally managed this with the publication of his *Analysis of the Statistical Account* for the whole of Scotland.[27]

The methodology Mackenzie used for his statistical studies followed Sinclair's model in many respects. This applied, firstly, to the selection of the geographical units to be inventorized, Mackenzie substituting the *parganas* surveyed by his teams for Sinclair's parishes. Here too, of course, uniformity was to be created in a broader context by working through a common list of data to be raised.[28] Among the 'Heads of Enquiry' that Mackenzie had been compiling for surveyors in South India since 1800[29] there are many categories that can be seen as direct equivalents to the lists Sinclair sent to his Presbyterian ministers. This applies in particular to information on topography, but also to categories such as agriculture, trade or climate. On the other hand, certain other points included, such as linguistic boundaries and the division of the population into castes, are clearly specific to the situation in South India.[30] Like Sinclair, Mackenzie saw describing smaller geographical units as a possible precursor to synthesized work that would combine material according to the same principles, thus providing an overview of larger regions. So he not only proposed creating a unified overview of all the areas acquired since 1799,[31] but even put forward the possibility of condensing the description of individual *parganas* into an overall picture of the Madras presidency.[32]

Despite these obvious similarities between Mackenzie's project and Sinclair's, there were also important differences, especially concerning how data was raised on the ground. They were both enterprises that could not succeed without local support and knowledge, but they were conducted under conditions that were poles apart. While Sinclair's ministers were a group of people generally well acquainted with local conditions, the situation was much more difficult for Mackenzie and his European assistants. Mackenzie insisted that while carrying out their cartographical work they should also produce a written description of each *pargana*, the more detailed the better, as he wrote to William Lantwar for instance,[33] and if possible to go beyond the essential information required in his lists.[34] Along with information that supplemented the cartographical material, (on location, size, topography and the internal structure of each *pargana*), further details on towns, villages, markets, fortifications and buildings of local importance such as temples or mosques were also to be included, likewise details on rivers and lakes, as well as woods, mountains, passes and roads. Mines and quarries were to be described in just as much detail as local products, right up to the quality of the ground and the cultivation methods used in the region.[35]

However, without knowledge of the local languages and as foreigners in the employ of new rulers, regarded with suspicion, the Europeans had limited room for manoeuvre. Mackenzie complained, for instance, that the population often reacted to the European surveyors with 'caution or shyness' and followed their work with 'friendless suspicions'.[36] This was all the more unfortunate since not all areas of knowledge regarded by Mackenzie as essential to his statistical description could be covered by observation alone. Although the surveyors, supported by the Company's military power, were in a position of relative strength, they were by no means always able to acquire all the data they regarded as relevant. Even if what remained of the Mysore state was de facto largely under British control, it was clear right from the start of the survey that the impression should not be given that the purpose of the surveys was connected to revenue, since this could have led to clashes with the still extant Rajah's administration. So questions about possible land ownership, or measurements and qualitative assessments of individual fields, essential for raising revenue, were not envisaged.[37] Although Mackenzie initially favoured an extension of his project to these questions, since he regarded them as closely connected with statistical studies,[38] such ideas increasingly retreated to the background as the years passed. After the defeat of Tipu Sultan the greatest danger to British rule in South India had certainly been overcome, but the Company continued to be involved in unpleasant and costly conflicts, such as local uprisings in Wynaad, armed conflicts with the *poligars*, or border disputes, for instance on the northern border.[39] In order to avoid further problems in Mysore, as in the Company's other territories, everything was now to be done to avoid provoking dissatisfaction and protest amongst the local population. For the survey this meant that any pressure applied to local officials to provide information should be kept to a minimum.

The example of the assistant Thomas Arthur shows very clearly that the surveyors' position was too weak for them to be able simply to insist on being given information. Arthur had joined the survey as an assistant in 1800 and in the same year was already carrying out his own investigations, though initially under Mackenzie's direct supervision. Arthur's impatient nature and – to put it politely – clumsy way of dealing with his Indian co-workers and the local population had already led to problems then, but without any serious consequences for the survey.[40] It was not until the beginning of 1803 – Arthur had just returned from several months' sick leave at the coast and due to lack of staff had been entrusted with surveying individual *parganas* on his own for the first time[41] – that difficulties arose, which his superiors no longer could or wished to ignore. The twenty-four-year-old, no doubt hoping to be rewarded for such good work, set about his task with great determination, but without taking any account of local sensitivities. When the local officials refused his request for more precise information about the size of the population in the *pargana*[42] he took it upon himself to carry out a sort of census, thereby clearly offending the rules of the purdah that applied to Muslim women and those belonging to higher castes.

Arthur's behaviour was a clear affront to the local *amildars* and they certainly did not let it go unnoticed. There were two elements to their reaction. Firstly, they chose the most obvious course, namely to deny Arthur any cooperation at all, which made it very difficult for him to make any progress; procuring the food he needed and also the vital support of local guides now became a problem. A second strategy proved to have even greater consequences and shows that the indigenous officials were very well aware that they could use the Company's internal structures to further their own interests. Their most important weapon here was a direct complaint to the offender's superior, at the highest level possible – a course already taken successfully by other interest groups in the Madras presidency.[43]

Right from the start of the survey, Purnaiya – the chief Minister in Mysore – had given Arthur the support of a *harkara*, who regularly informed the minister about Arthur's behaviour,[44] and so he learned of the proposed census at an early stage. Less than two weeks after Arthur had started his survey, Purnaiya sent his first complaint to the Mysore Resident, who forwarded it to Mackenzie on the same day.[45] The minister had not named any names, so the whole survey fell into disrepute, and, suitably alarmed, Mackenzie composed a letter to all his assistants exhorting them to avoid such actions in future and not to undertake anything without the agreement of the local officials.[46] Although there had been complaints about the surveyors before, this time the situation was particularly serious since Purnaiya's intervention with the Resident in Mysore meant that Mackenzie's immediate superior had been approached at the highest political level. However, whether or not the survey could continue depended on the Resident.

So it is hardly surprising that Mackenzie, having discovered that Arthur was the cause of the complaint, and despite their good personal relationship up till this point, told him in no uncertain terms that he was to avoid irritating the local officials ever again.[47] His tone became even sharper once it became clear that Arthur had no intention of behaving diplomatically.[48] In the meantime the conflict began to develop into a major affair. Arthur had initially agreed to stop putting any further pressure on the *amildars* if they were unwilling to give him the information he required; at the same time, however, he continued to complain about their lack of cooperation.[49] By August there were already new complaints, again caused by Arthur's attempts to establish the size of the population. Arthur responded with a complaint about the local population's lack of willingness to cooperate, which he sent direct to the Resident in Mysore – though without any success since Peile rejected his complaints and now forbade him to carry out any investigations connected with the population at all.[50]

Although Mackenzie also demanded once again that Arthur do his 'duty under authority' and follow the Resident's instructions[51] the damage had already been done. To start with Arthur was forbidden to have any further direct communication with the Resident and told not to extend his survey, as planned, to a border region considered particularly politically sensitive – Mackenzie ultimately had to carry out this work himself since it was 'work of more than usual delicacy'.[52] Despite the attempt to confine Arthur's work to less conflict-prone regions, complaints continued to be made and so, at the beginning of 1804, he was forbidden to carry out any work on his own without Mackenzie's direct supervision.[53] An investigation into the complaints carried out by Purnaiya focussed on three recurring shortcomings in particular: Arthur, it seemed, had paid too little for food, equipment and work carried out; had not paid at all for transport; and had personally behaved violently towards the locals.[54] Although the *harkara* Ramachandra Rao was held responsible for the first complaints and Arthur's recurring bouts of fever were accepted as an excuse for his uncontrolled behaviour so that initially he was allowed to carry out surveys independently again, with Mackenzie taking responsibility, this was still a severe blow to Arthur's career as a surveyor. After a further bout of serious illness in the summer of 1804, he was employed in Mysore once more until 1805,[55] but after renewed complaints of a similar nature he was ultimately withdrawn.[56]

Arthur's case – his exceptional lack of control and violence towards the local population – might be regarded as a one-off; although other surveyors were occasionally the subject of similar complaints, these were mostly without any serious consequences. Nonetheless, the case is a good example of how limited the surveyors' power over the local population was. They were neither able to raise their data by purely empirical means – in other words by directly counting the population – nor could they force the officials on the ground to provide them with the information they required. If they wanted to achieve their goals their relative powerlessness forced them to cooperate with the local elites. So statistical studies did not simply represent a process of gaining information and classification, but they also contained elements of interaction in which Indian actors played a major role. At an early stage Mackenzie recognized the potential offered by this interaction as a chance to realize his project.

Cooperation and *Karanam* Culture

During his time in Hyderabad, Mackenzie had already made extensive use of the chance to cooperate with Indian experts. Kavali Venkata Borayya had worked for him since they met, probably in 1796, and two years later, when more funds were available, he had employed a number of other Indian co-workers.[57] In Mysore, Borayya now worked as chief translator, initially in charge of four other Indian translators and writers.[58] With the new financial regulations in 1803, this staff of Indian co-workers was increased by one new appointee,[59] and then after the reforms of 1805 it was significantly expanded again. So, towards the end of the survey of Mysore, Mackenzie had the services of eleven Indian assistants altogether, paid by the government, who had command of the various languages written and spoken in the Madras presidency, including Kannada, Marathi, Telugu, ancient and modern Tamil as well as Sanskrit and Persian.[60]

This was Mackenzie's famous Indian staff, whose importance Nicholas Dirks was the first to point out. Although the Indian assistants mostly appear in the official accounts as translators or writers, their role went far beyond that of mediators between the British knowledge-producers and the precolonial elites, even though they were ideally suited to this task due to their knowledge of the local languages and customs.[61] They are best known for their contribution to Mackenzie's collection of historical documents – however, initially their most important contribution and the reason why they were paid for by government was compiling and translating statistical material. During the early years of the Mysore Survey Mackenzie had already seen how good the Indian assistants were at persuading the local officials to hand over documents;[62] but after the survey was restructured following Arthur's removal and Mather's retirement, when Anglo-Indian subassistants were made responsible for the geometrical part, most of the statistical part also became the Indian co-workers' remit. This division of labour was most apparent in the Ceded Districts, where Mackenzie provided each of the two teams of subassistants with one of his Indian co-workers 'who has had considerable experience of getting the different Accounts in the Districts Surveyed'.[63] Eventually the Surveying Department of Madras, founded in 1810, officially employed a number of Indians to collect geographical, historical and statistical material.[64]

In official correspondence Mackenzie sometimes referred to them as part of the 'machinery' without which the survey could not be conducted in the first place[65] and Mark Wilks, temporary Resident of Mysore and author of a historical work on South India, went so far as to call them Mackenzie's 'instruments', expertly chosen by him.[66] But although this sort of rhetoric seems to point to a fairly passive provision of information under Mackenzie's leadership, neither man had any hesitation in stressing that these co-workers had worked out the plan that made it at all possible to collect statistical and historical information.[67] Of the thirty-nine Indian co-workers identifiable by name[68] who worked for Mackenzie between 1796 and 1821 the Kavali brothers are undoubtedly the most well known.[69] Borayya played a leading role in conceptualizing the survey, and Mackenzie was so taken with his abilities that in his official reports he praised him to the heavens.[70] Borayya was about twenty years Mackenzie's junior and came from a family with long experience in diplomatic and administrative service. In his childhood and youth he had studied South Indian languages and Sanskrit, before, following the example of his elder brother, studying English and Persian to enter the service of the EIC as a scribe and translator.[71] Working for Mackenzie, in Hyderabad he at first officially took on the role of interpreter, and in Mysore that of chief translator. When Borayya died, in 1803 at the young age of twenty-six, his brother Kavali Venkata Lakshmayya, who had also been working for Mackenzie for some years, took over this role. He in turn was supported by his brother Kavali Venkata Ramaswami, who was promoted to become his official deputy in the following years.[72]

The Kavali brothers, with whom Mackenzie worked for almost twenty-five years, clearly had the greatest influence on the project, but a number of other people played an important role over the years. Narrain Row for instance, one of the most active co-workers as far as statistical studies were concerned, worked for Mackenzie from 1802 until his death in 1818.[73] Kistnaji and Dharmaiah, both immortalized with him in Hickey's portrait, worked with him for seventeen and twelve years respectively; Abdul Aziz worked with him for fourteen years. Each of these men had his own area of expertise: as *harkara*, Kistnaji advised Mackenzie on geographical matters; Abdul Aziz, a *munshi* (secretary), was mostly concerned with translating administrative documents from Persian, an ability that vitally complemented the other Indians' linguistic expertise;[74] and Dharmaiah was a Jain from Mysore and also a priest in a local temple.[75] He was one of the few people in South India who had command of Halegannada, an older form of Kannada, and proved to be invaluable in translating inscriptions from the ninth to the fourteenth century.[76]

So the question arises as to what the attraction was for these men in working for Mackenzie for so many years. Naturally money played a certain role at a time when traditional forms of patronage were increasingly curtailed by the unfolding power of the EIC. The Kavali brothers, for instance, even though they came from a well-known family, constantly struggled with financial problems, as Mackenzie himself later stressed:

> The four poor brothers when they came to my service were the younger of a numerous family that tho' of considerable respectability in their own class were absolutely ruined – they had no property whatever & all the pay I could afford for many years could little enable them to assist & support the Mother younger brothers & the families of three elder ruined brothers, from PS 15 to 20, 25 & finally 35 was the utmost they had & this was little enough to support 7 or 8 Families at Ellore Masulipatam & Madras; while these poor people travelled with me for several years. – The consequence was that when I went to Java I believe Letchmyah was the in debt for the means supporting this heavy Establishment. – At that time I believe he committed his first false step. – I had designed for him a certain commission in the Barrack Department which I thought would have made the Base of a Competency if well managed; but the poor man was not such an economist in his own affairs as he was in mine; & I think that his relations urged him to get this money invested in lands with the prospect of profit that was fallacious.[77]

Lakshmayya's and Ramaswami's financial difficulties seem to have been made even worse by clumsy dealings on the verge of illegality[78] but also by their sister Lakshmidevamma's debts. She had inherited a *zamindari* in the Kistna district from her late husband and relied on her brothers' support to pay the sums demanded by the government.[79] It seems that Mackenzie paid them more than he later realized. He had started by paying double, then two-and-a-half times the going rate to Borayya.[80] The other brothers were also relatively well paid, receiving twenty pagodas per month, which increased over the years to around eighty pagodas per month.[81] Although other long-time co-workers received considerably less – often only a tenth of this amount – they too profited from Mackenzie's system of paying bonuses for good achievements.[82] What is more, at the end of each year deserving co-workers received a special payment[83] and Mackenzie also offered them certain assurances beyond the time they worked for him, insisting, for instance, that they receive a pension after a long period of service.[84] In cases of death in service he supported the idea of pensions for the deceased's family.[85]

Despite these advantages of being employed by Mackenzie, some of which he financed from his own pocket, the pecuniary aspect alone cannot explain his co-workers' great commitment. Rather, the fact that they used their own initiative to such a high degree in their work for Mackenzie shows quite clearly that many of them could identify with the project. Among Mackenzie's co-workers were Hindus, Muslims, Jains and Christians. These people had not, of course, been chosen randomly – they all had a certain cultural background, certain linguistic knowledge and abilities which they could bring to the project. Phillip Wagoner has pointed out, however, that most of them were *niyogis*, a class of Brahmins who did not fulfil the role of religious specialists and scholars but undertook secular tasks in the precolonial administrations. The rise of the *niyogis* and similar Brahmin groups can be traced back to the eleventh century, but their dominant role at all levels of the administrations emerged largely at the time of the Vijayanagara Empire.[86]

Wagoner's discovery that many of Mackenzie's co-workers were *niyogis* is important because it allows us to understand the contribution of these groups to Mackenzie's statistical project against a deeper sociocultural background. Rao, Shulman und Subrahmanyam have described the rise of the *niyogis* and similar groups as part of a sociocultural process that fundamentally changed the intellectual landscape of South India.[87] Using the term commonly applied to the village scribes omnipresent from this time onwards they describe the new intellectual direction, borne along by literate elites, as *karanam* culture, explicitly without confining themselves to the bearers of the corresponding office. As they show, the rise of the literate classes was based on significant changes to South India's political culture from the seventeenth century onwards. From this time scribes employed in the administrations were no longer regarded as employees merely carrying out a task, but were increasingly perceived as political actors, giving them far greater status and influence. The reasons for this development were the increased use of Persian as the official language, the need for correspondence between small political units in various languages, the increasing complexity in state record-keeping and finally, in purely practical terms, the greater availability of paper and writing implements. *Karanams*, in Andhra generally recruited from the group of the *niyogis*, were famous for their command of various languages and dialects and not least for their calligraphical abilities.[88]

Mackenzie was well aware of the advantages of having staff with this sort of social and cultural background and sought to make best use of their linguistic, administrative and cultural expertise. In a memorandum concerning the revenue records to be found on the Deccan he dealt extensively with the 'Bramins to whom the whole of the Financial Department was usually committed', particularly with the *niyogis*: 'Neeyogee Bramins had been long employed in like manner, from the lower Offices of Accountants of Villages as an Hereditary Office to the Highest station of the Treasury'. He stressed that 'that Class whose speciality it was to keep … Records' could also be usefully employed in the Company's administration beyond working for his own project. This was particularly the case as these Brahmins were spread throughout almost the whole of South India and due to their common background were in a position to bring 'Provinces formerly regulated on different Systems' under 'one uniform System of Administration'.[89]

Rao and Subrahmanyam have also pointed out the fascinating self-perception of the *karanams* that went far beyond loyalty to one particular ruling class. They saw themselves as the people who wielded the actual power in the kingdoms. Their intelligence and their abilities in writing and language, as they put it in various texts, gave them the opportunity either to unite people or to separate them. They even ascribed to themselves the power to give the throne to an opponent of the reigning king. According to their self-confident credo, a kingdom's ministers were more important to its success and survival than the king himself.[90] The fact that despite all this they saw their role largely behind the scenes of power gave them a certain independence of political upheavals that assured their continued influence regardless of the rise and fall of various different rulers. It was not until the EIC gradually began to take over power in South India that their influence started to dwindle. Although they continued to exert control over many villages, the decline of many smaller kingdoms restricted their traditional path towards power and patronage.[91]

Many of them found jobs in the expanding Revenue Department; in 1818/1819 there were 28,746 'native revenue officers' in the Madras presidency alone.[92] Bhavani Raman has shown how dependent the Company's Revenue Department in South India was on these experts, since to start with all it had to work with were precolonial files.[93] A job with Mackenzie could perhaps seem particularly attractive since it meant not only that they could contribute their competence in dealing with precolonial files and their linguistic ability, but also because this could link up with their own intellectual traditions. For the *karanam* culture was not confined simply to carrying out administrative tasks and keeping records correctly, but found what must be its most important expression in the numerous texts recording the political, social and historical reality, mostly in prose form. It was based on the writer, one of whose key objectives was to be of use to the state: '[karanams] were writers in the true sense of the word as we understand it today'.[94] It is hard to ignore a certain similarity between the form of their writing and Mackenzie's descriptive statistics. Wagoner has shown that in essence *niyogis* shared Mackenzie's views about the survey, including how to organize knowledge production hierarchically, collecting knowledge on the ground, or the fundamental belief that a certain body of knowledge, including historical information, should be made available to the state.[95] Given the additional advantages provided by his Indian co-workers, due to their command of languages and knowledge of local traditions, it is hard to overestimate their influence. In particular they guaranteed that Mackenzie's statistical project was not based solely on European models but could also link up with the political and intellectual traditions of South India.

From Precolonial Archive to Statistical Memoir

Although many co-workers from other social and cultural backgrounds also contributed to this project, it was the *niyogis* who were mainly responsible for planning and carrying out the statistical studies. Thanks to their experience in the precolonial administrations they seem to have found it quite easy to fit in to Mackenzie's setup. They started off working directly under Mackenzie but soon formed a largely independent section within the survey team, which continued to constitute an important part of the Surveyor General's Department when it was founded in 1810. This section's organization varied little from other areas of the survey except that the correspondence was also written in various Indian languages; hierarchical channels of communication regulated how instructions were given, how the surveying was carried out and how reports were written.[96] As Mackenzie's direct subordinate, Kavali Venkata Lakshmayya held the highest position here.[97] Usually he was with Mackenzie or in the Madras office and conveyed instructions to the co-workers working in various regions on the ground, coordinated their procedures and received regular reports about their progress.[98] What is more, he was responsible for the finances and arranged, via Mackenzie, the payments needed by the assistants in the field – a task that was all the more important since costs were not only incurred for acquiring important documents and for the support of the local elites,[99] but copiers and scribes temporarily employed by the assistants also had to be paid.[100]

So Mackenzie had at his disposal an apparatus that allowed him to make systematic use of precolonial archives, particularly at a regional and local level. The idea of using the records kept by the previous states was not entirely new. Under Warren Hastings, for instance, a systematic assessment of local tax registers was started in order to get an adequate picture of the fiscal resources;[101] and in the 1780s London had specifically asked Company officials serving on outposts to examine regional archives.[102] In northern India most of these initiatives came to nothing, but in the south, starting with the work of James Grant, the first Resident in Hyderabad, a certain expertise developed in dealing with these archives,[103] which Read, Munro and Mather in Barramahal had also made use of.[104]

Mackenzie and his co-workers, using their knowledge of the archives, managed to develop a unified system to assess them, initially applicable to all the regions of South India and eventually to the whole of the subcontinent. Archives from various levels of the precolonial administration were used here. Probably the most important documents were those received from the revenue administration, either by the *amildars* or by their more localized assistants called *sheristadars*.[105] Two classes of files were of particular interest:[106] firstly, the *dehazadas*, already discussed, which provided an overview of the internal divisions and individual villages in each *pargana,* sometimes supplemented by information about the local irrigation systems, and in a few cases a list of all directly taxable items such as mills, smithies or markets (however, all archived data pertaining directly to revenue were explicitly excluded from Mackenzie's investigations);[107] secondly, *khaneh shumaries* were regularly made available here – population lists ideally drawn up annually, which generally contained details of the families and households as well as information about the caste they belonged to.[108]

These lists provided Mackenzie with information about the population that would otherwise have been virtually impossible to get hold of. His interest in it was based above all on the fact that he wanted to find out the actual size of the population in each *pargana* – he generally reckoned with four-and-a-half to five inhabitants in each house.[109] 'Where a regular Census is not attainable (as in this case from the prejudice of the Natives)', he wrote, 'it is presumed that this mode conveys a tolerably accurate idea of the actual state and progress of Populations'.[110] Despite the lack of accuracy he implied here, he stressed that these 'Accounts of the Population according to the Hindoo System' arranged according to castes also had their advantages because they were 'really very curious shewing at one view all the different tribes that form the subject of our Political regulations'.[111] Describing the population according to different groups of this sort was particularly useful, he went on, because it provided an overview of 'the relative proportion that the several Tribes and Classes Agricultural, Pastoral, Artists and Religions bear to each other and the whole'.[112] What is more, it made it possible for the British government to pick up its predecessors' practices:

An Enumeration of the several Castes & their numbers is to this day kept ... & I have no doubt is remnant of the Ancient System of Police or Financial Management: The several Castes, Tribes, Artisans & Classes of people being thus arranged under their respective Heads, who had interest in keeping a watchful eye over them;

perhaps no means could be more judiciously adopted to enforce a correct System of internal Police than following one sanctioned by the Laws and Customs of a people so very prejudiced in favour of their Ancient Ordinances.[113]

In Mackenzie's view *khaneh shumaries* gave the colonial state the opportunity to link up with precolonial practices and for this reason in later years he suggested that they be used systematically by the British authorities, a practice also followed in similar enterprises in other parts of India.[114] The way Mackenzie went about things shows quite clearly that he was not interested in delving more deeply into the question of 'castes' – he simply considered them to be related to one another hierarchically as occupational groups[115] – nor in organizing the diverse regional castes into a general supra-regional caste system as later attempted by the colonial state.[116] Nonetheless, use of the *khaneh shumaris* meant that classification of the population according to castes, even though initially conducted with reluctance, was included in the Company's archives for the first time – and with it the view of the social world preferred by India's literate classes.[117] In Mackenzie's view, however, it also presented an opportunity to link up with old Hindu traditions that had survived Muslim rule.

Along with these documents collected at the level of the *parganas*, Mackenzie's co-workers also had recourse to the archives of the ubiquitous village accountants called *shamboags* in Mysore. Their collections of texts, sometimes summarized under the term *kaifiyats*, whose significance for Mackenzie's collection has been pointed out by Rama Mantena in particular,[118] represented a treasure trove of information about the history and diverse aspects of the social and economic reality of individual locations, which Mackenzie's co-workers, schooled as they were in various languages and scripts, were all too eager to use. Francis Buchanan, who travelled Mysore and Canara about the same time as Mackenzie's surveys took place, described the materials he found with a village accountant in detail. There were verses containing medical knowledge, instructions for religious ceremonies, lists of local traders and population, accounts of contributions for the repair of a temple, grants of land and a number of revenue records. These disparate records, originating from different centuries, were completed by a chronicle written by succeeding generations, which detailed the political history – including the emergence of different rulers and administrators.[119]

Right from the start of the Mysore Survey the collection of *kaifiyats* formed an important part of the official work programme.[120] The hundreds of texts collected and compiled by Mackenzie's co-workers in the first two decades of the nineteenth century not only reflect his historical interests but above all were an essential component of the statistical project. The sociocultural background of the Indian co-workers clearly made access to the village scribes' archives much easier. Mackenzie did sometimes instruct his subassistants to get information about the available *kaifiyats* and to collect them immediately 'if they give them readily'.[121] But in general the Indian co-workers were responsible for this, since in regions not directly under British control in particular it was not always a simple matter. In Mackenzie's staff's correspondence and reports there are many references to the fact that as official envoys of the Company they were deeply mistrusted.[122] However, this does not mean that their investigations were generally unsuccessful. Difficulties tended to be an exception, which is why they were reported in detail while successful work was generally only mentioned briefly. For instance, after collecting the *khaneh shumaries* of twenty-two *parganas* Ananda Row wrote succinctly and to the point from Masulipatam in the Northern Circars: 'I am now also writing the particular Kyfeyats of each place'.[123]

When he reported that he was 'writing' the *kaifiyats* this certainly did not mean simply copying them: some new texts were also produced, based on local archives. Mackenzie's co-workers often composed these texts themselves using as sources not only archive material but sometimes also inscriptions or oral narratives. In some cases they also commissioned inhabitants of the villages in question to write them,[124] though presumably only people with experience of this sort of text. Texts were produced in the various languages of the Deccan and this not only took account of Mackenzie's statistical requirements, but was also in the tradition of *karanam* literature.[125]

The immediate result of assessing precolonial archives was an impressive collection of texts on topography, population and history. In the first years of the survey Mackenzie already had what he called a 'very satisfactory harvest' of *kaifiyats* and other documents.[126] Praising his survey later on, he said that he had used this favourable opportunity 'to procure every species of information that was attainable ...; for the purpose of illustrating the Resources and actual State of the Country, the Institutions, Customs and Manners of the Natives, their language and literature; the production and Manufactures of Ballaghaat; the Climate, the Soil & the State and mode of Agriculture &ca'.[127] Both originals and copies of many of these documents were included in what later came to be regarded as Mackenzie's private manuscript collection, which is why they have hitherto generally been seen in the context of his historical research.

However, combined with the surveyors' notes this material also formed the basis for statistical memoirs of each individual *pargana*.[128] This meant that, analogous to map drawing, the material collected first had to be subjected to a process of compilation and systematization. 'The Field Work is only a part of the Survey', Mackenzie stressed, '& it is not always recollected that it requires much time and labour to examine, reduce & combine the several parts; to make fair copies; to translate & combine the Memoirs &ca'.[129] So the material collected from the archives went through a process of transformation in which it was not only translated, but also adjusted to European notions of statistical and historical representation. *Kaifiyats* for instance were often abbreviated and transformed into a brief historical summary,[130] and where possible their chronological reliability checked by comparison with other material.[131] Other documents, such as *khaneh shumaries* on the other hand, were entered into the compendiums virtually unchanged.

Some of the statistical memoirs were compiled by Mackenzie's co-workers themselves. A good and very detailed example of this is the statistical description of Shikapoor in the Simoga region compiled by Kavali Venkata Lakshmayya. It begins with the information collected at *pargana* level consisting, along with the district's *dehazada* and the *khaneh shumari,* of data on religious and administrative buildings, on fortifications, passes and rivers, as well as on cultivated plots and taxable establishments. Then comes a description of the *pargana's* boundaries 'as communicated by the District Officers at Shikapoor', and finally of the district itself, 'compiled from enquiries on the spot'. This provides further information, for instance about the geographical location, the etymology of the place name, local products, flora and fauna, climate and life expectancy, language and script, notable buildings and the units of measurement used in the region. The description ends with the history of the *pargana* based on a *kaifiyat* prepared for Lakshmayya, which gives a chronological overview from the beginning of Shikapoor up to the British conquest.[132]

Just what an important contribution the Indian co-workers made in general to the statistical memoirs is demonstrated by comparing the memoirs of Travancore and Malabar attributed to Benjamin Swain Ward and Peter Conner.[133] In Travancore, Mackenzie had provided the two of them with an Indian assistant who was supposed to work on the statistical material,[134] while for the survey of Malabar, carried out after Mackenzie's death, this support was apparently no longer available. The memoir on Travancore contains long passages on the history of the region, population groups and religious establishments, but in his memoir on Malabar, Ward forgoes descriptions of 'history and antiquities, as also manners, customs, and distinctions of the various casts'. His references here to Buchanan's *Journey* and Hamilton's *India*,[135] stating that they contain all the necessary information, demonstrate how far behind Mackenzie's project he was; and what is more, when he stresses that these works are more reliable than those 'crude documents furnished by the natives', this could be taken as an attempt to justify the lack of content in his own work – though to some extent it could also be seen as lack of loyalty to Mackenzie.[136]

Another aspect of the statistical memoirs should also be highlighted. Comparison with journals compiled in the context of earlier surveys reveals the reorientation from purely military to administrative interests, similar to the way in which triangulation of individual *parganas* replaced route surveying in the sphere of cartography. Instead of the narrative description of a route in daily stages, specifically arranged to be particularly useful to marching army units, there was now a systematic overview in the form of a sort of inventory of each *pargana*.[137] In this way the traveller's view was replaced by that of the state, the 'view from nowhere' that characterizes modern maps and statistics.[138]

Although the statistical memoirs linked up with precolonial records and were sometimes compiled by Indian co-workers such as Lakshmayya, they also represented a significant change compared with earlier forms of administrative knowledge in India. By drawing together information previously archived locally, in comprehensive compendia available supra-regionally, they centralized state knowledge, something that had not happened in this form under the precolonial regime. Although the Mughal Empire did have written descriptions which could help to provide an overview of large sections of the empire, these were confined, as in the case of *Ain-i Akbari*, to fairly general accounts of the geography, the political situation, and data about revenue;[139] or as in the case of the *Daftar Asufiah* to a mere list of names of the administrative units and villages, with data on the annual tax revenue realized in the individual *parganas*.[140] However useful such compilations might have been, given the lack of geographical detail they were not sufficient for a central government to intervene without additional local expertise and access to local records. Not so Mackenzie's statistical memoirs, especially in combination with his maps. Anyone with access to this material could gain a detailed overview of the situation in a specific *pargana* independent of location, and on this basis make what at least seemed to be informed decisions about political, economic or social measures on the ground. Both in this function and in terms of content Mackenzie's memoirs anticipated the gazetteers of the later nineteenth century.[141]

Of course, in time it was these ever more refined forms of centralized information that the colonial regime later came to rely on when embarking on major projects conforming to specific notions of 'progress', such as building railways or dams, economic reforms and agronomic improvements.[142] In Mackenzie's day, however, governmental interventions of this sort were still an absolute exception. The most pressing question for a state striving for administrative control in the early nineteenth century was how to tax the country, and his surveys were only of limited use here.[143] This did not mean, however, that Mackenzie's statistical project was not also aimed at changing economic and sociocultural realities through state intervention. Indeed, the ideas on which his investigations were based could be seen as forerunners of the discourse on 'progress' and 'development' in the later nineteenth century.

The Means to Improvement

Despite the major role played by history in Mackenzie's project it was not aimed simply at guaranteeing continuity between the present and a precolonial past. Its objective was also to shape the future. In a broader and more abstract context his surveys can be seen as part of a trend also found in Early Modern European states to acquire ever new knowledge about territories' populations and everything connected with them, parallel and as a supplement to drawing maps[144] – a development Michel Foucault regards as closely connected with the 'governmentalization' of the state. From this perspective the new knowledge is closely tied in to a new sort of science of governance that recognizes population and economy as fields of intervention – this ultimately being the task of the 'governmental administration'.[145] And indeed it is statistics, even in their eighteenth-century descriptive form, which can be seen as one of the most important bases for such intervention.[146]

Some of the ideas regarding the role of the government arose from older mercantilist notions about state promotion of the economy; although with knowledge production new fields of intervention were certainly defined. However, a complete restructuring of Indian society was certainly never the aim. If, as David Scott would have it, the specific feature of 'colonial governmentality' was that it aimed at a radical transformation of Indian society,[147] then Mackenzie's project is more about a 'governmentality of the colonial transition' which, though it makes the state responsible for future developments, certainly does not envisage a clear break with the past. Mackenzie wanted to offer a perspective on India that was not nurtured purely by abstract universalist notions. This must also be one of the reasons why he conceived his surveys as a collective project in which the Indian co-workers also had considerable opportunity to introduce their own intellectual traditions. Of course, in Mackenzie's time this did not mean seeking to conduct a discussion about government aims within an Indian public[148] but rather a paternalistic, patronizing (or to use Foucault's terminology, 'pastoral') approach. As Kalpagam and Prakash argue, this can be seen as the most important characteristic of the governmentality of the colonial state far beyond the phase of transition.[149]

As Robb has shown, Mackenzie's vision of the future was clearly tied to notions of the state's responsibility.[150] In one of his best-known statements, repeated in several of his reports, Mackenzie wrote retrospectively about the origins of the Mysore Survey:

> At a moment when the attention of Government ... turned to the amelioration of the State of the Indian Subjects, the means of conciliating their minds, of exciting habits of industry & cultivating the arts of Peace under the security & milder influence of a fixed Rule, it was presumed that such investigations could not be viewed with indifference under the management of the Indian Company; since our best interests are involved in whatever tends to the acquisition of a more intimate knowledge of the Country and its resources & of the lights thence arising for the improvement of its Revenues and Commerce & the means of promoting the prosperity of a Population on a moderate computation of ten Millions of Native Subjects.[151]

The importance Mackenzie ascribes to his surveys here reflects Sinclair's conviction that the results of statistical investigations would provide a country with the 'means of its future improvement'.[152] In eighteenth-century terminology, 'improvement' initially referred to greater efficiency in agriculture, but it soon came to include ideas for promoting the economy in general, such as fishing or manufacturing, and also philanthropic goals such as moral improvement of the population through education. Peter Womack has shown that the semantic field encompassed by the term in the eighteenth century – social, aesthetic, moral, legal and religious improvement – can be understood as expressing the ideology of the economic elites insofar as it allowed etymologically and historically purely economic concepts of maximizing profit to appear to harmonize with the improvement of all life spheres.[153] Borne by the elites, the idea of improvement was so popular at this time in Scotland that historians have even described it as the 'age of improvement'.[154]

In numerous publications and practical initiatives enthusiasts like Sinclair sought to convert these ideas into reality[155] and his *Statistical Account of Scotland* can also be seen as the product of such enthusiasm. In the past, he argued, well-intentioned measures by statesmen were too often based on speculations produced only by study and were therefore destined to fail. Only knowledge of a society's 'internal structures' based on empirical information could enable the state to act in the right way.[156] 'The principle I maintain' he – who was carrying out agricultural experiments on his own estates – wrote,

> is this, that as no individual can improve his private property, without knowing exactly its extent, the soil of which it consists, the number of farmers by whom it is occupied, the state of buildings erected on it, the crops which it is capable of producing, the best means of cultivating it, &c. &c. &c. neither can any government improve a country, nor better the situation of its inhabitants, without entering into minute inquiries of a similar nature, for the purpose of at least removing all obstacles to improvement. For what is a nation but a great estate? What is a Country but a large farm? And the same principles that are applicable to the improvement of the one, must necessarily be calculated to promote the happiness and the interests of the other.[157]

It is hardly surprising that a neo-mercantilist approach of this sort that equated increasing the profit of a private agricultural business with improving living conditions within a state was welcomed with open arms by those in charge of a trading company and that in the early eighteenth century the EIC initiated a number of further statistical projects.[158] What is more, reference to the popular ideas of improvement also offered a new opportunity to justify the Company's territorial rule in India. A key element in the new concept of imperialism that began to carry weight around 1800 in Britain was the idea that the Empire was ultimately an enterprise for improving conditions in the supposedly backward colonies.[159]

Mackenzie occasionally adopted Sinclair's idea of the estate[160] and was also aware that his statistical investigations could potentially improve the EIC's image. He was, he wrote to Governor William Bentinck, most satisfied with the results of these investigations and was quite convinced 'that they will be equally so to many persons of extended views & enlightened minds in Britain & in Europe should they ever come under their view'.[161] But it would be wrong to assume that only neo-mercantilist rationality was in the foreground here or that he regarded his project purely in terms of its economic and propagandistic usefulness to the EIC. His perspective only becomes comprehensible against the backdrop of his general ideas about state and government, which most certainly applied to his Scottish homeland as well.

Mackenzie was convinced in principle that a strong government was a good thing. He rejected a fundamental change in the power structures. Like so many of his contemporaries he also rejected the democratic ideas of the French Revolution[162] and considered constitutional monarchy to be the most suitable form of government in Europe.[163] He was in favour of maintaining the traditional authorities: 'Happy shall I be', he wrote to Seaforth in light of the perceived threat posed by the French Revolution, '…to find you at home the chief, the landlord, of many happy Parishes, a Patriarch among your clan, a Legislator among your Countrymen'.[164] In India, as he saw things, the Company should act with authority since this was, after all, popular with the population. Looking back at history, he wrote in a memorandum about the precolonial power systems in South India, most of the Indian population believed that strong and energetic rule was better for the country than 'that mild accommodating spirit which however popular on a small scale is never sufficiently energetic to secure good Order & Stability'.[165]

For Mackenzie, however, guaranteeing order and stability was just the basis for further interventions which in Mysore, for instance, where there was a relatively sparse population[166] compared to the rest of India (due to the many wars), were to find expression in an active population policy. This was to involve measures for developing economy and infrastructure, ranging from setting up markets and warehouses, to establishing manufacturing, to promoting exports. By levying revenue, of course, the EIC itself could potentially profit from such a development as well – but Mackenzie stressed at the same time that it must also be in 'the Interests of the Natives'.[167]

Mackenzie had similar views about his Scottish home island, Lewis. Here too, he had written about ten years earlier, the first thing was to create conditions that would increase the size of the population, which would then stimulate production and the circulation of goods. In order to provide all the inhabitants with good prospects, manufacturing of sails and cloth should be established and Stornoway's relative proximity to the Baltic used to its advantage for importing hemp on favourable terms. Roads should be built and the farmers encouraged to use carts so that 'the poor women will be by degrees freed from the hardship of carrying the manure, peats &c. on their backs'. In particular, overseas trade and fishing must be promoted and it was especially important that the ships should belong to local traders so that the profits could remain on the island.[168]

This elaborate programme – it is not possible to go into all the details here – shows the extent to which Mackenzie was committed to the idea of 'improvement' but also that it was not just about increasing economic efficiency for the sake of the owners or the tax-levying authority. This becomes particularly clear from the context in which he felt compelled to convey these suggestions to his patron, Seaforth, since they were a direct reaction to Seaforth's idea of selling the whole parish of Uig, a desperately poor region in the west of Lewis, as a sheep farm.[169] Mackenzie was incandescent with rage about this proposal, which would have meant displacing about two thousand inhabitants,[170] and his letter to Seaforth was intended to help prevent this sale. He expressed his outrage even more clearly in a letter to Alexander Gillanders, his childhood friend: 'I thought the principle, that the true riches of a proprietor consist in a respectable tenantry had been so well understood, that I was not a little struck at seeing this notice'. John Sinclair's idea of increasing the rentability of estates by intensive sheep-rearing, he went on, may perhaps make sense in extremely sparsely populated areas, but he could not imagine that 'the inhabitants of that extensive Parish could [not] by degree be made more permanently useful to the Proprietor, than the precarious addition of rent which any Speculator may bring'. He recalled here in particular his traumatic experiences in the 1770s on Lewis with rent increases, famines and the subsequent mass emigration.[171]

He believed that both the Scottish landlord and the British government in India should forego radical measures for maximizing profit and aim instead for longer-term change in accord with the interests of the population. These interests, of course, could not be defined simply according to 'objective', supra-cultural criteria. The aim of his project, which included factors such as historical development and the specific geographical conditions, was to develop a programme of improvement that went beyond purely abstract ideas and was based on precise local knowledge. So his project in India pointed both to the past and to the future. On the one hand the EIC state should link up with existing South Indian institutions that were often centuries old, but on the other also play an active role in forging the future. For Mackenzie the statistical investigations were more than just a description of the present but played a key role in the project, in many ways, by creating a bridge between maintaining traditional ways of life and improving living conditions, between conservative wishes and progressive demands: in short, between past and future.

Thus, his project gave expression to far more than a purely 'defensive' or in Burke's sense 'conservative' approach. Such a characterization, which was applied to Mackenzie's contemporaries and friends Munro, Malcolm or Elphinstone, concentrates too much on the preservative element in their thinking while neglecting the progressive side. Martha McLaren has argued that the common ideas of these Scottish administrators can be described as an independent 'Scottish School of Thought' about the government of India, whose main point of reference was the intellectual traditions of the Scottish Enlightenment. In some ways similar to Burke, she says, they also stressed the need for continuity in India's political institutions but at the same time, especially influenced by Political Economy, they were keen to bring about economic and social change. In their eyes this should be brought about by the Indian population itself, stimulated by state intervention. According to their notion of progress Europe seemed to be more advanced than India in many ways, but this did not mean that the Indian population was not, in principle, capable of the same development, as was later maintained by conservative administrators, often using racist arguments. According to McLaren the Scottish School was thus an independent school between the conservative orientalists and the radically reformed Anglicists. While the former regarded Indian culture as essentially different and unfit for European-style development, the latter sought to restructure the country and its people completely according to purely theoretical principles.[172]

Like Mackenzie's project, with which it had much in common,[173] the Scottish School can also be seen as a typical expression of the transition phase in which the notions of continuity and change were often regarded not as absolute opposites but as complementary factors that served to legitimize British rule over the subcontinent. Despite ever more apparent attitudes that aimed at a radical transformation of Indian society, the notions on which the governmentality of transition was based had a lasting impact on the EIC state. On the one hand they guaranteed manifold continuities between British rule and its predecessors; on the other they flagged up the state's responsibility to play an active role in forging the future.

Notes

1. *Transactions of the Literary Society of Bombay* 3 (1823). For the society see Datta, 'James Mackintosh', 44f; Rendall, 'Scottish Orientalism', 49f.
2. 'Review of New Publications: Transactions of the Literary Society of Bombay ...', Vol. III', *Gentleman's Magazine* 95(2) (August/October 1825), 137.
3. A.F. Büsching, *Neue Erdbeschreibung*, 8 vols (Hamburg, 1760–1762). Partially translated into English with the title *A New System of Geography: In Which is Given, a General Account of the Situation and Limits, the Manners, History, ... of the Several Kingdoms and States. Carefully Translated from the Last Edition of the German Original*, 6 vols (London, 1762). For the

origin of the work see P. Hoffmann, *Anton Friedrich Büsching (1724–1793): Ein Leben im Zeitalter der Aufklärung* (Berlin, 2000), 145–68.

4. The third category mentioned by Büsching – what Mackenzie called 'political division' – was supposed to contain information about political structure, constitution and forms of religious organization. Mackenzie initially only wanted to deal with it marginally in the form of 'political statistics'. Cf. Colin Mackenzie, 'Plan of the Mysore Survey', 28 January 1800, BL/IOR/P/254/52, 729–45, here 730–39; and Büsching, *Neue Erdbeschreibung*, vol. 1, 25f. Unlike Mackenzie's survey, Büsching's idea of describing the earth was connected with religious notions.

5. Cf. Hoffmann, *Büsching*, 179–86; and M. Bowen, *Empiricism and Geographical Thought: From Francis Bacon to Alexander von Humboldt* (Cambridge, 1981), 155.

6. Sinclair, *Statistical Account*. For Sinclair as a model see Cohn, 'Transformation of Objects into Artifacts', 80; Wagoner, 'Precolonial Intellectuals', 790; and Vicziany, 'Imperialism, Botany and Statistics', 648f.

7. Josiah Webbe to Colin Mackenzie, 4 November 1799, NAI/SIR/SGO/3, 9f.

8. Sinclair considered Achenwall (falsely) to have invented the term 'Statistik': Sinclair, *Statistical Account*, vol. 20, lxxiii. For Achenwall's contribution see P. Streidl, *Naturrecht, Staatswissenschaften und Politisierung bei Gottfried Achenwall (1719–1772): Studien zur Gelehrtengeschichte Göttingens in der Aufklärung* (Munich, 2003), 123–36.

9. Before Sinclair's work there were only two publications in Britain that used the word 'statistical' in the title: *Political Geography: Introduction to the Statistical Tables of the Principal Kingdoms and States in Europe* (London and Dublin, 1789); and T.B. Clarke, *A Statistical View of Germany, in Respect to the Imperial and Territorial Constitution, Forms of Government, Legislation … With a Sketch of the Character and the Genius of the Germans, and a Short Enquiry into the State of their Trade and Commerce* (London 1790). Both referred explicitly to German models.

10. Cf. Sinclair, *Statistical Account*, vol. 20, xiii.

11. This made his project fundamentally different from William Petty's 'political arithmetic'. He considered Petty's contribution to be virtually irrelevant to his idea of statistical knowledge. Cf. Sinclair, *Statistical Account*, vol. 20, lxvii. For Petty see J. Mykkänen, '"To methodize and regulate them": William Petty's Governmental Science of Statistics', *History of the Human Sciences* 7 (1994), 65–88.

12. Cf. R. Vierhaus, 'Die Universität Göttingen und die Anfänge der Geschichtswissenschaft im 18. Jahrhundert', in H. Boockmann and H. Wellenreuther (eds), *Geschichtswissenschaft in Göttingen: Eine Vorlesungsreihe* (Göttinger Universitätsschriften, Series A: vol. 2) (Göttingen, 1987), 16. For the concept of 'university statistics' see K. Johanisson, 'Society in Numbers: The Debate over Quantification in 18th-Century Political Economy', in T. Frängsmyr, J.L. Heilbron and R.E. Rider (eds), *The Quantifying Spirit in the 18th Century* (Berkeley, Los Angeles and Oxford, 1990), 344–47; and S.J. Woolf, 'Towards the History of the Origins of Statistics: France 1789–1815', in S.J. Woolf and J.-C. Perrot, *State and Statistics in France 1789–1815* (Chur, London, Paris and New York, 1984), 83–85.

13. For the origins and development of mathematical statistics see for example R. Stone, *Some British Empiricists in the Social Sciences, 1650–1900* (Cambridge, 1997); S.M. Stiegler, *The History of Statistics: The Measurement of Uncertainty before 1900* (Cambridge, MA, and London, 1986); T.M. Porter, *The Rise of Statistical Thinking 1820–1900* (Princeton, 1986); and J.W. Tankard, *The Statistical Pioneers* (Cambridge, MA, 1984).

14. Cf. C.W. Withers, *Geography, Science and National Identity: Scotland since 1520* (Cambridge, 2001), 112–57; id., 'How Scotland Came to Know Itself: Geography, National Identity and the Making of a Nation, 1680–1790', *Journal of Historical Geography* 21(4) (1995), 371–97; R.L. Emerson, 'Sir Robert Sibbald, Kt, the Royal Society of Scotland and the Origins of

the Scottish Enlightenment', *Annals of Science* 45(1) (1988), 45f, 53f; and id., 'Science and the Origins and Concerns of the Scottish Enlightenment', *History of Science* 26(4) (1988), 33–66.

15. Sinclair, *Statistical Account*, vol. 1, viii–x.

16. Sinclair, *Statistical Account*, vol. 20, xviii.

17. Cf. J. Sinclair, *The Correspondence of the Right Honourable Sir John Sinclair, with Reminiscences of the most Distinguished Characters Who Have Appeared in Great Britain, and in Foreign Countries, during the Last Fifty Years*, 2 vols (London, 1831), vol.1, xxix.

18. D.J. Withrington, 'What Was Distinctive about the Scottish Enlightenment', in J.J. Carer and J.H. Pittcock (eds), *Aberdeen and the Enlightenment* (Aberdeen, 1987), 16.

19. Cf. J. Sinclair, *Analysis of the Statistical Account of Scotland; with a General View of the History of that Country and Discussions on important Branches of Political Economy*, 2 vols (Edinburgh, 1825–1826), vol.1, 68f; Mitchison, *Agricultural Sir John*, 141–49.

20. Cf. Mitchison, *Agricultural Sir John*, 134f.

21. Cf. Drayton, *Nature's Government*, 115f.

22. Colin Mackenzie, 'Second General Report on the Mysore Survey', 12 July 1803, NAI/SIR/REP/2, 17–35, here 33. Although this suggests that at the time of his appointment he was not familiar with the details of the relatively new *Statistical Account*, he was at least superficially familiar with Sinclair's work. Cf. Colin Mackenzie to Alexander Gillanders, 25 July 1794, NAS/GD/46/17/4, 448–55, here 453.

23. George Buchan to Colin Mackenzie, 19 January 1803, NAI/SIR/SGO/3, 91–93, here 91.

24. Cf. George Buchan to Postmaster General, 28 April 1804, NAI/SIR/SGO/90A, 40; 'Extract from the Minutes of Consultations in the Public Department', 17 February 1809, ibid., 41.

25. 'Extract of a General Letter ... dated February 9 1809', 367.

26. Sinclair, *Analysis*, vol. 1, 60. Sinclair was able to cite Dugald Stewart in order to legitimize his concept of knowledge (ibid. 59): 'It has been justly observed by a distinguished Philosopher that it is impossible to establish *solid general principles,* without previous study of particulars. Unless general principles will admit of practical application, however beautiful they may appear in theory, they are of far less value, than the limited acquisitions of the vulgar. The foundation of all human knowledge, therefore, must be laid in the examination *of particular facts*; and it is only so far as general principles are resolvable into these primary elements, that they possess either truth or utility'. Cf. D. Stewart, *Elements of the Philosophy of the Human Mind*, 3 vols (London and Edinburgh 1792–1827), vol. 1, 215.

27. Sinclair, *Analysis*; id., *Sketch of an Introduction to the Proposed Analysis of the Statistical Account of Scotland Containing Observations on the Nature and Principles of Statistical Enquiries, and the Advantages to Be Derived from Them* (London, 1802). For the plan of 1798 see Sinclair, *Statistical Account*, vol. 20, 12f.

28. Colin Mackenzie, 'General Heads of Instructions for the Geometrical & Geographical Survey of a Purgunnah or Hobely in Mysore', NAI/SIR/REP/2, 83f; see also id., 'Second General Report on the Mysore Survey, 12 July 1803', ibid., 17–35, here 33f; id., 'View of the Progress of the Survey of the Survey of Mysore and the Present State in January 1802', BL/OIOC/Mss Eur/F/228/39.

29. Colin Mackenzie, 'Hints or Heads of Enquiry for facilitating our Knowledge of the more Southern parts of the Deckan', 1800, BL/OIOC/Mss Eur/F/128/213.

30. Of Mackenzie's twenty-six categories eleven are identical with those of Sinclair, and another third, though in a different cultural context, certainly comparable. Cf. Colin Mackenzie, 'Hints or Heads of Enquiry for facilitating our Knowledge of the more Southern parts of the Deckan', 1800, BL/OIOC/Mss Eur/F/128/213; and Sinclair, *Statistical Account*, vol. 1, viii–x.

31. Colin Mackenzie, 'Second General Report on the Mysore Survey', 12 July 1803, NAI/SIR/REP/2, 17–35, here 33.
32. Colin Mackenzie, 'Memorandum of the Origin, Progress and Present State of the Geometrical and Statistic Survey of Mysore, to July 1st 1807', BL/Mss Add/14380, 34.
33. Colin Mackenzie to William Lantwar, 2 October 1809, NAI/SIR/SGO/90A, 122.
34. Cf. Colin Mackenzie to Michael Dunigan, 30 September 1809, NAI/SIR/SGO/90A, 117.
35. Cf. Colin Mackenzie, 'General Heads of Instructions for the Geometrical & Geographical Survey of a Purgunnah or Hobely in Mysore', NAI/SIR/REP/2, 83f.
36. Colin Mackenzie to Lieutenant P. Connor, 11 January 1816, NAI/SIR/SGO/573, 28f.
37. Cf. Colin Mackenzie to Barry Close, 9 November 1799, NAI/SIR/M/6, 27–32, here 28; Colin Mackenzie to John Warren, 5 September 1800, ibid., 176–79, here 177.
38. Cf. Colin Mackenzie to Barry Close, 24 October 1800, NAI/SIR/M/6, 211–14, here 212.
39. Cf. R.N. Yesudas, 'The English and the Tribals in Wayanad, 1799–1805', *Journal of Indian History* 64 (1986), 205–12; Beaglehole, *Munro*, 59–68.
40. Cf. Colin Mackenzie to Thomas Arthur, 19 November 1800, NAI/SIR/SGO/90, 233; also 14 December 1800, NAI/SIR/M/6, 229–31.
41. Colin Mackenzie to Thomas Arthur, 21 February 1803, NAI/SIR/M/6, 359f; id. to J.H. Peile, 24 February 1803, ibid., 365; id. to Thomas Arthur, 26 February 1803, NAI/SIR/SGO/90, 297f.
42. Other European assistants had similar problems in Mysore. It seems to have been easier for Mackenzie himself, who had most of the necessary enquiries carried out by his Indian co-workers: as he wrote to Munro, 'in Mysore the Amuldar and their servants are ready to do even more than I wish. It is a curious fact that Mr Warren and Mr Mather both complain of want of attention and information from the Amuldars in their respective Districts. – Mather in particular … supposes it is owing to his not being in the Company's Service – while I find everything go on smoothly in the Rajah's country'. See Colin Mackenzie to Thomas Munro, 29 April 1801, NAI/SIR/SGO/90, 390–92, here 392. See also Colin Mackenzie to Thomas Arthur, 6 May 1803, NAI/SIR/SGO/90, 301–3, here 302; also 17 June 1803, ibid., 304f.
43. Eugene F. Irschick, for instance, has shown that the local elites in the Madras Jaghire systematically made complaints to the superiors in order to undermine the position of the Collector, Lionel Place. Cf. Irschick, *Dialogue and History*, 51–53.
44. Cf. Edney, *Mapping an Empire*, 83, 329.
45. J.H. Peile to Colin Mackenzie, 9 March 1803, NAI/SIR/SGO/3, 433f. Arthur had only recently received his instructions: Colin Mackenzie to Thomas Arthur, 26 February 1803, NAI/SIR/SGO/90, 297f.
46. Colin Mackenzie to John Mather and Thomas Arthur, 16 March 1803, NAI/SIR/M/6, 368. Mackenzie initially suspected that Morison, who meanwhile had left, had caused the complaint. Cf. Colin Mackenzie to Thomas Arthur, 17 March 1803, NAI/SIR/SGO/90, 298; id. to J.H. Peile, 4 April 1803, NAI/SIR/M/6, 371.
47. Colin Mackenzie to Thomas Arthur, 17 April 1803, NAI/SIR/SGO/90, 298f.
48. Colin Mackenzie to Thomas Arthur, 6 May 1803, NAI/SIR/SGO/90, 301–3; also 17 June 1803, ibid., 304f.
49. Cf. Colin Mackenzie to Thomas Arthur, 3 July 1803, NAI/SIR/SGO/90, 305–7, here 306; also 8 August 1803, ibid., 307f.
50. J.H. Peile to Colin Mackenzie, 25 August 1803, NAI/SIRSGO/3, 437f; Colin Mackenzie to Thomas Arthur, 12 September 1803, NAI/SIRSGO/90, 309f.
51. Colin Mackenzie to Thomas Arthur, 26 November 1803, NAI/SIR/SGO/90, 312f, here 312.
52. Josiah Webbe to Colin Mackenzie, 10 December 1803, NAI/SIR/SGO/3, 453–55, here 353.

53. Translation from Extract of a letter from the Aumildar of Narsipoor addressed to the Dewan of Mysoor dated 15th Jan 1804', NAI/SIR/SGO/3, 469–71; Josiah Webbe to Colin Mackenzie, 24 January 1804, ibid., 461–66.

54. Cf. Mark Wilks to Colin Mackenzie, 29 March 1804, NAI/SIR/SGO/3, 473–78.

55. Cf. Colin Mackenzie to Thomas Arthur, 2 June 1804, NAI/SIR/M/18, 64.

56. J.H. Peile to Colin Mackenzie, 22 April 1805, NAI/SIR/SGO/3, 513f. For Arthur's dismissal and further career see also Phillimore, *Historical Records*, vol. 2, 376–80.

57. Cf. Colin Mackenzie, 'Establishment proposed for Captn. Mackenzie superintending the Mysore Survey for a Month of 30 days', NAI/SIR/M/6, 69f, here 69. Mackenzie also listed his Hyderabad staff here.

58. Cf. ibid., 70; Colin Mackenzie to Arthur Wellesley, 28 July 1800, NAI/SIR/M/6, 157–59.

59. Cf. Colin Mackenzie, 'Statement of the Establishment proposed for Major Mackenzie Superintendant of the Mysore Survey to commence from 1st October 1803 for a Month of 30 days, 21 December 1803, BL/IOR/F/4/280 (6426), 71f; B (FSG) to CD, 29 March 1804, ibid., 21–27. There is a copy of the statement in NAI/SIR/M/18, 40.

60. Cf. Colin Mackenzie to George Buchan, 23 February 1809, NAI/SIR/M/18, 263–66, here 266.

61. Dirks, 'Colonial Histories and Native Informants'. Later on Dirks himself went beyond the concept of the 'informant'. Cf. Dirks, *Castes of Mind*, 100.

62. Cf. for example Colin Mackenzie to Barry Close, 26 July 1800, NAI/SIR/M/6, 153–55; id. to Colonel Montresor, 28 July 1800, ibid., 159–62.

63. Colin Mackenzie to James Gahagan, 16 March 1809, NAI/SIR/SGO/90A, 53–55, here 55. See also id. to Michael Dunigan and Benjamin Ward, 15 March 1809, 49–52; id. to Gahagan, 9 May 1809, ibid., 58–60; id. to Kavali Venkata Lakshmayya, 27 January 1810, ibid., 85f; id. to Henry Hamilton and William Lantwar, 29 January 1810, ibid., 87f.

64. Cf. 'General Report on the State of the Surveying Department at Fort St. George and Draft reports of Progress for 1817 by Col. Colin Mackenzie, S.G. of India, 1816 and 1817', NAI/SIR/REP/3, Appendix 3 (1 August 1816), 37–76, here 68.

65. Colin Mackenzie to Mountstuart Elphinstone, 7 September 1818, NAI/SIR/SGO/435D, 9–11, here 10.

66. Mark Wilks to George Buchan, 4 March 1807, NAI/SIR/SGO/3, 565–71, here 570. There is a copy of the letter in BL/OIOC/Mss Eur/F 228/39.

67. Mackenzie stressed that the plan was 'entirely of their own & agreeable to ancient practice'. Likewise Wilkins, who stated that Kavali Venkata Borayya had had 'the merit of first tracing the outline of the plan which has been so successfully pursued'. Colin Mackenzie to Mountstuart Elphinstone, 7 September 1818, NAI/SIR/SGO/435D, 9–11, here 11; Mark Wilks to George Buchan, 4 March 1807, NAI/SIR/SGO/3, 565–71, here 570.

68. The most valuable information on this is in the following documents: 'Detailed List of the Establishment attached to the Superintendant of the Mysore Survey for the Month ending 30th April 1809 per Order of Government of 28th February 1809', NAI/SIR/SGO/90A, 213; 'Native Writers and Translators to the Collection of the late Col. Colin Mackenzie', 1822, BL/IOR/F/4/867 (22924), 198; 'Extra Native Writers in the Historical Department of the late Colin Mackenzie', ibid., 199 and the accounts for their costs: 'Messrs. Palmer and Co, Attornies to the Executive of the late Colonel Mackenzie to Charles Lushington', 19 October 1822, ibid. 155–77, here 175–77.

69. See Mantena, 'Kavali Brothers'; ead., *Origins of Modern Historiography*, 87–122; Rao, 'Pioneers of English Writing in India'; and J. Mangamma, *Book Printing in India with Special Reference to the Contribution of European Scholars to Telugu (1746–1857)* (Nellore, 1975), 251–64. In 1817 Mackenzie himself confirmed that he had employed four of the Kavali

brothers. Borayya, and another Kavali brother died while working for Mackenzie. Cf. Colin Mackenzie to John Riddell, 28 January 1817, NAI/SIR/SGO/573, 287–90, here 288.

70. See for example Colin Mackenzie, 'Second General Report on the Mysore Survey', 1803, NAI/SIR/REP/2, 34.

71. For details see the somewhat idealized biography later written in English by his brother Kavali Venkata Ramaswami, *Biographical Sketches*, 154f. See also Rao, 'Pioneers of English Writing', 3–5.

72. Lakshmayya had been working for Mackenzie since 1798, Ramswami since 1803. In a document of 1816 the latter is described as second 'Head Interpretor, Translator and Pundit'. Cf. 'Detailed List of the Establishment attached to the Superintendant of the Mysore Survey for the Month ending 30th April 1809 per Order of Government of 28th February 1809', NAI/SIR/SGO/90A, 213; and 'General Report on the State of the Surveying Department at Fort St. George and Draft reports of Progress for 1817 by Col. Colin Mackenzie, S.G. of India, 1816 and 1817', NAI/SIR/REP/3, Appendix 3 (1 August 1816), 37–76, here 73f.

73. Cf. Charles Lushington to Colin Mackenzie, 17 December 1819, NAI/SIR/SGO/9, 565; and Wagoner, 'Precolonial Intellectuals', 794.

74. At the beginning of the survey Mackenzie himself described the significance of a *munshi* as follows: 'I have in some measure provided for this by getting up a sensible Moor Man as a Mounshee who accompanied our Party to Hyderabad two years ago, as he is reckoned a good Persian Scholar, he will be useful in many respects & add a certain confidence to my Hindoo Servants while his attention will be also directed to these languages they are not conversant in'. Colin Mackenzie to Barry Close, 7 September 1800, NAI/SIRM/6, 179–82, here 180f. Abdul Aziz started working for Mackenzie in 1802.

75. Cf. M. Wilks, *Historical Sketches*, vol. 1, 510.

76. Cf. Colin Mackenzie, 'General Report on the State of the Surveying Department at Fort St. George and Draft reports of Progress for 1817', NAI/SIR/REP/3, Appendix 3 (1 August 1816), 37–76, here 72f, 75.

77. Cf. Colin Mackenzie to John Riddell, 28 November 1817, NAI/SIR/SGO/573, 287–90, here 288.

78. Cf. Mantena, 'Kavali Brothers', 130f; Dirks, 'Colin Mackenzie', 40f.

79. After various court cases between the family members, in 1841 the *zamindari* was allocated to Lakshmayya because of the money he had already paid. Cf. G. Mackenzie, *A Manual of the Kistna District in the Presidency of Madras* (Madras, 1883), 338f.

80. Cf. Colin Mackenzie, 'Establishment proposed for Captn. Mackenzie superintending the Mysore Survey for a Month of 30 days', NAI/SIR/M/6, 69f, here 70. Here Mackenzie proposes a monthly salary of 30 pagodas for Borayya, which he justifies as follows: 'The pay here proposed as Head Interpreter for Cavelly Boriah, a Bramin employed by me for several years, is suggested rather as a mark of approbation of the fidelity and attachment he is manifested with advantage to the publick duties I have been employed on & to defray the expence of several people occasionally assisting him; for he has been always paid by me from 20 to 25 Madras Pagodas per month tho' my allowances for Interpreter had been as stated here, only 10 Pag per Month'.

81. In 1809 Lakshmayya earned 40 pagodas and at the time of Mackenzie's death in 1821 300 Bengali rupis, a sum equivalent to more than 80 pagodas. Cf. 'Detailed List of the Establishment attached to the Superintendant of the Mysore Survey for the Month ending 30th April 1809 per Order of Government of 28th February 1809', NAI/SIR/SGO/90A, 213; and 'Native Writers and Translators to the Collection of the late Col. Colin Mackenzie', 1822, BL/IOR/F/4/867 (22924), 198.

82. Cf. Horace Hayman Wilson to Charles Lushington, 25 November 1822, BL/IOR/F/4/867 (22924), 149–54, here 152.

83. Cf. Kavali Venkata Lakshmayya to Charles Lushington, 1 June 1825, BL/IOR/F/4/867 (22925), 27–33, here 29.

84. By 1809, for instance, Lakshmayya had already been guaranteed a pension amounting to three quarters of his salary. By 1821 Mackenzie had managed to assure him of a pension equivalent to his full final salary, and six other co-workers half of their salary. Cf. George Buchan to Colin Mackenzie, 28 February 1809, NAI/SIR/SGO/3, 207f; and Horace Hayman Wilson to Charles Lushington, 3 January 1822, BL/IOR/F/4/867 (22924), 41–59, here 55f.

85. This was the case for the first time after Borayya's death, when Mackenzie himself intervened in an important official report to secure payment for his family. Other families were also paid pensions after bereavement, for example those of Narrain Row, Ramadoss and Venkaji. Before he left for Bengal, Narrain Row had already asked for this. Cf. Colin Mackenzie, 'Second General Report on the Mysore Survey', 12 July 1803, NAI/SIR/REP/2, 17–35, here 34; 'Extract of a Minute of the Right Honourable the GinC', 14 July 1817, NAI/SIR/SGO/7, 125f; Charles Lushington to Colin Mackenzie, 17 December 1819, NAI/SIR/SGO/9, 565; and Narrain Row to Colin Mackenzie, 31 December 1817, BL/OIOC/Mss Eur/Mack Misc/174.

86. Cf. Wagoner, 'Precolonial Intellectuals', 795. From the name suffix 'Row', Wagoner concludes a *niyogi* identity. On this basis eleven of the thirty-nine co-workers identifiable by name were *niyogi*, plus the four Kavali brothers.

87. V.N. Rao, D. Shulman and S. Subrahmanyam, *Textures of Time: Writing History in South India 1600–1800* (Delhi, 2001), 19–21, 93–139; V.N. Rao, 'Print and Prose: Pundits, Karanams, and the East India Company in the Making of Modern Telugu', in S. Blackburn and V. Dalmia (eds), *India's Literary History: Essays on the Nineteenth Century* (Delhi, 2004), 151f.

88. Cf. V.N. Rao and S. Subrahmanyam, 'Notes on Political Thought in Medieval and Early Modern South India', *Modern Asian Studies* 43(1) (2009), 201–4.

89. Colin Mackenzie, 'Memorandum of the Financial Records of the Deckan', 12 June 1809, BL/OIOC/Mss Eur/Mack Gen/44, 1–9, here 7, 9. Mackenzie explicitly mentions other groups too in this function, such as 'Mahratta Bramins' and Deshastas ('Dashest Bramins'). The fact that he had already been informed about these groups years earlier is evidenced by his notes of April 1803. See BL/OIOC/Mss Eur/Mack Gen/6, 12f. In 1828 Francis Whyte Ellis still considered it necessary to point out in his commentary on James Mills' *History of British India*, 3 vols (London, 1817), that the terms 'Brahmins' and 'priests' were certainly not interchangeable. According to him the *niyogis* in particular were exclusively involved with secular tasks. Cf. 'Analysis of the Code of Menu', *Asiatic Journal and Monthly Register for British India and its Dependencies* 26(152) (August 1828), 178f.

90. Cf. Rao and Subrahmanyam, 'Notes on Political Thought', 202–6; Rao, Shulman and Subrahmanyam, *Textures of Time*, 124–26.

91. Cf. Rao, 'Print and Prose', 150f; and Rao, Shulman and Subrahmanyam, *Textures of Time*, 111. For examples of the important role played by *niyogis/karanams* at village level in Andhra in the nineteenth century and beyond see R.E. Frykenberg, 'Village Strength in South India', in id. (ed.), *Land Control and Social Structure in Indian History* (Madison, Milwaukee and London, 1969), 227–47; M.A. Reddy, *Lands and Tenants in South India: A Study of Nellore District 1850–1990* (Bombay, Calcutta and Madras, 1996), 21–24.

92. Cf. 'Zemindary and Ryotwari Collections – Native Servants: General Return of Native Revenue Officers in the Pay of the Government of Madras, 1818–19', *Asiatic Journal and Monthly Register for British India and its Dependencies* 27(162) (1829), 679.

93. Cf. B. Raman, 'Tamil Munshis and Kacceri Tamil under the Company's Document Raj in Early-Nineteenth Century Madras', in Trautmann, *Madras School of Orientalism*, 211f.

94. Rao and Subrahmanyam, 'Notes on Political Thought', 202. Both authors see the *karanam* literature explicitly in the tradition of literature dealing with *niti*, which they translate as 'pragmatics', 'politics', 'statecraft'. Cf. ibid., 180f.

95. Cf. Wagoner, 'Precolonial Intellectuals', 798f.

96. Part of this correspondence was translated into English in order to give Mackenzie a degree of control. See BL/OIOC/Mss Eur/Mack Misc/172, 174 and the copious material in the *Translations:* BL/OIOC/Mss Eur/Mack Trans/12, 'Letters and Reports'. See also Wagoner, 'Precolonial Intellectuals', 792.

97. For a time, along with his brother Ramaswami, the linguistically gifted Lucius Rawdon Burke also deputized for him in this post, especially in 1817/1818 when Mackenzie had already moved to Calcutta while Lakshmayya had to stay in Madras due to financial and legal problems. However, this was clearly an exception, as demonstrated by a letter from Narrain Row expressing surprise at having received no response from Lakshmayya. Mackenzie subsequently bought Lakshmayya's freedom in December 1817. Cf. Narrain Row to Kavali Venkata Lakshmayya, 10 December 1817, BL/OIOC/Mss Eur/Mack Misc/174; id. to Lucius Rawdon Burke, 25 December 1817, ibid.; Colin Mackenzie to John Riddell, 23 November 1817, NAI/SIR/SGO/573, 283–86; also 28 November 1817, ibid., 287–90; 12 December 1817, ibid., 291f; and 23 December 1817, ibid., 293f.

98. By the end of 1805, for instance, Mackenzie's co-workers Narrain Row and Nitala Naina were writing regular reports on their progress; Narrain Row and Ananda Row also produced a joint report and for the later years there are a number of official reports. See for example BL/OIOC/Mss Eur/Mack Misc/172; 'Report of Narrain Row & Ananda Row for December 1805', BL/OIOC/Mss Eur/Mack Trans/12/12; 'Report of Narrain Row from April to August 1816', BL/OIOC/Mss Eur/Mack Trans/12/47; and 'Report made by S.N. Appavoo respecting the account &c. which he inquired in his 3rd Journey to Mahabaleeburam thro' Chingleputt & Patcheertam, from thence to Jagheer & Arcot Districts', [June–August 1816], BL/OIOC/Mss Eur/Mack Trans/12/59.

99. Nitala Naina wrote in 1807 for instance: 'I have no money for the different Historical expences & for me, you should please to send a bill for me otherwise I cannot live a moment in this country as I am not acquainted with anyone': Nitala Naina to Kavali Venkata Lakshmayya, 25 May 1807, BL/OIOC/Mss Eur/Mack Misc/172.

100. For instance when Narrain Row employed two scribes on his own initiative in about 1819, Mackenzie complained that he should have agreed it with Lakshmayya first. Cf. Narrain Row to Lucius Rawdon Burke, 25 December 1817, BL/OIOC/Mss Eur/Mack Misc/174.

101. The *amini* commission, tasked with carrying this out, was active for about two years from 1776 but its conclusions were not initially used for resetting the taxation rate. Cf. Travers, '"The Real Value of the Lands"'; and Mann, *Bengalen im Umbruch,* 191f, 195.

102. BL/IOR/H/46 (1), 1–5. The anonymous paper, dated to about 1780, was probably from the collection of the EIC historian John Bruce.

103. Cf. James Grant, 'Of the Northern Circars from a Political Survey of the Dekhin', 1784, BL/OIOC/Mss Eur/Mack Gen/47.

104. The survey documents show this quite clearly: John Mather, 'Records of the Barramahl & Salem &c. Districts – Section IInd, Geography', NAI/SIR/M/1, and the material in BL/OIOC/Mss Eur/Mack Gen/46, 171–385.

105. In Mysore these files were generally kept in the *kasbas* or main places of the *pargana*, and only occasionally in the subunits called *taroof.* Cf. Colin Mackenzie to John Warren, 24 April 1801, NAI/SIR/M/6, 258f.

106. Both *dehazadas* and *khaneh shumaries* were kept for fiscal purposes and were available in virtually all the *parganas* in India dealt with by surveys Mackenzie led. He specifically instructed his co-workers such as Benjamin Swain Ward (who was working with Narrain

Row) to accept the documents in the form customary in the field. Only occasionally, for instance if the registers were no longer being kept, did the documents have to be compiled again, as Nitala Naina reported. See Colin Mackenzie to Benjamin Swain Ward, 22 July 1809, NAI/SIR/SGO/90A, 72; and Nitala Naina to Kavali Venkata Lakshmayya, 1 August 1816, BL/OIOC/Mss Eur/Mack Trans/12/47, 94f.

107. Cf. Colin Mackenzie, 'Memorandum of the Origin, Progress and Present State of the Geometrical and Statistic Survey of Mysore, to July 1st 1807', BL/Mss Add/14380, 32. One of the most complete memoirs in this respect was 'Memoirs of a Geographical, Statistical and Historical Survey of the Mysore Dominions, commenced on the Partition of Mysore in 1799 with Maps, Vol VII containing The Province of Nugguar or Bidenoor Part II', NAI/SIR/M/7.

108. *Khaneh Shumaries* (rough lists of all houses) were clearly kept in all parts of the Mughal Empire and beyond. Cf. D. Bhattacharya and R.D. Roy, 'Khanasumari Records and the Statistical System of India', *Indian Historical Records Commission, Proceedings of the 45th Session* (1977), 227–37.

109. Cf. Colin Mackenzie, 'Statistic Remarks on the Population & Resources of the British Dependencies in Balla-Ghaat from Results of the Mysore Survey in 1802', NLS/Ms 11722 (I), 9f; id. to Mountstuart Elphinstone, 7 September 1818, NAI/SIR/SGO/435D, 10.

110. Colin Mackenzie, 'Memorandum of the Origin, Progress and Present State of the Geometrical and Statistic Survey of Mysore, to July 1st 1807', BL/Mss Add/14380, 32.

111. Colin Mackenzie to Mountstuart Elphinstone, 7 September 1818, NAI/SIR/SGO/435D, 10.

112. Colin Mackenzie, 'Memorandum of the Origin, Progress and Present State of the Geometrical and Statistic Survey of Mysore, to July 1st 1807', BL/Mss Add/14380, 32.

113. BL/OIOC/Mss Eur/Mack Gen/8, 125–32, here 129.

114. For instance in the presidencies of Bombay and Bengal. See for example R. Jenkins, *Report on the Territories of the Rajah of Nagpore. Submitted to the Supreme Government of India* (Calcutta, 1827), 19f; F. Buchanan Hamilton, *A Geographical, Statistical, and Historical Description of the District, or Zila, of Dinajpore, in the Province, or Soubah, of Bengal* (Calcutta, 1833), 67.

115. Here, of course, he saw one of the main differences between Indian and European societies. This difference, he said, was based on 'exclusive restriction of profession & of the occupations of life to Castes, with the profound respect & subserviency of the Several Classes of which the Nation is formed to the Superior Orders in gradation; all which at several periods was carried to an excess equally prejudicial to the rights of the prince & to the comfort of the people'. Colin Mackenzie, 'Memorandum on the Ancient Hindoo System of Government and its Vestiges in the South of the Peninsula', BL/OIOC/Mss Eur/Mack Gen/45, 1–11, here 5.

116. This is an important argument for Dirks, *Castes of Mind*, 117f, who stresses that castes were largely unimportant for the early colonial administration.

117. Cf., using later examples, N. Peabody, 'Cents, Sense, Census: Human Inventories in Late Precolonial and Early Colonial India', *Comparative Studies in Society and History* 43(4) (2001), 819–50. See also S. Guha, 'The Politics of Identity and Enumeration in India c. 1690–1990', *Comparative Studies in Society and History* 45(1) (2003), 148–67.

118. Cf. R.S. Mantena, 'The Question of History in Precolonial India', *History and Theory* 46(3) (2007), 404; ead., *Origins of Modern Historiography*, 125–30; and H.K. Sherwani, 'Contemporary Histories of the Qutb Shahi Dynasty of Golkonda', in M. Hasan (ed.), *Historians of Medieval India* (Meerut, 1968), 96f.

119. Cf. Buchanan, *Journey from Madras*, vol. 3, 170–73. Buchanan, who travelled in Canara, called these collections '*bahudunda*' and stated that they could be found with every village scribe. Cf. ibid, 166.

120. Cf. Colin Mackenzie to Barry Close, 7 September 1800, NAI/SIR/M/6, 179–82, here 181.

121. Colin Mackenzie to Michael Dunigan, 15 June 1810, NAI/SIR/SGO/90A, 132.

122. For a number of examples see Dirks, *Castes of Mind*, 102f; and id., 'Colonial Histories and Native Informants', 296–99.

123. Ananda Row to Colin Mackenzie, 15 November 1817, BL/OIOC/Mss Eur/Mack Misc/174.

124. See for example 'Kyfeyat or Historical Account of Cholaroya Patnam or Chola Maulega situated 3 Miles SW from Coombhaconum. Written by Ramiah aged 40 Years an Inhabitant of Cumbaconum; Sashachelliah aged 35 Years Inhabitant of Putt Erwar Grammam; Kistniah aged 95 Years Inhabitant of Chola Maulega. Translated by Baboo Row on the 5th July 1817', BL/OIOC/Mack Misc/77/17.

125. Cf. V. Rajagopal, 'Fashioning Modernity in Telugu: Viresalingam and his Interventionist Strategy', *Studies in History* 21(1) (2005), 48; and Rao, Shulman and Subrahmanyam, *Textures of Time*, 125.

126. Colin Mackenzie to Barry Close, 27 March 1801, NAI/SIR/M/6, 255f: 'the Kyfyats and accounts collected in the Districts; the harvest has been very satisfactory, but it will take time to arrange or abstract them'.

127. Colin Mackenzie, 'Memorandum of the Origin, Progress and Present State of the Geometrical and Statistic Survey of Mysore, to July 1st 1807', BL/Mss Add 14380, 1–38, here 31f. See also NLS/Ms 11722(i), 1–8.

128. The descriptions of each individual *pargana* in the Mysore Survey were compiled in seven volumes according to region. They became the model not only for the four-volume memoir of the Ceded Districts but also for numerous other memoirs of different regions in South India. Cf. Colin Mackenzie, 'Brief View of the Collection of notes observations and Journals of 31 years and of Collections of Manuscripts, Inscriptions, drawings &ca. for the last 19 years made by Colonel Mackenzie in India, exclusive of a considerable collection of Native Manuscripts in all Languages of India', [1813/14], BL/IOR/F/4/867 (22924), 60–139, here 66–68; for later memoirs see for example Colin Mackenzie to Stephen Lushington, 7 March 1820, BL/Mss Add/14380, 39–52, here 40–45.

129. Colin Mackenzie to C.R. Ross, 16 December 1815, NAI/SIR/SGO/573, 20–22, here 21.

130. Cf. Colin Mackenzie to Josiah Webbe, 21 November 1802, BL/IOR/F/4/152 (2598), 194–99, here 97. Copy in NAI/SIR/M/6, 354f.

131. Cf. Colin Mackenzie to Barry Close, 24 August 1800, NAI/SIR/M/6, 169; id., 'Second General Report on the Mysore Survey', 12 July 1803, NAI/SIR/REP/2, 17–35, here 25f.

132. Kavali Venkata Lakshmayya, 'Shikapoor', in 'Memoirs of a Geographical, Statistical and Historical Survey of the Mysore Dominions, commenced on the Partition of Mysore in 1799 with Maps, Vol VII containing The Province of Nugguar or Bidenoor Part II', NAI/SIR/M/7, 16–38, quotes from 23, 25. For a similar report by Lakshmayya see id., 'Remarks on the Mysore District', BL/OIOC/Mack Misc/117.

133. [P.E.] Conner and [B.S.] Ward, *Memoir of the Survey of the Travancore and Cochin States Executed under the Superintendance of Lieutenants Ward and Conner*, vol. 1. Reprinted with corrections and biographical sketch of Ward and Conner (Travancore, 1863; reprint, Trivandrum, 1994); eid., *A Descriptive Memoir of Malabar* (1905; reprint, Thiruvananthapuram, 1995).

134. Cf. Colin Mackenzie to Chief Sec. (FSG), 28 January 1816, BL/IOR/F/4/554 (13476), 335–60, here 340.

135. Buchanan, *Journey from Madras*; Hamilton, *Geographical, Statistical, and Historical Description*.

136. Conner and Ward, *Descriptive Memoir of Malabar*, 5.

137. However, in a broader context of history of knowledge a distinction can be made between travelogue and systematic geographical representation. See M. Edney, 'Reconsidering

Enlightenment Geography and Map Making: Reconnaissance, Mapping, Archive', in D.N. Livingstone and C.W. Withers (eds), *Geography and Enlightenment* (Chicago and London, 1999), 165–98; and R. Baasner, '"Unser Staatsgeographus ist beständig auf Reisen": Zur Ausdifferenzierung von Reisebeschreibung und Geographie 1750–1800', in M. Maurer (ed.), *Neue Impulse der Reiseforschung* (Berlin, 1999), 249–65.

138. J. Häkli, 'In the Territory of Knowledge: State-centred Discourses and the Construction of Society', *Progress in Human Geography* 15 (2001), 413.

139. Cf. Abu al-Fazl ibn Mubarak, *Ayeen Akkbery*, vol. 2, 1–171.

140. Cf. 'Translation of the Dafter Asuphia or Register of the Six Soobahs of Deckan as Registered Provincially under the Moghul Government from an Original Persian Mss, ... translated from the Original ... by Moonshees under the Direction of Major Mackenzie', BL/OIOC/Mss Eur/Mack Gen/43, 93–152.

141. The role of Mackenzie's work as a model for the later gazetteers is mostly under-estimated in favour of Francis Buchanan's later survey of Bengal, probably because unlike Mackenzie's work much of this was published. R.M. Martin, *The History, Antiquities, Topography, and Statistics of Eastern India ... in Relation to their Geology, Mineralogy, Botany, Agriculture, Commerce, Manufactures, Fine Arts, Population, Religion, Education, ... etc.*, 3 vols (London, 1838). Cf. R.C. Emmet, 'The Gazetteers of India: Their Origins and Development during the Nineteenth Century' (Master's thesis, University of Chicago, 1976), 42; and S.B. Chauduri, *History of the Gazetteers of India* (New Delhi, 1965), 48.

142. See D. Ludden, 'India's Development Regime', in N.B. Dirks (ed.), *Colonialism and Culture* (Ann Arbor, 1992), 247–87. For the connection between the forms of state knowledge and development regime in general see J.C. Scott, *Seeing Like a State: How Certain Schemes to Improve the Human Condition Have Failed* (New Haven, 1998).

143. See, however, the report by the Resident Mark Wilks on revenue in Mysore, partly based on data concerning the size of the territory raised by Mackenzie and his co-workers: M. Wilks, *Report on the Interior Administration, Resources, and Expenditure of the Government of Mysoor* (Fort William, 1805).

144. For an overview of research see L. Behrisch, 'Vermessen, Zählen, Berechnen des Raums im 18. Jahrhundert', in id. (ed.), *Vermessen, Zählen, Berechnen: Die politische Ordnung des Raums im 18. Jahrhundert* (Frankfurt and New York, 2006), 9–14.

145. Foucault, *Geschichte der Gouvernementalität*, 61–64. For more details on the relationship between governmentality and state knowledge production see the series of articles by U. Kalpagam: 'The Colonial State and Statistical Knowledge', *History of the Human Sciences* 13(2) (2000), 37–55; 'Colonial Governmentality and the "Economy"'; 'Colonial Governmentality and the Public Sphere in India', *Journal of Historical Sociology* 15(1) (2002), 35–58; and 'Cartography in Colonial India', *Economic and Political Weekly* 30(30) (1995), 87–98.

146. Cf. for example D. Schmidt, *Statistik und Staatlichkeit* (Wiesbaden, 2005).

147. Scott, 'Colonial Governmentality', 205.

148. For a similar argument see Mitchell, 'Knowing the Deccan', 155: 'That Mackenzie's focus was on collection rather than publication suggests that the constitution of political power during his lifetime did not rely centrally on a relationship with a public'.

149. Cf. Kalpagam, 'Colonial Governmentality and the "Economy"', 419f; Prakash, *Another Reason*, 126, 260 fn 11.

150. Cf. Robb, 'Completing "Our Stock of Geography"', 198–201.

151. Colin Mackenzie, 'View of the State of the Mysore Survey on 1st October 1803', NAI/SIR/REP/2, 239–53, here 250f; id., 'Memorandum of the Origin, Progress and Present State of the Geometrical and Statistic Survey of Mysore, to July 1st 1807', BL/Mss Add/14380, 1–38,

here 31f. See also the almost identical copy in NLS/Ms/11722(i), 1–8; Robb, 'Completing "Our Stock of Geography"', 201; Dirks, 'Colonial Histories and Native Informants', 290.

152. Sinclair, *Statistical Account*, vol. 20, xiii. Emphases in the original.

153. Cf. Womack, *Improvement and Romance*, 3, 174f.

154. N.T. Phillipson and R. Mitchison (eds), *Scotland in the Age of Improvement* (Edinburgh, 1970).

155. As an MP in the 1790s he played an important role in founding the British Wool Society, dedicated to improving the quality of British wool. Also at his initiative, in 1793, the Board of Agriculture and Internal Improvement was founded. As a semi-official institution this consisted of MPs and scientists and was concerned, amongst other things, with introducing new technologies into agriculture. See Mitchison, *Agricultural Sir John*; and G.E. Fussell, 'Impressions of Sir John Sinclair, Bart., First President of the Board of Agriculture', *Agricultural History* 25(4) (1951), 162–69.

156. Sinclair, *Analysis*, 61; id., *Sketch of an Introduction*, 12.

157. Sinclair, *Sketch of an Introduction*, 13.

158. For an overview see M. Mann, 'Collectors at Work: Data Gathering and Statistics in British India, c. 1760–1860', *Journal of the Asiatic Society of Bangladesh (Hum.)* 52(1) (2007), 57–84, and M. Thiel-Horstmann, 'Staatsbeschreibung und statistische Erhebungen im vorkolonialen und kolonialen Indien', in M. Rassem and J. Stagl (eds), *Statistik und Staatsbeschreibung in der Neuzeit vornehmlich im 16.–18. Jahrhundert* (Munich, Vienna and Zurich, 1980), 208–12. Both, of course, underestimate Mackenzie's role.

159. 'Central to the new species of British imperialism which emerged at the end of the [eighteenth] century is the idea that colonization was an enterprise of amelioration'. See Drayton, *Nature's Government*, 92.

160. Cf. Colin Mackenzie to Thomas Munro, 1 January 1819, BL/OIOC/Mss Eur/F/151/39, 268–75, here 270.

161. Colin Mackenzie to William Bentinck, 23 June 1805, BL/OIOC/Mss Eur/F/228/39, 13–16, here 15.

162. Cf. Colin Mackenzie to Seaforth, 4 September 1797, NAS/GD/46/17/4, 512–18, here 517.

163. Colin Mackenzie to Alexander Gillanders, 25 July 1794, NAS/GD/46/17/4, 448–55, here 454.

164. Colin Mackenzie to Seaforth, 4 September 1797, NAS/GD/46/17/4, 512–18, here 517.

165. Colin Mackenzie, 'Memorandum on the Ancient Hindoo System of Government and its Vestiges in the South of the Peninsula', BL/OIOC/Mss Eur/Mack Gen/45, 1–11, here 6f.

166. Colin Mackenzie, 'Statistic Remarks on the Population & Resources of the British Dependencies in Balla- Ghaat from Results of the Mysore Survey in 1802', NLS/Ms/11722,(i), 9f.

167. Colin Mackenzie to Merrick Shaw, 1 May 1804, NAI/SIR/M/18 61–65, quote 64. Cf. Robb, 'Completing "Our Stock of Geography"', 200f. The complete passage (63f) is as follows: 'The effects of restored Population under improved management in a state of tranquility & greater security will also for sometime hence [be] an important object of Observation & in what proportion the effect of increased cultivation following thereafter may operate to the advantage of the State in the increase of Revenue derived from the industry of the subjects. A Circulatory Medium, a Vent for the supraabundance of plentiful years, Marts and Entrepots of Manufactures & Produces will be found in the particularly necessary in an Inland Country possessing few meanings of transportation but by that of cattle. It will be therefore necessary that this increase of Cultivation be [illegibile: used?] by means of internal Arrangement to provide a due Vent by exportation & the erections of manufactures adopted to the Country & in the regulation of these having due regard to the Interest of the Company's Countries & of their Commerce will be matter of further discussion for which

data may be derived from the investigations of the Survey'. This is obviously a draft text; in the official version of the report this section is missing (BL/OIOC/Mss Eur/F/228/39, 1–3).

168. Colin Mackenzie to Francis Humberston Mackenzie, 21 July 1794, NAS/GD/46/17/4, 440–47, here 445–47.

169. The extent to which Seaforth's thoughts had moved in this direction is demonstrated by the draft of an advertisement for the sale of the parishes of Uig, Barvas and Loch. For Uig at least this intended sale was made public – Mackenzie knew about it from a newspaper. However, the sale never took place, as Finlay McKichan has shown. Cf. McKichan, 'Lord Seaforth and Highland Estate Management', 53. See also Richards, *History of the Highland Clearances*, vol.1, 200.

170. The Statistical Account for the 1790s gives the total population as 1898. See Sinclair, *Statistical Account*, vol. 19, 283.

171. Colin Mackenzie to Alexander Gillanders, 25 July 1794, NAS/GD/46/17/4, 448–55, here 452f.

172. Cf. McLaren, *British India and British Scotland*, 136, 241f, 249–54.

173. For instance, Mackenzie also stressed that his research was of use for 'rational speculations of Political Oeconomy'. See Colin Mackenzie to William Bentinck, 23 June 1805, BL/OIOC/ Mss Eur/F/228/39, 13–16, here 14.

Chapter 7

THE PAST IN THE PRESENT

A Comprehensive Project

When Ramachandra Guha, one of the leading Indian proponents of environmental history, pleaded for the social sciences to take an ecological turn in the 1990s and to make more of the relationship between society and environment,[1] one well-meaning critic pointed out that as far as the subcontinent was concerned this was not without a certain irony. To some extent, wrote Robert G. Varady, it was a call to link up with the colonial tradition of the gazetteers, since these had combined description of a region's natural features, for instance topography, climate, flora and fauna, with a view of the social world, from cultivation methods to local history, in an almost exemplary way. So these authors, he went on, had implicitly thematized the mutual dependence of environment and natural resources on the one hand and political structures on the other, and were thus, without realizing it, perhaps the first social ecologists.[2]

Indeed, for men like Mackenzie the extensive breadth of their descriptions of individual regions may have been less the product of theoretical reflection than of a notion that what was worth knowing was boundless, potentially excluding no aspect of the social and natural world. But behind the huge breadth of his project there was certainly more than an encyclopaedic 'totalizing concept of knowledge'.[3] Mackenzie's passion for climbing mountains[4] can perhaps be seen as a sort of key to his project. It points to a perspective on a landscape that seen from above appears as a 'great whole' and in which the traces of interaction between man and environment become visible in many forms. A whole series of statements about his project show that he was interested in the specific forms of interaction between culture and nature.[5] This means that he developed a sort of cultural-geographical view of things and concerned himself with the connections between the physical and cultural characteristics of landscapes. In his 'Memoir on the Various Modes of Watering Land' of 1793 he was already explaining regional differences in cultivation methods and irrigation techniques caused by differences in the quality of the earth and the climatic conditions.[6] But it was particularly in the 'Heads of Enquiry' that he circulated amongst his assistants at the beginning of the Mysore Survey that these connections became clear again and again: 'The Chains of Hills', he wrote here, 'form a remarkable feature of every country & particularly in this where the Climate, Seasons & Productions are so very materially affected by them & in a Political Light they are no less interesting in forming a natural boundary'. Sources, water courses and lakes, he said, were particularly interesting in a dry landscape and should also be seen in the context of religious edifices, such as temples dedicated to whichever deity was their protector. Again, the history of temples deserved special attention because they were most closely bound up with the general history of the country. And he went on to say that particular note should be taken of place names in the vernacular, since they regularly referred to specific qualities in the earth, and indeed to certain historical events.[7]

In this all-embracing approach, human history played a key role. For instance, the history of past empires could give clues to the geographical distribution of certain population groups, languages and religions.[8] And even at the local level particularities could be explained historically, for instance by more precise analysis of inscriptions found in situ that threw light on certain privileges and forms of land allocation and taxation.[9] Like nature, history determined the cultural and social forms of contemporary India; without historical knowledge a deeper understanding of specific regional features seemed impossible. The more we examine Mackenzie's numerous letters and reports, in which he describes and justifies his project, the more the impression emerges that there was a greater vision behind it which could, at the risk of being anachronistic, be described both as 'holistic' in the sense of cultural geography and also 'organic' in the sense of a sensitivity to the importance of specific historical developments for regional particularities. He sometimes speculated here on 'types or general rules of landscape or topography', as Robb states,[10] but he did little to work out such approaches theoretically, and it would perhaps be going too far to conclude from this that he wanted to reduce regional particularities to general characteristics within a comprehensive, 'objective' system of classification.

Although his maps and memoirs provided a picture of each individual *pargana* to a degree of detail previously unknown, they still only represented a compromise between the potentially limitless knowledge that could be gained about a territory and its inhabitants and what was possible in practical terms given the financial constraints and pressure of time. So, as we know, along with the cartographical and statistical parts of the survey Mackenzie and his co-workers developed a whole series of other activities which, though not designed to produce knowledge of direct use to the state, can still only be understood in the context of the project as a whole.

One of these, for example, was Mackenzie's collection of over 1,700 drawings, whose documentary nature has been pointed out by Jennifer Howes.[11] They deal with all aspects of the natural and cultural landscapes he and his co-workers passed through and which could not be adequately represented by a written description. Almost always labelled with place names, they depicted architectural details, agricultural implements and irrigation plants, rock formation of geological interest, fortifications, or even just general views of the landscape. Along with ethnographical drawings,[12] there are also – presumably to compensate for Heyne's departure to some extent – a whole series of natural-historical illustrations, mainly drawn by Indians and generally with details of the place and the vernacular names for animals and plants, which could later be used by natural historians to classify the various types according to European systems.[13] Mackenzie's interest in natural history is also manifested in his attempts to complete the mineral collection he started in the 1790s but which had already been severely decimated at the time through unfortunate circumstances.[14] Finally in this context, along with his collections of archaeological artefacts and over six thousand coins his famous and extremely impressive collection of original manuscripts and other material on the culture and history of South India should be also mentioned.

However clear the conceptual connection between the collections and Mackenzie's surveys, it is difficult to know where they fit in to the institutional context of the survey; they belong in a sort of grey area in which Mackenzie's private interests and official duties can barely be separated. On the one hand Mackenzie had already started some of these collections in the 1780s and 1790s, so the instigation of the Mysore Survey cannot be regarded as their starting point but more as an opportunity to extend and systematize them, while at the same time including them in a sensible way in an overall project. On the other hand this material remained in Mackenzie's possession until his death, from which his executors, Palmer and Co., concluded that the coins, illustrations and minerals were a private legacy created on Mackenzie's own initiative. So they decided 'to leave it to the pleasure of Government to accept or reject the same; or if the Government should deem it preferable, to transmit the coins &ca. to your Honble. Court, and leave the question regarding compensation entirely to your judgement and liberality'.[15]

Then again, of course, from the early years of the survey Mackenzie mentioned in his official reports that beyond the cartographical, statistical and historical material he was collecting numerous 'miscellaneous materials',[16] which he wanted to make available to the government once further work had been done with them. He used his official personnel to collect objects and prepare sketches and watercolours and sometimes also commissioned his subassistants to complete his mineral collection.[17] The draftsmen responsible for cartographical drawing, such as Cristian Ignatio, John Newman and John Mustie did many illustrations for him[18] – and in order to make the drawings he presumably used the materials provided for cartographical purposes. Above all, he constantly exhorted his subassistants to make sketches and drawings of 'any interesting part, Hill, Pagoda, Mosque &ca'.[19] The fact that he freely included such instructions in his official correspondence demonstrates the extent to which survey and collections were institutionally intertwined – in later years, however, he sometimes felt the need to point out that these were private requests which under no circumstances should lead to a dereliction of 'public duty'.[20]

In the light of all this, Archer's designation of Mackenzie's illustrations as 'semi-official' seems to be a quite apposite description of the smaller collections. What is much more difficult, of course, is to distinguish between 'private' and 'public' activities, where Mackenzie's historical collection is concerned. Dirks in particular has emphasized this distinction, not least in order to support his argument that Mackenzie's deep interest in Indian culture and history was to some degree at odds with the interests of the colonial state.[21] Mantena on the other hand stresses that those responsible in Madras promoted the project, and highlights the instrumental use the colonial state could expect from it, especially in questions of land law. At the same time, however, she too retains the dividing line when she describes Mackenzie as an 'amateur collector' and stresses his remarkable 'ability to navigate between his surveying duties and his historical investigations'.[22] Wagoner takes the opposite view when he argues that the historical investigations were quite obviously part of the statistical studies.[23]

This lack of clarity is partly attributable to Mackenzie himself, especially to the way he put it in his published letter to Johnston. Here he explained that although his historical collection rested on the 'basis of the lights originally obtained on the Mysore survey', it had been put together 'with the only burthen to government of the postage being franked, and the aid of some of the native writers'. In particular he declared that all the purchases made for the collection had been at his own expense.[24] The Directors partly recognized this at the conclusion of the Mysore Survey when they mentioned, to his satisfaction, that Mackenzie had added his investigations into the history, religion and antiquities to the survey on his own initiative, thereby exceeding what had originally been planned.[25]

Mackenzie undoubtedly used his own funds for his historical research, especially for the purchase and translation of manuscripts. In September 1800, for instance, he wrote a letter to Close, his superior, in which he asked permission to buy a copy of a rare book, adding that he would bear 'the expense of employing Transcribers for this & any other Pieces of the kind ... with much pleasure'.[26] But all this should not disguise the fact that in both organizational and financial terms the survey and the collection were closely intertwined. Mackenzie had already started the collection at the end of the 1790s, mainly due to his interest in Vijayanagara,[27] but at this time it was restricted to 'such notices as casually came in my way', in other words, chance discoveries.[28] It was not until the Mysore Survey had been set up that he started to go about collecting more systematically. In his original plan of 1800 he had already mentioned 'Enquiries into the Statistical History' as an important objective.[29] Even if the *kaifiyats* used for the statistical memoirs are the only things included in this category, it still means that a large proportion of the material in his historical collection was a direct product of his statistical project. At the same time, his co-workers were constantly acquiring new material so that in July 1800 he was already writing to Arthur Wellesley that his 'Enquiries in to the State & History of the Country increase every day with the other objects of the Survey'.[30] The fact that he regarded the historical investigations as part of the survey becomes even clearer in a letter of the same day to another officer from whom he hoped to receive valuable material: 'The present Survey not only comprehends the common Geographical Enquiries, but is also designed to throw as much light as possible on the Statistical History of the Country, its History, Production etc.', and he added: 'My view is to submit the whole of the materials I collect to the disposal of Government'.[31] The following year he wrote to the Resident that he had collected a wealth of material but would have to keep most of it back until it had been translated and put in order.[32] Finally, in his long report of July 1803 he gave the opinion, 'that a Statistic Investigation of the Country originally recommended in some measure included such narratives, as might convey any light on the subject', by which he meant, as he specified, the 'General history of the Country' far beyond the local histories he and his co-workers were collecting for the Statistical Memoirs.[33]

However, the fact that the historical investigations were becoming ever more extensive while those responsible in the Company were pressing for the survey to be brought to a rapid conclusion meant that new strategies were needed to justify the historical researches. Towards the end of 1802 he had already asked the Resident in Mysore officially whether a continuation of these investigations was basically wanted or not. At the same time, of course, he had suggested that 'the Investigation may be extended under the countenance of Government to embrace the whole of the Provinces under Survey'.[34] Again, in his report of summer 1803 he cautiously remarked that he would leave it to the government to assess the usefulness of his historical investigations,[35] but in the following report, of October of the same year, he was already suggesting that his collection of historical documents 'may be perhaps considered separately from the Principal Design'.[36] However, it seems that maintaining the historical investigations as a part of the survey met with support within government circles: less than two months later he must have received the news that the government was going to make additional funds available for his Indian co-workers.[37]

To what extent further strategies for carrying on with the historical research were sought behind the scenes, given the increasing criticism of Mackenzie's project from the military at this time, is ultimately impossible to say. There is some indication that support was given, however, as in January 1804 Mackenzie's friend George Buchan, chief secretary to the government in Madras, sent him a request from the Directors that had already been sent seven years earlier to leading administrative staff such as the Surveyor General of Bengal[38] and had been repeated in summer 1803. The Directors wrote:

> In order to enable the Company's Historiographer to complete a general History of the British Affairs in the East Indies ... we direct that such of our servants as may be in situations to promote this public Work be instructed to transmit ... such information on the Chronology, Geography, Government, Laws, Political Revolutions, the progressive Stages of the Arts, Manufactures and Sciences, and of the fine Arts, & particularly on the former & present state of internal and foreign Trade as they may be in stations to afford or may from time to time be able to collect.[39]

There is every reason to suppose that Mackenzie already knew about this directive, but the fact that it was now conveyed officially, combined with a special request regarding the survey's contribution,[40] gave him the opportunity to put his historical research on a new footing. It is possible that this was a way for Mackenzie to protect himself from the increasing criticism, and perhaps the intention was also to acquire further funding which, at a time when resources were tight, could only be expected in the form of a retrospective remuneration. In any case, Mackenzie's initial response was that because he knew of the Directors' interest, he had considered it his duty to include historical research in his survey right from the start. At the same time, however, he stressed that in so doing he was going above and beyond his official remit.[41]

Subsequently, of course, the term 'statistical history' was replaced in official correspondence and reports by 'Researches into the History and Institutions of the South of India carried on in concert with the Mysore Survey', which seemed to make the institutional connection between the collection and the survey much more flexible.[42] In his official reports Mackenzie now also stressed that the collection of historical material had been 'superadded to the original design ... with no expence to Government (save the indulgence of Postage approved of by Order October 1803) and the support and countenance of several private friends in the Judicial, Revenue & Diplomatic Departments in the several Provinces'.[43] Perhaps in order to make it clear to London, he now started to inform friends such as Henry Trail that he was mainly putting the collection of historical material together privately and at his own expense.[44]

Although Mackenzie was buying manuscripts from his own pocket, by the time of the 1804 request he could expect some compensation. Once the Directors had received more exact information about his activities, in 1808, they offered him the prospect of payment and an advance, so that he could feel positively encouraged to carry on with his collection.[45] Later on the executors of Mackenzie's estate even saw this as a sort of legal claim, using the Directors' correspondence to present it as the Company's obligation to buy the collection.[46] What is more, during Mackenzie's lifetime there was never any complete institutional separation of survey and collection. Mackenzie's official staff of Indian co-workers, even though sometimes supplemented by private employees, naturally continued to be totally involved with the historical collection. After his appointment as Surveyor General of Madras, in 1810, Mackenzie stressed that in this office he must also be responsible, at least to some extent, for historical material.[47] And he continued to use the surveys he was in charge of for collecting manuscripts: this was usually by the Indian co-workers but sometimes, if none of these were available, by the surveyors themselves.[48] It was only after Mackenzie's death, when his successor as Surveyor General, John Anthony Hodgson, wished to be relieved of the costs of the collection and the Indian co-workers involved with it, that it was finally separated from the Surveyor General's Department.[49]

Mackenzie's Historical Collection

At the time of his death, in 1821, Mackenzie's historical collection comprised 1,568 'literary' manuscripts in 14 languages and 15 alphabets; 264 volumes containing 1,070 'local tracts'; 8,076 copies of inscriptions; and 75 volumes of translations.[50] It was supplemented by the collection of historical coins and many drawings dealing with historical topics in the broader sense. Due to lack of a commentated inventory from Mackenzie's own pen, assessing the collection after his death has proved difficult ever since Horace Hayman Wilson first catalogued it in the 1820s.[51] However, it now seems clear that the way in which Mackenzie acquired his collection was by no means random or without any systematic plan, but was quite the opposite, as demonstrated by the detailed instructions he gave to his co-workers, telling them which places and pagodas they should visit and which manuscripts they could expect to find there.[52]

The most impressive evidence of his system is a whole series of memoranda that he circulated amongst EIC employees, beyond the circle of his direct staff. It is worth noting, for instance, that he prepared different circulars for the various regions of South India because he was aware of the differences in the sources available in the different regions.[53] Nothing, however, illustrates his knowledge better than his 'Memorandum on the Means of procuring Historical Materials regarding the South of India' of 1808, which represents detailed source information for the whole of the southern part of the subcontinent. Here he not only provides details of where certain types of sources were to be found, but – probably even more important from the point of view of the Company's employees – also about which institutions and groups of people had to be approached to gather them. Details of location are supplemented by chronological information; that is, Mackenzie explains which material can provide insights into which historical epochs. The basis for all this is a more precise categorization of the written sources into genres such as genealogies, chronological indices, popular legends, administrative files and temple chronicles.[54] This analysis of potential sources hardly meets today's standards, but it shows that a programme was systematically worked out that should produce a comprehensive body of sources on Indian history reaching back to the centuries before the birth of Christ. Generally speaking, Mackenzie's source material fell into three categories: manuscripts, inscriptions and evidence of the material culture.

The most famous part of Mackenzie's historical collection is formed by the manuscripts. Mackenzie's systematic assessment of precolonial archives arose from his statistical interest in the local history. Even at the start of the Mysore Survey, however, he already had interests that went far beyond this. The most diverse manuscripts were to be included in his research in order to supplement the historical information contained in the *kaifiyats* and to make corrections possible by comparing a variety of sources.[55] So he not only instructed his direct co-workers to collect all scripts that could contain historical information, but also made the same request of officers with whom he was friendly, and even of his superior, Close.[56] What is more, he sometimes tried to buy up relevant manuscripts that were in the possession of deceased Company employees.[57] However, his collection only grew slowly. In the second year of the Mysore Survey he informed Close that he had collected more than thirty 'different traditions relating to the History or Science of the Natives in Sanscrit, Canara or Marathi'.[58] Three years later he reported an extensive collection that he had organized according to regional criteria and language – Tamil, Marathi, Kannada, Telugu and Persian – to which he wished to add even more languages.[59] After another two years, in 1807, he was eventually talking of over four hundred manuscripts.[60]

At this point in time of course his staff of Indian co-workers had been working on the collection for years. Under Lakshmayya's leadership they were looking systematically at various regions of South India for significant material. They were selected for specific tasks according to which languages they knew, and in the areas allocated to them they visited temples, local officials and intellectuals who they thought might have relevant manuscripts. In some cases they managed to get hold of originals, though in most places of course they had copies made.[61] Since Mackenzie did not have to pay postal costs, they sent these to Lakshmayya by post and he archived them according to their regional provenance and language. The next logical step should have been to have them translated[62] but this only actually happened in very few cases: Mackenzie was deploying many of his Indian co-workers to collect manuscripts on the ground, so only a few translators were left for his archive. Thus it is understandable that while the total number of manuscripts went on growing until his death, the proportion translated continued to decrease.[63]

The help of co-workers with knowledge of languages and scripts was also indispensable in the second category in the collection of sources, namely the inscriptions, thousands of which they copied. These inscriptions on stone and copper, some attached to buildings, some freestanding or in the possession of private individuals, often included dates and above all documented the granting of privileges to religious establishments and private persons. Initially Mackenzie had regarded them primarily as a useful source for correcting chronological information in the *kaifiyats*,[64] but he soon came to see them as an important source in their own right. As he wrote in 1807, they were particularly valuable because they could not only contribute to establishing an accurate chronology, beyond any 'fabulous' stories typical of the Hindus' writings, but also because they could provide information about land rights and the state organization: 'It is in this respect', he wrote, 'as well as in the Genealogical and Historical deductions of the Races of the several Souvereigns, & in dates, that they are deemed valuable, as throwing considerable light on the Laws, Customs, & internal arrangements of the times as well as on Historical Events'.[65]

Mackenzie's collection of inscriptions should be regarded as an important pioneering achievement. At the beginning of 1807 he had already started to compile from his material 'a chronological series of the Inscriptions & Grants' that should offer 'excellent data' on the history of South India.[66] The index of over 1,100 inscriptions that Wagoner has discussed in detail and which Mackenzie sent to London[67] certainly shows more than any other document how intensively he and his co-workers examined the possibilities of arranging the material available to them in a source-critical way. In his introduction to it he not only describes his classification system in detail, including physical features, dating, content and intention, as well as language and type of script, but also develops a sort of diplomatic, in which he distinguishes between introductory formulae, keys to dating, and the specific content.[68]

The third part of the investigations consisted of unearthing the past through documenting and collecting the material culture. An important source-type here is antique coins: by examining the type of script used on them and dating them Mackenzie hoped to gain insights into the history of former empires,[69] and because coins of non-Indian provenance, for instance from China or the Roman Empire, were found, 'explanations ... of the connexion and extent of Commercial relations between the Eastern & Western Continents' were possible.[70] Some of these coins seem to have been owned by Indian collectors or lucky finders and could be bought from them;[71] others, Mackenzie was given by friends in the Company who had acquired them in a similar way.[72]

Occasionally, however, Mackenzie exhorted his co-workers to look for coins in specific places. Towards the end of the Mysore Survey, for instance, he heard that a great number of coins could be found near to so-called 'Pandoo Coolies', grave mounds from the centuries before Christ.[73] In the following years he himself, his subassistants and Indian co-workers were time and again busy digging in these tumuli.[74] In 1816/1817, for instance, Apavoo, with the help of a local British magistrate who let him have 'prisoners' to work for him, excavated an entire burial chamber near Madras, bringing out bones, stoneware and shards.[75] Although these investigations were unable to provide information about the age and importance of the mounds – this remained a mystery beyond Mackenzie's death[76] – they demonstrated not only the extent of his interests at this time, but also the comparative characteristics of his method: 'Information of the several places where they are found', he wrote briefly on this, '& a comparison of the circumstances attending them, can only explain their use & intention'.[77]

The main focus of Mackenzie's interest in India's material culture, however, was clearly the study and documentation of monuments. One place in which he had already developed an interest in the 1790s, and which he was never to lose sight of after a long visit in 1800,[78] was Vijayanagara. Although he already had an extensive collection of 'Plans, Drawings, Memoirs, Inscriptions and other Collections' for Vijayanagara in 1801,[79] he asked his co-workers, whenever they were in the vicinity, to collect further observations there – after all, he might have missed something.[80] Among the places documented most intensively over the years was the Buddhist Stupa in Amaravati, first thought to be a Jain temple,[81] and Mahabalipuram near to Madras.[82] Jennifer Howes, in particular, provides insight into the whole breadth of his interest in Indian architecture. She shows that Mackenzie and his co-workers created topographical views and sketches reworked later on, showing the course of his travels through the subcontinent. Then again, his collection contains numerous systematic sketches of sculptures and architectural details, often closely connected to translated descriptions of the iconography and history of the monument in question. It is certainly no coincidence that most of the illustrations were completed between about 1799 and 1810, when Mackenzie was in charge of the surveys of Mysore and the Ceded Districts.[83]

The overview given here is no replacement for intensive research into the provenance and further history of individual texts, as carried out so well by Wagoner and Kulke,[84] but it shows that in its breadth Mackenzie's approach clearly reflected the methods generally employed by European antiquarians: William Roy and Charles Vallancey are repeatedly mentioned as possible role models.[85] However, even a cursory glance at the three main areas of Mackenzie's historical collection and research – manuscripts, inscriptions and material culture – shows quite clearly what a substantial role was played by his Indian co-workers. It was their contribution that made it possible to assess the testimonies and heritage of South India – for instance by overcoming language barriers and understanding the various source genres – and finally to access relevant texts which would have been virtually inconceivable for Europeans without the Indians' help.[86] What is more, they were highly influential in choosing the objects worth documentation, as Howes has demonstrated for Mahabalipuram.[87] More than any other part of his collection the methods developed for the classification of inscriptions illustrate, as Philip Wagoner argues, the dialogic character of his research. With no command himself of South Indian languages or scripts, he was completely dependent here on the abilities of his co-workers: they were sometimes the only ones who made it possible to date the inscriptions and above all facilitated their integration into a broader context.[88]

Nevertheless the collection should not be regarded simply as a continuation and systematization of what already existed. Even though the contribution of the Indian assistants was vital for Mackenzie's project and guaranteed the survival of South Indian intellectual traditions, there is no getting away from the fact that these co-workers were strongly orientated towards Mackenzie's interests – Wagoner says of Narrain Row, for instance, that he had 'internalized' Mackenzie's positivist interest in chronology.[89] Mantena emphasizes even more strongly the power asymmetry in the collaboration, which ultimately set severe restrictions on the Indian intellectuals. While Mackenzie's project favoured certain European notions of reliable historical information over other traditions of historical narrative, in the medium term it led to a reconfiguration and 'disciplining' of the Indian tradition itself, which now, as Mantena tried to demonstrate using the *kaifiyats* written for colonial officials, sought to orientate itself even more towards the Europeans' positivist attitudes to historical 'facts'.[90] At the same time, she argues elsewhere, Mackenzie's collection led to a crisis in South Indian historiography by integrating the genuine forms of expression of Indian historical awareness into a 'colonial archive' that reduced India's historical texts to a role as a source for European historiographers, thereby delegitimizing them as an independent historical narrative.[91]

It may be that Mantena overestimates here the power of Mackenzie's project when she ascribes to it a sort of hegemonic position in South India's intellectual landscape, but what she has to say makes it clear that his documentation project, however much it was based on a desire to guarantee the survival of precolonial traditions, also always implied elements of transformation. This applies just as much to the relationship between precolonial spatial organization and cartographical logic as to the relationship between precolonial archives and statistical memoirs, and finally also to the relationship between South India's living historiographical tradition and Mackenzie's collection. It cannot be denied, however, that similar processes can also be observed in Europe, from the transformation of spatial concepts by cartography, to the integration of local knowledge into a centralized state body of knowledge, right up to the 'disciplining' of historical knowledge to accept forms orientated towards positivist notions.

Accessing India's History

The early nineteenth century had much to offer the British in the way of access to Indian history. Even if they took powerful ideas about historical developments with them to India, this did not mean that there was only one valid and recognized narrative of Indian history, be it the narrative of continuity, or loss and decline, or even of development. In fact, numerous approaches were available, some of which mutually supplemented one another, while at the same time leaving plenty of room for Indian ways of looking at history. In this respect Mackenzie's project can perhaps be regarded as typical of the production of historical knowledge at that time of transition, despite the publication, towards the end of his life, of James Mill's *History of British India* with its more dogmatic, though by no means uncontested, interpretation of the course of Indian history.[92]

The British attempts at accessing South India's history in the early nineteenth century were, at least in the Madras presidency, in many ways a collective project. The extent of collaboration and exchange that was usual here is manifested, for instance, in the papers and manuscripts John Leyden left behind before his abrupt departure from South India in 1805. Mackenzie took charge of this material, which had originally been stored in various different places.[93] With Leyden's permission Mackenzie not only compiled a complete list of all the manuscripts, but also had copies made of those he considered particularly significant. But permission was not granted to Mackenzie alone. He examined some of the material along with Ellis and John Malcolm; the latter was particularly interested in Persian documents and had completely free access to the collection.[94]

But it was undoubtedly Mackenzie's own collection that was the most important treasure trove of sources in the Madras presidency. He made his material available to numerous historians and orientalists who based their work on it extensively. Mark Wilks' *History of Mysore* is probably the best known example,[95] but many other contemporary works also demonstrate use of Mackenzie's sources. When Francis Whyte Ellis published a study of land rights in the Madras Jaghire along with his *sherishtadar*, Sankaraiah, they were able to present inscriptions from Mackenzie's collection as evidence of their theory.[96] Material from the collection also appeared in Kirkpatrick's *Select Letters of Tippoo Sultan* of 1811[97] and Alexander Campbell's *Grammar of the Teloogoo Language* of 1816.[98] What is more, the expertise of Mackenzie's Indian co-workers was often available to other researchers as well. Francis Whyte Ellis, who had been employed in important civilian posts in various provinces of the Madras presidency since 1806, was already supporting the work of Mackenzie's Indian co-workers at the time of the Mysore Survey,[99] and was perhaps, as Mackenzie himself later wrote, the first to become aware of the priceless value of his cooperation with Indian assistants.[100] In particular, Dharmaiah and his son Purshotamiah achieved a high degree of recognition in Madras: not only did Mark Wilks ask Dharmaiah for information when drafting the chapter on Jainism for his *History of Mysore*,[101] but Ellis was also familiar with his work.[102]

As is well known, Mackenzie did not write up his material into a major historical work of his own. The main reason for this was surely that he had doubts about his own capabilities as an author, presumably due to his lack of formal education. In fact, he considered his literary abilities to be fairly modest and even at the beginning of the Mysore Survey he made it clear in a letter to Kirkpatrick that no history of South India was to be expected from his pen. 'The idea [of a work on an earlier period elucidating the History and Customs of this Country] has been some time floating in my mind, but it will require an abler pen to dress them up to advantage'.[103]

But while Mackenzie was indeed providing 'raw material' to many orientalists and historians, this should not be seen as the sole aim of his collection. To see his antiquarianism as an end in itself would be to overlook not only the role attributed to history in his surveys but also the fact that behind his collection stood a research agenda that drew inspiration from various sources. For one thing his extensive reading guaranteed that he was well acquainted with the questions raised by contemporary European historiography; for another, his many and varied scientific contacts made it possible for him to link his own project closely with other scientific enterprises of the time.

Given the conventions of European historiography, chronology played an important role, as is evidenced by a series of papers covering the evolution of the various precolonial empires, including for instance the undated *Short View of the Great Revolutions of Government in the Dekan for 16 Centuries back*, in which seventeen different empires (including European rule) are listed and dated relatively precisely.[104] However, the European historiographical tradition had much more to offer than a positivist concentration on the history of events and Mackenzie was well aware of it. This is revealed, for instance, in some remarks he made to Kirkpatrick, in an attempt to persuade him to write a history of Haidar Ali and his son Tipu Sultan: 'the Life of Hyder & of Tippoo ... furnish a good subject to the Pen of the Philosophic Historian, the powers of the human mind uncultivated by letters or study, called forth into action by the exigencies of the times, and a new state founded on the ruins of weaker Ursupers, may be exemplified by the first'.[105] Setting aside the usual stereotypes about these South Indian rulers included in this passage, what he might have been getting at here is that a description of their character in terms of the humanist historiographical tradition with didactic intent could highlight virtues or vices that should be replicated or avoided. In its eighteenth-century 'philosophic' version this tradition meant that the characters described and their motivations should be placed in a specific cultural and historical context.[106] Above all, what becomes clear is that Mackenzie had little interest in a narration of history confined to political and military events and without more detailed historical analysis. He wrote in the same letter, for instance, that Kirkpatrick's work should offer an alternative to pieces he considered largely superfluous, such as Alexander Beatson's recent *View of the Origin and Conduct of the War with Tippoo Sultaun*, that were based solely on published state documents.[107]

A good way to approach the research agenda behind Mackenzie's collection is to look at the intellectual networks in which he operated. Almost needless to say, his Indian cooperators had a decisive role to play. Those who had family ties to the precolonial administrations came from a class that in South India functioned as 'appointed custodians of popular memory', as Sumit Guha puts it.[108] They undoubtedly influenced Mackenzie's view of the Hindus' traditional forms of government and the survival of many of their institutions under Islamic rule – an aspect that played a key role in Mackenzie's project. This is demonstrated, for instance, by the fact that, influenced by Borayya, his interest in the history of Vijayanagara in the 1790s became the starting point of his historical collection. Co-workers from a different religious sociocultural background could expand this perspective and indeed offer alternative narratives of Indian history; these included, for example, his Jain assistants such as Dharmaiah and Purshotamiah or, later in Bengal, Srinivasia.[109] In particular Dharmaiah, a Jain priest who knew Halegannada, considerably extended Mackenzie's understanding of the history of Indian religions. Mackenzie had employed him 'for particular purposes connected with the Institutions and History of the Country and especially for the first notices of the ancient or Halla Canara Language and Literature of the Upper Carnatic'.[110]

But again, there were also other sources of inspiration that might be seen as more closely connected with Mackenzie's own cultural background. Dirks once noted that Mackenzie's project should also be seen in the context of the widespread preoccupation with Scotland's Gaelic 'traditions' that emerged with the controversy over James MacPherson's *Ossian* poetry from the mid eighteenth century.[111] Societies such as the Highland Society of London founded in 1781, for instance, set themselves the task not only of authenticating the *Ossian* poetry, but also of collecting Celtic antiquities and maintaining old traditions, institutions and clothing.[112] Numerous related initiatives likewise attempted to protect the remnants of 'traditional' Scottish culture, for instance those around Walter Scott, by collecting ballads and poems.[113]

It can certainly be assumed that Mackenzie was well informed about these initiatives since they were also of great interest to the Scots in India. For instance, not only was a Gaelic version of the *Ossian* poetry published by the Highland Society of London in 1807, financed by donations from Madras,[114] but a branch of the society was also founded here in 1814, of which many of Mackenzie's friends and acquaintances were members.[115] And in London too some of his most important contacts, including members of the Seaforth family, played important roles in the society.[116] In his later years Mackenzie himself read Walter Scott's *Waverly* with enthusiasm and regarded it as an authentic report of great value: 'Waverly contains as far as it goes a full true & exact detail of all the events which took place in the Rebellion of 1745 when so many good & Honourable Countrymen ... were out', he confirmed to a friend.[117]

However, other influences might have been more important than Scottish 'romantic antiquarianism'. A circle of people with whom Mackenzie shared fundamental elements of his concept of history was the Scottish orientalists and historians grouped around the *Edinburgh Review*, which contained many of the group's most important publications.[118] Not only was the *Edinburgh Review* already giving his research fulsome praise in 1811,[119] but Mackenzie was also acquainted with many members of this group, including would-be historians John Malcolm[120] and Mountstuart Elphinstone,[121] and also orientalists such as John Leyden and William Erskine.[122] Many of them educated at Scottish universities, these men were mainly orientated to the philosophical historiography of the Scottish Enlightenment, in particular the theory of stadial development in human society. To put it simply, this meant studying the development of human societies in various stages of civilization which were then positioned on a scale of 'rudeness' to 'refinement'. In contemporary models Europe was at the top of the scale. Even William Robertson, who had great respect for the Hindus' achievements, described them as the first civilized nation and warned against treating them as an 'inferior race of men', was convinced of Europe's 'superior attainments in policy, science and arts'.[123] What was in dispute, of course, was exactly where Indian civilization should be positioned on the scale, assuming that this could be done objectively at all, given India's cultural multiplicity.[124]

Finally, Mackenzie was in contact with a number of orientalists who, since the 1780s, had organized themselves around the Asiatic Society in Calcutta and, in the second decade of the nineteenth century, around the Literary Society in Madras and the College of Fort St George.[125] Probably at the instigation of William Kirkpatrick, the Resident of Hyderabad, Mackenzie had been a member of the Asiatic Society of Bengal since the 1790s and from about 1800 had contact with such people as Charles Wilkins, who was head of the Company library in London, and H.T. Colebrooke.[126] Even more significant, however, are his contacts in the Madras presidency, where his project can be seen as part of what Trautmann has called the 'Madras School of Orientalism'.[127] Just how involved he was in the activities of the presidency's historians and orientalists is evidenced by the fact that he was one of the first in Madras actively to promote the founding of a society along the lines of the Asiatic Society – though its first meeting in 1809 came to nothing due to a lack of participants.[128] Many men around the society – including Thomas Strange or John Newbold[129] – were amongst his acquaintances.

As is well known, the orientalists in Calcutta celebrated their greatest success when they discovered the Indo-European language family,[130] while in Madras close cooperation between Europeans and Indians led to the finding that the South Indian languages, contrary to what was assumed by both Indians and Europeans alike, did not derive from Sanskrit, but formed what was regarded as the Dravidian language family.[131] Philology was naturally at the forefront of this research but in eighteenth-century understanding the study of history and the study of languages were not strictly separate from each other: not only were linguistic studies to be supplemented by historical ones,[132] but the study of language itself was regarded as a possible key to history. Quite a few linguists, including the British orientalists in India under the influence of William Jones, were convinced that comparative philology could provide insights into the deep historical relations between peoples – which is why Trautmann describes their project as an undertaking of 'linguistic' or, because of their biblical frame of reference, also 'Mosaic ethnology'.[133]

The interaction of these multifarious influences is surely manifested most clearly in the person of John Leyden, at one time a co-worker of Mackenzie's, who from 1804 was employed as a doctor and naturalist on the Mysore Survey. The son of a farmer and shepherd, he lived and studied mainly in Edinburgh from 1790, and as a member of its Literary Society and temporary editor of the *Edinburgh Magazine* had gained a firm place in the city's cultural life. He had also made a name for himself as a poet with a volume of poetry, *Scenes of Infancy*, into which he worked a great deal of folklore.[134] Travelling through the Scottish Highlands Leyden had also managed to collect ballads and antiquities and edited a rare text, the *Complaynt of Scotland*, a sixteenth-century political allegory.[135] Finally, along with Scott, he published the *Minstrelsy of the Scottish Border*, a collection of folkish ballads from the Anglo-Scottish border region which the two men supplemented with poetry of their own.[136]

At the same time, however, Leyden was a sort of eternal student at Edinburgh University where, in addition to medicine, he also studied humanities. The most influential figure here was Dugald Stewart, who represented the idea of stadial historiography in the form of his 'conjectural history'.[137] In the early years of the nineteenth century Leyden decided to go to India for career reasons. Although his original plan to be appointed directly to the College of Fort William initially failed,[138] like many other Scots of his generation he was able to enter the Company's service as a doctor. Even before he left for India in 1803 he had, by means of good contacts, been recommended to the returning governor of Madras, Lord Bentick, and so even while he was still in Britain he knew that in South India he would be given the opportunity to work as 'doctor, linguist, naturalist and antiquarian'.[139] The ideal post for Leyden was soon found: just a few months after his arrival in India, Mackenzie had been informed that soon a 'young man of extraordinary genius and Classical Scholar whose chief view is turned to the study of Languages, ... proficient in those Branches of General Knowledge that are cultivated at the academical Institutions at home' would be appointed to his survey as doctor and naturalist.[140] It is possible that a mutual friend, Mackenzie's former mentor Dr James Anderson, had originally put them in touch.[141] Leyden was officially appointed in January 1804 and by March he was already ready to leave Madras with Mackenzie.[142] The two men worked together for little more than a year because Leyden became seriously ill and had to be withdrawn,[143] but during this time he not only lived up to Mackenzie's expectations completely but also enriched the latter's research by adding ideas that had previously existed only in embryonic form.

John Leyden was a gifted linguist, though prone to exaggerate his own achievements enormously, which makes it difficult to assess them adequately. For instance, he reported to his father after less than a year in South India that he had already learned Tamil and Marathi and was just in the process of mastering Sanskrit, Telugu and Kannada.[144] There can be no doubt that during the Mysore Survey he was indeed doing intensive linguistic studies. He asked Kavali Venkata Ramaswami, who was apparently compiling a Kannada dictionary at Leyden's instigation, to send him versions of the alphabet and various scripts to help him learn the language.[145] His main interest, however, was not so much in mastering individual idioms as in comparative linguistics, and so he tried to arrange the Asian languages into three major groups, one of which should be represented by the languages of the Deccan.[146]

Given the short time they worked together and the fact that he joined the survey at a late stage, Leyden's influence on Mackenzie's project was necessarily limited, despite all the possibilities. But the breadth of his interests and the manifold intellectual influences that marked him show quite clearly that knowledge production in India in the early nineteenth century cannot be reduced to a single hegemonic approach. There seems to be little point in categorizing men such as Leyden or Mackenzie simply as representatives of the 'Enlightenment' or 'Romanticism'.[147] And while Mackenzie himself was always open to new ideas, at the same time his project was a source of inspiration to others. In particular it guaranteed that influential European stereotypes concerning India's historical development could be called into question by using new sources and placed into more complex contexts; his collection shows very clearly the extent to which Indian perspectives on history could also be taken into account here.

The Past and the Present

It is no coincidence that harking back to the 'celtic' cultural heritage of the Highlands took place in Scotland at a time when, in contemporaries' eyes, this heritage was in danger of disappearing as the region was being integrated into the social and economic edifice of Great Britain. So in essence the enthusiasm for Gaelic folklore represents a nostalgic project of remembering a supposedly lost past. Its most powerful expression was Walter Scott's regret for the disappearance of the 'traditional' way of life in the Highlands, as he puts it in the afterword to *Waverly*.[148] At the same time, however, this nostalgic distortion and romanticization of that way of life minimized its relevance for the present by representing the disappearance of Gaelic culture as an inevitable process.[149] And at the same time that the folklore movement emerged, the patriotic version of historiography prevalent hitherto, in which Scottish political and cultural independence took centre stage, was redefined by the Whig historians of the Scottish Enlightenment so that Scotland's past now appeared as an integrated part of a European history regarded as cosmopolitan.[150]

Idealizations of the past were of course not restricted to Scotland. In his *Dialogue and History* Eugene Irschick famously states that in the decades around the turn of the century in the Madras presidency a view of the present in South Indian emerged that made it seem like the product of a process of decline, particularly in the immediate vicinity of Madras, caused by the innovations of Muslim and European conquerors. This perception of the present was set against an idealized image of a past characterized by harmonious coexistence and economic prosperity. According to Irschick, European administrators and various groups of Indian inhabitants had contributed to this construction, and because normative significance was attributed to it, it became the yardstick by which the future under British rule was to be designed.[151]

In Mackenzie's collection there is much evidence for such an idealized construction of a Hindu past, especially in the many texts copied and compiled by his Brahmin assistants. The Vijayanagara Empire had a central role to play as a source of legitimation. This is hardly surprising as in South Indian popular memory the Empire was, with the notable exception of the Maratha regions, a central reference point. In particular many of the local histories collected by Mackenzie's co-workers show the extent to which invocation of Vijayanagara could be used to justify rights and privileges.[152] What is more, the empire often appears as an idealized version of a better Hindu past in these texts, characterized by its 'mild and benevolent Rule'.[153] Mackenzie himself confirmed that in many ways it was a government along the lines of the 'general system [that] had from time immemorial prevailed throughout India'.[154]

But even if idealized versions of the past found their expression in Mackenzie's collection, his project seen as a whole was by no means a project of nostalgia. Admittedly, sometimes he too felt the urge to protect what was getting lost, and for fear that further evidence might be destroyed he extended his collection to areas not touched by his official survey.[155] In marked contrast to Scotland's 'romantic antiquarianism', however, its aim was not to reconstruct a past that was over and done with, but it was supposed to reveal the relevance for the present of a past not yet finished. At the same time, Mackenzie's willingness to idealize the Indian past was also very limited. Of all the European historians William Robertson was surely the greatest proponent of the notion that at an early stage a harmonious social system was established in India with political institutions that took account of the needs of all its subjects. In his *Historical Disquisition concerning the knowledge the Ancients had of India* of 1791 Robertson had produced a history of the trade relations between Europe and India based on intensive study of European sources.[156] Mackenzie was already familiar with this work in the 1790s and the fact that in 1808 he was still claiming that the 'early state of Navigation and Commerce in these Countries' was one of his main interests, may suggest that his reading of Robertson's work had a lasting effect.[157] On the other hand his *Memorandum on the Ancient Hindoo Government* makes it clear that he had moved quite far away from the idea of original harmony: 'Of the Golden happy Age of the Hindoos', he wrote here, 'I am afraid like every other Sublunary happiness it depends more on comparison of the past than the feelings of the present, & that it recedes from the search the more we pursue'.[158]

Even though Mackenzie rejected some of Robertson's ideas, the historiography of the Scottish Enlightenment still retained greater significance for his understanding of history than the activities of the antiquarians around Walter Scott. The idea of a *history of manners*, reflected for instance in Robertson's long appendix on 'manners, … genius and institutions of the people of India' played a particularly important role here.[159] In very general terms, in the historiography of the Scottish Enlightenment the focus was not on autonomous historical actors but on the cultural conditions in which they acted and the, sometimes unintended, consequences of their actions. Customs, beliefs and institutions were understood and analysed here as an integrated system.[160] Such ideas were crucial for Mackenzie's research agenda, which focussed on:

> genius & manners of the people, the several Systems of Government & of Religion
> & … the predominant causes that influence their sentiments & opinions to this

day: lights will be thrown on the Tenures of Land, the original assessment of Rents & Revenues, & the condition of the people, the principles of the Clergy & middle classes & the genius & spirit of their Government prevalent in the Dekkan since Centuries: ... the use of such investigation in procuring authentic information of the condition & sentiments of Millions of subjects, will I hope confirm the Utility of this undertaking to the existing Government & prevent its being confounded with dry investigations into remote & obscure periods of antiquity of Legend & of Fable.[161]

One of the most important convictions of the historians and social theorists of the Scottish Enlightenment was that 'no theory of the social institutions or the forms of government would be satisfying unless it provided a viable account of how they were brought about'.[162] This was the very idea that Mackenzie embraced when working on the history of empires and dynasties in order to understand the historical dynamics that had led to the establishment of the contemporary forms of government in South India. The first thing of key importance here was to reconstruct the political history – understandably, since the Europeans knew little about it due to the supposed lack of reliable sources.[163] Mackenzie gives a comprehensive picture of the political developments in the late sixteenth and seventeenth centuries in a paper he wrote in 1815 for the Asiatic Society of Bengal, which was not published until more than twenty years after his death. Based on extensive sources he gives an exact overview here, unsurpassed by any at the time, of South India's political actors in the roughly 120 years after the fall of Vijayanagara.[164] Mackenzie's depiction is mainly geared towards the rise and fall of the small and large states of the time – but at the same time he is keen to raise key questions for his project regarding the continuities and changes in administration that accompanied the processes of political upheaval, in order to understand the structures of his day from a historically informed perspective.

In this context it was the history of how the sultanates of Bejapoor and Golconda were expanded that, in Mackenzie's view, had great influence on the 'intermixture of new arrangements with ancient customs' that characterized the present in South India.[165] In particular, he thought, their expansion was connected with the rise of sociocultural classes that shaped contemporary South Indian administrations and from which Mackenzie recruited most of his co-workers. In his essay Mackenzie demonstrates that in the various provinces different groups of 'secular Brahmins' had dominated the administration – in his opinion 'dessayet, Nizam Shahee or Marhatta Brahmins' in the Bejapoor area, but *niyogis* in Golconda.[166] The fact that the sultanates had set so much store by the 'acute and subtle genius of that class of their native subjects, which is so well accommodated to the arrangements of finance and political economy' he considered as the expression of a 'spirit moderate and mild, and well adapted to cherish agriculture'.[167] But even if this meant that they had transferred key spheres of their administration to Hindus, this was not to say that it was simply a continuation of older forms of administration: 'Thus the Carnatic on either side came to be administered in its revenues by two different classes of foreign Bramins, Marhatta and Tellinga, acting under the authority of a double Mohamedan Government, whose forms and documents then introduced are still erroneously recurred to as standards of the ancient system of financial administration in the Carnatic'.[168]

The starting point for Mackenzie's interest in history was his wish to understand the present, but given the changeful South Indian past this led him ever further into the depths of time. This is true, for instance, of Mackenzie's speculations on South Indian land rights, a pressing problem at the time in the Madras presidency. His undated 'Memorandum on the Ancient Hindoo System of Government', probably written between 1804 and 1809, provides good insight into his ideas. Along the lines of stadial historiography Mackenzie starts his overview with a speculative description of a pastoral Indian 'infant state'.[169] Even if remnants of this early condition could still be seen in certain isolated population groups, he wrote elsewhere,[170] in general its origins had turned into new forms of political organization due to population growth, forms in which an individual person could no longer take over power alone but in which territory had to be split into various subdivisions. Large empires, 'composed necessarily of jarring discordant principles', were, however, very difficult to hold together, so the history of India was a history of the rise and fall of consecutive dynasties:

> we find in every Hindoo Principality a gradual progression from an obscure beginning of hardihood & adversity of evil & danger to the acquisition & undisturbed possession of a Great Landed Property which the Master in occupying to advantage improves by good Management & promoting the prosperity of the people. From ease & affluence, in the natural course of things, ambition & Luxury arise, the one or the other involving him: & exciting the envy or attracting the Cupidity of his more powerful neighbours; his newly formed growing State soon falls prey to a more fortunate adventurer.[171]

All these empires had, he said, despite various differences, been based on certain fundamental principles which had also been retained to some extent under the rule of the sultanates and the Mughal Empire and had probably been characteristic of the whole of Asia: 'The Ancient Hindoo System of Government I conceive ... to have prevailed with various modifications down to the first Mahomedan Invasion; & thence, with greater variations perhaps, to the present times; this System indeed appears to have been general throughout Asia'.[172] The original pastoral society had had no need of land property: 'Custom the

Fountain of all Law strengthened these habits till inconveniences arose that were not felt in an Infant state'. So this was a fundamental characteristic of the old system, in which 'the Souvereign always appears to be considered the immediate Lord & Proprietor of the Soil.' Certain rights of the peasants, and particularly of the village communities had, however, been recognized in some form or other: 'a sacred regard to the right of occupancy was sanctioned & of the right in community of the ground of Villages & Townships; so that no land could be sold without the consent of the inhabitants; this seems to approach our idea of a perpetual or long Lease'. Along with this hereditary right of usage, however, little by little further changes took place which, although they can only be regarded as private property rights in a limited sense, did signify important modifications to the original system. Certain groups like the *poligars,* he went on, were particularly rewarded for military service, while it was religious institutions that had been able to acquire lasting land rights.[173]

Given the conventions of stadial history, it is hardly surprising that Mackenzie's account takes the form of a 'Narrative of Enlightenment', [174] in which cultural differences are represented in a temporalized form: 'while the obstinate adherence to Ancient customs enforced by the Laws, still preserve them in the Hindoo System, in Enlightened Europe the improvements in Legislation, & accommodation to the improved state of knowledge & ... separate what was perhaps originally the same'.[175] Stadial history not only provided a framework within which Indian history could be understood, but undoubtedly also included a key argument for justifying British imperialism in positioning Europe on the top of its scale of civilizations. Mackenzie, it seems, was not only aware of this but in some measure agreed with these ideas.

But if this sort of history provided a powerful framework for accessing South India's past, Mackenzie had of course much more to offer than rational speculation. His investigations could, for instance, provide evidence for the much discussed questions of whether there were forms of property in land in South India and, if so, where their origins lay, which his friends Mark Wilks, Thomas Munro or Francis Whyte Ellis were looking into so intensely.[176] Wilks stressed this aspect when explaining the value of Mackenzie's collection to the Directors: 'If it should be found practicable', he wrote, 'to trace by a series of authentic documents the history of landed property in the South of India, I imagine that no subject of superior interest and importance can be presented to the attention of a British Government'.[177] The British administration's 'historicist' orientation, its emphasis on ancient rights, laws and precedent, guaranteed here that Mackenzie's collection could be seen as a potentially important archive for the colonial state, housing a wealth of material on the basis of which manifold claims, from territorial issues to rights and privileges concerning revenue, could possibly be clarified.

However, it seems that Mackenzie himself was more interested in a general understanding of cultural norms than in how his investigations could be put to practical use. The breadth of his approach – based on the idea that all aspects of political institutions, culture and social life were interrelated – meant, of course, that Mackenzie's research went far beyond objects directly connected to the EIC's immediate interests. In many ways, his agenda not only overlapped with others' research, but far beyond that presented a research programme that characterized attempts by orientalists and historians to gain a better understanding of the history of South India for a long time to come. Nothing illustrates this better than the *Desiderata and Inquiries connected with the Presidencies of Madras and Bombay*,[178] disseminated by the Royal Asiatic Society from 1827 that had, if Mantena's dating is right, already been circulating in Madras twenty years earlier.[179] Although compiling these desiderata is commonly attributed to the society's secretary, Benjamin Guy Babington, Mackenzie's influence is quite obvious in this paper. Not only does it reflect the objects of his research in all their breadth, but many passages are also identical to a memorandum written by Mackenzie himself in 1808.[180] The published version of 1827 clearly states that the languages of South India are not derived from Sanskrit. A possible key role was attributed here to Purvada Halegannada as the putative 'parent' language of the south, and the value of Mackenzie's co-worker Dharmaiah, regarded as one of the last persons with command of this language, was stressed. Whether or not Dharmaiah had also influenced the formulation of linguistic questions is not clear – but while Mackenzie's *niyogi* co-workers were almost certainly not involved in the issue of the Dravidian language family,[181] he clearly participated in developing the idea of a South Indian past in which Sanskrit had not played a dominant role.

The origins of Mackenzie's interest in the South Indian languages are less closely connected with linguistic research than with his work on historical geography. Again, the starting point for Mackenzie's interest in history was the present. As Mackenzie said himself, his research had to be seen in the context of the numerous regional conflicts in South India at the time, in which historical territorial claims constantly played a role. At the forefront of the Third Mysore War, for instance, great attention had been paid to the question of whether the Rajah of Travancore had been able legally to acquire two forts from the Dutch to which Tipu Sultan also had a claim. What needed clarification here was whether and at what point in time they had belonged to the sphere of rule of a Rajah obliged to pay tributes to Tipu, since this was the basis of Tipu's claims.[182] Discussions of this sort certainly stimulated Mackenzie's interest in precolonial territorial organization, even though he was clearly not attempting to find concrete solutions in individual cases.

The wish to understand the historical emergence of the territorial structures of the present soon led Mackenzie to go far beyond the documents on the Mughals' organization of the Deccan such as the *Daftar Asufiah* and the *Haqiqatha-i-Hindustan* described in an earlier chapter. Probably influenced by his Indian co-workers he became convinced that the way in which the Islamic rulers subdivided their territory was very much along the same lines as the Hindus' older forms. His reference point here was the notion, going back to the Puranas, that the whole of India (or even a large part of Asia) was originally divided into countries called *desas*, which had formed the basis for future sub-divisions.[183] As Buchanan had discovered on his journey through Mysore, this idea was widespread amongst the Brahmins there, who could refer to inherited written documents which, though sometimes found to be contradictory, gave details about fifty-six *desas*.[184]

In 1800 Mackenzie was already stressing that an important objective for surveyors was to establish language boundaries since they could provide insight into 'the ancient extent of the dominions of the several nations ... [and] a distinct idea of the extent of each & their several branches would illustrate the more ancient history of the country'.[185] In the course of the survey the idea clearly seems to have taken root with him that language boundaries not only marked the borders of past empires but also that they were identical to the old *desas* and thus made it possible to reconstruct their exact location. Hardly surprisingly John Leyden in particular meticulously notes the language boundaries found during the survey in his journals,[186] but Mackenzie's other co-workers also seem to have fulfilled their duty so that Mackenzie had sufficient material available to make a 'philological' map, 'descriptive of extent of the various languages spoken in the 56 Desums or Hindoo Divisions of the Bharut Candum, or India'. Unfortunately it never reached London and to this day has never been found.[187] And despite decades of tirelessly collecting material Mackenzie and his co-workers never actually carried out the original plan to produce a work on the historical geography of the Deccan, accompanied by maps based on 'Hindoo works that may not be so readily come in the way of others' and comparing these with the writings of European authors in Antiquity.[188]

If awareness of the geographical spread of languages already forms a basis for the Dravidian theory, Mackenzie's main contribution to its formulation is surely that he supplemented the linguistic idea of language families by adding a historical perspective to the process of Sanskritization in South India. Two key aspects of this notion can also be found, long before Ellis published his 'Dravidian proof',[189] in his correspondence and drafts: firstly the idea of a social and cultural upheaval that took place in the history of South India; and secondly the idea that this was caused by a sort of colonization from the north. Mark Wilks suggests that Mackenzie's historical research indicates an 'Era of a great conquest of Canara & Malabar including Travancore ... by which the aborigines of the country were reduced to slavery, and the lands conferred on strangers'.[190] 'The Origin of the Slaves in Canara', Mackenzie himself wrote to

Munro, 'I presume you have heard there; they are said to be the aboriginal (or rather earlier) inhabitants, conquered by a new Souvereign who also introduced the Brahmins'.[191]

In particular the arrival of the Brahmins from the north is a topos that recurs again and again in Mackenzie's reflections on his collection. He seems to have recognized a connection between these events and religious upheavals in South India at an early stage, and so he was especially interested in the 'Religious Contentions that took place between the Brahmins, Jains & other Sects'.[192] This has to be seen against the backdrop of his research into the Jains which he had started during his stay in Ceylon and continued in Hyderabad.[193] With the Mysore Survey he had started to look at Jainism in greater detail. Early in 1800 he pointed out to Francis Buchanan that on his travels through Mysore he would have the opportunity to gather further information about them.[194] Of course, this would not be so easy, he said, since after the Brahmins had won the religious conflict with the Jains the latter had been burned, along with their books.[195]

Having also expressed his interest in the Jains in his circular of 1800,[196] a year later he suggested that, before the Brahmins arrived in South India, Jainism could have been the most widespread religion.[197] A few years later, having started his cooperation with Dharmaiah in 1804, he even became convinced that this applied to the whole of India and possibly even large sections of central Asia. He even thought it possible that the Indians described in classical Greek works could have been Jains.[198] It seems quite probable that Dharmaiah's opinion was influential here as he was convinced that Jainism had at some point been the uniform religion of India if not the whole world. Mark Wilks based his account of the persecution of the Jains on Dharmaiah's relations and manuscripts from Mackenzie's collection, even if he did not feel able to decide about the 'relative antiquity of the Jain and the bramins'.[199] Henry Thomas Colebrooke, with whom Mackenzie obviously communicated on this matter, expressly rejected the idea of an 'originally' Jain India – but despite being convinced that 'orthodox' Hinduism was very old, Colebrooke was prepared to concede the possibility that Jainism or Buddhism was the original religion of South India, only to be suppressed by the Hindus from the north.[200]

Mackenzie does not appear to have managed to develop a concrete theory about how the Brahminization of South India unfolded historically, despite discovering various aspects of it in the course of his investigations. But there is evidence to suggest that he took it to be a long process, ranging from the centuries BC, to the 'introduction of the doctrine of the Védes by the Chola Kings', to the removal of the last Jain ruler in Canara in the eleventh century and the bloody suppression of the Jains.[201] It is hard to overstate the influence of his ideas. His friend Wilks, who had a great talent for revealing the spectacular nature of these discoveries, put it like this:

> The religion of the Hindoos is usually represented as unchanged and unchangeable. Perhaps the religious history of Europe is scarcely more pregnant with revolution and unhappy contrary to another erroneous opinion. No Country on earth furnishes the records of such sanguinary persecution as those which have been achieved by the Bramins of India.[202]

It is certainly no coincidence that when Ellis was putting forth his theory of the Dravidian language family he used not only purely linguistic arguments but also historical ones very similar to Mackenzie's. 'When the ... [Brahmins from the North] established themselves in South India they found a native Literature already existing', he wrote, 'which though they introduced the language of science of the North [i.e. Sanskrit], they were compelled during their long contest with the *Jains*, to cultivate in their own defence'.[203] Alexander Campbell, in whose Telugu grammar the 'Dravidian proof' had been published for the first time, also assumed that in South India 'the introduction of Sanscrit words into this language' must have gone along with the spread of 'the religion of the Bramins'.[204] It must be stressed here that the idea that South India was subjugated by an invasion from the north is not simply speculation on the part of Mackenzie, Ellis or Campbell, but is based on the narratives and manuscripts collected by Mackenzie's co-workers. Even Horace Hayman Wilson, who was fairly sceptical about the Dravidian concept, confirmed that in many writings from the south there was proof that the 'brahmin Hindus' came from the north.[205]

Of course, the search for deep historical relationships between the peoples did not only lead to the philological knowledge so admired today but also to much speculation about the early history of humanity. Ideas about the 'celtic peoples' in Scotland, Wales and Ireland found expression in theories about the origins of the Skythians, Celts, Picts and Goths and their position in the peoples' family tree.[206] Quite often early connections with Asia and India were proposed, also, of course, in order to attribute a special role to the diverse Celtic peoples in the early history of Europe. Such theories can be found not only in the works of Charles Vallancey or in obscure linguistic pieces such as Edward Davies' *Celtic Researches*, of which Mackenzie possessed a copy,[207] but also for instance in publications such as Thomas Maurice's *Indian Antiquities* (the sixth volume of which contains a 'Dissertation on the Indian Origin of the Druids'),[208] and even in the *Asiatic Researches*, where Francis Wilford's essays are of particular note.[209] Even in the 1830s James Cowles Prichard, certainly the most prominent British ethnologist in the first half of the nineteenth century, produced a monograph arguing along similar lines.[210]

Mackenzie was one of those who took this theory very seriously. In a footnote to his description of the excavations in Amaravati (published posthumously) for instance, he made a connection between the ruins there and Druidism, whose religious ceremonies would have required similar edifices.[211] He had similar ideas about the grave mounds he discovered, as reported by the travel writer Maria Graham, who started her literary career with a description of her stay in India in 1810/1811.[212] She visited Mackenzie in Madras, where she was shown his collection. The two of them talked extensively about the grave sites and Graham reproduced what must be Mackenzie's most important ideas about them. Based on a certain similarity to Celtic grave sites in the British Isles he described them to her as 'Indian cairns'. The existence of these stone graves, he said, also to be found in Tartary, but especially in Britain, pointed to a connection between these peoples: 'one would be tempted to imagine that there must have existed, between the inhabitants of these remote nations, a connection sufficiently intimate to have transmitted similar customs to their descendants, although their common origins be forgotten'. As in the European past, Graham added, India also had its bards and *minnesingers* and some could still be seen today in South India.[213]

Mackenzie, who was clearly familiar with druid cairns from his Scottish homeland, repeated this theory to the Asiatic Society in 1819 when making it a gift of an urn found in a grave. As in his conversation with Graham, here too he pointed out the similarities between the grave mounds in Scotland and India. Also, based on what he had read, he stressed the fact that similar *tumuli* could be found in the whole of Asia, suggesting a common burial culture in Europe and Asia in early times – Mackenzie dated this to the time of the Roman Emperor Augustus, based on the discovery of a coin. He not only promised the society a detailed research report on this topic but also suggested that it should promote further research.[214]

Such ideas about the early history, which do actually place Mackenzie in close proximity to a romantic antiquarianism à la Charles Vallencey, merely represent a marginal aspect of his project. But at the same time they can also be seen as another piece in the mosaic that is Mackenzie's theory of a great cultural upheaval in India. The *tumuli*, it said in the report, were 'so indicative of a mode of sepulture entirely different from that followed by the present natives, the followers of the *Vedes,* that they evidently point to a change that has taken place since the age of Augustus'.[215] Naturally Mackenzie never actually presented the report to the society so details of his speculations cannot really be reconstructed. But here too it is clear that his research was by no means based on the idea of an 'eternal India'.

'What is now India', Robertson had written in 1791, 'always was there, and is likely to continue'.[216] In the course of his investigations Mackenzie had distanced himself from such ideas, if he had ever accepted them. He too was convinced of the longevity of certain Indian institutions, but for him this did not mean a virtually unchanged continuity of Indian culture over thousands of years. In order to understand the basic principles of India's government it was not enough for Mackenzie either to look for the roots of these principles in the far-off past, or indeed just to look at the present. In fact, the long period of time in between must be looked at, since the reality of contemporary India could only be understood against the backdrop of this historical change. Thus his project was not an exercise in 'essentializing' Indian culture,[217] and the main interest of Mackenzie the historian was the political and social dynamics of South India. As a good historian he emphasized both continuities and changes which, taken together, formed the basis for a complex present.

Mackenzie's surveys aimed, as has been argued in previous chapters, at understanding the present in order to mould the future – but in his eyes this had to include understanding the past as something that had moulded the present. If Indian institutions and forms of government were to constitute the basis of British rule, knowledge of their history was essential – but given the broad approach of 'philosophical history' this history could not be seen in isolation: society and economy, culture and religion, and indeed geography and nature were all factors that had to be taken into account. Moreover, if in the early years of his collection under the influence of people as different as Kavali Venkata Borayya and William Robertson, Mackenzie might have tried to search for sources of an idealized, 'original' Hindu past, under the influence of others such as Dharmaiah, he soon became convinced that such a past had hardly ever existed. Every past had its own past and the more he knew about South Indian history, it seems, the more he realized how little he knew. Stadial history, offering a theoretical framework, might have provided a possible master narrative of South India's history at least at some stage in his historical reflections – but for Mackenzie, the historian who characteristically footnoted his speculations, pure conjecture was certainly not enough. Out of all this grew the passionate effort to search for ever new sources, as is amply demonstrated by the size and diversity of his collection. So in a way Mackenzie did indeed become the prototype of a 'colonial antiquarian' but certainly not one who collected for collecting's sake alone. For him, history did not only provide a key to the present, but could also provide a key to shaping the future.

Notes

1. R. Guha, 'Introduction', in id. (ed.), *Social Ecology: Oxford in India Readings in Sociology and Social Anthropology* (New Delhi, 1994), 1–14.
2. R.G. Varady, 'Social Ecology: Oxford in India Readings in Sociology and Social Anthropology. Edited by Ramachandra Guha (Review)', *Journal of Asian Studies* 54(4) (1995), 1130.
3. T. Day, *Fluid Iron: State Formation in Southeast Asia* (Honolulu, 2002), 119.
4. He mentions this in a letter to Seaforth: Colin Mackenzie to Francis Humberston Mackenzie, 9 August 1796, NAS/GD/46/17/4, 485–95, here 492.

5. This is demonstrated, for instance, by the fact that in 1810, when two committees of the Asiatic Society were founded at John Leyden's instigation, one for natural history, medicine, 'Improvement of the arts' and 'whatever is comprehended in the general term of physics', and the other for literature, philology, history, antiquities and 'whatever is comprehended under the general term of literature', he naturally belonged to both of them. Cited from Grout, *Geology and India, 1770–1851*, 89.

6. Colin Mackenzie, 'Memoir on the Various Modes of Watering Land practised by the Natives of India. More particularly in the Provinces anciently designed under the names of Carnatic and Tallangana, wrote in April 1793', BL/OIOC/Mss Eur/Mack Gen/59, 63–81.

7. Cf. Colin Mackenzie, 'Hints or Heads of Enquiry for facilitating our knowledge of the more Southern parts of the Deckan, 1800', BL/OIOC/Mss Eur/F/128/213, para. 7.

8. Colin Mackenzie, 'Memorandum of the Financial Records of the Deckan', 12 June 1809, BL/OIOC/Mss Eur/Mack Gen/44, 1–9, here 7–9, id., 'Hints or Heads of Enquiry', BL/OIOC/Mss Eur/F/128/213, para. 10.

9. Colin Mackenzie, 'Introductory Memoir: Of the Use and Advantage of Inscriptions and Sculptured Monuments in illustrating Hindoo History', BL/OIOC/Mss Eur/Mack Gen/18A, 1–10.

10. Robb, 'Completing "Our Stock of Geography"', 198f.

11. Howes, *Illustrating India*. At the time of his death 2,815 illustrations were counted, many of them duplicates that were probably donated to the Asiatic Society of Bengal. Cf. M. Archer, *British Drawings in the India Office Library*, 2 vols (London, 1969), vol. 2, 473; Wilson, *Descriptive Catalogue*, vol. 2, ccxxiii; Public Letter from Bengal, 1 October 1822, BL/OIOC/F/4/867 (22924), 1–13; Horace Hayman Wilson to Stephen Lushington, 3 January 1822, ibid., 41–59; also 6 August 1822, ibid., 115–39; Lushington to Wilson, 22 August 1822, ibid., 140–145; Wilson to Lushington, 13 December 1822, ibid., 183–85; and 'Literary and Philosophical Intelligence', *Asiatic Journal and Monthly Register for British India and its Dependencies* 15(90) (1823), 581.

12. Discussed in detail by Howes, *Illustrating India*, 78–114.

13. Today these drawings are contained in three albums and some of them are complemented by Linnaean classifications. See BL/OIOC/NHD/37; 38; 46.

14. Mackenzie had to leave a large part of his collection behind after withdrawing from an attack by 'Maratha Freebooters'. Colin Mackenzie to Francis Humberston Mackenzie, 21 July 1794, NAS/GD/46/17/4, 440–47, here 444f; see also 9 August 1796, ibid., 485– 95, here 490.

15. Public Letter from Bengal, 1 January 1823, BL/IOR/F/4/867 (22924), 15–27; see also Messrs. Palmer and Co, Attornies to the Executive of the late Colonel Mackenzie to Lushington, 19 October 1822, ibid., 155–77.

16. Colin Mackenzie, 'View of the State of the Mysore Survey on 1st October 1803', NAI/SIR/REP/2, 239–53, here 253.

17. Cf. for example Colin Mackenzie to William Lantwar, 2 October 1810, NAI/SIR/SGO/90A, 122; id. to Henry Hamilton, 2 October 1810, ibid., 123f; also 18 December 1810, ibid., 137f.

18. All three belonged to Mackenzie's official staff. Cristian Ignatio worked for Mackenzie from 1801; John Newman from 1807 to about 1817; John Mustie is mentioned in 1816 as a draftsman paid by the Company. Cf. 'Detailed List of the Establishment attached to the Superintendant of the Mysore Survey for the Month ending 30th April 1809 per Order of Government of 28th February 1809', NAI/SIR/SGO/90A, 213; and Colin Mackenzie, 'General Report on the State of the Surveying Department at Fort St. George and Draft reports of Progress for 1817', NAI/SIR/REP/3, Appendix 3 (1 August 1816), 37–76, here 75.

19. Colin Mackenzie to Benjamin Swain Ward, 1 March 1810, NAI/SIR/SGO/90A, 18f; see also 5 January 1809, ibid, 5–7; id. to William Lantwar, 9 August 1810, ibid., 115; id. to Henry Hamilton, 15 November 1810 and 18 December 1810, ibid., 134, 137f; and

'Fieldbooks & Sketches. Survey in Mysore, Vellore & other Districts. By Messrs Ward, Hamilton and Lantwar, 1807–1808', NAI/SIR/FB/38.

20. Colin Mackenzie to Lieutenant Conner, 6 March 1816, NAI/SIR/SGO/573, 30–33, here 33.
21. Cf. Dirks, 'Colonial Histories and Native Informants', 294; id., 'The Invention of Caste: Civil Society in Colonial India', *Social Analysis* 25 (1989), 49.
22. Mantena, *Origins of Modern Historiography,* 3; for the support given to Mackenzie's project see ibid., 74–80.
23. Cf. Wagoner, 'Precolonial Intellectuals', 790 fn 10.
24. Mackenzie, 'Statement of the Literary Labours', 247.
25. Cf. 'Extract of a General Letter ... dated February 9 1809', 367; Colin Mackenzie to John Leyden, 9 October 1810, NLS/Ms 3380, 136–39.
26. Cf. Colin Mackenzie to Barry Close, 7 September 1800, NAI/SIR/M/6, 179–82, here 181.
27. Cf. Colin Mackenzie, 'Brief View of the Collection', BL/IOR/F/4/867 (22924), 60–139, here 72.
28. Colin Mackenzie to George Buchan, 28 February 1804, BL/OIOC/Mss Eur/F/228/39, No. 20.
29. Colin Mackenzie, 'Plan of the Mysore Survey and the Manner on which it is proposed to be executed', 1800, BL/IOR/P/254/52, 729–45, here 742. See also id. to Colonel Montresor, 28 July 1800, NAI/SIR/M/6, 159–62, here 162.
30. Colin Mackenzie to Arthur Wellesley, 28 July 1800, NAI/SIR/M/6, 157–59, here 158f.
31. Colin Mackenzie to Colonel Montresor, 28 July 1800, NAI/SIR/M/6, 159–62, here 161.
32. Colin Mackenzie to Barry Close, 27 June 1801, NAI/SIR/M/6, 276–78. See also 14 October 1801, ibid., 295–97, here 296; and 21 November 1802, BL/IOR/F/152 (2598), 94–99, here 97f.
33. Colin Mackenzie, 'Second General Report on the Mysore Survey', 1803, NAI/SIR/REP/2, 17–35, here 33.
34. Colin Mackenzie to Barry Close, 21 November 1802, BL/IOR/F/152 (2598), 94–99, here 97f.
35. Cf. Colin Mackenzie, 'Second General Report on the Mysore Survey', 1803, NAI/SIR/REP/2, 17–35, here 26.
36. Colin Mackenzie, 'View of the State of the Mysore Survey on 1st October 1803', NAI/SIR/REP/2, 251.
37. George Buchan to Colin Mackenzie, 19 November 1803, NAI/SIR/SGO/3, 91–93, here 92.
38. D. Campbell to Robert Hyde Colebrooke, 2 February 1798, NAI/SIR/SGO/574, 53f.
39. 'Extract of a General Letter from the Honble Court of Directors dated 9th May 1797', NAI/SIR/1/5, 24. Later on the Company's historian did actually publish a history, though without any knowledge of Mackenzie's material: see J. Bruce, *Annals of the East India Company: From Their Establishment by the Charter of the Queen Elizabeth to the Union of the London and East India Companies 1707–8,* 3 vols (London, 1810).
40. George Buchan to Colin Mackenzie, 7 January 1804, NAI/SIR/SGO/3, 99–102. For support from Buchan cf. Colin Mackenzie to Seaforth, 28 February 1809, NAS/GD/46/17/10, 521–24, here 522.
41. Colin Mackenzie to George Buchan, 28 February 1804, BL/OIOC/Mss Eur/F/228/39, No. 20, 27f.
42. Colin Mackenzie, 'Memorandum of the Origin, Progress and Present State of the Geometrical and Statistic Survey of Mysore, to July 1st 1807', BL/Mss Add/14380, 35; Colin Mackenzie to George Buchan, 28 February 1804, BL/OIOC/Mss Eur/F/228/39, No. 20; id. to Merrick Shaw, 1 May 1804, ibid., No 1; Colin Mackenzie to George Buchan, 27 November 1805, NAI/SIR/M/18, 135–37.

43. Colin Mackenzie, 'Memorandum of the Origin, Progress and Present State of the Geometrical and Statistic Survey of Mysore, to July 1st 1807', BL/Mss Add/14380, 36.
44. Colin Mackenzie to Henry Trail, 2 August 1805, BL/OIOC/Mss Eur/F/228/39.
45. 'Extract of a General Letter … dated February 9 1809', 368f.
46. Public Letter from Bengal, 1 January 1823, BL/IOR/F/4/867 (22924), 15–27.
47. Cf. Colin Mackenzie, 'Plan of Arranging the Surveyor General's Department & Generally all Surveys under the Presidency of Fort St. George', 29 November 1810, NAI/SIR/SGO/60, 3.
48. Cf. for example Colin Mackenzie to Lieutenant Conner, 11 January 1816, NAI/SIR/SGO/573, 28f.
49. Cf. Wilson, *Descriptive Catalogue*, vol. 1, xviii.
50. Cf. ibid., xxii–xxiv.
51. Dirks, 'Colonial Histories and Native Informants', 308–11, stresses this aspect in particular. See also Mantena, *Origins of Modern Historiography*, 141–47.
52. See for example Colin Mackenzie, 'Memorandum for Narrain Row to enquire at Beejanagoor, Anagoondy, Complee & Soodoor', 6 November 1809, NAI/SIR/SGO/90A, 80; id. to Kavali Venkata Lakshmayya, 27 January 1810, ibid., 85f; and Colin Mackenzie to William Lantwar, 2 October 1810, ibid., 122.
53. Colin Mackenzie, 'Queries particularly regarding Guzerat & the NW parts of India'; id., 'Heads of Historical Information more immediately applicable to the Southward, 20. Feb 1809' and id., 'Heads of Enquiry for Tanjore, November 1809', all BL/OIOC/Mss Eur/C/929.
54. Colin Mackenzie, 'Memorandum on the Means of procuring Historical Materials regarding the South of India', 14 February 1808, NLS/Ms 8955, 211–13.
55. Cf. Colin Mackenzie to Barry Close, 14 August 1800, NAI/SIR/M/6, 169.
56. Cf. for example Colin Mackenzie to: Alexander Walker, 14 March 1800, NLS/Ms 13602, 5–7; John Mather, 1 August 1800, NAI/SIR/M/6, 162; Captain Johnston, 8 October 1800, ibid., 193; Barry Close, 7 September 1800, ibid., 179–82, here 181; Johnston, 6 January 1801, ibid., 240f; and to Mather, 12 August 1801, NAI/SIR/SGO/90, 62.
57. For instance those of Captain Hathway, who had died in 1802. However, the price of six hundred pagodas for this collection was too expensive for him. Cf. Colin Mackenzie to William Morison, 16 January 1803, NAI/SIR/SGO/90, 213f; also 10 February 1803, ibid., 215–17; and 24 April 1803, ibid., 219–22.
58. Colin Mackenzie to Barry Close, 27 March 1801, NAI/SIR/M/6, 255f.
59. Colin Mackenzie to Merrick Shaw, 1 May 1804, NAI/SIR/M/18, 57–60. The letter cited is a draft. In the version Mackenzie sent he left out this passage presumably because he wanted to apply for more funds for this purpose and considered the timing to be unfavourable. Cf. Mackenzie to Shaw, 1 May 1804, BL/OIOC/Mss Eur/F/228/39, No. 1.
60. Mark Wilks to George Buchan, 4 March 1807, NAI/SIR/SGO/3, 565–71, here 567.
61. Cf. Dirks, 'Colonial Histories and Native Informants', 295–301.
62. Cf. for example Colin Mackenzie to William Kirpatrick, 14 October 1801, BL/OIOC/Mss Eur/F/228/19.
63. In later years Mackenzie was all too aware of this problem: 'A considerable body of information of the History & Antiquities of these Countries', he wrote, for instance, of his research in the Ceded Districts, 'are … secured but to arrange & translate them is not to be thought of at present; it may be sufficient to observe that enough is secured to throw a very considerable light on the Institutions & History of the Country'. Colin Mackenzie to George Strachey, 20 November 1815, NAI/SIR/SGO/573, 19f. See also Mackenzie to Stephen Lushington, 7 March 1820, BL/Mss Add/14380, 39–52, here 51f.
64. He stresses this in his second major report: Colin Mackenzie, 'Second General Report on the Mysore Survey', 1803, NAI/SIR/REP/2, 17–35, here 25. For the origins of this

collection see also: Mackenzie to William Kirkpatrick, 14 October 1801, BL/OIOC/Mss Eur/F/228/19.

65. Colin Mackenzie, 'Introductory Memoir: Of the Use and Advantage of Inscriptions and Sculptured Monuments in illustrating Hindoo History', BL/OIOC/Mss Eur/Mack Gen/18A, 1–10, here 4.

66. Cf. Colin Mackenzie to John Leyden, 30 April 1807, NLS/Ms 3380, 81–85, here 84; also 23 November 1807, ibid., 92–95, here 94.

67. Colin Mackenzie to Charles Wilkins, 25 October 1808, BL/OIOC/Mss Eur/Mack Gen/18, 275–78.; id., 'Register of a Collection of Ancient Sassanums or Grants and Inscriptions, on Public Monuments, Pillars & Temples; or on Grants preserved in private hands (under the two Descriptions of Silla or Stone and Tambra or Copper) issued by the several Governments that have prevailed in Balla-Ghaat. Collected in the Course of several Journeys through Mysore, Bednore & Canara from 1804 to 1807 with an Appendix containing Copies of FacSimilies, Translations & Drawings of some of the Inscriptions registered, as Specimens of the Manner in which they may illustrate the Ancient History, Government, Institutions, Laws, Civil & Religious Tenures & the State of Property in the Country', 12 October 1807; BL/OIOC/Mss Eur/Mack Gen/18A. Cf. Wagoner, 'Precolonial Intellectuals', 808f.

68. Colin Mackenzie, 'Introductory Memoir: Of the Use and Advantage of Inscriptions and Sculptured Monuments in illustrating Hindoo History', BL/OIOC/Mss Eur/Mack Gen/18A, 1–10.

69. Cf. Colin Mackenzie to John Mather, 5 June 1802, NAI/SIR/SGO/90, 89–91, here 89; id., 'Memorandum on the Means of procuring Historical Materials regarding the South of India', 14 February 1808, NLS/Ms 8955, 211–13, here para. 7, 11.

70. Colin Mackenzie, 'Brief View of the Collection', [1813/14], BL/IOR/F/4/867 (22924), 60–139, here 94.

71. Cf. for example Nitala Naina to Kavali Venkata Lakshmayya, 12 February 1808, BL/OIOC/Mss Eur/Mack Misc/172, 54–72; 'Particular Account of the Agriculture, Productions, Manufactures Commerce Imports & Exports with the Coins, Weights and Measures, and also an Account of the Soil, Seasons, Rains, Animals &c &c of the Tallook of Ahmednuggur in The Deckan from Enquires on the spot from Intelligent Natives in 1806', BL/OIOC/Mss Eur/Mack Gen/14, 7, 19f; 'Account of the Ancient Coins Drawing Images and Sculptures &c. Procured by the late Colonel McKenzie During his several Journeys in Deekhan Hindoostan & Java &ca.', BL/IOR/F/4/867 (22925), n.p.

72. Cf. for example [William] Garrow to Colin Mackenzie, 20 November 1808, BL/OIOC/Mss Eur/Mack Misc/171.

73. [William] Garrow to Colin Mackenzie, 24 December 1808, BL/OIOC/Mss Eur/Mack Misc/171.

74. Cf. Colin Mackenzie to Henry Hamilton, 15 November 1810, NAI/SIR/SGO/90A, 34; also 18 December 1810, ibid., 137f; and id. to Benjamin Swain Ward, 31 March 1810, ibid., 19f.

75. Cf. 'Report made by Apavoo in his Journey to Mahabalapooram and & from thence thro' the Jaghere & the Arcot District from October 1816 to May 29th 1817', BL/OIOC/Mss Eur/Mack Trans/12/60.

76. Cf. J. Babington, 'Description of the Pandoo Coolies in Malabar: With Four Drawings', *Transactions of the Literary Society of Bombay* 3 (1823), 324–30.

77. Colin Mackenzie to John Mather, 5 June 1802, NAI/SIR/SGO/90, 89–91, here 89; see also id, 'Memorandum on the Means of procuring Historical Materials regarding the South of India', 14 February 1808, NLS/Ms 8955, 211–13, here No. 7, 13.

78. He made this visit during an enforced interruption to the survey when most of the team were ill. Cf. Colin Mackenzie 'Second General Report on the Mysore Survey, 1803', NAI/SIR/REP/2, 17–36, here 19f.

79. Cf. Colin Mackenzie to Barry Close, 27 June 1801, NAI/SIR/M/6, 276–78, here 278. For the illustrations and plans see Howes, *Illustrating India*, 103–5.
80. Colin Mackenzie to Benjamin Swain Ward, 5 November 1809, NAI/SIR/SGO/90A, 7–9.
81. Cf. Howes, 'Colin Mackenzie and the Stupa of Amaravati'. See also Cohn, 'Transformation of Objects into Artifacts', esp. 88–91 and Mackenzie's description, published posthumously: [C. Mackenzie], 'Ruins of Amravutty, Depauldina and Durnacotta', *Asiatic Journal and Monthly Register for British India and its Dependencies* 15(89) (1823), 464–78.
82. J. Howes, 'Colin Mackenzie, the Madras School of Orientalism and Investigations at Mahabalipuram', in Trautmann, *Madras School of Orientalism*, 74–109; Howes, *Illustrating India*, 165–89.
83. Cf. Howes, *Illustrating India*, 115f.
84. H. Kulke, 'The Katakarajavamsavali: The Colonial Biography of Puri's Sanskrit Chronicle of the Year 1820', *Indian Historical Review* 38(1) (2011), 65–75; P.B. Wagoner, 'From Manuscript to Archive to Print: The Mackenzie Collection and Later Telugu Literary Historiography', in Trautmann, *Madras School of Orientalism*, 183–205.
85. Cf. W. O'Reilly, 'Orientalist Reflections: Asia and the Pacific in the Making of late Eighteenth-Century Ireland', *New Zealand Journal of Asian Studies* 6(2) (2004), 143–45; Mantena, *Origins of Modern Historiography*, 48; Howes, *Illustrating India*, 160f.
86. Cf. Mantena, *Origins of Modern Historiography*, 52–54.
87. Howes, 'Colin Mackenzie, the Madras School', 105f; ead., *Illustrating India*, 166.
88. Cf. Wagoner, 'Precolonial Intellectuals'.
89. Wagoner, 'From Manuscript to Archive to Print', 189f.
90. Mantena, *Origins of Modern Historiography*, 3–7, 147–49.
91. Cf. Mantena, 'Question of History', 398.
92. J. Mill, *The History of British India*, 3 vols (London, 1817).
93. Cf. Colin Mackenzie to John Leyden, 30 April 1807, NLS/Ms 3380, 81–85, here 81; also 10 May 1808, ibid., 98–100, here 98f.
94. Cf. Colin Mackenzie to John Leyden, 13 November 1809, NLS/Ms 3380, 115–19, here 115f.; J. Binney to Colin Mackenzie, 3 June 1809, BL/OIOC/Mss Eur/Mack Misc/171.
95. Cf. Wilks, *Historical Sketches*, vol. 1, x–xvi.
96. F.W. Ellis, *Replies to Seventeen Questions Proposed by the Government of Fort St. George Relative to Mirasi Right, with Two Appendices Elucidatory of the Subject* (Madras, 1818), for example xxxi, xl, xliv.
97. In the introduction Kirkpatrick expressly thanked Colin Mackenzie for his help. In particular Mackenzie's assistant, Meer Hussain Ali, was able to provide him with material. Cf. W. Kirkpatrick, *Select Letters of Tippoo Sultan to Various Public Functionaries Including His Principal Military Commanders, Governors of Forts and Provinces; Diplomatic and Commercial Agents … Together with Some Addressed to the Tributary Chieftains of Shânoor, Kurnool, and Cannanore, and Sundry Other Persons; With Notes and Observations, and an Appendix, Containing Several Original Documents Never Before Published* (London, 1811), 324, xi, xvi.
98. A. Campbell, *A Grammar of the Teloogoo Language: Commonly Termed the Gentoo, Peculiar to the Hindoos Inhabiting the Northeastern Provinces of the Indian Peninsula* (Madras, 1816), xiv.
99. Cf. Nitala Naina to Kavali Venkata Lakshmayya, 10 March 1806, BL/OIOC/Mss Eur/Mack Misc/172.
100. Colin Mackenzie to John Riddell, 17 April 1818, NAI/SIR/SGO/573, 318–24.
101. Wilks, *Historical Sketches*, vol. 1, 510.
102. Cf. Colin Mackenzie to John Leyden, 30 April 1807, NLS/Ms 3380, 81–85, here 84; also 10 May 1808, ibid., 98–100.
103. Colin Mackenzie to William Kirkpatrick, 14 October 1801, BL/OIOC/Mss Eur/F/228/19.

104. 'Short View of the Great Revolutions of Government in the Dekan for 16 Centuries back so far as they can be authenticated by Records, Manuscripts, Inscriptions, Coins &c. keeping clear of the Poetic and Fabulous Epochs', n.d., BL/OIOC/Mss Eur/Mack Gen/45, 9–11.

105. Colin Mackenzie to William Kirkpatrick, 12 July 1801, BL/OIOC/Mss Eur/F/228/19.

106. Cf. N. Hargraves, 'The "Progress of Ambition": Character, Narrative, and Philosophy in the Works of William Robertson', *Journal of the History of Ideas* 63(2) (2002), esp. 267f; N. Phillipson, 'Providence and Progress: An Introduction to the Historical Thought of William Robertson', in S.J. Brown (ed.), *William Robertson and the Expansion of Empire* (Cambridge, 1997), 57–59.

107. Colin Mackenzie to William Kirkpatrick, 12 July 1801, BL/OIOC/Mss Eur/F/228/19; Beatson, *View of the Origin and Conduct*.

108. S. Guha, 'The Frontiers of Memory: What the Marathas Remembered of Vijayanagara', *Modern Asian Studies* 43(1) (2009), 278.

109. For his contribution see for example [Srivinasia], 'Extracts from the Journal of a Learned Native Traveller of a Route from Calcutta to Gaya in 1820, Translated from the Original', *Oriental Magazine and Calcutte Review* 1 (1823), 769–75 and 2 (1823), 68–73. For authorship see H.H. Wilson, 'Account of the Foe Kúe Ki, or Travels of Fa Hian in India, Translated from the Chinese by M. Remusat', *Journal of the Royal Asiatic Society* 5(1) (1839), 131.

110. Colin Mackenzie, 'General Report on the State of the Surveying Department at Fort St. George and Draft reports of Progress for 1817', NAI/SIR/REP/3, Appendix 3 (1 August 1816), 37–76, here 72f.

111. N.B. Dirks, 'Is Vice Versa? Historical Anthropologies and Anthropological Histories', in T.J. McDonald (ed.), *The Historic Turn in the Human Sciences* (Ann Arbor, 1996), 43.

112. Cf. K. McNeil, *Scotland, Britain, Empire: Writing the Highlands, 1760–1860* (Columbus, 2007), 1–3. It was not until four years later that the Highland Society of Scotland was founded in Edinburgh. Although the 'preservation of the Language, Poetry and Music of the Highlands' was also on its agenda, it was mainly committed to a programme of improvement. Cf. H. Mackenzie (ed.), *Prize Essays and Transactions of the Highland Society of Scotland: To Which is Prefixed an Account of the Institution and Principal Proceedings of the Society*, 6 vols (Edinburgh, 1799–1824), vol. 1, iii.

113. For Scott's 'romantic antiquarianism' see for example I. Ferris, 'Melancholy, Memory and the "Narrative Situation" of History in post-Enlightenment Scotland', in L. Davis, I. Duncan and J. Sorensen (eds), *Scotland and the Borders of Romanticism* (Cambridge, 2004), 90; Y.S. Lee, 'A Divided Inheritance: Scott's Antiquarian Novel and the British Nation', *English Literary History* 64(2) (1997), 537–67; I. Ferris, 'Printing the Past: Walter Scott's Bannatyne Club and the Antiquarian Document', *Romanticism* 11(2) (2005), 143–57.

114. Cf. J. Sinclair, *An Account of the Highland Society of London, from its Establishment in May 1778, to the Commencement of the Year 1813* (London, 1813), 17, 45f; and Highland Society of London (ed.), *The Poems of Ossian in the Original Gaelic with a Literal Translation into Latin*, 2 vols (London, 1807).

115. Cf. *Calcutta Gazette*, 17 January 1814 and *Madras Courier*, 29 March 1814 in H.D. Sandeman (ed.), *Selections from Calcutta Gazettes of the Years 1806 to 1815 Inclusive, Showing The Political and Social Condition of the English in India upwards of fifty Years ago* (Calcutta, 1868), 345f, 353f.

116. From the Seaforth family the brothers Thomas and Francis Humberston Mackenzie, the latter of whom was chairman of the society for a time; also John Mackenzie 'of the Temple', first secretary and one of the founding fathers. Cf. Sinclair, *Account of the Highland Society*, 4f, 35, 39, 41, 62; for Colin Mackenzie's acquaintance with John Mackenzie see Colin Mackenzie to John Mackenzie, 14 February 1798, NAS/GD/46/17/4, 528f.

117. John Newbolt to William Erskine, 28 May 1815, NLS/Adv Mss/36.1.5, 359.

118. Cf. Rendall, 'Scottish Orientalism', 66f.

119. In connection with a review of Wilks' *Historical Sketches*. Cf. 'Review: Historical Sketches of the South of India, in an Attempt to Trace the History of Mysúr ... By Lieut. Col. Mark Wilks', *Edinburgh Review* 18(36) (1811), 343–70, esp. 348–50.

120. Malcolm was one of the most committed supporters of Mackenzie's historical research. Cf. John Malcolm to William Bentinck, 5 March 1807, NAI/SIR/SGO/3, 553–55; McLaren, *British India and British Scotland*, 66, 119–28.

121. However, Mackenzie only corresponded with Elphinstone in the last years of his life. Cf. Colin Mackenzie to John Riddell, 1 August 1818, NAI/SIR/SGO/573, 369–72, here 370.

122. For Erskine see Trautmann, *Languages and Nations*, 82–86; part of his correspondence in which Mackenzie plays a certain role in NLS/Adv Mss/36.1.5.

123. W. Robertson, *An Historical Disquisition Concerning the Knowledge which the Ancients Had of India; and the Progress of Trade with That Country prior to the Discovery of the Passage to It by the Cape of Good Hope: With an Appendix, Containing Observations on ... the Indians* (London, 1791), 335f. See also K. O'Brian, *Narratives of Enlightenment: Cosmopolitan History from Voltaire to Gibbon* (Cambridge, 1997), 136, 150f, 257.

124. Cf. Rendall, 'Scottish Orientalism', 60–64; McLaren, *British India and British Scotland*, 119–28.

125. Cf. H. Otness, 'Nurturing the Roots for Oriental Studies: The Development of the Libraries of the Royal Asiatic Society's Branches and Affiliates in Asia in the Nineteenth Century', *International Association of Orientalist Librarians Bulletin* 43 (1998), 9–17; Trautmann, *Languages and Nations*, 81–108, 116–30; id., 'Discovering Aryan and Dravidian in British India: A Tale of Two Cities', *Historiographia Linguistica* 31(1) (2004), 46–48.

126. For an overview of some of Mackenzie's contacts see Howes, *Illustrating India*, 55–77.

127. Wagoner, 'Precolonial Intellectuals', 788f, was the first to stress the connection between the two projects. See also Trautmann, 'Introduction', and *Languages and Nations*, esp. 210f.

128. Cf. Colin Mackenzie to John Leyden, 13 November 1809, NLS/MS 3380, 115–19, here 119.

129. For Newbold's role see 'Review: The Transactions of the Literary Society of Madras Part 1, London 1827', *Asiatic Journal and Monthly Register for British India and its Dependencies* 26(153) (1828), 332f; J. Gibbs, 'Archaeology in India', *Society of Arts Journal* 34 (1885/1886), 557.

130. W. Jones, 'On the Hindus: The third Anniversary Discourse', *Asiatic Researches* 1 (1788), 415–31. Cf. Trautmann, 'Discovering Aryan and Dravidian', 45.

131. For details see T.R. Trautmann, 'Hullabaloo about Telugu', *South Asia Research* 19(1) (1999), 53–70; id., 'Discovering Aryan and Dravidian', 39–42, 47f.

132. William Jones, for instance, was convinced that comparative linguistic research and other forms of historical investigation should complement one another. Cf. M.S. Dodson, *Orientalism, Empire and National Culture: India, 1770–1880* (Basingstoke, 2007), 26f.

133. Trautmann, 'Hullabaloo about Telugu', 54; id., *Aryans and British India*, 42–59. For the role played by Mosaic ethnology in the formation of European identities see C. Kidd, *British Identities before Nationalism: Ethnicity and Nationhood in the Atlantic World, 1600–1800* (Cambridge, 1999). 27–33.

134. J. Leyden, 'Scenes of Infancy; Descriptive of Teviotdale (1803)', in id., *The Poetical Remains* (London, 1819), 289–415. For Leyden as poet cf. N. Leask, 'Towards an Anglo-Indian Poetry? The Colonial Muse in the Writings of John Leyden, Thomas Medwin and Charles D'Oyly', in B. Moore-Gilbert (ed.), *Writing India 1757–1990: The Literature of British India* (Manchester, 1996), 58–63.

135. J. Leyden, *Tour in the Highlands and Western Islands, 1800*, edited by James Sinton (Edinburgh and London, 1903); J. Leyden (ed.), *The Complaynt of Scotland, Written in 1548 with A Preliminary Dissertation and Glossary* (Edinburgh, 1801).

136. W. Scott, *Minstrelsy of the Scottish Border Consisting of Historical and Romantic Ballads, Collected in the Southern Counties of Scotland; with a Few of Modern Date, Founded upon Local Tradition* (1801/1802), 5th edn., 3 vols (London and Edinburgh, 1812). For Leyden's contribution see vol. 1, cxxiii.

137. Cf. Rendall, 'Scottish Orientalism', 45f.

138. Although Leyden only claimed to have command of written Arabic and Persian, Alexander Fraser Tytler had supported his appointment; this failed, however, due to a surprising appointment to the post of College Superintendent. See John Leyden to Alexander Fraser Tytler, 13 June [1800/1801], NLS/Ms 3383, 120–23; Alexander Fraser Tytler to James Mackintosh, 25 June 1801, ibid., 128f. For the background see also Datta, 'James Mackintosh', 42.

139. John Leyden to 'My Dearest and only Love [Jesse]', 2 April 1803, NLS/Ms 3383, 130; see also id. to his father, 5 April 1803, NLS/Ms 3380, 54f.

140. Colin Mackenzie to J.H. Peile, 26 November 1803, NAI/SIR/SGO/90, 425–27, here 426.

141. Both were later involved at least indirectly in establishing a monument for the deceased Dr Anderson. After his arrival in India Leyden lived temporarily in Anderson's house, as Mackenzie had done. See Colin Mackenzie to John Leyden, 9 October 1810, NLS/Ms 3380, 140–43; and J. Morton, 'Memoirs of Dr Leyden', in J. Leyden, *The Poetical Remains* (London, 1819), xxxiv.

142. Cf. George Buchan to Colin Mackenzie, 14 January 1804, NAI/SIR/SGO/3, 95–97; B (FSG) to CD, 29 March 1804, BL/IOR/F/4/280 (6426), 21–27; CD to B (FSG), 23 October 1805, ibid., 39–41, John Leyden to his father, 23 March 1804, NLS/Ms 3380, 58f.

143. By early 1805 he already had to interrupt his work for reasons of ill health and six months later he stated that he was happy to get away from the 'fatiguing and dangerous service' of the Mysore Survey. Cf. John Leyden to Colin Mackenzie, 12 April 1805, NLS/Ms 3383, 218f; and Leyden to his father, 20 November 1805, NLS/MS 3380, 71f.

144. John Leyden to his father, 23 March 1804, NLS/Ms 3380, 58f. Reasonable doubts about Leyden's claim to know forty-five languages are raised in particular by J. Bastin in 'John Leyden and the Publication of the "Malay Annals" (1821)', *Journal of the Malaysian Branch of the Royal Asiatic Society* 75(2) (2002), 101–6.

145. Cf. Kavali Venkata Ramaswami to John Leyden, 18 July 1805, NLS/MS 3380, 64f.

146. He only published his analysis of the 'Indo-Chinese' language group; the descriptions of the other two remained unpublished. See J. Leyden, 'On the Languages and Literature of the Indo-Chinese Nations', *Asiatic Researches* 10 (1812), 158–289; cf. Trautmann, 'Hullabaloo about Telugu', 56f.

147. This is also how I understand the argument put forward in Dirks, 'Guiltless Spoliations'.

148. W. Scott, *Waverly; or `Tis Sixty Years Since* (1814), reprint edited by Claire Lamont (Oxford, 1986), 340. Cf. S. Makdisi, *Romantic Imperialism: Universal Empire and the Culture of Modernity* (Cambridge, 1998), 73.

149. This is one of the central arguments in Womack, *Improvement and Romance*. Pittock also argues that in Scott's presentation Scotland had become a 'museum of history and culture' without any political dynamics. See M. Pittock, *The Invention of Scotland: The Stuart Myth and the Scottish Identity, 1638 to the Present* (London and New York, 1991), 87.

150. Cf. C. Kidd, *Subverting the Scottish Past: Scottish Whig Historians and the Creation of an Anglo-British Identity* (Cambridge, 1993), 205–15; J.G.A. Pocock, *Barbarism and Religion: The Enlightenments of Edward Gibbon, 1737–1764*, 4 vols (Cambridge, 1999–2005), vol. 2, 280f; and M. Pittock, *Scottish and Irish Romanticism* (Oxford, 2008), 59–66.

151. Cf. Irschick, *Dialogue and History*, 67–114.

152. Cf. Guha, 'Frontiers of Memory', 273. In two texts about the Rajahs of 'Anagoondy' that were 'collected' for Mackenzie and later published, their descent from the rulers of

Vijayanagara is likewise mentioned to justify certain claims under British rule. Cf. 'History of the Anagoondy Rajahs, Taken from the Verbal Account of Timmapah, the Present Representative of that Family, at Camlapore, 10th January 1801. Communicated by Major Mackenzie', *Asiatic Annual Register or, View of the History of Hindustan, and of the Politics Commerce and Literature for the Year 1804* (London, 1806), 21–24; 'History of the Kings of Beejanagur and Anagoondy, from Enquires Made at Alputtun and Anagoondy, by Order of Major Mackenzie, in January 1801. Communicated by Major Mackenzie', ibid, 24–33.

153. 'Historical Accounts of Beedonoor or Caladee Samstanum', BL/OIOC/Mack Gen/6, 121–66, here 121.

154. C. Mackenzie, 'View of the Principal Political Events That Occurred in the Carnatic, From the Dissolution of the Ancient Hindoo Government in 1564 till the Mogul Government was Established in 1687, on the Conquest of the Capitals of Beejepoor and Golconda; Compiled from Various Authentic Memoirs and Original MSS., Collected Chiefly within the Last Ten Years, and Referred to in the Notes at the Bottom of Each Page', *Journal of the Asiatic Society of Bengal* 13(1) (1844), 422.

155. Cf. Notes by Colin Mackenzie, April 1802, BL/OIOC/Mss Eur/Mack Gen/6, No. 1e, 12f; Colin Mackenzie to William Bentinck, 23 June 1805, BL/OIOC/Mss Eur/F/228/39, No. 11, 13–15, here 15; id., 'Memorandum of the Origin, Progress and Present State of the Geometrical and Statistic Survey of Mysore, to July 1st 1807', BL/Mss Add/14380, 37.

156. Robertson, *Historical Disquisition*; Mackenzie already knew of Robertson's work in 1793 and probably owned the work in duplicate. Cf. D. Hill to Board of Superintendence to the College of FSG, 14 August 1816, BL/IOR/F/4/541 (12148), 23–26.

157. Cf. Colin Mackenzie to Charles Wilkins, 25 October 1808, BL/OIOC/Mss Eur/Mack Gen/18, 275–78, here 278.

158. Colin Mackenzie, 'Memorandum on the Ancient Hindoo System of Government', BL/OIOC/Mss Eur/Mack Gen/45, 1–11, here 6; see also Robertson, *Historical Disquisition*, for example 266, 268.

159. Robertson, *Historical Disquisition*, 255.

160. Cf. D. Francesconi, 'William Robertson on Historical Causation and unintended Consequences', *Storia della Storiografia* 36 (1999), 55; H.M. Höpfl, 'From Savage to Scotsman: Conjectural History in the Scottish Enlightenment', *Journal of British Studies* 17(2) (1978), 19–40.

161. Colin Mackenzie to William Bentinck, 23 June 1805, BL/OIOC/Mss Eur/F/228/39, No. 11, 14f.

162. Francesconi, 'William Robertson', 55. See also C.J. Berry, *Social Theory of the Scottish Enlightenment* (Edinburgh, 1997), 91, 113f; M. Schmidt, '"Conjectural History", and the Decline of Enlightenment Historical Writing', in U. Broich et al. (eds), *Reactions to Revolutions: The 1790s and Their Aftermath* (Berlin, 2007), 253f.

163. 'The Department of History in this Country', wrote his friend Mark Wilks, 'is so deformed by fable and anachronism, that it may [be] considered as an absolute blank in Indian literature'. Mark Wilks to George Buchan, 4 March 1807, NAI/SIR/SGO/3, 565–71, here 565f. See also Wilks, *Historical Sketches*, vol. 1, xv; and Dirks, 'Colonial Histories and Native Informants', 304.

164. Mackenzie, 'View of the Principal Political Events'. Historians still refer to this text as a 'classic' today. Cf. S. Subrahmanyam, 'Aspects of State Formation in South India and Southeast Asia, 1500–1650', *Indian Economic and Social History Review* 23 (1986), 358, fn 3.

165. Mackenzie, 'View of the Principal Political Events', 423.

166. Cf. ibid., 437, 440f. For a very similar description of these groups see Colin Mackenzie, 'Memorandum of the Financial Records of the Deckan', 12 June 1809, BL/OIOC/Mss Eur/Mack Gen/44, 1–9, here 7.

167. Mackenzie, 'View of the Principal Political Events', 434.

168. Ibid., 441.

169. Colin Mackenzie, 'Memorandum on the Ancient Hindoo System of Government and its Vestiges in the South of the Peninsula', BL/OIOC/Mss Eur/Mack Gen/45, 1–11, here 1. Mackenzie refers here to the material collected in southern India in the previous five years. This could either mean 1799, as the year in which the Mysore Survey started, or 1804, when the historical collection was put on a new financial footing.

170. Cf. Colin Mackenzie, 'Hints or Heads of Enquiry for facilitating our knowledge of the more Southern parts of Deckan', 1800, BL/OIOC/Mss Eur/F/128/213, para.11.

171. Colin Mackenzie, 'Memorandum on the Ancient Hindoo System of Government and its Vestiges in the South of the Peninsula', BL/OIOC/Mss Eur/Mack Gen/45, 1–11, 6.

172. Ibid., 1.

173. Cf. ibid., quotes 2, 1, 3.

174. Cf. O'Brian, *Narratives of Enlightenment*, 11; Pocock, *Barbarism and Religion*, vol. 1, 4.

175. Colin Mackenzie, 'Memorandum on the Ancient Hindoo System of Government and its Vestiges in the South of the Peninsula', BL/OIOC/Mss Eur/Mack Gen/45, 1–11, 5.

176. Wilks also deals with the topic in detail in his *Historical Sketches*, vol. 1, 104–98.

177. Mark Wilks to George Buchan, 4 March 1807, NAI/SIR/SGO/3, 565–71, here 568f.

178. 'Desiderata and Inquiries connected with the Presidencies of Madras and Bombay', *Asiatic Journal and Monthly Register for British India and its Dependencies* 24(141) (1827), 349–54, also reprinted, for instance, in *The Oriental Herald and Journal of General Literature* 14(45) (1827), 540–47; *Madras Journal of Literature and Science* 1(1) (1833), 44–52.

179. Cf. R.S. Mantena, 'Vernacular Futures: Orientalism, History, and Language in Colonial South India' (Ph.D. dissertation, University of Michigan, 2002), 58f; ead., *Origins of Modern Historiography*, 81; Trautmann, *Languages and Nations*, 177. Trautmann claims that Mackenzie himself was the author. Given that the author of the circular does not know whether Dharmaiah is still alive, but that the latter was still employed by Mackenzie in 1807, both the attribution and the date seem questionable at least.

180. Colin Mackenzie, 'Memorandum on the Means of procuring Historical Materials regarding the South of India', 14 February 1808, NLS/Ms 8955, 211–13.

181. In 1829, for instance, the *niyogi* Ramaswami was still writing that the South Indian languages derived from Sanskrit, cf. Mantena, *Origins of Modern Historiography*, 117.

182. Cf. J. Malcolm, *Political History of India from 1784 to 1823*, 2 vols (London, 1826), vol. 1, 68–70.

183. There is an early mention of this in Colin Mackenzie, 'View of the State of the Mysore Survey on 1st October 1803', NAI/SIR/REP/2, 239–53, here 250, fn, specifically stressing the continuity. See also Colin Mackenzie, 'Memorandum of the Financial Records of the Deckan', 12 June 1809, BL/OIOC/Mss Eur/Mack Gen/44, 1–9, here 2.

184. Cf. F. Buchanan, *Journey from Madras,* vol. 2, 304–6. If Buchanan referred to contradictions here, he later wrote that 'the Boundaries of these may be traced over all of India by consulting the learned, among whom to this day they are in general use, the modern names imposed by foreign invaders so often changing as to produce little impression'. F. [Buchanan] Hamilton, *Genealogies of the Hindoos, Extracted from Their Sacred Writings: With an Introduction and Alphabetical Index* (Edinburgh, 1819), 7f; see also 64f. Wilson mentions in Mackenzie's collection the Sanskrit *Desanirnaya* containing a description of the fifty-six *desams*. Cf. Wilson, *Descriptive Catalogue*, vol. 1, 131, No. III.

185. Colin Mackenzie, 'Hints or Heads of Enquiry for facilitating our knowledge of the more Southern parts of Deckan', 1800, BL/OIOC/Mss Eur/F/128/213, para. 10. See also Colin Mackenzie to Francis Buchanan, 5 June 1800, NAI/SIR/M/6, 119–21, here 121; and Wilks, *Historical Sketches*, vol. 1, 4f: 'The ancient divisions of the country may ... be traced with

greater probability by the present limits of spoken languages than by any other guide which is easily accessible'.

186. Cf. John Leyden, 'Journal from Madras to Seringapatam', June 1804, NLS/MS 3380, 178–82.

187. Colin Mackenzie, 'Brief View of the Collection' [1813/1814], BL/IOR/F/4/867 (22924), 60–139, here 79. The version of this manuscript held in London contains the note 'not rcvd' regarding this map.

188. Colin Mackenzie to John Leyden, 9 October 1810, NLS/Mss 3380, 140–43, here 141; see also id., 'Brief View of the Collection', BL/IOR/F/4/867 (22924), 60–139, here 74.

189. F.W. Ellis, 'Note to the Introduction', in Campbell, *Grammar of the Telloogoo Language*. Cf. Trautmann's detailed discussion of the grammar in 'Dr. Johnson and the Pandits: Imagining the Perfect Dictionary in Colonial Madras', *Indian Economic and Social History Review* 38(4) (2001), 375–97.

190. Mark Wilks to George Buchan, 4 March 1807, NAI/SIR/SGO/3, 565–71, here 567.

191. Colin Mackenzie to Thomas Munro, 28 January 1807, BL/OIOC/Mss Eur/F/151/9, 142–45, here 145. Slavery was indeed widespread in Canara. Cf. T. Sarkar, 'Bondage in the Colonial Context', in U. Patnaik and M. Dingwaney (eds), *Chains of Servitude: Bondage and Slavery in India* (Madras, 1985), 97–126, esp. 104f; and S. Vatuk, 'Bharattee's Death: Domestic Slave Women in Nineteenth-Century Madras', in I. Chatterjee and R.M. Eaton (eds), *Slavery and South Asian History* (Bloomington and Indianapolis, 2006), 210–33, esp. 215f.

192. Colin Mackenzie, 'Memorandum on the Means of procuring Historical Materials regarding the South of India', 14 February 1808, NLS/Ms 8955, 211–13, No. 3.

193. Cf. Colin Mackenzie to Francis Buchanan, 23 May 1800, NAI/SIR/M/6, 113–15, here 115; and Kavali Venkata Borayya and Mackenzie, 'Account of the Jains', 272–79.

194. Cf. Colin Mackenzie, to Francis Buchanan, 23 May 1800, NAI/SIR/M/6, 113–15, here 115. For Buchanan's interest in the Jains, see for example F. Buchanan, 'Particulars of the Jains Extracted from a Journal', *Asiatic Researches* 9 (1809), 279–86.

195. Colin Mackenzie to Francis Buchanan, 14 November 1800, NAI/SIR/SGO/90, 458f.

196. Colin Mackenzie, 'Hints or Heads of Enquiry for facilitating our knowledge of the more Southern parts of the Deckan, 1800', BL/OIOC/Mss Eur/F/128/213.

197. Colin Mackenzie to William Kirkpatrick, 14 October 1801, BL/OIOC/Mss Eur/F/228/19.

198. Colin Mackenzie to William Bentinck, 23 June 1805, BL/OIC/Mss Eur/F/228/39, No. 11, 15; id. to Charles Wilkins, 25 October 1808, BL/OIOC/Mss Eur/Mack Gen/18, No. 1, 275–78, here 275f.

199. Cf. Wilks, *Historical Sketches*, vol. 1, 508–12, quote 511.

200. H.T. Colebrooke, 'Observations on the Sect of Jains', *Asiatic Researches* 9 (1809), 301f.

201. Colin Mackenzie to William Bentinck, 23 June 1805, BL/OIOC/Mss Eur/F/228/39, No. 11, 13–15, here 15.; id., 'Statement of the Literary Labours', 315. For a critical assessment of Mackenzie's inability to date these events exactly see E.A. Kendall, 'Cooorumber and Chola, or Cholla Kings of the Carnatic', *Asiatic Journal and Monthly Register for British India and its Dependencies* 14 (79) (July 1822), 28f.

202. Mark Wilks to George Buchan, 4 March 1807, NAI/SIR/SGO/3, 565–71, here 569.

203. F.W. Ellis, *A Dissertation on the Malayalama Language* (1810; reprint, Thiruvananthapuram, 2005), 43.

204. Campbell, *Grammar of the Telloogoo Language*, xi, xx.

205. Wilson, *Descriptive Catalogue*, vol. 1, xxxif, liv–lxi.

206. Cf. Kidd, *British Identities before Nationalism,* esp. 200–10; J. Lennon, *Irish Orientalism: A Literary and Intellectual History* (Syracuse, New York, 2004), 95–102; and J. Leerssen, 'Celticism', in T. Brown (ed.), *Celticism* (Amsterdam and Atlanta, 1996), 1–20.

207. E. Davies, *Celtic Researches on the Origin, Traditions and Languages of the Ancient Britons: With Some Introductory Chapters on Primitive Society* (London, 1804), 146–50. For the significance of the *Celtic Researches* in terms of linguistics see D.R. Davis, 'Edward Davies, Paradigm Shift in Nineteenth Century Celtic Studies', in *History of Linguistics 1996: Selected Papers from the Seventh International Conference on the History of the Language Sciences*, 2 vols (Amsterdam and Philadelphia, 1999), vol. 1, 175–80; for Mackenzie's books see D. Hill to Board of Superintendance to the College of FSG, 14 August 1816, BL/IOR/F/4/541 (12148), 23–26.

208. T. Maurice, 'A Dissertation on the Indian Origin of the Druids and on the Striking Affinity which the religious Rights and Ceremonies anciently practised in the British Islands bore to those of the Brahmins', in id., *Indian Antiquities*, vol. 6. Mackenzie probably had a copy.

209. Cf. N. Leask, 'Francis Wilford and the Colonial Construction of Hindu Geography, 1799–1822', in A. Gilroy (ed.), *Romantic Geographies: Discourses of Travel 1775–1844* (Manchester and New York, 2000), 204–22.

210. J.C. Prichard, *The Eastern Origin of the Celtic Nations Proved by a Comparison of their Dialects with the Sanskrit, Greek, Latin and Teutonic Languages; Forming a Supplement to Researches into the Physical History of Mankind* (Oxford, 1831). See also T. Ballantyne, *Orientalism and Race: Aryansim and the British Empire* (Houndsmills and New York, 2002), 40; for Prichard's ethnology see esp. G.W. Stocking, *Victorian Anthropology* (New York and London, 1987), 47–53.

211. [Mackenzie], 'Ruins of Amravutty, Depauldina and Durnacotta', 469.

212. For Maria Graham see M.L. Pratt, *Imperial Eyes: Travel Writing and Transculturation* (London, 1992), 157; and A. Marchant, 'The Captain's Widow: Maria Graham and the Independence of South America', *The Americas* 20(2) (1963), 127–42, esp. 127–29.

213. M. Graham, *Journal of a Residence in India* (1811; reprint, New Delhi, 2000), 169.

214. Cf. 'Literary and Philosophical Intelligence', *Asiatic Journal and Monthly Register for British India and its Dependencies* 8(46) (October 1819), 354f.

215. Ibid., 355.

216. Robertson, *Historical Disquisition*, 261; see also 58, 267, 270.

217. The closest he came to such essentializations often associated with his generation of Indian administrators was perhaps in his ideas about the unbroken tradition of the village community as the core of Indian society, something that coincides with Munro's version of the 'village republic'. For a critical discussion see for example D. Ludden, 'Orientalist Empiricism: Transformations of Colonial Knowledge', in Breckenridge and van der Veer, *Orientalism and the Postcolonial Predicament*, 250–78.

Chapter 8

THE SURVEYOR GENERAL

Building Civil Structures

In the summer of 1809, for a brief moment British rule in South India seemed to be under threat as the conflict between military and civil government that had been on the cards for some time in the Madras presidency escalated. It developed into a more or less open mutiny in which virtually the entire EIC officer corps took part. The scale of the conflict had already become clear with the resignation of Commander-in-Chief Macdowell after Governor George Barlow refused him a seat in the governing council earlier in the same year, but the immediate cause was intervention by the civil government in affairs regarded by the military as internal: the most prominent was the suspension of several officers by the unpopular Governor, without due military procedure. This situation was exacerbated by a series of economizing measures that directly affected the officer corps' income and gave the impression that the Company's officers were being disadvantaged compared to their colleagues in the Royal Army.[1] Barlow's uncompromising attitude and the rumour that the Company's army was to be disbanded and replaced by royal troops[2] intensified the crisis considerably. By the summer of 1809 a number of garrisons were openly refusing to obey orders, for instance in Hyderabad, Masulipatam and Seringapatam, and in some cases this led to armed confrontations. Furthermore, about ninety per cent of the Company's officers refused to sign a declaration of loyalty to Barlow. The situation was only brought under control towards the end of the year with help from royal officers and especially due to the arrival from Bengal of Governor General Lord Minto, who granted a wide-ranging amnesty.[3]

The power struggle had, it seemed, been decided in favour of the civil authorities, and the response to the crisis of 1809 was far-reaching reforms

Notes from this chapter begin on page 274.

in the military sphere, also designed to secure the primacy of the civil govern-ment. The Commander-in-Chief of Bengal, General Hewett, was tasked with examining how the Company's army in the presidency was organized and, where necessary, with restructuring.[4] For Mackenzie, who had stopped carry-ing out surveying work in the field once the Mysore Survey was finished, these reforms were of immediate consequence. His appointment to the sinecure post of Barrack Master of Mysore in 1808 had not only guaranteed him a generous salary but also allowed him, along with coordinating the survey of the Ceded Districts, to turn his attention to his historical material, which he now ordered and partially translated. And indeed, his prospects seemed bright now since, after about twenty-five years' service to the Company, he had a large network of friends and supporters ranging from Governor Barlow, whom he had prob-ably known since the days of the 'Cornwallis family', via Calcutta, to London and the Court of Directors and the Board of Control.[5] But when the efficiency of all staff positions was checked two years later, personal obligations hardly played a role, so Hewett decided that Mackenzie's rather comfortable job as Barrack Master was unsustainable.[6] At the same time, however, the reform pro-posals included a reorganization of cartographic activities. In Hewett's report of summer 1810 he recommended appointing a Surveyor General who should be responsible for civil and some military surveys, while the Quarter Master General's responsibilities should be substantially reduced. The justification given for this proposal was that the sphere of cartography offered potential for economizing measures.[7]

So when Mackenzie heard about the abolition of his post in Mysore and sought a personal conversation with Barlow the Governor informed him, some-what abruptly, that as compensation he would be appointed Surveyor General.[8] Ironically, Mackenzie had long given up the idea that such an appointment could be useful for him. In fact, since 1805 he had been stressing in his private and official correspondence that he was no longer interested in a job of this sort.[9] He had told his friend Henry Trail that the position could hardly be lucrative for him and, what was more, that he no longer had the energy needed: 'The Appointment of Surveyor General if conferred now on me cannot answer … my purpose; the time is past for my arranging its duties with spirit; & the Salary appropriate to my Standing & Course of Service, would be too much for any of those Junior Claimants that will appear in Swarms to avail themselves of the application'.[10] But given the circumstances he had, of course, to accept the appointment, which was announced on 9 October 1810.

It is hardly surprising that he should be considered the appropriate person for this task given his long experience as a surveyor. Moreover, his promotion to Lieutenant Colonel in 1809 meant that he had reached one of the highest ranks in the EIC's army, and by 1810 he was third in the hierarchy of engineers in Madras.[11] Above all, however, Mackenzie was one of the few Company officers who had taken a clear stance on the side of the civil government during the 1809 mutiny. Not only had he signed the declaration of loyalty to Barlow, but at a critical point he was also one of fewer than ten Company officers who also signed a declaration of solidarity by the inhabitants of Madras.[12] Although he criticized the government in private, this was in keeping with his fundamental loyalty to the civil institutions: 'You may be assured of one thing', he wrote to his friend Leyden, 'that I shall always be found to range on the side of the legitimate Government'.[13]

Even if Mackenzie might not have been happy with the changes, they gave him the opportunity finally to settle his feud with the Military Department that had been going on since the Mysore years. Mackenzie's surveys were under direct control of the civil government, but the fact that in 1804 the task of administering cartographical material had, at the instigation of the Commander-in Chief, passed from civil institutions to the Quarter Master General posed a continuous threat to his project.[14] A special ruling allowed him to hold on to the documents connected with his surveys, but as the Directors had recently confirmed the Quarter Master General's right to archive them,[15] in summer 1810 Mackenzie still feared the end of his surveying system.[16] It was only the fact that he played for time that allowed him to keep back the Mysore Survey material until his own appointment as Surveyor General.[17]

Now, however, power relations were reversed. Even before being officially appointed, Mackenzie started to investigate all surveys in the presidency, a difficult task given the fact that surveying work had so far been carried out under both the military and different civil departments. Complying with the 'Orders of Government of the 9th Oct 1810', he wrote later,

> appointing me to the Office of Surveyor General then instituted under the Presidency for the express view of 'uniting under one fixed authority the whole of the unconnected Surveying Departments & for the providing more effectually for the preservation and arrangement of the extensive Surveys & other Geographical Materials under the charge of different Officers whose Duties were unconnected'; I conceived it my duty to turn my immediate attention towards obtaining the most authentic Information of the nature & intent of these Surveys to enable me to fulfil the objects required & answer the expectation of the Honble the Governor in Council in appointing me to this Office.[18]

However, Mackenzie's optimistic plan to present a report on the state of the Surveying Department before he took office came to nothing[19] since the military and also various other institutions failed to cooperate. The Revenue Department, for instance, seriously delayed the handover of material[20] and in Mackenzie's eyes even held back some of it.[21] When the government finally intervened in response to Mackenzie's complaints the Board of Revenue expressed its regret that the Surveyor General had no other aim 'than to endeavour to show that the orders in question had been misconceived or not sufficiently attended to by the Board'.[22]

The military establishment, of course, was even less prepared to give up responsibilities, but again Mackenzie proved to be uncompromising. Given the conflict still raging between military and civil government, it is not surprising that as it intensified holders of the highest offices on both sides became involved. As soon as the order of 9 October became known, the Quarter Master General, Valentine Blacker, had already started to develop a defence strategy, based in essence on the argument that unless his office had responsibility for mapping, the military's interests could not be represented.[23] He gained the support of Commander-in-Chief Auchmutty, who told the government that he especially approved of Blacker's plan to continue employing students from the Military Institution for cartographical work.[24] After more than two months of feuding Governor Barlow, to whom Mackenzie had appealed in person, finally intervened. He made the general order of October more specific, clearly restricting Blacker's responsibilities once again: firstly his staff should be reduced, secondly only very few surveys should take place under his supervision, and thirdly he was no longer allowed to make copies of the material.[25] Mackenzie's victory was almost total. Although there was a delay of several months before the documents were handed over,[26] when the decision was finally taken to set up a commission to review all the still-resistant Quarter Master General's material he was largely disempowered. 'The Committee have determined to meet at your office tomorrow at ten o'clock', a well-meaning member of the commission wrote in advance to Mackenzie: 'I hope we shall make "a good Report" and that we may retire with "Flying Colours"'.[27]

Once the Quarter Master General had been put in his place, Mackenzie had every opportunity to extend the responsibilities of his newly founded department. Fairly quickly he managed to gain control of the somewhat sparse geographical material held by others – sometimes by applying gentle pressure, as in the case of the Trigonometrical Survey.[28] Given the government's financial constraints, the most pressing task was to reduce costs and the easiest way this could be achieved was to improve coordination between the various different enterprises.[29] Edney rightly points out that it is virtually impossible to establish the actual costs of the surveys since they were accounted for in different departments. What is more, additional expenditure cannot be traced in retrospect, such as day-to-day material, instruments or officers' pay. Still, although Edney's estimate that Mackenzie's and Lambton's surveys in 1805/1806 alone swallowed up about 7.25 per cent of the entire non-military budget in Madras seems a bit high,[30] the absolute figures available show that these were certainly significant sums in terms of the EIC budget. The official accounts for Madras for 1800 to 1807 presented by the Company to the House of Commons list the Mysore Surveys separately and claim for them a relatively constant sum of slightly over twenty thousand pagodas per annum.[31] After meticulously studying the files for 1810, Mackenzie himself reckoned the total costs for all surveys in the presidency were about eighty-five thousand pagodas. A year later he had already managed to reduce the costs for all surveys by about forty per cent to around fifty thousand pagodas, a sum that remained fairly stable until 1815. There were, however, considerable shifts within this budget. While the costs for civil surveys actually rose in these five years, they fell by about thirty per cent in the military sphere. The military costs constituted more than fifty per cent when Mackenzie took office, but the proportion was just thirty-eight per cent in 1810/1811 and about twenty-nine per cent in 1815/1816.[32]

Mackenzie continued to employ military officers in leading positions and had, as a matter of fact, to make arrangements with the Madras Military Institution, but his preference for civil structures is also apparent in his staffing policy. In his office he relied in large measure on his experienced staff from earlier surveys: seven people were employed here for cartographical work, including, for instance, the scribe Lucius Burke or the draftsman Cristian Ignatio. Once the survey of the Ceded Districts was completed a number of Indian co-workers were also taken on, including Ramaswami, Dharmaiah, Purshotamiah, Abdul Aziz and Kistnaji. Lakshmayya officially took on the 'whole Management of the Native Establishment in directing the collection of the several Statistical Accounts & Mss'.[33]

Mackenzie was also able to expand his staff of Anglo-Indian subassistants. Although the civil surveying school had been disbanded when Mackenzie took office for reasons of cost, in 1810 of the forty-eight pupils and graduates not a single one decided to withdraw from service, as offered by the government.[34] Some of them were subsequently integrated into the Revenue Department,[35] but most remained in the Surveying Department. Mackenzie was convinced of the 'advantage to the public service of an Establishment of this kind' and regarded their dismissal as 'scarcely reconcilable to the Public engagements in rearing them'.[36] He now trained people in his own office, which presumably meant better quality since the school's curriculum had been confined to very rudimentary knowledge,[37] and the pupils' actual training had in any case only taken place during practical deployment. In 1815 Mackenzie had a total of twenty trained Anglo-Indian assistants, but only three military officers working for him,[38] and his highly qualified and relatively inexpensive staff were in demand all over India.[39]

It was more than a personal triumph for Mackenzie that he was able to start his draft regulations for the Surveyor General's Department, written in 1811, with a paragraph establishing that the Surveyor General should be directly answerable to the civil government and that the Commander-in-Chief of the army should be accorded the right of inspection only.[40] After years of struggle, it seemed, his idea of comprehensive surveying had finally triumphed over military interest. Mackenzie was now in a position not only to defend his system of surveying against its opponents but also to expand it to ever new regions. Needless to say, that is exactly what he did.

Extending the Survey

Following his appointment as Surveyor General Mackenzie was able to extend his system of surveying to large parts of South India. He now declared the Mysore Survey to be the 'Central Nucleus on which several Parts may depend' and as the 'Basis of further Operations & ... kind of Model Example'.[41] After Canara and the Ceded Districts the following years saw surveys in Soonda in the west and in the southern districts such as Tanjore or Coimbatoor. By the end of 1815 about half the Madras presidency had been surveyed using Mackenzie's system, including Mysore roughly seventy-five thousand square miles, about two-and-a-half times the size of Scotland. Geographical, statistical and historical memoirs had either been written or were being prepared for all these areas.[42] At the same time further surveys were either being planned or underway in Dindigul, Travancore, Wynaad, Pondicherry, Coorg, the Northern Circars and Hyderabad.[43] Under Mackenzie's supervision the well-trained Anglo-Indian surveyors carried out a large part of this work, while his large official Indian staff continued to collect statistical and historical information.[44]

Meanwhile, Mackenzie himself took the opportunity to try his system of surveying outside the subcontinent when staying in Java from 1811 to 1813. He had come there as Chief Engineer of an expedition caused by the threat of France's re-emergence as a power in Asia, after its annexation of the Netherlands. Large parts of the island of Java, ruled by the Dutch East India Company, had now fallen into Napoleon's hands and this meant a certain degree of control over important sea routes, unacceptable to the British, who sent a huge fleet from Madras in 1811.[45] Mackenzie's risky reconnaissance work – he not only compiled available material[46] but also landed several times on the island to reconnoitre possible landing stages[47] – proved to be instrumental for the conquest. The Dutch troops, who had initially withdrawn from Batavia, were easily overcome in August and September, but when most of the British troops returned to India in November 1811 Mackenzie was permitted to remain on the island.[48] In the following two years, only interrupted by military conflict with the Sultan of Yogyakarta in the island's interior, he pursued a project of knowledge production that in many ways resembled his surveys in India.

Mackenzie's experiences in Java seem in many ways to epitomize his Indian career. Once again his work in the Madras Surveying Department was interrupted by military duty, and once again military conquest opened up new geographical areas for enquiry. Due to his high standing in the EIC's hierarchy, however, from early on in Java he was part of the inner circle around Thomas Stamford Raffles, the newly appointed Lieutenant Governor.[49] Unlike the officials in London, Raffles regarded Java right from the outset as a long-term possession and possible core of the Empire in Indonesia; so he soon embarked on an ambitious reform policy designed not only to reorganize Batavia's administrative structures and social life along the lines of the British presidencies in India[50] but also to effect fundamental changes in the political and economic system left behind by the Dutch. For instance, he took measures to abolish slavery, forced services and delivery, as well as protective tariffs which he basically wanted to replace with a revenue system as in British India.[51]

Raffles and Mackenzie seem to have recognized their common interests at an early stage. The Lieutenant Governor not only shared Mackenzie's enthusiasm for culture, history and geography but also his friendship with John Leyden, who was originally intended to be appointed as Raffles' personal secretary.[52] After Leyden had died, in Batavia in August 1811,[53] together Raffles and Mackenzie set about looking through the manuscripts and papers he had left.[54] Soon Mackenzie was to become an active member of the Bataaviasch Genootschap, a society revived by Raffles under the English name Batavian Society and modelled on the Asiatic Society.[55] Raffles supported Mackenzie's urge to gain deeper knowledge about Java from the beginning. Soon after the conquest, on his own initiative Mackenzie had started to go through the former Dutch administration's files, now in a chaotic state due to the war, in search of geographical information. Soon he was able to persuade Raffles that it was worth examining the archives for material that was not just cartographical and he was subsequently made a member of a commission 'for the Purpose of Collecting and registering for the information of Government all Public Archives, Records, Plans, Surveys, or other Public Documents in the hands of the different Departments of the former Government'.[56]

Raffles' esteem for Mackenzie was most clearly expressed when he appointed him to head a commission tasked with examining the possibility of effectively regulating taxation of land ownership.[57] Raffles aimed at land reform, which in his view should include abolishing not only the Dutch monopoly economy but also seemingly feudal structures, and should also clarify the land right.[58] The work of the commission, consisting of Mackenzie and three Dutch members, went on for roughly eighteen months and was not easy. Communication between the individual members was not always satisfactory, partly because most of them did not speak English and Mackenzie had no command of Dutch. What is more, it had been decided to carry out the investigations separately in the island's various provinces. The complexity and regional differences in the system of land rights meant that the commissioners were constantly presenting independent reports which were so divergent that there was no chance of producing a uniform agenda. It also meant that no joint concluding report was ever produced.[59] In his own interim report Mackenzie presented fairly general ideas that clearly resembled his reasoning regarding the land system of South India – logically consistent as he speculated about a Hindu origin of Javanese institutions. He expressed his conviction that in principle, here too, all land belonged to the sovereign even though the smallholders also had certain claims which a British government could certainly not ignore.[60]

Mackenzie had initially hesitated to join the commission but accepted his appointment because, as he thought, 'being placed in a situation sufficiently respectable in the eyes of the inhabitants of the Island would give a degree of effect & facility to obtaining every species of knowledge of this important Colony that could not have been so readily acquired by the common measures of an occasional journey'.[61] Indeed, it seems he had been keen to extend his survey to Java from an early stage. On his own initiative he had brought with him two of his Anglo-Indian assistants, John Faulkner and John Malcolm, who remained on the island even after most of the British troops had left. Both were employed in surveying work but their contribution was less valuable than he had initially hoped for because, as he wrote, 'my object was frustrated'.[62] This probably refers to the fact that for reasons of economy Mackenzie had to abandon the idea of mapping Java according to his system: since the Dutch had started to map their possessions earlier in the century it was decided to follow up on their system with the existing staff even though Raffles, almost certainly under the influence of Mackenzie's expertise, judged it as 'somewhat deficient in accuracy of measurement and neatness of execution'.[63]

Even if the cartographical part of Mackenzie's survey could not be carried out in Java, his position allowed him to pursue large-scale statistical investigations. Mackenzie circulated a questionnaire amongst all the Europeans in charge that clearly resembled his 'Heads of Enquiry' in South India.[64] One of its successes was that Mackenzie could, as in Mysore, ascertain 'the population ... by actual enumeration by Houses and by families ... the authenticated Tables of which are annexed to the descriptive memoirs of Provinces'.[65] Raffles later repeatedly claimed that he had established the commission Mackenzie headed mainly for such investigations[66] – but this claim seems to be rather dubious and based more on the commission's results than on the Lieutenant Governor's initial expectations. Indeed, Raffles' own initial instructions to the commission were mainly restricted to questions concerning land tenure.[67] What is more likely is that Mackenzie reinterpreted its role following his own agenda. According to his own account he had distributed his statistical circular even before the commission had been instituted,[68] while another questionnaire, which focussed more on the question of land rights, was written two months later.[69] He undoubtedly had great influence on what research the commission undertook. This seems to be confirmed by the botanist Thomas Horsfield, who, careful not to diminish 'Raffles' merits, remarked that 'the instructions and powers afforded to Colonel Mackenzie were so ample and uncontrolled, that they enabled him to accumulate at a most favourable juncture, immediately after the conquest, a mass of information relating to the antiquities, history, internal administration, character, manners, and peculiarities of the Javanese, to an extent entirely surprising'.[70]

Like the statistical investigations, the historical enquiry also followed very similar patterns to those in South India, even though Mackenzie later deplored the difficulties resulting for both from a lack of staff comparable to his Indian co-workers.[71] However, he did have his multilingual long-time translator Lucius Rawdon Burke[72] as well as a number of Javanese translators and scribes by his side.[73] His high standing in the EIC's service during his travels for the commission allowed him to approach representatives of the Javanese political elites for manuscripts. The Adipati of Lasem, for instance, who was asked in particular for *babads* or chronicles, provided a text of this sort almost immediately and, as requested by Mackenzie, employed at least eight scribes to have it copied as quickly as possible.[74] A short time later Mackenzie particularly profited from access to the conquered Sultan of Yogyakarta's library. Of course he collected not only texts, but also large quantities of inscriptions and coins, while much was documented by drawings.[75] From time to time he interrupted other duties for days to carry out archaeological research himself.[76] So taken together, Mackenzie's activities in Java can clearly be seen as an extension of substantial portions of his system of surveying beyond the Indian subcontinent, as he himself later emphasized: 'the success of these investigations justify the hope, that considerable advantage may be derived from following up the same plan of research wherever the influence of the British government affords the same facilities, in the intervals of military occupations'.[77]

However, at the same time, he expressed his surprise at how little notice was taken of his work: 'I conceive I did a good Service in suggesting & drawing forth the Statistical, Political & Geographical Resources of these valuable Possessions – my work has been unnoticed in a degree that is astonishing even to myself'.[78] Once again he felt that he had not received the financial remuneration he deserved for his valuable services – but perhaps even more importantly, he felt that his contribution to British research in Java was not adequately honoured. Raffles, who had probably remained in charge of much of the material compiled by Mackenzie, drew extensively on it in his *History of Java*, but gave it only sparse and very general reference, and while he mentioned the 'zeal, talent and industrious research that characterized that officer' he still downplayed Mackenzie's role compared to his own.[79] For the first time, Mackenzie seemed annoyed about the fact that others were profiting from his work: 'the results of much that I suggested & actually conducted [is] now published to the world'.[80] This was probably even more frustrating since, due to the global conflict with France, the Directors had frequently forbidden the publication of Mackenzie's own maps and memoirs as they regarded them as sensitive geographical information.

On the Defensive

After the Directors had decided to create the post of a single Surveyor General for the whole of India,[81] early in 1815 both Calcutta and London, independently of one another, had determined that the job should go to Mackenzie.[82] Earlier in the same year he had been one of the first fifteen EIC officers to be made a Companion of the Order of the Bath.[83] This was the climax of Mackenzie's career, but also an important turning point: when he returned to Madras his project again seemed to be endangered, as time had worked against him. When he left Java in July 1813 he had not gone straight back to the presidency but after a stay in Calcutta had taken an extended leave of absence, for the first time in a career of thirty years with the EIC. Along with Lady Hood, Seaforth's oldest daughter and later heiress with whom he had grown up in Scotland, he embarked on a nine-month tour through North India taking in Benares, Lucknow, Delhi and Agra up to the Himalayas.[84] 'The Voyages & Journeys thro' Java', he later wrote to Lambton, 'were highly interesting; it was quite a new World, & in Hindoostan equally so, the rapid but extensive Journey ... will ever be remembered by me with gratification I cannot describe'.[85]

Just a few years later, however, he was having regrets about not returning earlier to Madras: 'I have not found things by any means so favourable to the Improvements I could have given', he wrote to his friend Munro in 1819 'from no want of attention I believe to me personally bent the *old Bane* of all Improvement, a too indulgent consideration to traversing plans & favourite Hobby Horses'.[86] During his stay in Java and his pleasant but unsystematic explorations in Northern India the situation in Madras that was so favourable to him in 1810 had greatly changed. Governor Barlow had been withdrawn in 1812, probably because of too close connections with Director Charles Grant – another supporter of Mackenzie – who came under attack in Britain.[87] For two years the Commander-in-Chief John Abercrombie had filled the post temporarily, before the Governor General's brother Hugh Elliot was appointed in 1814. All this meant that the climate of reform that had given momentum to Mackenzie's objectives three years earlier had faded. Officers William Morison and Benjamin Swain Ward, two of his co-workers from the Mysore Survey, had been in charge of the Surveyor General's Office during his absence, but it seems that they had not been able to carry out more than the absolutely essential tasks.[88] Meanwhile, the Quarter Master General had used the new situation to his advantage and had not transmitted newly produced cartographical material.[89] As Mackenzie asserted after his return,[90] the old feud continued, taking on ever more absurd forms: the military refused to provide him with urgently needed office material, which he then had to pay for temporarily out of his own pocket.[91] As a counterattack he then insisted that the military produce detailed reports of all surveying equipment in their possession.[92]

Problems immediately connected with Mackenzie's appointment were caused by the necessity to move the materials collected in Mackenzie's office to Calcutta, where the Surveyor General of India was to have his seat. Maps, memoirs and other documents had to be duplicated. In addition the Directors and diverse government offices had to be provided with maps and material. Duplication by hand was a difficult enough task in itself but it became all the more onerous because in 1811, when all the presidency's cartographical material had been transferred to Mackenzie's office, no time was allowed for looking through it and cataloguing it, and apart from that the archive had to change premises three times before 1815.[93] From summer 1815 onwards, to ease the situation Mackenzie drew on all available workers in Madras, where at times forty employees, amongst them twelve assistant surveyors and eighteen 'native writers', were involved in compiling, preparing and duplicating cartographical, statistical and historical material. In order that all co-workers could work continuously, additional tents were set up in the garden due to lack of space in the office.[94] It is quite understandable that at this time Mackenzie started to advocate the idea of a printed atlas.

Mackenzie's main problem, however, was neither the conflict with the Military Department nor the burden of copying materials, but the very content of the orders according to which the Directors had made his appointment possible. Although he would now be responsible for a greater geographical area, it actually meant fewer responsibilities for Mackenzie since the Directors had determined that the Surveyor General's duties should be confined to archiving and distributing cartographical material. The office-holder's main task would be to enter the results of new surveying in a general map. If new surveying were considered at the initiative of certain government departments, his sole task would be to write a report on what could be expected from them and this amounted to an almost complete loss of any involvement in planning. So the orders implied not only that in future the Surveyor General would no longer have his own staff of qualified surveyors, but also that Mackenzie's 'general uniform system' would be in danger. Moreover, even the administrative structures he had created in Madras seemed threatened as all remaining material was supposed to be transferred to the presidency's Chief Engineer, to whom one single additional draftsman would be allocated to carry out the work required.[95]

Mackenzie, of course, was certainly not prepared simply to give up his responsibilities. As he had done before, he reacted to these threats with a strategy of detailed information. Once again this led to a series of lengthy reports distributed within the administration.[96] Taken together, they clearly show the priorities he set between his arrival in Madras and his delayed departure for Calcutta in July 1817: firstly he wanted to keep responsibility for carrying out surveys, secondly, to secure the professional futures of those co-workers who could not accompany him to Bengal, and finally to retain the structures he created in Madras in the form of a department answerable to the Surveyor General of India.

The first of these objectives was, it seems, the easiest to accomplish. The practice common in India of interpreting the Directors' orders according to their general tenor offered various possibilities here.[97] The Directors' orders, Mackenzie argued, certainly seemed to imply that no new surveys should be conducted under the Surveyor General. On the other hand, thinking about the reasons why the Directors created the position in the first place, it must be obvious that this is not what they meant. Indeed, he went on, the fact that they wanted to set up a central authority must mean that what they actually wanted was to unify all such enterprises under one single body using one uniform system, especially since the usefulness of a comprehensive survey was generally recognized. Furthermore, continuation of his project was a practical necessity since there was in any case an obligation to continue to employ the assistants. The only way to use this to the government's advantage was, he said, to carry out more surveys.[98]

Based on such interpretation of the Directors' orders, Mackenzie's reports can be read as programmatic drafts for the continuation of his project. While the Madras Board was generally less than thrilled by their overwhelming length,[99] many of his suggestions were soon to be accepted.[100] This was true in particular of a series of proposals for further surveys to be conducted according to his system. The biggest and most important project within the British sphere of control seemed to him to be a survey of the Northern Circars – 'after 50 years possession, still wanting Survey'[101] – but the work should not be confined to this area; it should also extend to the Nizam's territory.[102] This, he said, had always been an 'object of solicitude with the Government of India', and was all the more necessary since the presence of a large number of British troops in the Nizam's territory demonstrated that the British interest was long term – seen by him, as in Mysore, as an important step towards direct rule.[103]

Mackenzie's second objective of securing the professional future of his co-workers and assistants was of a more personal nature since here his under-standing of a superior's responsibility mixed with the esteem he had developed for many of them over the years. For most of his Anglo-Indian assistants the continuation of surveys meant secure employment, so Mackenzie could confine himself to sorting out their financial claims from the time of his absence, which he sought to do to their advantage. Only in two cases of persons considered unfit for service did he recommend retirement on a government pension.[104]

European writers and draughtsmen such as C. Ignatio and John Newman had to leave the office, but Mackenzie insisted that they be put on half pay until transferred to other departments. For Lucius Burke, who had mastered eight Indian and four European languages and had been working with him for seventeen years, he suggested a provision similar to that granted to Burke's teacher, John Mather, sixteen years before.[105]

The case of the more than twenty Indian co-workers employed in the Surveyor General's Office, however, was more difficult, even though some of them – many were reluctant – were allowed to accompany him to Bengal. Mackenzie sought to achieve generous provision for them. His long-time colleagues Dharmaiah, Abdul Aziz and Kistnaji, advanced in age, were to get pensions of half their final salary, while for Lakshmayya he proposed full pay after leaving the service.[106] Some of his many translators engaged with statistical enquiries could continue their work, given the ongoing surveys. Mackenzie hoped that five others, including Ramaswami, could be transferred to the College of Madras with part of the historical collection, which he obviously wanted to use as a bargaining tool,[107] but this failed, probably because their sociocultural background was less appreciated there. While these co-workers were largely *niyogis*, who embodied the literary traditions of the *karanams* concerned with practical administrative tasks, the College preferred *pandits* from the sphere of courtly scholarship, who represented quite different literary traditions.[108] The administration in Madras was also somehow reluctant to accept his proposals, but in the end Mackenzie's efforts were generally successful and a comparatively generous arrangement was confirmed by government.[109]

Mackenzie was also successful in his third aim – the partial preservation of the structures he had created. This was perhaps the most difficult to achieve as the Directors' orders left little room for interpretation here: they had definitively determined that in all three presidencies concerned the office of Surveyor General was to be completely abolished. Clearly defying this order Mackenzie suggested that the Madras Surveying Department should carry on under an assistant. Of course, he had good reasons for this: given the difficulties in communicating between Bengal and Madras and the tendency of the Madras presidency to follow its own rules this would have led de facto back to the situation before reforms were initiated in 1810. Nevertheless, the Madras government was not convinced – it was only after a hard struggle that an Assistant Surveyor General was appointed in summer 1817.[110]

When making his plans Mackenzie had obviously assumed that they would be backed in full by the government and as early as January 1816 believed that he would soon be leaving.[111] In the months that followed, however, it became apparent that Governor Hugh Elliot was certainly not going to agree. As a reaction Mackenzie now argued that he had to write more reports before he could leave Madras because these would form the basis for further arrangements.[112] 'I see now how it stands', he wrote to a friend, '[and] it is by no means my wish or intention to go away before my Reports are given in. ... It would mortify me much to leave this work undone on which I have bestowed much pains'.[113] A ship intended to transport him and his material to Calcutta in summer 1816 left without him, after he had already postponed its departure for more than a month.[114] Years later Mackenzie was still complaining that it was Elliot's attitude alone that had kept him in Madras for so long.[115]

Both men played for time. Elliot initially refused to appoint the deputy Mackenzie wanted[116] and subsequently avoided direct correspondence with the Surveyor General,[117] only to reject his plans in their entirety once his departure seemed inevitable.[118] However, Bengal's dissatisfaction with his long absence now presented Mackenzie with a new strategy, which he certainly would not have accepted from any of his subordinates. Having been informed that only the Supreme Government had the powers to circumvent the Directors' orders he bypassed his superiors in Madras and turned directly to Calcutta, explained that the delay was due to issues that had not been clarified, and proposed the Scottish officer John Riddell for the position of Assistant Surveyor General.[119] The government in Madras was now compelled by Bengal to appoint him, at least temporarily, and also to provide for Mackenzie's co-workers, following his own suggestions.[120] In Madras there was understandable outrage about Mackenzie's behaviour – after all he had got Calcutta involved in the presidency's internal affairs – but the directives had to be followed. The government, however, expressed its barely concealed opposition by granting Riddell a ridiculously small salary,[121] and, what is more, soon forced him to communicate with the government via the military secretary: 'it is so impossible to account for that I can only be silent', was Mackenzie's reaction to this decision.[122] Nevertheless, when he left Madras in July 1817 Mackenzie could once again feel that he had prevailed in an administrative conflict: most of his ideas had been implemented and he had managed to retain most of his office's structures.

A 'Sea of Trouble'

On 17 July 1817 Mackenzie left Madras for the last time and arrived in Calcutta about two weeks later.[123] In his new function as Surveyor General he held such high office that his arrival was even announced in the official gazettes.[124] In Calcutta he was not an unknown; during his first visit four years earlier he had already moved in the highest circles. At an official reception Governor General Minto had even assured him of his 'warmest personal regard' and the 'highest degree of public esteem'.[125] The social life of the town, however, was very time-consuming. He wrote to a friend in Madras even a month after his arrival that so far he had been so caught up 'paying & receiving visits at this populous

Presidency' and paying the 'necessary attention to Official Authorities' that he had hardly been able to do anything else.[126] He was not only hobnobbing with the highest government officials but also with the town's famous orientalists and he regularly attended meetings of the Asiatic Society. His own scientific rank was not only acknowledged in Bengal by his election to the society's Committee of Papers,[127] but also in Britain. As one of the first British scientists in India he was elected *in absentia* to the Royal Society, in 1819, due to his knowledge in 'mathematics and several branches of natural knowledge'.[128]

Six years earlier, in Java, Mackenzie, who was about sixty, had married fifteen-year-old Dutch girl Wilhelmina Petronella Bartels – to the astonishment of his friends: 'however attractive she may be, and we may indeed judge of her power by its effects', Ellis, for instance, remarked, 'I do not fear that she "will overturn the other idols of his house" – they are too firmly established there to [be] easily expelled'.[129] The 'stiff but estimable Colonel' was, as the ever-derisive Seaforth heiress Mary Stewart Mackenzie, once Lady Hood, later reported, known for his 'disinclination to female society'.[130] There is no mention of an Indian female partner in Madras, in marked contrast to many of his friends,[131] and amongst the 'orphans' of the surveying school on record there is not a single little Mackenzie amongst the little Andersons, Rosses, Webbes and Malcolms. Of course, marriage could not do his reputation any harm; what is more, in the social life of Calcutta, where European women were rare, a young wife represented a certain attraction.[132] Although Mackenzie and his wife, whose sister lived with them to keep the young bride company during her husband's frequent absences, clearly did not have a very close relationship, they jointly maintained a household in Calcutta in which guests were no exception.

Even though it was important to participate in the time-consuming social life of Calcutta, Mackenzie still devoted himself to his new job with dedication. The post of Surveyor General of India may have been newly created, but Mackenzie had little opportunity to shape it because he had to start with the existing office in Bengal, which had never been a particularly efficient establishment. Robert Hyde Colebrooke, Surveyor General from 1794 until his death in 1808, had at least tried, during his more than fourteen years in post, to make what had previously been regarded as a sinecure into an efficient office, but he was so unsuccessful that he had left behind almost total chaos. Attempts to acquire suitable premises had failed,[133] likewise a request for urgently needed staff, which had ultimately led to the three assistant posts he had been granted since the 1780s being scrapped.[134] So despite the fact that the presidency had greatly expanded in area, during Colbrooke's later years in office hardly any surveying had been carried out.[135] Due to a shortage of staff he had increasingly found himself unable to provide the diverse government departments with maps[136] or to catalogue material arriving from other departments.[137] Eventually the financial situation had become so critical that he gave up his office's premises altogether and had to put the material in cheap storage.[138] Although there was some improvement under his successors – John Garstin and Charles Crawford – the chaos Colebrooke left behind was never really sorted out. The office may have been granted more finance and personnel[139] so that new surveys could be started,[140] but it remained more or less in a state of disorder until Mackenzie arrived.

So in 1817 Mackenzie took over an office consisting of little more than random material, a few scribes and draftsmen and a collection of largely unconnected orders regulating the department that had accumulated since the 1780s.[141] There were hardly any professional staff available in the presidency;[142] but Mackenzie was initially optimistic that he would manage to implement his general system in Calcutta nonetheless.[143] One of his first measures was to rent a house that had enough room for the material from Madras and Calcutta. The next was to bring some of his assistants and draftsmen from South India to Bengal: 'I want Scott & Hamilton for the Office as there is not a Soul here capable of doing what they can do'.[144]

However, just a few months after his arrival his optimism had largely evaporated. In the Calcutta Surveyor General's Department, he complained, there were 'nor orders nor regularity'. What little material existed was poor, and all that was being conducted were route surveys, while he himself had hardly any control over the surveyors who, as earlier in Madras, were answerable to the Quarter Master General. He had no idea what he was actually supposed to do as Surveyor General if he were not empowered to see to 'concert and arrangement'. Now for the first time during his career in India he thought of giving up:

> I almost repent that I ventured in this *sea of trouble* again, for 34 years one half of my time has been occupied in defending with one hand what was done by the other. – Now time & age & reflection steps in & checks what the ardent sanguine spur of youth & hope once would prompt to undertake – resistance formerly was but an additional stimulus to me to persevere in what was right and reasonable; & I hope on a cool review I never persevered in any other course. – Time is fleeting Munro, & it is high time for both of us to think of rest & tranquillity.[145]

Although Mackenzie now repeatedly stated that he would return to Britain as soon as various financial issues had been sorted out he continued to work diligently, attributing this to a sense of duty: 'a principle by which the whole course of my duty has been conducted [was] never to shrink from any duty wherein I might be considered usefully employed'.[146] He did at least manage to have the Surveyor General's Office transferred from the Military Department to the civil sphere;[147] since he was not prepared to share responsibilities with the military he did not want to employ any officers who were also answerable to the Quarter Master General.[148] At the same time, he asked Riddell to train up more boys from the orphans' school in Madras who could support him in Bengal, saying that they could live in his private house in Madras.[149] He wrote to government that it was essential, 'to have the Office and Department brought into a regular systematic Order & its duties well defined', before any more surveys could be carried out. He also complained about the Quarter Master General's incompetence: all he seemed to know about were route surveys.[150] In summer 1818 his fighting spirit was stirred once again, as he wrote to Riddell: 'I have had a great warfare to sustain & may still – but I am not to be dismayed'.[151]

But by the end of the year Mackenzie's energy was exhausted. From this time onwards his correspondence no longer contains any initiatives of his own but only complaints about the Quarter Master General, who was ordering surveys without informing him, or about the impossibility of introducing reforms as things stood.[152] Particularly irritating was the decision by the Governor General, the Marquess of Hastings, to remove Lambton's Great Trigonometrical Survey from the Surveyor General's control, although this was rescinded a short time later after intervention from London.[153] Even reports required by the government, for instance about the possibility of revenue surveys as conducted in Bombay or the chances of an optical telegraph connection between Calcutta and Madras, were constantly delayed or ignored,[154] although he never ceased to point out the advantages of his system of detailed surveys. In 1818 he had insisted that the surveyors who were supposed to investigate the planned telegraph line should be called 'inspectors', not surveyors, since all their job involved was an 'examination of the ground ... call it a *Survey*, if you please but not of that description of Surveys that is understood to contribute to a general knowledge of the Country'. In his eyes a 'real' survey of a region required 'regular analysis ... of its Geography, its statistics, its antiquities & history'.[155]

By now Mackenzie was in his late sixties and seriously ill. In his final years in Madras his health had already become unstable,[156] but it was not until the end of 1818 that it collapsed almost completely. In order to avoid the supposedly unhealthy air in Calcutta, in 1819 he bought or rented a house far outside the city, in Palta, and only travelled to the city now and again to sort out certain things in his office.[157] The following year saw him in Puri in Orissa for several months, which he hoped would improve his symptoms. As he had done before in Madras,[158] he used his leave of absence for archaeological enquiries – and along with the local official Andrew Stirling he commissioned a Sanskrit chronicle on Orissa.[159] During his final years it seems that archaeological inquiry and the collection of manuscripts did indeed become 'hobbies' as he no longer had the power to initiate systematic surveys. Going to Puri was his last major journey from Calcutta to the south. He would have liked to have travelled straight to the Madras presidency, 'a country ever dear to me',[160] where in his eyes he could have enjoyed the best and most healthy climate in India and 'the health-bringing sea breeze ... with more comfort & convenience', but it would have been difficult to carry out the business of his office from there.[161] Shortly after his return he again became seriously ill and died a few months later, on 8 May 1821.[162] One of his last letters, which he obviously dictated to an Indian scribe while bedridden, was to Thomas Turnbull, his long-time assistant and a former pupil of the surveying school. It can be seen as representative of the ideas that Mackenzie continued to enthuse about: he would like to send Turnbull to Tinnevelly, he had dictated:

> for the purpose of giving a descriptive Memoir of that province, which was omitted by ... the former Surveyors when the Map was made. I also am very desirous of getting accounts of the hill tribes of that Country & some notice of its history & the Inscriptions for which purpose Netal Naynah [Nitala Naina] has been attached & I hope you will be kind & protect him on my account.[163]

The ideas had stayed the same, but the indefatigable optimism and firm belief in the possibility of carrying out a meaningful project through sheer determination manifestly dwindled in Mackenzie's final years. A confidential letter to Thomas Munro at the beginning of 1819 shows how much he felt his ideas were threatened. He feared not only for his project of a detailed survey, but above all for the ideas implicit in it concerning the form the government of India should take. The letter is full of a sense of loss, not only the loss of friends who had died or returned to Europe but also the loss of certain ideas and values which, he believed, had characterized his generation:

> the labour & Researches of so many years begin to be viewed in doubt & hesitation; the Prime Movers in the Scene for 40 Years back have now all passed away & I am sorry to observe we have little to expect from the *Dandies* of the Present day. ... Even Lord Minto's Government is looked upon as an age past – the universal objects seem to live as comfortably & oeconomically as possible to save a fixed sum to retire on, while all care for the welfare of the Public is out of sight; among the Junior part indeed almost scouted.[164]

His own motives for coming to India were now forgotten in light of the many years he had spent striving for the 'welfare of the Public'. But his frustration cannot simply be explained as an old man's dislike of a young generation he considered to have no sense of duty and to be irresponsible and egoistic, nor by an increasing dislike for Calcutta, 'this opulent Capital of British Oriental Government', where the 'gay world' regarded his collections as 'Old Trumpery'.[165]

After nearly forty years in India, Colin Mackenzie had gradually started to doubt whether British rule was really the best thing for the country and its population. He remained convinced, he wrote, that the British government was better able to assure the people's freedom and possessions than any Indian regime. India seemed to him to be like the bankrupt estate of a family in conflict whose creditors had appointed an administrator to run the estate according to the law. In this sense, he said, British rule was right and its enemies should be repelled – 'parcere subjectis, debellare superbos' should be the motto.[166] This quotation from Virgil was a deliberate attempt to equate the British with the Roman Empire. But it also implies that rule brings with it responsibility[167] and it was precisely at this point that Mackenzie's doubts set in. Extension of British rule to further parts of India seemed to him to be only a matter of time, but the EIC was not capable of bearing the responsibilities this entailed:

> For undoubtedly in the progressive reduction of India from its Native States to Alliances supported by a Subsidiary Force which ultimately ends in provisional assumption of the territories first of our Enemies then of our Allies until at last it terminates in direct cession of the Provinces & assumption of the Management of the Revenue, it is incumbent on us to provide for the internal administration.[168]

The British were not at all prepared for this expansion; there was a lack of capable personnel and political will: 'To retain India, a downright Military Force & Restraint seems to be looked to, with the army of course this Doctrine will be ever prevalent'.[169] The militarism of British rule, which he could observe even more clearly in Calcutta than in South India, put him off and he feared that the new generation of officials would anchor it even more deeply in the EIC. The significance he attached to allocating all surveys to the civil sphere and the verve with which he fought for his ideas are quite understandable against this backdrop: 'Oh!', he wrote to his colleague, 'how many excellent fellows have passed since we met first at Nellore in 1787 – let us too, Munro, continue so to act as not to be forgotten altogether by our associates!'[170]

But his criticism was not aimed solely at the military. In his view the EIC's greatest mistake was that it excluded Indians from all high positions. India could never be governed properly unless locals were included in its administration. Thomas Munro is known to have shared this view – the two of them belonged to a minority who were unable to enforce their ideas. The colonial system lived increasingly from strict dividing lines between the cultures. Within the British ruling caste, overcoming these divisions remained the aim of just a small group. Colin Mackenzie, who owed his career to the Empire, never openly conceded that arguing in favour of Indian participation in rule while at the same time justifying the Empire on the basis of supposed civilizational superiority was ambivalent and often contradictory. Perhaps the dividing lines that in Europe, too, separated various segments of society from one another – advanced elites from the backward population, respectable gentlemen from climbers with humble origins, British reformers from Gaelic highlanders – seemed to him to be impenetrable. But Mackenzie never said anything specific about this. 'Time passes', now wrote the man known for his over-long reports to Munro, 'and Life is too short to go into long explanations'.[171]

His will, actually a combination of several versions written since 1811,[172] shows that he personally was certainly prepared to overcome colonial divisions. Mackenzie left behind a not inconsiderable amount of money; in fact, he was a rich man. His wife was to receive a large proportion of it, likewise his sister Mary, which made her the wealthiest inhabitant of Stornoway. Nor did he forget the needy in his hometown. He left smaller sums to his long-time Anglo-Indian scribe Lucius Burke, his sister-in-law and various friends. Finally, to his assistant Lakshmayya he left not only five per cent of the total amount, but also the proceeds of the sale of his collection, which after his death was bought by the EIC at a price of more than ten thousand pounds.[173] So in his last will Mackenzie clearly expressed once again the recognition and friendship that had bound him over the years to his most important colleague.

Notes

1. For the competition between the Royal Army and the Company army and between the armies in the individual presidencies cf. Peers, *Mars and Mammon*, 75–79; and id., 'Between Mars and Mammon', 392f.
2. For this rumour see J. Malcolm, *Observations on the Disturbances in the Madras Army in 1809: In Two Parts* (London, 1812), 22f. Indeed since the 1780s there had been constant debates in London as to whether the Company's troops should be totally replaced by the Royal Army. Cf. C.H. Phillips, *The East India Company 1784–1834* (Manchester, 1961), 54–59, 89f.
3. For the mutiny see T.A. Heathcote, *The Military in British India: The Development of British Land Forces in South Asia, 1600–1947* (Manchester, 1995), 63–66; and W.J. Wilson, *The History of the Madras Army*, 5 vols (Madras, 1882–1889), vol. 3, 235–94.
4. Cf. G. Hewett, *Private Record of the Life of the Right Honorable Sir George Hewett* (Newport, 1840), 60–65.
5. Cf. Colin Mackenzie to John Leyden, 13 November 1809, NLS/Mss 3380, 115–19, here 117f; also 9 October 1810, ibid., 136–39; Colin Mackenzie to Seaforth, 28 February 1809, NAS/GD/46/17/10, 521–24, here 523f; and Colin Mackenzie to Mrs Stewart Mackenzie, 24 March 1819, NAS/GD/46/17/51. Mackenzie's friends, Bannermann and Robinson, had been elected as Directors in 1808. Cf. Phillips, *East India Company*, 335–37.
6. For the new regulations for the barrack department and staff positions see Wilson, *History of the Madras Army*, vol. 3, 339f.
7. Cf. Edney, *Mapping an Empire*, 190f; and Phillimore, *Historical Records*, vol. 2, 298f.
8. Cf. Colin Mackenzie to William Lambton, 19 October 1810, NAI/SIR/SGO/90A, 34f.
9. Cf. Colin Mackenzie to Merrick Shawe, 25 June 1805, NAI/SIR/M/18, 121–24, here 124.
10. Colin Mackenzie to Henry Trail, 2 August 1805, BL/OIOC/Mss Eur/F/228/39. See also Mackenzie to Leyden, 13 November 1809, NLS/Ms 3380, 115–19.
11. In 1809 there were still three officers ahead of him on the list of engineers, namely the Chief Engineer Elisha Trapaud, William Norris and Walter C. Lennon. While Trapaud remained

in office during Mackenzie's lifetime, Lennon left in 1810 and Norris followed in November 1811. Cf. *The East India Register and Directory for 1809, Corrected to the 15th August 1809, Containing Complete Lists of the Company's Servants, Civil, Military and Marine, with Their Respective Appointments at the Different Presidencies in the East-Indies* (London [1809/1810]), 231; Phillimore, *Historical Records*, vol. 1, 348, 360; and *The East India Register and Directory for 1821, Corrected to the 28th February 1821, Containing Complete Lists of the Company's Servants, Civil, Military and Marine, with Their Respective Appointments at the Different Presidencies in the East-Indies* (London, [1821]), 258.

12. Cf. 'Madras Occurrences for August 1809', *Asiatic Annual Register, or a View of the History of Hindustan ... for the Year 1809* (London, 1811), 107f, 120. For the high-ranking officers' and civilians' refusal to sign the additional declaration of solidarity cf. Malcolm, *Observations on the Disturbances*, 111–13.

13. Colin Mackenzie to John Leyden, 13 November 1809, NLS/Mss 3380, 117. For Mackenzie's loyal attitude see also Mackenzie to Benjamin Swain Ward, 5 January 1809, NAI/SIR/SGO/90A, 5–7; also 10 September 1809, ibid., 77f.

14. James Stewart, 'Minute', 12 January 1804, BL/IOR/F/4/183 (3692), 5–21. Governor Bentinck agreed and stated that persons involved in practical surveys never had time for the work required. Cf. William Bentinck, 'Minute of the President', 24 September 1804, ibid., 35–46.

15. J.H. Peile to Mackenzie, 5 May 1810, NAI/SIR/SGO/3, 217f; also 10 May 1810, ibid., 221–26; and 10 July 1810, ibid., 229.

16. Cf. Colin Mackenzie to Benjamin Swain Ward, 17 July 1810, NAI/SIR/SGO/90A, 26–28.

17. He argued, for instance, that because he had not yet written a concluding report for the Mysore Survey he still needed the material. This was accepted. Cf. Colin Mackenzie to J.H. Peile, 11 July 1810, NAI/SIR/SGO/90, 104; and Peile to Mackenzie, 20 July 1810, NAI/SIR/SGO/3, 231.

18. Colin Mackenzie [to Government, March 1811] (draft), NAI/SIR/SGO/60, 51–59, here 51.

19. Cf. his provisional report of 29 November 1810: Colin Mackenzie, 'Prospectus of a Plan of Arrangement to be submitted for the Office of a Surveyor General, detailing its Objects, Duties, the Mode of conducting them, the Nature & Regulations of the Depot of Charts & the Estimated Expense of the Office with Proposals for regulating the Expense & conduct of the Existing Establishment & accelerating the effect & object of the Surveying Department', 29 November 1810, NAI/SIR/SGO/60, 3–22, here 3.

20. Some of his letters were even declared 'lost'. Cf. A.D. Campbell to Colin Mackenzie, 20 December 1810, NAI/SIR/SGO/319, 50–52, quote 52.

21. Colin Mackenzie [to Government, March 1811] (draft), NAI/SIR/SGO/60, 54, 59. This material is possibly the correspondence held today in BL/OIOC/Mss Eur/Mack Gen/58.

22. W. Oliver, Sec. B Rev. to Chief Sec. Gov., 29 April 1811, NAI/SIR/SGO/319, 48–50, here 49.

23. Valentine Blacker to Sir Samuel Auchmutty, 3 November 1810, BL/IOR/F/4/362 (9021), 51–61.

24. P.A. Agnew, Mil Sec (FSG) to J.H. Peile, B, 5 November 1810, BL/IOR/F/4/362 (9021), 49f.

25. George H. Barlow, 'Minute', 31 December 1810, BL/IOR/F/4/362 (9021), 5–42. Mackenzie had previously sent a note to Barlow via the Town Major, Barclay. See Robert Barclay to Colin Mackenzie [December 1810], BL/OIOC/Mss Eur/Mack Misc/171.

26. Cf. Colin Mackenzie to Sec. Gov., Mil. Dep., 19 January 1811, BL/IOR/P/257/15, 1666–78; and [William] Ornesby to Colin Mackenzie, 20 January 1811, BL/OIOC/Mss Eur/Mack Misc/171.

27. Gahagan to Colin Mackenzie, 11 February 1811, BL/OIOC/Mss Eur/Mack Misc/171.

28. Due to his knowledge of Lambton's work, when examining the Quarter Master General's material he had noticed that he too had successfully managed to keep some of the material

away from the military. Cf. Colin Mackenzie to William Lambton, 29 March 1811, NAI/ SIR/SGO/90A, 144f.

29. For instance, Thomas Munro had allocated up to a hundred co-workers to do surveying for an almost five-year survey of the Ceded Districts and spent around eighty thousand pagodas for this. But when he was supposed to present details of the size of the district to a Parliamentary commission he had to admit that he could only assess this very roughly as this was not a topographical survey and therefore did not take uncultivated land into account. Cf. Thomas Munro to B Rev. (FSG), 26 July 1807, in *The Fifth Report from the Select Committee on the Affairs of the East India Company*' (House of Commons Papers; Reports of Committees 1812 (377), VII, 1), Appendix 20, 783–94, here 783, 787; statement by Thomas Munro, 15 April 1813, *Minutes of Evidence taken before the Committee of the Whole House, and the Select Committee on the Affairs of the East India Company* (House of Commons Papers; Reports of Committees 1812–1813 (122) VII, 1), 167–75, here 170.

30. Cf. Edney, *Mapping an Empire*, 189. According to the accounts laid before Parliament, however, the expenses of 23,569 pagodas for 1805/1806 constituted only 0.29 per cent of the General Department's total outgoings of 8,039,078 pagodas. Cf. *Accounts, Presented to the House of Commons, from the East India Company, Respecting Their Annual Revenues and Disbursements, Trade and Sales, &c. for the Three Years, 1802–3, 1803–4, & 1804–5; Together with an Estimate of the Same for the Year 1805–6* (House of Commons Papers; Accounts and Papers 1807 (24), V, 447), 59–65.

31. The highest sum (23,569 pagodas) was reached in 1804/1805, the lowest (18,441 pagodas) in 1806/1807. Cf. *Accounts, Presented to the House of Commons, from the East India Company, Respecting Their Annual Revenues and Disbursements, &c. &c. &c.* (House of Commons Papers; Accounts and Papers 1801–1802 (126), V, 1), 33; *Resolutions Reported on Monday the 14th Day of March 1803, from the Committee of the Whole House, to Whom It Was Referred to Consider of the Several Accounts and Papers which Were Presented to the House, upon Tuesday Last, Relating to the Revenues of the East India Company; and to Whom Were Referred, the Several Accounts and Papers Relating Thereto, which Were Presented to the House Upon the 18th Day of June, in the Last Session of the Last Parliament* (House of Commons Papers; Accounts and Papers 1802–1803 (60), IX, 157), 61; *Accounts, Presented to the House of Commons, from the East India Company; Respecting Their Annual Revenue and Disbursements, Trade and Sales, &c. &c. &c.* (House of Commons Papers; Accounts and Papers 1803–1804 (111), IX, 53), 61; *Accounts, Presented to the House of Commons, from the East India Company; Respecting Their Annual Revenues and Disbursements, Trade and Sales, &c. &c. &c.* (House of Commons Papers; Accounts and Papers 1806 (158), XV, 1), 61; *Accounts, Presented to the House of Commons … for the Three Years, 1802–3, 1803–4, & 1804–5 …* (House of Commons Papers; Accounts and Papers 1807 (24), V, 447), 61; *Accounts, Presented to the House of Commons, from the East India Company, Respecting Their Annual Revenues and Disbursements, Trade and Sales, &c. for Three Years, According to the Latest Advices; Together with the Latest Estimate of the Same,* (House of Commons Papers; Accounts and Papers 1807 (54), V, 541), 63; *Accounts, Presented to the House of Commons, from the East India Company, Respecting Their Annual Revenues and Disbursements, Trade and Sales, &c. for Three Years, According to the Latest Advices; Together with the Latest Estimate of the Same,* (House of Commons Papers; Accounts and Papers 1808 (240), XIII, 59), 63.

32. Cf. Colin Mackenzie, 'A Statement of Expenses incurred Quarterly & Annually by the several Establishments considered to relate to the Surveying Department under the Presidency of Fort St. George reported to the Surveyor General from the formation of the Surveyor General's Office on 1st. December 1810, to the 1st of December 1815', NAI/ SIR/REP/3, 22f.

33. Colin Mackenzie to Chief Sec. (FSG), 1 August 1816, NAI/SIR/REP/3, 37–76, here 63, 70–73.

34. Cf. Thomas Gahagan to Chief Sec. Gov. (FSG), 10 December 1810, BL/IOR/F/4/362 (9021), 73–82; id. to President and Members of the Board of Revenue, 29 November 1811, ibid., 115–30; William Oliver, Sec. Rev. Dep. (FSG), to William Morison, 29 July 1811, NAI/SIR/SGO/319, 83f.

35. Cf. Colin Mackenzie, 'Abstract of the present Employment of the Revenue Surveying Establishments', 29 November 1810, NAI/SIR/SGO/60, 23.

36. Colin Mackenzie to Bayley, Act. Sec. Rev. (FW), 13 December 1816, BL/IOR/F/4/554 (13476), 385–400, here 386, 390.

37. When the school was set up the Directors had made it clear that they did not want any deep theoretical instruction. Cf. CD to B (FSG) Rev., 5 August 1796, BL/IOR/E/4/882, 718–26, here 725f. For this procedure, common under the Company in India, see S. Sangwan, 'Science Education in India under Colonial Constraints, 1792–1857', *Oxford Review of Education* 16(1) (1990), 81–95.

38. Cf. Colin Mackenzie to Chief Sec. Gov., 14 December 1815, BL/IOR/F/4/554 (13476), 147–245, here 158, 237f.

39. Especially for carrying out revenue surveys, which were now even planned in Bengal. Cf. Holt Mackenzie to Colin Mackenzie, 15 August 1815, BL/IOR/F/4/554 (13476), 400–6; E. Colebrooke and J. Deane to J. Lumsden, Vice President (FW), 1 August 1809, NAI/SIR/SGO/361, 239–42. For a similar enquiry from Bombay see W. Newnham, Sec. Gov. Bombay to D. Hill, 23 December 1817, NAI/SIR/SGO/8, 128f.

40. Colin Mackenzie, 'Draft of Regulations proposed for the Surveying Department at Madras', 1811, NAI/SIR/M/31, 5–19; William Thackeray to Colin Mackenzie, 29 January 1811, BL/IOR/F/4/362 (9021), 131–40, here 131.

41. Colin Mackenzie, 'Prospectus of a Plan of Arrangement to be submitted for the Office of a Surveyor General', 29 November 1810, NAI/SIR/SGO/60, 3–22, here 7.

42. Cf. Colin Mackenzie to Chief Sec. (FSG), 14 December 1815, BL/IOR/F/4/554 (13476), 147–245, here 194–99.

43. Cf. Colin Mackenzie to Chief Sec. (FSG), 1 August 1816, NAI/SIR/REP/3, 37–76, here 40–47.

44. Cf. Colin Mackenzie to Chief Sec. (FSG), 14 December 1815, BL/IOR/F/4/554 (13476), 147–245, here 162–64; also 28 January 1816, ibid., 335–60, here 336; 339f; 351–53; D. Hill, Sec. Gov., to Mackenzie, 23 February 1816, ibid. 370–77, here 373f; Mackenzie to James Garling, 18 April 1816, BL/IOR/F/4/555 (13477), 45–61, here 54.

45. Cf. J.S. Bastin, 'Introduction', in Thorn, *Conquest of Java*, xxf.

46. Colin Mackenzie, 'Memoir of the Present State of the Fortresses, Fortifications, Roads & Landing Places in Java. Compiled from different authorities, May 29th 1811. With a Military Map of Java exhibiting the different Roads, Posts, and other Relative Positions. Presented to the Commander in Chief on his arrival at Malacca June 1811', BL/OIOC/Mss Eur/Mack Priv/14, 19–35.

47. Cf. [Blakiston], *Twelve Years' Military Adventure*, vol. 2, 9–29; and Colin Mackenzie, 'Report of Proceedings on the North Coast of Java agreeable to the Instructions of His Excellency Sir J. Auchmutty Cin C &c.', 6th June 1811, BL/OIOC/Mss Eur/Mack Priv/14, 57–69.

48. Cf. 'Madras Public Consultations', 4 August 1815, BL/IOR/F/4/554 (13476), 77–89, here 86f.

49. For Raffles see J.S. Bastin, *Sir Thomas Stamford Raffles: With an Account of the Raffles-Minto Manuscript Collection Presented to the India Office Library [London] on 17 July 1969 by the Malaysia-Singapore Commercial Association* (Liverpool, 1969); id., *The Native Policies of Sir Thomas Stamford Raffles in Java and Sumatra: An Economic Interpretation* (Oxford, 1957).

50. Cf. R. van Niel, *Java's Northeast Coast: A Study in Colonial Encroachment* (Leiden, 2005), 231f; J.G. Taylor, *The Social World of Batavia: European and Eurasian in Dutch Asia* (Madison, Wisconsin, 1983), 96–113.

51. For Raffles' own description of his agenda see T.S. Raffles, *Substance of a Minute Recorded by the Hon. Thomas Stamford Raffles ... on the 11th February 1814; on the Introduction of an Improved System of Internal Management and the Establishment of a Land Rental on the Island of Java* (London, 1814).

52. Cf. Thomas Stamford Raffles to William Erskine, 10 September 1815, NLS/Ms 3380, 261–66.

53. Cf. Trautmann, 'Hullabaloo about Telugu', 57; [W. Scott], 'Biographical Memoir of John Leyden, M. D.', *Edinburgh Annual Register* 4(19) (1811), lxvii.

54. Both Raffles and Mackenzie withheld part of the manuscripts: Thomas Stamford Raffles to William Erskine, 10 September 1815, NLS/Ms 3380, 261–66; also 12 December 1815, ibid., 266f; Richard Heber to Colin Mackenzie, 8 October 1816, BL/OIOC/Mack Misc/171; Bastin, 'John Leyden and the Publication of the "Malay Annals"', 74f.

55. Founded in 1778, this scientific society enjoyed a period of lively activity in the 1780s, but then became largely insignificant. Raffles reformed it, following the model of the *Asiatic Society*. Cf. L. The and P. van der Veur, *The Verhandlingen van het Bataviaasch Genootschap: An Annotated Content Analysis* (Ohio, 1973), esp. 1–6.

56. 'Report and Journal of the Proceedings of Lieut. Colonel Colin Mackenzie, Chief Engineer on the Expedition to Batavia on the Island of Java, from October 1811 to June 1813', 14 December 1813, BL/OIOC/Mss Eur/Mack Priv/14, 215–62, here 215–19, quote 218f.

57. Thomas Raffles to Colin Mackenzie, F.J. Rothenbühler, J. Knops, P.H. Lawick van Pabst, 21 January 1812, BL/IOIC/Mss Eur/Mack Priv/14, 297–302. See also Bastin, *Raffles' Ideas*, 20–23.

58. Cf. Bastin, *Native Policies*, 9–12.

59. Cf. Bastin, *Raffles' Ideas* 123–26; and Niel, *Java's Northeast Coast*, 241–60.

60. Cf. Colin Mackenzie, 'Report, 12 August 1812', cited at length in Raffles, *Substance of a Minute*, 257–59, here 259. See also Bastin, *Raffles' Ideas*, 69f. For a critical assessment of the belief shared by many British officials that Java had a Hindu past see S. Tiffin, 'Raffles and the Barometer of Civilisation: Images and Descriptions of Ruined Candis in The History of Java', *Journal of the Royal Asiatic Society* 18(3) (2008), 341–60.

61. Colin Mackenzie, 'Report and Journal of the Proceedings of Lieut. Colonel Colin Mackenzie Chief Engineer on the Expedition to Batavia on the Island of Java from October 1811 to June 1813', 14 December 1813, BL/OIOC/Mss Eur/Mack Priv/14, 215–62, here 241.

62. Colin Mackenzie to William Morison, 6 September 1812, BL/IOR/F/554 (13476), 267–73 here 270f. See also Mackenzie to Chief Sec. (FSG), 1 August 1816, NAI/SIR/REP/3, 37–76, here 53f.

63. Cf. T.S. Raffles, *The History of Java*, 2nd ed., 2 vols (London, 1830), vol. 1, 6f. See also Phillimore, *Historical Records*, vol. 2, 293; and Mackenzie. 'Statement of the Literary Labours', 319.

64. 'Heads of Memoir of the Regentship or District of – in Java intended for obtaining a complete Geographical & Statistical view of the Island. Communicated for Circulation by Lieutt. Colonel Mackenzie', BL/OIOC/Mss Eur/Mack Priv/14, 303–09.

65. Colin Mackenzie, 'Brief View of the Collection of notes observations and Journals of 31 years and of Collections of Manuscripts, Inscriptions, drawings &ca. for the last 19 years made by Colonel Mackenzie in India, exclusive of a considerable collection of Native Manuscripts in all Languages of India', [1813/14], BL/IOR/F/4/867 (22924), 60–139, here 104f.

66. Raffles, *Substance of a Minute*, 5; id., *History of Java,* vol. 1, 171.

67. Cf. 'Raffles' Instructions to Mackenzie Land Tenure Commission, 14 January 1812', in Niel, *Java's Northeast Coast*, Appendix 21 (CD-ROM).

68. Cf. Colin Mackenzie, 'Report and Journal of the Proceedings of Lieut. Colonel Colin Mackenzie', 14 December 1813, BL/OIOC/Mss Eur/Mack Priv/14, 215–62, here 242.

69. 'Questionnaire of Mackenzie Commission, 15 February 1812' in Niel, *Java's Northeast Coast,* Appendix 22 (CD-ROM).

70. In a letter published in Raffles' widow's eulogy: Thomas Horsfield to Sophia Raffles, 31 December 1829, in S. Raffles, *Memoir of the Life and Public Services of Sir Thomas Stamford Raffles, F.R.S. &c. Particularly in the Government of Java 1811–1816, and of Bencoolen and its Dependencies, 1817–1824; With … Selections from his Correspondence* (London, 1830), 602–32, here 604.

71. Cf. Mackenzie, 'Statement of the Literary Labours', 320.

72. Cf. Colin Mackenzie to Chief Sec. (FSG), 1 August 1816, NAI/SIR/REP/3, 37–76, here 70–72.

73. One of whom, unnamed in the sources, later returned with him to Madras and then went back to Java at the EIC's cost. Cf. Lushington to Kavali Venkata Lakshmayya, 9 June 1825, BL/IOR/F/4/867 (22924), 33–37.

74. Cf. S. Kouznetsova, 'Colin Mackenzie as Collector of Javanese Manuscripts and Manuscript BL Mss Jav. 29', *Indonesia and the Malay World* 36 (106) (2008), 375–94, esp. 379–81, 376 fn 4.

75. Cf. C. Mackenzie, 'Statement of the Literary Labours', 319–23; also included in Mackenzie, 'Biographical Sketch' (1835), 354-64 under the title 'A General View of the Results of Investigations into Geography, History, Antiquities, and Literature, in the Island of Java, 10 November 1813', for the drawings see also Howes, *Illustrating India*, 192f.

76. Cf. Colin Mackenzie, 'Narrative of a Journey to Examine the Remains of an Ancient City and Temples at Brambana in Java. Extracted from a Journal kept by Colin Mackenzie', *Transactions of the Batavian Society for Science and Arts (Verhandelingen van het Bataviaasch Genootschap der Kunsten en Wettenschappen)* 7 (1814), 1–53.

77. Mackenzie, 'Statement of the Literary Labours', 248.

78. C. Mackenzie to Stewart Mackenzie, 24 March 1819, NAS/ GD/46/17/51.

79. Raffles, *History of Java*, vol. 2, cxlviii.

80. C. Mackenzie to Stewart Mackenzie, 24 March 1819, NAS/ GD/46/17/51. For Raffles' use of sources see D.E. Weatherbee, 'Raffles' Sources for Traditional Javanese Historiography and the Mackenzie Collections', *Indonesia* 26 (1978), 63–93.

81. 'Extract of a Separate Letter for the Honorable the Court of Directors in the Military Department dated 3. June 1814', NAI/SIR/1/5, 29–32, here 29.

82. CD to B (FW), Separate, 10 March 1815, NAI/SIR/SGO/7, 33; 'General Order by the Honorable the Vice President in Council, Fort William', 1 May 1815, ibid., 31f.

83. Cf. *The London Gazette* 17061 (16 September 1815), 1880 (www.thegazette.co.uk/ London/ issue/17061/page/1880, accessed 13 February 2017).

84. For this journey see Howes, *Illustrating India*, 196–208; and Phillimore, *Historical Records*, vol. 2, 83f, 89, 426f. They seem to have been joined by Lakshmayya at some point, as he took leave and Lady Hood later mentioned him as an acquaintance. Cf. Kavali Venkata Lakshmayya to William Morison, January 1814, NAI/SIR/SGO/567, 116; and Colin Mackenzie to Mary Stewart Mackenzie [Lady Hood], 24 March 1819, NAS/GD/46/17/51.

85. Colin Mackenzie to William Lambton, 3 May 1816, NAI/SIR/SGO/573, 44–46, here 45.

86. Colin Mackenzie to Thomas Munro, 1 January 1819, BL/OIOC/Mss Eur/F/151/39, 268–73, here 270.

87. Cf. P.J. Marshall, 'Barlow, Sir George Hilaro' *ODNB*.

88. Cf. Colin Mackenzie to John Riddell, 17 April 1818, NAI/SIR/SGO/573, 318–24. However, Mackenzie in his official correspondence praised Morison's work. Cf. Colin Mackenzie to David Hill, Sec. Gov., 22 July 1815, BL/IOR/F/4/554 (13476), 77–85.

89. Cf. Colin Mackenzie to Chief Sec. Gov., 14 December 1815, BL/IOR/F/4/554 (13476), 147–245, here 177–80, 220–22. Here the Quarter Master General made use of the fact that orders regarding the transfer of material – probably unintentionally – only extended to 1810. Cf. Mackenzie to [Josiah?] Marshall, 5 April 1816, NAI/SIR/SGO/573, 37f.

90. Cf. D. Hill to Colin Mackenzie, 10 May 1816, BL/IOR/F/4/555 (13477), 61–66.

91. Colin Mackenzie to Chief Sec. Gov. (FSG), 17 January 1816, BL/IOR/F/4/554 (13476), 309–15; W. Ormsby, Sec. Mil. B, to Mackenzie, 9 January 1816, ibid., 315f; D. Hill to Mackenzie, 6 February 1816, ibid., 316f; Mackenzie to Chief Sec. Gov., 26 September 1816, BL/IOR/F/4/555 (13477), 299–339, here 334–36.

92. Mackenzie stressed that the military was over-equipped with instruments: 'Among others there are … 42 Perambulators, 68 Brass Chains and 40 Plane Tables a number that can scarcely be required for a long time to come in any department'. Colin Mackenzie to Chief Sec. Gov., 26 September 1816, BL/IOR/F/4/555 (13477), 299–339, here 331–34, quote 332. See also D. Hill to Mackenzie, 11 November 1816, ibid., 345–48.

93. Cf. 'Account of Disbursement for House and Office rent for the Surveyor General's Office, Depot of Charts and instruments, and for the accomodation of the assistant Surveyors and Extra people employed in drawing, Writing & paid by Colonel C. Mackenzie from 1st December 1810 to 1st June 1815', BL/IOR/F/4/555 (13477), 277.

94. Colin Mackenzie to Chief Sec. (FSG), 1 August 1816, NAI/SIR/REP/3, 37–76, here 63–65.

95. Cf. 'Extract of a Separate Letter for the Honorable the Court of Directors in the Military Department dated 3 June 1814', NAI/SIR/30/1/5, 29–32, here 29–31.

96. Colin Mackenzie, 'A Statement of Expenses incurred Quarterly & Annually by the several Establishments considered to relate to the Surveying Department under the Presidency of Fort St. George reported to the Surveyor General from the formation of the Surveyor General's Office on 1st. December 1810, to the 1st of December 1815', NAI/SIR/REP/3, 22f; Colin Mackenzie to Chief Sec. (FSG), 14 December 1815, BL/IOR/F/4/554 (13476), 147–245; also 28 January 1816, ibid., 335–60; 1 August 1816, BL/IOR/F/4/555 (13477), 143–263 (NAI/SIR/REP/3, 37–76); and 26 September 1816, ibid., 299–339.

97. Cf. Bowen, *Business of Empire*, 194–208.

98. Colin Mackenzie to Chief Sec. Gov., 14 December 1815, BL/IOR/F/4/554 (13476), 147–245, here 183–87.

99. Cf. Public Letter from FSG, BL/IOR/F/4/554 (13476), 30 April 1816, 11–17, here 12.

100. Cf. D. Hill, Sec. Gov. (FSG), to Colin Mackenzie, 12 January 1816, BL/IOR/F/4/554 (13476), 299f; also 23 February 1816, ibid., 370–77; and 11 November 1816, BL/IOR/F/4/555 (13477), 345–48.

101. Colin Mackenzie to Chief Sec. Gov., 14 December 1815, BL/IOR/F/4/554 (13476), 147–245, here 214.

102. Mackenzie thus returned to his plan of 1811, which included a survey of both the Nizam's territory and that of the Marathas. Cf. Colin Mackenzie, 'Plan of Arranging the Surveyor General's Department & Generally all Surveys under the Presidency of Fort St. George', 19 November 1810, NAI/SIR/SGO/60, 6.

103. Colin Mackenzie to Chief Sec. Gov., 14 December 1815, BL/IOR/F/4/554 (13476), 147–245, here 218–22, quote 218.

104. Cf. Colin Mackenzie to Chief Sec. (FSG), 1 August 1816, NAI/SIR/REP/3, 37–76, here 49–61.

105. Cf. ibid., 70–72.

106. Cf. Ibid., 70. This suggestion was accepted, which is why H.H. Wilson proposed keeping him in the EIC's employ after Mackenzie's death – there would be no difference in cost. See Horace Hayman Wilson to Charles Lushington, 3 January 1822, BL/IOR/F/4/867 (22924), 41–59, here 55f.

107. Cf. Colin Mackenzie to Chief Sec. (FSG), 1 August 1816, NAI/SIR/REP/3, 37–76, here 74.

108. This applies particularly to the Telugu *pandits*. Cf. Rao, 'Print and Prose', esp. 147–51; and Mantena, 'Kavali Brothers', 146f.

109. 'Extract from the Minutes of The Right Honourable the Governor in Council', 29 July 1817, NAI/SIR/SGO/7, 128–30.

110. Cf. Edward Wood to Colin Mackenzie, 19 June 1817; NAI/SIR/SGO/7, 111.

111. Cf. Colin Mackenzie to Anthony Ferdinand Troyer, 9 January 1816, NAI/SIR/SGO/573, 27.

112. Colin Mackenzie, 'Memorandum of Business immediately on hand conceived to be necessary to close the Reports on the Surveying Department preparatory to the Surveyor General leaving this Presidency', 24 June 1816, BL/IOR/F/4/555 (13477), 129–39.

113. Cf. Colin Mackenzie to [Josiah?] Marshall, 5 April 1816, NAI/SIR/SGO/573, 37f.

114. Cf. Colin Mackenzie to [Josiah?] Marshall, 24 June 1816, NAI/SIR/SGO/573, 81f; Marshall to Mackenzie, 25 June 1816, ibid., 82f; Mackenzie to Marshall, 25 June 1816, ibid., 83f; id. to John Riddell, 26 June 1816, ibid., 91.

115. Colin Mackenzie to Thomas Munro, 1 January 1819, BL/OIOC/Mss Eur/F/151/39, 268–73, here 270. See also Colin Mackenzie to Mary Stewart Mackenzie, 24 March 1819, NAS/GD/46/17/51.

116. Cf. Colin Mackenzie to: [Josiah?] Marshall, 21 October 1816, NAI/SIR/SGO/573, 101; Cockrane, 31 October 1816, ibid., 102f; Marshall, 31 October 1816, ibid., 103–5; John Riddell, 21 March 1817, ibid., 129f; and to Marshall, 23 May 1817, ibid., 138f.

117. Cf. Colin Mackenzie to [Josiah?] Marshall, 4 December 1816, NAI/SIR/SGO/573, 115.

118. Cf. D. Hill, Sec. Gov. (FSG) to Colin Mackenzie, 27 January 1817; NAI/SIR/SGO/7, 45f; Edward Wood to Mackenzie, 25 April 1817, ibid., 79–81.

119. Colin Mackenzie to John Riddell, 6 June 1817, NAI/SIR/SGO/573, 143.

120. J. Young, Actg Sec. Gov. (FW) to Edward Wood, (FSG), 16 May 1817, NAI/SIR/SGO/7, 93–103, here 98–100; see also Colin Mackenzie to Wood, 16 June 1817, NAI/SIR/SGO/573, 144f.

121. Cf. Edward Wood to Colin Mackenzie, 19 June 1817, NAI/SIR/SGO/7, 111.

122. Colin Mackenzie to John Riddell, 16/19 July 1818, NAI/SIR/SGO/573, 358–63, here 359.

123. Colin Mackenzie to William Lambton, 15 July 1817, NAI/SIR/SGO/573, 148f; id. to Ward, 16 July 1817, ibid., 149.

124. Later, even as one of the most important events of the month: 'Asiatic Intelligence: Calcutta', *Asiatic Journal and Monthly Register for British India and its Dependencies* 5(26) (1818), 192.

125. At that time Mackenzie had delivered an address of loyalty by the Dutch inhabitants of Java. Cf. 'Calcutta Gazette, 2 September 1813', in Sandeman, *Selections from Calcutta Gazettes*, 306–9.

126. Colin Mackenzie to John Riddell, 28 August 1817, NAI/SIR/SGO/573, 271–75, here 271.

127. On 8 January 1820. Cf. 'Literary and Philosophical Intelligence', *Asiatic Journal and Monthly Register for British India and its Dependencies* 10(55) (July 1820), 81.

128. On 10 June. See RS/EC/1819/08 (https://collections.royalsociety.org/DServe. exe?dsqIni=Dserve.ini&sqApp= Archive&dsqDb=Catalog&dsqSearch=RefNo==%27EC%2F1819%2F08%27&dsqCmd=Show.tcl, accessed 13 February 2017). See also R.W. Home, 'The Royal Society and the Empire: The Colonial and Commonwealth Fellowship, Part 1: 1731–1847', *Notes and Records of the Royal Society of London* 56(3) (2002), 318.

129. Francis Whyte Ellis to William Erskine, 23 August 1813, NLS/Adv Mss/36.1.5, 80–87, here 84.

130. Shore, *Reminiscences of Many Years*, vol. 1, 351.
131. Munro, for instance, lived openly with his Indian female partner. Cf. Stein, *Munro*, 11f.
132. Cf. Marshall, 'British Society', 90.
133. Cf. Robert Hyde Colebrooke to Edward Hay, Sec. Gov., 13 March 1794, NAI/SIR/SGO/52, 43f; J.H. Harrington to Colebrooke, 16 June 1794, NAI/SIR/SGO/574, 26f; Colebrooke to John Lumsden, Chief Sec. Gov., 10 June 1803, NAI/SIR/SGO/54B, 219f; id. to J. Fombelle, 12 July 1804, ibid., 332f.
134. Cf. 'Extract from the Proceedings of His Excellency the Governor General in Council', 19 March 1801, NAI/SIR/SGO/574, 76; Robert Hyde Colebrooke to Francis Wilford, Thomas Wood and James Tillyer Blunt, 30 March 1801, NAI/SIR/SGO/54B, 32–34.
135. In 1806 only one officer had officially been made available for the surveys, in 1807 only two. See his annual reports: Robert Hyde Colebrooke to Thomas Brown, Chief Sec. Gov., 12 March 1806, NAI/SIR/SGO/54B, 432–34; also 12 March 1807, NAI/SIR/SGO/53A, 69–72.
136. Cf. Robert Hyde Colebrooke to Thomas Wood, 16 April 1801, NAI/SIR/SGO/54B, 35f; id. to Lieutenant. Colonel Gerard, Adj. Gen., 23 May 1801, ibid., 36; id. to Graeme Mercer, Sec. Gov., 2 May 1803, ibid., 202f; also 19 May 1803, ibid., 216f; id. to J. Fombelle, 12 July 1804, ibid., 332f; id. to A. Greene, Sec. Mil. Board, 25 January 1805, ibid., 362f; id. to John Lumsden, 12 March 1805, ibid., 369–72; id. to J. Dowdswell, Sec. Gov., 25 October 1806, NAI/SIR/SGO/53A, 43f.
137. Cf. John Garstin to: John Thornhill, Sec. Gov. Mil. Dep., 5 January 1809, NAI/SIR/SGO/53A, 204–6, here 204; and to Chief Sec. Gov., 13 May 1809, ibid., 245–50; see also Garstin to John Adam, Sec. Gov. Mil. Dep., 28 July 1809, ibid., 282–84.
138. Cf. John Garstin to John Hall, Paymaster to the Garrison, 21 April 1808, NAI/SIR/SGO/53A, 170.
139. Cf. John Garstin to: Thomas Brown, Chief Sec. Gov., 28 July 1807, NAI/SIR/SGO/54B, 483f; G. Dowdswell, Sec. Gov., 8 April 1808, NAI/SIR/SGO/53A, 168f; and to John Thornhill, 20 June 1808, ibid., 184f; see also Thornhill to Garstin, 24 June 1808, NAI/SIR/SGO/364, 38f.
140. Cf. Garstin's first annual report: John Garstin to John Adam, Sec. Gov. Mil. Dep., 15 June 1809, NAI/SIR/SGO/53A, 276–79. For a good overview of later enterprises see 'A List of all Surveyors with the Names of the Surveys on which they have been employed from January 1812 to 15th September 1816 with the number of Months for which allowances have been granted', NAI/SIR/SGO/370, 218f.
141. In 1815 Mackenzie had already insisted on receiving a copy of these regulations. Cf. Charles Crawford to Colin Mackenzie, 6 January 1815, NAI/SIR/SGO/370, 132–35; C.W. Gardiner, Sec. Gov. FSG to Crawford, 21 October 1814, NAI/SIR/SGO/6, 89; and Colin Mackenzie, 'Memorandum of the Heads under which some information is required regarding the mode of conducting the duties of the Surveyor General's Department, 20 November 1814,' BL/IOR/F/4/554 (13476), 263–70.
142. Although some of the engineers in the presidency had been able to gain practical experience working on the English Ordnance Survey, which the Surveyor General was informed about in detail, in Bengal they were given other duties. Cf. C.W. Gardiner, Sec. Gov., to Charles Crawford, 29 August 1813, NAI/SIR/SGO/5, 39; and Robert Dawson, 'Account of a Course of Instruction in Military Surveying, Sketching, Drawing &c given, on the Trigonometrical Survey under Command of Lieut. Colonel Mudge to Messrs. Ross, Macleod, Purton, Tate and Davidson, Cadets of the Honble. East India Company's Engineers; in the Year 1812, by Robert Dawson of H. M.'s Court of Royal Military Surveyors and Draftsmen', 24 October 1812, ibid., 41–47.

143. Cf. Colin Mackenzie to John Riddell, 28 August 1817, NAI/SIR/SGO/573, 271–75, here 272.
144. Colin Mackenzie to John Riddell, 28 November 1817, NAI/SIR/SGO/573, 287–90, here 287. See also 7 October 1817, ibid., 281f. Hamilton Scott and Burke arrived in Calcutta at the beginning of 1818. Cf. Mackenzie to Riddell, 17 April 1818, ibid., 318–24.
145. Colin Mackenzie to Thomas Munro, 24 December 1817, BL/OIOC/Mss Eur/F/151/57, 20f, here 21.
146. Colin Mackenzie to Lieutenant Colonel Young, Sec. Gov. Mil. Dep., 10 September 1818, NAI/SIR/SGO/435D, 15–21, here 20.
147. Cf. Sec. Gov. FW to Colin Mackenzie, 1 May 1818, NAI/SIR/SGO/8, 77.
148. Cf. Colin Mackenzie to Lieutenant Colonel Young, Sec. Gov. Mil. Dep., 30 September 1818, NAI/SIR/SGO/435D, 37f.
149. Colin Mackenzie to John Riddell, 1 August 1818, NAI/SIR/SGO/573, 369–72, here 370; see also Mackenzie to Mountstuart Elphinstone, Resident at Poonah, Calcutta, 7 September 1818, NAI/SIR/SGO/435D, 9–11, here 10. He was later allowed to train in the presidency: Lushington to Colin Mackenzie, 12 May 1820, NAI/SIR/SGO/10, 247–49; Mackenzie to Colonel Richards, 23 January 1821, NAI/SIR/SGO/435D, 117; id. to Lieutenant Buxton, 25 January 1821, ibid., 119f.
150. Colin Mackenzie to Lieutenant Colonel Young, Sec. Gov. Mil. Dep., 12 September 1818, NAI/SIR/SGO/435D, 23–28, here 24.
151. Colin Mackenzie to John Riddell, 1 August 1818, NAI/SIR/SGO/573, 369–72, here 372.
152. Cf. Colin Mackenzie to Lieutenant Colonel Young, Sec. Gov. Mil. Dep., 19 December 1818, NAI/SIR/SGO/435D, 53–55.
153. Cf. Lieutenant Colonel Young Mil. Sec. FW to Major John Craigie, [25 October?] 1817, NAI/SIR/SGO/7, 229–46; Colin Mackenzie to John Riddell, 11 April 1818, NAI/SIR/SGO/573, 313–18; CD to B (FW), Mil., NAI/SIR/1/5, 40.
154. Cf. Colin Mackenzie to Holt Mackenzie, 21 January 1821, NAI/SIR/SGO/435D, 115.
155. Colin Mackenzie to Lieutenant Colonel Young, Sec. Gov. Mil. Dep., 10 September 1818, NAI/SIR/SGO/435D, 15–21, here 18; see also 12 September 1818, ibid., 23–28, here 26.
156. Cf. for example Colin Mackenzie to [Josiah] Marshall, 5 January 1817, NAI/SIR/SGO/573, 125f; id. to John Riddell, 21 March 1817, ibid., 129f, also 28 August 1817, ibid., 271–75, here 271.
157. Cf. Colin Mackenzie to Lieutenant Colonel Young, Sec. Gov. Mil. Dep., 9 August 1819, NAI/SIR/SGO/435D, 92; id. to Lushington, 16 August 1819, ibid., 93.
158. For example when visiting the 'Seven Pagodas' near Madras in 1816/1817. Cf. Colin Mackenzie to [Josiah?] Marshall, 5 January 1817, NAI/SIR/SGO/573, 125f.
159. Cf. H. Kulke, 'Katakarajavamsavali', 69f.
160. Mackenzie, 'Narrative of a Journey to Examine the Remains at Brambana', 53.
161. Colin Mackenzie to Thomas Munro, 28 October 1820, BL/OIOC/Mss Eur/F/151/75, 160. For Mackenzie's judgement regarding the climate in Madras see also 24 December 1817, BL/OIOC/Mss Eur/F/151/57, 120f, here 121.
162. On the way to the lower stretch of the Hugli, where he hoped for better climatic conditions. Seriously ill, he had tried to work in his office until, based on a medical certificate, permission was given for him to leave. Cf. Colin Mackenzie to Lushington, Sec. Gov. FW, 14 March 1821; NAI/SIR/SGO/435D, 122; Lushington to Colin Mackenzie, 4 May 1821, NAI/SIR/SGO/11, 161.
163. Colin Mackenzie to Thomas Turnbull, 9 February 1821, NAI/SIR/SGO/435D, 123.
164. Colin Mackenzie to Thomas Munro, 1 January 1819, BL/OIOC/Mss Eur/F/151/39, 268–75, here 269.
165. Ibid., 268–69.

166. Ibid., 270.
167. 'tu regere imperio populos, Romane, memento / haec tibi erunt artes – pacique inponere morem / parcere subjectis et debellare superbos'. Aeneis VI, 851–53. (Vergil, Aeneis. Latin–German edited by Johannes Götte, Munich and Zurich 1988, 268).
168. Colin Mackenzie to Thomas Munro, 1 January 1819, BL/OIOC/Mss Eur/F/151/39, 269.
169. Ibid.
170. Ibid., 272.
171. Ibid., 269.
172. Cf. the four versions of the will in BL/IOR/L/AG/34/29/33.
173. Cf. Charles Lushington to Palmer & Co., 27 November 1822, BL/IOR/F/4/867 (22924), 177f.

EPILOGUE

About fifteen years after Mackenzie's death Alexander Johnston, meanwhile vice president of the Royal Asiatic Society, added another surprising detail to his version of Mackenzie's life story. When Mackenzie visited Madura in the early 1780s, Johnston now maintained, he and Johnston's parents formulated a plan to revive a traditional Hindu College said to have existed there in earlier times. Johnston reports that his father obtained a ruin, connected to the former college, from the Nawab of Arcot, and talks about grand architectural plans intended to mirror its future purpose: the teaching of mathematics. Mackenzie, he went on, had carried out the building work accordingly but when he was called away for other duties the project had to be abandoned.[1] However, according to a later district gazetteer, nine years earlier, in a letter to the Directors, he had merely declared that the 'Johnston house' was acquired by his father as a residence for his family. It was not until years later, it seems, that he mentioned the college for the first time in a letter. Here he described Mackenzie, who had never spent any significant period of time in Madura, as his 'early instructor', thus adding him to a list of two other illustrious names: Thomas Munro and the famous German missionary Christian Schwartz.[2]

Johnston's new details perhaps offer a key to understanding his confusing narratives as they seem to be directly connected with his personal interest in the house. When his family moved from Madura in 1787 the building was initially inhabited by various EIC civilian employees, and eventually sold by one of them to the Company in 1806. Twenty years later Johnston tried to get the house back and claimed that the sale was invalid as the building belonged to him as part of his parents' legacy. It was only after he had publicized the story of the Hindu college that his efforts met with partial success: even though they did not formally accept that he had any rights of ownership, the Directors stated that they were prepared to transfer the building to him as long as he used it as an educational facility – in fact, this never happened.[3] So it is quite conceivable that Johnston was using his narrative in an attempt to underpin his claim, and that he deliberately made it public in 1835 when the Indian education debate was approaching its zenith.[4]

Notes from this chapter begin on page 290.

If such motives are also imputed to Johnston's astonishing accounts of Mackenzie's early activities, then this might also explain their numerous inconsistencies. By stressing the role of his family – particularly of his grandfather Lord Francis Napier, but also of his parents – in instigating Mackenzie's research Johnston was able to stylize himself as a person very closely connected with this project and as a sort of 'heir' to it. This fits well with his claims, in all probability exaggerated, that he had been in regular communication with Mackenzie between 1802 and 1818 and had also had some influence on the scope of the collections.[5] Of course, all this gave Johnston, as vice president of the Royal Asiatic Society, additional authority for assessing the value of the collection, whose continuation and completion as proposed by Lakshmayya he advocated.[6] His interest in Mackenzie's project was undoubtedly genuine. During his years as Advocate General and Chief Justice, Johnston himself had made his own collection of legal texts intended to promote a legal system in Ceylon that took account of local cultural norms[7] and Mackenzie, who had visited the island in 1796, was able to provide him with valuable information.[8] Before Johnston returned to Great Britain, in 1817, Mackenzie sent him his autobiographical letter including the account of his collection, which could be used for further lobbying with the Directors in London.[9] In Johnston's subsequent descriptions of his relationship with Mackenzie, enriched again and again by new detail, a pattern is found that also emerges from other accounts given by him: while these narrations do have a certain a factual basis, he seems to have had a predilection for embellishing them with colourful and highly entertaining but less probable details.[10]

Johnston, however, did not only mould an enduring picture of Mackenzie's life story, but he also helped to ensure that Mackenzie's collections did not disappear into obscurity in the course of the nineteenth century. Even a superficial glance at the first volumes of the Royal Asiatic Society's journal as well as that of its Madras branch, the Madras Literary Society, is enough to demonstrate their significance for the activities of these British learned societies. Of course, this interest in Mackenzie's project was not confined to Europeans, and his former Indian co-workers continued to play an important role in South India's intellectual landscape. Thus, in nineteenth-century Madras the collection was ever present and even in Calcutta, where his activities were never esteemed as much as in the south, parts of the collection had a relevant afterlife. For instance, the archaeological finds constituted the first holdings of the India Museum in Calcutta founded in 1814[11] and his collection of coins served as an important source on which to build Indian numismatics.[12]

More importantly, from the point of view of the colonial state, after his death the survey itself remained an acknowledged means of producing knowledge, which remained characteristic of British rule over India. Although Mackenzie's system of mapping was soon overshadowed by the scientific brilliance of the

Great Trigonometrical Survey and the administrative requirements in broad sections of India were increasingly met by revenue surveys, the surveyors he had trained remained active in southern India for decades after his death, largely following his system; the *Atlas of India*, initiated by him in the course of the nineteenth century, was supplemented by ever more maps of individual regions;[13] and the statistical memoirs produced under his leadership remained an enduring benchmark. His administrative achievements and his permanent conflicts with the military were not without their consequences either: admittedly the Surveyor General's Office in Calcutta was soon restored to the military sphere but its counterpart in Madras remained under civilian control in the nineteenth century.[14] Despite the pessimism Mackenzie displayed in the last years of his life, and although his project was not carried on consistently in the form he wanted, his exertions were by no means inconsequential even though it is hardly necessary to mention that in the course of the nineteenth century the colonial state developed in a way that was quite different from Mackenzie's vision, for all its ambiguity.

In telling the story of Colin Mackenzie's life on these pages I have tried to avoid repeating the all-too-simple teleology so powerfully put forward by Johnston's narrative. Instead, I have told the story of a man who, like many of his Scottish contemporaries, went to India in the hope of making a quick fortune that would enable him to support his indebted father, build a house in his homeland, and live an independent life upon his return. In Madras, however, he ended up in a position where the planned return home repeatedly had to be postponed until eventually he died without ever seeing Stornoway again. As his hopes of making a rapid fortune were dashed soon after his arrival in India, it was initially the prospect of a successful, though also long career, and above all (in the last decades of his life) his unconditional belief in the usefulness of his project that postponed his return home again and again.

Mackenzie's unique life story cannot be understood without taking into account the more general context of early British rule in India. The forces and ideas that influenced his Indian career were relevant not only to him but to many of his British contemporaries in India and thus point to some more general characteristics of that period of transition. First of all, looking at Mackenzie's story offers an insight into the consequences the internal reforms initiated by the EIC in the late eighteenth century had on its administrative and military personnel. In the long careers they had to pursue much depended on complicated networks of interest and patronage – at the same time, however, they could play a highly significant role in configuring the EIC's administration, in Mackenzie's case even in building up the structures of an important government department.

Both the support and opposition that Mackenzie met, however, make it clear that the colonial administration during these years cannot be understood simply as a unified apparatus. The most significant fault line was the one between military and civil administration. It became visible not only in Mackenzie's continuous conflict with the army, but above all in the officers' mutiny of 1809 that ultimately allowed Mackenzie to build up civil structures for his surveying department. Of course, this is not to say that the period in question was a phase when the EIC was merely extending its civil administration – on the contrary, it was a phase of intense violence and warfare. For Mackenzie, his regular military assignments often meant that his activities were interrupted, but he was always prepared to accept the legitimacy of conquest. At the same time, warfare not only led to highly consequential decisions for his career but also opened up new geographical areas for the production of knowledge. The phase of transition in which his project came to fruition cannot simply be romanticized retrospectively as a phase of harmonious coexistence between Indians and Europeans.

However, it was a time when parts of the EIC's administration became convinced that to gain some legitimacy its power could not be based on rule by force alone. A new, interventionist understanding of 'government' was envisaged and Mackenzie's surveys can be regarded as an important contribution to this quest for governmentality. If they aimed at producing knowledge about territory and inhabitants that was to form a basis for sensible governmental intervention, this implied that such a production of knowledge had in itself to become a task for the state. Naturally, these ideas were not restricted to India, and it is certainly no accident that Mackenzie's mapping and inventorizing coincides with many similar projects for 'expanding the state internally' in Europe.

Rethinking British rule in India did not take place in an intellectual vacuum. Mackenzie's case points to the particular relevance of Scottish networks in India, not only as regards patronage structures but also in terms of intellectual influence. Men like James Anderson, who gave their advice to young Scots arriving in India, also spread ideas derived from Scottish universities, while a large number of Scottish historians and orientalists were highly influential in formulating basic ideas about India's culture and history. Notions of 'improvement' met here with 'philosophical' approaches to the past, and while these ideas in relation to India were arguably formulated in a much less dogmatic way than in later decades, and men like Mackenzie were open to many additional influences, they still proved to be an important point of reference for thinking about continuity and change. These ideas alone cannot explain the way in which Mackenzie's surveys developed, but over the years they certainly remained relevant.

Producing knowledge about India generally meant far more than merely projecting European ideas on to the colonial territory, and Mackenzie's surveys are one of the most shining examples of this. The expertise of the Indian co-workers ensured that precolonial structures formed a basis for his surveys just as much as European ideas; so the system of mapping followed during the surveys was predicated on a profound knowledge of precolonial territorial structures, while statistical memoirs largely rested upon the contents found in precolonial archives. If the expertise of *niyogis* was indispensable for such forms of administrative knowledge, historical enquiry left ample space for differing voices, as demonstrated, for instance, by Dharmaiah's role in formulating the idea of a pre-Brahmin South Indian past. All in all, the project can certainly not be used as an example of irreconcilable differences between colonial European and precolonial Indian forms of knowledge.

However, just as the colonial state that emerged around of the turn of the century was not, despite its 'historicist' tendencies, simply a continuation of what had been there before, the project also included important aspects of change. Territory was ordered according to the rules of geometrical cartography, local archives transformed into a centralized body of knowledge pertaining to a centralized state, and historical narratives in many cases organized according to a positivist approach to chronology. Whether such processes should be regarded as specifically 'colonial' is a question of perspective, though it should be noted again that similar developments could be observed in contemporaneous Europe. Perhaps Mackenzie's contribution to structures specifically colonial should be sought elsewhere. The maps and statistical and historical memoirs produced under his supervision represented the foundations of a seemingly 'knowledgeable' colonial state that to some extent was able to dispense with the help of the local experts so essential for Mackenzie's project, to develop less cooperative forms of knowledge production, and to draw much stricter boundaries between colonized and colonizers.

One final aspect of Mackenzie's project should be emphasized here. I have argued in this book that Mackenzie's investigations should be seen as an integrated project whose component parts were not only brought to fruition within a largely unitary structure in terms of administration, personnel and finance, but were also so ineluctably bound together in terms of content that there seems little point in trying to make a clear distinction between 'private' and 'official' interests. Despite being documentary, in many respects the unity of this project was based less on a purely encyclopaedic, additive understanding of knowledge than on a sort of 'cultural geographical' approach in which topography and natural history, political and religious history, and the interaction between nature and humans offered the most important key to understanding a complex present. Even if he sometimes emphasized the unbroken continuity of certain cultural forms, in unearthing the past he did not aim to present a romantic transfiguration of India's past but was essentially geared towards forging the future.

In this respect it might be connected to another, arguably more general transition described by Reinhart Koselleck. Implicitly confining his analysis to Europe, he has argued that in the decades around the turn of the eighteenth century the sense of the acceleration of time caused by important social and intellectual changes led to stronger emphasis on the singularity of historical experience and a clearer line of separation between 'space of experience' and 'horizon of expectation'.[15] The rethinking of the relationship between past and future during these decades took on many forms, some of which were also deeply influential in configuring perceptions about the meaning of British rule over India: Burkean conservatism may be mentioned here as well as the enthusiasm for 'improvement' of men like John Sinclair, and of course the theoretization of modernization so central to the reflections of Scottish Enlightenment thinkers. For Mackenzie himself, who had witnessed the radical transformations taking place in the Scottish Highlands in his youth, this changing relationship between past and future was less an issue of rational speculation than of personal experience. In a way, with his project he sought to find his own answer to the challenge, an answer that was neither purely conservative nor radically progressive. Aiming simultaneously to guarantee continuity and to promote change through the production of knowledge, his vision of a truly comprehensive survey was based on a particular urge to retain the unity between past, present and future.

Notes

1. 'Proceedings of the Anniversary Meeting May 1835', xi–xiii. This narrative was also propagated further, for instance by H. Caunter and W. Daniell, *The Oriental Annual, or Scenes in India, Comprising Twenty-Two Engravings from Original Drawings by William Daniell, R.A., and a Descriptive Account by the Rev. Hobart Caunter, B.D.* (London, 1836), 39–41.
2. Cf. W. Francis, *Madura* (Madras District Gazetteers), 2 vols (Madras, 1906), vol. 1, 262f. 'Proceedings of the Twenty-Sixth Anniversary Meeting of the Society, Held on the 12th of May, 1849', *Journal of the Royal Asiatic Society of Great Britain and Ireland* 11 (1849), iif.
3. Cf. Francis, *Madura*, vol. 1, 262–64. At the initiative of P.F. Campbell Johnston, Alexander's son, a scholarship was set up in 1872 at Madras University, financed by letting out the house.
4. For details see Zastoupil and Moir, 'Introduction'.
5. Cf. Johnston, 'Statement by Alexander Johnston, 19 July 1832', 254–56, para. 1929, 1932. Johnston and Mackenzie met briefly in about 1807 and probably kept up some correspondence, but I could find no evidence that Johnston had any greater influence. For the meeting see: Colin Mackenzie to Alexander Johnston, 9 September [1807?], NYPL/MssCol/1578, Dossier 5. My thanks to Mr Weatherly Stephan of the New York Public Library, who gave me access to this document in electronic form.
6. Cf. Johnston, 'Statement by Alexander Johnston, 19 July 1832', 256f, para. 1936–1938.
7. Cf. S. Sivasundaram, *Islanded: Britain, Sri Lanka, and the Bounds of an Indian Ocean Colony* (Chicago and London, 2013), 107–14, 118–22; and T. Nadaraja, *The Legal System of Ceylon in its Historical Setting* (Leiden, 1972), 15, 62, 183f. For Johnston's own account of his policy in Ceylon and his proposals for the government of India cf. 'Statement by Alexander

Johnston, 6 July 1832', in *Minutes of Evidence taken before the Select Committee on the Affairs of the East India Company and also an Appendix and Index,* 6 vols ([London, 1832]), vol. 4, 136–84.

8. Mackenzie supported Johnston by sending him a paper on southern Indian marriage ceremonies, which Johnston, according to his own account, used for legally regulating marriages in Ceylon and later published: see C. Mackenzie, 'An Account of the Marriage Ceremonies of the Hindus and Mahommedans, as Practised in the Southern Peninsula of India', *Transactions of the Royal Asiatic Society of Great Britain and Ireland* 3(1) (1831), 170–84, esp. 170.

9. Cf. Johnston, 'Statement by Alexander Johnston, 19 July 1832', 254f, para. 1930.

10. Johnston's own life story contains more quite extraordinary details. One such is the astonishing story of the 'Heart of Montrose', a family relic that, during his lifetime, was lost or stolen several times in most adventurous ways, but somehow always returned to the family, only to be lost for good in the confusion of the French Revolution. Cf. Alexander Johnston to 'My Dear Daughters', 1 July 1836, in Napier, *Life and Times of Montrose*, 501–6.

11. T. Guha-Thakurta, 'The Museumised Relic: Archaeology and the first Museum of Colonial India', *Indian Economic and Social History Review* 34(1) (1997), 29.

12. See H.H. Wilson, 'Description of Select Coins, from Originals or Drawings in the Possession of the Asiatic Society', *Asiatic Researches* 17 (1832), 559–606.

13. Cf. Edney, 'Atlas of India 1823–1947'.

14. Cf. Phillimore, *Historical Records*, vol. 3, 303.

15. Cf. Koselleck, '"Space of Experience"'.

BIBLIOGRAPHY
PRIMARY SOURCES

Unpublished Sources

1. British Library, London [BL]

1.1 Manuscripts [Mss Add]

12564–13915 *Volumes and Maps presented by the Representatives of the late Marquess Wellesley*
BL/Mss Add/13582; BL/Mss Add/13663

14380 *Copies of Papers relating to the Survey of India*

37274–37318 *Wellesley Papers*
BL/Mss Add/37275

40714–40716; 42069–42082 *Hamilton and Greville Papers*
BL/Mss/Add 40715; BL/Mss Add/42071

1.2 India Office Records [IOR]

B *Minutes of the East India Company's Directors and Proprietors, 1599–1858*
BL/IOR/B/98

E *East India General Correspondence*

E/4 *Correspondence with India, 1703–1858*
BL/IOR/E/4/880, BL/IOR/E/4/881; BL/IOR/E/4/882; BL/IOR/E/4/883;
BL/IOR/E/4/884

F *Board of Control General Records, 1784–1858*

F/4 *Board Collections, 1796–1858*

BL/IOR/F/4/17 (754); BL/IOR/F/4/18 (757); BL/IOR/F/4/18 (758); BL/IOR/F/4/78 (1750); BL/IOR/F/4/152 (2598); BL/IOR/F/4/165 (2829); BL/IOR/F/4/183 (3692); BL/IOR/F/4/260 (5707); BL/IOR/F/4/275 (6129); BL/IOR/F/4/280 (6426); BL/IOR/F/4/362 (9021); BL/IOR/F/4/541 (12148); BL/IOR/F/4/554 (13476); BL/IOR/ F/4/555 (13477); BL/IOR/F/4/636 (17424); BL/IOR/F/4/867 (22924); BL/ IOR/F/4/867 (22925)

H *Home Miscellaneous Series, c. 1600 – c. 1900*
BL/IOR/H/46; BL/IOR/H/91; BL/IOR/H/255; BL/IOR/H/256/1; BL/ IOR/H/446

L *Departmental Records*

L/AG/34 *Records of the Official Agent to the Administrators General in India and of the Estates and Wills Branch, 1714–1950*
BL/IOR/L/AG/34/23/209; BL/IOR/L/AG/34/29/33

L/MAR/B *Marine Department Records (Ships' Logs, 1702–1856)*
BL/IOR/L/MAR/B/27/Q

L/MIL/9 *Military Department Records, 1707–1957 (Records Relating to Entry into the Service, 1753–1940)*
BL/IOR/L/MIL/9/255

P *Proceedings and Consultations of the Government of India and of the Presidencies and Provinces, 1702–1945*
BL/IOR/P/243/9; BL/IOR/P/253/11; BL/IOR/P/254/41; BL/ IOR/P/254/52; BL/IOR/P/256/29; BL/IOR/P/257/15; BL/ IOR/P/259/56

X *India Office Reference Collection (Map Collections, c. 1700–1960)*
BL/IOR/X/595/1–2; BL/IOR/X/596/1–3; BL/IOR/X/597; BL/ IOR/X/598; BL/IOR/X/599; BL/IOR/X/600; BL/IOR/X/601/1–2; BL/ IOR/X/602/1–2; BL/IOR/X/2065; BL/IOR/X/2066; BL/IOR/X/2108, 1–7; BL/IOR/X/2110/1–5; BL/IOR/X/2297/1–2; BL/IOR/X/2298; BL/IOR/X/2302; BBL/IOR/X/2314/1–20; BL/IOR/X/2315/1; BL/ IOR/X/3948; BL/IOR/X/3949; BL/IOR/X/9599

1.3 Oriental and India Office Collections [OIOC]

Mss Eur *Private Papers/Manuscripts in European Languages*

C/929 *Miscellaneous papers, probably strays from the Mackenzie Collection*

D/1058 *Sir James Lillyman Caldwell Papers*

D/1073 *Typescript copies of personal letters from James Rennell to Rev. Gilbert Burrington*

F/87–89 *Elphinstone Collection*
BL/OIOC/Mss Eur/F/88/402

F/128 *Sutton Court Collection*
BL/OIOC/Mss Eur/F/128/213

F/151 *Munro Collection*
BL/OIOC/Mss Eur/F/151/8; BL/OIOC/Mss Eur/F/151/9; BL/OIOC/Mss Eur/F/151/39; BL/OIOC/Mss Eur/F/151/57; BL/OIOC/Mss Eur/F/151/75

F/218 *Verelst Collection*
BL/OIOC/Mss Eur/F/218/103

F/228 *Kirkpatrick Collection*
BL/OIOC/Mss Eur/F/228/19; BL/OIOC/Mss Eur/F/228/39

Mack Gen *Mackenzie General Collection*
BL/OIOC/Mss Eur/Mack Gen/6; BL/OIOC/Mss Eur/Mack Gen/8; BL/OIOC/Mss Eur/Mack Gen/14; BL/OIOC/Mss Eur/Mack Gen/18; BL/OIOC/Mss Eur/Mack Gen/18A; BL/OIOC/Mss Eur/Mack Gen/43; BL/OIOC/Mss Eur/Mack Gen/44; BL/OIOC/Mss Eur/Mack General/45; BL/OIOC/Mss Eur/Mack Gen/46; BL/OIOC/Mss Eur/Mack Gen/47; BL/OIOC/Mss Eur/Mack Gen/58; BL/OIOC/Mss Eur/Mack Gen/59; BL/OIOC/Mss Eur/Mack Gen/60; BL/OIOC/Mss Eur/Mack Gen/61; BL/OIOC/Mss Eur/Mack Gen/68; BL/OIOC/Mss Eur/Mack Gen/69

Mack Misc *Mackenzie Miscellaneous Collection*
BL/OIOC/Mss Eur/Mack Misc/77; BL/OIOC/Mss Eur/Mack Misc/117; BL/OIOC/Mss Eur/Mack Misc/136; BL/OIOC/Mss Eur/Mack Misc/171; BL/OIOC/Mss Eur/Mack Misc/172; BL/OIOC/Mss Eur/Mack Misc/174

Mack Priv *Mackenzie Private Collection*
BL/OIOC/Mss Eur/Mack Priv/14

Mack Trans *Mackenzie Translations*
BL/OIOC/Mss Eur/Mack Trans/12

Orme *Orme Collection*
BL/OIOC/Mss Eur/Orme/OV/6

NHD *Natural History Drawings*
BL/OIOC/NHD/37; BL/OIOC/NHD/38; BL/OIOC/NHD/46

WD *Western Drawings*
BL/OIOC/WD/576; BL/OIOC/WD/600; BL/OIOC/WD/633; BL/OIOC/WD/634; BL/OIOC/WD/736; BL/OIOC/WD/856; BL/OIOC/WD/2709

1.4 Biographical Notes compiled for R.H. Phillimore, Historical Records of the Survey of India (bound typed manuscript)

BL/OIR 354.54

2. National Archives of India, New Delhi [NAI]
Survey of India Records [SIR]

1/5 *Orders from Court of Directors respecting the Surveyor General's Department, 1788–1853*

FB *Fieldbooks*
NAI/SIR/FB/38

J *Journals*
NAI/SIR/J/3; NAI/SIR/J/8

M *Memoirs*
NAI/SIR/M/1; NAI/SIR/M/3; NAI/SIR/M/6; NAI/SIR/M/7; NAI/SIR/M/10; NAI/SIR/M/12; NAI/SIR/M/14; NAI/SIR/M/18; NAI/SIR/M/22; NAI/SIR/M/31

SGO *Surveyor General's Office*
NAI/SIR/SGO/3; NAI/SIR/SGO/5; NAI/SIR/SGO/6; NAI/SIR/SGO/7; NAI/SIR/SGO/8; NAI/SIR/SGO/9; NAI/SIR/SGO/10; NAI/SIR/SGO/11; NAI/SIR/SGO/52; NAI/SIR/SGO/53A; NAI/SIR/SGO/54B; NAI/SIR/SGO/60; NAI/SIR/SGO/90; NAI/SIR/SGO/90A; NAI/SIR/SGO/171b; NAI/SIR/SGO/319; NAI/SIR/SGO/361; NAI/SIR/SGO/364; NAI/SIR/SGO/370; NAI/SIR/SGO/435D; NAI/SIR/SGO/567; NAI/SIR/SGO/573; NAI/SIR/SGO/574

REP *Reports*
NAI/SIR/REP/2; NAI/SIR/REP/3

3. National Archives of Scotland, Edinburgh [NAS]

3.1 Exchequer and Treasury [E]

E/504 *Customs Records: Collectors' Quarterly Accounts*
NAS/E/504/33/1; NAS/E/504/33/2

3.2 General and Particular Registers of Sasines [RS]

RS/38 *Particular Register of Sasines etc for Inverness, Ross, Sutherland and Cromarty: Second Series*
NAS/RS/38/12

3.3 Private Papers [GD]

GD/46 *Papers of the Mackenzie Family, Earls of Seaforth (Seaforth Papers)*
NAS/GD/46/13/99; NAS/GD/46/15/25; NAS/GD/46/15/269; NAS/GD/46/17/4; NAS/GD/46/17/10; NAS/GD/46/17/51

GD/427 *Papers of the Gillanders Family of Highfield*
NAS/GD/427/44; NAS/GD/427/91; NAS/GD/427/150; NAS/GD/427/153; NAS/GD/427/211; NAS/GD/427/213; NAS/GD/427/214; NAS/GD/427/216, NAS/GD/427/225; NAS/GD/427/226

3.4 Records of the Board of Customs and Excise [CE]

CE/1 *Scottish Board of Customs, Minute Books*
NAS/CE/1/17

CE/3 *Scottish Board of Customs. Establishment Books*
NAS/CE/3/13/2; NAS/CE/3/13/3

CE/86 *Stornoway Outport and District Records*
NAS/CE/86/2/1; NAS/CE/86/2/2; NAS/CE/86/2/3

4. National Library of Scotland, Edinburgh [NLS]

4.1 Advocates' Manuscripts [Adv Mss]

36.1.5.–36.1.7b *William Erskine*
NLS/Adv Mss 36.1.5

4.2. Manuscripts [Mss]

11001–13496 *Minto Papers*
NLS/Ms 11722

13601–14195 *Walker of Bowland Papers*
NLS/Ms 13602

3380–84 *Leyden and Morton Correspondence and Papers*
NLS/Ms 3380; NLS/Ms 3383

8942–8989 *Foreign Mission Records of the Church of Scotland*
NLS/Ms 8955

5. **New York Public Library [NYPL]**

    MssCol 1578 *Alexander Johnston Papers*

6. **Southampton University Library [SUL]**

Wellington Papers [WP]

    1   **General Correspondence and Memoranda, 1790–1832**
         SUL/WP/1/58; SUL/WP/1/124

    3   **India Letter Books 1798–1805**
         SUL/WP/3/3/100

Published Sources and Contemporary Writings (up to 1858)

Abu al-Fazl ibn Mubarak. *Ayeen Akkbery or Institutes of the Emperor Akber.* Translated by
    Francis Gladwin. 3 vols. Calcutta, 1783–1786.
*Accounts, Presented to the House of Commons, from the East India Company, Respecting Their
    Annual Revenues and Disbursements, &c. &c. &c.* (House of Commons Papers; Accounts
    and Papers 1801–1802 (126), V, 1).
*Accounts, Presented to the House of Commons, from the East India Company; Respecting Their
    Annual Revenue and Disbursements, Trade and Sales ,&c. &c. &c.* (House of Commons
    Papers; Accounts and Papers 1803–1804 (111), IX, 53).
*Accounts, Presented to the House of Commons, from the East India Company; Respecting Their
    Annual Revenues and Disbursements, Trade and Sales, &c. &c. &c.* (House of Commons
    Papers; Accounts and Papers 1806 (158), XV, 1).
*Accounts, Presented to the House of Commons, from the East India Company, Respecting Their
    Annual Revenues and Disbursements, Trade and Sales, &c. for the Three Years, 1802–3,
    1803–4, & 1804–5; Together with an Estimate of the Same for the Year 1805–6* (House
    of Commons Papers; Accounts and Papers 1807 (24), V, 447).
*Accounts, Presented to the House of Commons, from the East India Company, Respecting Their
    Annual Revenues and Disbursements, Trade and Sales, &c. for three Years, According to
    the Latest Advices; Together with the Latest Estimate of the Same,* (House of Commons
    Papers; Accounts and Papers 1807 (54), V, 541).
*Accounts, Presented to the House of Commons, from the East India Company, Respecting Their
    Annual Revenues and Disbursements, Trade and Sales, &c. for Three Years, According to the
    Latest Advices; Together with the Latest Estimate of the Same* (House of Commons Papers;
    Accounts and Papers 1808 (240), XIII, 59).
Aitchison, C.U. (ed.). *A Collection of Treaties, Engagements and Sanads relating to India and
    Neighbouring Countries,* 14 vols. Calcutta, 1929–1933.
'Analysis of the Code of Menu'. *Asiatic Journal and Monthly Register for British India and its
    Dependencies* 26(152) (August 1828), 174–80.
Anderson, J. *Five Letters to Sir Joseph Banks … on the Subject of Cochineal Insects, Discovered
    at Madras.* Madras, 1787.
——— . *A Sixth Letter to Sir Joseph Banks.* Madras, 1787.

———. *A Seventh, Eighth and Ninth Letter to Sir Joseph Banks.* Madras, 1787.

———. *A Tenth Letter to Sir Joseph Banks.* Madras, 1787.

———. *An Eleventh Letter to Sir Joseph Banks.* Madras, 1787.

———. *The Continuation of Letters on the Progress and Establishment of the Culture of Silk, on the Coast of Coromandel.* Madras, 1792.

———. *The Conclusion of Letters on the Culture of Silk, with Additional Accounts of both Kinds of Bread Fruit Trees and the Distribution of Nopal.* Madras, 1792.

———. *Miscellaneous Communications.* Madras, [1795].

———. *Letters, &c.* Madras, 1796.

Anderson, W. *The Scottish Nation, or the Surnames, Families, Literature, Honours and Geographical History of the People of Scotland*, 3 vols. Edinburgh, 1862f.

The Annual Register, or a View of the History, Politics and Literature, for the Year 1783. London, 1785.

'Asiatic Intelligence: Calcutta'. *Asiatic Journal and Monthly Register for British India and its Dependencies* 5(26) (February 1818), 189–97.

'Asiatic Intelligence: Calcutta Miscellaneous: Deaths'. *Asiatic Journal and Monthly Register for British India and its Dependencies* 12(71) (November 1821), 504–6.

'Asiatic Intelligence: Madras: Deaths'. *Asiatic Journal and Monthly Register for British India and its Dependencies* 5(25) (January 1818), 89.

'The Atlas of India: Published by the East India Company'. *Asiatic Journal and Register for British India and its Dependencies* 27(162) (June 1829), 723f.

Babington, J. 'Description of the Pandoo Coolies in Malabar: With Four Drawings'. *Transactions of the Literary Society of Bombay* 3 (1823), 324–30.

Beatson, A. *A View of the Origin and Conduct of the War with Tippoo Sultaun; Comprising a Narrative of the Operations of the Army under the Command of Lieutenant-General George Harris, and of the Siege of Seringapatam.* London, 1800.

'Behaviour of Great Ladies in Town to their Country-Acquaintance, in a Letter from Elisabeth Homespun'. *The Mirror* 53 (26 July 1779). Reprinted in *The Mirror: A Periodical Paper, Published at Edinburgh in the Years 1779 and 1780*, 3 vols. Edinburgh, 1781, vol. 2, 146–55.

Bell, A. *The Madras School or Elements of Tuition, Comprising the Analysis of an Experiment in Education, Made in the Male Asylum, Madras, with is Facts, Proofs and Illustration.* London, 1808.

The Bengal Calendar for the Year 1789: Including a List of the Hon. and United East-India Company's Civil and Military Servants on the Bengal Establishment, &c. Including Also Those at Madras, Bombay, Fort Marlborough, China, and St. Helena, A New Edition, Corrected at the East-India House. [London], [1789].

The Bengal Calendar & Register, for the Year One Thousand Seven Hundred & Ninety; Containing Complete and Accurate Lists of the Honorable East India Company's Servants, on the Bengal Establishment, Upon a New and More Extensive Plan than any ever before. London, 1790.

The Bengal Obituary or, A Record to Perpetuate the Memory of Departed Worth, Being a Compilation of Tablets, and Monumental Inscriptions from Various Parts of the Bengal and Agra Presidencies, to Which Is Added Biographical Sketches and Memoirs of Such as Have Pre-eminently Distinguished Themselves in the History of British India since the Formation of the European Settlement to the Present Time. Calcutta, 1851.

The Bengal or East-India Calendar, for the Year MDCCXCV: Including a List of the Hon. and United East-India Company's Civil and Military Servants on the Bengal Establishment, &c. Also Those at Madras, Bombay, Fort Marlborough, China, and St. Helena. London, 1795.

Bennett, W. '*The Excellence of Christian Morality: A Sermon Preached before the Society in Scotland for Propagating Christian Knowledge at their Anniversary Meeting*. Edinburgh, 1800.

'Biographical Memoir of Colonel Mackenzie, C.B., Late Surveyor General of India'. *Asiatic Journal and Monthly Register for British India and its Dependencies* 12(72) (December 1821), 537–40.

[Blakiston, J.]. *Twelve Years' Military Adventure in Three Quarters of the Globe: Or, Memoirs of an Officer who Served in the Armies of His Majesty and of the East India Company, Between the Years 1802 and 1814, in Which Are Contained the Campaigns of the Duke of Wellington in India, and His Last in Spain and the South of France*, 2 vols. London, 1829.

Browne, J. *A History of the Highlands and of the Highland Clans*, 4 vols. Glasgow, 1835–1838.

Bruce, J. *Annals of the East India Company: from Their Establishment by the Charter of the Queen Elizabeth to the Union of the London and East India Companies 1707–8*, 3 vols. London, 1810.

Brüggemann, L.W. *A View of the English Editions, Translations and Illustrations of the Ancient Greek and Latin Authors, with Remarks*. Stettin, 1797.

Buchanan, F. *A Journey from Madras through the Countries of Mysore, Canara, and Malabar, Performed under the Most Noble Marquis Wellesley, Governor General of India, for the Express Purpose of Investigating the State of Agriculture, Arts and Commerce; the Religion, Manners, and Customs; the History Natural and Civil, and Antiquities, in the Dominions of the Rajah of Mysore, and the Countries Acquired by the Honourable East India Company, in the Late and Former Wars, from Tippoo Sultaun*, 3 vols. London, 1807.

———. 'Particulars of the Jains Extracted from a Journal'. *Asiatic Researches* 9 (1809), 279–86.

———. *Journal … Kept during the Survey of the Districts of Patna and Gaya in 1811–1812*. Edited and Introduced by V.H. Jackson. Patna, 1925.

———. *Journal … Kept during the Survey of the District of Shahabad in 1812–13*. Edited and Introduced by C.E.A.W. Oldham. Patna, 1926.

[Buchanan] Hamilton, F. *Genealogies of the Hindoos, Extracted from their Sacred Writings: With an Introduction and Alphabetical Index*. Edinburgh, 1819.

Buchanan Hamilton, F. *A Geographical, Statistical, and Historical Description of the District, or Zila, of Dinajpore, in the Province, or Soubah, of Bengal*. Calcutta, 1833.

Büsching, A.F. *A New System of Geography: in Which is Given, a General Account of the Situation and Limits, the Manners, History, … of the Several Kingdoms and States: Carefully Translated from the Last Edition of the German Original*, 6 vols. London, 1762.

———. *Neue Erdbeschreibung*, 8 vols. Hamburg, 1760–1762.

Campbell, A. *A Grammar of the Teloogoo Language: Commonly Termed the Gentoo, Peculiar to the Hindoos Inhabiting the Northeastern Provinces of the Indian Peninsula*. Madras, 1816.

Campbell, J. *A Political Survey of Britain: Being a Series of Reflections on the Situation, Lands, Inhabitants, Revenues, Colonies, and Commerce of This Island*, 2 vols. London, 1774.

Caunter, H. and W. Daniell. *The Oriental Annual, or Scenes in India, comprising Twenty-Two Engravings from Original Drawings by William Daniell, R.A., and a Descriptive Account by the Rev. Hobart Caunter, B.D.* London, 1836.

'Chronicle'. *Annual Register, or a View of the History, Politics, and Literature, for the Year 1773.* 2nd edn. London, 1775, 65–202.

Clarke, T.B. *A Statistical View of Germany, in Respect to the Imperial and Territorial Constitution, Forms of Government, Legislation … With a Sketch of the Character and the Genius of the Germans, and a Short Enquiry into the State of their Trade and Commerce.* London, 1790.

'Col. Colin Mackenzie'. *Gentleman's Magazine* 91(2) (October 1821), 378.

Colebrooke, H.T. 'Observations on the Sect of Jains'. *Asiatic Researches* 9 (1809), 287–322.

'Colonel C. Mackenzie'. *New Monthly Magazine and Literary Journal* 3(12) (December 1821), 642.

'Colonel Madan'. *Gentleman's Magazine* 100(1) (May 1830), 470f.

'Consequence to Little Folks of Intimacy with Great Ones, in a Letter from John Homespun'. *The Mirror* 12 (6 March 1779). Reprinted in *The Mirror: A Periodical Paper, Published at Edinburgh in the Years 1779 and 1780*, 3 vols. Edinburgh, 1781, vol. 1, 89–96.

'Copy of Sir Alexander Johnston's Evidence Relating to the Mackenzie Collection'. *Journal of the Royal Asiatic Society of Great Britain and Ireland* 2(2) (1835), xxx–xxxiii.

'Correspondence between Andrew Ross Esqr. at Madrass and George Andrew Ram Esqr. at Tanjore, on the Subject of Furnishing Water to the Northern Circars', in A. Dalrymple (ed.), *Oriental Repertory*, vol. 2(3). London, [1795?], 457–63.

[Dalrymple, A.]. *A Short Account of the Gentoo Mode of Collecting the Revenues, on the Coast of Choromandel.* London, 1783.

Dalrymple, A. 'Introduction to the Second Number', in id. (ed.), *Oriental Repertory*, vol. 2(2). London, [1794?], i–iv.

———. 'On Watering the Northern Circars', in id. (ed.), *Oriental Repertory*, vol. 2(3). London, [1795?], 33–60.

Davies, C. (ed.). *The Private Correspondence of Lord Macartney, Governor of Madras (1781–85).* London, 1950.

Davies, E. *Celtic Researches on the Origin, Traditions and Languages of the Ancient Britons: With Some Introductory Chapters on Primitive Society.* London, 1804.

'Deaths'. *Blackwood's Edinburgh Magazine* 22(133) (December 1827), 767–70.

'Debate at the India House, 28 September 1825'. *Oriental Herald and Journal of General Literature* 7 (October–December 1825), 380–89.

Debrett, J. *The Peerage of the United Kingdom of Great Britain and Ireland*, 13th improved edn, 2 vols. London, 1820.

'Description of a Visit of a Great Lady to the House of a Man of Small Fortune, in a Second Letter from Mr Homespun'. *The Mirror* 25, (20 April 1779). Reprinted in *The Mirror: A Periodical Paper, Published at Edinburgh in the Years 1779 and 1780*, 3 vols. Edinburgh, 1781, vol. 1, 193–203.

'Desiderata and Inquiries Connected with the Presidencies of Madras and Bombay'. *Asiatic Journal and Monthly Register for British India and its Dependencies* 24 (141) (1827), 349–54.

'Desiderata and Inquiries Connected with the Presidencies of Madras and Bombay'. *The Oriental Herald and Journal of General Literature* 14(45) (September 1827), 540–47.

'Desiderata and Inquiries Connected with the Presidencies of Madras and Bombay'. *Madras Journal of Literature and Science* 1(1) (1833), 44–52.

Dirom, M. *A Narrative of the Campaign in India Which Terminated the War with Tippoo Sultan in 1792.* London, 1793.

'Domestic Transactions'. *Royal Magazine or Gentleman's Monthly Companion* (October 1761), 213–17.

East India Company (ed.). *Copies and Extracts of Advices to and from India, Relative to the Cause, Progress, and Successful Termination of the War with the Late Tippoo Sultaun, Chief of Mysore, the Partition of His Dominions in Consequence Thereof; and the Distribution of the Captured Property Found in Seringapatam.* [London],1800.

The East India Kalendar, or, Asiatic Register for Bengal Madras, Bombay, Fort Marlborough, China and St. Helena for the Year 1791: On a More Extensive Plan than Any Hitherto Offered to the Public. London, 1791.

The East India Kalendar, or, Asiatic Register for Bengal Madras, Bombay, Fort Marlborough, China and St. Helena for the Year 1793: On a More Extensive Plan than Any Hitherto Offered to the Public. London, 1793.

The East India Kalendar, or, Asiatic Register for Bengal Madras, Bombay, Fort Marlborough, China and St. Helena for the Year 1794: On a More Extensive Plan than Any Hitherto Offered to the Public. A New Edition. London, 1794.

The East India Kalendar, or, Asiatic Register for Bengal Madras, Bombay, Fort Marlborough, China and St. Helena for the Year 1796: On a More Extensive Plan than Any Hitherto Offered to the Public. A New Edition. London, 1796.

The East India Kalendar, or, Asiatic Register for Bengal Madras, Bombay, Fort Marlborough, China and St. Helena for the Year 1797: On a More Extensive Plan than Any Hitherto Offered to the Public. A New Edition. London, 1797.

The East India Kalendar, or, Asiatic Register for Bengal Madras, Bombay, Fort Marlborough, China and St. Helena for the Year 1798: On a More Extensive Plan than Any Hitherto Offered to the Public. A New Edition. London, 1798.

The East India Kalendar, or, Asiatic Register for Bengal Madras, Bombay, Fort Marlborough, China and St. Helena for the Year 1800: On a More Extensive Plan than Any Hitherto Offered to the Public. A New Edition. London, 1800.

The East India Register and Directory for 1809, Corrected to the 15th August 1809, Containing Complete Lists of the Company's Servants, Civil, Military and Marine, with Their Respective Appointments at the Different Presidencies in the East-Indies. London [1809–1810].

The East India Register and Directory for 1821, Corrected to the 28th February 1821, Containing Complete Lists of the Company's Servants, Civil, Military and Marine, with Their Respective Appointments at the Different Presidencies in the East-Indies. London, [1821].

'The East Indies'. *London Literary Gazette or Journal of Belles Lettres, Arts, Sciences &c.* 817 (15 September 1832), 586–88.

Ellis, F.W. *A Dissertation on the Malayalama Language.* 1810. Reprint edited by Puthusseri Ramachandranam, Thiruvananthapuram, 2005.

———. *Replies to Seventeen Questions Proposed by the Government of Fort St. George Relative to Mirasi Right, with Two Appendices Elucidatory of the Subject.* Madras, 1818.

———. 'Note to the Introduction', in A.D. Campbell, *Grammar of the Telloogoo Language Commonly Termed the Gentoo: Peculiar to the Hindoos Inhabiting the North Eastern*

Provinces of the Indian Peninsula. 1816. 3rd edn., Madras, 1839. Reprint, New Delhi and Madras, 1991, 1–31.

'Extract of a General Letter from England in the General Department dated February 9 1809 to the Government of Fort St. George'. *Madras Journal of Literature and Science* 2(9) (1835), 364–69.

Fay, E. *Original Letters from India (1779–1815).* Edited by E.M. Forster, 2nd edn. London, 1986.

The Fifth Report from the Select Committee on the Affairs of the East India Company. (House of Commons Papers; Reports of Committees 1812 (377), VII, 1).

Fort William-India House Correspondence and Other Contemporary Papers Relating Thereto, vol. 2: Public Series 1757–1759, Edited by H.N. Sinha. Delhi, 1957.

Fort William-India House Correspondence and Other Contemporary Papers Relating Thereto, vol. 3: Public Series 1760–1763. Edited by R.R. Sethi. Delhi, 1968.

Fort William-India House Correspondence and Other Contemporary Papers Relating Thereto, vol. 5: Public Series 1767–69. Edited by Narenda Krishna Sinha. Delhi, 1949.

Fort William-India House Correspondence and Other Contemporary Papers Relating Thereto, vol. 10: Public Series 1786–88. Edited by Raghubir Sinh. Delhi, 1972.

Fullarton, W. *A View of the English Interests in India; and an Account of the Military Operations in the Southern Parts of the Peninsula, during the Campaigns of 1782, 1783, and 1784: In Two Letters.* London, 1787.

General Orders by Government, Fort St. George, Twelfth July M.DCC.XCVI. Madras, 1796.

'General Orders by Government, Fort St. George, 24 December 1800'. *Asiatic Annual Register, or a View of the History of Hindustan and of the Politics, Commerce and Literature of Asia for the Year 1801.* London, 1802, 54f.

Graham, M. *Journal of a Residence in India.* 1811. Reprint, New Delhi, 2000.

[Greville, C.F.]. *British India Analyzed: The Provincial and Revenue Establishments of Tippoo Sultaun and of Mahomedan and British Conquerors in Hindostan, Stated and Considered,* 3 vols. London, 1793.

Hamilton, W. *A Geographical, Statistical, and Historical Description of Hindostan,* 2 vols, London, 1820.

Herodot, *Histoire d'Hérodote traduite du Grec, avec des Remarques historiques et critiques, un Essai sur la Chronologie d'Hérodote, et une Table géographique par M. Larcher,* 7 vols. Paris, 1786.

Hewett, G. *Private Record of the Life of the Right Honorable Sir George Hewett.* Newport, 1840.

Heyne, B. *Tracts, Historical and Statistical, on India; with Journals of Several Tours through Various Parts of the Peninsula: also, An Account of Sumatra in a Series of Letters, by Benjamin Heyne, M.D., F.L.S, Member of the Asiatic Society of Calcutta, and the learned Societies of Bombay, Berlin, &c., and Surgeon and Naturalist on the Establishment of Fort St. George.* London, 1814.

Highland Society of London (ed.). *The Poems of Ossian in the Original Gaelic with a Literal Translation into Latin,* 2 vols. London, 1807.

'History of the Anagoondy Rajahs, Taken from the Verbal Account of Timmapah, the Present Representative of that Family, at Camlapore, 10th January 1801. Communicated by Major Mackenzie'. *Asiatic Annual Register or, View of the History of Hindustan, and of the Politics Commerce and Literature for the Year 1804.* London, 1806, 21–24.

'History of the Kings of Beejanagur and Anagoondy, from Enquires Made at Alputtun and Anagoondy, by Order of Major Mackenzie, in January 1801. Communicated by Major Mackenzie'. *Asiatic Annual Register or, View of the History of Hindustan, and of the Politics Commerce and Literature for the Year 1804.* London, 1806, 24–33.

Hodges, W. *Travels in India, during the Years 1780, 1781, 1782 & 1783.* London, 1793.

Homer. *The Iliad and Odyssey of Homer, translated into English blank verse, by W. Cowper,* 2 vols. London, 1791.

'Importance of British India to the Merchants and Manfacturers of Great Britain'. *Saturday Magazine* 127 (28 June 1834), 241–43.

'Influence of the Neighbourhood of a Rich Asiatic, in a Letter by John Homespun'. *The Lounger* 17 (28 May 1785). Reprinted in *The Lounger: A Periodical Paper, Published at Edinburgh in the Years 1785 and 1786. By the Authors of The Mirror,* 3 vols., 4th edn. London, 1788, vol. 1, 156–63.

Jenkins, R. *Report on the Territories of the Rajah of Nagpore: Submitted to the Supreme Government of India.* Calcutta,1827.

Jervis, T.B. 'Memoir on the Origin, Progress, and Present State of the Surveys in India'. *Journal of the Royal Geographical Society of London* 7 (1837), 127–43.

Johnston, A. 'Statement by Alexander Johnston, 6 July 1832', in *Minutes of Evidence Taken before the Select Committee on the Affairs of the East India Company and Also an Appendix and Index,* 6 vols. [London, 1832], vol. 4: Judicial, 136–84.

———. 'Statement by Alexander Johnston, 19 July 1832', in *Minutes of Evidence Taken before the Select Committee on the Affairs of the East India Company and Also an Appendix and Index,* 6 vols. [London, 1832], vol. 1: Public, 254–57.

'Jonathan Scott Esq. LLD'. *Gentleman's Magazine* 99(1) (May 1829), 470f.

Jones, W. 'A Dissertation on the Orthography of Asiatic Words'. *Asiatic Researches* 1 (1788), 1–56.

———. 'On the Hindus: The Third Anniversary Discourse'. *Asiatic Researches* 1 (1788), 415–31.

Kavali Venkata Borayya and C. Mackenzie, 'Account of the Jains: Collected from a Priest of this Sect; at Mudgeri. Translated by Cavelly Boria, Brahmen, for Major Mackenzie'. *Asiatic Researches* 9 (1809), 244–86.

Kavali Venkata Ramaswami, *Biographical Sketches of Dekkan Poets, being Memoirs of the Lives of Several Eminent Bards, both Ancient and Modern, Who Have Flourished in Different Provinces of the Indian Peninsula.* Calcutta, 1829.

Kearsley, C. *Kearsley's Complete Peerage, of England, Scotland and Ireland; Together with an Extinct Peerage of the Three Kingdoms.* London, 1794.

Kendall, E.A. 'Cooorumber and Chola, or Cholla Kings of the Carnatic'. *Asiatic Journal and Monthly Register for British India and its Dependencies* 14 (79) (July 1822), 28f.

Kimber, E. *The New Peerage; or, Ancient and Present State of the Nobility of England, Scotland, and Ireland: Containing a Genealogical Account of all the Peers,* 2nd edn., 3 vols. London, 1778.

Kirkpatrick, W. *A Vocabulary, Persian, Arabic and English; Containing Such Words as Have Been Adopted from the Two Former of Those Languages, and Incorporated into the Hindvi.* London, 1785.

———. *Select Letters of Tippoo Sultan to Various Public Functionaries Including his Principal Military Commanders, Governors of Forts and Provinces; Diplomatic and Commercial Agents ... Together with Some Addressed to the Tributary Chieftains of Shânoor, Kurnool,* and Cannanore, and Sundry Other Persons; With Notes and Observations, and an Appendix, Containing Several Original Documents Never Before Published*. London, 1811.

Knox, J. *A Tour through the Highlands and Hebride Islands in MDCCCLXXXVI*. London, 1787.

Lambton, W. 'An Account of a Method for Extending a Geographical Survey across the Peninsula of India'. *Asiatic Researches* 7 (1803), 312–35.

'The Late Colin Mackenzie C.B'. *East India Military Calendar Containing the Services of General and Field Officers of the Indian Army: By the Editor of the Royal Military Calendar* 3 (1826), 310–31.

Leyden, J. (ed.). *The Complaynt of Scotland, Written in 1548 with A Preliminary Dissertation and Glossary*. Edinburgh, 1801.

———. 'On the Languages and Literature of the Indo-Chinese Nations'. *Asiatic Researches* 10 (1812), 158–289.

———. 'Scenes of Infancy; Descriptive of Teviotdale (1803)', in J. Leyden, *The Poetical Remains*. London, 1819, 289–415.

———. *Tour in the Highlands and Western Islands, 1800*. Edited with a Bibliography by James Sinton. Edinburgh and London, 1903.

'Literary and Philosophical Intelligence'. *Asiatic Journal and Monthly Register for British India and its Dependencies* 8(46) (October 1819), 354–63.

'Literary and Philosophical Intelligence'. *Asiatic Journal and Monthly Register for British India and its Dependencies* 10(55) (July 1820), 81–84.

'Literary and Philosophical Intelligence'. *Asiatic Journal and Monthly Register for British India and its Dependencies* 15(90) (June 1823), 581–84.

Loch, D. *Essays on Trade, Commerce, Manufactures and Fisheries in Scotland, Containing Remarks on the Situation of Most of the Sea-Ports*, 3 vols. Edinburgh, 1778.

Lower, M.A. 'Memorial of the Town, Parish and Cinque-Port of Seaford, Historical and Antiquarian'. *Sussex Archaeological Collections Relating to the History and Antiquities of the County* 3 (1854), 73–150.

Mackenzie, C. 'Account of the Construction of the Plan of the Roads from Nellore to the Western Passes, and to Ongole, &c., Measured in 1788 by Colin Mackenzie Practitioner-Engineer', in A. Dalrymple (ed.), *Oriental Repertory* 1(1). London, [1791?], 57–64.

———. 'The History of the Cummum Tank from Relation of Senabella Fackier', in A. Dalrymple (ed.), *Oriental Repertory*, vol. 2(2). London, [1794?], 333*f.*

———. 'Source of the Pennar River' in A. Dalrymple (ed.), *Oriental Repertory*, vol. 2(2). London, [1794?], 335*f.*

———. 'Account of the Pagoda at Perwuttum: Extract of a Journal by Captain Colin Mackenzie. Communicated by Major Kirkpatrick'. *Asiatic Researches* 5 (1799), 303–14.

———. 'Account of the Pagoda at Perwuttum: Extract of a Journal by Captain Colin Mackenzie. From the Fifth Volume of the Asiatic Researches. *New Annual Register, or General Repository of History, Politics and Literature for the Year 1799*. London, 1800, 144–50.

———. 'Map of the Dominions of the late Tippoo Sultaun exhibiting their Partition among the Allied Parties and the Rajah of Mysore, according to the Partition Treaty of Mysore concluded the 22nd June 1799, by Captain Colin Mackenzie of the Engineers', in A. Beatson, *A View of the Origin and Conduct of the War with Tippoo Sultaun;*

Comprising a Narrative of the Operations of the Army under the Command of Lieutenant-General George Harris, and of the Siege of Seringapatam. London, 1800, 248–49.

———. 'Remarks on Some Antiquities on the West and South Coasts of Ceylon. Written in the Year 1796'. *Asiatic Researches* 6 (1801), 425–54.

———. 'Narrative of a Journey to Examine the Remains of an Ancient City and Temples at Brambana in Java. Extracted from a Journal kept by Colin Mackenzie'. *Transactions of the Batavian Society for Science and Arts* (*Verhandelingen van het Bataviaasch Genootschap der Kunsten en Wettenschappen*) 7 (1814), 1–53.

———. 'Statement of the Literary Labours of the Late Colin Mackenzie, C.B. (Originally Communicated to the Asiatic Journal)'. *Asiatic Journal or Monthly Register for British India and its Dependencies* 13(75) (March 1822), 242–49 and 13(76) (April 1822), 313–25.

———. 'Ruins of Amravutty, Depauldina and Durnacotta'. *Asiatic Journal and Monthly Register for British India and its Dependencies* 15(89) (1823), 464–78.

———. 'An Account of the Marriage Ceremonies of the Hindus and Mahommedans, as Practised in the Southern Peninsula of India'. *Transactions of the Royal Asiatic Society of Great Britain and Ireland* 3(1) (1831), 170–84.

———. 'Biographical Sketch of the Literary Career of the Late Colonel Colin Mackenzie, Surveyor General of India; Comprising Some Particulars of his Collection of Manuscripts, Plans, Coins, Drawings, Sculptures &c. Illustrative of the Antiquities, History, Geography, Laws, Institutions, and Manners of the Ancient Hindus; Contained in a Letter Addressed by Him to the Right Honourable Sir Alexander Johnston V.P.R.A.S &c. &c.'. *Journal of the Royal Asiatic Society of Great Britain and Ireland* 1(2) (1834), 333–64.

———. 'Biographical Sketch of the Literary Career of the late Colonel Colin Mackenzie, Surveyor General of India; Comprising some Particulars of his Collection of Manuscripts, Plans, Coins, Drawings, Sculptures &c. Illustrative of the Antiquities, History, Geography, Laws, Institutions, and Manners of the Ancient Hindus; Contained in a Letter Addressed by Him to the Right Honourable Sir Alexander Johnston V.P.R.A.S &c. &c.'. *Madras Journal of Literature and Science* 2(8) (1835), 262–90 and 2(9) (1835), 354–69.

———. 'View of the Principal Political Events That Occurred in the Carnatic, From the Dissolution of the Ancient Hindoo Government in 1564 till the Mogul Government was Established in 1687, on the Conquest of the Capitals of Beejepoor and Golconda; Compiled from Various Authentic Memoirs and Original MSS., Collected Chiefly within the Last Ten Years, and Referred to in the Notes at the Bottom of Each Page'. *Journal of the Asiatic Society of Bengal* 13(1) (1844), 421–63 and 13(2) (1844), 578–609.

Mackenzie, H. (ed.). *Prize Essays and Transactions of the Highland Society of Scotland: To which is prefixed an Account of the Institution and Principal Proceedings of the Society.* 6 vols. Edinburgh, 1799–1824.

Mackenzie, R. *A Sketch of the War with Tippoo Sultaun; or, a Detail of Military Operations, from … 1789, until the Peace … in February 1792,* 2 vols. Calcutta, 1793–1794.

Macleod, A.M. 'A Highland Parish of the Last Century'. *Good Words* 32 (1891), 237–40.

'Madras Occurrences for August 1809'. *Asiatic Annual Register, or a View of the History of Hindustan … for the Year 1809.* London, 1811, 106–23.

Malcolm, J. *Observations on the Disturbances in the Madras Army in 1809: In Two Parts.* London, 1812.

——. *Political History of India from 1784 to 1823*, 2 vols. London, 1826.

'Marjory Mushroom's Account of Her Life in Town. Hardships to be Endured by a Disciple of the Ton'. *The Lounger* 56 (25 February 1768). Reprinted in *The Lounger: A Periodical Paper, Published at Edinburgh in the Years 1785 and 1786. By the Authors of The Mirror*, 3 vols., 4th edn. London, 1788, vol. 2, 200–8.

Marshall, P.J. (ed.). *Problems of Empire: Britain and India 1757–1813.* London, 1968.

——. (ed.). *Writings and Speeches of Edmund Burke, vol. 6: India, The Launching of the Hastings Impeachment, 1786–1788.* Oxford, 1991.

——, (ed.). *Writings and Speeches of Edmund Burke, vol. 7: India, The Hastings Trial, 1789–1794.* Oxford, 2000.

Martin, M. *A Description of the Western Isles of Scotland: Containing a Full Account of their Situation, Extent, Soil, Product, Harbours.* London, 1703.

Martin, R.M. (ed.). *The Despatches, Minutes and Correspondence of the Marquess Wellesley, K.G., during his Administration in India*, 5 vols. 1836/37. Reprinted in Delhi, 1984.

——. *The History, Antiquities, Topography, and Statistics of Eastern India ... in Relation to their Geology, Mineralogy, Botany, Agriculture, Commerce, Manufactures, Fine Arts, Population, Religion, Education, ... etc.*, 3 vols. London, 1838.

Maurice, T. *Indian Antiquities: or, Dissertations, relative to the Ancient Geographical Divisions, the Pure System of Primeval Theology, the grand Code of Civil Laws, the Original Form of Government, and the Various and Profound Literature, of Hindostan. Compared, throughout, with the Religion, Laws, Government, and Literature, of Persia, Egypt, and Greece. The Whole Intended as Introductory to, and Illustrative of, the History of Hindostan.*, 5 vols. London, 1793f.

[Member of the Highland Society in London]. *The Necessity of Founding Villages Contiguous to Harbours for the Effectual Establishment of Fisheries on the West Coast of Scotland and the Hebrides.* London, 1786.

'Members of the Asiatic Society, 1797'. *Asiatic Researches* 5 (1799), 427f.

'Memoir of Dr Walker', in W. Jardine, *The Naturalist's Library, II: Ornithology, vol. XII, III.* Edinburgh, London and Dublin, 1842, 17–49.

Mill, J. *The History of British India*, 3 vols. London, 1817.

Minutes of Evidence Taken before the Committee of the Whole House, and the Select Committee on the Affairs of the East India Company (House of Commons Papers; Reports of Committees 1812–1813 (122) VII, 1).

'The Monthly Chronologer: Scotland'. *London Magazine: Or, Gentleman's Monthly Intelligencer* 42 (July 1773), 363.

Morton, J. 'Memoirs of Dr Leyden', in J. Leyden, *The Poetical Remains.* London, 1819, i–xcii.

Mossner, E.C. and I.S. Ross (eds). *The Correspondence of Adam Smith* (The Glasgow Edition of the Works and Correspondence of Adam Smith, vol. 6), 2nd edn. Oxford, 1987.

Muller, J. *The Attac and Defence of Fortified Places: In Three Parts: Illustrated with Twenty-five Large Copper-Plates*, 2nd edn. London, 1757.

——. *A New System of Mathematics Containing Plane Geometry; General Investigation of Areas, Surfaces, and Solids; Greatest and Least Quantities; Trigonometry; Logarithms;*

Motion, Uniform, Compound, Accelerated, Retarded, Projectiles, Application: To which is Prefixed the First Principles of Algebra, by Way of Introduction. London, 1769.

Napier, M. *Memoirs of John Napier of Merchiston, his Lineage, Life, and Times, with a History of the Invention of Logarithms.* Edinburgh and London, 1834.

———. 'Introduction', in id. (ed.). *De Arte Logistica Joannis Naperi Merchistonii Baronis Libri qui supersunt.* Edinburgh, 1839, iii–xciv.

———. *The Life and Times of Montrose Illustrated from Original Manuscripts, Including Family Papers; With Portraits and Autographs.* Edinburgh, 1840.

'Narrative of a Country Family Raised to Sudden Affluence by the Arrival of a Son from India, and of the Taxes to which the Enjoyment of Its Wealth Is Subject, in a Letter from Marjory Mushroom'. *The Lounger* 36 (8 October 1785). Reprinted in *The Lounger: A Periodical Paper, Published at Edinburgh in the Years 1785 and 1786. By the Authors of The Mirror*, 3 vols, 4th edn. London, 1788, vol. 2, 1–8.

'Narrative of the Happiness of a Virtuous and Benevolent East Indian; in a Letter from John Truman'. *The Lounger* 44, 3 December 1785, Reprinted in *The Lounger: A Periodical Paper, Published at Edinburgh in the Years 1785 and 1786. By the Authors of The Mirror*, 3 vols, 4th edn. London, 1788, vol. 2, 74–84.

The New Statistical Account of Scotland, by the Minsters of the Respective Parishes, under the Superintendence of a Committee of the Society for the Benefit of the Sons and Daughters of the Clergy, 15 vols. Edinburgh, 1845.

Nichelson, W. *Sundry Remarks and Observations, Made in a Voyage to the East-Indies … with the Necessary Directions for Sailing to and from India, and into the Several Ports and Harbours Thereof.* The Second Edition, with Additions. London, 1773.

Political Geography: Introduction to the Statistical Tables of the Principal Kingdoms and States in Europe. London and Dublin, 1789.

Prichard, J.C. *The Eastern Origin of the Celtic Nations Proved by a Comparison of their Dialects with the Sanskrit, Greek, Latin and Teutonic Languages; Forming a Supplement to Researches into the Physical History of Mankind.* Oxford, 1831.

'Proceedings of the Anniversary Meeting of the Royal Asiatic Society Held on Saturday, the 9th of May 1835'. *Journal of the Royal Asiatic Society of Great Britain and Ireland* 2(2) (1835), ix–xx.

'Proceedings of the Anniversary Meeting of the Royal Asiatic Society Held on Saturday, the 9th of May 1835'. *Madras Journal of Literature and Science* 4 (12) (1836) 168–81.

'Proceedings of the Anniversary Meeting of the Royal Asiatic Society Held on the 6th of May 1837'. *Journal of the Royal Asiatic Society of Great Britain and Ireland* 4(2) (1837), xvii–xlvi.

'Proceedings of the Twenty-Sixth Anniversary Meeting of the Society, Held on the 12th of May, 1849'. *Journal of the Royal Asiatic Society of Great Britain and Ireland* 11 (1849), i–xxiii.

Raffles, S. *Memoir of the Life and Public Services of Sir Thomas Stamford Raffles, F.R.S. &c. Particularly in the Government of Java 1811–1816, and of Bencoolen and its Dependencies, 1817–1824; With … Selections from his Correspondence.* London, 1830.

Raffles, T.S. *Substance of a Minute Recorded by the Hon. Thomas Stamford Raffles … on the 11th February 1814; on the Introduction of an Improved System of Internal Management and the Establishment of a Land Rental on the Island of Java.* London, 1814.

———. *The History of Java*, 2nd edn., 2 vols. London, 1830.

Rennell, J. *Description of the Roads in Bengal and Bahar.* London, 1778.

————. *A Bengal Atlas: Containing Maps of the Theatre of War and Commerce on that Side of Hindoostan: Compiled from the Original Surveys; and Published by Order of the Honourable the Court of Directors for the Affairs of the East India Company.* [London], 1781.

————. *Memoir of a Map of Hindoostan; or the Mogul's Empire: with an Examination of Some Positions in the Former System of Indian Geography; and Some Illustrations of the Present One: and a Complete Index of Names to the Map.* London, 1783.

————. *Memoir of a Map of Hindoostan; or the Mogul Empire: with an Introduction, Illustrative of the Geography and Present Division of that Country; and a Map of the Countries Situated between the Heads of the Indian Rivers, and the Caspian Sea. ... To which is Added, an Appendix ...* The Second Edition. With Very Considerable Additions, and Many Corrections: and a Supplementary Map. London, 1792.

————. *Memoir of a Map of the Peninsula of India; from the latest Authorities Exhibiting its Natural and Political Divisions ... the Latter, Conformable to the Treaty of Seringapatam, in March 1792.* London, 1793.

————. 'The Journals of James Rennell, First Surveyor General of India'. Edited by T.H.D. LaTouche. *Memoirs of the Asiatic Society of Bengal* 3 (1914). 95–248.

Resolutions Reported on Monday the 14th day of March 1803, from the Committee of the Whole House, to Whom It Was Referred to Consider of the Several Accounts and Papers which Were Presented to the House, upon Tuesday Last, Relating to the Revenues of the East India Company; and to Whom Were Referred, the Several Accounts and Papers Relating Thereto, which Were Presented to the House Upon the 18th Day of June, in the Last Session of the Last Parliament, (House of Commons Papers; Accounts and Papers 1802–1803 (60), IX, 157).

'Review: Historical Sketches of the South of India, in an Attempt to Trace the History of Mysúr, ... By Lieut. Col. Mark Wilks'. *Edinburgh Review* 18(36) (1811), 343–70.

'Review of New Publications: Transactions of the Literary Society of Bombay ..., Vol. III'. *Gentleman's Magazine* 95(2) (August/October 1825), 137–40, 335–37.

'Review: The Transactions of the Literary Society of Madras Part 1, London 1827'. *Asiatic Journal and Monthly Register for British India and its Dependencies* 26(153) (1828), 332f.

Ritter, C. *Erdkunde von Asien*, vol. IV, I, Section 2. Berlin, 1836.

Robertson, W. *An Historical Disquisition Concerning the Knowledge which the Ancients Had of India; and the Progress of Trade with That Country prior to the Discovery of the Passage to It by the Cape of Good Hope: With an Appendix, Containing Observations on ... the Indians.* London, 1791.

Ross, C. (ed.). *Correspondence of Charles, first Marquis Cornwallis,* 3 vols. London, 1859.

Sandeman H.D. (ed.). *Selections from Calcutta Gazettes of the Years 1806 to 1815 Inclusive, Showing the Political and Social Condition of the English in India upwards of Fifty Years Ago.* Calcutta, 1868.

[Scott J.]. *An Historical and Political View of the Decan, South of the Kistnah; Including a Sketch of the Extent and Revenue of the Mysorean Dominions, as Possessed by Tippoo Sultaun, to the Period of his Latest Acquisitions of Territory.* London, 1791.

Scott, W. *Minstrelsy of the Scottish Border Consisting of Historical and Romantic Ballads, Collected in the Southern Counties of Scotland; with a Few of Modern Date, Founded upon Local Tradition.* 1801/1802. 5th edn., 3 vols. London and Edinburgh, 1812.

————. *Waverly; or `Tis Sixty Years Since.* 1814. Reprint edited by Claire Lamont. Oxford, 1986.

[Scott, W.]. Biographical Memoir of John Leyden, M.D. *Edinburgh Annual Register* 4(19) (1811), xli–lxviii.

Seely, J.B. *The Wonders of Elora, or The Narrative of a Journey to the Temples and Dwellings Excavated out of a Mountain of Granite and Extending Upwards of a Mile and a Quarter*, 2nd edn. London, 1825.

Shaw, L. 'The Family of Brodie', in id., *The History of the Province of Moray … By the Reverend Mr Lachlan Shaw, Minister of the Gospel at Elgin*. Edinburgh, 1775.

Shore, J., Lord Teignmouth. *Sketches of the Coasts and Islands of Scotland and of the Isle of Man: Descriptive of the Scenery of Those Regions*, 2 vols. London, 1836.

———. *Reminiscences of Many Years*, 2 vols. Edinburgh, 1878.

Sinclair, J. *The Statistical Account of Scotland drawn up from the Communications of the Ministers of the Different Parishes*, 21 vols. Edinburgh, 1791–1799.

———. *Sketch of an Introduction to the Proposed Analysis of the Statistical Account of Scotland Containing Observations on the Nature and Principles of Statistical Enquiries, and the Advantages to be Derived from Them*. London, 1802.

———. *An Account of the Highland Society of London, from its Establishment in May 1778, to the Commencement of the Year 1813*. London, 1813.

———. *Analysis of the Statistical Account of Scotland; with a General View of the History of that Country and Discussions on Important Branches of Political Economy*, 2 vols. Edinburgh, 1825–1826.

———. *The Correspondence of the Right Honourable Sir John Sinclair, with Reminiscences of the most Distinguished Characters Who Have Appeared in Great Britain, and in Foreign Countries, during the Last Fifty Years*, 2 vols. London, 1831.

[Srinivasia]. 'Extracts from the Journal of a Learned Native Traveller of a Route from Calcutta to Gaya in 1820, Translated from the Original'. *Oriental Magazine and Calcutte Review* 1 (1823), 769–75 and 2 (1823), 68–73.

Stewart, D. *Elements of the Philosophy of the Human Mind*, 3 vols. London and Edinburgh 1792–1827.

Stewart, D. Earl of Buchan, and W. Minto. *An Account of the Life, Writings and Inventions of John Napier of Merchiston*. Perth, 1787.

Stocqueler, J.H. *The Oriental Interpreter and Treasury of East India Knowledge: A Companion to the Handbook of British India*. London, 1848.

Sullivan, J. *Tracts upon India; Written in the Years, 1779, 1780, and 1788… With Subsequent Observations*. London, 1794.

Supplementary Despatches and Memoranda of Arthur, Duke of Wellington, 15 vols. London, 1858–1872.

'Surveys in India'. *Asiatic Journal and Monthly Register for British India and its Dependencies* 27(157) (January 1829), 56.

'Table of Pay and Allowances for a Month of Thirty Days, to the Officers in the Madras Establishment', *General Orders by Government, Fort St. George, Twelfth July M.DCC. XCVI*. Madras, 1796, 13.

Tavernier, J.B. *The Six Voyages of John Baptiste Tavernier, Baron of Aubonne, through Turkey, into Persia and the East-Indies, for the Space of Forty Years Giving an Account of the Present State of those Countries …: to Which is Added, a New Description of the Seraglio Made English by J.P.; Added Likewise, A Voyage into the Indies, &c. by an English Traveller, Never Before Printed, Publish'd by Dr Daniel Cox*. London, 1677.

Taylor, W. *Catalogue Raisonnée of Oriental Manuscripts in the Library of the (Late) College, Fort St. George, Now in Charge of the Board of Examiners*, 3 vols. Madras, 1857–1862.

Teroovercadoo Mootiah, 'A Historical and Chronological Journal, of the Life of Teroovercadoo Mootiah, Together with Notes to the Terms Therein Occurred, and Also with a Letter to Mr Ross Thereunto Prefixed, Jan. 24, 1795', in A. Dalrymple (ed.), *Oriental Repertory* 2(4). London, [1797?], 559–76.

Thévenot, J. de, *The Travels of Monsieur de Thevenot into the Levant: In Three Parts. Viz. into I. Turkey. II. Persia. III. The East-Indies. Newly Done out of French*. London, 1687.

'Third Letter from Marjory Mushroom, Giving an Account of Her Feelings on Her Return to the Country'. *The Lounger* 62 (8 April 1786). Reprinted in *The Lounger: A Periodical Paper, Published at Edinburgh in the years 1785 and 1786. By the Authors of The Mirror*, 3 vols, 4th edn. London, 1788, vol. 2, 253–62.

Thorn, W. *The Conquest of Java: Nineteenth-century Java Seen through the Eyes of a Soldier of the British Empire*. [1815] Edited by John Bastin. Hong Kong 2004.

Transactions of the Literary Society of Bombay 3. 1823.

Vergil, *Aeneis*. Latin–German edited by Johannes Götte, Munich and Zurich 1988.

Walker, J. 'Report to the Assembly 1765, Concerning the State of the Highlands and Islands'. *The Scots Magazine* 28(12) (1766), 680–89.

———. 'An Oeconomical History of the Hebrides or Western Islands of Scotland' (1763). *Transactions of the Gaelic Society of Inverness* 24 (1899–1901), 120–39.

Wellesley, R. 'Copy of the Letter, Dated the 19th of July 1804, from the Governor General in Council of Bengal, to the Government of Fort St. George, Relative to the Interior Government of the Country, and the Provision of Goods for the Company's Investment', in *Papers relating to East India Affairs, ordered, by the House of Commons, to be Printed, 12 May 1813*, [London, 1813], 91–103.

Wilks, M. *Report on the Interior Administration, Resources, and Expenditure of the Government of Mysoor*. Fort William, 1805.

———. *Historical Sketches of the South of India in an Attempt to Trace the History of Mysore*, 3 vols. London, 1810–1817.

Wilson, H.H. *A Descriptive Catalogue of the Oriental Manuscripts and Other Articles Illustrative of the Literature, History, Statistics and Antiquities of the South of India, Collected by the Late Lieut.-Col. Colin Mackenzie, Surveyor General of India*, 2 vols. Calcutta, 1828.

———. 'Description of Select Coins, from Originals or Drawings in the Possession of the Asiatic Society'. *Asiatic Researches* 17 (1832), 559–606.

———. 'Account of the Foe Kúe Ki, or Travels of Fa Hian in India, Translated from the Chinese by M. Remusat'. *Journal of the Royal Asiatic Society of Great Britain and Ireland* 5(1) (1839), 108–40.

'Zemindary and Ryotwari Collections – Native Servants. General Return of Native Revenue Officers in the Pay of the Government of Madras, 1818–1819'. *Asiatic Journal and Monthly Register for British India and its Dependencies* 27(162) (1829), 679.

Secondary Sources (from 1859)

Ahuja, R. 'Unterwegs zur Kolonialmetropole: Madras in der zweiten Hälfte des 18. Jahrhunderts', in D. Rothermund (ed.), *Periplus 1996: Jahrbuch für Außereuropäische Geschichte*. Münster, 1996, 61–75.

———. *Die Erzeugung kolonialer Staatlichkeit und das Problem der Arbeit: Eine Studie zur Sozialgeschichte der Stadt Madras und ihres Hinterlandes zwischen 1750 und 1800* (Beiträge zur Südasienforschung, vol. 183). Stuttgart, 1999.

Anderson, B. *Imagined Communities: Reflections on the Origin and Spread of Nationalism.* Revised edn. London and New York, 2006.

Anderson, G.M., W.F. Shughart II and R.D. Tollison. 'Adam Smith in the Customhouse'. *Journal of Political Economy* 93(4) (1985), 740–59.

Anjaneyulu, M.S.R. 'The English Acquisition of Chicacole Circar'. *Journal of Indian History* 56(1–3) (1983), 127–34.

Archer, M. *British Drawings in the India Office Library*, 2 vols. London, 1969.

———. *India and British Portraiture, 1770–1825*. London, 1979.

Armstrong, G.G. 'The Port of Madras for Three Hundred Years', in *The Madras Tercentenary Commemoration Volume*. London, Bombay, Calcutta and Madras, 1939, 209–16.

Arnold, D. 'European Orphans and Vagrants in India in the Nineteenth Century'. *Journal of Imperial and Commonwealth History* 7 (1979), 104–27.

———. *Science, Technology and Medicine in Colonial India* (The New Cambridge History of India pt. 3 vol. 5). Cambridge, 2000.

———. *The Tropics and the Travelling Gaze: India, Landscape and Science 1800–1856.* Delhi, 2005.

Baasner, R. '"Unser Staatsgeographus ist beständig auf Reisen": Zur Ausdifferenzierung von Reisebeschreibung und Geographie 1750–1800', in M. Maurer (ed.), *Neue Impulse der Reiseforschung*. Berlin, 1999, 249–65.

Baily, T.G. 'Review: Camanistan i Shu'arā by Lachmi Narayan Shafiq, Edited by Abdul Haq, Aurungabad 1928'. *Bulletin of the School of Oriental Studies* 5(4) (1930), 927f.

Ballantyne, T. *Orientalism and Race: Aryansim and the British Empire.* Houndsmills and New York, 2002.

Barrow, I.J. *Making History, Drawing Territory: British Mapping in India, c. 1756–1905.* New Delhi, 2003.

Barrow, I. and D.E. Haynes. 'The Colonial Transition: South Asia, 1780–1840'. *Modern Asian Studies* 38(3) (2004), 469–78.

Bastin, J.S. 'Colonel Colin Mackenzie and Javanese Antiquities'. *Bijdragen tot de Taal-, Land en Volkenkunde* 109 (1953), 273–75.

———. *Raffles' Ideas on the Land Rent System in Java and the Mackenzie Land Tenure Commission* (Verhandelingen van het Koninklijk Instituut voor Taal-, Land- en Volkenkunde, vol. 14). s-Gravenhage, 1954.

———. *The Native Policies of Sir Thomas Stamford Raffles in Java and Sumatra: An Economic Interpretation.* Oxford, 1957.

———. *Sir Thomas Stamford Raffles: With an Account of the Raffles-Minto Manuscript Collection Presented to the India Office Library [London] on 17 July 1969 by the Malaysia-Singapore Commercial Association.* Liverpool, 1969.

————. 'John Leyden and the Publication of the "Malay Annals" (1821)'. *Journal of the Malaysian Branch of the Royal Asiatic Society* 75(2) (2002), 101–6.

————. 'Introduction' in W. Thorn, *The Conquest of Java: Nineteenth-century Java seen through the Eyes of a Soldier of the British Empire.* [1815] Edited by John Bastin. Hong Kong, 2004, xiv–xxiv.

Bayly, C.A. *Indian Society and the Making of the British Empire* (The New Cambridge History of India, pt. 2 vol.1). Cambridge, 1988.

————. *Empire and Information: Intelligence Gathering and Social Communication in India, 1780-1870.* Cambridge, 1996.

Bayly, S. *Saints, Goddesses and Kings: Muslims and Christians in South Indian Society, 1700-1900.* Cambridge, 1989.

Beaglehole, T.H. *Thomas Munro and the Development of Administrative Policy in Madras, 1792-1818.* Cambridge, 1966.

Behrisch, L. 'Vermessen, Zählen, Berechnen des Raums im 18. Jahrhundert', in id. (ed.), *Vermessen, Zählen, Berechnen: Die politische Ordnung des Raums im 18. Jahrhundert.* Frankfurt and New York, 2006, 9–14.

Berry, C.J. *Social Theory of the Scottish Enlightenment.* Edinburgh, 1997.

Bhattacharya, D. and R.D. Roy. 'Khanasumari Records and the Statistical System of India'. *Indian Historical Records Commission, Proceedings of the 45th Session* (1977), 227–37.

Biggs, M. 'Putting the State on the Map: Cartography, Territory and European State Formation'. *Comparative Studies in Society and History* 41(2) (1999), 374–405.

Black, J. *British Foreign Policy in an Age of Revolutions, 1783–1793.* Cambridge, 1994.

Blake, D.M. 'Colin Mackenzie: Collector Extraordinary'. *British Library Journal* 17(2) (1991), 128–50.

Bourdieu, P. 'Ökonomisches Kapital, Kulturelles Kapital, Soziales Kapital', in R. Kreckel (ed.), *Soziale Ungleichheiten.* Göttingen, 1983, 183–98.

————. 'Die biographische Illusion', in id., *Praktische Vernunft: Zur Theorie des Handelns.* Frankfurt/Main, 1988, 75–83.

Bourne, J.M. *Patronage and Society in Nineteenth-Century England.* London, 1986.

Bowen, H.V. 'British India, 1765–1813: The Metropolitan Context', in P.J. Marshall (ed.), *The Oxford History of the British Empire, vol. 2: The Eighteenth Century.* Oxford and New York, 1998, 540–44.

————. *The Business of Empire: The East India Company and Imperial Britain, 1756–1833.* Cambridge, 2006.

Bowen, M. *Empiricism and Geographical Thought: From Francis Bacon to Alexander von Humboldt.* Cambridge, 1981.

Breckenridge C.A. and P. van der Veer (eds). *Orientalism and the Postcolonial Predicament: Perspectives on South Asia.* Philadelphia, 1993.

Brewer, J. 'Servants of the Public', in id. and E. Hellmuth (eds), *Rethinking Leviathan: The Eighteenth-Century State in Britain and Germany.* Oxford, 1999, 127–47.

Brittlebank, K. *Tipu Sultan's Search for Legitimacy: Islam and Kingship in a Hindu Domain.* Oxford, 1997.

Brooke J. and L. Namier (eds). *The House of Commons 1754–1790,* 3 vols. London, 1964.

Bryant, G.J. 'Officers of the East India Company's Army in the Days of Clive and Hastings'. *Journal of Imperial and Commonwealth History* 6(3) (1978), 203–27.

————. 'Scots in India in the Eighteenth Century'. *Scottish Historical Review* 64(1) (1985), 22–41.

————. 'Indigenous Mercenaries in the Service of European Imperialists: The Case of Sepoys in the Early British Army, 1750–1800'. *War in History* 7(1) (2000), 2–28.

Buisseret, D. (ed.). *Monarchs, Ministers, and Maps: The Emergence of Cartography as a Tool of Government in Early Modern Europe*. Chicago, 1992.

Bumsted, J.M. *The People's Clearance: Highland Emigration to British North America, 1770–1815*. Edinburgh, 1982.

Burke, B. *A Genealogical and Heraldic Dictionary of the Landed Gentry of Great Britain and Ireland*, 2 vols., 4th edn. London, 1862f.

Cain, R.J.P. *The Cadastral Map in the Service of the State: A History of Property Making*. Chicago and London, 1984.

Callahan, R. *The East India Company and Army Reform, 1783–1798*. Cambridge, MA., 1972.

Carey, P. 'Changing Javanese Perceptions of the Chinese Communities in Central Java, 1755–1825'. *Indonesia* 37 (1984), 1–47.

Carnall G. and C. Nicholson (eds). *The Impeachment of Warren Hastings: Papers from a Bicentenary Commemoration*. Edinburgh, 1989.

Chauduri, S.B. *History of the Gazetteers of India*. New Delhi, 1965.

Cohn, B.S. 'The Transformation of Objects into Artifacts, Antiquities and Art in Nineteenth-Century India', in id., *Colonialism and its Forms of Knowledge: The British in India*. Oxford, 1996, 76–105.

Colley, L. *Britons: Forging the Nation 1707–1837*. London, 1994.

Conner, [P.E.] and [B.S.] Ward. *Memoir of the Survey of the Travancore and Cochin States Executed under the Superintendance of Lieutenants Ward and Conner*, vol. 1. Reprinted with Corrections and Biographical Sketch of Ward and Conner. Travancore, 1863. Reprint, Trivandrum, 1994.

————. *A Descriptive Memoir of Malabar*. 1905. Reprint, Thiruvananthapuram, 1995.

Cook, A.S. 'Establishing the Sea Routes to India and China: Stages in the Development of Hydrographical Knowledge', in H.V. Bowen, M. Lincoln and N. Rigby (eds), *The Worlds of the East India Company*. Woodbridge, Suffolk, 2002, 119–36.

Cooper, R.G.S. *The Anglo-Maratha Campaign and the Contest for India: The Struggle for Control of the South Asian Military Economy*. Cambridge, 2003.

Coull, J.R. 'The Development of Herring Fishing in the Outer Hebrides'. *International Journal of Maritime History* 15(2) (2003), 21–42.

Craib, R.B. 'A National Metaphysics: State Fixations, National Maps, and the Geo-Historical Imagination in Nineteenth-Century Mexico'. *Hispanic American Historical Review* 82(1) (2002), 33–68.

————. *Cartographic Mexico: A History of State Fixations and Fugitive Landscapes*. Durham and London, 2004.

Crowley, J.E. 'Neo-Mercantilism and the Wealth of Nations: British Commercial Policy after the American Revolution'. *Historical Journal* 33 (2) (1990), 339–60.

Das, S.K. *Sahibs and Munshis: An Account of the College of Fort William*. Calcutta, Allahabad, Bombay and Delhi, 1978.

Datta, K. 'James Mackintosh, Learned Societies in India, and Enlightenment Ideas', in J.J. Carer and J.H. Pittcock (eds), *Aberdeen and the Enlightenment*. Aberdeen, 1987, 40–51.

Davis, D.R. 'Edward Davies, Paradigm Shift in Nineteenth Century Celtic Studies', in *History of Linguistics 1996: Selected Papers from the Seventh International Conference on the History of the Language Sciences*, 2 vols. Amsterdam and Philadelphia, 1999, vol. 1, 175–80.

Day, T. *Fluid Iron: State Formation in Southeast Asia*. Honolulu, 2002.

Desmond, R. *The European Discovery of the Indian Flora*. Oxford, 1992.

Devine, T.M. 'Landlordism and Highland Emigration', in id. (ed.), *Scottish Emigration and Scottish Society*. Edinburgh, 1992, 84–103.

———. *Clanship to Crofters' War: The Social Transformation of the Scottish Highlands*. Manchester and New York, 1994.

———. *Scotland's Empire 1600–1815*. London, 2003.

Devine, T.M. and J.M. Mackenzie (eds). *Scotland and the British Empire* (Oxford History of the British Empire Companion Series). Oxford, 2011.

Dirks, N.B. 'The Invention of Caste: Civil Society in Colonial India'. *Social Analysis* 25 (1989), 42–52.

———. 'Introduction: Colonialism and Culture', in id. (ed.), *Colonialism and Culture*. Ann Arbor, 1992, 1–25.

———. 'Colonial Histories and Native Informants: Biography of an Archive', in C.A. Breckenridge and P. van der Veer (eds), *Orientalism and the Postcolonial Predicament: Perspectives on South Asia*. Philadelphia, 1993, 211–32.

———. 'Guiltless Spoliations: Picturesque Beauty, Colonial Knowledge and Colin Mackenzie's Survey of India', in C.B. Asher and T.R. Metcalf (eds), *Perceptions of South Asia's Visual Past*. New Delhi, 1994, 279–313.

———. 'Foreword' in B.S. Cohn, *Colonialism and its Forms of Knowledge: The British in India*. Oxford, 1996, ix–xvii.

———. 'Is Vice Versa? Historical Anthropologies and Anthropological Histories', in T.J. McDonald (ed.), *The Historic Turn in the Human Sciences*. Ann Arbor, 1996, 17–51.

———. *Castes of Mind: Colonialism and the Making of Modern India*. Princeton and Oxford, 2001.

———. 'Colin Mackenzie. Autobiography of an Archive', in T.R. Trautmann (ed.), *The Madras School of Orientalism: Producing Knowledge in Colonial South India*. Oxford and New York, 2009, 29–47.

Dodgshon, R.A. 'Coping with Risk: Subsistence Crisis in the Scottish Islands and Highlands, 1600–1800'. *Rural History* 17(1) (2004), 1–25.

Dodson, M.S. *Orientalism, Empire and National Culture India, 1770–1880*. Basingstoke, 2007.

Dodwell, H.H. 'The Carnatic, 1761–84', in id. (ed.), *The Cambridge History of India, vol. 5: British India 1497–1858*. Cambridge, 1929, 273–94.

Donnelly, T. 'The King's Custom Administration in Aberdeen, 1750–1815'. *Northern Scotland* 16 (1996), 187–98.

Drayton, R. 'Knowledge and Empire', in P.J. Marshall (ed.), *The Oxford History of the British Empire, vol. 2: The Eighteenth Century*. Oxford and New York, 1998, 231–52.

———. *Nature's Government: Science, Imperial Britain, and the 'Improvement' of the World*. New Haven and London, 2000.

Drescher, H.W. *Themen und Formen des periodischen Essays im späten 18. Jahrhundert: Untersuchungen zu den schottischen Wochenschriften The Mirror und The Lounger*. Frankfurt am Main, 1971.

———. 'Introduction', in id. (ed.), *Literature and Literati: The Literary Correspondence and Notebooks of Henry Mackenzie*, 2 vols. Frankfurt am Main, 1989–99, vol. 1, 29–39.

Edney, M. 'The Atlas of India 1823–1947. The Natural History of a Topographic Map Series'. *Cartographica* 28(4) (1991), 59–91.

———. 'British Military Education, Mapmaking, and Military "Map Mindedness" in the later Enlightenment'. *Cartographic Journal* 31(1) (1994), 14–20.

———. 'Mathematical Cosmography and the Social Ideology of British Cartography, 1780–1820'. *Imago Mundi* 46 (1994), 101–16.

———. *Mapping an Empire: The Geographical Construction of British India, 1765–1843.* Chicago and London, 1997.

———. 'Reconsidering Enlightenment Geography and Map Making: Reconnaissance, Mapping, Archive', in D.N. Livingstone and C.W. Withers (eds), *Geography and Enlightenment.* Chicago and London, 1999, 165–98.

Elliott, J.H. *Empires of the Atlantic World: Britain and Spain in America 1492–1830.* New Haven and London, 2006.

Emerson, R.L. 'Science and the Origins and Concerns of the Scottish Enlightenment'. *History of Science* 26(4) (1988), 33–66.

———. 'Sir Robert Sibbald, Kt, the Royal Society of Scotland and the Origins of the Scottish Enlightenment'. *Annals of Science* 45(1) (1988), 41–72.

Emmet, R.C. 'The Gazetteers of India: Their Origins and Development during the Nineteenth Century'. Master's thesis, University of Chicago, 1976.

Escolar, M. 'Exploration, Cartography and the Modernization of State Power'. *International Social Science Journal* 151 (1997), 55–75.

Ethé, H. *Catalogue of Persian Manuscripts in the Library of the India Office,* 2 vols. Oxford, 1903–1937.

Evelynola, E. *The Organization of the English Customs System 1696–1786.* Newton Abbot, 1968.

Farrington, A.J. *Catalogue of East India Company Ships' Journals and Logs 1600–1834.* London, 1999.

Ferris, I. 'Melancholy, Memory and the "Narrative Situation" of History in post-Enlightenment Scotland', in L. Davis, I. Duncan and J. Sorensen (eds), *Scotland and the Borders of Romanticism.* Cambridge, 2004, 77–93.

———. 'Printing the Past: Walter Scott's Bannatyne Club and the Antiquarian Document'. *Romanticism* 11(2) (2005), 143–57.

Fisher, M.H. 'Indirect Rule in the British Empire: The Foundations of the Residency System in India (1764–1858)'. *Modern Asian Studies* 18(3) (1984), 393–428.

———. 'The Resident in Court Ritual, 1764–1858'. *Modern Asian Studies* 24(3) (1990), 419–58.

———. *Indirect Rule in India: Residents and the Residency System 1764–1858.* Delhi, 1991.

Förster, S. *Handelsmonopol und Territorialherrschaft: Die Krise der East India Company 1784–1813* (Kleine Beiträge zur europäischen Überseegeschichte vol. 9). Bamberg, 1991.

———. *Die mächtigen Diener der East India Company: Ursachen und Hintergründe der britischen Expansionspolitik in Südasien, 1793–1819.* Stuttgart, 1992.

Foucault, M. 'Governmentality', in G. Burchell, C. Gordon and P. Miller (eds), *The Foucault Effect: Studies in Governmentality.* Chicago, 1991, 87–104.

———. *Geschichte der Gouvernementalität I. Sicherheit Territorium, Bevölkerung: Vorlesung am College du France 1977–1978.* Edited by M. Sennelart. Frankfurt am Main, 2004.

Francesconi, D. 'William Robertson on Historical Causation and unintended Consequences'. *Storia della Storiografia* 36 (1999), 55–80.

Fraser, T.G. 'India 1780–86', in P. Roebuck (ed.), *Macartney of Lisanoure, 1737–1806*. Belfast, 1983, 154–215.

Frenzel, C.A. *Major James Rennell, der Schöpfer der neueren englischen Geographie: Ein Beitrag zur Geschichte der Erdkunde.* Leipzig, 1904.

Francis, W. *Madura* (Madras District Gazetteers), 2 vols. Madras, 1906.

Fry, H.T. *Alexander Dalrymple (1737–1808) and the Expansion of British Trade.* London, 1970.

Fry, M. *The Dundas Despotism.* Edinburgh, 1992.

Frykenberg, R.E. *Guntur District 1788–1848: A History of Local Influence and Central Authority in South India.* Oxford, 1965.

———. 'Village Strength in South India', in id. (ed.), *Land Control and Social Structure in Indian History.* Madison, Milwaukee and London, 1969, 227–47.

———. 'The Social Morphology of Madras', in K. Ballhatchet (ed.), *Changing South Asia*, 5 vols. London, 1984, vol. 3, 21–41.

Furber, H. *Henry Dundas: First Viscount Melville 1742–1811. Political Manager of Scotland, Statesman, Administrator of British India.* London, 1931.

———. 'Trade and Politics in Madras and Bombay', in A. Siddiqi (ed.), *Trade and Finance in Colonial India, 1750–1860.* Oxford, Delhi and New York, 1995, 66–98.

———. 'The United Company of Merchants of England trading to the East Indies, 1783–96', in id. *Private Fortunes and Company Profits in the India Trade.* Edited by Rosane Rocher. Aldershot, 1997, 138–47.

Fussell, G.E. 'Impressions of Sir John Sinclair, Bart., First President of the Board of Agriculture'. *Agricultural History* 25(4) (1951), 162–69.

Fyfe, A. *Science and Salvation: Evangelical Popular Science Publishing in Victorian Britain.* Chicago and London, 2004.

Garg, B.R. *Charles Grant: The Forerunner of Macauley's Educational Policy.* Ambala, Cantt, 2003.

Gascoigne, J. *Sir Joseph Banks and the English Enlightenment: Useful Knowledge and Polite Culture.* Cambridge, 1994.

———. *Science in the Service of Empire: Joseph Banks, the British State and the Uses of Science in the Age of Revolution.* Cambridge, 1998.

———. 'The Royal Society and the Emergence of Science as an Instrument of State Policy'. *British Journal for the History of Science* 32(2) (1999), 171–84.

Gibbs, J. 'Archaeology in India'. *Society of Arts Journal* 34 (1885/1886), 555–64.

Gilbert, A.N. 'Recruitment and Reform in the East India Company Army, 1760–1800'. *Journal of British Studies* 15(1) (1975), 89–111.

Gogate P.P. and B. Arunchalam, 'Area Maps in Maratha Cartography: A Study in Native Maps of Western India'. *Imago Mundi* 50 (1998), 126–40.

Gole, S. *Early Maps of India.* New Delhi, 1976.

———. *India within the Ganghes.* Delhi, 1983.

———. *A Series of Early Printed Maps of India in Facsimile*, 2nd edn. Delhi, 1984.

Gordon, S. and J.F. Richards. 'Kinship and *pargana* in Eighteenth Century Kandesh'. *Indian Economic and Social History Review* 22(4) (1985), 371–98.

Gosh, D. *Sex and the Family in Colonial India.* Cambridge, 2006.

Gray, M. 'The Kelp Industry in the Highlands and Islands'. *Economic History Review*, 2nd ser., 4(2) (1951), 197–209.

Grout, A. 'Geology and India, 1775–1805: An Episode in Colonial Science'. *South Asia Research* 10(1) (1990), 1–18.

———. 'Geology and India, 1770–1851: A Study in the Methods and Motivations of Colonial Science'. Ph.D. dissertation, School of Oriental and African Studies, London, 1995.

Grove, R.H. *Green Imperialism: Colonial Expansion, Tropical Island Edens and the Origins of Environmentalism, 1600–1860*. Cambridge, 1995.

Guggerli D. and D. Speich. *Topografien der Nation: Politik, kartografische Ordnung und Landschaft im 19. Jahrhundert*. Zurich, 2002.

Guha, R. *A Rule of Property for Bengal: An Essay on the Idea of the Permanent Settlement*. Paris, 1963.

Guha, R. (ed.). *Social Ecology. Oxford in India Readings in Sociology and Social Anthropology*. New Delhi, 1994.

Guha, S. 'The Frontiers of Memory: What the Marathas Remembered of Vijayanagara'. *Modern Asian Studies* 43(1) (2009), 269–88.

———. 'The Politics of Identity and Enumeration in India c. 1690–1990'. *Comparative Studies in Society and History* 45(1) (2003), 148–67.

Guha-Thakurta, T. 'The Museumised Relic: Archaeology and the first Museum of Colonial India'. *Indian Economic and Social History Review* 34(1) (1997), 21–51.

Habib, I. *An Atlas of the Mughal Empire: Political and Economic Maps with detailed Notes, Bibliography and Index*. Delhi, Oxford and New York, 1982.

———. 'Introduction: An Essay on Haidar Ali and Tipu Sultan', in id. (ed.), *Confronting Colonialism: Resistance and Modernisation under Haidar Ali and Tipu Sultan*. London, 2002, xvii–xlvii.

Hackman, R. *Ships of the East India Company*. Gravesend, 2001.

Häkli, J. 'In the Territory of Knowledge: State-centred Discourses and the Construction of Society'. *Progress in Human Geography* 15 (2001), 403–22.

Hannah, M.G. *Governmentality and the Mastery of Territory in Nineteenth-Century America*. Cambridge, 2000.

Harfield, A. *British and Indian Armies in the East Indies 1685–1935*. Chippenham, 1984.

Hargraves, N. 'The "Progress of Ambition": Character, Narrative, and Philosophy in the Works of William Robertson'. *Journal of the History of Ideas* 63(2) (2002), 262–82.

Harley, J.B. 'Maps, Knowledge, and Power', in D. Cosgrove and S. Daniels (eds), *The Iconography of Landscape: Essays on the Symbolic Representation, Design and Use of Past Environments* (Cambridge Studies in Historical Geography vol. 9). Cambridge, 1988, 277–312.

———. 'Deconstructing the Map'. *Cartographica* 26(2) (1989), 1–20.

Hawes, C.J. *Poor Relations: The Making of a Eurasian Community in British India 1773–1833*. Richmond, 1996.

Heathcote, T.A. *The Military in British India: The Development of British Land Forces in South Asia, 1600–1947*. Manchester, 1995.

Hechter, M. *Internal Colonialism: The Celtic Fringe in British National Development, 1536–1966*. London, 1975.

Hemingway, F.R. *Gódávari* (Madras District Gazetteers). Madras, 1907.

Hind, R.J. 'The Internal Colonial Concept'. *Comparative Studies in Society and History* 26(3) (1984), 543–68.

Hintze, A. *The Mughal Empire and its Decline: An Interpretation of the Sources of Social Power*. Aldershot, Hampshire, and Brookfield, Vermont, 1997.

Hoare, M.R. *The Quest for the True Figure of the Earth: Ideas and Expeditions in Four Centuries of Geodesy*. Aldershot and Burlington, Vermont, 2005.

Hoffmann, P. *Anton Friedrich Büsching (1724–1793): Ein Leben im Zeitalter der Aufklärung*. Berlin, 2000.

Home, R.W. 'The Royal Society and the Empire: The Colonial and Commonwealth Fellowship, Part 1: 1731–1847'. *Notes and Records of the Royal Society of London* 56(3) (2002), 307–32.

Höpfl, H.M. 'From Savage to Scotsman: Conjectural History in the Scottish Enlightenment'. *Journal of British Studies* 17(2) (1978), 19–40.

Hotts, S. 'Alexander Beatson', in A.W. Skempton, *A Biographical Dictionary of Civil Engineers in Great Britain and Ireland, vol. 1: 1500–1830*. London, 2002, 47f.

Howes, J. 'Colin Mackenzie and the Stupa of Amaravati'. *South Asian Studies* 18 (2002), 53–65.

———. 'Colin Mackenzie, the Madras School of Orientalism and Investigations at Mahabalipuram', in T.R. Trautmann, (ed.), *The Madras School of Orientalism: Producing Knowledge in Colonial South India*. Oxford and New York, 2009, 74–109.

———. *Illustrating India: The Early Colonial Investigations of Colin Mackenzie 1784–1821*. Oxford, 2010.

Huggan, G. *Territorial Disputes: Maps and Mapping Strategies in Contemporary Canadian Fiction*. Toronto, Buffalo and London, 1994.

Ingram, E. *Commitment to Empire: Prophecies of the Great Game in Asia, 1797–1800*. Oxford, 1981.

———. 'Empire Building as Career-building: The Wellesleys in India'. *Consortium on Revolutionary Europe: Selected Papers* (1998), 453–61.

Irschick, E.F. *Dialogue and History: Constructing South India, 1795–1895*. Berkeley, Los Angeles and London, 1994.

Jaireth, S. 'Close Encounters of the Colonial Kind or Looking for Colin Mackenzie's Pandits'. *Social Alternatives* 20(4) (2001), 55–60.

Jarvis, R.C. 'The Archival History of the Customs Records' in F. Ranger (ed.), *Prisca Munimenta: Studies in Archival and Administrative History*. London, 1973, 202–14.

Jayewardene-Pillai, S. *Imperial Conversations: Indo-Britons and the Architecture of South India*. New Delhi, 2007.

Johanisson, K. 'Society in Numbers: The Debate over Quantification in 18th-Century Political Economy', in T. Frängsmyr, J.L. Heilbron and R.E. Rider (eds), *The Quantifying Spirit in the 18th Century*. Berkeley, Los Angeles and Oxford, 1990, 343–61.

Kain R.J.P. and E. Baigent. *The Cadastral Map in the Service of the State: A History of Property Mapping*. Chicago, 1992.

Kalpagam, U. 'Cartography in Colonial India'. *Economic and Political Weekly* 30(30) (1995), 87–98.

———. 'Colonial Governmentality and the "Economy"'. *Economy and Society* 29(3) (2000), 418–38.

———. 'The Colonial State and Statistical Knowledge'. *History of the Human Sciences* 13(2) (2000), 37–55.

———. 'Colonial Govermentality and the Public Sphere in India'. *Journal of Historical Sociology* 15(1) (2002), 35–58.

Katten, M. 'Manufacturing Village Identity and its Village: The View from Nineteenth-Century Andhra'. *Modern Asian Studies* 33(1) (1999), 87–120.

Kejariwal, O.P. *The Asiatic Society of Bengal and the Discovery of India's Past 1784–1838*. Delhi, 1988.

Kidd, C. *Subverting the Scottish Past: Scottish Whig Historians and the Creation of an Anglo-British Identity*. Cambridge, 1993.

———. *British Identities before Nationalism: Ethnicity and Nationhood in the Atlantic World, 1600–1800*. Cambridge, 1999.

Kincaid, D. *British Social Life in India 1608–1937*. Port Washington and London, 1971.

Kivelson, W. *Cartographies of Tsardom: The Land and its Meanings in Seventeenth Century Russia*. Ithaca and London, 2006.

Konvitz, J.W. *Cartography in France 1660–1848: Science, Engineering, and Statecraft*. Chicago and London, 1987.

———. 'The Nation-State, Paris and Cartography in Eighteenth- and Nineteenth-Century France'. *Journal of Historical Geography* 16(1) (1990), 3–16.

Kosambi M. and J.E. Brush. 'Three Colonial Port Cities in India'. *Geographical Review* 78(1) (1988), 32–47.

Koselleck, R. '"Space of Experience" and "Horizon of Expectation": Two Historical Categories', in id., *Futures Past: On the Semantics of Historical Time*. Translated and with an Introduction by Keith Tribe. New York, 2004, 255–75.

Kouznetsova, S. 'Colin Mackenzie as Collector of Javanese Manuscripts and Manuscript BL Mss Jav. 29'. *Indonesia and the Malay World* 36(106) (2008), 375–94.

Kulkarni, A.R. 'Source Material for the Study of Village Communities in Maharashtra'. *Indian Economic Social History Review* 13(4) (1976), 513–23.

Kulke, H. 'The Katakarajavamsavali: The Colonial Biography of Puri's Sanskrit Chronicle of the Year 1820'. *Indian Historical Review* 38(1) (2011), 65–75.

Kumar, D. 'The Evolution of Colonial Science in India: Natural History and the East India Company', in J.M. MacKenzie (ed.), *Imperialism and the Natural World*. Manchester, 1990, 51–66.

———. *Science and the Raj, 1857–1905*. Delhi, 1995.

Landwehr, A. *Die Erschaffung Venedigs: Raum, Bevölkerung und Mythos 1570–1750*. Paderborn and Munich, 2007.

Lawson P. and J. Phillips, '"Our Execrable Banditti": Perceptions of Nabobs in Mid-Eighteenth-Century Britain'. *Albion* 16(3) (1984), 225–41.

Leask, N. 'Towards an Anglo-Indian Poetry? The Colonial Muse in the Writings of John Leyden, Thomas Medwin and Charles D'Oyly', in B. Moore-Gilbert (ed.), *Writing India 1757–1990: The Literature of British India*. Manchester, 1996, 52–85.

———. 'Francis Wilford and the Colonial Construction of Hindu Geography, 1799–1822', in A. Gilroy (ed.), *Romantic Geographies: Discourses of Travel 1775–1844*. Manchester and New York, 2000, 204–22.

Lee, Y.S. 'A Divided Inheritance: Scott's Antiquarian Novel and the British Nation'. *English Literary History* 64(2) (1997), 537–67.

Leerssen, J. 'Celticism', in T. Brown (ed.), *Celticism*. Amsterdam and Atlanta, 1996, 1–20.

Lennon, J. *Irish Orientalism: A Literary and Intellectual History.* Syracuse, New York, 2004.

Leonard, K. 'The Hyderabad Political System and its Participants'. *Journal of Asian Studies* 30(3) (1971), 569–82.

Lewis, B. 'The Mysore Kingdom at AD 1800: Archaeological Applications of the Mysore Survey of Colin Mackenzie', in C. Jarrige and V. Lefèvre (eds), *South Asian Archaeology 2001: Proceedings of the Sixteenth International Conference of the European Association of South Asian Archaeologists, held in Collège de France, Paris, 2–6 July 2001,* 2 vols. Paris, 2005, vol. 2, 557–65.

Lewis B. and C.S. Patil. 'Chitradrurga: Spatial Patterns of a Nayaka Period Successor State in India'. *Asian Perspectives* 42(2) (2003), 267–86.

Love, H.D. *Vestiges of Old Madras, 1640–1800: Traced from the East India Company's Records Preserved at Fort St. George and the India Office and Other Sources,* 3 vols. 1918. Reprinted in New York, 1968.

Ludden, D. 'Patronage and Irrigation in Tamil Nadu: A Long-term View'. *Indian Economic Social History Review* 16(3) (1979), 347–65.

———. *Peasant History in South India.* Princeton, 1985.

———. 'Agrarian Commercialism in Eighteenth Century South India: Evidence from the 1823 Tirunelveli Census'. *Indian Economic Social History Review* 25(4) (1988), 493–519.

———. 'India's Development Regime', in N.B. Dirks (ed.), *Colonialism and Culture.* Ann Arbor, 1992, 247–87.

———. 'Orientalist Empiricism: Transformations of Colonial Knowledge', in C.A. Breckenridge and P. van der Veer, (eds), *Orientalism and the Postcolonial Predicament.* Perspectives on South Asia. Philadelphia 1993, 250–78.

MacDonald, D. *Lewis: A History of the Island.* Edinburgh, 1978.

Macinnes, A.I. *Clanship, Commerce and the House of Stuart, 1603–1788.* East Linton, 1996.

Mackenzie, A. *History of the Mackenzies with Genealogies of the Principal Families of the Name,* new revised and extended edn. Inverness, 1894.

Mackenzie, G. *A Manual of the Kistna District in the Presidency of Madras.* Madras, 1883.

MacKenzie, J.M. 'Essay and Reflection: On Scotland and the Empire'. *International History Review* 15(4) (1993), 714–39.

———. *Empires of Nature and the Natures of Empire: Imperialism, Scotland and the Environment.* East Linton, 1997.

Mackenzie, W.C. *Colonel Colin Mackenzie: First Surveyor-General of India.* Edinburgh and London, 1952.

Mackillop, A. 'Fashioning a "British" Empire: Sir Archibald Campbell of Inverneil and Madras', in A. Mackillop and S. Murdoch (eds), *Military Governors and Imperial Frontiers c1600–1800: A Study of Scotland and Empires.* Leiden and Boston, 2003, 205–31.

———. 'Europeans, Britons and Scots: Scottish Sojourning Networks and Identities in India, c.1700–1815', in A. McCarthy (ed.), *A Global Clan: Scottish Migrant Networks and Identities since the Eighteenth Century.* London, 2006, 19–47.

———. 'Locality, Nation, Empire. Scots and the Empire in Asia, c.1695–c.1813', in T.M. Devine and J.M. Mackenzie (eds), *Scotland and the British Empire* (Oxford History of the British Empire Companion Series). Oxford, 2011, 54–83.

Madan, P.L. *Indian Cartography: A Historical Perspective.* Delhi, 2001.

Makdisi, S. *Romantic Imperialism: Universal Empire and the Culture of Modernity.* Cambridge, 1998.

Mangamma, J. *Book Printing in India with Special Reference to the Contribution of European Scholars to Telugu (1746–1857).* Nellore, 1975.

Mann, M. *Flottenbau und Forstbetrieb in Indien 1794–1823.* Stuttgart, 1996.

——. *Bengalen im Umbruch: Die Herausbildung des britischen Kolonialstaates 1754–93.* Stuttgart, 2000.

——. 'Mapping the Country: European Geography and the Cartographical Construction of India, 1760–90'. *Science, Technology and Society* 8 (2003), 25–46.

——. 'Collectors at Work: Data Gathering and Statistics in British India, c. 1760–1860'. *Journal of the Asiatic Society of Bangladesh (Hum.)* 52(1) (2007), 57–84.

Mantena, R.S. 'Vernacular Futures: Orientalism, History, and Language in Colonial South India'. Ph.D. dissertation, University of Michigan, 2002.

——. 'The Question of History in Precolonial India'. *History and Theory* 46(3) (2007), 396–408.

——. 'The Kavali Brothers: Intellectual Life in Early Colonial Madras', in T.R. Trautmann (ed.), *The Madras School of Orientalism: Producing Knowledge in Colonial South India.* Oxford and New York, 2009, 126–50.

——. *The Origins of Modern Historiography in India: Antiquarianism and Philology, 1780–1880* (Palgrave Studies in Cultural and Intellectual History). New York, 2012.

Marchant, A. 'The Captain's Widow: Maria Graham and the Independence of South America'. *The Americas* 20(2) (1963), 127–42.

Markham, C.R. *A Memoir on the Indian Surveys.* London, 1878.

——. *James Rennell and the Rise of Modern English Geography.* London, Paris and Melbourne, 1895.

Marshall, P.J. *The Impeachment of Warren Hastings.* Oxford, 1965.

——. *East Indian Fortunes: The British in Bengal in the Eighteenth Century.* Oxford, 1976.

——. 'Masters and Banians in Eighteenth-Century Calcutta', in B.B. Kling and M.N. Pearson (eds), *The Age of Partnership: Europeans in Asia before Dominion.* Honolulu, 1979, 191–214.

——. *Bengal: The British Bridgehead: Eastern India 1740–1828* (The New Cambridge History of India pt. 2, vol. 2). Cambridge, 1987.

——. 'British Society in India under the East India Company'. *Modern Asian Studies* 31(1) (1997), 89–108.

Martin, J. 'An Engineer in the Mysore War of 1791–1792'. *Journal of the Society for Army Historical Research* 22(90) (1944), 324–38.

McGilvary, G. *Guardian of the East-India Company: The Life of Laurence Sulivan.* London and New York, 2006.

——. *East India Patronage and the British State: The Scottish Elite and Politics in the Eighteenth Century.* London and New York, 2008.

McIver, E. *Memoirs of a Highland Gentleman Being the Reminiscences of Evander McIver of Scourie.* Edited by George Henderson. Edinburgh, 1905.

McKichan, F. 'Lord Seaforth and Highland Estate Management in the First Phase of Clearance (1783–1815)'. *Scottish Historical Review* 86(1) (2007), 50–68.

McLaren, M.P. *British India and British Scotland, 1780–1830: Career Building, Empire Building & a Scottish School of Thought on Indian Governance.* Akron, Ohio, 2001.

McNeil, K. *Scotland, Britain, Empire: Writing the Highlands, 1760–1860*. Columbus, 2007.

Mersey, V. *The Viceroys and Governors-General of India, 1757–1947*. London, 1949.

Michael, B.A. 'Separating the Yam from the Boulder: Statemaking, Space, and the Causes of the Anglo-Gorkha War of 1814-1816'. Ph.D. dissertation, University of Hawaii, 2001.

―――. 'Making Territory Visible: The Revenue Surveys of Colonial South Asia'. *Imago Mundi* 59(1) (2007), 78–95.

Miller, D.P. 'Joseph Banks, Empire and "Centers of Calculation" in late Hanoverian London', in D.P. Miller and P.H. Reill (eds), *Visions of Empire: Voyages, Botany, and Representations of Nature*. Cambridge, 1996, 21–37.

Mills, L.A. *Ceylon under British Rule 1795–1932: With an Account of the East India Company's Embassies to Kandy 1762–1795*. London, 1964.

Misra, B.B. *The Central Administration of the East India Company 1773–1834*. Manchester, 1959.

Mitchell, L. 'Knowing the Deccan: Enquiries, Points, and Poets in the Construction of Knowledge and Power in Early-Nineteenth-Century South India', in T.R. Trautmann (ed.), *The Madras School of Orientalism: Producing Knowledge in Colonial South India*. Oxford and New York, 2009, 151–82.

Mitchison, R. *Agricultural Sir John: The Life of Sir John Sinclair of Ulbster, 1754–1835*. London, 1962.

―――. 'Scotland 1750–1850', in *The Cambridge Social History of Britain, 1750–1850*, 2 vols. Cambridge, 1990, vol. 1, 155–207.

―――. 'The Government and the Highlands, 1707–45', in R. Mitchison and N. Phillipson (eds), *Scotland in the Age of Improvement*. Edinburgh, 1996, 24–45.

Mitter, P. 'The Early British Port Cities of India: Their Planning and Architecture circa 1640–1757'. *Journal of the Society of Architectural Historians* 45(2) (1986), 95–114.

Morris, H. *The Governors-General of British India*. 2 vols. 1907. Reprinted in New Delhi, 1984.

Mosse, D. *The Rule of Water: Statecraft, Ecology, and Collective Action in South India*. New Delhi, 2003.

Mukherjee, N. *The Ryotwari System in Madras, 1792–1827*. Calcutta, 1962.

Murdoch, A, *The People Above: Politics and Administration in Mid Eighteenth-Century Scotland*. Edinburgh, 1980.

Mustafa, M. 'The Shaping of Land Revenue Policy in Madras Presidency: Revenue Experiments – the Case of Chittoor District'. *Indian Economic and Social History Review* 44(2) (2007), 213–36.

Mykkänen, J. '"To methodize and regulate them": William Petty's Governmental Science of Statistics'. *History of the Human Sciences* 7 (1994), 65–88.

Nadaraja, T. *The Legal System of Ceylon in its Historical Setting*. Leiden, 1972.

National Archives of India (ed.). *Catalogue of Memoirs of the Survey of India, 1773–1866*. New Delhi, 1989.

Neild-Basu, S. 'The Dubashes of Madras'. *Modern Asian Studies* 18(1) (1984), 1–31.

Neild, S.M. 'Colonial Urbanism: The Development of Madras City in the Eighteenth and Nineteenth Centuries'. *Modern Asian Studies* 13(2) (1979), 217–46.

Niel, R. van, *Java's Northeast Coast: A Study in Colonial Encroachment*. Leiden, 2005.

Noyce, F. 'A Striking Episode in Madras History', in *The Madras Tercentenary Commemoration Volume*. London, Bombay, Calcutta and Madras, 1939, 97–106.

O'Brian, K. *Narratives of Enlightenment: Cosmopolitan History from Voltaire to Gibbon*, Cambridge, 1997.

O'Reilly, W. 'Orientalist Reflections: Asia and the Pacific in the Making of late Eighteenth-Century Ireland'. *New Zealand Journal of Asian Studies* 6(2) (2004), 127–47.

Otness, H. 'Nurturing the Roots for Oriental Studies: The Development of the Libraries of the Royal Asiatic Society's Branches and Affiliates in Asia in the Nineteenth Century'. *International Association of Orientalist Librarians Bulletin* 43 (1998), 9–17.

Parker, J.G. 'The Directors of the East India Company, 1754–1790'. Ph.D. dissertation, University of Edinburgh, 1977.

———. 'Scottish Enterprise in India, 1750–1914', in R.A. Cage (ed.), *The Scots Abroad: Labour, Capital, Enterprise, 1750–1914*. London, Sydney and Dover, 1985, 191–219.

Peabody, N. 'Cents, Sense, Census: Human Inventories in Late Precolonial and Early Colonial India'. *Comparative Studies in Society and History* 43(4) (2001), 819–50.

———. 'Knowledge Formation in Colonial India', in D.M. Peers and N. Gooptu (eds), *India and the British Empire*, (Oxford History of the British Empire Companion Series). Oxford, 2012, 75–99.

Peers, D.M. 'Between Mars and Mammon: The East India Company and Efforts to Reform its Army, 1796–1832'. *Historical Journal* 33(2) (1990), 385–401.

———. *Between Mars and Mammon: Colonial Armies and the Garrison State in India 1819–1835*. London and New York, 1995.

———. 'State, Power, and Colonialism', in D.M. Peers and N. Gooptu (eds), *India and the British Empire* (Oxford History of the British Empire Companion Series). Oxford, 2012, 16–43.

Phillimore, R.H. *Historical Records of the Survey of India*, 4 vols. Dehra Dun, 1949–58.

Phillips, C.H. *The East India Company 1784–1834*. Manchester, 1961.

Phillips, J. 'Parliament and Southern India, 1781–83: The Secret Committee of Enquiry and the Prosecution of Sir Thomas Rumbold'. *Parliamentary History* 7(1) (1988), 81–97.

Phillipson, N. 'Providence and Progress: An Introduction to the Historical Thought of William Robertson', in S.J. Brown (ed.), *William Robertson and the Expansion of Empire*. Cambridge, 1997, 55–73.

Phillipson, N. and R. Mitchison (eds). *Scotland in the Age of Improvement*. Edinburgh, 1970.

Pinch, W. 'Same Difference in India and Europe'. *History and Theory* 38(3) (1999), 389–407.

Pittock, M. *The Invention of Scotland: The Stuart Myth and the Scottish Identity, 1638 to the Present*. London and New York, 1991.

———. *Scottish and Irish Romanticism*. Oxford, 2008.

Pocock, J.G.A. *Barbarism and Religion: The Enlightenments of Edward Gibbon, 1737–1764*, 4 vols. Cambridge, 1999–2005.

Porter, T.M. *The Rise of Statistical Thinking 1820–1900*. Princeton, 1986.

Powell, A.A. *Scottish Orientalists and India: The Muir Brothers, Religion, Education and Empire* (Worlds of the East India Company 4). Woodbridge, Suffolk and Rochester, NY, 2010.

Prakash, G. *Another Reason: Science and the Imagination of Modern India*. Princeton, 1999.

Prasad, S.N. *Catalogue of Historical Maps of the Survey of India.* New Delhi, 1975.

Pratt, M.L. *Imperial Eyes: Travel Writing and Transculturation.* London, 1992.

Raghavan, M.D. 'Some old Madras Houses', in *The Madras Tercentenary Commemoration Volume.* London, Bombay, Calcutta and Madras, 1939, 113–21.

Raj, K. 'Colonial Encounters and the Forging of New Knowledge and National Identities: Great Britain and India, 1760–1850'. *Osiris* 15 (2000), 119–34.

————. 'When Human Travellers become Instruments: The Indo-British Exploration of Central Asia in the Nineteenth Century', in M.-N. Bourguet, C. Licoppe and H.O. Sibum (eds), *Instruments, Travel and Science: Itineraries of Precision from the Seventeenth to the Twentieth Century.* London and New York, 2002, 156–88.

Rajagopal, V. 'Fashioning Modernity in Telugu: Viresalingam and his Interventionist Strategy'. *Studies in History* 21(1) (2005), 45–77.

Raman, B. 'Tamil Munshis and Kacceri Tamil under the Company's Document Raj in Early-Nineteenth Century Madras', in T.R. Trautmann (ed.), *The Madras School of Orientalism: Producing Knowledge in Colonial South India.* Oxford and New York, 2009, 209–32.

Ranson, C.W. 'The Growth of the Population of Madras', in *The Madras Tercentenary Commemoration Volume.* London, Bombay, Calcutta and Madras, 1939, 317–24.

Rao, N.V. 'Pioneers of English Writing in India: The Cavally Telugu Family'. *Annals of Oriental Research* 18(2) (1963), 1–33.

Rao, V.N. 'Print and Prose: Pundits, Karanams, and the East India Company in the Making of Modern Telugu', in S. Blackburn and V. Dalmia (eds), *India's Literary History: Essays on the Nineteenth Century.* Delhi, 2004, 146–66.

Rao, V.N. and S. Subrahmanyam. 'Notes on Political Thought in Medieval and Early Modern South India'. *Modern Asian Studies* 43(1) (2009), 175–210.

Rao, V.N., D. Shulman and S. Subrahmanyam. *Textures of Time: Writing History in South India 1600–1800.* Delhi, 2001.

Razzell, P.E. 'Social Origins of British Officers in the Indian and British Home Army, 1758–1962'. *British Journal of Sociology* 14(3) (1963), 248–60.

Reddy, D.S. 'The Ryotwari Land Revenue Settlements and Peasant Resistance in the "Northern Division of Arcot" of the Madras Presidency during Early British Rule'. *Social Scientist* 16(6/7) (1988), 35–50.

Reddy, M.A. *Lands and Tenants in South India: A Study of Nellore District 1850–1990.* Bombay, Calcutta and Madras, 1996.

Reitan, E.A. 'Popular Cartography and British Imperialism: The Gentleman's Magazine, 1739–1763'. *Journal of Newspaper and Periodical History* 2(3) (1986), 2–13.

Rendall, J. 'Scottish Orientalism: From Robertson to James Mill'. *Historical Journal* 25(1) (1982), 43–69.

Rice, B.L. *Mysore: A Gazetteer compiled for Government.* Revised edn. 2 vols. London, 1887. Reprint, New Delhi, 2001.

Richards, E. 'How Tame were the Highlanders During the Clearances?'. *Scottish Studies* 17(1) (1973), 35–50.

————. *A History of the Highland Clearances: Agrarian Transformation and the Evictions, 1746–1886,* 2 vols. London and Canberra, 1982–1985.

Riddy, J. 'Warren Hastings: Scotland's Benefactor?' in G. Carnall and C. Nicholson (eds), *The Impeachment of Warren Hastings: Papers from a Bicentenary Commemoration.* Edinburgh, 1989, 30–57.

Rieu, C. *Catalogue of Persian Manuscripts in the British Museum*, 3 vols. London, 1879–1883.

Robb, P. 'Completing "Our Stock of Geography" or an Object "Still More Sublime". Colin Mackenzie's Survey of Mysore'. *Journal of the Royal Asiatic Society* 8(2) (1998), 181–206.

Rutnam, J.T. *The Early Life of Alexander Johnston (1775–1849), Third Chief Justice of Ceylon*. Colombo, 1988.

Rymer, L. 'The Scottish Kelp Industry'. *Scottish Geographical Magazine* 90(3) (1974), 142–52.

Said, E. *Orientalism*. New York, 1979.

Sangwan, S. 'Science Education in India under Colonial Constraints, 1792–1857'. *Oxford Review of Education* 16(1) (1990), 81–95.

———. 'Natural History in Colonial Context: Profit or Pursuit? British Botanical Enterprise in India 1778–1820', in P. Petitjean and C. Jami (eds), *Science and Empires: Historical Studies about Scientific Development and European Expansion*. Dordrecht, Boston and London, 1992, 281–98.

———. 'Reordering the Earth: The Emergence of Geology as a Scientific Discipline in Colonial India'. *Indian Economic and Social History Review* 31(3) (1994), 291–310.

———. 'The Strength of a Scientific Culture: Interpreting Disorder in Colonial Science'. *Indian Economic and Social History Review* 34(2) (1997), 217–49.

Sarkar, T. 'Bondage in the Colonial Context', in U. Patnaik and M. Dingwaney (eds), *Chains of Servitude: Bondage and Slavery in India*. Madras, 1985, 97–126.

Satyanarna, A. *History of the Wodeyars of Mysore (1610–1748)*. Mysore, 1996.

Schendel, W. van, 'Introduction', in id. (ed.), *Francis Buchanan in Southeast Bengal (1798): His Journey to Chittagong, the Chittagong Hill Tracts, Noakhali and Comilla*. Dhaka, 1992, ix–xxv.

Schlögl, D. *Der planvolle Staat: Raumerfassung und Reformen in Bayern, 1750–1800*. Munich, 2002.

Schmidt, D. *Statistik und Staatlichkeit*. Wiesbaden, 2005.

Schmidt, M. '"Conjectural History", and the Decline of Enlightenment Historical Writing', in U. Broich, H.T. Dickinson, E. Hellmuth and M. Schmidt (eds), *Reactions to Revolutions: The 1790s and Their Aftermath*. Berlin, 2007, 231–62.

Schrikker, A. *Dutch and British Colonial Intervention in Sri Lanka, 1780–1815: Expansion and Reform*. Leiden and Boston, 2007.

Scott, D. 'Colonial Governmentality'. *Social Text* 43 (1995), 191–220.

Scott, H.L. *Military Dictionary: Comprising Technical Definitions; Information on Raising and Keeping Troops; Actual Service, including Makeshifts and Improved Matériel; and Law, Government, Regulation, and Administration relating to Land Forces*. 1861. Reprinted in New York, 1968.

Scott, J.C. 'Patron-client Politics and Political Change in Southeast Asia'. *American Political Science Review* 66(1) (1972), 91–113.

———. *Seeing Like a State: How Certain Schemes to Improve the Human Condition Have Failed*. New Haven, 1998.

Shaw, J. *The Management of Scottish Society, 1707–64: Power, Nobles, Lawyers, Edinburgh Agents and English Influence*. Edinburgh, 1983.

Sherwani, H.K. 'Contemporary Histories of the Qutb Shahi Dynasty of Golkonda', in M. Hasan (ed.), *Historians of Medieval India*. Meerut, 1968, 84–97.

Singh, S.B. *European Agency Houses in Bengal (1783–1833)*. Calcutta, 1966.

Sivasundaram, S. *Islanded: Britain, Sri Lanka, and the Bounds of an Indian Ocean Colony*. Chicago and London, 2013.

Skrine, F. *Life of Sir William Wilson Hunter, K.C.S.I., M.A. LL.D., Vice-President of the Royal Asiatic Society, etc.* London, New York and Bombay, 1901.

Smith, J.C. *Annals of Lodge Fortrose A.F. & A.M. No. 108: Compiled from the Lodge Records*. Toronto, 1905.

Srinivasachari, C.S. *History of the City of Madras: Written for the Tercentenary Celebration Committee*. Madras, 1939.

Steadman, J.M. 'The Asiatick Society of Bengal'. *Eighteenth-Century Studies* 10(4) (1977), 464–83.

Stein, B. *Thomas Munro: The Origin of the Colonial State and his Vision of Empire*. Delhi, 1989.

Stern, P.J. 'From the Fringes of History: Tracing the Roots of the English East India Company-state', in S. Agha and E. Kolsky (eds), *Fringes of Empire: Peoples, Places, and Spaces in Colonial India*. New Delhi, 2009, 19–44.

———. *The Company-State: Corporate Sovereignty and the Early Modern Foundations of the British Empire in India*. Oxford, 2011.

Steuart, A.F. 'Miss Katherine Read, Court Paintress'. *Scottish Historical Review* 2 (1904), 38–46.

Stiegler, S.M. *The History of Statistics: The Measurement of Uncertainty before 1900*. Cambridge, MA, and London, 1986.

Stocking, G.W. *Victorian Anthropology.* New York and London, 1987.

Stokes, E. *The English Utilitarians and India*. Delhi, Bombay, Madras and Calcutta, 1959.

Stone, R. *Some British Empiricists in the Social Sciences, 1650–1900*. Cambridge, 1997.

Streidl, P. *Naturrecht, Staatswissenschaften und Politisierung bei Gottfried Achenwall (1719–1772): Studien zur Gelehrtengeschichte Göttingens in der Aufklärung*. Munich, 2003.

Subrahmanyam, S. 'Aspects of State Formation in South India and Southeast Asia, 1500–1650'. *Indian Economic and Social History Review* 23 (1986), 357–77.

———. *Courtly Encounters: Translating Courtliness and Violence in Early Modern Eurasia*. Cambridge, MA, 2012.

Sumpter, R.M. *Patronage and Politics in Scotland, 1707–1832*. Edinburgh, 1986.

Sutherland, L.S. 'Lord Macartney's Appointment as Governor of Madras, 1780: The Treasury in East India Company Elections'. *English Historical Review* 90(356) (1975), 523–35.

Sutton, J. *Lords of the East: The East India Company and its Ships 1600–1874*. London, 1981.

Sweet, J.M. 'Instructions to Collectors: John Walker (1973) and Robert Jameson (1817); with Biographical Notes on James Anderson (LL.D.) and James Anderson (M.D.)'. *Annals of Science* 29(4) (1972), 397–414.

Symonds, J. 'Toiling in the Vale of Tears. Everyday Life and Resistance in South Uist, Outer Hebrides, 1760–1860'. *International Journal of Historical Archaeology* 3(2) (1999), 101–22.

Tankard, J.W. *The Statistical Pioneers*. Cambridge, MA, 1984.

Taylor, J.G. *The Social World of Batavia: European and Eurasian in Dutch Asia*. Madison, Wisconsin, 1983.

The Madras Tercentenary Commemoration Volume. London, Bombay, Calcutta and Madras, 1939.

The, L. and P. van der Veur. *The Verhandlingen van het Bataviaasch Genootschap: An Annotated Content Analysis.* Ohio, 1973.

Thiel-Horstmann, M. 'Staatsbeschreibung und statistische Erhebungen im vorkolonialen und kolonialen Indien', in M. Rassem and J. Stagl (eds), *Statistik und Staatsbeschreibung in der Neuzeit vornehmlich im 16.–18. Jahrhundert.* Munich, Vienna and Zurich, 1980, 205-13.

Thomas, A.P. 'The Establishment of Calcutta Botanic Garden: Plant Transfer, Science and the East India Company, 1786–1806'. *Journal of the Royal Asiatic Society* 16(2) (2006), 165-77

Thorne, R.G. (ed.). *The House of Commons 1790–1820,* 5 vols. Warburg, 1986.

Tickell, A. 'Negotiating the Landscape: Travel, Transaction, and the Mapping of Colonial India'. *Yearbook of English Studies* 34 (2004), 18–30.

Tiffin, S. 'Raffles and the Barometer of Civilisation: Images and Descriptions of Ruined Candis in The History of Java'. *Journal of the Royal Asiatic Society* 18(3) (2008), 341–60.

Tomlinson, B.R. 'From Campsie to Kedgeree: Scottish Enterprise, Asian Trade and the Company Raj'. *Modern Asian Studies* 36(4) (2002), 769–91.

Trautmann, T.R. *Aryans and British India.* Berkeley, Los Angeles and London, 1997.

———. 'Hullabaloo about Telugu'. *South Asia Research* 19(1) (1999), 53–70.

———. 'Dr Johnson and the Pandits. Imagining the Perfect Dictionary in Colonial Madras'. *Indian Economic and Social History Review* 38(4) (2001), 375–97.

———. *Languages and Nations: The Dravidian Proof in Colonial Madras.* New Delhi, 2003.

———. 'Discovering Aryan and Dravidian in British India: A Tale of two Cities'. *Historiographia Linguistica* 31(1) (2004), 33–58.

———. 'Introduction', in id. (ed.), *The Madras School of Orientalism: Producing Knowledge in Colonial South India.* Oxford and New York, 2009, 1–25.

——— (ed.). *The Madras School of Orientalism: Producing Knowledge in Colonial South India.* Oxford and New York, 2009.

Travers, R. 'Death and the Nabob: Imperialism and Commemoration in Eighteenth-Century India'. *Past and Present* 196(1) (2007), 83–124.

———. *Ideology and Empire in Eighteenth Century India.* Cambridge, 2007.

———. '"The Real Value of the Lands": The Nawabs, the British and the Land Tax in Eighteenth-Century Bengal'. *Modern Asian Studies* 38(3) (2004), 517–558.

Tyson, R.E. 'Landlord Policies and Population Change in North-East Scotland and the Western Isles'. *Northern Scotland* 19 (1999), 63–74.

Varady, R.G. 'Social Ecology: Oxford in India Readings in Sociology and Social Anthropology. Edited by Ramachandra Guha' (Review), *Journal of Asian Studies* 54(4) (1995), 1129–31.

Vatuk, S. 'Bharattee's Death: Domestic Slave Women in Nineteenth-Century Madras', in I. Chatterjee and R.M. Eaton (eds), *Slavery and South Asian History.* Bloomington and Indianapolis, 2006, 210–33.

Vibart, H.M. *The Military History of the Madras Engineers and Pioneers from 1743 up to the Present Time,* 2 vols. London, 1883.

Vicziany, M. 'Imperialism, Botany and Statistics in Early-Nineteenth Century India: The Surveys of Francis Buchanan 1762–1829'. *Modern Asian Studies* 20(4) (1986), 625–60.

Vierhaus, R. 'Die Universität Göttingen und die Anfänge der Geschichtswissenschaft im 18. Jahrhundert', in H. Boockmann and H. Wellenreuther (eds), *Geschichtswissenschaft in Göttingen: Eine Vorlesungsreihe* (Göttinger Universitätsschriften, Series A: vol. 2). Göttingen, 1987, 9–29.

Wagoner, P.B. 'Precolonial Intellectuals and the Production of Colonial Knowledge'. *Comparative Studies in Society and History* 45(4) (2003), 783–814.

―――. 'From Manuscript to Archive to Print. The Mackenzie Collection and Later Telugu Literary Historiography', in T.R. Trautmann (ed.), *The Madras School of Orientalism: Producing Knowledge in Colonial South India*. Oxford and New York, 2009, 183–205.

Walch, G.T. *The Engineering Works of the Gódávari Delta: A Descriptive and Historical Account: Compiled for the Madras Government*, 2 vols. Madras, 1896.

Wallach, B. 'British Irrigation Works in India's Krishna Basin'. *Journal of Historical Geography* 11(2) (1985), 155–73.

Washbrook, D.A. 'India, 1818–1860: The Two Faces of Colonialism', in A. Porter (ed.), *The Oxford History of the British Empire, vol. 3: The Nineteenth Century*. Oxford and New York, 1999, 395–421.

―――. 'The Colonial Transition in South India, 1770–1840'. *Modern Asian Studies* 38(3) (2004), 479–516.

Weatherbee, D.E. 'Raffles' Sources for Traditional Javanese Historiography and the Mackenzie Collections'. *Indonesia* 26 (1978), 63–93.

Webster, A. 'The Strategies and Limits of Gentlemanly Capitalism: The London East India Agency Houses, Provincial Commercial Interests, and the Evolution of British Economic Policy in South and South East Asia 1800–50'. *Economic History Review* 59(4) (2006), 743–64.

Whatley, C.A. *Scottish Society 1707–1830: Beyond Jacobitism, towards Industrialisation*. Manchester, 2000.

White, H. 'The Historical Text as Literary Artifact', in id., *Tropics of Discourse: Essays in Cultural Criticism*. Baltimore and London, 1986, 81–100.

Wickremesekera, C. *'Best Black Troops in the World': British Perceptions and the Making of the Sepoy 1746–1805*. New Delhi, 2002.

Wilson, J.E. 'Anxieties of Distance: Codification in Early Colonial Bengal'. *Modern Intellectual History* 4(1) (2007), 7–23.

Wilson, K. *The Island Race: Englishness, Empire and Gender in the Eighteenth Century*. London and New York, 2003.

Wilson, W.J. *The History of the Madras Army*, 5 vols. Madras, 1882–1889.

Withers, C.W. 'Education and Anglicisation: The Policy of the SSPCK toward the Education of the Highlander, 1709–1825'. *Scottish Studies* 26 (1982), 37–56.

―――. *Gaelic in Scotland 1698–1981: The Geographical History of a Language*. Edinburgh, 1984.

―――. *Gaelic Scotland: The Transformation of a Culture Region*. London and New York, 1988.

―――. 'How Scotland Came to Know Itself: Geography, National Identity and the Making of a Nation, 1680–1790'. *Journal of Historical Geography* 21(4) (1995), 371–97.

———. *Geography, Science and National Identity: Scotland since 1520.* Cambridge, 2001.

Withrington, D.J. 'The S.P.C.K. and Highland Schools in Mid-Eighteenth Century'. *Scottish Historical Review* 41(132) (1962), 89–99.

———. 'What Was Distinctive about the Scottish Enlightenment', in J.J. Carer and J.H. Pittcock (eds), *Aberdeen and the Enlightenment.* Aberdeen, 1987, 9–19.

Wolffhardt, T. 'Inseln am Rande Europas: Zeit, Entwicklung und Tradition auf Lewis und Harris, Äußere Hebriden', in A. Fischer-Kattner et al. (eds), *Schleifspuren: Lesarten des 18. Jahrhunderts: Festschrift für Eckhart Hellmuth.* Munich, 2011, 237–54.

Womack, P. *Improvement and Romance: Constructing the Myth of the Highlands.* Basingstoke and London, 1989.

Wood, P. 'Science in the Scottish Enlightenment', in A. Broadie (ed.), *The Cambridge Companion to the Scottish Enlightenment.* Cambridge, 2003, 94–116.

Woolf, S.J. 'Towards the History of the Origins of Statistics: France 1789–1815', in id. and J.-C. Perrot, *State and Statistics in France 1789–1815.* Chur, London, Paris and New York, 1984, 79–194.

Yesudas, R.N. 'The English and the Tribals in Wayanad, 1799–1805'. *Journal of Indian History* 64 (1986), 205–12.

Zastoupil L. and M. Moir, 'Introduction' in eid. (eds), *The Great Indian Education Debate: Documents relating to the Orientalist-Anglicist Controversy, 1781–1843* (London Studies on South Asia vol. 18). Richmond, 1999, 1–72.

Online Resources

The London Gazette (https://www.thegazette.co.uk/, accessed 13 February 2017).

Oxford Dictionary of National Biography (http://www.oxforddnb.com/, accessed 13 February 2017).

Royal Society – Fellowship Directory (https://royalsociety.org/fellows/, accessed 13 February 2017).

INDEX

Abdul Aziz, 189, 259, 267
Abercrombie, John, 264
Abul al-Fazl ibn Mubarak, 159
Achenwall, Gottfried, 181
Adam of Woodstone, William, 65
Adipati of Lasem, 263
Ain-i Akbari, 159, 197
Amaravati, 224, 240
amildars
    conflicts with, 125f, 185f
    refusal of cooperation in the Ceded Dis-
        tricts, 165
    support for surveyors, 125, 163, 193
Ananda Row, 195
Anderson, Alexander and John, agents, 65
Anderson, Alexander, teacher at Stornoway,
    32, 83n146
Anderson, James, 64, 231, 288
    and networks of natural historians, 69f
    and proposals on irrigation in the North-
        ern Circars, 102, 104
    employs Indian co-workers, 72, 94, 104
    initiatives for the 'public welfare', 71f
    instructs Mackenzie in mineralogy, 70
antiquarianism
    colonial, 8f
    in Scotland, 228f, 232f
    Mackenzie's, 9, 106, 224, 227, 241f
Archer, Mildred, 218
Army. *See* East India Company (EIC): army;
    military; Royal Army
Arnold, David, 68
Arthur, Thomas, 126
    appointed assistant on the Mysore Survey,
        122, 185
    complaints about, 125, 185–87
    counts population, 185
    illnesses, 127, 128, 187

surveys boundaries, 158, 165
withdrawn from Mysore Survey, 131, 187
Asiatic Society of Bengal
    as model for a learned society at Madras,
        230
    as model for Batavian Society, 261
    Mackenzie as member of Committee of
        Papers, 269
    Mackenzie becomes member, 95, 229f
    Mackenzie gives papers to, 234, 241
Atlas (ship), 50f
Atlas of India, 169, 265, 287
Auchmutty, Samuel, 258
Aurungabad, 160, 161

babads, 263
Babington, Benjamin Guy, 237
Bangalore, 127
Banks, Joseph, 12, 21n60, 69, 72
Barlow, George, 255–58 passim, 264
Barramahal, 101, 121, 157, 193
Barrow, Ian, 155
Bastin, John Sturgus, 7
Battle of Polilur, 53
Beatson, Alexander
    as Mackenzie's competitor, 98
    career, 66f
    tank survey in Northern Circars, 102
    *View of the Origin and Conduct of the War
        with Tippoo Sultaun,* 228
Bejapoor, 234
Bentinck, William Lord, 129f, 200
    grants Mackenzie extra allowance for
        establishment, 128
    on Mackenzie's self-perception, 135
    points out Mackenzie's achievements,
        130, 135
Blacker, Valentine, 258

Blake, David M., 7, 135
Board of Control, 15, 63, 256
Bombay (town), 52
Bombay presidency, 136
boundaries
    landmarks marking, 163, 164, 170
    local knowledge needed to identify, 163
    mapping of, 162f, 164f
    of Mysore, 117, 119f, 125, 156, 164f
    part of local understandings of space, 170
    surveyors settling local conflicts on, 164f
Bourdieu, Pierre, 4
Breckenridge, Carol, 13
Brodie, Alexander, 67
Brodie, James, 64, 67
Buchan, George, 220
Buchanan, Francis
    commissioned to make enquiries in My-
        sore, 120
    cooperation with Mackenzie, 120, 239
    description of village accountant's archive,
        194
    *Journey from Madras through the Countries
        of Mysore*, 196
    on Hindu geography, 238, 252n184
    support of British expansion, 120,
        139n22
Burke, Edmund, 54, 202, 290
Burke, Lucius Rawdon
    accompanies Mackenzie to Java, 263
    joins Mysore Survey, 133
    pension suggested for, 267
    provided for in Mackenzie's will, 274
    role in Surveyor General's Office, 209n97,
        259
Büsching, Anton Friedrich, 180f

Calcutta, 15, 50, 70, 95, 229, 230, 264,
    265, 268, 271, 286
    as a centre of patronage, 63f, 256
    botanical gardens in, 69
    British government at, 264, 268
    Mackenzie's departure for, 266, 268
    militarism at, 273
Calcutta (city), 52
    Mackenzie on, 268f, 272
    Mackenzie's household at, 269

social life at, 268f
supposed unhealthiness of, 271
Call, John, 97
Campbell, Alexander
    Grammar of the Teloogoo Language, 227,
        240
Campbell, Archibald, 57
    and Scots in Madras, 26, 41n17
Canara, 117, 135
    becomes part of EIC's territory, 118
    Buchanan's travel to, 194
    Jain rulers, 239
    Mysore Survey extended to, 136, 260
    slavery in, 238
Canara (language), 133, 222, 228
Cape Colony, 50, 88
cartography
    and genesis of modern state and its terri-
        tory, 154f, 169f
    and imperialism, 154
    as yardstick for character of EIC's rule,
        87f
    logic of European, 15, 166, 170, 225f,
        289
    military interest in, 86
Carwar, 117
Ceded Districts
    atlas of, 167–69
    boundaries, 125, 164f
    revenue survey of, 276n29
    survey of, 136f, 188, 224, 256, 259, 260
Ceylon, 50, 94, 239
    British conquest of, 60, 61, 88, 92
    Johnston Chief Justice in, 286
    Mackenzie's article on geography and
        antiquities, 95f
    Mackenzie's hopes to be appointed Chief
        Engineer and Surveyor General of,
        111n67
Chicacole, 102f. *See also* Northern Circars
Clive, Edward, 127
Close, Barry, 163, 218, 222
    member of the Mysore commission, 117
    promoted by Wellesley, 119
Cohn, Bernard S., 7, 8
Coimbatoor, 55, 118, 260
Colebrooke, Henry Thomas, 230, 239

Colebrooke, Robert Hyde, 97, 269f
  praise for Mackenzie's achievements, 162
College of Fort St George, 70, 229, 267
College of Fort William, 119, 231
colonial knowledge, 14
colonial transition, 10–12, 14f, 198, 202,
  226, 287–89
Coorg
  boundary of, 165
  Rajah of, 156
  survey of, 260
Coote, Eyre, 53
Cornwallis, Charles, 57, 65, 119
  appoints Mackenzie 'Surveyor to the
    Nizam's Detachment', 96
  appreciation of Mackenzie's work during
    Third Mysore War, 61
  'family', 63, 256
  plans to extend Permanent Settlement to
    South India, 100
Corps of Guides, 66
Court of Directors, 130, 218, 221, 236,
  265, 285, 286
  and Madras politics, 53
  and Wellesley, 119
  cuts allowances for Mysore Survey, 128
  patronage, 26, 39, 63, 256
  praise for Mackenzie's work, 135, 183
  regulations concerning surveys and maps
    in India, 98, 257, 264, 265f
  remunerations for achievements in India,
    72, 97, 135
  request for historical information, 220
Curnoul, Nabob of, 93

Daftar Asufiah, 160, 161, 197, 238
Dalrymple, Alexander, 104
  on EIC's responsibilities for irrigation
    systems, 101f
  Oriental Repertory, 58, 95, 106
Davies, Edward, 240
Deccan, 52, 92, 100, 117, 162
  languages of, 195, 231
  revenue records, 191
  territorial organization of, 158–61, 237f
dehazadas
  as basis for mapping, 166
  as basis for statistical description, 196

as testimonies of ancient territorial organi-
    zation, 163f, 177n78
  causing confusion, 163
  provided by *amildars*, 163, 193
Dharmaiah
  employed at Surveyor General's Office,
    259
  command of Halegannada, 189, 228, 237
  influence on Mackenzie, 228, 237, 239,
    242, 289
  pension proposed for, 267
  portrayed by Hickey, 2–4
  recognition at Madras, 227, 252n179
Dindigul
  Mackenzie's survey of fortress, 55
  survey of, 260
Dirks, Nicholas, 7, 8, 16, 187, 218, 228
Drayton, Richard, 13
dubashes, 51, 126
Dundas, Henry, 38, 49n125, 54, 66, 67,
  182
Dunigan, Michael, 134

East India Company (EIC). *See also* Court
  of Directors; patronage
  Anglo-Indian employees, 134
  army, 2, 25, 39, 55, 59, 61, 63, 255f
  careers within, 66f
  character of rule, 86, 100f, 272f
  crisis and reform, 53f, 56f
  economic interests, 12f, 72, 199f
  Indian employees, 94, 191
  interest in statistical knowledge, 199f
  profitability of employment with, 24f
  Scots in, 25–27
Edney, Matthew, 7, 86, 129, 155, 157, 258
Elliot, Hugh, 264, 267f
Ellis, Francis Whyte
  and Mackenzie's Indian co-workers, 227
  Dravidian proof, 238, 240
  examination of Leyden's papers, 226
  interest in land rights, 226, 236
  on Mackenzie's marriage, 269
  use of inscriptions collected by Macken-
    zie, 226f
Elphinstone, Mountstuart, 94, 202, 229
Erskine, William, 229

Faulkner, John, 262
First Mysore War, 53
Fleming, Captain G., 162
Fort St George. *See* Madras
Foucault, Michel, 11, 198
Fourth Mysore War, 61, 66, 102, 106f, 117, 119, 136
France
    global conflict with Britain, 52, 53, 60, 88, 98, 260, 264
    revolution, 200
Fraser Tytler, Alexander, 25
Freemasons, 69, 83n146

Gaelic
    'traditions' recovered, 228f, 232
    as Mackenzie's mother tongue, 27, 32
    attack on culture, 10, 29
    replacement of, 29f
    version of *Ossian* financed from Madras, 229
Ganjam, 102. *See also* Northern Circars
gazetteers, 197, 215
geographical positions, 157, 158, 168, 174n37
Ghauts, 105, 118
Gillanders, Alexander, 33, 201
Gillanders, George, 28, 33, 38
    and Murdoch Carn Mackenzie's debts, 36
    and Stornoway Customs, 33f, 37
    position of power, 31
    Proposals for Improving the Island of Lewis, 30f
Gladwin, Francis, 159
Godavery, 102
Golconda, 91
Golconda (sultanate of), 234
Goldingham, John, 113n105, 132
Gooty, 104
governmentality, 11f, 198, 202, 288
Graham, Maria, 241
Grant, Charles, 66, 130, 135, 264
Grant, James, 193
Great Trigonometrical Survey, 155, 170, 258, 271
    as celebrated scientific project, 157, 286f
    cost, 258

initially planned as coming in support of Mysore Survey, 157
    regarded as part of the Mysore Survey by Rennell, 129
Greville, Charles Francis, 130
    British India Analyzed, 101, 104
    contact with Seaforth family, 39
    on Madras government's responsibilities, 101–2
    part of networks of natural historians, 69f
Guha, Ramachandra, 215
Guha, Sumit, 228
Guntoor, 94. *See also* Northern Circars
    EIC takes possession of, 58
    Mackenzie's planned survey of, 59

Haidar Ali, 53, 118, 227
Hamilton, Henry, 134, 270, 283n144
Hamilton, Walter
    Geographical, Statistical, and Historical Description of Hindostan, 196
Haqiqatha-i-Hindustan, 160f, 238
harkaras, 2
    corps of, 94
    Mackenzie on, 94
    on Mysore Survey, 122, 186f (*see also* Kistnaji, Ramachandra Rao)
    role downplayed by Rennell, 94, 110n51
    working with Mackenzie, 2, 93f, 163
Harley, John Brian, 154
Harris, George, 79n87, 117
Hastings, Francis Rawdon, 271
Hastings, Warren, 11, 13
    and Scottish applicants, 26
    impeachment, 54
    systematic assessment of local tax registers under, 192
Havillard, Thomas de, 131
Hewett, George, 256
Heyne (Heine), Benjamin, 125, 217
    appointed to Mysore Survey, 122
    background, 141n51
    conflict with Mackenzie, 127
    leaves Mysore Survey, 127
    plans botanical garden at Bangalore, 127

Hickey, Thomas
    portrait of Colin Mackenzie, 2, 6, 189
Highland Regiments, 25, 37, 39, 63
Highland Society of London, 228f
    branch opened in Madras, 229
historicism
    as doctrine of British rule in India, 100f,
        236, 289
    Mackenzie's agenda based on, 105f, 161f,
        165f, 194
historiography
    and positivism, 225f, 227f, 289
    and Scottish Enlightenment, 229, 232,
        233f, 236, 242
    changes in on Scotland, 232
    delegitimation of South Indian, 225
    influences on British of South India,
        226–30
    Mackenzie Collection as starting point of
        modern in India, 7, 8, 225f
    narrative structures of, 4
    on British surveying projects in India, 7
    philosophical, 229, 242, 288
    stadial, 229, 230, 235f, 242
Hobart, Robert, 72, 91, 97, 103, 130
Hodges, William, 50f
Hodgson, John Anthony, 221
Holland, John, 58
Howell, William, 134
Howes, Jennifer, 7, 8, 94, 95, 217, 224, 225
Huggan, Graham, 154
Hyderabad, 62, 92, 95, 100, 106, 122, 136,
    159, 187, 239, 255
    British Resident at, 88, 89, 94, 95, 98,
        117, 193, 229 (*see also* Grant, James;
        Kennaway, John; Kirkpatrick, William)
    French Corps stationed at, 88
    invasion plan by Mackenzie, 91
    Mackenzie's map and accompanying
        memoir, 97, 98f, 160, 162f
    Mackenzie's surveys at, 88–94, 132, 136,
        156
    route maps produced by Mackenzie,
        89–91
    survey of in 1816, 260
Hyderabad (town), 89, 91
    British corps stationed near, 88

weir systems, 91

Ignatio, Cristian, 218, 243n18, 259, 267
improvement, 288, 290
    as justification of EIC's rule, 199f
    ideology of, 30, 199
    Mackenzie's ideas on, 40, 106, 198–201
    of Lewis, 28–30, 31, 200f
    of the Northern Circars, 101
    statistical knowledge as basis for, 198f
    to be brought about by science, 71f
India Act (1784), 54
inscriptions
    as historical sources, 95, 195, 222, 223f
    collection of, 2, 221, 223f, 263, 272
    giving evidence of land rights and privi-
        leges, 216, 226f
    Halegannada translated by Dharmaiah,
        189
    index of, 135, 223, 225
Inspector of Revenue Surveys (Madras), 101
internal colonialism, 29, 44n48
irrigation
    calls for EIC to be responsible for, 101–
        03, 105
    department responsible for, 98, 103f
    described in Journals and Memoirs, 89
    EIC's inconsistent attitude towards, 102
    facilities mapped, 157, 168
    included in survey, 122, 181, 193
    Mackenzie on in South India, 104–07
    pictured in Mackenzie's collection, 217
    poor state of in the Northern Circars,
        102f
    regional differences explained by differing
        geographical conditions, 216
    survey in the Northern Circars, 102, 132
Irschick, Eugene, 232

Jainism
    chapter on in Wilks' *History of Mysore*,
        227
    Mackenzie's research on, 4, 9, 17n13,
        224, 239
    seen as original religion of South India,
        239

Jains
among Mackenzie's assistants, 2, 189, 190, 227, 228,
as rulers of Canara, 239
conflict with Brahmins, 239f
temple statue removed by Mackenzie, 135
Java, 264, 269
British conquest of, 60, 92, 260
Mackenzie's investigations on, 7, 260–64
under British administration, 262f
Johnston, Alexander
inconsistencies of his narrative, 18n19, 55, 286
interest in Mackenzie's collection, 286
on Mackenzie's reasons to go to India, 4–6, 32f, 36
on Mackenzie's visit to Madura, 55, 285
publication of Mackenzie's autobiographical letter, 4
Johnston, Samuel, 55
Jones, William, 99, 230

kaifiyats, 194–96, 219, 222, 223, 225
Kalpagam, U., 198
Kavali brothers, 188f, 206fn69, 208n86.
See also Kavali Venkata Borayya; Kavali Venkata Lakshmayya; Kavali Venkata Ramaswami
Kavali Venkata Borayya, 10
accused of being in possession of a stolen horse, 125
chief translator on Mysore Survey, 187
educational background, 188
influence on Mackenzie, 94, 96, 100, 188, 206n67, 228, 242
pay, 189, 207n80
Kavali Venkata Lakshmayya
as head of Indian co-workers, 188, 192, 222f, 259
financial difficulties, 189
pay, 189, 207n81
pension proposed for, 267
portrayed by Hickey, 2
proposes to continue Mackenzie's collection, 286
provided for in Mackenzie's will, 274

statistical description of Shikapoor by, 196f
time working for Mackenzie, 207n72
Kavali Venkata Ramaswami, 188f, 231, 259, 267
Keating, Michael, 103
Kennaway, John, 94, 160
khaneh shumaries, 193f, 195, 196
Kirkpatrick, William, 94, 122, 130, 229
as Wellesley's confidant, 130
knowledge of Persian, 160
member of the Mysore commission, 117
network of Indian co-workers, 94, 160
provides Mackenzie with materials, 160f
Select Letters of Tippoo Sultan, 227f
transfers a paper by Mackenzie to Asiatic Society of Calcutta, 95
Kistna, 95, 102, 104, 117
Kistna (district), 189
Kistnaji, 2, 189, 259, 267
König, Johann Georg, 69
Koselleck, Reinhart, 10, 289f
Kulke, Hermann, 224
Kyd, Alexander, 97

Lachmi Narayan Shafiq, 160f
Lakshmidevamma, 189
Lambton, William, 129, 131, 157f, 258, 264, 271
Lantwar, William, 133, 134, 150n184, 184
Lewis (Island), 35, 36, 201
emigration, 30f, 33, 45n60
famine, 30f
Mackenzie's ideas for improvement of, 200f
part of Seaforth's estate, 27
programme of improvement, 28–30
resistance to socioeconomic change, 30
Lewis, Barry, 169
Leyden, John, 66, 71, 238, 257
and Scottish Enlightenment, 229, 230f
as linguist, 231
dies in Batavia, 261
literary activities in Scotland, 230
manuscripts and papers, 226, 261
naturalist on Mysore Survey, 127, 231
Literary Society of Bombay, 180

Macartney, George, 55, 57
Macdowell, Hay, 255
Macfarlane, Walter, 181
Mackenzie 'of the Temple', John, 65,
  248n116
Mackenzie Collections, 2
  beginnings of, 55, 217, 219, 228
  coins, 217, 223f, 263, 286
  compensation for, 217, 220f
  conceptual connection with surveys, 9,
    215–17
  drawings, 7, 55, 95, 217f, 263
  in recent historiography, 7, 8f, 218
  inscriptions, 223, 263, 272
  institutional connection with surveys,
    217–21
  manuscripts, 194f, 218–21, 222f
  minerals, 217, 218
  potentially valuable archive for colonial
    state, 236
  research agenda, 242
  systematic plan for, 221f
  used by historians and orientalists, 226f
Mackenzie commission (Java), 261–63
Mackenzie of Coul, Alexander, 63
Mackenzie of Strickathrow, 31, 34, 36
Mackenzie, Alexander, 32
Mackenzie, Colin
  accused of inappropriate behaviour during
    the Mysore Survey, 125f
  and Indian languages, 93f
  appointment to EIC, 39
  autobiographical letter to Alexander John-
    ston, 4, 36, 218, 286
  belief in meritocratic principle, 57, 62
  birth, 27, 42n26
  death, 272, 283n162
  education, 32f, 45n71, 70
  enthusiasm for science, 68, 71, 72
  Gaelic as mother tongue, 32
  garden house at Madras, 69
  'holistic' approach, 215f
  house in Stornoway, 27
  illnesses, 89, 92f, 126, 136, 271f
  income, 36, 60, 78n71, 96, 97, 128f, 134,
    135, 137, 144fnn114–115, 256

  leaves of absence from Stornoway cus-
    toms, 37f
  on Brahminization of South India,
    238–40
  on British government in India, 105f,
    161f, 200, 201, 272–74
  on early connections of Celtic peoples
    with Asia, 240f
  on European assistants, 132
  on First Coalition War, 88
  on French Revolution, 200
  on territorial organization of South India,
    160, 161, 237f
  on writing a history of South India, 227
  participation in wars, 55, 59, 60f, 260
  reading, 70f
  reasons to go to India, 36f, 48n116
  self-teaching, 32, 70f
  specialization as surveyor, 58f, 62, 86
  transfers of money to his family, 1f, 37,
    135f
  will, 274
  wish to return to Britain, 27, 60, 96f, 270
Mackenzie, Francis Humberston, 28, 57, 62,
    64, 70, 71, 101, 130, 200, 264, 269
  acquaintances in India, 63, 81n111
  as Mackenzie's most important contact in
    London, 64
  correspondence with Mackenzie, 62f, 65,
    88, 93, 96, 99, 201
  expulsions from the Highlands in his
    name, 45n60
  knows Mackenzie from his youth, 33
  member of the Highland Society of Lon-
    don, 229, 248n116
  plans selling the parish of Uig, 201,
    214n169
  probable support of Mackenzie's appoint-
    ment to the EIC, 38f
  recommendations for Mackenzie, 55, 65f
  unhappy about Mackenzie's departure for
    India, 48n116
Mackenzie, Henry, 24
Mackenzie, Mary, 1, 27, 32, 274
Mackenzie, Mary Stewart, Lady Hood, 65,
    264, 269
Mackenzie, Murdoch 'Carn', 33

financial situation, 36f
    postmaster in Stornoway, 27, 36, 42n28
Mackenzie, William Cook, 7, 16, 60
MacPherson, James, 228
Madan, Charlotte, 63
Madan, William James, 63
Madras (presidency)
    as different from Bengal, 14, 100
    Board, 58, 129, 266
    Board of Revenue, 103, 257f
    discussions about legitimate forms of Brit-
        ish rule in, 100f
    escalating conflict between civil authori-
        ties and military, 255f
    in 1783, 52–54
    Indian revenue officers, 191
    languages spoken in, 187
    posts dealing with cartographical tasks in
        1798, 98
    revenue systems, 100f
    Scots in, 26, 41n17, 64, 67
    surveys in, 86, 260 (*see also* Ceded Dis-
        tricts: survey of)
    Tank Department, 103f
Madras (town)
    as Mackenzie's home from home, 68f
    in 1783, 50–52
    social life, 69f, 93
Madras Engineers, 55f, 256
    duties, 56, 60
    Mackenzie joins, 55
    promotion and pay, 59f, 78n71
    qualifications, 55
    reforms by Patrick Ross, 56
    relation to civil and military authorities,
        55f
Madras Jaghire, 53, 86, 102, 113n98,
    205n43, 226
Madras Literary Society, 229, 286
Madras Male Asylum, 132
Madras Military Institution, 131, 258
Madras Observatory, 70
Madras School of Orientalism, 7, 8, 230
Madura, 104
    Mackenzie's visit to, 18n19, 55, 285
Malcolm, John, 26
    and 'Scottish School of Thought', 202

and historiography of the Scottish En-
    lightenment, 229
    interest in Persian documents, 226
    praises results of Mysore Survey, 135
    promoted by Wellesley, 119
    secretary of the Mysore commission, 117
Malcolm, John, assistant of Mackenzie, 262
Mangalore, 117
Mantena, Rama, 7, 8f, 194, 218, 225, 237
maps. *See also* cartography
    adequacy of Mackenzie's, 169
    and linear boundaries, 155
    archiving of, 58, 257f, 265
    as 'colonial texts', 170
    as expression of ideologies, 154, 155
    circulation limited, 98, 263f
    drawing of as possibility to enhance career
        prospects, 97
    drawn by *harkaras*, 94
    drawn for the Mysore commission, 118,
        137fn6
    duplication of, 58, 133, 169, 265
    early maps drawn by Mackenzie, 58
    of Barramahal by Mather, 157
    of Bengal, 86 (*see also* Rennell: Bengal
        Atlas)
    of Hyderabad by Mackenzie, 89–91, 92,
        97f
    of Madras presidency requested by Court
        of Directors, 58
    'philological' by Mackenzie, 238
    reflecting military interests, 87f
    resulting from Mysore Survey, 129, 130,
        134f, 155
    resulting from Survey of the Ceded Dis-
        tricts, 166–68
    route maps, 87, 89–91
    uniformity of Mackenzie's, 168
    view from nowhere expressed in, 197
Maratha Wars, 131
Marathas, 53, 117
    and partition of Mysore, 118
    British boundaries with, 156
    knowledge of Tipu's territories, 160
    popular memory of Vijayanagara Empire,
        232
Mather, John, 123, 158, 164
    career, 121

contribution to the Mysore Survey, 131f
illnesses, 126f, 128
influence on planning the Mysore Survey, 121f, 157
relationship to Mackenzie, 121
retirement and pension, 132, 134, 188, 267
revenue survey of Salem and Barramahal, 101, 121, 193
Maurice, Thomas, 240
Maxwell, Hamilton, 63
McLaren, Martha P., 10, 62, 202
Medows (sometimes Meadows), William, 65
memoirs
    accompanying general maps, 98
    geographical, statistical and historical, 15, 129, 135, 195–97, 211n128, 216, 219, 226, 260, 262, 264, 265, 272, 287, 289
mercantilism, 11, 13, 198
    neo-mercantilism, 12, 21n61, 199f
Michael, Bernardo Ammedeus, 155, 162
militarism, 11f
    Mackenzie on, 273
military
    conflict with civil government, 255
    department's feud with Mackenzie, 257, 258, 259f, 264f
    influence on decision making, 12
    influence on Mysore Survey, 156
    interest in cartography, 86, 87f
    objectives of Mackenzie's surveys in Hyderabad, 91f
    opposition to Mackenzie's surveys, 128, 130f, 134, 220
    protection of surveyors and instruments, 123, 184
military fiscalism, 11f, 86, 106
Mill, James
    History of British India, 226
Minto, Gilbert Elliot, Earl of, 65, 130, 255, 268, 272
Morison, William, 122 131, 264
Mughal Empire
    Mackenzie's view on continuity of older administrative forms under, 161, 164, 235

territorial organization, 159, 161, 237f
Munro, Thomas, 11, 26, 94, 132, 165, 238f, 264, 270, 272, 273, 274, 285
    and 'Scottish School of Thought', 202
    handles complaints against Mackenzie, 125f
    interest in land rights, 236
    long connection with Mackenzie, 143n82
    member of the Mysore commission, 117
    promoted by Wellesley, 119
    revenue survey of Salem and Barrmahal, 101, 121, 193
Mustie, John, 218, 243n18
Mysore
    as competitor of the EIC in South India, 53, 100 (*see also* Haidar Ali; Tipu Sultan)
    botany and geology, 120, 127
    boundaries of, 117, 119, 125, 156, 164f
    British Resident, 119, 123, 129, 131, 135, 163, 165, 186, 188, 219 (*see also* Close, Barry; Malcom, John; Webbe, Josiah; Wilks, Mark)
    fever rages among population, 126f
    list of *parganas* or *taluks* compiled by Marathas' and Nizam's delegations, 160
    Mackenzie as Barrack Master of, 135, 256
    maps and memoirs of, 134f, 169
    partition of, 118, 136, 156, 158, 160, 164
    Rajahs of, 53, 118f, 127, 136, 163, 184f
    territorial organization, 161, 176n60
    under British control, 118f, 184, 266
Mysore commission, 117f, 121, 160
Mysore Survey
    as part of general survey of South India, 136f, 158f, 183f, 260
    as seminary of practical surveys, 132–34
    based on precolonial territorial organization, 156f, 160–62, 183
    conflicts with local administrators and population, 125f, 185–87
    cost, 258f
    demilitarization, 132, 134
    documentation, 123f, 129f, 257
    European assistants, 121f, 132 (*see also* Arthur, Thomas; Heyne, Benjamin;

Mather, John; Morison, William; Warren, John)
extension of, 136f, 260
Indian staff, 121, 122f, 124, 187–89
initiated by Wellesley, 119f
interrupted by illnesses, 126f
Mackenzie appointed superintendent, 61, 119f
Mackenzie's lobbying for, 129–31
materials resulting from shipwrecked, 130
method of mapping, 156f
misunderstood in London, 129
opposition to in Madras, 129, 130f, 257
organization, 121, 123f, 124f, 131–34
pay and allowances, 123, 128f
results, 134f
scope of, 12, 119f, 127f, 182f, 183f, 216–21
uniformity of method, 156, 158f, 183

Napier John, 33
Napier, Francis, 32f, 36, 55, 286
Narrain Row, 188f, 225
Narsing Row, 126
Nawab of Arcot, 53, 285
Newbold, John, 230
Newman, John, 218, 243n18, 267
niyogis
among Mackenzie's Indian co-workers, 190, 192, 208n86, 237, 267, 289
and *karanam* culture, 190–92
Mackenzie on, 191, 234
Nizam of Hyderabad, 53, 58
administration of, 94, 99, 160f, 163
and partition of Mysore, 118, 125, 136, 160
as British ally, 88, 117, 156
mistrust of British surveying work, 88f, 91, 162
North, Frederick (Lord North), 54
Northern Circars, 91, 94, 101, 159, 195
acquired by the EIC, 53, 58
famine, 102, 104
irrigation of, 102f, 104, 105
survey of, 260, 266
tank survey of, 103f, 132

Oakeley, Charles, 66
orientalism, 13
Orissa, 53, 271
Ossian, 228f
first Gaelic version financed from Madras, 229

Palighaut
Mackenzie's survey of fortress, 55
Palmer & Co., 217
parganas
as basis for cession of territory, 159f, 161
as basis of Mackenzie's surveys, 156f, 158f, 161, 183f
as part of Mughal Empire's territorial organization, 159
descriptions and memoirs of, 184, 195–97, 211n128, 216
Mackenzie on registers of, 163
mapping of, 157f, 162f, 164f, 166–68, 169, 170, 216
seen as continuation of older territorial units, 161f, 164
Parliament, Great Britain, 4, 24, 26, 28, 38, 39, 53, 54, 61, 64, 67, 119
patronage, 49n128
and Scottish networks, 25, 62f, 64, 288
careers based on, 62, 66f
EIC as source of, 26, 39
Indian forms of, 94, 189, 191
Mackenzie's dependence on, 34, 38f, 60, 62–66, 130, 135, 256, 287
of science by EIC, 12f, 68, 182
structures within the EIC, 10, 27, 60, 62, 63f, 287
Peile, J.H., 186
Permanent Settlement, 11, 100
Philippines, 60
Phillimore, Reginald Henry, 7, 39
Pigot, George, 53f
Pitt, William, 66
Pittman, Gibbon, 103
place names
as historical sources, 96, 216
etymology, 166, 196
transcription of, 98f, 166
Pondicherry, 52, 60, 260

Prakash, Gyan, 12, 198
precolonial archives
    systematically used for Mackenzie's sur-
        veys, 193–96
    use for revenue administration, 166, 192f
Prichard, James Cowles, 240
Prince of Wales Island (Penang), 127
prize money, 61, 79fn87
Proby, Mary, 63
Puri, 271
Purnaiya, 118, 163, 165, 186
Purshotamiah, 227, 228, 259

Quarter Master General, 256, 257f, 264f,
    270f

Raffles, Thomas Stamford, 261–63
    History of Java, 263f
Rai Mansaram, 161
Raidroog, *amildar* of, 125f
Ramachandra Rao, 186f
Raman, Bhavani, 191
Rao, Velcheru Narayana, 190, 191
Read, Alexander, 101, 121, 193
Regulating Act (1773), 54, 57
Rendall, Jane, 10
Rennell, James
    Bengal Atlas, 86, 176n66
    career, 24f
    Memoir of a Map of Hindoostan, 159
    on Mysore Survey, 129, 145fn126
    self-taught, 87
    survey of Bengal, 86, 139fn28
    Surveyor General of Bengal, 97, 139fn28
    underplays the role of *harkaras*, 110n51
    wealth, 41n9
revenue surveys, 287
    Bombay, 271
    Madras, 101, 106 (*see also* Barramahal)
Reynolds, Charles, 97, 108n12
Riddell, John, 268, 270f
Robb, Peter, 7f, 68, 129, 166, 169, 198, 216
Robertson, William, 35, 229, 241, 242
    Historical Disquisition, 70, 233
Ross, Andrew, 102, 104, 106
Ross, James, 132, 133f
Ross, Patrick

as Chief Engineer, 56, 59
    encouragement of Mackenzie, 56, 57f,
        58f, 64, 67, 70
    extension of Fort St George, 52, 56
    in Madras social life, 69
    initiatives to appoint Surveyor General,
        58, 96, 111n68
route surveys
    as standard in Bengal, 162, 270, 271
    by Mackenzie, 58, 88, 89–91, 156
    methodology, 86f
    practical advantages, 87
    preparing further expansion, 88, 91
    reflecting the interests of early Company
        rule, 87f, 106, 155, 196
Roxburgh, William, 69, 102, 104
Roy, William, 224
Royal Army, 25, 26, 55, 56, 64, 122, 255
Royal Asiatic Society, 4, 237, 285, 286
Royal Society, 12, 269
Rumbold, Thomas, 53, 54

Salem, 101, 121
Sankaraiah, 226f
Sauters, Doctor, 126
science
    as instrument of the state, 12, 13
    Mackenzie's interest in, 70–72
Scott, David, 11f, 198
Scott, Jonathan, 106
Scott, Walter, 230
    'romantic antiquarianism', 229, 232
    Waverly, 229, 232
Scott, William, 149fn184, 270
Scottish Enlightenment, 10, 182, 202, 229,
    232, 233f, 290
Seaforth family, 27. *See also* Mackenzie,
    Francis Humberston
    Colin Mackenzie relative of, 27, 42n27
    Thomas Frederick Humberston Macken-
        zie, 37, 38, 39, 229, 248n116
    integration into British elite, 27f
    Kenneth Mackenzie, First Earl, 28, 30,
        31, 32, 34, 38
    under financial pressure, 28
Second Mysore War, 51, 53, 55,
Seely, John, 2

Seringapatam, 104, 122, 128, 255
Shikapoor, 196
Shulman, David, 190
Sibbald, Sir Robert, 181
Simoga, 196
Sinclair, John, 38, 290
    attempts to extend statistical project, 182
    Mackenzie on his ideas of increasing rent-
        ability, 201
    on methodology of statistical enquiry, 183
    on statistical knowledge as basis for im-
        provement, 199
    organization of statistical enquiry, 182,
        184
    Statistical Account of Scotland, 181f, 199
Smith, Adam, 38, 69
Smith, Archibald, 34
Society in Scotland for the Propagation of
    Christian Knowledge (SSPCK), 30, 32
Sravana Belgula, 4
Srinivasia, 228
statistical enquiry
    as governmental, 180
    as material part of Mackenzie's surveys,
        182
    based on systematic use of precolonial ar-
        chives in Mackenzie's surveys, 193–96
    concept of popularized on the British
        Isles, 181
    differences between Mackenzie's and Sin-
        clair's, 182, 183f
    EIC's interest in, 182
    requiring local cooperation, 182, 184, 187
    responsibility of Indian staff in Macken-
        zie's surveys, 188
    scope of, 181
    traditions of, 181
Stein, Burton, 101
Stewart, Dugald, 204n26, 230
Stirling, Andrew, 271
Stornoway, 1f, 6, 27, 69, 201, 274, 287
    economy and society, 28f, 31
    Freemasons at, 83n146
    Mackenzie comptroller of customs at,
        33–36, 124
    post office, 27, 31, 33, 36
    programme of improvement for, 28, 29
    schools, 32, 45n71

Strange, Thomas, 230
Stuart (sometimes Stewart), James, 131
subassistant surveyors. *See also* Howell,
    Willam; Lantwar, William; Ross, James;
    Scott, William; Summers, James; Ward,
    Benjamin Swain
    regular structure of promotion for, 133f
    responsible for geometrical part of Survey
        of Ceded Districts, 188
    sociocultural background, 132, 134
    training during Mysore Survey, 132f
Subrahmanyam, Sanjay, 190, 191
Sullivan, John, 100
    Tracts upon India, 101f, 104
Summers, James, 134
surveying school (Madras), 132, 133, 134,
    259, 269, 272
Surveyor General of Bengal, 97, 98, 124,
    162, 220, 269f
Surveyor General of Bombay, 97, 112n85
Surveyor General of Ceylon, 111n67
Surveyor General of India, 7, 137, 264, 269
    duties of, 265
    Mackenzie appointed, 2, 62, 264
    office of, 221, 269–71, 287
Surveyor General of Madras, 13, 183,
    department of, 221, 259f, 266f, 287
    gains control of surveys in Madras presi-
        dency, 257f
    Indian staff, 192, 221, 260, 267
    initiative to appoint Military Surveyor
        General, 98, 99
    initiatives to appoint, 58, 66, 96f, 97f,
        256
    Mackenzie appointed, 62, 131, 221, 256
    responsibility for historical materials, 221
    surveys planned and carried out under,
        260, 266
Surveyor to the Nizam's Detachment
    de Havillard appointed, 131
    Mackenzie appointed, 61, 62, 96
    Mackenzie's salary as, 96, 97, 128,
        144fnn114–115
    Mackenzie's work as, 88, 89–91, 92f
surveys. *See also* route surveys; revenue sur-
    veys
    institutionalization as an instrument of
        the state, 7, 12, 13, 106, 286f

as collection of data needed for effective administration, 155

as symbolic claim to rule, 153f

comprehensive advocated by Mackenzie, 99, 106f, 137, 198, 271

cost of in Madras presidency, 258f

military reduced under Mackenzie's responsibility, 259

Teroovercadoo Mootiah, 72, 104

Third Mysore War, 55, 59, 60, 61, 62, 63, 88, 100, 117, 160, 237

Tipu Sultan, 53, 55, 60, 61, 66, 100, 117, 118, 158, 160, 165, 185, 227, 237

Topping, Michael, 105

appointed Superintendent of Tank Repairs, 103, 114n128

plan for watering the countries between Kistna and Godavery, 102

reports on state of the tanks in the Northern Circars, 103

training of Anglo-Indian boys, 132

Trail, Henry, 130, 136, 220, 256

Trautmann, Thomas, 6, 7, 230

triangulation. *See also* Great Trigonometrical Survey

Mackenzie's method of mapping based on, 89, 156f, 157f, 196

use of during route surveys, 87, 89

Tulloch, Brodie & Co., 65

Turnbull, Thomas, 154, 272

Vallancey, Charles, 224, 240

Varady, Robert G., 215

Veer, Peter van der, 13

Venkat Row, 126

Vicziany, Marika, 120

Vijayanagara, 190, 219, 224, 228, 232, 234

Vizagapatam. *See* Northern Circars

Wagoner, Phillip, 7, 8, 190, 192, 218, 223, 224, 225

Ward, Benjamin Swain, 134, 149fn184, 150n185, 196, 264

Ward, Francis Swain, 51, 73n7

Warren, John, 122, 128, 131

Washbrook, David, 14, 100

Webbe, Josiah, 129

Wellesley, Arthur, 60f, 66, 91, 117, 121, 219

Wellesley, Henry, 117

Wellesley, Richard, 65, 66, 117, 120, 122, 128, 129, 130, 137n1, 181, 182

appoints Mackenzie superintendent of Mysore Survey, 119f

on future state of Mysore, 118f

patronage of Great Trigonometrical Survey, 129

points out Mackenzie's achievements, 130

promotion of officers with knowledge of Indian languages, 119

Wellington, Arthur. *See* Wellesley, Arthur

West Indies, 37, 56

White, Hayden, 4

Wilford, Francis, 240

Wilkins, Charles, 230

Wilks, Mark

History of Mysore, 226f

interest in land rights, 236

on Jainism, 239

on Mackenzie's Indian co-workers, 188

on Mackenzie's research, 238, 240f

praises results of Mysore Survey, 135

Wilson, Horace Hayman, 221, 240

Womack, Peter, 199

Wood, Thomas, 97

Wynaad, 118, 185, 260

Yogyakarta, Sultan of, 60, 260, 263